Underground Front

Underground Front

The Chinese Communist Party in Hong Kong

Second Edition

Christine Loh

Hong Kong University Press
The University of Hong Kong
Pok Fu Lam Road
Hong Kong
https://hkupress.hku.hk

© Christine Loh 2018

ISBN 978-988-8455-79-9 (*Hardback*)
ISBN 978-988-8455-73-7 (*Paperback*)

All rights reserved. No portion of this publication may be reproduced or transmitted in any form or by any means, electronic or mechanical, including photocopying, recording, or any information storage or retrieval system, without prior permission in writing from the publisher.

British Library Cataloguing-in-Publication Data
A catalogue record for this book is available from the British Library.

Digitally printed

This book is dedicated to the historians and social scientists whose work on Hong Kong studies has inspired me to try to write this book, and to the archivists who are continuing to fight for good records and archival management so that important archival materials can be made available from generation to generation.

Contents

Abbreviations	viii
Preface to the Second Edition	x
Preface to the First Edition	xi
Introduction: The Chinese Communist Party in Hong Kong	1
1. Party Supremacy and Hong Kong	15
2. The Chinese Communist Party Tools of Co-optation and Persuasion	27
3. The Earliest History of the Chinese Communist Party in Hong Kong: From 1920 to 1926	42
4. Purge, War, and Civil War: From 1927 to 1948	53
5. Hong Kong to the Chinese Communist Party: From 1949 to 1965	78
6. The Cultural Revolution and the Riots of 1967: From 1966 to 1976	99
7. The Taking Back of Hong Kong: From 1977 to 1984	125
8. The Shaping of Post-Colonial Hong Kong: From 1983 to 1989	145
9. Passage to Reunification: From 1990 to 1997	171
10. Reunification, Patriotism, and Political Disorder: From 1997 to 2017	202
Appendix I: Survey of Public Opinion about the Chinese Communist Party 2007	245
Appendix II: The VIPs Invited to Witness the Signing of the Sino-British Joint Declaration	251
Appendix III: Members of the Basic Law Drafting Committee and Basic Law Consultative Committee	254
Appendix IV: Olympic Torch-Bearers 2008	258
Notes	263
Biographies	326
Bibliography	341
Chinese Publications	351

Abbreviations

Anti-Persecution Committee	Hong Kong-Kowloon All Sectors Anti-Persecution Committee
BAAG	British Army Aid Group
Beijing or Central Authorities	CCP and the Chinese government
BLCC	Basic Law Consultative Committee
BLDC	Basic Law Drafting Committee
Branch Bureau (South China Bureau)	Hong Kong Central Branch Bureau (renamed the Central South China Bureau)
CCP Central Committee	Central Committee of the Chinese Communist Party
CCP Hong Kong	The Chinese Communist Party's Hong Kong and Macao Affairs Work Committee in Hong Kong
CCP	Chinese Communist Party
CDO	City District Office
CIA	Central Intelligence Agency
CPPCC	Chinese People's Political Consultative Conference
DAB	Democratic Alliance for the Betterment of Hong Kong (subsequently renamed Democratic Alliance for the Betterment and Progress of Hong Kong)
Foreign Office	The Foreign and Commonwealth Office
FTU	Federation of Trade Unions
HKAA	Hong Kong Affairs Advisors
HKSAR	Special Administrative Region of Hong Kong
JLG	Joint Liaison Group
KMT	Kuomintang
Liaison Office	Liaison Office of the Central People's Government in the HKSAR

Abbreviations

NPC	National People's Congress
OMELCO	Office of the Members of the Executive and Legislative Councils
PC	Preparatory Committee
PWC	Preliminary Working Committee
SC	Selection Committee
SCNPC	Standing Committee of the National People's Congress
UMELCO	Unofficial Members of the Executive and Legislative Councils
Xinhua Hong Kong	Xinhua News Agency (Hong Kong Branch)

Preface to the Second Edition

Since the publication of the first edition in 2010, there have been many events that allowed me to observe the Chinese Communist Party's activities in Hong Kong. This edition ends in 2017, soon after the reunification passed its twentieth year. I have had the benefit of reading new publications about CCP history and activities in Hong Kong, some of which have commented on my first edition. Where corrections are due, I have made them in this edition. I am pleased that the first edition provoked others to write about the CCP in Hong Kong.

I am grateful to Hong Kong University Press for giving me the opportunity to update the book. This edition goes into greater depth on the party's view on "one country, two systems", "patriotism", and "elections", as well as the post-1997 governance and political system in Hong Kong, and where challenges lie. Britain's presence has faded and the People's Republic has become prominent. A generational change has taken place on the Mainland, and also in Hong Kong. The Mainland has made significant advances in many areas, whereas Hong Kong people seem to feel "stuck". The younger generations in Hong Kong find the politics of the Mainland unappealing. It seems a segment of young people in Hong Kong reject the Mainland. Yet they will have to reconcile with Hong Kong being an inalienable part of China. The next phase of the life of the Hong Kong Special Administrative Region might be about the process of reconciliation but the mighty CCP has to also admit that the political order it has put in place in Hong Kong has flaws.

This writing project has always been about telling the story of the CCP in Hong Kong, which must include the party's outlook and perspectives. This is especially relevant after the reunification since Hong Kong is a part of the People's Republic and there is no escaping that Beijing has "comprehensive jurisdiction". Yet Hong Kong's struggle to find wiggle room to exercise its autonomy is also understandable. We must be thankful that the political transition has been peaceful even if there were many moments of frustration. May cool heads and strong hearts continue to guide our national and local leaders.

Any factual mistakes, misperceptions, and misinterpretations in this edition are entirely my own.

Christine Loh
August 2017

Preface to the First Edition

This is an outsider's view of the ultimate insider issue. It is impossible to know how the Chinese Communist Party functions without being a party member. The reason I wrote this book is simply that I have always had a fascination for the Chinese Communist Party.

When I was very young, I heard from my Cantonese nanny how China was very poor and the Communists were "bad like everyone else". That is not an untypical attitude about authority among the *laobaixing*—the common folk. My father, who came to Hong Kong from Shanghai in 1951, said the Nationalists (Kuomintang) were corrupt and bad, the Communists were supposed to be better, but they messed things up. My nanny's nephew swam across shark-infested waters to search for a better life in colonial Hong Kong, and he once told me that the Communists were "good but became bad". By the time of the Cultural Revolution, the less said about the Communists the better—China had gone mad. I remember riots and bombs in 1967 in Hong Kong. My mother and stepfather talked about leaving but things calmed down soon and no one around me talked about the Communists again for a very long time.

When I was a teenager in the late 1960s, I used to spend afternoons during summer holidays watching Mainland movies in a Wanchai cinema that is now gone. There were never many people in there. The movies were fascinating because Mainland movies were about the "revolution" and the glorious Chairman Mao Zedong. China seemed quite fantastical. It was certainly unlike the Chinese society of Hong Kong that I knew. Then in 1972, when US president Richard Nixon went to China, there was a flurry of worldwide interest about the Chinese Communists and from then I was hooked. I wanted to know more about them. At university, I read up on communist literature. I admired Karl Marx's writings—and still do, and see Marx and Friedrich Engels's *The Communist Manifesto* as a great piece of political writing. However, I didn't like Vladimir Lenin, but Mao Zedong's collected works were quite mesmerising. However, studying in genteel England then and connected to British Hong Kong, Maoism seemed unreal.

Communist China became real for me only in 1980 when I lived in Beijing for about six months. The people I met were warm, but officialdom was not only highly bureaucratic but on formal occasions—like before the start of each business negotiation—stultifying. A senior apparatchik would recite party orthodoxy. Since then, I have travelled to many places on the Mainland and have met many people, some of whom were party members. I have had many discussions with Mainland friends about modern Chinese history, the party's view of things, and of course the future of the People's Republic of China. Having been a member of the Hong Kong Legislative Council from 1992 to 1997 and 1998 to 2000, I had a sideways view of the activities of the Chinese Communist Party in Hong Kong, which brought back my childhood fascination. Since then, my work in policy research has enabled me to learn more about national politics, as well as China's political and party structures. I believe it is essential to understand aspects of the Leninist state to understand China and the Chinese Communist Party.

As I said, this is an outsider's view of the story of the Chinese Communist Party in Hong Kong. I do not claim this to be history—this is merely a condensed story. What I have attempted to do is to use published sources and a few chats here and there to write a short story of the party's activities that related to Hong Kong from 1921. I believe no one has yet done this. For the earliest period of communist history in Hong Kong, there is no better reference source than Chan Lau Kit-ching's *From Nothing to Nothing*. For information on the East River guerrillas, I am grateful to have had sight of Chan Sui-jeung's manuscript on the East River Column, which is now published. I have also relied on Xu Jiatun's autobiography, which I have referred to as memoirs in the footnotes rather than by its Chinese title, as well as the writings of Huang Wenfang, who worked for Xinhua Hong Kong and whom I knew and had several long chats with many years ago.

Those who have helped me may not wish to be acknowledged here, as unfortunately party matters are still considered "sensitive" in Hong Kong. I do need to thank Colin Day, former publisher of Hong Kong University Press, for his interest in my work and his tolerance of repeated delays in meeting deadlines. He has also helped to edit my manuscript and provided a much-needed eagle eye. I am also most grateful to Yan Yan Yip for putting together the appendices and for helping with footnotes, and Iris Chan for checking and rechecking biographical details. I need to thank the National Endowment for Democracy for providing partial initial funding so that I could hire a research assistant to plough through materials more quickly, and to my family for providing the remaining resources so that I could finish this writing project. My research assistant, Allan Man, was extremely patient with me and tolerant of my inadequacies. Anyone else would probably have given up. Michael DeGolyer of the Hong Kong Transition Project was willing to include a few questions about how the Hong Kong public saw the Chinese Communist Party in one of his surveys, for which I am also grateful. I am also grateful for the assistance from the staff of the Public Record Office, the Information Services Department, and to the *South China Morning Post* for information and use of photographs.

Preface to the First Edition

There will likely be criticisms from some quarters that this writing project represents making a mountain out of a molehill or that this is an exercise supported by "foreign forces". I hope if there are such critics that they will be willing to read it with an open mind. I seek to tell a story, not to discredit the Chinese Communist Party. Scholars will no doubt find many gaps, but I hope this effort can still make an interesting read for the general reader. One day when party archives are fully open, there will be much more for scholars to write about. Any factual mistakes, misperceptions, and misinterpretations are entirely my own.

Christine Loh
December 2009

Introduction

The Chinese Communist Party in Hong Kong

Writing about the Chinese Communist Party (CCP) in Hong Kong used to be a much more sensitive subject than it is today. In the first edition of this book, it was noted that the CCP remained a subject to be avoided because its presence was still a "secret", although one that everyone had known about for a very long time. Nowhere else in the world was there a political system where the ruling party remained an underground organisation as in the Hong Kong Special Administrative Region (HKSAR). Twenty years after the reunification, the party has become much more visible and visibly active in Hong Kong. There should no longer be any issue to openly discuss party history, structure, policies, and activities. The party also wants Hong Kong to understand its values and outlook, which needs open discussion.

The story of the CCP and Hong Kong was one of secrecy and contradiction that goes back even before the party was founded in 1921. As a result of nineteenth-century "unequal treaties" that forced the Qing government to cede and lease territories to Britain, Hong Kong was seen merely to be under temporary British administration and China would recover the lost territory "when the time was ripe". The Kuomintang (KMT) had thought it would recover Hong Kong after World War II but could not. After 1949, the CCP was willing to wait a long time to resolve the question of Hong Kong because it served China's purpose to continue to live with the contradiction of claiming sovereignty but tolerating British de facto control.[1] The story of the CCP in Hong Kong is the tale of how the party dealt with that contradiction. From the time of the birth of the CCP, Hong Kong served as a very useful and fairly secure haven for party members and friends to stage revolutionary and political activities, including communications, propaganda, united front activities, fundraising and intelligence gathering. Hong Kong was also a good place for the Mainland in terms of trade, loans, investments, and gifts from compatriots.

The Hong Kong question was complex because it concerned both foreign and domestic policies that required careful consideration on many fronts. In taking back Hong Kong in 1997, the CCP created the concept of "one country, two systems" (initially meant for Taiwan) to allow the HKSAR room to be different. This solution was in fact characteristic of Chinese policy since the 1920s. On regaining formal sovereignty over Hong Kong, the CCP was willing to allow the HKSAR to retain a "high degree of autonomy" for at least 50 years after 1997. In other words, the CCP sought to retain both sovereignty and the benefits arising from the status quo. However, having taken back sovereignty in 1997, the CCP also had to shoulder the responsibility of administration it entailed. The latter half of this story describes how that responsibility required the CCP to a great extent to accept capitalism and the Hong Kong way of doing things. However, while the party appreciates that Hong Kong needs to function differently from the Mainland, its basic instincts, which are Leninist in nature, make it difficult for the party apparatus not to over-extend its reach into the city's public affairs. The sharpest point of departure between the party's way and Hong Kong's way arises from their different governing experience. Hong Kong's colonial past, though authoritarian, was underpinned by the rule of law in the Western liberal tradition, whereas the Mainland's experience stems from traditional authoritarian rule, and Leninism that gives the CCP supremacy.

From the party's point of view, it can claim success for decolonising Hong Kong. After all, "pro-government forces" now dominate the political structure as a result of the party's hard work in co-opting the Hong Kong elites and helping the patriotic camp to win elections so that a new political order emerged after 1997. There is a price to success however. The pro-government forces, a mixed bag, naturally want their interests to be protected, but the selfishness of some and the incompetence of others give the CCP multiple headaches. The CCP might even acknowledge in private that the pro-government forces are unruly and that Hong Kong has a dysfunctional political system dominated by corporatist vested interests that the people see as unfair. As the system was designed to give conservative forces dominance, the party should not be too surprised that the Hong Kong community continues to demand one-person-one-vote. The CCP had to rely on naked power to press home the message in 2004 through a constitutional interpretation by the Standing Committee of the National People's Congress (SCNPC) that Hong Kong must be more patient in achieving universal suffrage. Nevertheless, by 2007, the party indicated that it could accept one-person-one-vote for the election of the chief executive in 2017 and for the Legislative Council possibly by 2020. The important opportunity for 2017 was unfortunately lost when legislators voted the proposal down in 2015 amidst much drama on the floor of the legislature, and against the backdrop of Hong Kong society having experienced a number of major mass movements.

The CCP was not unaware that the ground was shifting in Hong Kong. In 2007, the then General Secretary of the CCP, Hu Jintao, noted in his report to the 17th National Party Congress in respect of implementing the "one country, two systems" policy that it was a "major task the party faced in running the country". To ensure the long-term prosperity and stability in Hong Kong and Macao, he noted the party was presented with a set of "new circumstances", which indicates that at the very top of the power structure, governing Hong Kong well had become a test of the party's governing capability.[2] The new challenge and situation was interpreted by the United Front Department to mean Hong Kong's local problems and the many conflicts among interest groups.³ Moreover, the United Front Department clarified how the CCP saw the situation:

> Since the Reunification a high degree of autonomy has been successfully implemented through "one country two systems" . . . and "Hong Kong people ruling Hong Kong". Furthering development and a harmonious society have become a consensus of different sectors in Hong Kong society . . . However, there are new situations and problems: "One Country, Two Systems" is a brand new topic. Capitalism is practiced in Hong Kong . . . while the Mainland mainly practices socialism. There is no precedent to deal with the relationship between the two. There is no previous experience that could be referred to. Hong Kong's economy is experiencing restructuring, and in addition, there are the impacts of incidents such as the Asian Financial Crisis and SARS. Hong Kong's economic, social and livelihood problems are inter-related and the interests involved are relatively complex. These are all the problems that need to be addressed to maintain Hong Kong's long-term stability. It is a test of our party's leadership and governing capacity.⁴

The reference to the interrelated economic, social, and livelihood problems is a reference to the many conflicts among interest groups. In January 2008, an essay in the Central Party School's influential publication, *Study Times*, revealed that to meet the challenge the party created a second governing team of Mainland cadres and government officials to manage Hong Kong affairs. The essay by Cao Erbao, then head of research of the Liaison Office—the CCP office in Hong Kong, discussed the training and deployment of the team and said that it should carry out its work in Hong Kong openly as a legitimate team.⁵ That was an important signal. The CCP would have to "come out" in Hong Kong, even if not yet in name (Chapter 10).

Six Phases of the CCP Story

The story of the CCP in Hong Kong can be said to have six distinct phases since 1921, when the party was established on the Mainland.

The first phase begins in 1920 with the earliest Marxist publication started by three intellectuals. Marxism's initial attraction to them was that it seemed to offer specific ideas on how to address social problems. This phase runs from the early 1920s to 1949, when the party assumed power on the Mainland. This period includes dramatic strikes and boycotts, the story of the East River guerrillas during World War II, the spill over to Hong Kong of the bitter civil war fought between the KMT and CCP on the Mainland, and the close connection between party activities in Hong Kong and Guangdong. The CCP could have tried to take back Hong Kong after the war but it decided as a matter of strategy to leave it in British hands because it served party interests (Chapters 3 and 4).

The second phase covers the immediate period after the CCP assumed power in 1949 and up until the start of the Cultural Revolution. By the 1950s, the CCP had become Mao Zedong's party. He had turned Marxism into the ultimate political truth. Ideology was enforced by mass political campaigns and non-believers were dealt with harshly. While land reform was imposed in Guangdong, Hong Kong became a sanctuary for those who managed to escape. This phase includes the impact of the Korean War on Hong Kong and a range of incidents that were a direct legacy of continuing conflicts between the KMT and CCP (Chapter 5).

The third phase is the decade of the Cultural Revolution between 1966 and 1976. The 1967 riots were perpetrated by CCP members in Hong Kong. What was extraordinary was Zhou Enlai's role in protecting Hong Kong to the best of his ability because he believed in the colony's continuing usefulness to the CCP. His efforts were the signals to the British that the 1967 riots did not have Beijing's full backing. By the end of the riots, the CCP's apparatus in Hong Kong was almost completely destroyed with the Hong Kong community turning away from Marxism–Maoism totally (Chapter 6).

The fourth period covers the early part of the Deng Xiaoping era. Once China decided to take back Hong Kong at the end of 1981, it was vital for the CCP to work out how it was going to resume sovereignty and create its own post-colonial establishment. The party concluded the Sino-British Joint Declaration and began to draft a post-1997 constitution for Hong Kong called the Basic Law. A senior cadre, Xu Jiatun, was sent to plan for the resumption of sovereignty. He launched a new propaganda and united front campaign in Hong Kong that targeted the tycoons and economic elites so that they could be won over to the side of the CCP and away from the departing British (Chapters 7 and 8).

The fifth phase is the post-Tiananmen period, when the CCP faced many difficulties in reviving its credibility. The party thought the British might have second thoughts about giving up Hong Kong. In the final five years of colonial rule, the CCP had to deal with the last governor of Hong Kong whose push for modest democratic reform roused suspicion that the British wanted to make post-1997 politics hard to manage for the Chinese. The local party machinery went all out to counter that "sinner for a thousand years"—Chris Patten—although it had limited success in denting the governor's popularity with the public (Chapter 9).

The last phase deals with the first two decades of the HKSAR. Hong Kong's post-colonial establishment—a creation of the CCP—was based on a two-prong design: first, by packing tycoons, their children, and their nominees into a political structure dominated by voting blocks of vested interest to select the chief executive and to fill half the seats of the Legislative Council; and second, to beef-up a major pro-government political party—the Democratic Alliance for the Betterment and Progress of Hong Kong (DAB)—as well as support patriotic groups and individuals to be politically active so that they could dominate the political structure. However, the CCP has given itself the unenviable task of mediating and perpetuating their various interests. Despite the dominance of the pro-government forces, the CCP apparatus in Hong Kong failed to save the first chief executive, Tung Chee Hwa (1997–2005), who resigned before completing his second term. His successor,

Donald Tsang (2005–2012), a career civil servant, was expected to do better but ended his term being even less popular than his predecessor. Worse, after he left office he was prosecuted and convicted of misconduct in public office for failure to disclose a conflict of interest. Leung Chun Ying (2012–2017), the third and least popular chief executive, became the focus of constant and intense bashing. The last chapter of this book covers the period from 1997 to 2017—the sixth phase, when the younger generations in Hong Kong created a new rhetoric of "localism" but some crossed the line of the CCP's tolerance by calling for "self-determination" and "independence".

Two Interwoven Issues

Dealing with capitalism

This first decade of post-1997 coincides with the start of a new century when the CCP stopped referring to itself as a "revolutionary party".[6] Instead, it practises "capitalism under CCP leadership".[7] In the past, it was the party's job to lead the revolution. Today, it is the party's leadership that will bring about market reform. In other words, the words and policy goals have changed, but not the supreme status of the CCP in China. Indeed, the supremacy of the party remains a key regime value (Chapter 2).

Hong Kong's electoral design may well have given the party comfort about how to manage capitalism on the Mainland. By managing the leading capitalists, the CCP could manage capitalism. It would involve tolerating exploitation for the sake of prosperity and stability, and balancing the vested interests of various groups. Hong Kong's constitution, the Basic Law, was designed to embed vested interests into the electoral system through subsectors and functional constituencies.

From the early 1980s, CCP leaders had to focus on how socialist China could deal with capitalist Hong Kong. Deng Xiaoping promised that Hong Kong could continue to "race horses and go dancing" after 1997. He also stressed that as long as a person supported China regaining sovereignty over Hong Kong, it did not matter what kind of belief he or she held. Feudalism and even slavery could be tolerated. In other words, socialist China was prepared to tolerate even the worst exploitation in Hong Kong under its one country, two systems principle, and that the policy would not change for 50 years. Indeed, the CCP was ready to accept inequality on the Mainland too. Deng Xiaoping had said in the 1980s that in the early days of economic reform, some people could get rich first. Two decades later, the rich had to be integrated into the party.

In 2001, Jiang Zemin promoted the idea that the party must open its door to "new classes" signalling the end of Marxist class struggle. He championed the Three Represents ideology as one of the ruling theories of the CCP to legitimise the inclusion of capitalists and private entrepreneurs into the party.[8] According to official surveys, 33.9 percent of private entrepreneurs were party members in the mid-2000s; and a decade later, 40 percent of private entrepreneurs were party members.[9] A probable reason why the percentage is so high is that when the state-owned enterprises were privatised in the earlier days, their leading managers and cadres frequently became the proprietors and senior executives of the repackaged corporations. In more recent times, entrepreneurs and young people join the party because it provides access and latent advantages. Thus, to an important extent, the CCP membership of the new business class reflects the CCP's involvement in the creation of private enterprise. By 2014, the private sector produced at least two-thirds of China's gross domestic product.[10]

The Mainland's wide wealth gap between urban and rural communities became a cause for concern.[11] The Three Represents ideology is meant to strengthen the CCP's authority and legitimacy. Party leaders probably believe that through the party system they can rein in the capitalists when necessary to ensure that they are not overly exploitative. Perhaps they also believe that since the party can manage almost anything with adequate planning why not capitalism and markets too? After all, there are now millions of party members working in the private sector.[12] The CCP's united front successes in Hong Kong might have resulted in its added confidence that capitalism can be managed via managing the capitalists. Indeed, as Xu Jiatun observed, capitalists' political inclinations usually follow their business interests and so they can be brought under control by providing the right incentives or disincentives.

The rich and poor divide in Hong Kong is now among the widest in the world.[13] Beijing's attempt in the past to maintain prosperity may well have contributed to stretching the wealth gap. When the colonial administration sought to increase welfare spending in 1995, a deputy director of the Hong Kong and Macau Affairs Office described it thus: "It's like a Formula One car [referring to Hong Kong] which is going to crash and kill all six million people [what additional welfare would do]."[14] Tung Chee Hwa blamed the colonial administration for having increased social spending and sought to downplay his own fiscal expansion in 1998.[15] By 2012, Leung Chun Ying acknowledged the wide wealth gap and made fighting poverty a key plank of his administration.

Another complaint in Hong Kong, especially during the terms of office of Tung Chee Hwa and Donald Tsang, is "business—politics collusion", which shows the public's doubt over how the public interest can be safeguarded when economic vested interests are embedded into the political system. The choice to co-opt mainly rich businessmen to draft the Basic Law in the 1980s and into the post-reunification ruling establishment led to their interests being given political priority. Today, the CCP faces the same dilemma as the British. Without allowing the people of Hong Kong to choose their own local leaders, who else could be found to endorse and perpetuate the political system except the business elites? The CCP essentially decided to retain the colonial system because it was a tried and tested way to maintain central control.

The HKSAR government perceived devising policy as balancing interests. When Donald Tsang ran for re-selection in 2007, his campaign materials made clear that: "I will encourage government officials to change their mindset, from that of policy formulator to that of interest coordinator."[16] In making policy, officials would coordinate "interests" above all else. Perhaps Tsang was influenced by Hu Jintao's statement at the 17th National Party Congress that there was a "new situation" in the maintenance of the long-term stability and prosperity of Hong Kong, as well as the United Front Department's explanation of what Hu Jintao meant. As noted earlier in this chapter, the party's view of the "new situation" had to do with Hong Kong's local problems and conflicting interests. The United Front Department's explanation may have inspired Tsang to focus on interest coordination. In this light, the general public was just one stakeholder among many. Moreover, Tsang put his government's role of coordinating interests ahead of policy formulation. In other words, his administration's policies were interests-dependent, and the interests were those entrenched in the Hong Kong political system. Therefore, having majority support among the key political stakeholders became the deciding consideration in the formulation of government policy.[17] Taking an "interest coordination" approach might be considered politically pragmatic for the HKSAR government but it prevented better policies being made and in any event it did not make politics smoother for Donald Tsang. A new phenomenon arose post-2013 for Leung Chun Ying. The Legislative Council became mired in wide and extended filibustering, preventing government business from getting done. Governance could no longer be described as "efficient"—a positive aspect that Hong Kong had previously been able to assert.

Managing elections

Since the post-1997 political system in the HKSAR includes elections and the Basic Law states the "ultimate aim" is universal suffrage, there is no way for the CCP not to manage elections. Managing elections is about who gets elected. The outcome to date has been active management of the election of the chief executive and other elections. The party's blueprint is to ensure the chief executive is a trusted person, and that pro-government forces make up the majority in local political bodies and "anti-China" elements will not get too far. The assumption is that the "patriots" embedded in the system will support the HKSAR government.

So far, the chief executive has been someone chosen by the CCP. In direct geographical elections to the Legislative Council, the results are mixed. The pro-democracy camp captured the majority of the votes even though the proportional voting system limited the number of seats it won. In functional elections, the pro-government camp has always dominated especially in the constituencies that provide for corporate voting. However, the Article 23 legislation on national security, so important to the CCP, had to be withdrawn in 2003 under public protest. Instead, it led to the downfall of Tung Chee Hwa. Moreover, the HKSAR government does not feel it is able to practise executive-led government in the sense that it can always command enough votes in the legislature. The hodgepodge of groups that make up the pro-government coalition embodies a variety of interests that cannot be regarded as a majority party in power. Even bills that were unrelated to constitutional development failed—such as on copyright and medical council reform—due to extended filibustering in 2016. Despite the CCP's hard work, Hong Kong became hard to govern. The proposal for the 2017 chief executive election by universal suffrage failed in 2015—but the CCP is probably not unhappy about that.

The New Political Order

A key part of taking back Hong Kong for the CCP was to build a new political order there with a set of regime values based on Beijing's definition of "one country, two systems". The new hegemony of beliefs and ideology had to be frequently repeated post-reunification. The people of Hong Kong seem to keep forgetting them. There are several features of this new ideology.

- Acceptance of China's sovereignty over the HKSAR. The HKSAR is subordinate to Beijing, and a high degree of autonomy does not mean full autonomy.
- Implementation of the Basic Law, including respecting the fact that the HKSAR has an executive-led (not legislative-led) political system.
- Consideration of Beijing's interests, views and concerns, especially as they relate to national security so as to prevent the HKSAR from being used as an anti-China base by "foreign forces".
- The HKSAR is to be governed by "patriots" who share the regime values of the new political order.[18]

The chief supporters and advocates of the new political order are the business elites, rural interests, the old-time leftists, and others who have reoriented their beliefs and ideology towards China. The chief opposition consists of the pro-democracy politicians and advocates who are considered by the CCP to be steeped in Western political ideals, who want to bring full democracy to Hong Kong—a departure from how the Central Authorities see how one country, two systems should work.

The new political order and its values are rejected by the younger generations in Hong Kong. The unexpected Occupy and Umbrella Movements in 2014 galvanised the young and their Hong Kong-centric orientation (i.e., localism), which challenged not only the pro-government camp but also the traditional democrats. The young people of Hong Kong find the entire establishment outdated and disappointing. Worse, a poll in July 2016 showed one in five Hong Kong residents, especially those who were younger and better educated, preferred "independence" for Hong

Kong after 2047.¹⁹ For the CCP, the ugly head of an independent Hong Kong must be quashed (Chapter 10).

"Coming Out" Party

The CCP presence in Hong Kong under British rule was hidden behind a wholesale tea company during the war years, and then sheltered from 1946 behind the curtains of a news agency. Party members have revealed that when they joined the party in the past they were taken to Guangzhou to process the formalities for admission, which required the applicant to provide detailed background information. Members' files were kept in a two-storey building at Xiaobei Huayuan (小北花園) in Guangzhou where CCP Hong Kong had an office. As part of the initiation process, a new member would attend briefings.²⁰ It is unclear how someone from Hong Kong joins the CCP today but there must be some similarity to the process on the Mainland, where one has to apply and be recommended to join the party, disclose personal and family information, take courses and tests, be on probation for a period of time, and pledge to implement party decisions.

Is it finally time for the CCP to "come out" in Hong Kong? After all, Li Hou of the Hong Kong and Macao Affairs Office in Beijing has already stated in 1986 that the CCP has always been in Hong Kong.²¹ Yet, the only times when the CCP and its operation was discussed at some length in public prior to 1997 were during two motion debates in 1995 and 1997 in the Hong Kong Legislative Council. An assemblage of what was said then provides a useful reminder of just how many of the political elites in Hong Kong knew about the existence of the CCP but most of them did not wish to consider whether the party should operate in the open or not after reunification.²²

> [The] ruling party in China is the Communist Party which is represented by the Xinhua News Agency in Hong Kong . . . Is there anyone who does not know that the Chinese Communist Party's representative organ has already been existing in Hong Kong?
>
> Will the CCP rule over Hong Kong? If it did, it would have to go through the process of election. (Allen Lee, Liberal Party, 1995; 1997)
>
> I find it difficult to understand why such a motion has been moved . . . unless it is to create maximum worry among already worried Hong Kong residents, the vast majority of whom have already indicated clearly their wish to stay out of politics . . . If there is a communist cell in Hong Kong . . . it apparently has not caused any instability so far. . . . (Elsie Tu, 1995)
>
> We all know that the existence of the Communist Party . . . in Hong Kong is the result of historical development . . . this motion . . . is not justified in terms of jurisprudence. (Philip Wong, 1995)
>
> I feel that the local people are not that afraid of the CCP. (Tam Yiu Chung, DAB-FTU, 1995)

> We believe that if the Chinese Communist Party continues to carry out covert activities in Hong Kong, the confidence of the people of Hong Kong will be consequently be undermined. (Frederick Fung, Association for Democracy and People's Livelihood, 1995)
>
> [the] operation of the Chinese Communist Party started long time ago and has existed for a long time. Hong Kong people all know the operation and the nature of the New China News Agency . . . All along, the Chinese Communist Party has been operating in the form of an underground party in Hong Kong and its activities are not conducted openly . . . After the handover in 1997, the activities of the Communist Party will increase rather than decrease. (Anthony Cheung, Democratic Party, 1997)
>
> to hold discussion on this topic now will . . . only confuse the public. There is nothing to worry about. (Ip Kwok Him, DAB, 1997)
>
> We also have Chinese Communist Party members in Hong Kong. Again, so what? (David Chu, Hong Kong Progressive Alliance, 1997)

In December 1996, Tung Chee Hwa was asked how he would handle the relationship with Xinhua Hong Kong—in other words the CCP—if he were selected to be the first chief executive. Tung sidestepped the question by saying that he understood many Hong Kong people worried that Xinhua Hong Kong would become the "king of kings" in Hong Kong in future but he did not believe it would happen because the Central Government would respect one country, two systems.[23]

Rumours of who are party members among the post-1997 elites have been raised in Hong Kong from time to time. For example, an academic said in a seminar in Hong Kong in May 1997 that he believed there were four underground party members in Tung Chee Hwa's then Executive Council.[24] Another report noted that a political advisor to Tung was an active leftist student involved in the riots in 1967 and a party member.[25] There was yet another report that claimed that the then Secretary for Justice, and a member in the Central Policy Unit, were also local CCP members.[26] Questions were asked directly of Tsang Yok Sing, a founding member and former chairman of the DAB, and president of the Legislative Council (2008–2016), whether he was a party member. His answer is illuminating as to how the CCP likely sees its place in Hong Kong society:

> In fact, since the founding of the DAB, I have been asked [whether I am a CCP member] many times . . . I can say frankly, I have never answered this question. The reason is, Hong Kong people's attitude to the concept of the Communist Party is very negative. (*South China Morning Post*, 8 October 2008)[27]
>
> On being asked whether he was a CCP member: "I am so disappointed that you asked me about this. It is only a small issue. It is no big deal." (*South China Morning Post*, 4 February 2009)[28]

Indeed, Hong Kong people have known about the existence of the CCP in Hong Kong for a long time and are desensitised to the party's involvement in local politics probably because they know they must accept it. Part and parcel is the known fact that the nation is a one-party state. A survey conducted by the Hong Kong Transition Project in 2007 (see Appendix I) for the first edition of this book showed that there was 44 percent overall satisfaction with the Chinese government ruling China as a whole. Veteran NPC member Ng Hong Man's assessment was that many Hong Kong people thought positively about the Chinese economy and China's rising global status, but they disapproved of the widespread corruption and the lack of personal liberty and democracy on the Mainland.[29] As regards the CCP and Hong Kong, 47.1 percent of the survey respondents believed the CCP understood Hong Kong people's views while 41.2 percent did not think so. The rest were unable to offer a view. The responses also showed Hong Kong people knew the CCP influenced Hong Kong political affairs quite substantially:

Concern about CCP interference in Hong Kong affairs: 50.9 percent of the respondents said they were not worried about CCP interference in Hong Kong affairs, while 36.2 percent ranged from slightly worried to somewhat worried. There were 9.9 percent who were very worried, and 3.1 percent who did not know.

CCP influence over HKSAR government: 12.5 percent felt there was a great deal of interference, 39.1 percent felt the CCP was "somewhat" interfering, 20.2 percent thought interference was "not so much" while 7.2 percent thought there was no interference from the party; 18.3 percent were unable to express a view.

One aspect of the 2007 survey that deserves highlighting still is about party membership in Hong Kong. The majority of the respondents preferred not to know.

CCP membership declaration: On being asked whether CCP membership in Hong Kong should be declared, 36.1 percent of the respondents supported transparency and 2.8 percent thought declaration should be made in the future. However, 46.8 percent felt things should "continue as they are"—that is for party membership not to be declared. Of the remaining respondents, 1.5 percent thought the subject was "too sensitive", while 12.7 percent did not know.

A survey in 2016 asked respondents on their level of trust in the Chinese government as part of a survey on Hong Kong's political development. Answers were given on a scale from 0 to 10 (0 being no trust at all; 10 being having total trust; and 5 being so-so). The largest group was level 5 (22.5 percent), followed by level 0 (18.5 percent), with an overall mean of 4.36.[30]

The CCP had obviously discussed how it should function in Hong Kong post-1997. Xu Jiatun, who was the head of the party in Hong Kong from 1983 to 1990, noted that:

After 1997, the leading organ of the Work Committee [i.e., CCP] should exist openly. But the grassroots organisations of the party should continue to play a secret role. Moreover the Work Committee should be separated from [Xinhua Hong Kong] and be renamed the Hong Kong Region Work Committee. It should be run openly. However, after the return of sovereignty over Hong Kong to China, it is unreasonable that the Communist Party, the ruling party of China, will still be an underground party in Hong Kong whose activities are regarded as unlawful. Since the DAB was formed, we can arrange for all or a large number of members of the underground party to join the DAB to preserve their roles as party members, and the DAB's platform will be their programme of action. All in all, this sensitive issue within the party and the society of Hong Kong must be discussed and resolved now, as 1997 is approaching.[31]

Xu Jiatun's view was understandable—when Hong Kong would become Chinese territory, the ruling party should no longer demean itself by functioning as an underground party. Nevertheless, he envisaged grassroots organisations of the CCP would continue to play a secret role post-1997. If the party were to operate openly, but its grassroots bodies, such as trade unions, youth groups, and women's groups, would not reveal themselves as party organs, then in effect only some party members would acknowledge their party membership while allowing others to continue to hide it. Xu's views were prescient. It would prove to be the case (Chapter 10).

The underground nature of the CCP in Hong Kong arose out of complicated history. Prior to reunification it suited both the British and Chinese sides to keep a veil drawn over the existence of the CCP in Hong Kong. Hong Kong was British territory to the British and Chinese territory to the Chinese. The situation was made more difficult by the KMT and its past activities in the colony. Yet, Hong Kong was not torn apart by the longstanding conflicts between the KMT and CCP, and between China and the Western powers. Quiet accommodations were reached. Official silence on the part of the British about the CCP was one notable example of omissions that were considered necessary prior to 1997 in order to hold the colony together. The attempt to raise the subject for discussion in the Legislative Council in 1995 and 1997 ran into a complete stonewall from the colonial administration, and at the same time caused the leftist camp to go into almost hysterical overdrive. The veil of silence made it impossible, or at least extremely awkward, to say anything about the party in Hong Kong prior to 1997. However, this habit has extended beyond 1997 to the reunified HKSAR.

Omissions and evasions have taken a toll on public discourse. Perhaps it could be said in the past that to acknowledge and talk about the ideological contradictions running through Hong Kong in public was to revive them but with the colonial era having ended more than two decades ago, it cannot possibly still be so. On the Mainland, CCP leadership is pervasive. The party is embedded throughout the Chinese government structure and the management of state-owned enterprises, as well as many other types of mass institutions, such as trade unions and universities. It should be entirely appropriate for Hong Kong people to openly discuss party policies towards the HKSAR and how the party operates in Hong Kong. It is no secret that the CCP carries out extensive propaganda and united front work in Hong Kong, and that it has a large structure that is coordinated and led today by the Liaison Office of the Central People's Government in the HKSAR (Liaison Office). It is well-organised, well-funded, and politically active, including in elections. The people of Hong Kong know the CCP is there wielding considerable day-to-day influence in the affairs of the HKSAR government.

The CCP releases figures from time to time on membership so we know there are nearly 90 million members in total by 2016. However, since the party is an underground organisation in Hong Kong, there is no authoritative information on the number of party members there. In the mid-1980s, there were apparently about 6,000 members according to Xu Jiatun with about half being local members from Hong Kong and the rest from the Mainland.[32] According to other sources, figures in the region of 15,000 and 28,000 had been suggested for the period around 1997.[33] Yet another estimate was that between 1983 and 1997, some 83,000 Mainland officials with changed names and false identities have entered Hong Kong as part of a covert scheme to groom a political force in Hong Kong so as to promote Beijing's long-term interests. The logic of creating this fifth column was described to have emanated from Beijing's "underlying fears, suspicion and distrust" (Chapter 9).[34] Whatever may be the true number of party members in Hong Kong, the number is likely to be rather large by now. Perhaps this is why nearly 47 percent of the respondents to the 2007 survey mentioned above preferred not to know: because they realised they might find the truth disconcerting.

This is precisely the issue. Continuing to operate the CCP in Hong Kong in secret can only cause unnecessary discomfort. Hong Kong people already accept the CCP's undoubted authority in leading the affairs of state. What Hong Kong people want is the party's willingness to enable Hong Kong to function with a high degree of autonomy including being able to pursue and achieve the "ultimate aim" of universal suffrage provided for in the Basic Law. For nearly four decades now, Hong Kong people have come to see the pursuit of greater democracy as an important way to guarantee their freedoms, sustain open government, and underpin good governance. The executive-led system based on functional elections is not seen to be able to deliver good governance. The essential issue between Hong Kong and Beijing lies at the crux of how the party sees these goals can be achieved.

The CCP had promoted universal suffrage in its early days. However, its view today is that democracy could spell the end of one-party rule and also throw China into chaos, as politicians resort to social and ethnic divisions to mobilise votes. Beyond losing elections, the party elites are biased against the working and peasant classes, who would have a good chance to win power under the Western "bourgeois" model of universal suffrage, but workers and peasants are considered unsuitable to hold power because they are poorly educated. Matters are further complicated by the Mainland's historical experience. On occasions when the CCP has allowed public discussion of its performance, the people's negative reaction had been too uncomfortable to bear, such as during the Hundred Flowers Campaign, and the brief Democracy Wall period. Deng Xiaoping tried to rationalise the hostility to democracy on the grounds of the low educational standards of the nation—which he then applied to Hong Kong in a well-known speech.[35]

Chinese leaders do not regard liberal democracy as the path for China. In fact, they see their success since the 1980s as demonstration that authoritarian regimes can be effective in improving people's lives and the CCP has earned performance legitimacy. They see the rise of China is a great unfolding drama led by the party, and that economic growth has to be coupled with active diplomacy to transform Chinese power and influence around the world. Hong Kong was extremely important to China in the 1980s and 1990s, when it was the crucial gateway for trade, capital, and investment but that dependency has dropped significantly. Today, CCP leaders feel they need to assert and repeat the party's values and regime outlook in Hong Kong and to stamp out talk about self-determination and independence, lest such dangerous ideas stoke similar ones elsewhere in the country. They also wish to show their tolerance has limits. To the younger generations in Hong Kong, whose values are liberal, the party's rhetoric and values are unattractive. They are dissatisfied with unfair politics. They hope for a sign that the political system can be revamped—so that there can be better policies for society to progress. As the vast majority of Hong Kong people accept Hong Kong is a part of the People's Republic of China, and the noise of self-determination and independence will likely die down, the CCP will still have to face the question of the efficacy of the current political system that has entrenched certain vested interests and whether that can promote good governance, social equity, and a competitive economy in Hong Kong.

1
Party Supremacy and Hong Kong

The key regime value of the Chinese Communist Party that Hong Kong has to contend with is the supremacy of the party. Marxism as a set of economic theories has never received much interest and attention in Hong Kong, and in any event, by 1984, China's own economic reforms were beginning to depart from them. Thus, it was not Marxism that the party wanted to impart to Hong Kong but the regime's views and values, which are rooted in the Leninist concept of party supremacy, more commonly referred to as "party leadership". As noted in the Introduction, the one country, two systems principle that applies to the HKSAR emphasises "one country". To enjoy the second system, the people of Hong Kong must accept party leadership.[1] The party's worldview and its beliefs form the backdrop against which it makes decisions about Hong Kong. This translates into a new political order where political life in Hong Kong can be seen through the party's activities in managing the media, controlling key appointments to public bodies, supporting the post-1997 administration, giving its preferred candidates a helping hand at elections, and having a governing team of Mainland officials and cadres to ensure the one country, two systems project is successfully implemented.

Party-Government Structure

The Constitution of the People's Republic of China states that supreme power rests with the National People's Congress (NPC), with the Standing Committee of the National People's Congress (SCNPC) being the most important. However, it also provides that the CCP is the leading force in the country. In order to ensure the party's leadership in government, the CCP has a system whereby the party and government structures run in parallel to each other. In addition, there is a party group system that is embedded in each government body. When the term the Central Authorities (*Zhongyang*) is used, it refers to this party-government structure at the top, which is situated in Beijing. Thus, at each level of government—the centre, province, municipality, city, county, township, and autonomous regions—there is a full array of party groups with the party having committees, branches, and cells embedded within the government organs. The party organ supervises the government of the corresponding level. This organisation principle also applies to the NPC, the Chinese People's Political Consultative Conference (CPPCC), the courts and public prosecution, state-owned companies, trade unions, and other mass organisations, and is no different in the HKSAR where Mainland organisations are concerned.[2]

Figure 1 China's parallel system of power[3]

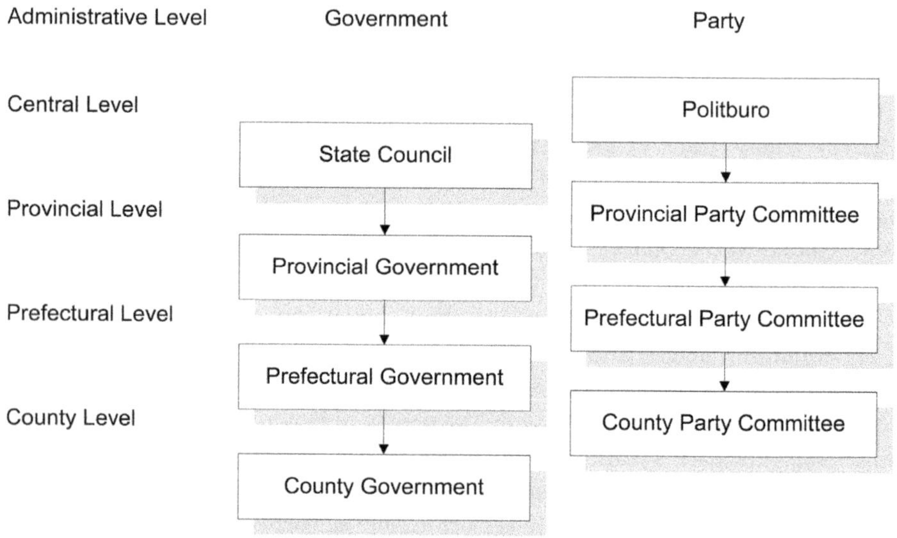

Administrative Level	Government	Party
Central Level		Politburo
	State Council	
Provincial Level		Provincial Party Committee
	Provincial Government	
Prefectural Level		Prefectural Party Committee
	Prefectural Government	
County Level		County Party Committee
	County Government	

China's governing principle is that the party makes policy and the government carries it out. The People's Liberation Army is a core component of the party system and not the government system. The army is ranked on par with the State Council, the government's highest level of authority. This means the government does not control the army. Instead, the military answers to a party organ, the Military Affairs Commission. In other words, the party controls both the government and the army.

Figure 2 The party group system in government bodies[4]

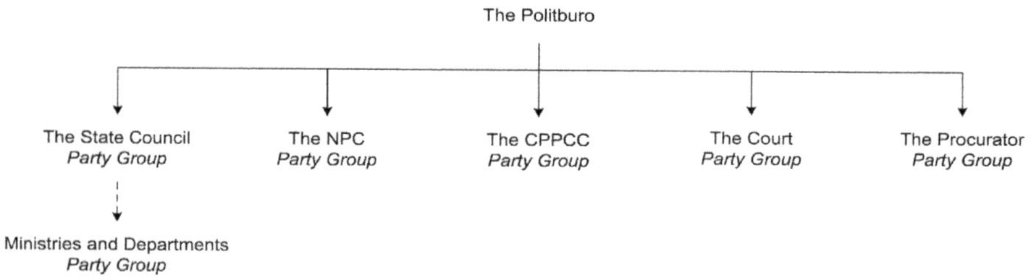

The Politburo
- The State Council Party Group
  - Ministries and Departments Party Group
- The NPC Party Group
- The CPPCC Party Group
- The Court Party Group
- The Procurator Party Group

Figure 3 The party group system in mass organisations[5]

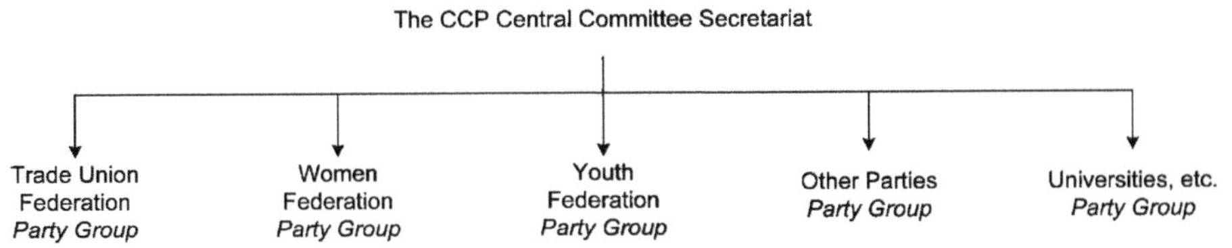

```
                    The CCP Central Committee Secretariat
    ┌───────────────┬───────────────┬───────────────┬───────────────┐
    ↓               ↓               ↓               ↓               ↓
Trade Union      Women          Youth         Other Parties   Universities, etc.
Federation     Federation     Federation      Party Group      Party Group
Party Group    Party Group    Party Group
```

The CCP Constitution stipulates that the National Party Congress and the CCP Central Committee elected by the National Party Congress are the party's highest decision-making organs. Party congresses occur approximately every five years and one of their key tasks is to set a new term of the CCP Central Committee.[6] Another crucial aspect of a party congress is the Political Report delivered by the highest ranking party member, the general secretary. The Political Report serves to establish the party's line in all major policy areas until the next congress. The hierarchical nature of the party system is designed to give the leaders in Beijing the power to set the national agenda. The highest central body for this purpose is the Politburo of the CCP. The 18th Party Congress had a 25-member Politburo, likewise the 19th Party Congress. The Politburo's Standing Committee is the most powerful body in the entire party system. The Standing Committee of the 18th Party Congress only had 7 members, as does the Standing Committee of the 19th Politburo. Generally, each Politburo member also holds a substantive position in the party. The Politburo is nominally appointed by the CCP Central Committee. The Central Committee arising from the 18th Party Congress had 205 members and 168 alternate members comprising of leading cadres throughout the country,[7] while the 19th Central Committee had 204 members and 172 alternate members. In reality, the Politburo determines the list of nominees to the CCP Central Committee. The CCP Central Committee meets in plenary sessions (known as *plenums*) at least once every year. Most day-to-day policy-making for the party is left with the Politburo and its Standing Committee. The Politburo is served by the Secretariat of the CCP Central Committee, which is a permanent party bureaucracy and is headed by the general secretary.

The dozen or so CCP Central Committee departments and committees have responsibility for specific areas and feed into Politburo decision-making. Important organs include the Organisation Department, United Front Department, and Propaganda Department.[8] All three departments are core organs of the party. The Organisation Department deals with personnel appointments. The Propaganda Department interacts with a large number of party and government departments and bodies to explain the party line and sustain party image. The United Front Department is the party's face in Chinese society. It coordinates with all kinds of official and societal bodies and activities. Chapter 2 discusses propaganda and united front work to provide a context for the discussion of these activities in subsequent chapters. There is also the Central Commission for Discipline and Inspection, which looks after the party's internal rules and regulations, including fighting corruption.

The CCP Central Committee usually designates a senior party leader to oversee important areas. Thus, Qian Qichen, the former Politburo member and foreign minister, looked after Hong Kong matters for some years straddling the transition. The CCP Central Committee may also form Leadership Small Groups for specific areas of work, and the one on Hong Kong and Macao affairs has existed for many years. After the massive demonstration in Hong Kong in 2003 against the passage of the Article 23 national security legislation, the reassessment of the party's Hong Kong policy was chaired by Politburo member Zeng Qinghong. Other Politburo members who have overseen Hong Kong matters post-1997 include Xi Jinping and Zhang Dejiang. Moreover, there is also the Work Committee which supervises the political life and discipline of all party members in the central party machinery. At each lower level, a party committee exercises power. Thus, the next level below the central level is the Provincial Party Committee, followed by the Municipal Party Committee and so on.

In Hong Kong, prior to 2000, the party's organ operated out of Xinhua Hong Kong sharing the same office location in Happy Valley. Its real name was the Hong Kong and Macao Work Committee of the CCP (CCP Hong Kong).[9] Since January 2000, the physical location of the Xinhua News Agency as a news organisation has been separated from the location of the party organ. The Xinhua News Agency now befits its name. The party and government organ is now the Liaison Office of the Central People's Government in the HKSAR. The Liaison Office, located in the Western District, is responsible for coordination work with Mainland organisations in Hong Kong including the People's Liberation Army, which has been stationed in Hong Kong since 1997, and the Office of the Commissioner of the Ministry of Foreign Affairs, which is responsible for dealing with foreign affairs related to the HKSAR. As discussed in Chapter 10, the Liaison Office continues the party's work in post-reunification Hong Kong.

The top government organ in China, the State Council, functions like a cabinet and is headed by the premier, who is also a member of the Standing Committee of the Politburo. The State Council includes various ministries and commissions. In the case of Hong Kong, the State Council's Hong Kong and Macao Affairs Office has been the most important government organ.[10]

Despite the hierarchical and authoritarian nature of the Chinese governing system, actual authority is fragmented as a result of multiple reporting lines that run through the party structure, the government structure and the provinces, municipalities and other regions and areas. Thus, officials—referred to as functionaries or cadres (who may or may not be party members although almost all are members), who carry out party or government policies and programmes in any given office, have to answer to a range of bosses within different structures and places, and work out who has priority on a particular matter. The cadre core is considered the elite that provide leadership for the masses.[11] Lines of criss-crossing authority are exceedingly complex, as well as cumbersome, providing plenty of opportunities for one actor to frustrate policy implementation, especially since officials and units of the same bureaucratic rank cannot issue binding orders to each other. This was the case between the State Council's Hong Kong and Macao Affairs Office and Xinhua Hong Kong between 1983 and 1989, when Xu Jiatun was the director of Xinhua Hong Kong. His rank within the party was equivalent to that of Ji Pengfei, the head of the Hong Kong and Macao Affairs Office, and both were members of the CCP Central Committee although Ji would enjoy greater prestige having once been foreign minister. Turf battles continued with their successors Lu Ping and Zhou Nan (Chapters 8 and 10).

The CCP controls career mobility for the party and non-party elites who run the extensive public sector in China. This responsibility covers government positions, the legislature, judicial and procurator positions, and even positions in trade unions, youth leagues, women's federations, universities, and the state-controlled bodies. It uses the *nomenklatura* system as a way to lock party, government, and public sector officials into a tight web of control. The *nomenklatura* consists of two separate lists: one is a list of key positions and the other is a list of positions to be reported to a higher authority. Tens of thousands of positions appear on the two combined lists. Taken together, the lists extend central party control to deputy bureau chief-level in all central and provincial-level organs. The system distributes the authority to make appointments and dismissals among a number of different party organs, each controlling an array of positions. The interlocking nature of the Chinese governing system between party and government further consolidates party control.[12]

This web of political control from the Mainland extends formally into Hong Kong. The party has the authority to vet the appointments and dismissal of all significant leadership positions in Mainland organisations and all state-controlled companies operating in Hong Kong, including the appointments of Hong Kong deputies to the NPC, provincial and local congresses, as well as the national and local CPPCC. Post-1997, the Basic Law provides that the chief executive has to be formally appointed by the Central People's Government (Article 45), and that the positions of secretaries (ministers), deputy secretaries of departments (the most senior civil servants), directors of bureaux, the commissioner of the Independent Commission Against Corruption, director of audit, commissioner of police, director of immigration, and commissioner of Customs and Excise are also formally appointed by the Central People's Government upon the nomination of the chief executive (Article 48(5)). This means that post-1997 these positions have become a part of the *nomenklatura* system.[13]

The problems of the Chinese bureaucratic system and how to deal with intra-rank conflicts could be seen in the means by which Jiang Zemin, who was the

Chinese leader in power during the handover years, prohibited heads of CCP organs and their equivalents in government ministries, provinces, and municipalities from interfering in the affairs of Hong Kong. The prohibition was implemented through the careful placing of the position of the HKSAR chief executive within the Chinese party and state bureaucracies. The chief executive carries the rank of a vice-premier or state councillor, which is one grade above that of a minister or provincial governor. The Mainland only has four vice-premiers and five state councillors. Moreover, the HKSAR has a rank equivalent to that of the Mainland's special municipalities (Beijing, Tianjin, Chongqing, and Shanghai), whose party chief carries Politburo rank. Furthermore, Beijing has so far been careful in not putting a cadre in place to head CCP Hong Kong post-1997 who would carry a more senior rank than that of the chief executive (Chapter 10).

Handling Hong Kong Affairs

Once the Politburo has made a decision, the State Council implements it. In the case of Hong Kong affairs, once the Politburo has made a decision, there are two ministries within the State Council that are involved in carrying it out. The Hong Kong and Macao Affairs Office is responsible for overall administration. Under the Ministry of Foreign Affairs, the Office of Hong Kong and Macao Affairs was responsible before reunification for dealing with Britain and Portugal respectively.[14] After 1997, the Foreign Ministry remains involved and set up the Office of the Commissioner of China's Ministry of Foreign Affairs in Hong Kong to handle foreign affairs matters (Chapter 10). In addition, since 2000, the Liaison Office is the most important party-government organ in Hong Kong. Prior to 2000, the organ was publicly known as the New China News Agency, Hong Kong Branch (Xinhua Hong Kong) but it was really the Hong Kong and Macao Work Committee (referred to hereafter as CCP Hong Kong). The news agency was first set up in 1946. In 1949, when the CCP took power on the Mainland, Xinhua Hong Kong became a low-ranking divisional arm of the State Council to help with business transactions involving Hong Kong. In 1978, it was upgraded to a bureau-level organisation and placed under the newly formed Hong Kong and Macao Affairs Office under the State Council. After 1983, Xinhua Hong Kong was given full provincial grade in anticipation of the workload for the recovery of sovereignty.[15] However, after 1989, it was downgraded once more before being turned into the Liaison Office in 2000. There may well be further changes in the future (Chapters 4 and 10).

Lenin's Legacy

What became the party and state structures of communist states were developed under Vladimir Lenin's (1870–1924) rule in the Soviet Union, and the Chinese party structure was modelled on Leninist lines. Like its Russian counterpart, Chinese

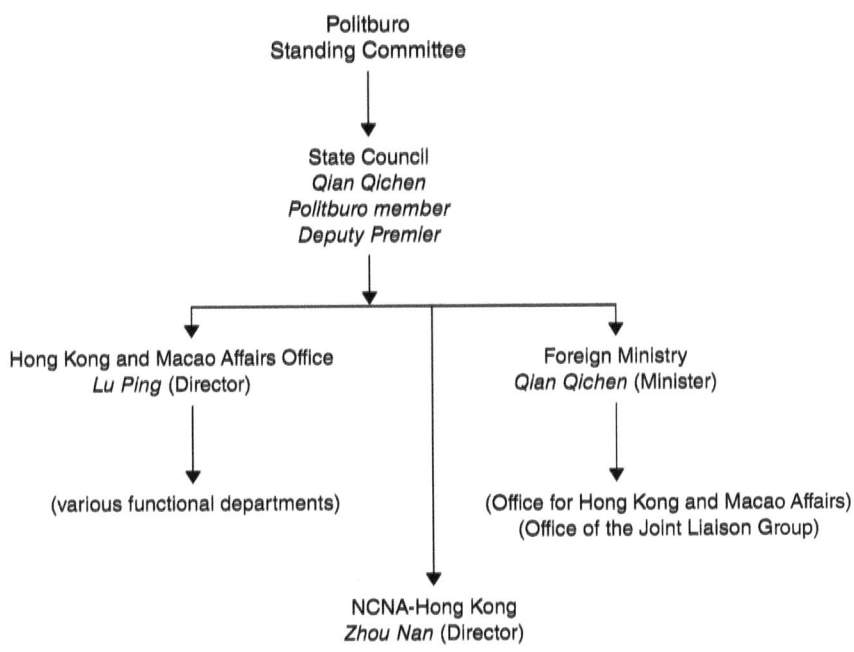

Figure 4 Handling of Hong Kong affairs prior to 1997[16]

communism was and is still based on dialectical materialism, the supremacy of the communist party, and a secret police.[17]

Lenin thought Russian workers could not develop by themselves the necessary political consciousness to create a revolution and that they needed an organisation through which professional revolutionaries would lead them. The party was the organisation to implement revolutionary change. The professionals were the party elites, the party acted as the vanguard of the proletariat (people), and the term "democratic dictatorship of the people" refers to the right of the party to permanent revolutionary leadership—in other words, to permanent rule. The term "dialectical materialism" in Leninism-speak means the responsibility of the party to do what it deems appropriate to "accelerate the march of history", which is the ultimate victory of communism.[18] "Marxism-Leninism" was coined after Lenin's death by Josef Stalin (1878–1953) who wanted to redefine Marxism in terms of his interpretation of Leninist theory and practice, in order to legitimise his ideological authority and policies.

In China, the history of the CCP is inseparable from the person of Mao Zedong until his death in 1976. He was a highly charismatic leader. Mao Zedong Thought is a variant of Marxism-Leninism, which sought to solve the problem of how to start a communist revolution in an overwhelmingly rural society. Marxism-Leninism did not regard the peasantry as the powerful revolutionary force that Mao believed was essential in China's circumstances. Mao was also concerned with creating a revolutionary movement while simultaneously waging war against the Japanese invasion. Mao noted that Lenin came to power as Russia agreed to end its war with Germany through massive concessions. Thus, compromising with the KMT was essential for the CCP to pursue its ultimate goals.

Maoism embodied Mao's thoughts on the politics, organisation, and strategy of revolutionary struggle. His vision was for the party to lead the Chinese peasantry to national transformation through an agrarian revolution. He emphasised the importance of "revolutionary mass mobilisation" to achieve socialism including using armed struggle and guerrilla tactics. Mao was the acknowledged leader of the Chinese Revolution because he was able to articulate ideas and mobilised a huge number of followers. Indeed, Mao's contribution to Marxism-Leninism was his ability to mobilise Chinese peasants to the communist cause. It was Mao who succeeded in turning to the peasantry and drew strength from China's rural vastness. He had the gift for understanding the aspirations of potential followers and of addressing them, as well as the charisma to activate and channel the energy of millions. Maoist China established the party structure and tools to enable the CCP to operate and then govern after 1949, the legacy of which remains today. The CCP structure is a well-oiled machine and a phenomenal piece of political machinery. Public life at every level in China is dictated by the party. Party leadership has been elevated to a way of life in the People's Republic. Looking back at China's history under the CCP, there were periods when endless time was spent in criticism, self-criticism, study groups, struggle meetings, and rectification campaigns designed to assert group purpose over individual thought. In implementing permanent class struggle—a key Maoist concept—there were interminable efforts after 1949 to root out corruptive "rightist" forces. This was the main justification for the Great Proletarian Cultural Revolution, when Mao called upon the people to wrest control from party and government officials, such as Deng Xiaoping, who had supposedly veered off the socialist path and became corrupt.

> **Marxist-Leninist Vocabulary**
>
> **Democratic Dictatorship of the People:** Right of the party to permanent revolutionary leadership.
>
> **Dialectical Materialism:** The action of the party to do what it deems fit to "accelerate the march of history" towards communism.
>
> **Historical Materialism:** claims to know the way history is moving and Communism is the path which the CCP leads.
>
> **Democratic Centralism:** is communist democracy and is the fundamental organisational and leadership system of the CCP. No cadre is allowed to place himself above party organisations.

> **Bourgeois Mentality:** Attitude that is focused on conventional respectability, property values, and capitalist pursuits that is exploitative in nature.

To carry out class struggle, the CCP had to evolve tools to do so. First of all, Marxism provided a whole new vocabulary for translation into Chinese, all of which was not easy to understand. Perhaps they appeared fashionable in the early days but doctrines such as "dictatorship of the proletariat", "dialectical materialism", "historical materialism", and "democratic centralism" became thought-terminating clichés. There were essential courses at party schools and study groups. Complex human problems were compressed into highly reductive phrases. These became the start and finish of any ideological analysis. During the thought reform period, discussed in Chapter 5, for instance, the phrase "bourgeois mentality" was used to dismiss individual expression, alternative ideas and balance in political judgments. Leninist-speak was loaded, relentlessly judging, and operated by the party to serve whatever was the cause of the day.[19] As Chapters 4 and 5 show, not only were national top leaders purged, but a number of party leaders connected to Hong Kong were also purged during the Cultural Revolution for their alleged bourgeois mentality and related failings. Today, the CCP mission is to "build socialism with Chinese characteristics" or "market socialism". The party's basic line is to build China into a strong and prosperous state by "taking economic development as the central task" and "adhering to the Four Cardinal Principles", which are to stay on the socialist road, continue with the people's democratic dictatorship, observe the leadership of the CCP, and hold-up Marxism-Leninism, Mao Zedong Thought, Deng Xiaoping Theory, and other contributions from recent and current leaders, such as Jiang Zemin's Three Represents, Hu Jintao's Scientific View of Development, and Xi Jinping's Chinese Dream. In political life, it is also necessary to uphold the party's basic line—that is, not deviate from party policies and decisions; "to seek truth from facts", which refers to using solutions that work;[20] "serve the people wholeheartedly", which expresses the moral ideal of unselfishness required of cadres, and "uphold democratic centralism", which reinforces party discipline.

Democratic centralism is the guiding principle for intra-party life. It is in effect an internal consultation system. Hong Kong had its first taste of how it works during the Basic Law drafting process (Chapter 8). The process for the selection of the chief executive of the HKSAR has the flavour of democratic centralism (Chapters 9 and 10). It is useful to remember that Leninist democratic centralism tolerates no opposition and competition because it is a one-party state vision of politics. The word "democratic" refers to the party internal consultation process. The party has a highly hierarchical structure. It is divided into cells which meet regularly to evaluate members' work and to make suggestions about how to improve it, and to evaluate the party's positions and make suggestions for change. These suggestions are taken by the cell leader to section meetings (made up of the cell leaders and other leading cadres in an area, and by section leaders to the CCP Central Committee. The party leadership decides on new positions (a new line) which all members are then bound to put into practice. Democratic centralism forces everyone to speak up. At cell meetings, each person must express his or her opinions, including openly voicing any disagreements. However, once a decision is made, "centralism" prevails and the decision must be implemented without deviation. On the Mainland, democratic centralism supposedly means a system of politics for all and not only for the party elites. Supporters of democratic centralism also argue that it forces people to evaluate themselves and listen to the evaluation of others. In defence of communist democracy, "bourgeois democracy", as practised in the West, is said to encourage politicians to hide their failures and for the political elites to exploit the people.[21] Democratic centralism may be said to combine the advantages of discipline without giving up the free airing of views and discussion but it has proven to be risky, as people who voiced politically incorrect ideas proved vulnerable for the views they expressed during consultation, such as during the Hundred Flowers campaign, Cultural Revolution, and other campaigns.[22] Moreover, the CCP continues to believe open, public, political debate and competition to be dangerous because they could result in chaotic politics and therefore social instability. This view is one that has been proffered to Hong Kong as a reason for slowing down democratic reform.

The application of Marxist-Leninist language and the creation of the democratic centralism structure within the CCP are meant to create a homogenous outlook among party members since ideology and discipline are so important for the party. Another party management tool was its class theory, which was the foundation of Chinese communism under Mao Zedong. He categorised Chinese society into various classes and ascribed certain political characteristics to each of them. There were the landlord class and comprador class, the middle bourgeoisie, the petite bourgeoisie, the semi-proletariat, the proletariat, and peasants. In good Soviet bloc tradition, in order to keep tabs on the people so as to be able to find out who was politically reliable and who not, the party developed extensive archives and personal dossier systems. A personal dossier contains detailed information about a particular person's family and past history and records of performance and attitudes. Apart from the usual biographical information of an individual, the Chinese dossier contains a lot of other information about family links, relationships, and political correctness. In the personal dossier of a typical urban worker, there would be academic reports from primary school to university, assessment reports by teachers, professional qualifications, work reports, employment records, assessments by supervisors and peers, membership of organisations including CCP membership and assessments, and any other information available about the individual. There are two copies of the dossier for every adult, one held by the person's work unit and the other by the local Public Security Bureau, the police in China. When the state was the sole employer in China, the work unit was where political campaigns were carried out. Indeed, the work unit was the fundamental link created under the

Chinese communist system to handle the relationship between the state and society. For an ordinary person, it is not easy to see one's own file. He or she has to seek the help of a party member, and then altering the file for correction is even more complicated because only special cadres can make alterations. A black mark anywhere could cause a lifetime of trouble during the Mao era since so much depended on it, including having to get the permission of one's work unit for travel, marriage, having children, divorce, and change of workplace. The fate of an individual in terms of career, employment benefits, and social services could be controlled by the CCP leadership within the work unit. The dossier was the forum upon which administrative decisions were made by the state relating to an individual. There was no escape by changing jobs because the dossier was where the transfer from one work unit to another would be authorised. Deng Xiaoping's reforms to the work unit system broke the tradition of categorising people according to their class and family origins in 1983, and by 2000, much of the oversight power of work units over their workers has been abolished. As economic reform continues with the state shrinking as the principal employer in the country, the personal dossier system has become less and less important, as there are a large and growing number of private sector jobs. At the end of 2017, there were over 65 million individually owned businesses and over 27 million private enterprises, which employed over 340 million people.[23] Nevertheless, the extensive dossiers on citizens remain for now.

In Hong Kong no such files exist, although there are many bits of information on all Hong Kong residents that are held by different government departments and public bodies. These are generated where an individual has had to deal with such organisations. Examples are driving licence applications, social welfare records, and hospital records. Also records of a private nature are held by private organisations. The Personal Data (Privacy) Ordinance passed in 1996 allows an individual to ask whether an organisation holds personal data pertaining to him or her and to apply for access, but this law does not apply to the CCP organs in Hong Kong yet, if it ever will. One Hong Kong legislator had the audacity to use this Ordinance to ask the Director of Xinhua Hong Kong whether his agency held a file on her (Chapter 10).

As for party members' dossiers, with nearly 90 million members today, the task of keeping their files is daunting. Reports in the 1980s showed that one person is designated to work on keeping the dossiers of every 1,000 members.[24] The number of keepers of such dossiers must be large even today with the advance of computer technology. The local party committees are responsible for keeping the dossiers of lower ranking members. According to Xu Jiatun, the files of CCP Hong Kong, presumably including those of party members in Hong Kong, were kept in Guangzhou at the No. 8 Office of the Guangdong Provincial Party Committee, where Xinhua Hong Kong's office was during his time.[25] This has been corroborated by a former party member.[26] The CCP Central Committee is responsible for the dossiers of members with ranks of vice-ministers and deputy heads of provincial organisations.

The dossiers of prominent non-party members are kept by the United Front Department and its subsidiaries.

Civil Society

In Hong Kong, civil society groups are a part of daily life and have been for a long time. In 2014, Hong Kong had over 34,600 registered non-government organisations (NGOs).[27] Despite the attempts to control the political structure post-1997, Hong Kong has not turned into a place of a single official vision. Indeed, civil society is offering alternative and competing ideas to those of the HKSAR government; and the Hong Kong public is willing to fund them on many issues. Nevertheless, the amendment of the Societies Ordinance by the Provisional Legislature in 1997 reflects Mainland worries about anti-China influence (Chapter 10). Non-government groups are only slowly evolving on the Mainland, where there are over 500,000 registered NGOs and many more that are unregistered. The CCP is ambivalent about NGOs. While they help address many issues, such as poverty alleviation, education, public health, environmental protection, labour problems, and disaster relief, the party is concerned about potential challenges to its rule. In 2017, a tough law passed the previous year to regulate foreign NGOs took effect and is estimated to affect 10,000 overseas NGOs operating in China, including ones from Hong Kong. The new law would enable the authorities to weed out foreign NGOs that they find troublesome.[28]

2
The Chinese Communist Party Tools of Co-optation and Persuasion

One of the most important tools of the Chinese Communist Party is the "united front". Originally developed in the early days of the party, it is a strategy to unite with all forces that could be united with the CCP in order to fight a common enemy. It is thus a co-optation strategy to bring as many people on side as possible, and coupled with propaganda, these were, and remain, the essential hand-in-glove tools to win the "hearts and minds" of the Hong Kong community throughout much of the time that the party has been active there. While propaganda work provides the substance and materials of the party line on various issues, united front work targets people of influence to bring them on-side so that they could accept the party line or at least not object to it. United front and propaganda work are placed at the heart of the CCP's metabolism. The United Front Department and the Propaganda Department are two of the CCP Central Committee's core organs.

The success of the united front in Hong Kong during the transition years was helped by the certainty that China was going to resume sovereignty in 1997. United front work prior to 1997 focussed on promoting "patriotism", making people comfortable with China's resumption of sovereignty, emphasising the paramount importance of good communication between Beijing and Hong Kong, and that achieving democracy was not viable in the short term. Post-1997, the emphasis shifted to instilling a sense of nationalism among Hong Kong people, that "harmony" in politics would bring the "stability" necessary for economic advancement, and more significant democratic reform might be possible in the future if Hong Kong people became sufficiently patriotic. Working alongside united front efforts is the extensive propaganda system, which involves itself in many areas, such as culture, media, publishing, education, religion and sports, all helping to create a new political order to realise the CCP's vision for one country, two systems.

United Front Work: Get Up Close and Personal

United front work is about building personal relationships with a large group of non-party folks. It is heavy-manpower work requiring great patience and a large bevy of people to cultivate relations with all sorts of people in Hong Kong. Since personal relationships are very important in this line of work, the party often uses its best people for those contacts that are considered the most valuable. They would even pay attention to the target's birthday and other anniversaries to ensure gifts were sent and well-wishes delivered so that the friendship could be cemented. They would invite them to travel to the Mainland and to meet important people so as to give the target a sense that the authorities valued the relationship. It is vital that the target is made to feel important. Over time, trusted relations can be built but it is primarily professional in nature.

Intellectuals and artists have always been targets of the united front because they are valuable to propaganda work. They are seen as agents who can shape the message into something ordinary people can understand and associate with. The party has a long record in running study groups, organising classes and schools. It has also been publishing everything from leaflets, posters, journals, magazines and newspapers, producing films, songs, operas, as well as using the arts to promote its ideas. As can be seen in various chapters of this book, the CCP has engaged in all these activities in Hong Kong for a considerable period of time.

In CCP-speak, "intellectuals" include managers, administrators, technicians and experts. These people are often influential as models for other groups because as knowledgeable people they are considered to have social authority. In its battle for power with the KMT prior to 1949, the CCP built alliances with intellectuals and artists to help isolate the nationalists. By winning over more intellectuals to the revolutionary cause, the party could more successfully influence other groups to join in. In terms of its strategy to take back Hong Kong, cultivating the intellectuals in Hong Kong has also been one of the tactics.

The CCP may be said to have had five major united front episodes since its founding, with the fifth being the absorption of Hong Kong in 1997 and Macao in 1999, and thus most relevant to this book. For the sake of completeness, all five phases are noted below:

> **Phase I and Phase II—Draw strength through alliances:** The CCP had to enter into various alliances—"fronts"—because it was relatively weak and needed to build strength through collaboration with others. These were times to show willingness to negotiate and compromise because the communists were a minority. The first phase was between 1924 and 1927 when the KMT and CCP cooperated to fight the warlords during the Northern Expedition, and the second phase saw them banding together once more to fight the Japanese between 1936 and 1945. The "First United Front" and "Second United Front" are touched upon in Chapters 3 and 4. Chapter 4 enumerates many of the united front and propaganda activities in Hong Kong in order to support and raise funds for revolutionary activities on the Mainland, as well as establishing connections in various fields, such as culture, media and education, and establishing the Xinhua News Agency as the de facto presence of the CCP in Hong Kong in 1946.

Phase III—Transitional co-optation: After 1949, the CCP sought to achieve communism on the Mainland. In the early days, the party still needed time to train-up their own people and thus there were good reasons to be conciliatory, but it was also a time to use thought reform based on self-criticism and re-education to transform society. By 1957, Mao Zedong felt the transition had been sufficiently completed and the party could assert power. This stage then morphed into the Cultural Revolution. Throughout this period the CCP was busy with united front and propaganda activities in Hong Kong, with the Hong Kong communists provoking the riots of 1967 (Chapters 5 and 6).

Phase IV—Win back support: In 1979, a fourth united front was designed to give support to modernisation. Former allies and many others had to be rehabilitated from Cultural Revolution purges. United front work was necessary to bring about "socialism with Chinese characteristics". This is discussed in Chapter 7. This phase dovetailed with cultivating the Overseas Chinese elites, including those in Hong Kong, to assist China's modernisation by investing and setting up enterprises on the Mainland. This phase also overlapped with Phase V to take back capitalist Hong Kong as negotiations started with the British government in the early 1980s.

Phase V—Win over capitalists, stop independence advocacy: In order to resume sovereignty in 1997, a massive fifth united front campaign had to be rolled out in Hong Kong to build alliances with all manners of groups, but in particular with the political and economic elites of the day so as to win their loyalties. The "landlord", "comprador" and "bourgeoisie" classes were all to be actively cultivated. Anyone who supported reunification was a patriot even if they opposed socialism. Their self-interests also opened them to manipulation. Those who were co-opted were invited to sit on important bodies to legitimise the transition process to Chinese rule. Winning over capitalists is discussed in Chapters 8 and 9; Chapter 10 deals with the united front against independence advocacy.

It can be seen that it was at times of crisis or directional change that the role of ideas was most important to the party. After all, it is the strength of inspiring ideas that enable people to put up with inconveniences and make sacrifices for a better tomorrow. These are the junctures when heavy doses of propaganda and united front work were felt to be essential. Even those who could not be won over, work could still be focussed on ensuring that they remained neutral because their withdrawal would help to defeat the opposition. In other words, potential opposition could be neutralised. The united front strategy for Hong Kong was one of co-optation as well as exclusion. Co-optation may be defined as the process of formally incorporating individuals or groups into decision-making or consultative processes. The target may be helpful as an informant, adviser or committee member.[1] Those who were considered "representative" of key interest groups were targeted to be brought on-side as a matter of priority.

Anyone with influence can be useful to the CCP. For example, in united front work, there is no separation of church and state. Religious bodies in Hong Kong are seen to represent interests and they are seen to have influence over believers. Thus, representatives from various religions have been given seats on the Election Committee that selects the chief executive of the HKSAR as part of the CCP's united front strategy. In the mid-1980s, when united front work intensified, the most important targets were the political elites—the appointees to the Executive and Legislative Councils, the economic elites—the tycoons—and then the intelligentsia and the technical-managerial professionals. The party looks at representation not in terms of formal representation (i.e. public consent) but influence. The purpose of the strategy was to influence the outlook and decisions of leaders in various fields in Hong Kong because the party regarded them as important shapers and influential agents of its governing values and beliefs. Moreover, the united front enabled the targeted groups to grow accustomed to the fruits of their membership in the post-reunification establishment so that they have a stake in maintaining it. This was the inclusive side of the strategy.

There was also an excluding side that sought to sideline opposition voices. In classic united front fashion, anyone who could be brought on-side would be since it was best to minimise opposition than to fight them. Those who continued to oppose, however, became the enemy and the focus of attack for being "unpatriotic". For those who were co-opted—the "patriots", the price for basking in the new status was also to share the burden of the new ruling authority in maintaining the new status quo. The most influential individuals were given greater say in the drafting of the post-1997 constitution—the Basic Law—for example, whereas the less influential were given advisory positions or used for window-dressing. There was also a concerted effort to bring on-side former government officials, presumably because they could provide advice on how Hong Kong was administered and also, should there be a need, they could be asked to manage things post-1997. How the united front worked in Hong Kong during the transition years is explained in Chapters 8 and 9. Soon after 1997, it was necessary to continue the united front to nurture a new generation of pro-government supporters in Hong Kong, since those who had been co-opted from around 1984, when the Sino-British Joint Declaration was signed, were reaching retirement age. The next generation had to be organised differently because they had to face elections. Moreover, after more than a decade of Chinese rule, the younger generations felt Hong Kong was losing its identity, giving rise to "localism", and some even called for "self-determination" and "independence", which the party must quash. This last phase is discussed in Chapter 10.

Co-optation Bodies

A discussion about the united front would not be complete without touching upon the Chinese People's Political Consultative Conference and the National People's Congress because there has been a long tradition of appointing Hong Kong people to them as part of China's political co-optation strategy. In the past, leading pro-China left-wing figures from the labour, education, cultural and patriotic business sectors were appointed to serve in China's political institutions as representatives of Hong Kong compatriots. Apart from the national CPPCC and NPC, appointments were also made to provincial and municipal CPPCCs and local people's congresses. Between 1984 and 1997, China became much more active in co-opting Hong Kong elites from outside the traditional left-wing circles. Appointments to the CPPCC have been used as a way to cultivate people the CCP wanted to bring on-side. After all, there is no doubt about what the terms of reference of the CPPCC are:

> The Chinese People's Political Consultative Conference is an organisation of the united front of the Chinese people, an important institution of multi-party cooperation and political consultation under the leadership of the Communist Party of China, a major form for carrying forward socialist democracy in the political life of the country. Unity and democracy are two major themes of the Chinese People's Political Consultative Conference . . . The National Committee of the Chinese People's Political Consultative Conference shall be composed of the Communist Party of China, the various democratic parties, public personages without party affiliation, people's organisations, ethnic minority groups and people of all walks of life, compatriots of the Hong Kong Special Administrative Region, the Macao Special Administrative Region and Taiwan, returned overseas Chinese and specially invited personalities, who are divided into a number of sectors.[2]

The existence of this body pre-dated the establishment of the People's Republic. After World War II, there was a brief moment in time when the KMT and CCP agreed to an armistice and held talks in 1945 on post-war political reforms via a Political Consultative Conference, where other smaller parties were invited to join. This agreement to form such a conference was included in a wider agreement known as the Double Ten accord. The first assembly was held in Chongqing from 10 to 31 January 1946 with representatives from various groups but trust broke down between the KMT and CCP and civil war ensued (Chapter 4). After gaining control of most of the Mainland, the CCP organised a new consultative conference in September 1949 inviting delegates from various parties to attend and discuss constructing a new state with the CCP playing the leading role. This conference was then renamed the CPPCC, holding its inaugural meeting on 21 September 1949. It became the official manifestation of the united front with the mission to:

> realise New Democracy, oppose imperialism, feudalism, and bureaucratic capitalism and establish an independent, democratic, peaceful, united, prosperous, and strong new China. To this end, we unite with the democratic classes and

nationalities in the country and Overseas Chinese as well as form the great people's united front. It is not only the Chinese Communist Party which has been struggling for the last twenty-eight years to achieve this goal; the democratic parties, people's organisations, regions, troops and minorities nationalities, Overseas Chinese and democratic personages likewise favour and support it.[3]

In effect, the first conference was a quasi-constitutional body playing the role of a constitutional convention. It enabled party leaders, leading members of other smaller political parties who were the CCP's allies against the KMT, and representatives of mass groups to interact within an institutional framework. The CPPCC's 1949 Common Programme served as the state constitution until superseded by the 1954 Chinese Constitution. At the first CPPCC meeting, it also approved the new national anthem, flag, capital city, and state name, and created the first government. During the early years, the CPPCC was also the de facto legislature until the NPC was created and took over the role the CPPCC had played.

The major function of the CPPCC is to conduct political consultation. The national CPPCC usually has over 2,200 members and its Standing Committee usually has about 300 members.[4] The chairman of the CPPCC is usually the fourth ranking member of the Politburo. Members are selected through consultation and recommendation. The Standing Committee decides through consultation on the number of members and the candidates. The usual practice of the membership mix of the CPPCC is to adhere to a one-to-two ratio of CCP members to non-party members. Thus, if one CCP member is added to the CPPCC, two non-party members must also be added. A portion of the national CPPCC members are top local officials who at the time of appointment were reaching the retirement age limit of 65; some were the leaders of ministries and commissions in the CCP Central Committee while others were the CPPCC chairpersons and vice-chairpersons at the local levels. For example, Chen Zuoer, after retiring as the deputy director of the Hong Kong and Macao Affairs Office was appointed to the CPPCC Standing Committee in 2008.[5] There are also members from the military and religious groups, as well as the descendants of some notable persons. There has also been an increase in members from Hong Kong and Macao.

In 2005, Tung Chee Hwa was made a vice-chairman of the national CPPCC after he resigned as the chief executive of Hong Kong. Tung had been a member of the Eighth CPPCC in 1993, when 84 individuals from Hong Kong were appointed to the national CPPCC, but stepped down when he became chief executive in 1997. In March 2017, Leung Chun Ying was made a vice-chairman even though he had not yet finished his term of office. There were 124 Hong Kong appointees to the 12th national CPPCC.[6] As can be seen in Chapter 9, there are now many Hong Kong appointees to provincial and local people's political consultative conferences. This co-opts the lesser elites into the party's united front bodies. In accepting membership to the CPPCC, those who are not party members are nevertheless expected to uphold the leadership of the CCP. This obligation was not always understood by the Hong Kong appointees, as one declared: "When I was appointed as a delegate to the CPPCC, no one told me that my obligation was to uphold the leadership of the Party."[7]

Dealing with patriotic appointees takes great patience, however. An example of this could be glimpsed from the two statements made during the March 2009 NPC and CPPCC meetings in Beijing. The first was Xi Jinping telling NPC deputies from Hong Kong that they should lead the public in tackling the financial crisis by offering ideas and suggestions to the HKSAR government. The second was in a closed-door meeting between Li Guikang, deputy director of the Liaison Office, and CPPCC members from Hong Kong, when Li revealed that his office had reach a 10-point agreement with the Hong Kong administration on measures to enhance the participation of CPPCC members in local affairs. These included appointing them to public bodies and setting-up some kind of working mechanism to help them participate in local affairs. Both the Liaison Office and the HKSAR government later denied the existence of such an agreement.[8] It is unclear what led to those statements. Perhaps they were in response to CPPCC and/or NPC members complaining that their views were not being sought on Hong Kong affairs. While some of them hold positions in the HKSAR political structure, such as serving on the Executive Council or Legislative Council, and are deeply involved in local affairs, it would be difficult to have any kind of formal institutional arrangements to involve CPPCC deputies as a whole under the one country, two systems principle. The same goes for NPC deputies. Furthermore, CPPCC and NPC members have so far not been regarded by the Hong Kong community as providing the intellectual force required to articulate the many complex issues relating to post-1997 governance and Mainland–Hong Kong relations, precisely because they are seen as united front mouthpieces. Unless and until they no longer carry that perception, and unless they wish to play a genuine role in deliberation and debate, they will continue to play the role of merely "explaining" the Mainland's views. This is the inhibiting and debilitating legacy of the united front.

> **Persuasion vs. Propaganda**[9]
>
> Persuasion is a form of communication involving interaction in which the receiving party adopts a change in a given attitude or behaviour because he believes that such a change will fill a need or desire.
>
> Propaganda is a form of communication involving a deliberate and systematic attempt to shape perceptions, structure cognitions, and direct behaviour to achieve, through the manipulation of symbols, a purpose that is advantageous to the communicator.

CCP-Style Persuasion

In English, if the word "persuasion" is considered neutral, then "propaganda" is a word that carries heavy negative sentiments because it connotes bias and untruth. This is presumably why the Propaganda Department changed its English name to the Publicity Department although the old name is still by far the more often used. The Chinese word for propaganda does not carry the same negative connotations that it does in English. The Chinese meaning is "to spread information" or "to broadcast". Nevertheless, the Chinese people are skilled decipherers of official-speak. The party certainly understands how important propaganda is. Emphasis on the correct use of terms on politically sensitive topics is an effective way of constraining public debate and resisting social change. Since the Tiananmen crackdown in 1989, propaganda work has become the very "life blood" of maintaining the CCP's ongoing legitimacy and hold on power.[10]

Carrying out propaganda work

The use of propaganda in China versus official-speak elsewhere is not just a matter of language but a matter of major differences in political systems. While every political system and government provides official information that ranges from data, facts and straight forward information to messages that are constructed to persuade, rally, deflect or serve propaganda purposes—more commonly referred to nowadays as "spin"—it is the Leninist system that puts propaganda at the institutional and spiritual core of the one-party structure (Chapter 1). At the apex is a top party cadre who oversees propaganda work, and the central-level Propaganda Department is directly supervised by the CCP Central Committee. The propaganda system "is the most extensive and, arguably, the most important of all CCP-controlled bureaucratic systems in China".[11] The work of the department today has been described thus:

> We are a department in charge of political work . . . We mainly provide spiritual impetus, intellectual support and positive public opinion for [China's] economic development. We aim to make party policies become the masses' conscious actions and kindle the masses' positive thinking and creativity, to unite all forces which can be united, arouse all positive elements, transform negative forces into positive forces and mobilise them to throw themselves into economic construction, reform and opening-up.[12]

The extensive propaganda system consists of four parts: the network of cadres and offices installed throughout the party-state bureaucracies and state-owned enterprises; within the People's Liberation Army; within the state-run education, sports, science, technology, health, culture and media sectors; and all mass organisations such as labour unions, youth and women groups, universities, government-operated NGOs, and non-government ones (which are required to register with the

Ministry of Civil Affairs that is under the leadership of the Propaganda Department on ideological issues).

The party has historically divided propaganda work into "internal" (directed at the Chinese people) and "external" (directed at foreigners, Overseas Chinese and the outside world); and into four types—political, economic, cultural, and social. The Propaganda Department and its sister unit, the Office of Foreign Propaganda, are supervised by a handful of senior party—government figures in the party-state propaganda system under two leading groups with some overlapping membership. The CCP Central Committee Secretariat coordinates and facilitates linkages between the various organisations involved in propaganda work.

Controlling the media[13]

The CCP has a deep understanding of the use of propaganda. Even pre-dating the formation of the party in 1921, the communists had to learn how to disseminate a new ideology—Marxism—in China. Lenin thought newspapers were the best collective propagandists, agitators and organisers. If he were alive today, he would no doubt include the electronic media and new communication means through the Internet, mobile phones, text messaging, and social media as well. It was no accident that in 1937, the party decided to establish its own news agency—the Xinhua News Agency; in 1948, it created the *People's Daily*, so it has its own mouthpiece; and in 1958, Beijing Television was created as the party's broadcaster, which in 1978 changed its name to China Central Television. In terms of organisational arrangements today, the Xinhua News Agency is an institution of the government's State Council; and the *People's Daily*[14] is an organ of the CCP Central Committee. The directors of both organisations are members of the CCP Central Committee. Xinhua owns many other publications. China Central Television is under the control of the government's State Administration of Radio, Film and Television. These key media agencies do not have editorial independence, although in recent years they have had more leeway in some aspects of programming so as to produce more popular programmes for the public, but it would be a mistake to equate increased commercialisation of the Chinese media with the decline of either the CCP or its propaganda efforts.[15] Essentially, their news reporting and programming follow guidelines provided by the Propaganda Department. In other words, the party controls content, while the government supervises operation. As for journalists, Liu Yunshan, a former head of propaganda, made it clear that: "one of the primary tasks of journalists is to make the people loyal to the Party".[16] Moreover, as explained in Chapter 1, the *nomenklatura* system gives authority to the Propaganda Department to appoint and remove publishers, chief editors and other key officials to media bodies.

Shaping the message

During the Mao Zedong era, official-speak was designed to perpetuate revolution so that China could become a modern communist state. Today, it is designed to maintain the political status quo and promote the CCP's regime values. The new approach is to emphasise the CCP's legitimacy through its ability to make China economically strong and its people prosperous. Scholars have noted that in giving-up socialism, the CCP realised it faced a threat to its legitimacy. In response, the regime replaced its ideological legitimacy to lead the revolution with not only performance legitimacy provided by strong economic development, but also nationalist legitimacy, such as hosting the Olympic Games in Beijing in 2008 and for Chinese athletes to sweep many gold medals. A major setback was 4 June 1989, after which the party had to launch an extensive education campaign. The campaign appealed to patriotism to ensure loyalty in a population that had many domestic discontents. In order to maintain authoritarian control at a time when Marxist-Leninist ideology was becoming obsolete, the party warned of the existence of hostile international forces in the world trying to hold China back.[17] For example, in January 1994, Jiang Zemin warned at the national annual meeting on propaganda work that: "The international community is steadfastly opposed to China becoming strong and powerful and will never give up its plot to 'Westernise' and break-up China" and that work on "patriotic collectivist and social education" must support each other.[18] This has essentially remained a key task for on-going propaganda work.

Propaganda work in Hong Kong

These have also been key propaganda messages in Hong Kong—the HKSAR could do even better economically with the opening-up of the Mainland and appropriate party-government policies. Hong Kong people needed to be made more patriotic, however, which makes cultural exchanges and patriotic education important.

An example of the use of cultural means could be seen in 2004 in the way that the Mainland media reported the display of a Buddhist treasure in Hong Kong:

> A high-profile display of the finger bone relic of the Sakyamuni Buddha—one of the most sacred relics in Buddhism—is expected to "inject a proud feeling and patriotism," a prominent Buddhist master said in Beijing . . . At a news conference, Master Sheng Hui, executive deputy director of the Mainland Buddhist Association, described Hong Kong Buddhism as a branch of the religion on the Mainland. The bond between the two organisations has always been close, he said. "This showcase event is approved by the central government, and that shows it cares very much about the Hong Kong people" Sheng said. . . . Kok Kwong, chairman of the Hong Kong Buddhist Association, said . . . he hoped the exhibition of the holy relic will encourage peace, patriotic compassion and national unity in Hong Kong.[19]

It is noteworthy what the chief executive, Tung Chee Hwa, also said: "On behalf of the HKSAR government and the people of Hong Kong, I express heartfelt gratitude to the central government for granting special permission for the Buddha's finger relic . . . to be displayed in Hong Kong."[20] He also noted that local Buddhist followers and all citizens were privileged to have the rare opportunity to see such sacred and precious assets and that the welcoming ceremony for the relic and other treasures was not only a gala event for the Buddhist community, but also a good deed advocating peace, virtues and social harmony in Hong Kong.[21]

On the same occasion, Liu Yandong, the then head of the CCP Central Committee's United Front Department, who was sent to Hong Kong for the unveiling ceremony the press that the display of the relic indicated that:

> the central government's respect and care for Hong Kong Buddhism community and Hong Kong people. She said the exhibited national treasures represented China's long history and splendid culture and she believed that every Chinese people would be proud of those cultural relics. She said, since Hong Kong's return to the motherland, the central government has made all the efforts to ensure the prosperity and stability of Hong Kong and happiness and well-being of the Hong Kong people. She emphasised that "if the family lives in harmony, all affairs will prosper". With the support from the central government and led by the HKSAR government headed by chief executive Tung Chee Hwa, Hong Kong compatriots will surely make Hong Kong a splendid city so long as they work together with one heart.[22]

All the key messages were there—"inject a proud feeling and patriotism"; Beijing "cares very much about the Hong Kong people" and since the reunification has "made all the efforts to ensure the prosperity and stability of Hong Kong"; the exhibition would "encourage peace, patriotic compassion and national unity in Hong Kong"; and Hong Kong people needed "to work together with one heart" with Beijing under the leadership of the Hong Kong chief executive. The timing of the display was important. In 2003, the HKSAR's clumsy push for passing national security legislation led to a massive demonstration and calls for democratic reform. The CCP saw what happened as a threat to stability that had to be dealt with resolutely. With meticulous and secret planning, the party stunned Hong Kong in April 2004 with the announcement that the SCNPC would provide a Basic Law interpretation to rule out Hong Kong achieving universal suffrage for the election of the chief executive and the legislature in 2007 and 2008 respectively (Chapter 10). After making such an aggressive move, soothing and education was felt to be necessary and thus using the display of the Buddhist relic to promote harmony and unity was a specially organised event to show the party's care for Hong Kong.

In terms of propagating patriotic education, the 2007 Policy Address of the HKSAR chief executive, Donald Tsang, provides an excellent example of government plans, although Tsang would not have anticipated at the time that it would lead to the first mass movement for his successor Leung Chun Ying in 2012. The relevant section, entitled "National Education", is worth quoting full:

> The decade following Hong Kong's return to the motherland has seen a growing sense of national identity in our community. To prepare ourselves for the next decade, we must have a better understanding of our country's development and a stronger sense of our national and cultural identity. If Hong Kong people make their life and career plans from the perspective of national development, both individual citizens and the community at large will surely have a brighter future.
>
> At the welcoming banquet the HKSAR Government hosted on 30 June this year, President Hu Jintao earnestly advised that "we should put more emphasis on national education for the youth in Hong Kong and promote exchanges between them and the young people of the Mainland so that they will carry forward the Hong Kong people's great tradition of loving the motherland and loving Hong Kong".
>
> The future lies with our young people. In the interest of our country's development and the continued success of "One Country, Two Systems" the HKSAR Government will make every effort to promote national education. In particular, we will attach great importance to promoting national education among our young people, so that they grow to love our motherland and Hong Kong, aspire to win honour and make contributions for our country, and have a strong sense of pride as nationals of the People's Republic of China.
>
> The promotion of national education is an undertaking of the whole community. The HKSAR Government will work closely with various sectors in the community, in particular the education sector, to enhance our young people's awareness and understanding of our country's development, the land and the people, the history and the culture. This can be done through different means and channels, such as classroom teaching, teacher education, extra-curricular activities and exchanges with young people from the Mainland. The objective is to foster among young people a sense of affinity with our motherland and heighten their sense of national pride and identity.
>
> We will give more weight to the elements of national education in the existing primary and secondary curricula and the new senior secondary curriculum framework to help students acquire a clearer understanding of our country and a stronger sense of national identity. The Government will also encourage more schools to form flag guard teams and to stage more national flag-raising ceremonies, and subsidise more Mainland study trips and exchange programmes for youths. We will rally the efforts of various sectors to bring about synergy in enhancing the overall effectiveness of national education.[23]

When will Hong Kong people be considered sufficiently patriotic? According to Ma Lik, a former chairman of the DAB, patriotism was the prerequisite for universal suffrage meaning, among other things, that people must stop thinking of what happened in Tiananmen Square on 4 June 1989 as a "massacre". He reckoned that, at the rate Hong Kong was moving, it would take until 2022 for the public to have experienced enough "national awareness education" to accept CCP rule and thereby win the right to directly elected local government. Still, some progress had been made. Initially, he thought the appropriate date would be 2047.[24] A mark of the first 20 years post-reunification was the repeated need to remind Hong Kong people about the importance of being patriotic (Chapter 10).

Propaganda techniques

Propaganda is about influencing language, thought and emotions. Once this is done, there is less need for direct censorship. Thus, much effort is spent on using the right (i.e., official) definitions and terminologies in public discourse. Some of the use of propaganda may appear crude, but when they are applied constantly through the media that the party controls and are repeated by its supporters, repetition can be overwhelming. Even if the public recognises that the propaganda messages for what they are, it becomes clear what is politically correct and what is not, and with patriotic education focussed on young people, the propaganda system seeks to reap a long-term harvest of influencing young minds. How the techniques have been used in Hong Kong is illustrative:

> **Repetition for assurance:** This technique is simple and basic. By repeating a well-chosen slogan, an idea takes on form because it can be easily repeated by many people. For example, the slogan "stability and prosperity" was most often repeated prior to 1997 to reassure the Hong Kong community that everything would be fine.
>
> **Intentional vagueness:** Broad generalities are useful to clinch a deal, leaving details to be worked out. Since the devil is in the details, workability and public acceptability depend on the final details. The policy of granting the HKSAR "a high degree of autonomy" was in effect a cleverly designed slogan to give a sense that the HKSAR would enjoy day-to-day autonomy without interference from the Mainland.
>
> **Personal attack and labelling:** Attacking the opponent personally rather than his or her argument, aims to identify flaws or weakness in the opponent, and so weaken public trust in or arouse prejudice towards him or her. By labelling some people in the democratic camp in Hong Kong as "always opposing" it aimed to show that those people were constantly unreasonable. When the party was at its most furious, unforgettable labels were used, such as "sinner of a thousand years", a label Chinese officials gave to Chris Patten, the last governor of Hong Kong. Those who are called "patriots" are right-minded and those who are "unpatriotic" are "anti-China" or "running-dogs of the British".
>
> **Alleging a sex scandal:** A man may be accused of having mistresses or that he visits prostitutes. If the target is a woman, she may be described as having loose morals.

Diverting from substance: Labelling also diverts the attacker away from having to address the opponent's argument. For example, a certain person may be said to be "anti-China" but no evidence is produced to support the attack.

Demonising the opposition: By putting the opposition, whether individuals or groups, in a bad light, such as that they are ignorant, inexperienced, rude or unacceptable to those in power, the aim is to project them as unworthy of public support. Thus, by saying that certain democrats were unacceptable to Beijing there was in fact no more that needed to be said. The people should know those named would never get very far in political life.

"Some people" or "few people" argument: By claiming that some people, or only a few people, are disagreeing or causing trouble, this tactic aims to deny that there may be a large number of people who disagree.

One of the key responsibilities of the Propaganda Department is to issue regular rulings and briefings on the correct definitions and terminologies to be used through directives and notices, as well as, through the use of the law, to require the media to consult the propaganda authorities in specific circumstances, such as when there is a disaster and in cases of high sensitivity.[25] Thus, propaganda work affects not only how news is reported but also the language used for public discourse. The fruit of the party's propaganda efforts can be seen in the way party members and those affiliated with the party articulate various issues where there are party lines to take. Examples include submissions to the HKSAR Government on legislating national security legislation under Article 23 of the Basic Law, and on the various rounds of public consultation on constitutional development since 2004 (Chapter 10).

Propaganda in Action

In 2003, the CCP published a *Practical Manual for Party Propaganda Work*, which provides a fascinating look at how the party sees an essential part of its work today.[26] The principles in the book are applied throughout the party's propaganda work, and thus are also relevant to how it is done in Hong Kong.

President Hu Jintao, the general secretary of the CCP, wrote the foreword to the book showing its importance. The manual states that the goal of party propaganda is to mould generation after generation to understand the socialist cause. Propaganda must serve the party and give proper guidance to the people. It should fill society since the object of a propaganda message is to get it continually out to the people by using many different means, such as through books, movies, periodicals and the Internet, so that they can reinforce one another. Propaganda should be positive—news reporting should hold to a "positive principle" by balancing praise and exposing problems. In other words, it should not overdwell on problems, particularly problems that are hard to solve. Readers should have a positive feeling after hearing the reports and believe that problems are being dealt with by the authorities. The manual stresses that development is China's Number One task and that it is the key to solving most of the country's problems. The manual observes that the Internet is having greater impact on the people's thinking. Moreover, it notes that people outside the Mainland are always plotting to infiltrate China ideologically; so the party needs to strengthen its management of news websites and other types of websites because ideological strength is important to China's overall national strength.[27] The manual also notes that preparing the people for a change in the party line is "an art form". The manual warns that change must be introduced gradually and subtly, so as not to create stress among the people because of the capacity of the masses to accept change. Once the party has changed a party line, propaganda should intensify so that it penetrates everywhere.[28]

The manual contains an interesting section on feeding propaganda to foreigners, noting that it is a different task from domestic work because the targets and their backgrounds are different. Foreigners are useful to spread propaganda overseas, so the manual warns that foreigners should be given what they can accept and care must be taken that what they see and experience in China will help to build a good image of China internationally. Moreover, it is essential to take gentler and subtler approaches with foreigners, avoiding the use of slogans or saying things that may cause disagreement. It is best to present facts in such a way that foreigners are enabled to draw their own conclusions. Explain what the foreigner does not understand, even if it means over simplifying things if need be.[29]

The manual also contains a section on religious propaganda. It starts by acknowledging that while the principle of religious freedom should be respected, it is also necessary to strengthen the education of the people, especially young people, in dialectic materialism, which in Leninism-speak means the action of the party to do what it deems fit to "accelerate the march of history" towards communism (Chapter 1). The manual explains that the roots of religion will remain for a very long time and the party has no alternative but to implement a policy of religious freedom. Nevertheless, through education in socialist culture and civilization, the roots of religion can be weakened over time. The party should not use words that offend believers and if there is any doubt on what to do, officials should contact the United Front Department. Religious publications should be closely monitored.[30]

3

The Earliest History of the Chinese Communist Party in Hong Kong

From 1920 to 1926

The story of the Chinese Communist Party in Hong Kong may be said to begin with three men who started the irregular *Zhenshanmei Magazine* in 1920. Lin Junwei (alias Lin Changchi) was a school inspector with the Education Department, Zhang Rendao was a graduate of the well-known high school, Queen's College, and Li Yibao was a primary school teacher. They wanted to report on labour issues and introduce basic Marxist principles to a wider audience. Some time at the end of 1920, they made a special effort to meet Chen Duxiu on the boat Chen was travelling on from Shanghai to Guangzhou as it passed through Hong Kong. Inspired and encouraged by Chen, the three men established the Marxism Research Group at Mengyang Primary School in Happy Valley where Li Yibao was teaching.[1]

Chen Duxiu went on to become the CCP's first party secretary after founding the party in Shanghai together with Li Dazhao. They also created the Socialist Youth League. Other party branches sprung up in Beijing, Guangzhou, Changsha, Wuhan, Jinan, and Japan. The First Party Congress was held in Shanghai on 23 July 1921 with 13 delegates (including Mao Zedong) representing 59 party members. The early party branches were highly energetic and quickly became organised to propagate Marxism, especially among youth, workers and peasants, and expanded their network to more provinces. Marxism's appeal was that it seemed to offer coherent theses on the accumulation of capital and the exploitation of workers. It was unsurprising that intellectuals and students should be attracted by the new ideology.

Lin Junwei, Zhang Rendao, and Li Yibao formed links with the CCP's Guangdong-based organisation. Being teachers, they were able to attract a number of students to the study group. Their activities were carried out in the name of the New China Students Club Hong Kong Sub-branch,[2] which by 1923 became the Chinese Socialist Youth League, Hong Kong Special Branch, coming under the Guangdong Socialist Youth League.[3] As the Chinese Socialist Youth League was the only CCP-related organisation in Hong Kong in the early days, it represented both the party and the league in effect.[4] Achievements were modest since members lacked resources and expertise.[5] This state of affairs continued up until mid-1924 when the CCP Central Committee decided to set up a party structure in Hong Kong. In November 1924, when the reorganisation took effect, seven local league members were considered eligible to join the CCP and they made up the party in the colony.[6]

The earliest days of the CCP presence in Hong Kong was a part of the story of the party getting established and surviving as a political organisation. Naturally, Hong Kong, a small colonial outpost, was never the party's main focus. Its eyes were always firmly on Mainland China. Not surprisingly, the CCP's activities in the colony were ad hoc in nature and dictated by the fast-changing environment on the Mainland. Nevertheless, Hong Kong provided an extremely useful base for the party to organise support for the communist cause.

Hong Kong, an Inspiration

Hong Kong was in fact an inspiration for the emergent socialist movement on the Mainland. The most extensive labour strike in the history of modern China was sparked in the British colony of Hong Kong. The 1920s was a time of worldwide labour dissatisfaction. Workers in Hong Kong and the Mainland were not unaware of labour strikes in other parts of the world, which were a direct result of worker discontent aggravated by the economic dislocations brought on by World War I.[7] The nineteen-day strike from March to April 1920 by the Chinese Mechanics Institute was a momentous occasion. Many of its members were skilled workers, who were not easy to replace. They asked repeatedly for a 40 percent pay rise to offset inflation and resorted finally to a strike with 9,000 of them leaving Hong Kong for Guangzhou, where the cost of living was lower. Their withdrawal brought life to a standstill in Hong Kong. The employers had no choice and agreed to a 32 percent pay increase, whereupon the mechanics returned to resume work. The successful strike was the first coordinated industrial protest in Hong Kong's history and caught the attention of the early Chinese Marxists.[8]

The mechanics strike pre-dated the founding of the CCP on the Mainland. The strike showed the interconnected socio-economic dynamics between Hong Kong and Guangdong, as well as their connectedness to ideas and events overseas. Hong Kong was already globally linked. Its longstanding trading and seafaring activities had brought its people into contact with activities and conditions elsewhere in the world. There were to be more and larger strikes to come in Hong Kong marking important milestones in the history of the CCP.

Guangdong and Hong Kong have always been close and inseparable, and thus the work of the communists in Guangdong and Hong Kong was likewise intimately linked. With only a handful of CCP members in the colony and a limited capacity to act, the Hong Kong communist structure in the early days "was essentially an offshoot of the Guangdong structure"[9] and most of the CCP's impact on Hong Kong originated from Guangdong. The importance of that closeness during the various labour protests in the 1920s will be seen later in this chapter. Indeed, the interwar years in Hong Kong saw many strikes and boycotts—workers had genuine grievances that the Chinese compradors and European taipans, as well as the colonial authorities, chose to ignore for too long. On the whole, the wealthy Chinese merchants were conservative in outlook, easily alarmed by social changes and reform movements. Yet, the obvious injustice at the time of the relative social positions of the British and the Chinese, and of employers and workers, did not turn the people of Hong Kong against colonialism altogether despite their strong sense of Chinese nationalism. The politics of the Mainland was just too divided and volatile. For all its imperfections, Hong Kong was a safe haven for people of all types and shades to pursue their dreams and beliefs.

However, the pragmatism of the Hong Kong Chinese to get on with life in Hong Kong was not enough to win the trust of either colonial authorities or the British *hongs*. The British knew they were imperial trespassers and thus suffered from a constant "siege mentality".[10] Indeed, to survive in Hong Kong, they needed to separate themselves from the Chinese. The Chinese were barred from living on the Peak for example by the Peak District Reservation Ordinance 1904 and Peak District (Residence) Ordinance 1918; the Chinese were kept out of the Hong Kong Club and other recreational establishments frequented by the Europeans. There was naturally no thought of giving the Chinese any kind of political representation. Not only were the Hong Kong Chinese barred from involvement in policy-making, they were mostly also excluded from carrying out policies. Up until the 1950s, the cadets who held all the most senior jobs in the Hong Kong civil service were recruited in Britain; and even the lower-ranking jobs in many government departments were held by Europeans.[11]

In Hong Kong's colonial society, the British could never be completely relaxed that they had local Chinese support, and the Hong Kong Chinese could never quite depend upon the British to fight for their interests. The British and the Mainland authorities dealt with each other as sovereign powers. When British power was in ascendant, the British behaved as conquering imperialists and China had to reluctantly accommodate but remained unhappy and disgruntled. To the Chinese, Hong Kong was Chinese territory and its people were compatriots. To the Hong Kong Chinese, they had managed to carve out a reasonable life in Hong Kong but who could speak for them? This is a question that resonates still today. Just as the British did not then feel they could fully trust the people of Hong Kong, Beijing's distrust today arises not from ethnic differences but from a vast ideological divide. The history of Hong Kong is one with multiple currents and complex nuances, which the CCP probably still has difficulty understanding.

The Hong Kong Seamen's Strike 1922

During the first major labour event, the Seamen's Strike of 1922, the CCP had no formal structure in Hong Kong so it could not claim credit for it, but the strike became a notable milestone in party history nevertheless because the key labour organisers did subsequently join the party.

Chinese seamen banded together in 1921 to fight for better wages and working conditions from shipping companies. They were particularly unhappy with the very large gap between their pay and that of non-Chinese seamen, which was very much higher. They asked for pay rises of between 15 percent and 35 percent, which employers twice turned down.[12] The seamen were also held hostage to an extremely unfair contract hiring system that took a large chunk of their already low wages. Eventually, they formed a new Chinese Seamen's Union[13] and began a strike on 13 January 1922 when a third pay rise demand was ignored by the *hongs* Butterfield and Swire and Jardine Matheson.[14] It started with 1,500 deck hands and stokers stopping work. A week later, the number of strikers rose to 6,500 and by the end of the month some 30,000 workers, including pilots, tallymen, lighter-men, carriers, stevedores, wharf coolies, cargo labourers and others, had joined the strike.[15] The earlier strikers were almost all Cantonese, but as events escalated, seamen of Shanghai, Ningbo, and Zhejiang origins who had their own unions refused jobs vacated by the Cantonese. This was probably due to the communists in Shanghai helping to persuade workers to support the strike in Hong Kong.

The strike paralysed shipping, traffic, and production, and caused food prices to rise, when the price of rice was already high.[16] The British colonial administration and the Chinese compradors tried to intervene to settle the dispute without success. By 16 January, the authorities deemed it necessary to declare martial law and armed guards were placed at strategic points to preserve order, although contemporaneous reports showed the strike was carried on in an orderly manner.[17] By the end of the month, over 10,000 seamen had left Hong Kong for Guangzhou, where they were sympathetically received by both the head of the fledgling Guangdong military administration under Chen Jiongming, as well as his rival, Sun Yat-sen. Chen wanted to enhance his popularity as he anticipated there would soon be a political showdown with Sun.[18] The union sent more and more workers across the border, partly to prevent disorder in Hong Kong and partly to reduce the financial burden of subsidising the striking workers since the cost of living was lower in Guangzhou.[19]

On 1 February, with the support of the Hong Kong Chinese business elites, the colonial authorities proscribed the union and sought to close it down on the ground that its activities caused widespread distress. Two other unions were also declared unlawful. Things quickly boiled over into a general strike involving more than 50,000 workers, including cooks, domestics, bakers, pastry chefs, office boys, delivery men, dairymen, tramway workers, rickshaw pullers and general coolies, bank clerks and other workers.[20] The Chinese staff of Government House serving the governor also walked out.[21] The government retaliated by issuing and rushing through in one day the Emergency Regulations Bill giving it powers to prohibit posters and public gatherings, censor mail, conduct body searches, and raid private premises, such as the union's office. By the end of the month, some 120,000 workers had joined the strike.

In order to prevent more workers leaving the colony, the Hong Kong administration suspended train services to Guangzhou. Political tension heightened on 4 March when 2,000 domestic workers decided to walk from Hong Kong to Guangzhou. When they tried to break through the guarded cordon at Shatin set up to prevent them from leaving Hong Kong, the British used Indian troops supporting the police to fire at the crowd attempting to depart.[22] Government reports noted that five strikers were killed and several were wounded.[23] This incident, referred to as the Shatin Massacre, aroused considerable public ill-feelings towards the colonial administration and resulted in more strikes and a paralysed Hong Kong.

An economic strike had been turned into a major political confrontation. The shipping companies and colonial administration had to back down following negotiations among the seamen, their employers, and the Guangzhou and Hong Kong authorities. An agreement with the union on pay was reached with wage increases averaging about 30 percent and the seamen returned to work on 6 March. Chen Jiongming and Sun Yat-sen were also keen to see the disruptions stopped as they hoped to gain financial assistance and diplomatic recognition for the military administration through Hong Kong and were thus anxious to avoid offending the British.[24] The speed with which the workers went back to work showed the strike was much more of an economic rather than a political struggle. The ban against the Chinese Seamen's Union was also lifted. Despite the seamen's victory, inflation would erode their pay gains. While they were also promised money as partial compensation for lost wages, it was never in fact paid.[25]

The Seamen's Strike was important for another reason beyond its large scale. The Chinese business elites were no longer able to play the role of mediator between Chinese workers and foreigners because they could not look beyond their own commercial interests. Moreover, the Seamen's Strike was the first time the CCP intervened in Hong Kong affairs although it played a minimal role. While some of the union leaders, most notable Su Zhongzheng and Li Weimen, became CCP members by the time of the next strike, they were not party members at the time of the Seamen's Strike.[26] At the start of the strike in January 1922, the CCP Guangdong Branch was still in its infancy. It had only been set up after the CCP's First Party Congress had been held in Shanghai in July 1921. The branch saw the strike as an opportunity to further party work in Guangdong, and organised various activities to support the Hong Kong strikers. For example, it mobilised public support for the strike in Guangzhou, issued 3,000 copies of the *Manifesto to the Seamen*, set up a support committee to receive the strikers and to provide for them, and dissuaded Ningbo seamen from going to Hong Kong to take up jobs left by the strikers. The CCP activists in Guangdong "were simply too few, too poor, too inexperienced and too unknown" to do very much more.[27]

Nevertheless, from the CCP's perspective, the Seamen's Strike is considered significant in party history. The truth may be that at the time the strike inspired party members more than communism inspired the strikers, and with the passage of time, the episode became hailed as a political struggle against imperialism and colonialism.[28] It was also significant that it was the first time that the colonial administration and local business elites felt seriously threatened. Moreover, the success of the strike further emboldened workers and other labour disputes followed.[29]

To the last, Governor Reginald Stubbs (governor from 1919 to 1925) believed that the Seamen's Strike was a conspiracy organised by Sun Yat-sen and the KMT in Guangzhou under Soviet influence to undermine the colonial regime in Hong Kong.[30] While the KMT subsidised the strikers' livelihood and provided accommodation when they relocated across the border, the strike in Hong Kong was a locally organised affair. Moreover, the right-wing within the KMT did not support further strikes, as they had close ties with local businessmen. Anti-communist sentiments were particularly strong among the Chinese merchants in Hong Kong, whose commercial interests were affected. They felt the unions "had strong Bolshevist support", the "government could not retreat one inch" in negotiating with the strikers, and urged "the suppression of all labour guilds".[31] The colonial authorities regarded the Chinese businessmen as representing responsible local opinion, while the truth was they ignored the grievances of, and had little sympathy for, the plight of the seamen. From then on, the Chinese business elites and the colonial administration became staunchly anti-communist and anti-union.

Guangzhou–Hong Kong Strike-Boycott, 1925–1926

At the start of the Guangzhou–Hong Kong Strike-Boycott in 1925, there were not many CCP members in Hong Kong and they did not have much organisational capacity in Hong Kong. Nevertheless, with KMT funding and CCP orchestration, the impact was massive. It ended sixteen months later only because the KMT was ready to ease off. It was in fact a complex period of time with many things in flux. Sun Yat-sen's death in March 1925 led to a jockeying for power within the KMT. The KMT's and CCP's interests on the Mainland soon diverged. In Hong Kong, while there was a strong sense of nationalism and social justice among the Chinese that needed to be aired, the people also wanted order so that they could get on with their lives. In a contested environment, the difficult choices people made were often seen as a contest between their loyalty to a foreign administration that did not understand or trust them, and their fear of fast-changing politics on the Mainland that were uncertain and violent.

The dramatic chain of events started in February 1925 in Shanghai when workers at the Japanese-owned Naigai No. 8 Cotton Mill went on strike because a Japanese overseer had beaten a female worker. The numbers of strikers swelled to more than 35,000, as workers from 20 other Japanese-owned mills joined in. On 15 May, a worker vs. management confrontation at the No. 7 mill resulted in the shooting and killing of worker Gu Zhenghong, who was a CCP member. The party seized the chance to organise a large-scale event. On 28 May, the party decided to mobilise workers and students to launch an anti-imperialist demonstration on 30 May in the British-controlled International Settlement, the day of Gu's memorial service. On 30 May, protesters and Sikh policemen under the command of a British inspector came to blows on Nanjing Road. Shots were fired killing several people and wounding dozens more.[32] The police also made many arrests. The incident provoked a massive outburst of anti-British sentiments and Chinese nationalism, which gave the CCP the opportunity to call an immediate general strike on 1 June. When the strike started, there were further shootings and deaths leading to many more workers joining the strike in the International Settlement over the next few days.

Indignation over the events in Shanghai reverberated throughout China. The CCP in Shanghai saw this incident as an opportunity to strengthen their political position and instructed the CCP branches in different cities to mobilise the public to support the strike in Shanghai. Against this background, the CCP in Guangdong began to agitate as news reached Guangzhou and Hong Kong. By then, Su Zhaozheng and Li Weimin had joined the CCP and became the chief agitators in the Strike-Boycott.[33] The KMT backed calls for an immediate general strike and sponsored a joint operation between the KMT and CCP. Both parties could see political gains for them in exploiting anti-foreign themes. The CCP "worked as the hand inside the glove of the left wing of the KMT" and without KMT money the strike would have collapsed within a short time.[34] Thus, unlike the Chinese Seamen's Strike, this time the CCP Branch in Guangdong was deeply involved in every aspect of the Strike-Boycott.

The strike started in Hong Kong on 18 June, when 80 percent of the senior students from Queen's College absented themselves. Most of the senior students in the Yaumati Government School did the same thing the following day.[35] On 19 June seamen, tramway men and printers led the walk out and left for Guangzhou. The CCP formed a small party core to arrange food and accommodation for them.[36] On 21 June, students from Queen's College also left for Guangzhou. On 23 June, during a march through Shaji in the foreign concession of Shamian Island, in which Zhou Enlai participated, British and French troops opened fired killing 52 people and injuring over 170 demonstrators.[37] Another veteran communist, Liu Shaoqi, was also in Guangzhou. Anger was at a fever-pitch in Guangzhou after the shootings. The incident referred to as the Shaiji Massacre, provoked many more workers in Hong Kong who were working for foreign firms in machine-building, telegraphing, catering and other jobs to join the strike.[38] As anti-British anger swept through Hong Kong, many more workers and their families left for Guangzhou. Among the early strikers were servants working in the exclusive residences on the Peak, where Chinese could not live.

It is worth pausing here to emphasise one point. China's most famous and able revolutionaries joined the CCP in the 1920s when they were young. Some of them, such as Mao Zedong, Zhou Enlai, Deng Xiaoping, Ye Jianying, and Liao Chengzhi, remained in political life for a very considerable time and their views and assumptions influenced policies for many decades.

Through the arrangements of the KMT's finance chief, Liao Zhongkai, a Hakka, the CCP received considerable funds to support the Hong Kong strikers in Guangzhou. Liao was a left-wing KMT leader and supported the strikers enthusiastically. The right-wing of the KMT had called unsuccessfully for limited strikes. Patriotic overseas Chinese also sent funds to support the strikers. The KMT seized casinos, opium dens and other unoccupied places and used them to accommodate the Hong Kong strikers. Liao's son—Liao Chengzhi—became a member of the CCP and would play an important role in the war effort against the Japanese and in the resumption of sovereignty over Hong Kong one day (Chapters 4 and 7).

In response to the rising anti-British sentiments and to show toughness to the nationalists, the Hong Kong government severed economic relations with Guangzhou. Under the direction of the CCP in Guangdong, the various unions representing Hong Kong and Mainland workers that were under its influence convened a conference in Guangzhou. The purpose was to form the Guangzhou–Hong Kong Strike Committee which would be under the CCP's national organ in the labour movement, the All-China Federation of Trade Unions. Su Zhaozheng became the chairman of the Strike Committee, which had numerous subcommittees in charge of armed defence, picketing and other activities.

It is noteworthy that the Hong Kong strikers, in addition to supporting the cause of other Chinese workers on the Mainland, also had their own demands. They called for freedom of expression, equality of treatment for Chinese and non-Chinese, universal suffrage to elect the legislature, improvement of working conditions, lower housing rents; and freedom to live anywhere in the colony.[39] In other words, they had grievances over the privileges of foreigners and demanded equal treatment. These demands were probably the first time ever in Hong Kong history that the people of Hong Kong demanded liberalisation of the political system. Interestingly, at a later stage of the Strike-Boycott, the CCP leadership considered that these demands were unrealistic and should not to be further pursued at that time.[40]

The strike severely affected the daily life of Hong Kong. Economic activities ground to a halt. The city was paralysed. Food prices began to soar as markets closed. Refuse was not collected. Large scale withdrawal of capital from banks almost led to the collapse of the banking system, had the authorities in Hong Kong not stepped-in to arrange a special loan of HK$30 million to keep local businesses going until normal trade could resume.[41] Within two days of the strike starting, the colonial authorities called on volunteers to keep essential services running. The call initially was made to Europeans because the authorities did not trust the Chinese, but a belated call for Chinese volunteers was made and over 2,000 men came forward, with another 1,000 ready to help.[42] The success of the call for local volunteers surprised the British. The government also invoked emergency powers to counter communism and anti-British propaganda attacks. The Counter-Propaganda Bureau was set up to influence thinking locally and outside Hong Kong, including in Britain, that the problem was linked to the rising tide of Bolshevism and not due to any serious grievance in Hong Kong.[43] In mid-1925, the Chinese newspaper *Industrial and Commercial Daily* was founded as an anti-propaganda tool with government subsidy. Its editorial aim was to show the chaos in Guangdong as the result of communist agitators. The paper was considered a highly successful tool to promote "anti-Red" sentiments.[44]

The Chinese Chamber of Commerce, merchant guilds and the Tung Wah Hospital Committee, representing local business interests in Hong Kong, threw their support behind the colonial administration and all blamed the "Bolsheviks". By the end of July, the worst was considered over as workers begun to trickle back to the colony from Guangdong. By September 1925, most of the workers who stayed in Hong Kong had returned to work. After all, few could afford to have no income for an extended period of time.[45]

But just as a sense of normality was returning, events were about to enter a new intense phase—the Strike Committee in Guangdong called for a boycott of all British goods and a ban on ships using Hong Kong. It issued a set of regulations which only allowed ships belonging to countries other than Britain and Japan to enter the ports of Guangdong and the ships must not have visited Hong Kong first. The export of foodstuffs and raw materials to Hong Kong was also expressly prohibited by the regulations.[46] The Strike Committee formed picket platoons at the ports to search all incoming ships to Guangdong for British goods and goods imported from Hong Kong, and ships from Hong Kong and Britain were not allowed to enter any of the ports in Guangdong. The Whampoa Academy arranged the supply of arms and ammunitions to the pickets and provided special training to them.[47]

The Strike-Boycott reduced Hong Kong's two-way trade by about half in 1925 as compared to the previous year.[48] There was also a sharp drop in tax revenue. Many businesses closed, which also affected the banking sector badly.[49] There were reports of intimidation of workers to get them to strike and prevent them from returning to Hong Kong.[50] This resulted in the formation of the secret Labour Protection Bureau by the colonial authorities. Its job was to protect workers from intimidators and launch counter-attacks on the intimidators. An ex-pirate called Liang Weichen, who had also been a former general in the ousted Chen Jiongming's army, was found most suitable for the job. The band of 150 special policemen—thugs—put together for the secret mission apparently did "excellent work".[51]

Governor Stubbs did not cope well with the crisis. He became increasingly frustrated with the troublesome regime in Guangdong and even tried to find ways to subvert it.[52] By November, Stubbs had been replaced by Cecil Clementi (governor 1925–1930), a Cantonese speaker, who understood Chinese affairs better, although he also believed the authorities in Guangdong were out to ruin Hong Kong. Nevertheless, he was willing to engage the KMT leaders in dialogue through using local Chinese go-betweens in March 1926 when the opportunity arose.[53] By then, the relationship between the KMT and CCP was running into trouble after Sun Yat-sen's death. The boycott was costly to keep up and the KMT had other priorities as it was preparing to launch the Northern Expedition.[54] Meanwhile, Clementi had worked hard to cultivate the loyalty of the local elites. Shrewdly, in 1926, he appointed the first ethnic Chinese person Chow Shouson to be one of two unofficial members of his advisory cabinet, the Executive Council, both to show a new relationship between the colonial administration and the Chinese population, as well as to reward Chow.[55] Chow, together with Robert Kotewall, who was half Chinese and half Parsee, were two of the administration's closest local advisers during the Strike-Boycott. They in effect orchestrated Hong Kong counter-propaganda campaign. When Chow stepped down from the Executive Council in 1936, Kotewall filled his place until the Japanese invasion of Hong Kong in 1941.[56] Interestingly, Chow and Kotewall were vilified after World War II for allegedly cooperating with the Japanese. Both had been asked to work with the Japanese by the leading members of the former colonial administration within a week of Hong Kong's surrender, so as to promote friendly relations between the Chinese and the conquerors. The primary concern then was to restore public order,[57] and Hong Kong's Chinese elites were used as go-betweens to minimise bloodshed and consolidate Japanese rule.[58]

With Sun Yat-sen gone by March 1925, a period of intense jockeying for position within the KMT followed to determine who would lead the party. After Liao Zhongkai was assassinated in August, power eventually fell to Chiang Kai-shek, who was the commander-in-chief of the KMT army. Chiang had observed at that time that: "British power in the Orient had passed its peak."[59] By March 1926, Chiang had ousted his competition. He curbed the power of the CCP within the united front and also disarmed the pickets of the Strike Committee, although he returned the arms thus confiscated to the CCP. After the Northern Expedition was launched in the summer of 1926, Chiang let the communists exhaust themselves from fighting, while he planned their demise using his longstanding association with the Shanghai gangsters. Many communists were killed over the next several months.[60] The KMT-CCP alliance was no longer needed. It became politically desirable for Chiang to promote national reunification instead of anti-imperialism. The Soviet Union, now led by Josef Stalin (1878–1953), preferred to see the KMT succeed because it thought the nationalists had the better chance to unify China. So he asked the CCP not to keep up the boycott against Hong Kong to ensure the British would not be able to use that as an excuse to intervene with the Northern Expedition. Meanwhile, Clementi's strategy was to show that he was both willing to negotiate with the KMT and show force, but in early September, just as negotiations were proving difficult, as the KMT was fighting at Wuchang, Clementi got Whitehall to send Royal Navy gunboats to clear pickets from the wharves in Guangzhou. There was in fact no fighting as pickets dispersed quickly.[61] Negotiations resumed and a compromise settlement was reached.[62] The boycott was formally lifted on 10 October 1926, the same day that Wuchang was taken by the KMT.

The Strike-Boycott is considered an important political achievement of the CCP's early history as it significantly bolstered its influence in China. For the CCP branch in Guangdong, it used the Strike-Boycott as an opportunity to expand membership. The total membership of the CCP and Chinese Socialist Youth League in Guangdong had increased from about 700 just before the Strike-Boycott to more than 7,000 by the end of it, though the quality of the new recruits was considered questionable.[63]

From Hong Kong's perspective, the Strike-Boycott involved a large number of workers. Some reports noted 250,000 of them had joined the strike during the period, which represented about a third of the colony's population.[64] The events undermined the business confidence and that affected Hong Kong's prosperity for years afterwards.[65] Politically, the Strike-Boycott made the ordinary people of Hong Kong painfully aware that radicalism could be costly. The public was punished by the Strike-Boycott as their normal living was seriously dislocated. Many Hong Kong strikers also suffered as they were not taken back by their former employers.[66] The colonial government also thwarted unionism. Several leftist labour unions including the Chinese Seamen's Union were proscribed and their leaders arrested. New legislation was enacted to prohibit unions from being affiliated with an organisation outside the colony, and to outlaw strikes with political causes. These anti-union measures were only relaxed after the Second World War.[67] In sum, the Strike-Boycott made trade unions "impoverished and unpopular" and they were "little more than friendly societies concerned more with the provision of funeral expenses for the dead than the improvement of the condition of living".[68] The labour movement in Hong Kong was basically halted for the next two decades after the Strike-Boycott. The events of the 1920s did not secure for the workers' concessions in response to their political demands. In the years following 1926, the British administration in Hong Kong took steps to prevent the insurgence of Mainland-inspired political activity.

From 1925 onward, the press in Hong Kong was subject to censorship, and in 1927 the authorities suppressed a dozen of the principal Chinese trade unions. Particular efforts were made to forestall any further annoyance from the CCP. Two of the banned unions, the General Labour Union of Hong Kong and the Chinese Seamen's Union, were well known for their communist leanings. A special Anti-Communist Squad in the police devoted itself to the hunting down of Communist Party members. By 1935 the police felt able to report contentedly that the colony was free from organised Communism.[69]

4
Purge, War, and Civil War
From 1927 to 1948

It is far from well known that there was a period of time when the Chinese Communist Party Guangdong headquarters was in the British colony of Hong Kong nor is the very important role that it played common knowledge. The party's activities in Hong Kong entered a new phase in 1927 when Chiang Kai-shek embarked on the Party Purification Movement against CCP members all over China, throwing the communists into disarray. The ferocious purge started in mid-April, first in Shanghai and then Guangzhou. Many important CCP members or suspected activists were arrested and most of them executed.[1] Many of those who were lucky enough to escape the purge fled to Hong Kong—the nearest shelter outside the jurisdiction of the KMT. The CCP's establishment in Guangdong was almost completely broken. Indeed, the CCP leadership decided to relocate the CCP Guangdong Branch's headquarters from Guangzhou to Hong Kong in order to escape the KMT's relentless pursuit. The relocation lasted until 1936, when the party re-established itself in Guangdong once again.

The party in Hong Kong during this period of time was extraordinarily active, with the bulk of its work focussed on supporting the communist movement on the Mainland. For example, on 1 August 1927, when the CCP carried out the first military action in its history to overthrow the local KMT administration at Nanchang, the CCP Guangdong headquarters in Hong Kong was asked by the CCP Central Committee to provide support to the CCP troops when they reached the East River and, after the failure of the uprising, Hong Kong was instructed to receive communist fugitives from the Mainland.[2] Later, the Hong Kong–based headquarters was also actively involved in the planning and instigating of the Guangzhou uprising in December 1927 to establish a communist government in South China. Again, the uprising failed with more than 6,000 communists losing their lives.[3] These uprisings were ordered and financed by the Soviets, all of which failed and caused many deaths. Indeed, they weakened the young party considerably. It is fair to say that the heavy Soviet influence at that time was "catastrophic for the CCP".[4] After the Guangzhou uprising, the CCP Guangdong headquarters in Hong Kong continued to direct most of its efforts to reviving the communist movement in Guangdong.

The various waves of CCP members who had escaped to Hong Kong faced a difficult life there. Governor Cecil Clementi was hostile towards the CCP in light of his experience with the Strike-Boycott of 1925–1926 discussed in Chapter 3. He formed a close relationship with the KMT authorities to suppress CCP activities. In the party's terminology, CCP members experienced a period of White Terror during the late 1920s to 1930s in Hong Kong. Many of them were arrested by the colonial government relying on KMT intelligence and then deported to Guangdong. The CCP hideouts in Hong Kong were frequently raided by the police. The colonial government even allowed KMT secret agents to carry out activities in Hong Kong to find communists. By the end of 1934, the CCP's establishment in Hong Kong was basically thinned out and activities essentially ground to a halt.[5] Despite the harassment of the communists by the colonial authorities, Ho Chi Minh (1890–1969) managed to found the Vietnamese Communist Party in Hong Kong in February 1930.[6]

During this period of time, though the CCP Guangdong headquarters was stationed in Hong Kong, it was hardly possible to promote communism. Moreover, Hong Kong people were simply not very interested. The violent though short uprising in Guangzhou perpetrated by the communists and the equally bloody retaliation by the KMT created a tremendous sense of fear in Hong Kong that the spat between the parties could engulf the colony. People came to the conclusion that it was best to stay away from political radicalism. The silence of apathy seemed a good strategy under the circumstances.[7] The business elites supported the colonial administration's tough stance against the communists.[8] It was a dark and difficult period for the CCP in Guangdong and Hong Kong—the party was nearly completely shattered.

It is also worth noting that the British and Governor Clementi thought that the New Territories were economically and strategically important to the colony and if it was returned to China one day, Hong Kong Island and Kowloon could not be sustained. After the Strike-Boycott of 1925–1926, Clementi thought about the 99-year lease on the New Territories and believed that the British should offer attractive terms to the nationalists to buy the freehold, but Whitehall was too preoccupied to give the idea much consideration.[9] It would be interesting to ponder what might have happened had the British managed to persuade the KMT to sell the leasehold on the New Territories to them. Although it seems doubtful that the nationalists would have seriously entertained the idea, as can be seen from Chiang Kai-shek's attempt to regain Hong Kong after World War II from Britain (see below).

Japanese Invasion, 1937–1945

Timing is everything in life. On 7 July 1937, the Marco Polo Bridge incident ignited World War II in Asia.[10] The invasion of China by the Japanese saved the CCP from obliteration by the skin of its teeth. Many major coastal cities like Shanghai, Nanjing and Guangzhou quickly fell to the disciplined Japanese army.[11] The invasion brought a respite from the KMT's campaign to eliminate the communists. The communists retreated into the interior in the 1930s through a series of escapes walking through eleven provinces covering 6,000 miles, culminating in what became known as the Long March.

Notwithstanding their deep mutual animosity, the KMT and CCP were forced by circumstances to collaborate once more in a Second United Front to fight Japan. The KMT-CCP collaboration was preceded by one of history's most bizarre episodes—the Xian Incident. While in Xian to plot fighting the CCP, Chiang Kai-shek was kidnapped on 12 December 1936 by Zhang Xueliang, a warlord supposedly allied with the KMT. Zhang apparently wanted the two parties to unite to defeat the Japanese, and thought Chiang had to be got rid of as Chiang was reluctant to cooperate with the CCP. Chiang was saved through the extraordinary intercession of Zhou Enlai. The Soviets and even some communists worried about what could happen with Chiang gone. There was no leader then with Chiang's stature to forge a united front even if he was reluctant. A bargain was struck. In return for his release, Chiang agreed to stop attacking the CCP and join forces with the communist to fight the Japanese instead.[12] With the KMT's attention focussed elsewhere, the communists managed to regroup, and their contribution during the war gained them a degree of international recognition by the end of World War II. Indeed, Mao Zedong claimed that the communists had 1.2 million members, commanded 910,000 troops[13] and controlled much of the countryside north of the Yangtze by then.[14]

By September 1938, the Japanese were pushing south. The fall of Shanghai and Nanjing were terrible ordeals. After the fall of Nanjing in the winter of 1937, for at least six weeks, the Japanese Army raped, pillaged and executed both prisoners of war and civilians. While estimates vary, it is generally accepted that at least 250,000 men, women and children were killed. The wealthy were able to flee before the arrival of the Japanese. The people who suffered were the city's poor.

By October, the Japanese had landed on the coast of Guangdong. Guangzhou fell after just nine days of fighting. Half a million refugees from the Mainland flooded over to Hong Kong seeking safety.[15] The war was then at Hong Kong's doorstep. Things were getting far too close for comfort.

Up until the start of the Pacific War in December 1941, Hong Kong was a war-free zone as the British adopted a neutral stance towards the Sino-Japanese War. The colonial administration had to navigate delicate sensitivities. Its natural sympathies were with China, and it did not want to clamp down on the activities of the local Chinese attempting to aid fighting on the Mainland. Yet, it could not afford to upset Japan or ignore British government policy, which had declared Hong Kong as a neutral zone in September 1938.[16] Thus, the Hong Kong authorities not only had to prohibit certain activities, such anti-Japanese public meetings, but also censored Chinese newspapers for opposing Japan. It also turned down requests by the Chinese Unofficial Members of the Legislative Council to send relief money to the Mainland, nor was the Hong Kong Red Cross permitted to send personnel there. However, the authorities turned a blind eye to both the nationalists and communists funnelling resources to the Mainland through the colony.[17]

Eighth Route Army Hong Kong Office

During the war years with Japan, Hong Kong was extremely important to both the CCP and KMT. In January 1938, the colonial government allowed the CCP to set up a local liaison office.[18] It was as a result of Zhou Enlai's negotiations with Archibald Clark-Kerr, the British ambassador (1882–1951) in Chongqing. Under the guise of a wholesale tea company called Yue Hwa Company at 18 Queen's Road Central, the CCP set up what was in effect the Eighth Route Army Hong Kong Office in the colony. The Office was headed by Liao Chengzhi under the direction of Zhou Enlai, who had become the head of the CCP Central Southern Bureau by then. The main task of the Office was to act as a purchasing agency for the CCP, as well as to use the special political and geographic circumstances of Hong Kong to conduct united front work in Hong Kong, Macao and among the overseas Chinese to gain sympathy and support for the fight against the Japanese.[19] Liao Chengzhi would head the State Council's Hong Kong and Macao Affairs Office one day and play an important part in the resumption of sovereignty over Hong Kong (Chapter 7).

The Hong Kong police raided the Yue Hwa Company on 11 March 1939 and arrested a number of staff as a result of its anti-Japanese activities. The company was closed until Zhou Enlai protested to the British ambassador in Chongqing. Those arrested were released and all documents seized were returned. However, under strong Japanese pressure, the Hong Kong government was forced to have the company closed later that year. Nonetheless, Liao Chengzhi and his colleagues continued to operate covertly and it was an open secret to one and all in Hong Kong that they were still the CCP's Eighth Route Army Hong Kong Office.[20]

The communists continued to engage in many types of activities in Hong Kong. Firstly, they encouraged artists and writers to rally to the anti-Japanese cause. They formed the Chinese National Anti-Japanese Literary Association Hong Kong Branch and the Hong Kong Youth Literature Study Association in 1939 and 1940 respectively to organise programmes and events. The CCP on the Mainland organised writers and journalists to go to Hong Kong to publish anti-Japanese newspapers and magazines.[21] Filmmakers from Shanghai co-produced anti-Japanese war films together with the Hong Kong local movie industry.[22] Secondly, the Eighth Route Army Hong Kong Office used Hong Kong as a base to raise funds for the war effort. Their work secured donations in cash and in kind from overseas Chinese.[23] With his family connections and extensive network of friends, Liao Chengzhi did well for the resistance. Thirdly, Song Qingling, widow of Sun Yat-sen, was an ally. Song's special political status on the Mainland, as well as internationally, made her extremely useful. She formed the Defend China League in Hong Kong in June 1938 and was quite successful in rallying support for the resistance. Liao Chengzhi's mother, who came from a well-known family joined the League and helped to raise funds for her son's cause.[24]

The party also performed various quasi-military tasks to support guerrilla forces in Guangdong, including running relief efforts and recruiting fresh forces to send to the war zones. The CCP in Hong Kong drew on their connections with the labour unions in Hong Kong, such as the Chinese Seamen's Union, to organise the resistance. A principal organiser and secretary of the Seamen's Union, Zeng Sheng, began to recruit Hong Kong volunteers to cross over to Guangdong to form a guerrilla movement behind Japanese lines. The recruits were mainly driven by a sense of nationalism to fight Japan and not by communism. In Malaya, Singapore and Indonesia alone, there were over 2.3 million overseas Chinese, who proved crucial to China in its war effort. It was relatively easy to mobilise the overseas Chinese because many of them were of Hakka origin with their home counties in the Pearl River Delta region of Guangdong.[25]

Guerrillas and war

On 12 October 1938, the Japanese landed in Daya Bay in Guangdong and defeated the nationalist army. The next day, a band of 120 guerrilla fighters came together in the East River area in order to put together another fighting force. They were driven by a sense of patriotism rather than communism to resist the Japanese. With the fall of Guangzhou, the Overseas Chinese formed a special association in order to send representatives on an inspection tour of the Pearl River Delta region with the help of Liao Chengzhi, himself a Hakka. After the tour, young people from Southeast Asia, particularly those of Hakka origin, were recruited to join service teams to engage in propaganda and relief work. The Hakka and other Cantonese recruits would become the most active Chinese guerrilla fighting force in the neighbourhood of Hong Kong and the Pearl River Delta during the rest of the war. By December 1938, the Huizhou-Baoan People's Anti-Japanese Guerrilla Force and the Dongguan-Baoan-Huizhou People's Anti-Japanese Guerrilla Force had come to life. They got some weapons from the KMT but were not well-endowed in resources and materials.[26]

When Poland was invaded in September 1939, Britain declared war on Germany and Hong Kong became a part of Britain's war effort. Hong Kong was already a part of China's war effort, even though the colony was technically neutral. Besides being a functioning port, a new industry had also sprung into life to produce gas masks, helmets and other wartime supplies for China. Up until then, around 60 percent to 70 percent of the war materials reaching the KMT from overseas went through Hong Kong. In order to speed up war supplies, the nationalists brought their administrative infrastructure to Hong Kong. In 1939, there were a total of 32 KMT organs operating in Hong Kong on what the British Foreign Office described as an "official and semi-official" basis. Indeed, the KMT treated Hong Kong as an offshore retreat where they could go for weeks and months at a time.[27] The KMT also published its own newspaper to drum up support for the war effort.[28]

The Japanese army occupied Hong Kong on Christmas Day 1941. The guerrillas were already in Hong Kong, having begun operations by early 1941, initially without the knowledge of the Hong Kong government. Their commander was Cai Guoliang. They infiltrated the New Territories with the goal of organising villagers in preparation for the Japanese invasion. When the guerrillas first arrived, they were thought to be bandits. The guerrillas needed to win the confidence of the village elders to gain the villagers' cooperation. As the guerrillas proved effective in controlling the real bandits, they were gradually able to take over village administration. Despite the danger, many villagers joined the fighting for they had a common cause against the Japanese. The villagers were hardy folks, knew the terrain well and made a good fighting force.

The Japanese took Hong Kong because it was a useful prize. The excellent harbour provided a crucial anchorage for Japanese shipping. Moreover, essential war materials could no longer be delivered so easily to the Chinese troops on the Mainland. After the fall of Guangzhou, when the Kowloon–Guangzhou rail route was severed, innumerable junks in Hong Kong had smuggled materials to support fighting on the Mainland. Tokyo estimated that the junks were channelling as much as 6,000 tons of munitions across the border each month. The Japanese believed that by capturing Hong Kong, the war effort on the Mainland would be severely weakened.[29]

Despite the fact that the Battle for Hong Kong lasted only eighteen days, the Japanese did not gain firm control over the whole of the territory. They were able to control the urban areas, but the rural parts of the New Territories were another matter altogether. The rugged countryside was hard to secure because the terrain allowed the guerrillas to continue active undercover activities. Thus, the CCP never had to cease its operation in Hong Kong during the war years.[30]

The guerrilla forces in Guangdong did not make life easy for the Japanese either. After a few years of fighting, they had become disciplined and seasoned soldiers with the talented Zeng Sheng as their general and commander-in-chief. Zeng had been the secretary general of the Hong Kong Seamen's Union. The guerrillas followed Mao Zedong's fighting strategy closely. They had an elite core made up of well-trained fighters; a part-time rank-and-file group made up of recruits whose main responsibility was to defend their own village area; and auxiliaries, who supported troops by acting as couriers, runners and labour units.[31] Up until December 1943, the guerrilla forces were under KMT command as part of the united front. However, on 2 December 1943, the CCP Central Committee declared that five guerrilla fighting units in the Pearl River Delta would go under communist command instead and be known as the East River Column, Guangdong People's Anti-Japanese

Guerrilla Corps.[32] By 1943, the East River guerrillas had a total strength of about 5,000 full-time soldiers divided into six detachments.[33]

Cai Guoliang's detachment mainly operated in the Mirs Bay–Sai Kung area but it had also managed to penetrate into parts of urban Kowloon. This unit turned out to be highly competent and because of its unique abilities, it was given the designation of the Hong Kong–Kowloon Independent Brigade on 3 February 1942. A founding ceremony was held at a church at Wong Mo Ying Village in Sai Kung.[34] On 2 December 1943, this Brigade became one of the fighting units put under CCP command. Thus, the New Territories became a sub-area of the Guangdong guerrillas, with each sub-area under the supervision of three officers—the military command, a political officer and a liaison officer.[35] The resistance would not have worked without the cooperation of the villagers, who provided food and shelter, and helped with the escape of prisoners and civilians.

Children as young as ten years old were trained as runners. They were known as "little devils". These kids were tough. The intelligence work of the guerrillas could not have been done without them. The boys usually worked on their own and the girls in pairs. With the agreement of their parents, these runners learnt about the importance and absolute secrecy of their work, and were expected to give their lives to the cause if necessary. Some were caught and died but none of them ever betrayed the resistance. They were trained with the system of codes of triangles and crosses. A runner with a message with three crosses and three triangles had to run at top speed to deliver it. In the city, children were also used to work in espionage. These "little rats" provided information about Kai Tak airport. The children could move around easily and were regarded as a nuisance by the Japanese. The guerrillas trained them to measure the thickness of walls and to memorise the layout of the entire area in order to be able to draw a diagram of the area. They were also trained to remember the numbers of aeroplanes, and the runways inside, as well as the directions for take-offs. This information was passed on to the Allies after clearance by the CCP headquarters. There were many stories about the quick wits and bravery of these children. Women guerrillas also played an important role in Hong Kong. Some worked as runners, and others in the military units, but most of them worked in radio communications, intelligence, propaganda, as well as taking care of necessities for the military units. The women usually worked in pairs and carried their messages hidden in their hair or food baskets.[36]

The guerrillas' activities helped the war effort in three crucial ways. The first was to help people escape capture during the early days of the occupation. Soon after the fall of Hong Kong, Zhou Enlai directed the East River guerrillas to evacuate prominent Chinese writers, journalists and political activists who were friends of the CCP to "Free" China—those areas not occupied by the Japanese. There were two routes for the escape at the end of 1941 and early 1942. The East Route went from Ngau Tze Wan to Sai Kung to Mirs Bay and then to Dameisha and from there to

Huiyang. The West Route started in Shanghai Street, then to Castle Peak Road, Tai Po, Yuen Long, Lok Ma Chau, and across to Meilin and Baishilong.[37]

Liao Chengzhi had left Hong Kong in January 1941 via the East Route but was sent back subsequently to help important people trapped in Hong Kong to escape, including Song Qingling and Liao's own mother. These people were brought to China by the Communications Unit of the guerrillas dressed as refugees. Liao Chengzhi and others were able to escape on 5 January 1942. Approximately 800 persons left Hong Kong with the assistance of the communists over a three-month period.[38] The guerrillas' organisation skill was impressive, as they managed to slip people out under the noses of the Japanese.

In addition, the guerrillas also rescued and smuggled British and Allied Prisoners of War (POWs) to safety. On 9 January 1942, the first group of POWs escaped under the leadership of Lt. Col. Lindsay Ride, with the help of Francis Lee Yiu Piu, who made arrangements with the guerrillas. They went by boat and on foot, and were hidden, housed and fed by the New Territories villagers and were eventually led across the border by the Communications Unit. Subsequently, Ride established the British Army Aid Group (BAAG) in South China to help escapees and to smuggle medicines into the POW camps in Hong Kong.[39] The Brigade provided crucial intelligence for the BAAG. The success of BAAG was also the success of the guerrillas because they linked the POW camps with the outside world.[40] After 1942, there were few escape attempts by the POWs because of fear of reprisals of those who were left behind. From then on, the cooperation between the guerrillas and the Allies was mainly in espionage, sabotage and the smuggling of medical supplies to the POWs and to civilian camps. They continued to help civilian refugees who fled from Hong Kong into Free China.[41]

By 1944, rescue missions were mainly of downed Allied airmen who were bombing Hong Kong. There were many stories, such as that of Lt. Donald W. Kerr of the 14th Squadron of the US Air Force whose aeroplane was shot down during a bombing raid of Kai Tak airport in February 1944. He was rescued by a thirteen-year-old little devil. Together with a translator, the three of them spent more than 20 days dodging the Japanese and hiding in caves. Kerr was brought safely to the guerrilla headquarters in Huiyang across the border. About a hundred foreigners including Britons, Dutchmen, Belgians, American air force personnel and Indian soldiers were saved. The successful escapes earned the CCP much good will and bolstered its reputation. The guerrilla assistance was considered so important that in March 1945, the US Navy sent personnel to consult with the East River Detachment in preparation for an Allied landing in south China.[42]

In the area of espionage, two stories illustrate the kind of work carried out in Hong Kong. A guerrilla agent, Li Cheng, infiltrated the headquarters of the Intelligence Department of the Kempeitai (Japanese Military Police). Even after the guerrillas successfully bombed the railway bridge at Argyle Street in April 1944, Li was still able to pass an enemy map of Hong Kong, Kowloon and the New

Territories to the headquarters of the East River Detachment, who in turn passed it on to the Americans. On 13 July 1945, an emergency order came from the Kempetai Intelligence Headquarters to seal off all roads and shipping in order to eliminate the Inner City Unit of the guerrillas. Li Cheng was able to get the warning to the members of the unit in time. Li worked for a total of three years and eight months for the Japanese, which was the entire period of the occupation.[43]

In the case of Ya Wen, she was instructed to observe all movements of boats in the harbour with a pair of binoculars smuggled to her. The binoculars were taken apart, and brought to her on two separate trips. She was instructed to mark down all the buoys and label them and observe the type of boats. The information she gave was transmitted to her own unit and forwarded to the US Air Force for the bombing of shipping in the harbour.[44]

Another crucial activity was to harass the Japanese at every opportunity. Indeed, the totality of their efforts amounted to far more than just flea bites and they imposed visible pressure on the Japanese. For example, the Hong Kong–Kowloon Independent Brigade sent handgun units to attack the Japanese bases, cut off the Japanese supplies and ambush traitors. There were two aspects to the harassment: firstly, by propaganda activities, such as producing anti-Japanese leaflets and posters, distributing them widely, to the fury of the Japanese, in front of their military offices; and secondly, by finding sabotage opportunities to throw hurdles in the way of the Japanese. For example, in 1944, using air raids as an excuse, agents in the Kowloon Dockyard sounded sirens at least once a week so workers would scatter, thereby slowing down the Japanese production system. The bombing of the No. 4 railway bridge in Kowloon in 1944 was accomplished by a civil servant with the Department of Water Works. The explosives were brought to the city, piece by piece from the New Territories by women guerrillas dressed as hawkers selling firewood and children dressed as cowherds. To fight the Japanese in the waters, the Brigade destroyed the marine supplies of the Japanese troops.[45]

Who would take back Hong Kong?

Hong Kong lay inside the Allied powers' China theatre, which covered the whole of China, Indo-China and Thailand, Chiang Kai-shek became the supreme commander of this theatre in January 1942. Chiang sought to use the war to end the "unequal treaties". With the support of the United States, he instructed the Chinese ambassador to Britain, Wellington Koo,[46] to propose to Britain in mid-1942 that it should give up Hong Kong, or at least the leased New Territories. The British knew the United States, under President Franklin Roosevelt, was not keen on assisting Britain in the restoration of its Empire after the war. The Foreign Office had even suggested that Hong Kong was already a lost cause, so that a gesture of cession would demonstrate to the Americans that the British were not fighting the war for the reactionary purpose of preserving the British Empire.[47] The question of Hong

Kong's future became the subject of an intense internal debate within the British government in 1942. The Colonial Office did not want to give-up the colony and it won Winston Churchill's support (prime minister, 1941–1945 and 1951–1955). A compromise between Britain and the KMT was eventually reached, where China merely informed Britain that the Chinese government "reserves its rights" to raise the issue "for discussion at a later date".[48] Moreover, the Chinese elites in Hong Kong made clear to Whitehall that they preferred British to Chinese rule after the war.

Knowing that Chiang Kai-shek wanted to regain Hong Kong, a Hong Kong Planning Unit was formed in 1943 in London to plan the future civil administration once Hong Kong was recaptured from the Japanese, so that the British could, by regaining physical possession as soon as possible, foil Chiang's effort. Up until November 1943, Roosevelt was still assuring Chiang that the United States would help him recover Hong Kong. However, by 1944, the United States had softened its position on restoration of the British Empire because it was better to keep Britain strong as a bulwark against the Soviet Union. Also the Americans had become disappointed with Chiang's military efforts in China. Harry Truman (US president, 1945–1953) had become president after Roosevelt passed away in April 1945. The United States no longer insisted that Hong Kong had to be handed back to China after the war, as Truman was less motivated than his predecessor to push decolonisation because on balance, it was better for the United States to keep the British strong in the region. Once the British realised this, they were not about to give Hong Kong up, and it became important to dash to recover Hong Kong once the Japanese surrendered.[49]

At the end of the World War II, after Japan surrendered on 14 August 1945, the general arrangement among the Allies was for the Japanese forces within China, Taiwan and French Indo-China north of the 16-degree north latitude to surrender to Chiang Kai-shek. This should have included Hong Kong. However, the British government did not see such an arrangement to be in its interest, because Britain wanted to restore British jurisdiction over its Asian colonies and wanted no hiccups, despite Chiang's assurance that he would not try to retake Hong Kong after accepting the surrender.[50] To ensure Chiang would keep his word, Britain made it known that it would accept Japanese surrender irrespective of the Allies' operational theatres arrangement. Chiang sought to resolve the matter diplomatically. After rounds of tussling, the final compromise was that Rear Admiral Cecil Harcourt would represent both Britain and Chiang when receiving the surrender from the Japanese, and that the acceptance of the surrender would only take place after Chiang had formally accepted the same for China. Harcourt's fleet was already at Subic Bay in the Philippines and thus could reach Hong Kong quickly.

Why did Chiang acquiesce to an arrangement he was clearly unhappy with? Most likely, his hands were already very full. He had to work out the acceptance of the surrender on the Mainland. Although there were KMT troops in the south that could have been put into action, as Britain did not want to give up Hong Kong,

Chiang might well have had to fight to regain it. Perhaps he did not want to risk the possibility of losing, which would have discredited him. Besides, he needed the support of both Britain and the United States to remain an important player on the world stage. Chiang certainly did not want the communists to use the opportunity to expand their influence. In fact, by late August, nationalist troops were on the move towards Hong Kong, but the KMT claimed that it was not going to take Hong Kong but wanted to prevent the communists from doing so.[51] Unsurprisingly, some Mainland historians put the blame on Chiang and the KMT for not taking Hong Kong back then.[52] However, there is a case to be made that Chiang was so determined to prevent the communists from doing so, that it was better to allow the British to recapture it.[53]

The KMT wanted Japanese soldiers everywhere to surrender to KMT soldiers. Likewise, the CCP saw no reason why they should not disarm Japanese soldiers in areas under its control. While the KMT issued a directive to its soldiers that the communists should not deal with the Japanese, the CCP sent out its own order to communist forces that they should demand Japanese soldiers surrender to them. From the moment that Japan surrendered, the KMT and CCP in effect started to fight each other again.

Oddly enough, the CCP ended up playing a role in the Japanese surrender in Hong Kong but the communists did not seize the territory for itself. Before the arrival of British forces, the Hong Kong–Kowloon Independent Brigade was the only military force in the territory.[54] Its units took control of Tai Po and Yuen Long and all the other market towns in the New Territories, as well as the outlying islands. In most cases, the Japanese gave up or fled as soon as the communists showed-up. The guerrillas got the villagers to organise local administrations and self-defence forces. They collected for their own use ammunition and supplies that the Japanese left behind. Extra supplies were sent to Guangdong to their guerrilla comrades. They gave no signs of wanting to impede the British taking control of Hong Kong. The result was that the mutual suspicion and animosity between the KMT and CCP had in effect cancelled each other out on this occasion, and Hong Kong fell back into the hands of the eager British.[55]

As news of Japan's surrender spread in the Stanley prisoner of war camp, the senior British officer kept there, Franklin Charles Gimson (1890–1975, the Colonial Secretary who unluckily arrived in Hong Kong a day before the Japanese invasion), approached the Japanese commandant to say that he would take charge pending the arrival of British troops. Gimson knew that was what he had to do because the British government, through the British ambassador in Chongqing and via the BAAG and others, had relayed a message to him to assume administration of Hong Kong as soon as he could, so that a token British presence could be re-established. This was important to foil any move from Chiang Kai-shek to recover Hong Kong or give the communists a chance. He appointed himself as the acting governor of Hong Kong once the Japanese conceded, and then asked the Japanese to help with maintaining order.⁵⁶ When Cecil Harcourt and British soldiers finally arrived on 30 August 1945 and control was handed to them, Harcourt declared a military government by proclamation the following day with himself as its head, and Gimson as lieutenant governor. On 16 September 1945, Harcourt formally accepted the Japanese surrender in Government House.

When the Hong Kong–Kowloon Independent Brigade negotiated with the British concerning its role, an understanding was reached that the CCP would be allowed to continue a presence in Hong Kong by setting up a liaison office, and that its members would be guaranteed the freedom of travel and publication, as long as they did not carry out "unlawful" activities.⁵⁷ Huang Zuomei, also known as Raymond Wong, was the CCP-British go-between. Fang Fang was another prominent guerrilla at the time, who would direct guerrilla activities in Guangdong, Guangxi and Jiangxi from Hong Kong during the civil war until 1949. The liaison office, initially set up at 172 Nathan Road, Kowloon, would eventually morph into the Xinhua News Agency, Hong Kong Branch with Huang Zuomei as its second director. The first director was Qiao Guanhua, who also spent time in Hong Kong during the war years.⁵⁸

After the surrender in September 1945, since the British did not have enough soldiers to maintain law and order in the territory at that time, they asked the guerrillas to help. The guerrillas agreed and left some troops behind until the 30 June 1946 to police Sha Tau Kok, Yuen Long, and Sai Kung. Nevertheless, the Brigade's main body of soldiers moved north of the Shenzhen River to the Mainland. A British-funded self-defence unit was then set up in the New Territories, which functioned until the autumn of 1946.⁵⁹ When the Brigade withdrew from Hong Kong on the 28 September 1945, they issued a moving message, ending thus:

> Farewell, our beloved Hong Kong compatriots. Today, we shall depart Hong Kong. But our care and concern for your happiness and liberty remains unchanged. You have experienced a long period of suffering. We hope that the Hong Kong government shall give you adequate relief and to assist you in rebuilding your business and improve your livelihood. We hope that your glorious struggle will earn the well-deserved respect from the international community. Today, we shall withdraw. But our hearts are with you forever.⁶⁰

Guangdong was a sideshow in the overall Chinese civil war as the hard battles were fought in Northern China. The guerrillas from the Hong Kong–Kowloon Independent Brigade fought the KMT from October 1945 in Guangdong. In one of the many skirmishes that were fought in Shenzhen, it was reported that a hundred guerrillas were killed and over thirty seriously injured. What was interesting was that many of those injured were transported by the Brigade to a hospital in Kowloon for treatment. The East River guerrillas eventually went to Shandong to continue fighting the KMT.

Huang Zuomei, the interpreter and director of international relations for the East River Column, was considered by the British to be an agent of the BAAG. He was invited by the British government to join the victory parade in London in May 1946 and was awarded a medal by King George VI for courage during the war and given an MBE.⁶¹ The relationship between the CCP and the colonial government could be said to have reached a high point.

Having recovered Hong Kong, the British needed to re-establish authority. They had outlawed the KMT in the colony before the Japanese occupation, but it had to be accepted after the World War II. Most crucially, it was the ruling party in China. On the whole, the KMT also saw it in its interest to cooperate with the British authorities in Hong Kong and not to stir up trouble there.⁶² At the same time, the CCP adopted a low profile. The communists did not want to cause trouble for the British either. The party never lost sight of the bigger picture: its concern was on the Mainland. Its goals were to promote the united front against the KMT, to support guerrilla activities in Guangdong, and to use the colony as a contact point internationally.⁶³ When the British military administration was replaced by a civil government in 1946, the British could focus on rebuilding its support base among the local elites without interference from the KMT and CCP. Most of the former business and professional elites were brought back to serve the British colonial administration, and in return, the elites worked doubly hard to restore British rule. The symbiotic need was strong on both sides.⁶⁴

The return of Mark Young (governor, 1941 and 1946–1947) on 1 May 1946 to resume the governorship that he had surrendered in December 1941 provided a brief spell of democratic talk in Hong Kong. Young proposed a plan to increase political representation that was accepted by Whitehall but with the change of governor in July 1947, the Young Plan was dropped, as his successor, Alexander Grantham (governor, 1947–1957), had very different ideas. As Hong Kong would not be independent, he thought it did not need the same kind of reform that other colonies would need to prepare for independence. Moreover, colonial administrators were concerned that elections could turn Hong Kong into an electoral battleground between the KMT and CCP as civil war broke out on the Mainland, and the British government was not insisting on constitutional change.⁶⁵ The people of Hong Kong were grateful that the local economy had picked up and they were not embroiled in more fighting.

The Guerrillas Then and Now

Fang Fang became a vice-chairman of the Guangdong provincial CCP after 1949 and was responsible for imposing the party's land reform but was considered too soft on the locals. He was accused of the dual fault of refusing to learn from the country's land reform experience and defying his superiors by promoting "localism"—euphemism for not following central orders. To protect Fang and others,

Ye Jianying accepted responsibility as the most senior cadres in the province, and both Fang and Ye had to make self-criticisms. Many cadres were demoted or lost their jobs in Guangdong. Fang was then further demoted, and eventually dismissed from all his party posts. Through the efforts of fellow Chaozhou clansmen who held senior positions at the Overseas Chinese Commission in Beijing, Fang was posted there in 1955 to serve as the deputy director. Ye Jianying was extremely unhappy about the purges in Guangdong although there was not much that he could do at the time. During the Cultural Revolution, discussed in Chapter 6, Fang Fang and many people like him were accused of having foreign connections. Fang was arrested in December 1966, detained, tortured and died after five years in 1971. It was only in the 1994 that the party acknowledged that the accusations and punishments against Fang Fang were wrong.[66]

As for the other East River guerrillas, Zeng Sheng became deputy provincial governor of Guangdong and mayor of Guangzhou in 1960 and was regarded as having done a good job. However, he was arrested in 1967 in Beijing, beaten and incarcerated until 1974. It was extreme irony that his alleged fault was having been an agent of the imperialists and a "bandit" during the war. Zeng was appointed vice-minister of transport in October 1975, became minister in 1979, retired in 1983 and died in Guangzhou in 1995. Of the East River Guerrillas, Tan Gan worked in Xinhua Hong Kong from its earliest days until his retirement in the early 1990s; Chen Daming went on to do party work in Beijing but was transferred to Xinhua Hong Kong to take up the post of deputy director in 1982 when the Sino-British negotiations over the future of Hong Kong began; and Yang Qi was purged in the 1950s but subsequently transferred to Xinhua Hong Kong to head the regular news section. In 1982, Yang became the secretary general at Xinhua Hong Kong before becoming the publisher of *Ta Kung Pao* in 1984. He retired in 1992.[67]

As of 1997, there were estimated to have been about 300 members of the Hong Kong–Kowloon Independent Brigade still living in Hong Kong, about 130 on the Mainland and some also in Macao. The organising committee for the reunification celebrations invited former brigade members to join the activities. Moreover, chief executive Tung Chee Hwa held a reception for them in August 1997 after which the HKSAR government begun to compile a list of brigade members who died in action and eventually added 115 names to the Roll of Honour at the City Hall Memorial Shrine in October 1998. Members of the brigade and their surviving spouses were accorded the same treatment as other veterans in pension entitlements from 1999.[68] There is still much good historical research work of this period waiting to be done. Besides the archives of the Hong Kong Public Record Office and the British archives, the Hong Kong University Library also has records left by Lt. Col. Lindsay Ride of the BAAG.[69]

War Ends, War Begins

The Chinese people were exhausted after eight years of Japanese occupation. The war had disrupted their lives enormously. There were vast numbers of traumatised and destitute people with no help in sight. Families had been separated, and the scars of war were deep. The economy was in tatters, and hyperinflation would soon set in. Chiang Kai-shek's government faced the daunting task of re-establishing administration, restarting industry and dealing with famine in several parts of the country. Post-war recovery and reconstruction was a Herculean task. The last thing China needed was more bloodletting.

There was a brief moment of hope that the KMT and CCP could find a way to coexist. The CCP's realism about the relative weakness of the communists—although much recovered since 1927—led Mao Zedong and Zhou Enlai to travel to Chongqing in August 1945 to negotiate a power-sharing deal with Chiang Kai-shek and the KMT. Chiang had issued an invitation to them to meet in Chongqing as he was also under pressure from many quarters to negotiate with the communists.[70] The CCP controlled about 20 percent of China's land mass and perhaps a third of the population, mainly in the rural parts of North China.[71] After 43 days of talks, the two sides agreed to adopt a policy of peace, national reconstruction, cooperation and to avoid civil war. But it would come to naught. Neither side could agree terms for the creation of a coalition government and how to unify their respective troops into a national force. President Truman tried unsuccessfully to prevent civil war by sending special envoy General George C. Marshall (1880–1959) to reconcile differences. He became disillusioned with both sides. By then, the KMT and CCP were eager to have a face-off, taking China towards chaos. The civil war started on 26 June 1946. However, the end—victory for the CCP—was not a foregone conclusion.

The CCP's military history notes that the communists' strategy was to sap the effective strength of the KMT first before engaging in major battles.[72] The communists had perfected guerrilla operations fighting the Japanese. They adapted ideas from Sun Zi (544–496 BC), which Mao Zedong articulated in his famous essay "On Guerrilla Warfare" in 1937.[73] The civil war had three distinct phases. The first stage between July 1946 and June 1947 was a war by gradual attrition. The strategy was to draw the KMT army units far into Manchuria in the northeast and deep into Shanxi in central China thus splitting-up the enemy's army. The People's Liberation Army deliberately gave up Yenan (Yan'nan) in March 1947 without contest, withdrew into the countryside, and would only take on the enemy where it could win due to having numerical superiority, such as when the enemy troops were dispersed or isolated.[74] The second stage was aimed at preserving its own strength, but eroding that of the enemy's in limited, well-chosen counter-offensives while extending the range of engagements. The communists saw an opportunity to attack the KMT troops in Manchuria in the autumn and winter of 1947. The success of the CCP in the north was watched from afar by the rest of China. The increase in the power of the CCP set off "seismic shifts in Chinese society" bringing new recruits to the communist cause.[75] By then, the CCP had a compelling ideology that resonated with the people who had suffered so long, a charismatic leader in Mao Zedong, and now an ability to assert authority over the less-than-endearing KMT. By the late summer of 1948, the CCP had 2 million troops, reaching parity in numbers with the nationalists. Many CCP soldiers were defectors from the KMT. It was time to go on the final stage—to be on the offensive, as enemy soldiers had become not only physically tired, but the KMT had become highly unpopular as a result of its cruelty to dissenters and widespread corrupt practices. Meanwhile, infighting within the KMT resulted in Chiang Kai-shek being pushed out of office in January 1949. Within a mere five more months of fighting, the communists had won.[76] On 1 October 1949, Mao Zedong proclaimed the establishment of the People's Republic of China from the Gate of Heavenly Peace in Beijing. In December, Chiang Kai-shek, who was holding out in Chengdu, climbed aboard an aeroplane on a foggy day and flew to Taiwan to rule China from there. Chiang intended to return one day in triumph to win back the Mainland, while the communists continue to regard Taiwan as unfinished business left over from history.

Hong Kong's Role during the Civil War

During the civil war, Hong Kong, under British administration was useful to the CCP primarily because it was not under KMT control.[77] To the CCP, Hong Kong's relatively liberal political environment provided significant strategic value, as it could be used as an operational base to facilitate war against the KMT in South China. The Hong Kong population was not its main target. The CCP cultivated relations with British officials and took care not to challenge British sovereignty in Hong Kong.

The CCP understood the importance of combining overt and covert activities. While it conducted open propaganda and mass mobilisation work, its underground activities collected intelligence and penetrated organisations it wanted to influence. Zhou Enlai was the party's master organiser and he recognised Hong Kong's undoubted usefulness. After the first phase of the civil war had begun, senior party members were sent to Hong Kong from the latter half of 1946 to use the colony to support CCP activities.[78] Zhou noted in December that the role of Hong Kong had become more important, not only in relation to its activities in Guangdong, Guangxi and among the Chinese communities in Southeast Asia, but also for liaison with Europe and United States. Zhou saw the need to resolve how better to use Hong Kong so that the party's overt and covert activities could be properly coordinated.[79] The CCP Central Committee's solution made on 16 January 1947 was to set up a Hong Kong Central Branch Bureau in Hong Kong. Its major tasks would be to drive propaganda campaigns against Chiang Kai-shek and the United States (which was supporting the KMT) as well as facilitate guerrilla fighting on the Mainland.[80] The secretary for the Branch Bureau was the guerrilla leader Fang Fang. The Hong Kong Central Branch Bureau, formally established in May 1947, was placed under the direct leadership of the CCP Central Committee, but operationally it was to take direction from the Shanghai Central Branch Bureau, although in effect communication and direction mainly came from the CCP Central Committee.[81] The geographic scope of the Branch Bureau's work was extensive and regional in nature, covering CCP activities in Guangdong, Guangxi, Fujian, Hunan, Yunnan, and Guizhou. In February 1949, the Branch Bureau in Guangzhou was renamed the CCP Central South China Bureau to reflect its regional nature. Within this structure were several committees and groups—there was a municipal work committee responsible for covert CCP work in the large cities of the various provinces; a rural armed forces work committee, an organisational work unit, and small groups to manage overseas Chinese work, united front work, cultural work, finance and economic work, and youth and women's work. There were also various local party committees, which supervised the underground CCP work in small cities and rural areas.[82] In addition, a Hong Kong Work Committee was also set up to manage a range of activities in Hong Kong and South China. The open activities included united front work to bring people to the side of the communist cause, such as publishing journals and newspaper, cultural activities, and connecting to youths, workers, women and the Overseas Chinese communities, as well as foreign affairs. It also carried out covert intelligence gathering work.[83]

Within this structure, the party devised guerrilla warfare, organised cadres and supporters to receive military training and mass mobilisation skills in Hong Kong, after which they were dispatched to various rural areas in southern China to instigate military struggles against the nationalists. From 1946 until the end of 1948, about 3,000 people went through training for the communist cause.[84]

Another important task at the time was to build relations with people who had arrived in Hong Kong to get away from the KMT. These groups included members of smaller parties, intellectuals and youths who had come under KMT pressure. Others who fled the Mainland, such as business people, were worried about the growing political instability.[85] The CCP considered them important targets to build a broad alliance against the enemy. The party invited them to discussions and meetings to explain CCP policies so as to gain their support.[86] For example, it was important for the CCP to cultivate prominent political figures like General Li Jichen and He Xianging, both former high-ranking KMT members, who broke with the nationalists and formed the KMT Revolutionary Committee in Hong Kong with the goal of overthrowing Chiang Kai-shek. Another target was the China Democratic League, a small political party formed by intellectuals and proscribed by the KMT. The league decided at a meeting in Hong Kong in January 1948 to form an alliance with the CCP.[87] Many of these non-CCP political figures returned to the Mainland after the founding of People's Republic of China in 1949 and were allowed to play various political roles in the CCP regime. In General Li's case, he became a vice chairman of the Standing Committee of the NPC in 1954.[88] The party's aim was to use them to serve the communist cause. In examining papers obtained by the Hong Kong Police after a raid of the home of a leading CCP member in Hong Kong at the time, the British had the following observations: "They will be used, but if they are given any place in a so-called Coalition Government they will have to enter on the Communist Party's terms and they will be allowed no policy of their own. There is clearly no intention to allow an opposition Party outside the Government."[89]

During the civil war period, Hong Kong had an important role in promoting propaganda work, the aim of which was to stoke anti-KMT sentiments and spread the CCP's political ideas back into South China. To promote "cultural hegemony", a Press Committee and a Culture Committee were set up under the Hong Kong Work Committee to carry out extensive united front and propaganda work in the education, journalism, literature and arts sectors in Hong Kong. The CCP always recognised the importance of intellectuals, who had strong skills in the use of language for publication, as well as using cultural and educational activities for mass mobilisation.

The communists established secondary schools with financial support from sympathetic businessmen and had its members become teachers. This arrangement, on the one hand, helped to propagate communist ideology among young people, and at the same time, enabled CCP members to earn a living in Hong Kong.[90] Together with members of the various democratic parties, the communists formed Dade College in Tuen Mun in October 1946 in a handsome weekend house. The creation of a college followed instructions from Zhou Enlai that there was a need to provide a base for cadres and sympathisers who had gone to Hong Kong. Many famous left-wing intellectuals taught at the college, such as Qian Jiaju, Guo Moruo, and Mao Dun. Its students came from the Mainland, among the guerrillas in Guangdong, and from communist parties in Southeast Asia. There were few students from Hong Kong. Of the 250 students in 1948, only 10 percent were local recruits. Numbers from Hong Kong were dismal because young people in the colony were assessed to have suffered from "Hong Kong head . . . an ideological syndrome that included arrogance, a selfish and city-oriented view, as well as a tendency to forget their Chinese identity and to despise their own culture".[91] Intensive training in Marxism was provided and the students were then sent to the Mainland. In 1949, the Hong Kong government cancelled the school's registration because it was accused of acting as a training centre for CCP cadres and pursuing activities inconsistent with Hong Kong's security interests. During its short history, Dade College trained more than 740 students.[92]

The party invested in newspapers and magazines because it was well aware that these publications were the major means to spread ideas. The CCP-controlled *Zheng Bao*, *Huashang Bao*, *Jingji Daobao*, *Guangming Bao*, *Renmin Bao*, *Wen Wei Po*, *Yuanwang Zhoukan*, and *Qunzhong Zhoukan*. The English bi-monthly journal, *China Digest*, was also published to appeal for support from overseas. Though these publications had their own editorial focus, in general, they spread anti-KMT messages and drummed up support for the communist cause.[93] The CCP cadres met regularly with the editorial staff of other local newspapers, like the *Huaqiao Ribao* and *Xingdao Ribao* to persuade them to adopt a sympathetic stance towards the CCP position.[94] A number of music, drama, and literature clubs were also formed to cultivate relations with people in arts and culture.[95]

> **Xinhua News Agency and Hong Kong**
>
> 1937—Xinhua News Agency established in Yenan.
> 1947—Xinhua News Agency (Hong Kong Branch) established.
> 1st Director—Qiao Guanhua (喬冠華), 1947–1949.
> 2nd Director—Huang Zuomei (黃作梅), 1949–1955.
> 3rd Director—Liang Weilin (梁威林), 1958–1977.
> 4th Director—Wang Kuang (王匡), 1978–1982.
> 5th Director—Xu Jiatun (許家屯), 1983–1989.
> 6th Director—Zhou Nan (周南), 1989–1997.
> 7th Director—Jiang Enzhu (姜恩柱), 1997–2002.
> NCNA (Xinhua Hong Kong) renamed the Liaison Office in 2000.
> 8th Director—Gao Siren (高祀仁), 2002–2009.
> 9th Director—Peng Qinghua (彭清華), 2009–2012.
> 10th Director—Zhang Xiaoming (張曉明), 2012–2017.
> 11th Director—Wang Zhimin (王志民), 2017–present.

CCP Structure and Xinhua News Agency

One of the most important decisions made by the CCP in relations to Hong Kong was to create the Xinhua News Agency, Hong Kong Branch in November 1946—the agency's first office outside the Mainland. The decision was made by Zhou Enlai, then the party secretary of the South China Bureau. This agency eventually became the Chinese quasi-diplomatic mission and CCP organ in the colony up until 1997.

The Xinhua News Agency was first founded in April 1937 at Yenan, the CCP headquarters from 1936 to 1947. Its first director was Liao Chengzhi. It became the official voice of the party, as well as a news agency and broadcasting station. Its mission was to sway public opinion to support the communist cause. During the Sino-Japanese War, it set up branch offices in various provinces, and began English broadcasting in September 1944 in order to appeal for overseas support.[96]

The Hong Kong agency's first director, Qiao Guanhua, was also the then party secretary of the Hong Kong Work Committee,[97] and would one day lead China's delegation to the United Nations, and then become foreign minister. His son, Qiao

Zhonghuai, would also work at Xinhua Hong Kong in the 1980s (Chapter 7). When Xinhua was first established in Hong Kong, it only had a staff of 15 split into three groups of five. The first consisted of the members of the Hong Kong administrative office of the East River Column, the second was in charge of the underground radio station run by the South China Bureau, and the third was made up of the five people in the editorial office of the former *Cheng Pao* (the party newspaper in Hong Kong then). A key task was to play the role of the CCP's mouthpiece in South China by preparing Chinese and English press statements for the local press and foreign correspondents stationed in Hong Kong. Qiao liaised with the colonial authorities on behalf of the CCP whenever necessary. From its earliest days, Xinhua Hong Kong was a quasi-diplomatic channel for government exchange. Owing to Qiao's special position, foreign correspondents frequently approached the agency for information about China and CCP policies, and through these contacts, the agency could in turn gather information about how the West saw events on the Mainland. Xinhua Hong Kong was conducting "united front work on an international level".[98] The strength of the communist presence in Hong Kong then was unknown but it had been estimated at about 5,000 supporters.[99]

CCP-British Relations

CCP's activities in Hong Kong reached an unprecedented level during the early period of the civil war. The CCP was well aware that their existence in Hong Kong to a very large extent depended on the tolerance of the British. Reportedly, Mao Zedong told a British journalist in 1946:

> China has enough trouble . . . for us to clamour for the return of Hong Kong. I am not interested in Hong Kong; the Communist Party is not interested in Hong Kong; it has never been the subject of any discussion among us. Perhaps ten, twenty or thirty years hence we may ask for a discussion regarding its return, but my attitude is that so long as Chinese are not treated as inferior to others in the matter of taxation and a voice in the Government, I am not interested in Hong Kong, and will certainly not allow it to be a bone of contention between your country and mine.[100]

On another occasion while speaking to journalists about Hong Kong, Mao said: "We are not going to demand for the return of Hong Kong at the present moment. China has a big territory, and many places have not yet been governed well. Why on earth do we have to prioritise to deal with such a small territory? In future, the Hong Kong issue could be resolved by consultative methods."[101]

Thus, a guiding principle of the CCP's work in Hong Kong during the civil war period was that, while facilitating the party's activities on the Mainland, it should avoid conducting any activities harming the interests of Hong Kong. Thus, the party would not organise labour or student movements to unsettle the territory.[102] Also, there were reports that when some local activists suggested promoting the idea of returning Hong Kong to Chinese rule in their printed materials, they were censured by the party.[103] In fact, in 1948 when there were communist activities in Malaysia, another British colony in Asia, the CCP in Hong Kong quickly issued a public statement to distance itself from those activities. The comments made by the British afterwards were illuminating:

> In so far as Hong Kong is concerned, their [CCP] line is to avoid incurring the displeasure of the authorities and this has been in fact the basis of the Communist Party's activities in Hong Kong over the past year. Hong Kong as a base from which to direct activities abroad is too valuable to be frittered away in local activities which might result in the banning or even expulsion of the Party with its leaders.[104]

Further, the improved relationship between the CCP and the British government during World War II also made the British more tolerant towards the CCP in Hong Kong. The British were impressed by the CCP's war effort against the Japanese and its achievements on the Mainland, and they had become disillusioned with the KMT's governing ability.[105] Moreover, the British had problems with Chiang Kai-shek and the KMT over the future of Hong Kong. As Qiao Guanhua noted: "On the one hand, [Britain] had a highly-strained relationship with Chiang Kai-shek. On the other hand, it did not refuse us (the CCP)."[106] This attitude contributed to the neutral stance adopted by the British towards the Chinese civil war and resulted in the colonial authorities in Hong Kong not curbing CCP's activities there.

The CCP's united front work played a significant role in shaping a favourable British policy towards China. During World War II, Zhou Enlai emphasised improving the Sino-British relationship, as he considered Britain an important political power in international politics and that China must promote friendship with it in order to resist Japan. Zhou took the initiative to cultivate relations. He invited British officials, journalists and other influential figures to visit the CCP headquarters at Yenan.[107] He was also particularly keen on building friendships with the British diplomatic representatives in China. In particular, he kept in regular contact with Sir Horace Seymour (British ambassador, 1942–1946) and eventually befriended Seymour. CCP-British relations were also helped by Song Qingling's friendship with Lady Seymour. During Seymour's term as ambassador, he made several favourable reports about the CCP to the Foreign Office that influenced British policy. Seymour advised the Foreign Office that the correct policy to follow was neutrality and non-intervention in the Chinese civil war.[108]

Thus, between 1946 and 1948, the CCP did not pose a challenge to the government of Hong Kong. There was an incident concerning the Walled City that had some importance, but it was clear that the CCP did not want to cause trouble. The legal status of this small part of Kowloon was an unsettled element of British administration in Hong Kong. Upon Chinese insistence, the 1898 Convention of Beijing that ceded Kowloon to the British, provided for an area of about 6 acres to enable Chinese administration to continue. In 1899, the British claimed by means of issuing an Order-in-Council to incorporate the area into the colony. While the Chinese never recognised the unilateral revision, they could not physically claim jurisdiction there. Through the years, the Walled City became a world of its own. It was crowded, dilapidated, a constant fire hazard, a crime spot and inhabited by the poor. In 1947, the colonial authorities decided to clear the Walled City for redevelopment, a move that would have affected the 25,000 residents there. On 27 November, the government gave them two weeks' notice to vacate. The residents organised themselves to resist the development and requested help from the KMT government, a move that bought them more time. However, the Hong Kong authorities charged them with squatting on Crown land. On 12 January 1948, the government lost patience and sent in the police, but they bungled the clearance by opening fire. One resident died and dozens were injured. While things had to be settled between the KMT and the British, the CCP avoided adding fuel to the fire. The CCP-controlled newspapers expressed sympathy for the residents throughout and heaped criticisms on the KMT. Even after the shootings, they merely expressed regret and said the Hong Kong government was wrong not to give more time to negotiations. Assurances were also passed on to the British that the CCP did not intend to cause trouble.[109]

Nevertheless, the British became less tolerant toward CCP activities in Hong Kong in the later stage of the civil war. In May 1948, British assessment of the political development in China was that the CCP might eventually defeat the KMT and dominate the whole of China. As far as Hong Kong was concerned, the British worried that, in case Guangdong fell to the communists, the "communists could be expected to exploit the opportunity of directing and assisting vigorously the subversive activities of Chinese Communist groups in Hong Kong".[110] This worry was also clearly reflected by Governor Alexander Grantham:

> It still remains the policy of the Communists in Hong Kong to lie low and to avoid a head-on collision with the administration which would hamper their more overt activities . . . How long this policy will be maintained depends entirely on circumstances, but, as the Communists advance south of the Yangtze, a change to a more active attitude of hostility may be anticipated, and at any moment a decision by the Communists higher command to turn to the direct offensive [might also be anticipated]. This would mean strikes internally and possibly guerrilla or direct military attack externally.[111]

From 1948, in anticipation of possible internal subversive activities, the colonial authorities began to tighten the control over the CCP in Hong Kong. CCP activists and supporters came under increasingly surveillance, and residences of CCP leaders, such as Fang Fang, Lian Guan, and Zhang Bojun were raided by the police. CCP-controlled publications like *Zheng Bao* and *Huashang Bao* were also regularly inspected by the political branch of the colonial government and personnel of these publications interrogated.[112] The colonial government also enacted legislation to restrain CCP activities. For example, in 1948 the Education Ordinance was amended to the effect that any school organised for political purposes would be banned. Dade College was consequently shut down in February 1949. The Registration of Persons Ordinance, Expulsion of Undesirable Persons Ordinance and Emergency Regulations Ordinance were either enacted or amended so that the security authorities were empowered to search, detain, arrest and remove troublemakers from Hong Kong. The Societies Ordinance was also amended to require all local societies to register with the government, which had the power to refuse registration on the grounds of affiliation with a political organisation outside Hong Kong. The authorities regarded this amendment as:

> An essential measure, not only to forestall a demand for the establishment by the Chinese Communist Party of an office in Hong Kong, but also to control the infiltration, under respectable disguise, of Communists. There is no intention of suppressing political activity for the benefit of the Colony, but only political activity which has no relation to the Colony and merely projects external troubles and quarrels into the life of Hong Kong.[113]

The colonial government knew that the Chinese Democratic League and the KMT Revolutionary Committee were important CCP's allies in Hong Kong and would be affected under the new legislation.[114] Further, another 38 leftist social clubs were also refused registration, thus becoming unlawful.[115] The amendment of the Societies Ordinance had far-reaching implications for the CCP in Hong Kong. Since it could only operate openly in Hong Kong with the approval of the colonial government, the amendment forced them to continue working as an underground political party in Hong Kong after the establishment of the PRC in 1949, and this underground nature has continued until the present day.

Though the colonial government viewed communism as a "political menace" and "extreme vigilance is exercised in order that no subversive movements may be hatched underground",[116] it did not want to provoke the communists into outright hostility. The British worried that "if there is a serious deterioration in relations between the colonial government and the Chinese authority in control of South China, strong economic pressure may be brought to bear by boycotting the colony, by interfering with the passage of its supplies from South China, and by fomenting strikes within the colony".[117] Most likely, the economic difficulties brought by the Strike-Boycott in 1925–1926 still haunted colonial officials.

There would be one more incident before the communists defeated the KMT that affected relations with the British. On 20 April 1949, the British frigate, HMS *Amethyst*, was en route from Shanghai to take supplies to the British embassy in Nanjing. When it was about 160 miles up the Yangtze River it was fired upon by communist troops as they were preparing to launch an attack on KMT forces across the river. There were many deaths and injuries. The captain of the warship was injured and soon died from his wounds. Subsequent attempts by the British Far Eastern Fleet to rescue the *Amethyst* resulted in serious damage to the rescue ships.

In May 1949, in a private meeting with the US ambassador to China, a top CCP official demanded that, as part of the settlement for the dispute over the *Amethyst*, the British should agree to discuss the question of Hong Kong. The point was made moot when the ship managed to slip away at night under the command of a new captain, after which the CCP did not raise the issue again either directly or indirectly. By the time the ship escaped on 30 June, it had in effect been under arrest by the communists for more than three months.[118]

Xu Jiatun wrote about this incident in his memoirs:

> On 1 April 1949, the People's Liberation Army crossed the Yangtze River, took Nanjing and other large and smaller cities, and seized strategic posts at the lower reaches of the river. At that time, the British warship, HMS *Amethyst* was guarding the waters nearby in support of KMT troops. Deng Xiaoping and Liu Bocheng gave an order to blockade the Yangtze intending to hold the *Amethyst* at bay. Edward Youde got wind of the information. The British embassy instructed him to notify the vessel to make a sortie on the night of 22 April. Young Edward was later commended for his exploits.[119]

Edward Youde would become governor of Hong Kong in 1982. In 1949, he was the attaché at the British embassy in China. In fact, Youde was dispatched to negotiate for the ship's release with the communists. He trekked through communist-controlled territory for a day and a half, but by the time he reached the Yangtze the ship had already escaped, although he was still commended for his effort.[120] Xu Jiatun thought Youde was an intelligence officer, which was unlikely in view of the fact that he was overtly the attaché. Perhaps Xu's assumption was based on Chinese practices that someone of Youde's position would also be in intelligence. Soon after Youde took over as governor, he would meet Xu Jiatun, the director of Xinhua Hong Kong, who was the political commissar of the 88th Division under the 29th Army commanding a battalion to cross the Yangtze on 21 April 1949. Xu and his division were forging ahead at night on 22 April toward the eastern front at Wuxi. Xu recalled that his division did not know until the next day that the *Amethyst* had managed to flee.[121] The ship escaped to Hong Kong.

Britain had not expected the attack and felt humiliated. Although Britain did not believe that was a certain sign at the CCP would soon attack Hong Kong, military reinforcements were sent to beef up the garrison in the colony, increasing the strength from a few thousand to 30,000 soldiers supported by tanks, fighter aircrafts and a naval unit. The unhappy *Amethyst* incident led to further crackdowns in Hong Kong of left-wing groups and activities.[122]

A Volcanic Phenomenon

Despite the shelling of HMS *Amethyst*, a significant feature of the CCP activities in Hong Kong during the civil war period was its flexibility over the problem of the sovereignty of Hong Kong, although there were occasional rumblings of discontent. With anti-imperialism and anti-colonialism as two of the CCP's main political doctrines, it should have sought to challenge the British over Hong Kong. However, the CCP were willing to put the issue aside. CCP members were in fact instructed to leave the question of Hong Kong alone and focus on South China:

> We had to make a trade-off in the struggle [between us and KMT]. Openly, we could not oppose the KMT to recover Hong Kong otherwise we would be put in a passive political position; but if the KMT recovered Hong Kong our party would also be put in a very disadvantageous position. If we could have a firm start in Hong Kong, we may then use it. Therefore, the CCP Central directed us to use the contradictions between the KMT, Britain and United States, as well as the foundation laid down by us in the Sino-Japanese War, to force the British colonial government to make a few concessions under which favourable conditions would be created to facilitate the [CCP] members to conduct activities, and to make Hong Kong an operational base for the democratic movement in South China.[123]

Politburo member Peng Zhen explained that it would be "unwise" for the CCP "to deal with the problem of Hong Kong rashly and without preparation".[124] That flexible and pragmatic approach continued to be adopted by the CCP after 1949 and lasted until early 1980s when Sino-British negotiation over the future of Hong Kong commenced. Nevertheless, British officials felt Hong Kong was "living on the edge of a volcano" which could erupt at any time.[125] Governor Grantham noted that: "The attitude of the Chinese authorities towards Hong Kong was a combination of passive hostility with occasional outbursts of active unfriendliness."[126] Rumblings would occur on several occasions in the 1950s, and violently in 1967.

5
Hong Kong to the Chinese Communist Party
From 1949 to 1965

Between 1949 and the eve of the Cultural Revolution, the colony of Hong Kong was an active united front and propaganda centre of the Chinese Communist Party. Hong Kong was also useful for the party to gather intelligence. The party could have made a move to take back the colony but Mao Zedong and Zhou Enlai made a calculated decision that Hong Kong should be left in British hands because it could serve the party's interest better that way during the early years of the founding of the People's Republic. In the eyes of the CCP, the Kuomintang, and its key backer, the United States, would cause trouble from time to time, thus vigilance on the part of the CCP was essential to ensure their activities in Hong Kong could not subvert the Mainland.

The CCP's policy to leave Hong Kong in British hands and to maintain good relations with Britain could be seen right from the time when the communists were about to win the civil war. In December 1948, the head of Xinhua Hong Kong, Qiao Guanhua, told the British that CCP policy was not to take the colony by force when it came to power in China, and the party would not agitate for the return of Hong Kong.[1] This was verified in April 1949 through confidential party documents obtained by the Hong Kong Police in a raid on the home of Fang Fang which confirmed that the CCP did not have any intention to recover Hong Kong after it had occupied South China. The CCP was prepared to deal with the question of Hong Kong separately from the other issues that had an international dimension. The British noted that:

> A deduction of even greater importance that appears to emerge is a CCP decision *not* to molest Hong Kong following the capture of Kwangtung. Hong Kong is not only *not* included in the plans for Kwangtung but is deliberately excluded. Its problems are analyzed separately from those of its hinterland.[2]

With the establishment of the People's Republic of China, Mao Zedong, the chairman of the CCP, became state president. Zhou Enlai was appointed as the premier and foreign minister (a post he held until 1958 but even after that, he continued to play a crucial role in charting China's foreign policy). Zhou's attitude was to take into consideration the actual conditions, exploit differences among others where beneficial to China, and compromise if necessary so as to win time.

China did not take back Hong Kong for good reason. During the final stage of the civil war, what the CCP was most concerned about was whether the United States would intervene militarily to support the KMT. Zhou Enlai saw the risk that recovering Hong Kong then could arouse great opposition from the West and provide Western powers with an excuse of military intervention in the civil war. As such, when the People's Liberation Army reached Shenzhen in October 1949, it was instructed not to advance across the border.[3]

The first instruction from Beijing to the CCP members in Hong Kong came from Zhou Enlai just a few days after 1 October 1949 and the founding of People's Republic. Zhou laid down specific directions to CCP Hong Kong: the party would not try to liberate Hong Kong in the meantime but would continue to operate in Hong Kong; the party should start a broad patriotic united front to establish connections with different kinds of people, including those who opposed the communists; and party members had to tolerate British rule and capitalism in Hong Kong and should not try to change the existing system.[4] These directions were probably the first time that the newly established CCP regime confirmed to local CCP members that it wished to maintain the status quo, though without a comprehensive plan on how to use Hong Kong.

In the spring of 1950, when Huang Zuomei, the second head of Xinhua Hong Kong, visited Beijing, Zhou Enlai articulated a detailed Hong Kong policy to him. Zhou said that: "China's Hong Kong policy was part of the overall strategic plan for the East-West struggle" and "should not be assessed by a narrow principle of territorial sovereignty". The United States and Britain had conflicting interests in the Far East and had vast differences in their policy towards China.[5] The British were more tolerant of the People's Republic—Britain recognised the new government in January 1950. The British view was that Hong Kong was Britain's best hope in doing business with China since British firms could no longer operate on the Mainland after 1949.[6] Moreover, it was also longstanding British policy to deal with governments that had established control. Washington, however, saw China as a potential menace and was worried about Hong Kong's role in supplying both the military and economic needs of North Korea, the Soviet Union, and China.[7]

Despite Britain's recognition of the People's Republic and awareness of the need to maintain good relations with the Chinese, the British looked at the security problems of Hong Kong in 1949 with some apprehension. The CCP could destabilise the colony if it wished. Governor Alexander Grantham knew he needed to reassure the business community that Britain was determined to maintain its position in Hong Kong. In the ensuing years, the colonial administration passed the Societies Ordinance to prohibit all societies which were branches of, or affiliated with, foreign political parties. In other words, the CCP and the KMT became outlawed organisations. Other laws were passed to ban politically-inspired strikes, allow deportation of undesirable aliens, and close communist-controlled schools. These were the Emergency (Principal) Regulations, which could be brought into operation one by one.⁸ The Societies Ordinance also outlawed organisations in Hong Kong that were created by the KMT for operations against the communists. The triad society known as the 14K, which also engaged in criminal activities, was originally formed for such a purpose in Guangzhou before the communist victory in 1949 and later migrated to Hong Kong.⁹

CCP's Hong Kong Policy Apparatus

China's one-party system entails the CCP making policy, which is then carried out by the government, with party members holding both party and government posts concurrently. From 1949 to 1957, China's policy towards Hong Kong was primarily devised by the CCP Central Committee's Foreign Affairs Leading Group in which Zhou Enlai was the chairman and Chen Yi the deputy chairman. On important issues, such as on Hong Kong, Zhou would have consulted closely with Mao Zedong. The decisions of this body were then put to the State Council's Foreign Affairs Staff Office, headed by Chen Yi with Liao Chengzhi as the first deputy head. The Staff Office had a number of small groups, including the Hong Kong and Macao Group and the Propaganda Group, both of which had responsibilities for matters relating to Hong Kong. Li Hou, who would have a long career dealing with Hong Kong until 2008, was the deputy chairman of the Propaganda Group in 1950s.¹⁰

The policy apparatus relevant to Hong Kong matters went through numerous structural rearrangements between 1949 and 1957. Shortly before the founding of the People's Republic of China, Qiao Guanhua, the first head of Xinhua Hong Kong, was transferred back to Beijing. With his transfer, duties for the party work committee in Hong Kong were taken over by the CCP's South China Bureau in Wuhan. Ye Jianying was one of the party secretaries of the South China Bureau. Huang Zuomei, the East River guerrilla discussed in Chapter 4, was sent to Hong Kong as the special envoy of the South China Bureau. At the same time, Huang was appointed as the director of Xinhua Hong Kong. In 1952, the South China Bureau was reorganised and established a new Hong Kong and Macao Work Committee in Guangzhou.¹¹ Its first secretary was Qu Mengjue, also the party secretary of Guangdong, and the second secretary was Wang Kuang, who would one day be the director of Xinhua Hong Kong (Chapter 7). Instructions from the State Council's Foreign Affairs Staff Office were first conveyed to the State Council's Overseas Affairs Committee and then through the Guangdong Provincial Party Committee to the Hong Kong and Macao Work Committee for implementation.¹²

In 1955, Zhou Enlai requested the British government to allow China to set up a Chinese Foreign Affairs Envoy's Office in Hong Kong. The British suggested that China establish a consulate instead. This was unacceptable as it would imply China acknowledged Hong Kong as part of British territory. Governor Grantham strongly opposed the idea of a special Chinese presence because he believed such an arrangement would bolster the CCP's united front activities and there would be endless disputes as to the political functions of the Chinese representative: "There is no room for two governors in Hong Kong."[13] The Chinese made similar requests in succeeding years but to no avail.[14] Thus, Beijing looked to use Xinhua Hong Kong more intensively instead. Britain's refusal to allow Beijing to set up a special office in Hong Kong resulted in two outcomes: firstly, the Chinese government had to continue to use Xinhua Hong Kong to perform a quasi-official role in the colony up until 1997. Secondly, the Hong Kong colonial administration would not have a direct communication channel between Beijing and Hong Kong, and such a channel might have given Hong Kong more "diplomatic stature and possibly more bargaining leverage as a virtual third party dealing with both London and Beijing".[15]

In terms of party organisation and work, when Mao Zedong visited Guangdong in 1956, he criticised the CCP's work in relation to Hong Kong as unsatisfactory and that the CCP organ responsible for Hong Kong should not be stationed on the Mainland. Mao saw no reason why Hong Kong work should be done from Guangzhou and not more directly.[16] Mao's criticism led to a number of structural changes. Firstly, CCP Hong Kong moved back to the colony from Guangzhou and operated inside Xinhua Hong Kong once more with Liang Weilin (a former East River guerrilla leader) as the head. Just prior to going to Hong Kong, Liang was the director of the Education Department of Guangdong. Interestingly, the CCP Hong Kong's deputy, Huang Shimin, remained in Guangzhou. Perhaps this was an accommodation to the Guangdong party agencies that the second-in-command would stay across the border. Secondly, all the party's work in Hong Kong was centralised under the direction of CCP Hong Kong. Thirdly, the State Council's Foreign Affairs Staff Office would directly communicate with CCP Hong Kong without going through either the State Council's Overseas Affairs Committee or the Guangdong Provincial Party Committee.[17] From the time of Liang Weilin, Xinhua Hong Kong shed its principal function as a news agency and channel for government exchange in the colony to become the shop front from which the CCP operated.[18]

East-West Struggle

China's entry in the Korean War (1950–1953) to fight the United States was decisive in more ways than one. Beyond keeping North Korea's Kim Il-Sung in power, the war forced Beijing, Pyongyang, and Moscow into closer alliance but made China's rapprochement with the West, especially Washington, impossible. In fact, Beijing's participation in the Korean War had the effect of extending the Cold War to Asia.[19]

Although China was unenthusiastic about becoming involved in Korea as it was challenging enough to deal with national reconstruction, the Chinese felt they had no choice but to side with North Korea and the Russians. From the American perspective, communism was on the move: "There can be little doubt but that Communism, with China as one spearhead, has now embarked upon an assault against Asia with immediate objectives in Korea, Indo-China, Burma, the

Philippines, Malaya and with medium-range objectives in Hong Kong, Indonesia, Siam, India and Japan."[20] Thus, even before the United States had got a mandate from the United Nations to assemble a force to defend South Korea, President Truman ordered American forces into action. After three years of fighting, the Korean War ended in a truce that left China and the United States deeply suspicious of each other.

In December 1950, the United States slapped on a trade embargo against China, which involved a total ban on all commercial and financial transactions (which was to last until 1971). A partial embargo was imposed by the United Nations in May 1951 on exports to China of strategic goods and materials. Thus, China became isolated from world markets. The United States ignored Hong Kong's political status as British territory. All American exports to Hong Kong were banned unless licensed, which was granted on a case-by-case basis. Transhipments to China via Hong Kong were reduced to a trickle, seriously hurting the colony's trade. The colonial administration had to lobby Washington to treat Hong Kong differently from the rest of China. By 1952, the United States agreed to a degree of relaxation, but further relaxation was only allowed in 1953 after fighting stopped in Korea. Nevertheless, Hong Kong had to adopt a range of re-export controls demanded by the United States.[21]

The United States set up a large consulate in Hong Kong partly to ensure Chinese goods did not move on to the American market via the colony in some way, and vice versa.[22] The decisions of American inspectors illustrated perverse Cold War–inspired logic that also provided moments of high farce. Governor Grantham provided an example of Hong Kong's frustration: "The classic example is that of dried ducks. These ducks were processed in Hong Kong and then exported to America. Many of them came from eggs laid in China and bought to Hong Kong to hatch. Were the ducks from these eggs communist ducks or true-blue British ducks?"[23] The solution found was mind-twisting but comical. Provided an inspector was present when the eggs hatched and could rubberstamp the ducklings' feet, and an inspector could stamp the matured ducks before slaughter, the ducks could be dried and exported to the United States. Shrimps faced a similar predicament. If caught in Hong Kong waters, might they have begun life in communist waters? No administration solution could be found and so all shrimp exports to the United States from Hong Kong were banned.[24]

The Korean War was particularly lucrative for the indigenous villagers of the New Territories however, as they provided a lifeline to China and the CCP for obtaining scarce products:

> many became very rich. The trade embargo against China gave many the opportunity to smuggle illegal goods into China. This was quite simple since there was only a small, symbolic fence marking the Sino–Hong Kong border, so it was easy to get back and forth . . . Smuggling took place all along the border from Kat O in Mirs Bay, to Lok Ma Chau and on to Yuen Long. Everything that was needed in China was smuggled—tyres, petrol, medicine, even engines for aircraft![25]

China's Attitude: Exploit Differences

Beijing's view of Hong Kong was that: "if Hong Kong remained in British hands, the CCP could hold the initiative" and could "influence Britain so it would not, and dared not, follow the US's China policy and its Far East arrangements too closely". Thus, China could "widen and use the Anglo-American contradictions" for its own benefit. In other words, China would exploit their differences. In these circumstances, "Hong Kong possesses a lot of benefits and functions" for China. The CCP could start "the largest and broadest possible patriotic united front work" in Hong Kong to support China's struggle against the United States and facilitate economic development. Besides, Hong Kong could serve as a window for China to the outside world and as "an outpost to break the blockade and embargo imposed on China by the American-led Western coalition".[26] Zhou Enlai instructed Huang Zuomei that CCP Hong Kong must recognise this "great strategic significance" and should try their best to "preserve the status quo of Hong Kong, including the British colonial economic and capitalist systems".[27] This policy was later articulated by the CCP, as "making full use of Hong Kong in the interest of long-term planning", which basically remained unchanged for the next 40 years.[28]

Thus, while the Mainland represented a direct challenge to British rule, Hong Kong's survival in British hands depended on whether it remained useful to the Mainland. Most importantly, Hong Kong continued to import food, raw materials and other products from the Mainland despite the trade embargoes. Then, as Hong Kong's export manufacturing business grew over time, rapid industrial expansion resulted in greater and greater imports from the Mainland.[29] The tiny British-run colony provided China and the CCP with a reliable stream of funds to finance national development, and for that, it was worth putting ideology aside.[30]

In 1957, Zhou Enlai further elaborated how Hong Kong could be used by the CCP to facilitate China's economic development:

> In order to survive and develop, Hong Kong has to strictly abide by the capitalist system and this is advantageous to us . . . Hong Kong should be converted as a useful port to our economy . . . In the course of our socialist building, Hong Kong could become an operation base for us to establish overseas economic connections, and through Hong Kong we could attract foreign investment and foreign exchange.[31]

In terms of political strategy, Zhou believed Hong Kong could become an "observatory" and "communication centre" for China to gather information from the West and to make friends.[32] In other words, Zhou saw from the start that Hong Kong was not only important to China's economy, but also for the CCP's propaganda and united front work, and intelligence gathering.

By 1959, the Hong Kong authorities noted the CCP machinery was making fewer attempts to undermine its authority. Governor Robert Black (1958–1964) ascribed the change to worsening external relations between China and the Soviet

Union, and also with India, while internally, the Great Leap Forward was collapsing. It was a time for the CCP to refrain from making enemies unnecessarily. In particular, there was no reason to alienate Britain since there were economic advantages to be derived from the continued existence and prosperity of Hong Kong. Indeed, the Chinese were

> realistic enough not to allow ideological considerations to deter them, and they have, on the whole, refused to be drawn by Russian attempts to needle them on the grounds that their policy over Hong Kong . . . is inconsistent with their professed views . . . Communist organisations in Hong Kong have shown similar restraint, clearly as a result of instructions. The leftwing Federation of Trade Unions has confined their main public activities to more or less genuine trade unions matters and has refrained from anti-Government agitation . . . Similarly, the leftwing schools have avoided clashes with authority, and the political indoctrination of pupils has been on a limited scale and has not been specifically directed against Government.[33]

Black noted in 1964 that: "Our present relations with China are probably as satisfactory as it is reasonable to expect between a Colonial administration and a Communist state."[34]

Issue of Sovereignty

Although the CCP showed flexibility on the question of Hong Kong's sovereignty, it was not without limits. The CCP did not distinguish between the secession of Hong Kong and Kowloon to Britain and the lease on the New Territories. It considered all three treaties signed in the nineteenth century governing the status of Hong Kong, Kowloon and the New Territories were "unequal" and therefore not binding.[35] As such, Hong Kong belonged to China and it would be "recovered one day". The presence of the British in Hong Kong continued only because China tolerated them out of practical need and Beijing retained the right to exercise sovereignty over Hong Kong at any time.[36] The logic of this position meant that in the CCP's view, Britain had never had sovereignty of Hong Kong and any unilateral political reforms relating to decolonisation, democratisation and increasing autonomy would be an infringement of China's sovereignty over Hong Kong.

Further, the CCP also laid down ground rules for Britain's continued presence in Hong Kong. When Governor Grantham paid an unofficial visit to Beijing in 1955, Zhou Enlai warned that Britain's presence would only be tolerated if Hong Kong was not used as an anti-communist base; any activity which undermined the People's Republic must be prevented in Hong Kong; and the colonial administration must protect the Chinese government's representatives and organisations in the territory.[37] The understanding between the British and Chinese governments on the rules of conduct for Hong Kong endured through the late 1950s and the early 1960s, despite the turmoil on the Mainland as a result of the various political campaigns.

Mao Zedong apparently gave this policy his direct blessing in 1959 that: "It is better to keep Hong Kong the way it is, we are in no hurry to take it back, it is useful to us right now."[38]

Political Rumblings

Despite the generally cordial Sino-British relations, there were occasional rumblings. The KMT was a great irritant, and Taiwan was and remains a "great wound" to the CCP.[39] From time to time, Hong Kong was reminded that there was unfinished business between the KMT and CCP and, as discussed in Chapter 4, the colony was at risk from the fallout of this conflict.

Sensitivities flared in December 1949 during a Sino-British dispute over whether the People's Republic or Taiwan had rights to 71 aeroplanes that had been transferred to Hong Kong in the summer of that year as a result of the CCP occupying Shanghai during the final stage of the civil war. The KMT argued that they should be impounded so they could not be used by the communists to invade Taiwan. They also established an American company and transferred titles of all the aeroplanes to that company and litigation begun in Hong Kong as to who had the rightful claim to them. In February 1950, the Supreme Court awarded all the aircraft to China, Britain having recognised the People's Republic the month before. The United States exerted pressure on the British not to hand over the aeroplanes to China, threatening to cut off Marshall Aid and military assistance. Under instructions from Whitehall, the Hong Kong authorities used every administrative means to detain the aircraft for several months. KMT agents then blew up seven of the aircraft. The court decision was appealed and the Judicial Committee of the Privy Council in London ruled in 1952 that the aeroplanes belong to the American company. The CCP could have made a much bigger fuss than it did but "it chose to stomach the injury and injustice because it did not wish to upset its relations with Britain".[40] Since the aircraft could by then no longer in fact fly, that was probably also a factor in the CCP's decision.[41] In the midst of the controversy over the aeroplanes, a more serious incident took place in April 1951. Under very strong American pressure, the British requisitioned a Chinese tanker, the SS *Yung Hao*, in Hong Kong. Beijing regarded it as a blatantly unfriendly act—one even more so than over the aircraft—because the ship was not a war vessel and its ownership was indisputably Chinese. Beijing retaliated by requisitioning most of the properties of the Shell Company on the Mainland.[42]

On 11 April 1955, the *Kashmir Princess*, a chartered aircraft owned by Air India, exploded in mid-air and crashed into the Pacific Ocean after refuelling in Hong Kong while en route to Jakarta carrying Chinese and other delegates to the Bandung Conference. Huang Zuomei was on board and was one of the sixteen people killed. An Indonesian inquiry reported that a time bomb was responsible for the crash and it was highly probable that the bomb was installed in Hong Kong. The Hong Kong authorities offered money for information on suspects and questioned 71 people connected with the servicing of the aeroplane. When police began to focus on a janitor who worked at the airport named Chow Tse-ming, he escaped to Taiwan. The true target was thought to have been Zhou Enlai. The official explanation for the change of his travel plan at the last minute was that he had appendicitis and needed an operation.[43] After the *Kashmir Princess* incident, the Mainland intensified its intelligence work relating to Taiwan. There was apparently even a plot to assassinate Mao Zedong and other party leaders one year during the National Day celebration in Tiananmen, but Chinese agents in Hong Kong intercepted intelligence and the Taiwan agents were arrested after crossing the border.[44]

On 10 October—the Double Tenth anniversary—in 1956, disorder broke out after what seemed to have been a minor incident. On the morning of the anniversary of the 1911 Revolution celebrated by the KMT as China's national day, a manager removed some Republic of China flags in a resettlement estate that residents had put up on a wall. Though the manager was acting upon building regulations, a crowd gathered and demanded that the flags be allowed to be posted again. The situation became tense and the police were called in. The crowd got larger and violence broke out with some stoking from triads. Stores and offices owned by pro-communist sympathisers, particularly those in Tsuen Wan, were looted and damaged. At first, the colonial authorities refrained from taking tough action in the hope that tempers would subside, but things got worse, as the pro-nationalist supporters turned into an out-of-control mob. They stormed premises, perpetrated attacks and killed a number of people. The Hong Kong police had to scale up its response. A curfew was declared that afternoon and the government called in the troops to deal with the disturbances, after which the rioting eased. The violence took twelve days to subside, at the end of which 59 people were dead, including the wife of the Swiss Consul who was burnt to death in a car that got into the way of the mob, and 443 people were injured. Six thousand arrests were made and in the subsequent trials, four people were convicted and sentenced to death.[45] After the 1956 riots, the British *charge d'affaires* in Beijing was summoned twice by Zhou Enlai and Vice-Foreign Minister Zhang Hanfu to receive complaints about the British allowing mob action of "cold-blooded murders and looting by KMT agents" in Hong Kong, and that the British had colluded with the KMT under American direction. Zhou went as far as saying that the Chinese government reserved the right to make demands of the Hong Kong government in the future although he did not provide specifics.[46]

CCP Work in Hong Kong

Despite the general concern among the CCP leadership that Hong Kong could be used as a base for anti-CCP intrigue, Liao Chengzhi, who looked after the daily operation of CCP work concerning Hong Kong, laid down directions for local members in Hong Kong. As recollected by Liang Weilin, Liao said in 1958 that:

Do not indoctrinate the Hong Kong public with socialist education. It is not correct to adopt the Mainland's way of doing things in Hong Kong ... the struggle against Britain has to be reasonable, advantageous to us and limited.[47] You have to distinguish the situation between the Mainland and Hong Kong. Your task is not to recover Hong Kong. Instead, your task is to use Hong Kong fully. Unless Hong Kong is in serious chaos, we are not going to consider the recovery of Hong Kong in the next 10 years. Therefore, your work has to adopt a long term perspective and should not make the situation too tense, and over-expose yourself in Hong Kong. You need to struggle against Britain, but have to stop before going too far. You have to keep a cool head and should not be overly heated.[48]

Moreover, it was emphasised that the party's propaganda work in Hong Kong and Portuguese-held Macao should be careful not to infringe local policies and laws and the local political and cultural norms had to be taken into account.[49]

Several obvious messages could be distilled from these various statements: firstly, the CCP in Hong Kong should operate in a manner different from that on the Mainland; secondly, its activities should avoid creating conflict with the colonial administration; and thirdly, party members should abide by local laws and norms. Liao Chengzhi once joked with Li Zisong, the former chief editor of *Wen Wei Po*, that those who broke the law and were deported to the Mainland would be spanked.[50]

United Front Work

The CCP in Hong Kong focussed on the local population to counter the influence of the KMT, as well as to ensure that the British or the other foreign powers would not be able to turn Hong Kong into a subversive base against the CCP.[51] Zhou Enlai had instructed the CCP machinery in Hong Kong to make as many friends with as many people as possible, including foreigners living in the colony. Liang Weilin revealed that conducting united front work in Hong Kong was the most important task during his 20 years in office. He recalled that Zhou Enlai regularly reminded him that the CCP should do a good job in united front work in Hong Kong in order to "unite with different kinds of friends in ordinary times so that we can ask for help when necessary". As such, CCP Hong Kong considered united front work as "the basis and starting point of various tasks".[52] The party carried out a wide range of activities. United front work included influencing foreigners, the local elites and the working class, strengthening media influence, and providing education in Mainland-funded schools.

International outreach through Hong Kong

In 1957, the Marco Polo Club was founded by lawyer Percy Chen, a CCP supporter, as a way for the CCP to connect with people it wished to exchange views with.

Chen was born in Trinidad. He studied at University College in London and did his legal apprenticeship at the Middle Temple. In 1926, he went to China and felt he "had come home". His father, Eugene Chen, was the KMT's foreign minister and Percy Chen was given a job at the ministry. Percy Chen became increasingly disappointed with the KMT and eventually supported the CCP instead. In 1947, he established a private law practice in Hong Kong. The Marco Polo Club was a dinner club with a select membership. These included mainly foreign businessmen, journalists, trade representatives and consular officers. There were no membership fees to pay although they paid for their meal when they came. Invitation reminders came in the form of a simple postcard mailed once a month to members. The card requested their presence at cocktails, a European-style formal dinner, and a screening of Chinese films on the last Thursday of each month in a private dining room of the Mandarin Hotel. Percy Chen did not allow Americans to dinner gatherings until 1972 because of poor relations between China and the United States. This was the world's only social organisation in which Westerners could mix regularly and informally with officials of the People's Republic of China. The main attraction for the Westerners, Japanese and others was the opportunity to sound out, over whisky and soda, representatives from Xinhua Hong Kong and the Bank of China on the latest developments in the Mainland. In the 1970s, usually about 30 CCP cadres attended the dinners.[53]

Tycoons and workers: Cultivate high and low

One of the jobs of the united front machinery was to explain Mainland policies along the correct party line, so that misunderstandings could be clarified. The CCP successfully cultivated local business tycoons like Richard Charles Lee Ming Chak, who was a member of the Executive Council and the Legislative Council,[54] Mok Ying Kwai, who was from a prominent comprador family,[55] Ho Yin, who was influential in Macao,[56] and Henry Fok Ying Tung, who violated the UN-imposed trade embargo during the Korean War by smuggling steel and rubber to China.[57] Mok became a committed communist supporter and was deported by the British to Guangdong in 1952. He and Fok would be appointed to help draft the post-1997 constitution (Chapter 8). These contacts also helped the party to make important connections with other prominent figures in Hong Kong. Trips were arranged for important contacts to visit the Mainland to meet Chinese leaders. Liang revealed that these influential business and social figures enabled him to connect with other people and so facilitated the party's united front work. Contacts were also made with ethnic Chinese civil servants in the colonial administration although they could not be invited to travel to the Mainland as non-official contacts could.[58]

Apart from the elites, the united front also targeted the working class. Xinhua staff regularly visited the squatter and temporary housing areas and provided assistance to them in order to win hearts and minds. They were also active within labour unions and sought to cultivate union leaders.[59] The local CCP carried out its work primarily through the Hong Kong Federation of Trade Unions (FTU) founded in 1948 and its friendly unions. According to the Registrar of Trade Unions' Report, there were more than 90,000 workers affiliated with the FTU and its sister bodies in 1962.[60] A confidential government report then noted that the FTU "aim(s) to unite all Hong Kong workers in support of the communist cause and to recruit more members for affiliated unions in view of increased efforts by right-wing unions to counteract left wing influence in the labour movement".[61] Providing free schooling for the children of workers and providing medical services were common methods to recruit union members.[62]

The left-wing unions organised study groups regularly. For example, in 1960 there was a political study campaign among left-wing unions. Political study groups were formed to study Volume IV of the *Selected Works of Mao Zedong*, and members of the study groups were the leading office bearers and active members of the FTU and its affiliated unions.[63] Union leaders were invited to visit the Mainland to meet Chinese officials to give a sense that they were valued. For example, on a particular visit to Beijing in the 1960s, the unionist delegation was seen by both Chen Yi and Liao Chengzhi. When they talked in their meeting about the scheme for re-issuing identity cards in Hong Kong, Liao commented that it was a measure for the colonial government to control local Chinese more easily and to those people who chose to claim British nationality under the scheme, Liao chose not to criticise them but said that "efforts should be made to unite and educate them". Liao also said that the Chinese government "had never recognised Hong Kong, Kowloon and the New Territories as British territory, but that the present status of Hong Kong was favourable to the Chinese government for reason of trade and contact with people of other countries, and for obtaining materials which are badly needed in China".[64]

Get them early, get them young

The provision of education in Mainland-funded schools became the most serious cause of friction between the local CCP and the colonial administration in the 1950s and 1960s.[65] Recruiting young people to join the CCP's cause was important, although Beijing could have exploited the situation even more in light of the fact that there was a strong desire on the part of parents to send their children to school, and yet no universal provision of education for the young in Hong Kong. Those who lost out because of this government failure were the children of working-class and poor families, including the largely illiterate fishing community, who could not afford to pay for school.

In 1950, there were estimated to have been approximately 150,000 students in the colony attending registered schools and only a third of them received government support. By the mid-1950s, the school population had increased to nearly 300,000. While the total enrolment of Hong Kong students at leftist schools is not known, it has been estimated at 10,000 to 20,000 in the mid-1950s, which would have been about 4 percent of the total student body.[66] In 1960, there were estimated to have been about 20 leftist schools in Hong Kong and about 3 percent of the overall student body were studying at them. At the secondary school level, approximately 11 percent of Hong Kong high school students were studying at CCP-controlled schools. The colonial administration described these schools as "real hard-core" institutions with "little doubt that they served as indoctrination centres for communist youth cadres".[67] At the same time, there were also a large number of unregistered schools operated by left-wing trade unions. In January 1959, reports from the Education Department showed that there were as many as 1,263 such schools, accommodating some 60,000 to 70,000 pupils.[68] The CCP also did youth work. The most famous leftist youth group was the After-School Social Club.[69]

Contemporaneous government documents showed that the local CCP would give instructions to the teachers on the correct line to follow on such issues as the Great Leap Forward and other CCP policies. Teachers were also instructed to keep in close touch with students' parents and cultivate friendship with teachers in non-communist schools.[70] The colonial authorities had various methods to curb communist infiltration of education. For example, the Director of Education regularly sent officials to inspect the communist schools, and if a school was found to have persistently breached the education regulations, the government would withdraw financial aid to the school. The Director of Education could also refuse to register a teacher if he or she was found to have been educated in a communist environment. The colonial government also used town planning legislation to stop the expansion of communist schools.[71] Another measure was the use of building safety legislation to shut down communist schools, where they were found to have been in breach, such as in the case of the Chung Wah Middle School in 1958, where the first Chief Executive of the HKSAR Tung Chee Hwa studied.[72] The principal of Pui Kiu Middle School was deported for using the school for propaganda purposes.[73] The tussle between the colonial government and the local CCP in the education sector only became less vigorous following the decline of communist schools after the riots in 1967.

Trade unions

In comparison with the CCP's activities in the education sector, there were less open conflicts between the left-wing labour unions and the colonial government though the unions were closely monitored. The authorities were always concerned about the unions' continuous stressing of the need to "strengthen the unity of the workers and to consolidate their position through improved welfare conditions" because such a policy "is unlikely to bring the local left-wing labour movement into direct conflict with the government. But if these efforts to increase unity are successful, they would produce a left-wing labour movement that would be more formidable to deal with should the FTU's policy change back to more aggressive tactics".[74]

Propaganda and Party Mouthpieces

Propaganda work was also a vital aspect of party activities. The party's propaganda work in Hong Kong was carried out mainly through several CCP-controlled newspapers. These included *Wen Wei Po, Ta Kung Pao, New Evening Post, Ching Pao Daily*, and *Hong Kong Commercial Daily*. These newspapers had their own specific editorial interests and targeted readership. *Wen Wei Po* and *Ta Kung Pao* were directed by the local CCP and charged with the specific task of reporting news about China in a positive fashion. The director of Xinhua Hong Kong would hold discussions with the editorial staff to decide what to report and how to report Mainland news. As such, they had limited editorial freedom. *Wen Wei Po*'s targeted readers were the Hong Kong general public, whereas *Ta Kung Pao* aimed to attract readers from business circles and among intellectuals. For *Ching Pao Daily* and *Hong Kong Commercial Daily*, their editorial direction was to conduct propaganda targeting Taiwan. These newspapers were quite successful up until the Cultural Revolution. Their total circulation figures occupied about one-third of the overall local newspaper market[75] but the local party's propaganda work did run into conflict with the colonial administration from time to time, the most significant occasion being the 1 March Incident in 1952.

The prelude to the incident started on 21 November 1951 when a fire broke out in the squatter settlement of Tung Tau Village, immediately northeast of the Walled City of Kowloon. Some 5,000 huts were destroyed and the estimated number of people left homeless varied, ranging from about 12,000 to 25,000.[76] In the aftermath of the fire, trade unionists joined the fire victims to organise relief for the victims but the unionists were subsequently deported in January 1952. In the meantime, various organisations in Guangzhou also started to collect money for the victims seeing the fire as a good publicity and propaganda opportunity. In February, the Guangzhou organisations inquired through Ko Cheuk Hung, the chairman of the Hong Kong Chinese General Chamber of Commerce, whether the Hong Kong government would allow a Comfort Mission from Guangzhou to visit the victims in Hong Kong to give them money. They did not seek the help of the FTU because it was too closely associated with the communists. The government refused permission. From the colonial authorities' perspective, the outcome of the mission "was not difficult to foresee . . . fiery speeches would be made against imperialists, aid would have been promised from Mother China . . . Rioting would have broken out."[77] Through the intercession of Percy Chen, permission was granted on the basis that delegation members would not come as a mission, but only as representatives of donors and would not make any public political speeches. Ko and Chen wanted to help the victims, but they would not have wanted any incident because they could be deported for causing trouble.[78]

The delegation bringing HK$102,040.81 was scheduled to arrive on 1 March 1952. On the day, a serious disturbance broke out:

> Thousands of Communist-led students and workers marching along Nathan Road . . . attacked police, servicemen and Europeans, overturned and burned vehicles, and smashed property in a roaring riot . . . The crowd had gathered at the Kowloon Railway Station in Tsimshatsui around noon in order to await the expected arrival of the Canton "comfort" mission to the Tung Tau Village fire victims. When the mission failed to arrive, having been denied entry into the Colony, the crowd started its parade, waving banners and shouting slogans. The mood of the paraders grew uglier as they marched, and disturbances broke out.[79]

The delegation was to have been met at the border on a special railway coach by a welcoming reception headed by Mok Ying Kwai, in his capacity as a senior member of the Chinese General Chamber of Commerce. The special coach did not cross the border on the morning of 1 March for reasons that were never clarified. The delegation informed the Chinese General Chamber of Commerce before noon that they would not be arriving and an announcement was made to the press. Nevertheless, the news obviously did not reach the 10,000 people gathered at Tsim Sha Tsui. The crowd was finally told at 3 pm that the train was not coming and people begun to disperse peacefully. It was only when a large group reached the Jordan Road junction, half a mile from the rail station that an incident occurred. Eyewitness accounts indicated that a police vehicle inadvertently ran into the crowd, injuring a girl. The police officers involved exchanged abusive shouts with the crowd and confusion ensued. Armed police arrived shortly thereafter, tear gas was used and rioting broke out. When the crowd reached Mong Kok, a policeman found himself surrounded by the crowd and he opened fire, killing one person and injuring two people. It took another two hours to restore order. By the end, more than a hundred people were arrested, and twelve people eventually deported.[80]

Ta Kung Pao, *Wen Wei Po*, and *New Evening Post* published articles supporting the protesters and criticising the colonial authorities. The government retaliated by arresting the publishers and prosecuted them for incitement. *Ta Kung Pao* reprinted an article from the *People's Daily* (the CCP's national newspaper) criticising the Hong Kong government. The colonial authorities got a court order to stop publication of the paper for six months. Eventually, Beijing was forced to intervene and the Foreign Ministry made a strong protest to the British government in May 1952. The British wanted to de-escalate matters and allowed *Ta Kung Pao* to publish again in June 1952. Charges against *Wen Wei Po* and *New Evening Post* were dropped.[81]

It is noteworthy that the top party leaders had given clear instructions that the left-wing newspapers in Hong Kong were to conduct "patriotic education" on Hong Kong people and they should be distinguished from those "socialist education" newspapers on the Mainland. Liao Chengzhi once said that:

> We have two types of newspaper. One type conducts socialist education to serve the socialist building of the country. This is the Mainland's type of newspaper. Another type is those we run in Hong Kong and overseas . . . our newspaper for overseas Chinese should adopt patriotism as its basic direction . . .
>
> Is it possible for us to run a socialist newspaper in Hong Kong? It is impossible and also unnecessary . . . the task of our newspapers in Hong Kong is to conduct patriotic education . . . the larger circulation the better . . . the newspapers should target the vast majority of population in Hong Kong and Macao . . . be what they love to read and what they could understand . . . our newspapers should not disengage from the majority of the Hong Kong people.[82]

To emphasise the point that Beijing did not want the Hong Kong left-wing newspapers to sound like party mouthpieces, Chen Yi also vividly stated that "if we want you to run a party newspaper in Hong Kong, we better do it by asking the *People's Daily* to set up a new division to publish the *People's Daily* in Hong Kong".[83] However, the CCP controlled newspapers in Hong Kong generally adopted a revolutionary approach in their editorial direction, probably because many of those involved were passionate about the anti-imperialist cause, but perhaps also to ensure that they could not be accused of having made ideological mistakes. As recalled by Liang Weilin, Zhou Enlai complained that the Hong Kong Xinhua News Agency almost turned *Ta Kung Pao* into the *People's Daily*.[84]

Intelligence Gathering

Hong Kong's unique geographic location and liberal environment made it a useful intelligence gathering centre for the West to find out about the CCP during the Cold War. Indeed, Hong Kong was the "best listening post" into "Red China". Hong Kong was a base for agents from the Mainland and Taiwan, and served as "one of the few places where the two sides could rub elbows, and, if the situation called for it, pass on communications to each other's governments".[85]

In late 1949, the United States' Central Intelligence Agency (CIA) set up a listening post within the United States Consulate. Shortly thereafter, when the embassy was closed in Beijing, American reporting work on China shifted entirely to Hong Kong and personnel was significantly increased in the 1950s. Hong Kong was an excellent place to debrief travellers or people returning from the Mainland for information about China.[86] A United States declassified CIA report in 1960s showed that CIA agents infiltrated groups in Hong Kong with connections to the CCP and that Hong Kong was an important operation point along with Paris, Stockholm, Algiers, Dar es Salaam and Mexico.[87] Infiltrated organisations included the Bank of China and the China Resources Corporation.[88] The Chinese government frequently described Britain as a "stooge of the United States" by allowing Hong Kong to be used as a base for American imperialism to subvert China.[89]

At the same time, Hong Kong was also used by the CCP as its most important window to obtain intelligence about the West. As the CCP did not have a worldwide network of contacts, it depended heavily on intelligence gathered in Hong Kong to double-check information collected elsewhere in the world.[90] According to Xu Jiatun, the director of Xinhua Hong Kong from 1983 to 1990, the CCP had already built a relative good intelligence network in Hong Kong by the 1960s. Secret agents were dispatched to Hong Kong from various Mainland authorities, including those involved in public security, national security and military affairs. Intelligence agents worked from Xinhua Hong Kong or used Mainland enterprises as cover. Xu disclosed that the CCP had successfully infiltrated the senior level of the colonial administration, as well as the Taiwan intelligence network, in Hong Kong. For example, in 1955, the CCP discovered that Taiwan secret agents planned to assassinate Zhou Enlai by planting a bomb on the *Kashmir Princess*, as discussed above. In 1961, Tsang Chui For, an assistant superintendent of police, was found to be a secret agent. After he was exposed, he was deported to the Mainland where he was given a provincial-level official post and appointed as deputy chairman of the Standing Committee of the Guangdong People's Congress, as well as becoming a member of the national CPPCC.[91] According to Xu, intelligence personnel were spread into all sectors of the community, and most of them were Cantonese. However, the CCP intelligence network in Hong Kong was basically wiped out by the colonial administration during the Cultural Revolution–inspired riots in 1967.

Hong Kong's Left: "Pathetic and Lovely"

The local CCP members in Hong Kong at times failed strictly to observe the policies from Beijing designed to ensure they did not overreact and would always observe the limits of the law. For example, the 1 March Incident in 1952 was initiated by local CCP and not endorsed by Beijing.[92] In the education sector, communist controlled schools adopted Mainland's education methods, such as organising "study groups", that forced the colonial administration to take suppressive measures. Another illuminating example happened in 1953 when the pro-Beijing businessmen in the Chinese General Chamber of Commerce demanded that the People's Republic of China's national flag be raised in the chamber's premises on National Day. At the time, the chamber was made up mainly of politically moderate businessmen, with some radical members from both the communist as well as nationalist camps. The controversy over hoisting of the flag led to deep, open, division among the membership.

Undeniably, suppression by the colonial government easily provoked the local CCP into adopting a radical course of action. The radical left inclination was also partly due to its lack of the international strategic vision that the CCP top leaders had, and that made them fail to appreciate the importance of not destabilising Hong Kong. Their radical approach did not advance their work in Hong Kong and at times bothered Beijing. In 1959, in a meeting of the State Council's Foreign Affairs Staff Office, Chen Yi expressed his disapproval towards the CCP in Hong Kong and tactfully commended their "radical left" behaviour as "pathetic and lovely".[93] Chen's worries about the radical left approach of local CCP were subsequently proved to be correct during the riots in Hong Kong in 1967.

Mainland Campaigns

Zhou Enlai and those party leaders responsible for Hong Kong and foreign policies were extraordinary men with cool heads and steady hands. They had a clear view of the greater cause that would serve the party's interest with Hong Kong left in British hands, and so, as long as the British understood the limits of China's tolerance, life in the colony could continue. Despite the restraint on party activities in Hong Kong, just across the border in Guangdong life had turned upside down from 1949, first with the implementation of land reform that marked China as a communist state. The Hong Kong community always had a sense of unease about the new regime as a steady flow of escapees found their way to the colony. The people living in Hong Kong knew that life on the Mainland was not what propaganda made it out to be. Their relatives in Guangdong asked for food parcels to be sent, and on trips back to their ancestral villages, Hong Kong people could see for themselves the dire conditions in communist China.

> **Major National Campaigns**
>
> **1950–1952:** Land Reform
> **1950–1951:** Suppression of Counterrevolutionaries
> **1951–1952:** Three Antis and Five Antis; Thought Reform of Intellectuals
> **1953–1956:** Agricultural Collectivization
> **1957:** Hundred Flowers; Anti-Rightist Movement
> **1958–1961:** Great Leap Forward
> **1966:** Cultural Revolution

Mao Zedong's vision of the New China was the total transformation of society. He was impatient for its realisation. Bourgeois thinking had to be eliminated through re-educating the people, and once communism was firmly established, proletarian ideology would dominate.[94] The new state used ideology and "correct thinking" to justify policies and behaviour. Everyone had to go through "thought reform". Intellectuals in particular were required to confess their "wrong" views and accept CCP ideology as the correct thinking. The people were compelled to meet regularly in their places of work or neighbourhoods to study correct thinking. Moreover, Mao's social transformation required new battle lines to be drawn to eliminate those who were seen to be standing in the way. Despite the hopeful beginning, the new nation would soon be embroiled in political campaign after political campaign causing enormous suffering. Fortunately, Hong Kong was shielded from the devastating consequences by its colonial status. Indeed, the colony became a sanctuary for the torrents of refugees from the Mainland. The early land reform campaign wiped out the landlord-gentry tradition of rural China. Landlords had their land confiscated and redistributed. They had to stand summary trails and many were executed. The new socialist rural order was made up of party cadres supported by middle peasants, who could own their own land to operate small family farms.[95] A number of party members with Hong Kong links were prominent officials in Guangdong during the land reform period. Ye Jianying was appointed Guangdong's first party secretary, Fang Fang was made one of three vice-chairmen, and many others, such as Zeng Sheng, who fought as guerrillas, were given important positions. Fang Fang was also the director of the provincial land reform committee in the party. Their view was that there was a need to take the unique circumstances of Guangdong into account in implementing land reform.

The Pearl River Delta was highly commercialised, with smaller landholdings than was the case in northern China. Many of the landlords in fact owned small plots of land, which they farmed themselves. Furthermore, as most of the overseas Chinese came from Guangdong, many of them bought land so they could return for retirement. Moreover, all those people who had fought as guerrillas or supported the fighters during the war and civil war needed to be protected. Ye and Fang did not want to turn on them. Ye Jianying insisted that the aim of land reform was to eliminate landowners as a class, but not eliminate the landowners as individuals. How land reform should proceed in Guangdong became a point of contention with Mao Zedong. In June 1952, Mao accused those responsible in Guangdong for the unsatisfactory pace in implementing land reform. Fang Fang was replaced and Ye Jianying was transferred to work in Beijing. Fang's successor, Tao Zhu proved much more efficient, some would say ruthlessly so. Tao and Deng Xiaoping had a good working relationship during the 1950s and early 1960s. Deng also got to know the young cadre from Henan, Zhao Ziyang, who worked under Tao, and who helped to direct land reform at the time. When Tao was promoted in 1965, Zhao was put in charge of Guangdong. One day Zhao would become premier overseeing the Sino-British negotiations for the return of Hong Kong working closely with Deng Xiaoping.[96]

The brutal Suppression of Counter-revolutionaries Campaign in 1950–1951 targeted former KMT elements, "imperialists" and "reactionaries". It involved mass trials and public executions.[97] The Three Antis and Five Antis campaigns of 1951 and 1952, supposedly anti-corruption drives, also targeted capitalists and those whose loyalty to the CCP was felt to be suspect.[98] While the Thought Reform Campaign, a psychological coercion campaign, aimed at professors, sought to remould intellectual discourse along Marxist-Leninist lines.[99] There were also continuous efforts to "liberate" the masses from the influence of "bourgeois ideology and raise their socialist consciousness" through using united front strategies.[100]

Those campaigns generated substantial resentment within the party and among the people. The brief Hundred Flowers Campaign of 1956–1957 was designed to ameliorate the negative impact by allowing people to speak out about the policies of the government and the party. Initially, Mao displayed open support for it, saying: "Our society cannot back down, it could only progress . . . criticism of the bureaucracy is pushing the government towards the better." People were encouraged to voice their criticisms as long as they were "constructive" ("among the people") rather than "hateful and destructive" ("between the enemy and ourselves").[101] By July 1957, Mao decided the complaints were non-constructive and had reached an uncontrollable level, as they not only showed widespread resentment against the regime, but also raised fundamental questions about communism. A halt had to be called.[102] Those who voiced criticisms came under suspicion and were eventually rounded up during the Anti-Rightist Campaign and accused of being counter-revolutionaries.[103] Future premier, Zhu Rongji (premier, 1998–2003) was one of the many people who were purged for his criticisms of Mao's policies. To boost agricultural and industrial production, Mao pushed yet another campaign—the Great Leap Forward (1958–1961) that was supposed to allow China to industrialise rapidly and catch up with the West, but led to widespread famine instead. By the end of 1962, millions of people had perished.[104] At the same time, a programme of agricultural collectivisation started. Farming families were organised into communes so that the country could become a truly communist nation. Collectivisation was expedited in 1955, and by the end of 1958 almost all of China's rural population had been reorganised into communes.[105]

Between 1949 and 1965, large numbers of refugees from China found their way to Hong Kong, including those with previous KMT connections, businessmen—the "capitalists"—and ordinary folks—the "bourgeoisie". Many people from Shanghai fled to the colony too and re-established their lives and businesses there, which gave an additional boost to the economic capacity of Hong Kong. Hong Kong's population at the end of 1949 stood at 1.86 million. By the end of 1952, the colony's population had risen to 2.18 million as a result of high local birth rate as well as people coming from the Mainland. The border between Hong Kong and the Mainland was closed in 1956, but many refugees still made it through. By the end of 1957, the population had increased to nearly 2.8 million. The border had to be better sealed in 1968, making it harder to cross. Nevertheless, by the end of 1960, Hong Kong's population had risen to 3.128 million. By the end of 1965, Hong Kong had 3.625 million people.

Prelude to Revolution

Hong Kong survived the disruptions suffered during the Korean War. Entrepôt trade was supplanted by new export manufacturing industries fuelled by both entrepreneurs and workers from the Mainland, who found refuge in the colony. The 1950s and 1960s were characterised by strong motivation of Hong Kong people to advance. Social mobility was high and people worked extremely hard to rebuild their lives.[106]

On the Mainland, Mao Zedong stepped down as chairman of the People's Republic of China in 1959, taking responsibility for the disastrous Great Leap Forward, although he retained the position as the chairman of the CCP. Liu Shaoqi, who assumed Mao's position as head of state, and Deng Xiaoping, who was party secretary of the CCP, were charged to adopt emergency measures to revive the economy. In the 1960s, de-collectivisation started and by the summer of 1962, there were signs of economic recovery. Liu, Deng and other leaders, such as Chen Yun and Peng Dehuai advocated well thought-out policies over political campaigns to advance development—communism could not be achieved in one go. Mao feared that economic rehabilitation would steer China away from revolution. In his mind, it was necessary to attack the internal enemies with revisionist tendencies to keep the revolution alive. Mao did not like what he had seen in the Soviet Union and feared China would go the same way if nothing was done to stay on the revolutionary path. In his view, Nikita Khrushchev (1894–1971) had veered away from communism in the Soviet Union through dismantling Stalin's policies. Mao also did not like how Soviet-US relations were developing. He believed Khrushchev no longer viewed the imperialist United States as "evil" but only as a rival.[107] Mao begun to criticise Soviet revisionism, raising the drumbeat that China must stick to its communist ideological commitment. Mao had backing from his wife Jiang Qing and Lin Biao in pushing his line of thinking. The stage was set for another major campaign to ensure China stayed on the revolutionary course. The Great Proletarian Cultural Revolution was about to begin.

6
The Cultural Revolution and the Riots of 1967
From 1966 to 1976

The 1967 riots were a critical event in the history of the Chinese Communist Party in Hong Kong. They were the most radical and violent act challenging British rule since the labour strike-boycott of 1925–1926. While there was much social discontent over relative deprivation in Hong Kong, which erupted in April 1966 over a proposed rise in Star Ferry fares, the riots that then ensued lasted less than a week. The 1967 riots were different—they went on for eight months, at the end of which the CCP establishment was largely destroyed by the colonial administration, and the sympathy of Hong Kong people lost.

China's Cultural Revolution can be said to have three stages. The first began in 1966 and ended in April 1969.[1] This was the time when Hong Kong was most involved, as a result of the communist-inspired riots in 1967 and 1968 orchestrated by the CCP in Hong Kong. The second period, from April 1969 to October 1973, saw the rise and fall of Lin Biao and the consolidation of the power of the Gang of Four. After the riots, the Hong Kong government went through a period of reform in order to strengthen its credibility and legitimacy. The people also went through a period of reflection about their sense of identity in relation to Hong Kong. The third period of the Cultural Revolution ended with the death of Mao Zedong in September 1976 followed by the arrest of the Gang of Four on 6 October.[2] By then, Hong Kong people identified strongly with their city and increasingly less with the Mainland.

All the major events of this period of history have been documented, but there are still relatively few scholarly analyses, although more work can be expected as the British archives for that period are now open. This chapter looks at the 1967 riots and the activities of the CCP in Hong Kong.

The Great Proletarian Cultural Revolution

The disturbances in Hong Kong need to be seen within the context of what happened on the Mainland. The revolution was launched by Mao Zedong to reassert his authority, rid China of "liberal bourgeois" elements and continue "class struggle". The first bell of the Cultural Revolution was rung on 1 June 1966, when the

CCP's official newspaper, the *People's Daily*, stated that all "imperialists", "people with affiliations with imperialists" and "imperialist intellectuals" must be purged. On 8 August, the party's Central Committee passed a decision to push "a new stage in the development of the socialist revolution in our country, a deeper and more extensive stage".³ The decision stated that:

> Although the bourgeoisie has been overthrown, it is still trying to use the old ideas, culture, customs and habits of the exploiting classes to corrupt the masses, capture their minds and endeavour to stage a comeback. The proletariat must do the exact opposite: it must meet head-on every challenge of the bourgeoisie in the ideological field and use the new ideas, culture, customs and habits of the proletariat to change the mental outlook of the whole of society. At present, our objective is to struggle against and overthrow those *persons in authority* who are taking the capitalist road, to criticise and repudiate the reactionary bourgeois *academic authorities* and the ideology of the bourgeoisie and *all other exploiting classes* and to transform education, literature and art and all other parts of the superstructure not in correspondence with the socialist economic base, so as to facilitate the consolidation and development of the socialist system.⁴ [author's italics]

Mao Zedong concluded that the revolution had yet to eliminate the bourgeoisie in society. Even more troubling to Mao was his perception that the CCP had lost its revolutionary zeal and party leaders had gone soft. He feared China would go the way of the Soviet Union, as it was doing under Nikita Khrushchev, and become "revisionist". He then began to lay the groundwork to eliminate the highest ranks of the party hierarchy. Over the next few years, apart from Zhou Enlai and a few others, the purge touched all the leading cadres, war heroes and veteran revolutionaries, including all those who had worked alongside Mao for decades. No one's record was beyond question. The Cultural Revolution evolved into waves of purges, during which a very large number of party and government officials were denounced and removed from office.

In order to bring down the party hierarchy, Mao bypassed it to reach out to radicals to do his bidding, and to appeal to students and youths to root out exploitation and energetically "destroy the old and bring in the new". Privilege, position and hierarchy must be denounced. He believed young people could best protect his revolutionary legacy and those who were disloyal to him must be got rid of. He encouraged the young to act on their instincts. Educational establishments were considered too elitist and were closed down. Cultural sophistication, scholarship, expertise and professionalism were devalued. Instead, the *Little Red Book* of Mao's quotations, published in millions of copies, was all one needed to know. Culture and the arts should only serve the revolution. Art objects with no revolutionary value were considered useless. Many priceless cultural relics were destroyed, such as the Confucius Temple in Qufu in Shandong.

Groups of youths, who banded together into shock forces of Red Guard, encouraged others to criticise those deemed politically suspect.⁵ Family members, friends, colleagues, teachers and neighbours were not spared. Many people suffered the most heart-wrenching public humiliation. There was widespread looting and destruction of homes and properties. The Red Guards supported Mao's call to create a classless society where no one was better than anyone else. The Red Guards also turned their anger on foreigners. Britain was a special case because of its presence on Chinese territory with the colony of Hong Kong. Red Guards burnt down the British Mission in Beijing in August 1967, which was the most serious incident to take place in foreign affairs that year.[6] During the height of the Cultural Revolution, the normal functions of the organs of the government and the CCP on both central and local levels were paralysed.[7] Indeed, between mid-1966 and 1971, the CCP had become dysfunctional. Revolution and governance can never be expected to sit well together.

The first sign that political upheaval was brewing on the Mainland reached Hong Kong in May 1966—travellers reported that the mayor of Beijing, Peng Zhen, one of China's top cadres, had been dismissed. Wall-posters were also spotted proclaiming that the defence minister, Lin Biao, was Mao Zedong's most loyal supporter. Rumours abounded that there was a power struggle between Mao and Lin on the one side, and Liu Shaoqi, Deng Xiaoping, and Zhou Enlai on the other side. By August 1966, the Cultural Revolution movement had broken out in Beijing and quickly spread throughout the country. The news of events in China caused concern in Hong Kong although life in the colony remained stable. Businessmen visiting the Canton Trade Fair in October and November that year reported doing little business, as negotiations were hampered by endless lectures from the hosts on Mao Zedong Thought. At about that time, news reached Hong Kong that Liu Shaoqi had been disgraced.[8]

Green Light for Red Riots

Zhou Enlai, through Liao Chengzhi, had initially conveyed a message to CCP Hong Kong that the Cultural Revolution would not spread to the colony, as the campaigns only targeted the bourgeoisie and anti-revolutionaries on the Mainland. It was also made clear that any revolutionary activities in Hong Kong would jeopardise the foundation and network established by the CCP there.[9] In October 1966, when Hong Kong party members visited Beijing to celebrate National Day, Liao Chengzhi repeated the same message to them.[10] However, there had already been an early sign that things might not remain calm for Hong Kong. In September, Red Guards in Guangdong had renamed Hong Kong as the "Expel-the-Imperialists City" and thought they won a propaganda victory when a Hong Kong official spokesman said that letters from the Mainland to Hong Kong using the new name would be delivered.[11] While the renaming of Hong Kong bordered on the farcical it showed that British administration could not completely shield Hong Kong from revolutionary excesses.

Events moved quickly on the Mainland. Revolutionary fervour became increasingly intense. Hong Kong party members and supporters considered what they should do despite what Zhou Enlai and Liao Chengzhi told them. They watched from afar purge after purge of high-ranking cadres and officials in Beijing. No one wanted to make an ideological mistake at what was obviously a risky time. Self-preservation was the priority.[12] The local CCP leaders did not want to be recalled to the Mainland, which had been the fate of other cadres stationed overseas. Although there was no way for the party to force them to leave Hong Kong if they had not wanted to go, as their livelihood depended on the party, they had to be careful.[13]

There was also the example of Macao to take into account—should similar action be emulated in Hong Kong? In November 1966, leftists in Macao took advantage of a trivial dispute over an attempt by the police to demolish an illegal extension that had been built on the grounds of a leftist school to organise demonstrations. On 3 December, students tried to prevent the demolition and claimed they were beaten by the police. The next day, students joined with the Federation of Trade Unions in Macao to demonstrate against the Portuguese colonial government. Protesters read out the *Thoughts of Mao Zedong* and sang revolutionary songs before the governor's house. On 5 December, as the rioters became unruly, Governor Nobre de Carvalho ordered Portuguese troops to fire on rioters killing several demonstrators. A curfew was imposed. The Chinese moved gunboats into Macao's territorial waters and Beijing accused the Portuguese of practicing "fascist atrocities" against the Chinese people of Macao. Rioters stormed the governor's residence. The Portuguese soon gave in. They accepted the leftists' demands to make a public apology for killing protesters and to pay compensation.[14]

The CCP Hong Kong sent members to Macao to learn what happened there, and they returned keen to get into the act in Hong Kong, seemingly having forgotten the instructions from Zhou Enlai and Liao Chengzhi.[15] The British watched events closely. The British realised that the Portuguese Government in Macao not only lost control but "they never really got it back".[16] Having lost control, Portugal offered to hand Macao back to China but the Chinese refused it. The British would be unwilling to share power informally with China, as Portugal was willing to do. In 1974, Portugal made a second attempt to give Macao back, which was likewise refused. It was only in 1986 after the question of Hong Kong was settled that China was ready to negotiate the settlement of Macao.

By March 1967, the British felt trouble was brewing in Hong Kong—a string of labour disputes started to occur and the left-wing press began to accuse "agents of Taiwan and American imperialism" of oppressing Chinese workers in Hong Kong.[17] Governor David Trench (1964–1971) said at an off-the-record press briefing in London that the Red Guards' aim was "to Macao us".[18]

To the leftists in Hong Kong, political developments in Beijing appeared to require them to take action. By May 1966, the Central Cultural Revolution Group, initially formed in Beijing with the endorsement of the Politburo to draft policy documents, became effectively Mao Zedong's personal provider of alternative information. By August, it became the campaign headquarters of the Cultural Revolution and quickly grew into a large bureaucracy occupying several buildings at Diaoyutai. By February 1967, it replaced the Politburo and CCP Central Committee Secretariat for all their duties. By then, the party organisation had been shattered by the various purges.[19] The ascendancy of radicals—led by Jiang Qing—and their control of the Central Cultural Revolution Group must have been noted by the leftists in Hong Kong.

Moreover, radicals in Beijing also left their mark on foreign affairs. The Central Cultural Revolution Group insisted on the global dissemination of Mao Zedong Thought. Chen Yi, the foreign minister, got into trouble for resisting and had eventually to make a self-criticism.[20] Red Guard liaison stations were created within the ministry to oversee its work. During this turbulent period, the radicals also abolished the government's State Council's Foreign Affairs Staff Office, which had day-to-day responsibility for Hong Kong matters, and replaced it with a new Foreign Affairs Revolutionary Leading Small Group. The radicals attacked former Staff Office personnel and transferred them to various other departments. Liao Chengzhi, the Staff Office's first deputy, was forced to step aside and eventually purged and thrown into prison in 1968. Most of the staff members who looked after Hong Kong and Macao affairs were transferred to the Western Europe Bureau of the Ministry of Foreign Affairs.[21] The Revolutionary Leading Group became the direct supervising organ of CCP Hong Kong.

While Zhou Enlai remained in office, the leftists in the colony were unclear whether he still had full control over Hong Kong affairs.[22] In January 1967, the Foreign Affairs Revolutionary Leading Group issued a directive to CCP Hong Kong, asking members to "rectify" the "wrong rightist line", which Chen Yi and Liao Chengzhi had to endorse, and "go back to the revolutionary path again".[23] It became obvious that Zhou's position was also at risk.[24] That was the green light radical leftists in Hong Kong had been waiting for to launch revolution in the colony.

Another point to note was that, while the Ministry of Foreign Affairs in Beijing had been weakened by the radicals with the result that it paid less attention to Hong Kong, the Guangdong Provincial Military Management Committee had become more involved in the colony's affairs. The Committee's No. 2 Small Group became responsible for providing assistance to local cadres and chaperoned visitors—mainly from unions, schools and other leftist organisations—from Hong Kong and Macao. Some scholars believe the No. 2 Small Group must have played a key role in the organised disturbances during the Cultural Revolution in Hong Kong.[25]

Both Sides Prepared for Trouble

The ensuing riots of 1967 were orchestrated by CCP Hong Kong working from the Xinhua Hong Kong office. The director of Xinhua Hong Kong at the time was Liang

Weilin and his deputy was Qi Feng—both of whom would have great longevity at Xinhua Hong Kong serving for another decade, as will be seen in Chapter 7. It should be noted that Xinhua Hong Kong was not immune from running into trouble with the radicals in Beijing. Two of its deputy directors, Zhu Wanping and Liang Shangyuan were purged and dismissed. For example, Liang, who worked on overseas Chinese affairs, was accused of having connections with Taiwan. Their posts in Hong Kong were not filled until 1973, which probably weakened communication between Beijing and Hong Kong during those years.[26]

As the CCP members and supporters got ready for action in the colony, the Hong Kong administration was well prepared to meet trouble, although senior officials did not think there was imminent serious danger in early 1967. They only became concern in early April after street riots broke out.[27] In terms of preparedness, the colonial authorities benefited from police reforms introduced after the riots of October 1956. With the Star Ferry riots in 1966, the authorities were just beginning to realise the extent of social frustration and alienation among the underprivileged class.[28] The toll from the 1956 riots—59 deaths, 443 people hospitalised, and 1,740 court convictions for a week of trouble—was high. Nevertheless, the authorities had a chance to test police preparedness and, taking lessons from those riots, made further improvements. Police officers received regular anti-riot training, the police had three companies of anti-riot officers on stand-by at any one time, and further reinforcements could be brought in quickly. The authorities also observed what happened in Macao in December 1966 and took lessons from it. When the confrontation started in 1967, the Hong Kong government "had in place an organised, equipped, well-trained and efficient anti-riot police".[29] Indeed, the toll from the 1967 was low compared to that from the previous year. Despite eight months of protracted clashes between police and protestors and almost 1,200 bomb incidents during 1967, total casualties in Hong Kong were 51 deaths, 848 people injured, and 2,077 convicted by the courts.[30]

Early conflicts

There had been a string of seven major labour disputes in March and April 1967 in shipping, taxi, textile, and cement companies, which the Hong Kong authorities noted, but did not think indicated that there was imminent danger. The prelude to the riots was a particular industrial dispute over work conditions at the Hong Kong Artificial Flower Works in late April 1967. Condition in the factory was Dickensian, like many others—no better but no worse.[31] Scuffles only occurred after factory management responded with a lockout and wholesale dismissal of workers. While the origin of the dispute did not appear to have been perpetrated by the CCP-dominated leftist unions, poor handling by factory management provided the CCP with the opportunity to politicise matters.[32] Attempts to settle the disputes were deliberately frustrated. Rowdy demonstrations then ensued, designed to intimate the management.³³ It was at that time that the secretary for defence, Jack Cater, was made deputy colonial secretary (special duties) to tackle the mobilisations. This unit met every day in 1967 to brief the governor. Cater would one day become chief secretary of Hong Kong.

Disturbances started on May Day—1 May 1967, also referred to as International Labour Day—in the large factory in San Po Kong, where there were 686 workers. The dispute was still ongoing after a week, and on 6 May:

> A group of dismissed workers from the Hong Kong Artificial Flower Works . . . were picketing the factory premises and, ignoring repeated warnings from the police, they persisted in illegally trying to prevent the removal of goods by the management. The police finally intervened and arrested 21 men. It was a minor incident; there was little or no violence and no one was seriously injured. It was, however, enough to provoke an immediate reaction; headlines appeared in the communist newspapers denouncing the government and accusing the police, in the most violent terms, of persecution and of brutally attacking unarmed workers.³⁴

The FTU defined the 6 May incident as a "planned, organised and premeditated suppression of the patriotic workers and compatriots" by the police.³⁵ On 11 May, the conflict escalated. Leftist supporters were mobilised to go to the factory to express support for the workers there, and they tried to break into the factory. The police were called in again. Indeed, all policemen were called to duty that day as thing got more unruly. By evening, the crowd had grown substantially and some rioters started to pelt the police with stones and bottles. The police responded with clubs, wooden bullets and tear gas. The unrest spread to the nearby Tung Tau Resettlement Estate, and the entire East Kowloon area was placed under curfew that evening. More than 100 people were arrested. On 12 May, Liao Chengzhi chaired a meeting in Beijing to discuss what was happening in Hong Kong. The vice foreign minister, Luo Guibo, was also present. They both had reservations about promoting confrontation in the colony but a decision was made to assist the struggle.³⁶ In the meantime, on 12 and 13 May, the leftist groups in the colony organised a series of demonstrations in both Kowloon and Hong Kong Island, and violent clashes between the demonstrators and the police continued. Buses were set alight, government offices were looted, buildings were burnt and property damaged. More arrests were made. Order was only restored on 14 May.

The editorial of *Ta Kung Pao* labelled the violent conflict as an aggressive act committed by the colonial administration against the local Chinese.³⁷ Other CCP-controlled newspapers likewise fiercely condemned the action of the Hong Kong authorities. The colonial authorities looked at the CCP's efforts this way:

> In May the communists had under their control all the machinery required for a full-scale propaganda campaign. Their three newspapers, *Ta Kung Pao*, *Wen Wei Po* and the *New Evening Post*, were well established and had a good circulation and they were backed up by about six other papers which not only followed their lead

but at times ran to excesses of wild invention of their own. They had ample printing facilities for other propaganda material and the men and equipment for newsreel production. They also enjoyed considerable encouragement and assistance from . . . [Xinhua Hong Kong] . . . This agency was largely responsible for directing the propaganda campaign . . . as could be seen from the identical reports of incidents that regularly appeared in communist papers . . . It was also responsible for producing distorted accounts of the events in Hong Kong for the consumption of the authorities in Peking. Its highly-coloured and wildly exaggerated reports undoubtedly played a large part in inflaming opinion in China against the Government of the Colony. In their campaign the communists employed every theme and every weapon, from deliberate distortion of facts and falsification of photographs to the spreading of rumour and the fabrication of non-existent incidents. Rumours put about ranged from the possible but untrue—rice shortages, power or water stoppages—to the widely improbable—as for example the stories which appeared in minor communist newspaper, complete with photographs and maps, of Chinese gunboats approaching the Colony. Communist reporters and photographers were present at every incident to produce their versions of events; and in many cases demonstrations were organised solely for publicity purposes . . . [Another] propaganda medium was posters. These appeared from the start of the confrontation . . . reaching their height at the end of May and the beginning of June. Posters and slogans appeared everywhere, both ashore and afloat.[38]

The colonial authorities saw the rising propaganda efforts were aimed at enlisting active support from Beijing.[39] The "workers" demanded that all the protesters arrested at the San Po Kong disturbances should be released; compensation should be paid; responsible parties should be punished; and a written apology should be made to all the Chinese people living in Hong Kong.[40] On 15 May, China's Ministry of Foreign Affairs issued a statement demanding that the British government instruct the Hong Kong administration to stop all "fascist atrocities", free those who had been arrested, and demanded that the authorities immediately accept all the workers' demands. The *People's Daily* published a commentary warning the colonial authorities that they had to "stop before it is too late".[41] Luo Guibo also presented the British *charge d'affaires* in Beijing with a formal protest. CCP Hong Kong received a message from Yao Dengshan, the head of the Foreign Affairs Revolutionary Leading Small Group, that it had Beijing's full support in continuing the struggle in Hong Kong.[42] The message was a significant morale booster, which induced the leftists to step up action.

The British tried to assess China's real intention on Hong Kong so as to be able to interpret the verbal support for the disturbances from the ministry and Mainland media. There was confusion over whether there was about to be intervention from the Mainland. Cater's impression was that "it was quite obvious that Beijing, especially Zhou Enlai, did not like the trouble made by the leftists in Hong Kong" and that the struggle campaign was a local effort.[43]

On 16 May 1967, various leftist organisations from business, education, labour, film and other sectors banded together to form the Hong Kong–Kowloon All Sectors Anti-Persecution Struggle Committee. It was created to give a semblance of widespread unity among people from all walks of life—a standard united front tactic. The Committee was supposed to be the command centre for planning, organising and commanding the people's struggle but in reality it was CCP Hong Kong that made all the important decisions and orchestrated the struggle behind the scene.[44] The Committee had seventeen members with Yeung Kwong, the FTU leader at the time, as chairman.[45] When the Committee was launched, Yeung's speech on the occasion referred to the colonial authorities oppressing the Chinese and urged the people to find inspiration in Mao Zedong Thought to "escalate the struggle to a higher level until victory is achieved against the British imperialist capitalists".[46] The Committee issued similar demands to those made by the Foreign Ministry.[47]

With Beijing's message of support, the leaders of CCP Hong Kong mobilised hundreds of supporters from various leftist organisations to demonstrate outside Government House, where the governor lived and worked. For several days after 16 May, there were large crowds on Upper Albert Road in front of Government House. The demonstrators chanted communist slogans, sang revolutionary songs, waved placards, made speeches and plastered the gates of Government House with posters of quotes from Mao Zedong.

Large loudspeakers were also placed on the roof of the Bank of China Building in Central, broadcasting communist propaganda. The police proved quite creative in countering the noise by setting up on the roof of the Information Services Department across the road even more powerful loudspeakers playing popular music and Cantonese opera to drown out the propaganda.[48] The resulting din made the area of Statue Square unbearable for the three days that the contest between left-wing forces and the Hong Kong authorities lasted.[49] The use of loudspeakers for broadcasting was eventually banned in late May.

According to contemporary reports, the protesters at Government House behaved in a surprisingly orderly fashion:

> As it was already lunch time, the demonstrators knocked-off and returned an hour later to resume chanting until five o'clock, when they all went home. The only casualty was the governor's pet poodle, which went frantic with indignation and had to be removed from the scene.[50]

A deal had in fact been made. There had been secret communication between the police and left-wing leaders that there could be demonstrations in front of Government House if protesters remained peaceful.[51] However, a request to meet the governor on 17 May was turned down.

Another report showed an amusing side to the protest:

> Government House was plastered with posters. The governor had to use the back gate. But the Hong Kong Government was brilliant. They did things like putting

up special notices for those who were coming to protest. A number of leading pro-communists were also fat-cat communists and would turn up in their expensive Mercedes cars. So a notice was put out saying: "Petitioners' car park this way."[52]

Less amusing, a million protesters marched past the British Mission in Beijing on 17 May calling upon the British to leave Hong Kong. A mass rally held the next day at a sports stadium in Beijing drew 100,000 people including senior leaders, such as Zhou Enlai and Chen Yi. In Shanghai, rioters broke into and destroyed the home of the British diplomatic representative.[53] Soon thereafter, Zhou Enlai called a meeting to discuss Hong Kong. Chen Yi, Liao Chengzhi, and Luo Guibo were present. Zhou complained about the methods used by the leftists in Hong Kong. Their actions represented provocation to the British and Zhou questioned whether the colonial authorities would tolerate them. To continue the struggle appropriately, he ordered that a special Hong Kong–Macao office be created to provide leadership for Hong Kong and Macao matters. He probably also saw this as a counterweight to the radical Revolutionary Leading Group. Luo was made head of this unit, which was staffed by people with foreign affairs experience.[54] Zhou Enlai's role during the riots was the most interesting and enigmatic of all, which will be discussed later in this chapter.

Increased fervour

Apparently, there were some concerns expressed within the leftist camp that the daily protests at Government House could easily turn violent. The voices of caution were criticised by Liang Weilin and Qi Feng as "rightist"—there was no need to be "afraid to struggle, afraid to win".[55] Indeed, things took a violent turn on 22 May, as thousands of protestors headed towards Government House for what had become their daily vigil. The protesters were asked by the police to split up into smaller groups before continuing on. They refused and clashed with the police. The leftists then sparked riots in various parts of the territory. The police used tear gas and wooden bullets in retaliation and arrested 167 of the rioters. The left-wing press reported several hundred injuries and called what happened the Bloody May 22 Incident. The editorial of *Wen Wei Po* accused the colonial administration of having carried out bloody suppression that resulted in a massacre.[56] Xinhua Hong Kong alleged that 200 people had been killed or injured.[57]

CCP Hong Kong sent a ten man delegation to Beijing to meet the new Hong Kong–Macao unit. In discussion about how to continue the struggle, Beijing cadres thought it unrealistic to demand the British surrender unconditionally. It would require exerting comprehensive pressure on the British, and ideas on how to do that were considered unworkable. For example, cutting off or reducing food and water supplies to Hong Kong would only harm the compatriots, and anything involving the army to cause problems at the border was inappropriate. A consensus emerged that the struggle in the colony had to be waged mainly by the Hong Kong people against the colonial authorities. In meetings on 24 and 27 May, Zhou Enlai warned against using an "overly leftist" approach in handling the struggle in Hong Kong. He maintained that any struggle against the colonial authorities must be done within the limit of established policy—it must be "reasonable, advantageous and restrained".[58] In another meeting on 30 May, Zhou Enlai rejected the idea from the Hong Kong delegation to attack and kill some Hong Kong police officers because the police were corrupt and unpopular in the colony. Other plans included organising three rounds of strikes. The first would be from 10 June involving 80,000 to 100,000 workers, with transport workers forming the backbone so that they could bring transport and traffic to a standstill. The second wave of strikes could then be expanded to include 300,000 to 400,000 workers to put pressure on the authorities, with a third and final general strike aimed at paralysing Hong Kong as during the Strike-Boycott in 1925–1926 (Chapter 3). Zhou Enlai and Liao Chengzhi were doubtful the leftists could involve such large numbers of strikers and pull things off. Zhou thought that in the worst case, Beijing could be forced to take back Hong Kong prematurely and that would not serve China's interest. While the plans were to be revised by the leaders in Beijing, the Hong Kong delegation was sent back to the colony and told that they could act on their ideas first while Beijing considered revisions.[59]

Thus, starting from the end of May, leftists began to organise a series of stoppages and strikes in different trades trying to cause a breakdown of the city's public transport, as well as water and electricity supplies.[60] Another problem for Hong Kong in 1966 and 1967 was that below average rainfall led to a shortage of water. So Hong Kong wanted to buy more water from Guangdong, but a request for an additional supply from Guangdong went unanswered. To save water, ever tighter rationing was implemented: supply in Hong Kong had to be limited to four hours every four days in the summer of 1967. Heavy rains in August and September eased the situation.[61] The water issue would not be resolved until on 1 October 1967, when the contract came up for renewal and when Zhou Enlai got back full control of foreign affairs, which also signalled the easing of confrontation in Hong Kong.[62] Much would happen before then.

On 3 June, the editorial of the *People's Daily* in Beijing condemned the British in very harsh terms and encouraged compatriots in Hong Kong to mobilise the masses to fight imperialism:

> Hong Kong is ruled by thoroughly appalling British imperialism, it is the enemy of four million Hong Kong compatriots, it is the enemy of . . . the Chinese . . . in the past 100 years or so, British imperialism committed every crime in Hong Kong, and should be held accountable for the monstrous sins! . . . At present, the task placed before the patriotic Hong Kong compatriots is to press ahead and persevere in the struggle against British violence so as to win a great victory. To achieve this, it is necessary to boldly arouse the masses. With the working class as the nucleus,

all patriotic and anti-imperialist forces in Hong Kong that can be united should be united and the ranks for struggle against British violence continuously consolidated and expanded.[63]

The editorial was "one the strongest condemnations of Hong Kong by the PRC in the 17 years of its existence and was seen as a veiled threat which had the intention of unsettling the authorities in the Colony".[64] The effect of the editorial was that it further stirred up the anti-British fervour of the leftists in Hong Kong. They believed that the party leaders in Beijing must have abandoned the previously cautious policy, and that China was ready to take back Hong Kong very soon. The revolutionary passion in the leftist camp surged to a high level.[65] Their hope was not so much to defeat the authorities in the street but to show that the British might no longer have the stamina to hold on since Britain had an overall policy of decolonisation.[66]

The colonial authorities stepped up efforts to deal with the disturbances. Emergency regulations were introduced to prohibit the display of inflammatory posters that had slogans like "Hang David Trench". Police carried out searches of leftist bookshops, banks, department stores and cinemas, and confiscated weapons and inflammatory materials. Violent conflicts frequently occurred during these searches and seizures. On two occasions, three leftists were killed. They became "martyrs" and the leftists declared that the "blood debts can only be repaid by blood".[67] In protest, Liang Weilin, the head of CCP Hong Kong, sent a message to the governor that if the colonial administration did not apologise, it "would be destined to be beaten to death by Hong Kong patriotic compatriots and the Chinese people".[68]

In June 1967, CCP Hong Kong rolled out a new campaign to initiate a labour strike, business boycott, and school strike. At the time, the Chinese government owned more than 50 department stores, a number of other smaller shops, publishing houses, restaurants, the Bank of China and eight smaller banks, two insurance companies and three financial syndicates.[69] The aim of the campaign was to turn Hong Kong into a "dead port", shake the foundation of colonial rule and undermine it enough so that the British would surrender.[70] Agitators tried to persuade food sellers to stop selling food but it was hardly practical since everyone, including the leftists, had to eat. On 13 June, the Guangdong authorities staged a token one-day stoppage of food supply to Hong Kong.[71] On 24 June, 60,000 workers from more than 20 trades including marine and land transport, docks, textile industry and public services answered the appeal of the leftist camp to go on a general strike. Some of the workers were government employees or employees of British-owned enterprises. On 27 June, 20,000 students from 32 left-wing schools boycotted classes. On 28 June, while the food strike was supposed to start, Guangdong ignored it and kept sending food to the border. As businesses with close Mainland connection started a four-day boycott the next day, the food importers among them would not receive the food from Guangdong leaving provisions piling up at the border.

The Hong Kong government's assessment was that the leftist actions in the colony were the result of local initiatives and not the product of a well thought-out policy from Beijing. The disposition of the People's Liberation Army in Guangdong, and the intelligence that the British had, supported such a view.[72] Indeed, enormous efforts were made on the Mainland side to maintain food supplies to Hong Kong throughout the trouble period despite transport difficulties as a result of the disruptions by the Red Guards. This shows the various forces that were at play behind the scene on the Mainland.[73]

The leftist press claimed that more than 200,000 people had joined the boycott.[74] The campaign was declared a victory. At a meeting on 1 July, Yeung Kwong said that it had caused the colonial authorities to suffer "dizziness and headaches", and its "power and prestige had been significantly discredited".[75] However, the truth was the campaign neither created the expected effect of paralysing Hong Kong nor unsettling the ruling basis of the colonial government. The campaign failed to garner wide support. In comparison to Hong Kong's total working population then of 1.5 million, the impact brought about by 60,000 strikers was relatively minor. Thoughtful people in the leftist camp had questioned whether the strike-boycott was wise, as it would have the most serious impact on the working class and small businesses. In fact, by the end of June, the strike-boycott began to run out of steam. On 2 July, the food embargo was lifted.

The peak of violence

On 8 July 1967, armed militia crossed the border from the Mainland side to Sha Tau Kok and shot up the police post there, killing five policemen. With continuous shootings, the police officers needed reinforcement, as there were still many of them holed up in their post. In fact, gangs had already swarmed across the border and caused trouble on 24 June. On that earlier occasion, the District Office and the Gurkha commander tried to negotiate and had to sign an apology to end the incident. On the second occasion however, things were much more worrying:

> There was no knowing whether this was a local initiative or the beginning of a proper invasion . . . A decision to send in the army to retake the police post . . . required approval in London over a weekend. It took the whole day to get it, during which time the Gurkhas were formed up just short of the border. When approval eventually arrived, the militia were found to have retreated. From that time, the army took over control of the border until shortly before the handover of Hong Kong to China when the police returned.[76]

Jack Cater believed Zhou Enlai had not approved the incident at Sha Tau Kok. According to Cater:

Beijing told us to "hold on" and that they would help. But then they were also in chaos. There were also riots and most of the provinces in China had serious problems. They could not do anything for us at that time.[77]

The Hong Kong government concluded that the incident, though serious, was not an attempt at armed invasion of the colony as no regular People's Liberation Army unit was involved. The incident was likely organised and executed locally by radical elements in the immediate vicinity across the border.[78] However, the leftist press depicted the Sha Tau Kok incident as a show of support from Beijing for the anti-imperialist struggle in Hong Kong. Moreover, a veteran leftist claimed that a large number of Red Guards in Guangdong were in fact prepared to rush over the border to liberate Hong Kong. They were only stopped by a just-in-time telephone call from Zhou Enlai.[79]

As the impact of the strike campaigns had been disappointing, the leftists became increasingly militant, perhaps out of desperation. On 9 July, 150 leftists clashed with the police in the Western District during which one rioter and one policeman were killed. The death of the policeman, who was stabbed, was hailed by *Jing Pao* as "butchering live a yellow skin dog". On the same day, another crowd of 300 leftists was engaged in a serious violent conflict with the police in North Point. They destroyed a tram station, attacked public vehicles passing by and set fire to a public bus. The police retaliated by firing tear gas and raiding several leftist strongholds in North Point. The riot lasted until midnight. Over the next few days, there were more riots and attacks on the police by the leftists, usually by hurling stones and splashing acidic liquids. Some leftists also attempted to persuade the Chinese serving in the police force to join their cause. The Anti-Persecution Committee praised the violent acts of the leftists and encouraged them to continue, and "to point the knife towards the British-Hong Kong fascists and their followers, and attack them without mercy".[80]

In face of the increasing use of violence, the Hong Kong government was determined to crack down hard on the leftists. On 12 July 1967, the acting colonial secretary stated in the Legislative Council that:

> we are now entering a new phase of violence and perhaps terrorism, for there is nothing so degraded that these men will not stoop to . . . We are convinced and determined now that the [time has] come to grasp and retain the initiative in this contest, we have no [doubt] that in doing so we shall have the whole-hearted support of the vast majority of the community, and we have no doubt of the final outcome. Meanwhile it is a time to be alert and resolute and steadfast.[81]

That night, the government imposed a curfew on Hong Kong Island and Kowloon. At the same time, Governor David Trench had decided he needed to replace the then Police Commissioner Edward Tyrer, whom he found not tough enough to deal with the confrontation. Tyrer was retired the next day.[82] The police, with the back-up of the British Army, carried out a series of raids on known or suspected leftists' strongholds. For the next three weeks, the police continued to raid the premises of left-wing unions, schools, stores and theatres, clocking up over 60 places. The police found and seized a large number of weapons and illegal materials. In one particularly dramatic operation, which involved more than a thousand policemen and soldiers, helicopters from a British aircraft carrier were used to land police officers and soldiers on the roof of a 27-storey building, while more officers and soldiers attacked at ground level at the same time. After that, the leftists covered the roof of the Bank of China Building with barricades to prevent it from also being used as a helicopter landing platform.[83] There was resistance to most of the raids, which resulted in five deaths and 1,500 arrests according to leftist sources.[84]

The Hong Kong government also started to arrest well-known and influential leftist leaders in the territory. For example, Tang Bingda, a key committee member of the Anti-Persecution Struggle Committee and treasurer of the Chinese General Chamber of Commerce, was apprehended. Famous leftist movie stars Fu Qi and Shi Hui were detained and Ling Wanyan, headmaster of the left-wing Sai Kung Public School, was removed.

On 20 July, the Hong Kong government brought in sweeping additional emergency powers while continuing to raid left-wing premises. New regulations made it an offence to spread "false reports or false statements either verbally or in writing likely to cause public alarm or despondency". Courts were empowered to hold criminal trials from which the public could be excluded so as to prevent witness intimidation. Other emergency regulations dealt with the power to seize weapons, oblige people to provide names and addresses to police officers on demand, disperse assemblies, prevent obstruction of the armed forces in the course of performing their duties, prohibit unlawful meetings, and protect official vehicles. On 28 July, another three emergency regulations were passed authorising the police to arrest and detain "conspirators and instigators" who took care to remain in the background, and using others to do their work for them.[85]

The totality of the Hong Kong government's action hit the leftists hard but they were not about to give up yet. Under the direction of CCP Hong Kong, they decided to retaliate by planting bombs throughout the city. There was a sense that they had to escalate the level of violence. In any event, they had no better idea at the time according to Liang Shangyuan, the former deputy director of the Xinhua Hong Kong.[86] Planting bombs was something the leftists had already done. The bombs were homemade devices using gunpowder extracted from firecrackers.[87] On 12 July, two bombs they planted had exploded in the New Territories and Kowloon respectively but no one was hurt on those occasions. On 20 July, the Anti-Persecution Struggle Committee called on its supporters to be "bolder" and "ignite a few more flares" and "open up a few more battlegrounds".[88] On 26 July, nine bombing incidents happened in various places causing numerous injuries. The Committee applauded that bombs "blossomed everywhere" and that they "seriously disturbed, exhausted and highly embarrassed" the authorities.[89] More bombs, mixed with hoaxes, were planted by the leftists until the end of 1967. According to government statistics, the police defused some 8,000 bombs or suspected explosive devices, in which more than 1,100 bombs were real, during the riots. As students from leftist schools became involved in the disturbances, the Hong Kong government saw the communist-dominated schools as "centres for storage and disseminations of inflammatory literature and even for the manufacture of bombs, both simulated and real".[90] On 27 November 1967, a student from the Chung Wah Middle School was injured in an explosion that happened in his school laboratory while, as alleged by the police, he was making bombs. For this reason, the police raided and closed the school afterwards, evoking a protest from Beijing. Tung Chee Hwa, the first chief executive of the HKSAR, studied at Chung Wah Middle School in the early 1950s. The school principal, Wong Jo Fun, was arrested and detained by the police during the 1967 riots.[91] Bombs were also sent in parcels to recipients in British companies like the Hong Kong and Shanghai Banking Corporation and Jardine Matheson.[92]

The bombs were a serious concern for both the authorities and the Hong Kong public. The bombs had killed, maimed and injured many innocent people including children. As bombing persisted, the government banned all firecrackers so that bombs could not be made using the gunpowder. The bombings were seen as inexcusable terrorist acts by the community. Communist sympathisers were referred to in derogatory terms, like "lefties" or "leftist jackass" by ordinary folk.[93] The extremists among the leftist camp used assassination as the means to continue their campaign. On 24 August, Lam Bun, a popular radio talk show host on Commercial Radio, noted for his condemnation of the leftists, was killed as he was driving to work. A death squad pretending to be road maintenance workers poured gasoline over Lam's car and set it, and Lam, on fire. He was burned to death. Lam's cousin who was also in the car was seriously burnt and died in hospital several days later.[94] The killers have never been caught. After the killing, a leftist newspaper, the *New Evening Daily*, published an article that afternoon listing the "crimes" Lam had supposedly committed.[95] It was also reported that a number of prominent figures who had voiced opposition against the riots, for example, Kan Yuet Keung (senior member of the Legislative Council and member of the Executive Council), Louis Cha (chairman of *Ming Pao*), Chung Sze Yuen (chairman of the Federation of Hong Kong Industries) and Henry Luk Hoi On (editor of the rightwing newspaper *Chun Pao*) were on a death list.[96] A direct legacy of the murder of Lam Bun is the still running radio drama *18th Floor Block C* on Commercial Radio. The show was launched in the wake of the riots but the programme became inseparable from what happened to Lam and continues to commemorate the spirit of speaking out against what is wrong in society.[97]

The end of violence

On 19 July, Hsueh Ping, supposedly a reporter at the Xinhua News Agency, was sentenced to two years' imprisonment by a Hong Kong court in connection with rioting.[98] On 19 August 1967, the police raided three left-wing newspapers and arrested the publishers, editors-in-chief, and printers for publishing false and seditious materials.[99]

> [T]he arrest of the publishers and the banning of the three newspapers, the *Tin Fung Yat Po*, the *Hong Kong Evening News* and the *Afternoon News* were not simply because they were leftwing press, but because they told people to plant bombs in the streets. They were acting the violence, and were much more extreme.[100]

Wen Wei Po criticised the police action as "thoroughly fascist, thoroughly persecutory" and demanded the immediate release of the editors. The arrests incited the radicals in Beijing. On 20 August 1967, the Ministry of Foreign Affairs issued an ultimatum to the British government demanding the lifting of the ban on the newspapers and release of those arrested in Hong Kong within 48 hours, which the British refused to do. To the British, meeting the demands would amount to a total surrender. At the same time, the *People's Daily* issued commentaries on two consecutive days attacking British colonialism in Hong Kong. On 22 August, the Red Guards demonstrated in front of the British Mission in Beijing and then set it on fire.[101] British diplomatic personnel were beaten when they escaped from the building, which was almost completely burned down. One of those beaten was Percy Cradock,[102] who would one day return to Beijing as ambassador (1978–1984), where he would open and lead the negotiations on the future of Hong Kong.

Although Zhou Enlai no longer had full control over foreign affairs, he was furious at what happened and condemned the radicals as "uneducated" and "anarchistic". As the incident was a serious diplomatic violation, Zhou sought and got the consent of Mao Zedong to make an official apology to the British government and undertook that China would rebuild the mission building. Mao was taken aback by what happened, which sparked an important turning point in the events of the Cultural Revolution.[103] Mao also realised that by then the Mainland economy was reaching crisis point—industrial output fell 14 percent and foreign trade contracted by about 10 percent. China needed Hong Kong for its ability to generate foreign currency to help overcome its economic problems brought on by the political upheavals,[104] and could not pour funds into sustaining the riots there. In this light, it can be seen that the hard currency obtained by China through exports to Hong Kong was extremely valuable. The revolution caused acute disruption to China's domestic economy. If it were not for the financial connection with Hong Kong, the CCP's supply of money would have been seriously reduced.

Thus, by early September 1967, the tone in Beijing changed, even though the leftists in Hong Kong had wanted to continue using bombs, expand the strike campaign and launch a fishing boat demonstration off the coast of Hong Kong.[105] Zhou

Enlai regained control over foreign affairs, and the leaders of the revolutionary faction involved in the British Mission burning were either punished or removed from office.[106] From the perspective of the Hong Kong government, Beijing was not about to resume Hong Kong hastily, or support the leftists unreservedly. For the local leftists, this incident gave them a clear message that they would not have full backing from Beijing to unseat the colonial government. In fact, when the news of Zhou's apology reached CCP Hong Kong, they found it hard to swallow, as it in effect rejected their struggle to topple the colonial authorities. They disseminated the news in a low-key manner.[107] Sino-British relations showed an improvement. By the end of September, the British ambassador to the United Nations made clear that Britain supported China's admission to the international body.[108]

In any event, the leftists' efforts in Hong Kong were not getting anywhere, but the visit of Lord Shepherd (1918–2001, minister of state, Foreign and Commonwealth Office, 1967–1970) on 13 October prompted another wave of violence. The police paid informers for information about where bombs were being made and the identities of those who would plant bombs. The number of bomb incidents dropped. The authorities continued to raid the leftists' premises, which was highly disruptive. Funds for sustaining strikes were running out. Many striking workers, who had been dismissed by their employers, were dissatisfied with the strike pay they were receiving. Allegedly, some of the most loyal strikers were given free theatre tickets instead of strike pay.[109] Some of the strikers had become so hard-up that they were forced to appeal to the government for assistance. Mainland-controlled banks and department stores started to remove propaganda posters from their premises, as they were eager to win back lost business and customers.[110]

At the end of October 1967, Zhou Enlai reportedly summoned the senior cadres from Hong Kong, including Liang Weilin and Qi Feng, to Beijing and criticised them severely that they had committed a mistake of "extreme leftism". They were ordered to stop agitation in Hong Kong.[111] Indeed, their stay in Beijing for two months was Zhou Enlai's way to have "their heads cool down".[112] The struggle thus petered out by January 1968. Indeed, the immediate result of the riots was the exact opposite of its intended purpose—the disturbances had increased the legitimacy of the colonial authorities. It is worth noting that Liang and Qi were not made accountable beyond Zhou's reprimand. Liang continued as the director of Xinhua Hong Kong until December 1977. Qi also remained as the deputy director until the mid-1980s when he retired.

The bravery and steadfastness of the police force in Hong Kong was rewarded with many commendations and the right to add the word "Royal" to the name of the force was granted by Queen Elizabeth II in 1969, in recognition of its distinguished service during the riots.

Impacts of the 1967 Riots

Eight months of disturbances had caused anxiety, distress, inconvenience and economic loss to the Hong Kong community. During 1967, there was a net decrease in total bank deposits amounting to HK$243 million. At the end of the year, total deposits stood at HK$8,162 million, compared to HK$8,405 million at the end of 1966.[113] Trading at the Hong Kong stock market had to be temporarily suspended twice during the turbulent period. Stock prices declined across the board and started to recover only in January 1968.[114] Despite the disturbances, Hong Kong still managed a 17 percent increase in the value of domestic exports and 14 percent in re-exports.[115]

The vast majority of the Hong Kong community did not rally behind the leftists' cause to unseat British administration. They could see that if the Red Guards ran Hong Kong, they would have to adhere to Maoist ideology and living standards would drop. However, the riots of 1966 and 1967 made blindingly obvious the existence of many unattended social problems in Hong Kong, in particular, in the areas of labour, housing and education. This prompted the colonial government to carry out a series of social reforms to improve the quality of administration and the living conditions of the working class. Hong Kong had grey industrial slums, where workers laboured very long hours in unsafe and unhealthy conditions, in which the young, uneducated, workers felt frustrated by their limited prospects. While the government had made substantial efforts to resettle refugees and squatters with a massive public housing programme since the Shek Kip Mei fire in December 1953—the next major fire after the Tung Tau fire in 1951 discussed in Chapter 5—social and educational amenities had not kept up with the huge post-war population growth. Jack Cater acknowledged that "if not for the riots, I do not think that the government will carry out any reforms".[116] The appointed political elites that populated the Executive and Legislative Councils and the government's various advisory committees did very little to push social reform. They preferred to keep taxes low and social welfare minimal.[117] Thus, the recommendations from the government-appointed Commission of Inquiry to create social insurance and benefits programmes were rejected by both the colonial officials and their appointees.[118]

The succeeding five years after the riots was a time when political, social and economic conditions in Hong Kong had to be re-examined and the riots strengthened the hand of those who called for reform, which included professionals in social, medical and educational work. On the political side, the Hong Kong government placed the problem on the "serious lack of communication between the government and ordinary people in town",[119] not the distribution of power. Thus, the political solution was to create a mediating local-level structure between the government and the community in the urban areas in order to improve public relations. This mirrored the District Offices in the New Territories. Ten District Offices were set up in mid-1968:

They will be as accessible as possible to those living in their Districts, and they will keep in touch with all local organisations. They will be required to assess the overall impact of government policies on the people of their districts and to explain these policies, as well as the difficulties and the achievements of the government to ordinary people. Although they will not at first be required to carry out many executive functions they will be responsible for advising on the co-ordination of public services. They will consider whether there should be any variation in emphasis in government policies in the Districts and they may initiate proposals for changes in policies or for new policies when the need for these becomes apparent from the feeling of the public. They will be expected to get to know the problems and conflicts and trends of public thinking in their districts before attitudes have been struck. We hope that their work will strengthen the ability of the Government to give all the people who live here a fair share of those services which the community can afford.[120]

In its political aim, the City District Office scheme proved quite effective in extending the government's communication network into the lower strata of Hong Kong society.[121] It was subsequently supplemented by the establishment of many more consultative and advisory bodies, which involved "the administrative absorption of politics" designed to co-opt the elites to shore up support for the colonial authorities,[122] as well as to make Chinese an official language alongside the use of English. Another minor reform of a political nature was to give the office of the Unofficial Members of the Legislative Council slightly greater leeway to redress grievances after rejecting the establishment of an Ombudsman.[123]

The riots also exposed the poor employment conditions of the local work force. In the 1960s, many Hong Kong workers worked a 12-hour day, seven days per week. They had low job security and little bargaining power. Working conditions were basic. On 14 February 1968, the commissioner of labour announced a series of legislative proposals to be implemented in phases concerning a long list of items in the areas of labour's welfare, health and safety.[124] Two labour advisers from Britain were invited to go to Hong Kong to assist in setting up a labour tribunal and improving the laws regulating trade unions. Nevertheless, it took until 1973 before all the various labour legislative proposals were enacted into laws.[125]

The riots also forced the colonial government to review the poor education situation in Hong Kong. In 1967, more than 150,000 children of primary school age were unable to attend school and only 39 percent of the 10 to 14-year-old group and 13 percent of the 15 to 19-year-old group could attend secondary schools. By 1971, it was estimated that there would be 2 million people in Hong Kong below the age of 19, which would create even greater strains on the already inadequate education system.[126] In 1971, the government undertook to provide free primary education for all eligible children, and in 1979, nine years of free and compulsory education was provided so that children must stay in school until the age of 15.

The riots of 1967 made the Hong Kong community reflect upon their sense of identity. The elites were not about to support the leftists but neither did most other groups. No one wanted Hong Kong to be run by the Red Guards. In mid-May 1967, 98 local organisations pledged their support for the Hong Kong government to suppress the rioters. These ranged from business and trade associations to professional bodies, schools, and *kaifong* (neighbourhood) associations. Several days later, more than 300 social organisations published a joint statement in two Chinese newspapers to support efforts of the colonial government in restoring law and order. The people even suggested tougher action than the government wanted against the leftists "because they were really frightened about the Communists".[127] The Heung Yee Kuk, a traditional rural organisation representing the interests of the indigenous inhabitants of the New Territories, also made a public statement against the actions of the leftists.[128]

A local consciousness also began to emerge in the rest of Hong Kong society. From late 1947 to the end of 1965, the population of Hong Kong had increased from 1.80 million to 3.625 million as a result of a high local birth rate and migrants from the Mainland. The new arrivals were mainly poor refugees with no sense of belonging to Hong Kong and yet most of them were not about to return across the border. Even between the two years of 1966 and 1967, Hong Kong's population increased by some 135,000 people. Between 1968 and 1976, when Mao Zedong died and the Gang of Four lost power, the population increased to over 4.55 million.

Impact of the Riots on the Local CCP

Undoubtedly, the leftists were the biggest loser after the riots. A large number of underground CCP members and party sympathisers were arrested and imprisoned during the riots. A vast majority of the underground network of the CCP was exposed and destroyed by the Hong Kong government. The intelligence efforts built up by the CCP inside the colonial government and various social sectors almost completely disintegrated. Further, the CCP's intelligence efforts towards Taiwan in Hong Kong were seriously damaged and did not fully recover until the 1980s.[129]

In terms of financial loss, the riots were expensive for the CCP. Reports noted that the Anti-Persecution Struggle Committee, acting on behalf of the party, paid a subsidy of HK$480 a month to strikers. Those who planted hoax bombs received HK$40 and those who planted a real bomb received HK$200 per planting.[130] The Committee did not have unlimited funds to keep shelling out. Contemporaneous news reports noted that by the end of July 1967, the riots had cost the CCP at least HK$260 million, including HK$200 million in lost trade, HK$40 million in loss of local business and HK$20 million dollars in providing an advance to the Anti-Persecution Struggle Committee to whip up trouble.[131] A contemporaneous report noted that:

> (the local leftists) had made wrong decisions in the struggle campaign, misused the "struggle fund" remitted to them from Peking, badly miscalculated the extent

of popular support, caused heavy losses to China trade and business in Hong Kong, supplied Peking with poor intelligence, failed in their propaganda work in Hong Kong for the past seventeen years and put stories in the leftwing newspapers from the rest of the press in Hong Kong.[132]

The riots also changed the course of life for many of the leftists. Many strikers remained unemployed for a long time as they were dismissed by employers. Their enthusiasm for the communist cause turned into frustration. Many severed their ties with the leftist camp. Morale in the camp, especially among the workers, hit rock bottom.[133] The leftist trade unions lost significant ground in Hong Kong. They turned inward and seldom involved themselves in social affairs. The self-imposed isolation from Hong Kong society remained unchanged up until the mid-1980s.[134]

For many youngsters, who were inspired by the communist cause, their lives were changed forever. Florence Leung Mo Han, who was a CCP member and president of the Hok Yau Club—a peripheral party organisation established in 1949 in Hong Kong to recruit young people—regretted that their futures were ruined.[135] The Tsang family provides a vivid example and there are many such cases. Tsang Tak Shing, the secretary for home affairs (2007–2015), was a high school student at the time of the riots. In September 1967, he was sentenced to two years' imprisonment for distributing seditious materials at school. He lost the opportunity to go to university and, after he was released from jail, he worked at *Ta Kung Pao* up until the 1990s, when he was appointed into the Central Policy Unit in 1998 by Tung Chee Hwa. His younger sister, Tsang Lai Yu, aged 15 then was jailed for a month for participating in the riots. She later worked in a leftist newspaper as a public relations manager.[136] Elder brother, Tsang Yok Shing, the founding chairman the DAB, and president of the Legislative Council (2008–2016), although he graduated with a first class honours from the University of Hong Kong in 1968, decided to give up further studies and taught at a leftist school for almost three decades.

Tsang Yok Sing remembered the riots thus:

> The Government handled the riots in a very high-handed, colonial manner. I felt that it was protecting the interests of the capitalists, and, in doing so, suppressing the workers. I personally knew many of the people, the workers and trade unionists, involved in the violence, and they were very good people . . . The prevailing view now is that the police acted with a great deal of restraint at the time, and that people in the leftist camp were just a violent mob . . . This is not true, and the Government's firm action was neither necessary nor justified . . . The greatest shock during that time was the imprisonment of my siblings. My brother . . . was a Form 6 student at St Paul's, and was a timid boy . . . He was sent to Stanley Prison which was then full of trade unionists and non-violent workers . . . A couple of months later, my fifteen-year-old sister was also arrested. She was a Form 3 girl at Belilios Public School. She was in the playground with thirteen other girls, and when the school bell rang they refused to go back to the classroom. I cannot quite remember what they were asking for, but anyway the headmistress decided they were making

trouble. She called the police, and all fourteen were tried, found guilty of breaching the emergency legislation in force during 1967, and sent to the women's prison at Lai Chi Kok for one month . . . It was also a very difficult period for me. After my brother's arrest, I was shunned at university . . . My experience drove me more to the other side. I worshipped Mao Zedong and he became my idol.[137]

Tsang Yok Sing's views were echoed by Andrew Li Kwok Nang, a young reporter then, and Chief Justice (1997–2010). He had interviewed many of those arrested during the disturbances and examined the reports of about a hundred of them. Li also traced the roots of the unrest to social inequality. He also found Hong Kong youngsters then to be disillusioned about their future prospects. Li quoted from one interview that he felt was representative:

> If the labour dispute had been dealt with fairly and justly by the Labour Department, everything would have been fine. Instead the Hong Kong British sent in the police to deal with a labour dispute, and they beat fellow Chinese. The Hilton or Garden Road incident marked a turning point. Fellow Chinese went to stage an orderly demonstration but they were beaten up by the cunning police. After this, it became a radical and political struggle.[138]

The most serious impact on CCP Hong Kong was on its united front work. The violence used during the riots turned Hong Kong people off many things associated with communist China for a generation. There was a distinct leftist phobia after the riots. For example, Xinhua Hong Kong employees were uncomfortable with disclosing who they worked for fearing they would be ostracised. There was a time when Hong Kong people referred to Xinhua workers as all born in the Year of the Tiger with "man eating" instincts.[139] Many of the Xinhua Hong Kong staff up until the early 1980s were underground party members who lost their normal jobs during the riots.[140] The party's united front work remained stagnant until Liang Weilin stepped down as director of the Xinhua Hong Kong in December 1977 and Liao Chengzhi regained power in Beijing over Hong Kong affairs in 1978. Liao Chengzhi had been purged but was released from detention in 1972.

Various indicators show the loss of credibility of the leftist cause. The circulation rate of the major leftist newspapers dropped drastically after the riots. For example, the circulation of *Ta Kung Pao* and *Wen Wei Po* fell from more than 100,000 to just 10,000 per day each.[141] For a time, many shoppers did not want to patronise the Mainland department stores. People could not even tolerate the extension of a leftist school in their district, as can be seen from the open letter to the authorities written by the villagers at Yuen Long opposing the extension of the Hon Wah Middle School:

> The facts are that illegal weapons were found by the police in the school and its students were instructed to throw bombs . . . these acts angered both God and Man and are not permissible in the world . . . after the struggle failed, Hon Wah Middle School immediately changed its appearance with evil hidden intent and tried to

ignite the fire again . . . our villagers are used to peaceful living for generations, if troublemakers were allowed to study here and spread wicked "struggle" beliefs . . . they will for sure create a lot of noise and disturbances, and causing villagers to be afraid and feel uneasy when sleeping and eating, and endanger the safety of our district.[142]

As Tsang Yok Sing noted, the leftists felt ostracised from mainstream society:

> They read patriotic newspapers, went to cinemas that showed patriotic pictures, shopped at patriotic stores that sold only Chinese products, joined patriotic unions, and sent their children to patriotic schools . . . these loyalists felt obliged to spring to the defence of the PRC whenever she was under attack. They would stand by their motherland for better or for worse . . . like any relatively closed community, they had a subculture of their own . . . Members of this leftist community were strictly excluded from the British colonial establishment.[143]

Interesting disclosures

A central figure during the 1967 riots was Zhou Enlai. He has been described as the "perfect revolutionary" because he "almost never made a mistake. This was the key to his ongoing success over many decades and throughout turbulent times." When he was caught between titanic political forces, Zhou would try to "find the middle way", resort to absurd "rhetorical babble" whenever necessary, and he "took Mao Zedong's political temperature at every opportunity to make sure that he had found the middle ground", taking pains not to antagonise people from different camps.[144]

In May 1967, Zhou faced a serious threat to his political survival when there was an attempt to drag him down.[145] Conscious of the danger, Zhou felt he had to act extremely carefully. He could not condemn the leftists in Hong Kong. He sought to both encourage and restrain the riots at the same time. He ordered that an ad hoc office on Hong Kong affairs at the Foreign Ministry be set up so that he could watch and influence decisions. He approved or supported all the key actions mentioned in this chapter—the Foreign Ministry statement, attended the mass rally at the sports stadium, and the mass rally in front of the British mission in Beijing. Zhou did not stop the plans for the strikes that were supposed to paralyse the colony. In July, he told the commander of the Guangzhou Military Region in a private conversation that it was not in China's interest to use force. On 17 August, the radicals wanted to attack Chen Yi, which was in effect an attack on Zhou. Zhou was so enraged that day that he suffered a heart attack. With him indisposed, China's foreign affairs spun out of control. On 22 August, when demonstrators sought to take over the British Mission in Beijing, Zhou made sure security forces from the Beijing Garrison were sent to protect the mission and its staff, but to no avail. It was after the burning of the mission that Zhou showed his fury by summoning all concerned for a dressing down. When Mao Zedong showed how upset he was over what happened, Zhou seized the opportunity to change the course of political direction, marking an important turning point in the Cultural Revolution.[146]

Disclosures by people with CCP connections are also illuminating. According to Liang Shangyuan, shortly after the 22 May Bloody Incident, Zhu Wanping, the other deputy director at the time, visited Beijing to ask for instructions from Zhou Enlai. Zhou told him that what the leftists were doing in Hong Kong was forcing the Central Government "to ride the horse". Furthermore, during the riots, Zhou prohibited the People's Liberation Army from crossing the border to Hong Kong and no weapons and bombs were allowed to be sent. Thus, Zhou had no intention to change the "making full use of Hong Kong in the interest of long-term planning" policy, let alone use violent means to recover Hong Kong. In Liang's view, the CCP Hong Kong had to take responsibility for the riots of 1967. While they knew Zhou's views, the local leftists wanted to create an irreversible situation in Hong Kong so that Beijing would be forced to accept it.[147] Zhu and Liang were both labelled as anti-revolutionary subsequently and purged. In Liang's case, when he returned to the Mainland in 1968, an unnamed source in Hong Kong informed Beijing that he was a spy for Taiwan. He was imprisoned and only released in 1973 when Zhou Enlai asked to review his case.[148]

A party official, who was responsible for party propaganda work in Hong Kong during the riots, shared Liang Shangyuan's interpretation of events. According to him, the riots were initiated by the local leftists egged on by radicals in Beijing. Zhou Enlai approved the activities but he was never really supportive of the struggle in Hong Kong. When Zhou met Liang Weilin and Qi Feng at the end of 1967, Zhou made it clear that the leftist confrontation was contradictory to the Central Government's policy towards Hong Kong.[149] Some leftists wished that by adopting increasingly violent means, the struggle in Hong Kong could be escalated to a power struggle on the international level between China and the United States and Britain.[150]

In reflecting upon the 1967 riots afterwards, some veteran leftists described the struggle as a farce and a power struggle.[151] They felt they had been used and they regretted what they did.[152] Others were disappointed that their "patriotic behaviour" was never officially recognised and felt that they were owed an explanation from the local CCP and the Central Government in Beijing.[153] Their voicing of their sense of injustice probably resulted in Tung Chee Hwa's extending to several of the activists during the riots an invitation to the Mid-Autumn Festival party held in Government House in September 1997. In 1999, several prominent local leftists were awarded medals or appointed as Justice of the Peace for their contribution to the society. In 2001, upon the nomination of the FTU, Yeung Kwong, the chairman of the Anti-Persecution Committee, was awarded the Grand Bauhinia Medal. Yeung's award created substantial controversy in Hong Kong, as he was considered to have been one of the key personalities of the 1967 riots.

Resolution on CCP History

How should the CCP explain the maelstrom of the Cultural Revolution when so very many people suffered so terribly and the country experienced a severe setback? Overall, the Cultural Revolution remains a frightful memory because it left so many enduring physical, emotional and psychological scars. Issued on the CCP's 60th anniversary in 1981, the *Resolution on Party History* stated that the Cultural Revolution was initiated and led by Mao Zedong, and that it was an episode in party history that was "comprehensive in magnitude and protracted in duration". The Cultural Revolution did not conform to Marxism-Leninism or China's reality. Mao was "a leader labouring under a misapprehension". The party claimed that Lin Biao and Jiang Qing took advantage of Mao's errors and committed many crimes "behind his back". The party's Central Committee also admitted that:

> The theories and practices of the Cultural Revolution were totally erroneous. The Cultural Revolution did not constitute a revolution or social progress in any sense, nor could it possibly have done so . . . The Cultural Revolution was responsible for the most severe setback and the heaviest losses suffered by the Party, the state and the people since the founding of the People's Republic.[154]

Leading scholars of this period of Chinese history continue to ask why party leaders of considerable ability, experience, toughness, and prestige failed to restrain Mao when he ran amok. There is as yet no thoroughly researched answer.[155]

No wonder Chief Executive Donald Tsang aroused so much controversy from all quarters on 12 October 2007, when he described the Cultural Revolution as an "extreme form of democracy" on a radio show when discussing Hong Kong's constitutional development.[156] Tsang was taken to task for two reasons. Firstly, he dared to suggest that an inevitable result of democracy would be extremism; and secondly he ignored the fact that during the Cultural Revolution, and especially in 1967, Hong Kong people had refused the invitation to join in the riots. He had to make a public apology the following day to stop further public condemnation.[157]

On the fiftieth anniversary of the 1967 riots in 2017, more than a hundred leftist workers and their families went to the Wo Hop Shek Public Cemetery to commemorate "heroes" who died during the riots and were buried there. An FTU representative was present at the fiftieth anniversary memorial. The 67 Synergy Group has been organising the annual memorial since 2011.[158] Thinking about the past remain painful for those who suffered. Yet, this period of time in Hong Kong's history is one that deserves much more research so as to enable the community to develop an interpretation of the events of that era and what significance they hold for Hong Kong to reflect on its present and future.

7

The Taking Back of Hong Kong

From 1977 to 1984

There were two central issues surrounding Chinese Communist Party activities in Hong Kong between 1977 and 1984. The first was for Hong Kong to facilitate China's goal of rapid modernisation and the second was the party's decision to take back Hong Kong in 1997. These were both extremely important to the CCP and Hong Kong matters had the very highest level of attention within the party. Hong Kong would indeed prove to play a very useful role in China's economic reform with the longstanding policy of "making full use of Hong Kong in the interest of long-term planning" remaining relevant. However, on the resumption of sovereignty over Hong Kong, the party would be forced to contend with the issue of democratic reform. What may be the most significant legacy of how the British sought to deal with the transition negotiations, which ultimately resulted in the Sino-British Joint Declaration in 1984, was its final-hour attempt to introduce direct elections. This created deep distrust with the Chinese which would colour the debate on constitutional reform for years to come.

Deng Xiaoping and the CCP were sceptical of democracy.[1] He refuted the argument that democracy was what China needed.[2] Deng believed democracy would bring chaos to the country. Indeed, the limits of the party's political tolerance needed to be spelt out. The party put forward the Four Cardinal Principles in 1979 that would guide future policies. The principles were: keeping to the socialist road, upholding the dictatorship of the proletariat (later changed to "upholding the people's democratic dictatorship"), upholding Marxism-Leninism and Mao Zedong Thought, and upholding the leadership of the CCP. Essentially, they amount to one thing—the dominance of the CCP in Chinese politics.[3]

Nevertheless, Deng Xiaoping would devise a "one country, two systems" formula for reunification of the country that entailed the maintenance of capitalism for a considerable period of time. Moreover, for the sake of reunification, Deng was prepared to say the Four Cardinal Principles did not apply to Hong Kong. In reality, there could be no escaping from the CCP of course. Deng said what the party expected from the people of Hong Kong was "patriotism". A patriot was defined as someone who loved the motherland, loved Hong Kong and supported the resumption of sovereignty. As such, he or she would need to think seriously about the responsibilities involved, especially to have a better understanding of China, which would lead them to support the party's leadership of the country. In the case of Hong Kong, a patriot could be excused for any kind of economic belief:

> A patriot is one who respects the Chinese nation, sincerely supports the motherland's resumption of sovereignty over Hong Kong and wishes not to impair Hong Kong's prosperity and stability. Those who meet these requirements are patriots, whether they believe in capitalism or feudalism or even slavery.[4]

Deng Xiaoping's view of the difference between socialism and capitalism is important to note. Deng said in 1992 that: "The essence of socialism is liberation and development of the productive forces (land, labour and capital), elimination of exploitation and polarisation, and the ultimate achievement of prosperity for all."[5] In other words, since capitalism accepted inequality and exploitation, China would accept it in the case of Hong Kong.

On the economic front, Deng Xiaoping wanted China to make up for lost time as quickly as possible. His development vision in 1978 was a new Long March to turn China into a "modern, powerful socialist country before the end of this [20th] century".[6] Deng supported ambitious ideas. China's new Open Door Policy in 1978 included promoting international trade and investment. China earmarked four southern cities as Special Economic Zones—Shenzhen, Zhuhai, Shantou, and Xiamen, to take advantage of their geographic proximity to the overseas Chinese communities of Hong Kong, Macao, and Taiwan in order to attract their investments to set up export manufacturing joint ventures. Deng also recognised there was a need to reform the uncompetitive state-owned enterprises. He coined the term "market socialism with Chinese characteristics" to distinguish what China was attempting to do from capitalism.

Deng Xiaoping's reforms and how they impacted Hong Kong and the Sino-British negotiations on China's resumption of sovereignty over Hong Kong are well-documented by many publications. This chapter deals with the shaping of the CCP's policy on the taking back of Hong Kong and the party's strategies to win hearts and minds of the Hong Kong community during the negotiations period. In the months before the Sino-British Joint Declaration was concluded, the CCP's united front efforts focused on cultivating community support for the Chinese position although the people of Hong Kong were firmly shut out of the negotiation process.

Revive CCP Work in Hong Kong

To promote economic modernisation, the tempo and style of work for the CCP in Hong Kong would need to change. After the 1967 riots, the work of Xinhua Hong Kong had become stagnant. A makeover was necessary for it to play a reinvigorated role. After all, China was embarking on all sorts of new economic and financial experiments, such as allowing Hong Kong–based Mainland enterprises to invest in stocks, foreign currency and property in the colony. China was also going to start making substantial investments in Hong Kong in real estate, construction, shipping and banking. The era of Deng Xiaoping was one that involved making capitalistic practices respectable again. China's new interest in economic development would create much excitement in Hong Kong, as it meant the end of hardcore communism and the beginning of potentially interesting business opportunities.[7]

Personnel changes at Xinhua Hong Kong were necessary to deal with the task of using Hong Kong to assist China in its modernisation. It was time for Liang Weilin to go. He had served as the director of Xinhua Hong Kong for some 20 years, and was a key figure associated with the 1967 riots, a period of time that had become decidedly passé. Notwithstanding that, he must have done a reasonably good job to have survived so long. He was transferred back to the Mainland to become the deputy governor of Guangdong in December 1977. A new director had to be found.

In the meantime, Beijing needed to restructure responsibility for its Hong Kong work. Deng Xiaoping gave Liao Chengzhi this task. Liao, who had a long association with Hong Kong, was Beijing's expert on the colony. He was purged during the Cultural Revolution, but rehabilitated in 1972 and eventually made a member of the CCP's Central Committee. It was also decided in May 1978 that the State Council—the highest organ of state power and administration—would set up a new Hong Kong and Macao Affairs Office with Liao as the head. Li Hou, who had long experience in working on Hong Kong matters, as was seen in Chapter 5, together with Lu Ping, were his principal assistants in the new office.[8] The existence of the new Hong Kong and Macao Affairs Office was however not made public until 1982, perhaps to avoid raising questions and speculation in Hong Kong and Britain about China's intentions concerning the colony. Its first task was to strengthen transportation links between the Mainland and Hong Kong so that business travel could be made more convenient.[9] In those days, there was no direct train. Travellers going from Hong Kong to the Mainland had to get out of the train on the Hong Kong side of the border and walk across a bridge to get on another train on the Mainland side. There was no link by boat or air. The first direct contacts were chartered flights in 1979 from Shanghai bringing hairy crabs to Hong Kong.[10]

Thus, Liao Chengzhi was the most important person in the CCP on Hong Kong matters since he was not only the acknowledged expert on the territory, but also a member of the CCP Central Committee with responsibility for Hong Kong, and he headed the Chinese government's body looking after Hong Kong. He remained arguably the most influential Chinese leader on Hong Kong matters up until he died in 1983.

In July 1978, Wang Kuang, who was the director of the Central Publication Bureau and a well-known writer and former journalist, arrived in Hong Kong to become the new director of Xinhua Hong Kong.[11] As can be seen from Chapter 5, Wang had been handling Hong Kong work since the early 1950s. In 1978, he became the most senior cadre of CCP Hong Kong and thus also China's chief representative in Hong Kong.

Figure 5 Hong Kong and Macao Affairs Office[12]

The Hong Kong and Macao Affairs Office

The State Council's Hong Kong and Macao Office was established to:

1. Organise the Hong Kong and Macao Work Committee and relevant departments to research and determine policies and proposals to solve the 1997 Hong Kong and Macao problems so that the departments and offices within the next 15 years can solve the Hong Kong and Macao problem and carry out the necessary preparation work.
2. Carry out investigation and research work, grasp Hong Kong and Macao political and economic trends, and in a timely fashion report on them to the CCP Central Committee and State Council.
3. Assist the CCP Central Committee to manage the following work of the Hong Kong and Macao Work Committee: (a) upper-level united front work; (b) worker and student basic-level mass work; (c) news media, publishing, film etc, patriotic propaganda, cultural and educational work; and (d) party and youth league work and cadre work.
4. With the relevant central departments, manage China's (a) economic work; (b) foreign affairs matters; (c) Taiwan affairs; (d) Overseas Chinese affairs and tourism; (e) exchange relations in culture, sports, academic and science and technology; all in relations to Hong Kong and Macao, as well as investigate and approve the setting-up of organisations by various regions and departments and their sending of personnel to Hong Kong and Macao.
5. Leading the work of the Liaison Office station in Guangzhou.

In other words, the person who held the position of director became the public face of the CCP and the Chinese government in the territory. Wang had six deputy directors. Its office was relocated from Wan Chai to a 22-storey building in Happy Valley.[13] During Wang Kuang's time, Xinhua Hong Kong had about 100 staff most of whom were natives of Guangdong, and the CCP's leadership in the colony consisted of about 40 people, including not only those within Xinhua Hong Kong but also the key cadres in Mainland enterprises.[14]

Structurally, the CCP in Hong Kong consisted of three parts. The first one was the local organisation. Its members were directly accountable to Liao Chengzhi. The second part was made up of various CCP organs. Its members were cadres sent by these organs, such as from the CCP Central Committee, Central Military Commission, and units from the provinces and municipalities. The third part consisted of members sent by the Overseas Chinese Affairs Commission. According

Table 1 Members of CCP Hong Kong[15]

Secretary General	Director of Xinhua Hong Kong
Deputy Secretaries General	Six Deputy Directors of Xinhua Hong Kong Chief of Bank of China Group Chief of China Resources Group Chief of China Merchant Group Chief of China Travel Services, etc.
Secretary	Secretary of Xinhua Hong Kong
Standing Committee	Consisted of the above members
Members	Leading members of other important Mainland bodies in Hong Kong. Representatives from the ministries directly concerned with national security were also represented in this category.

to the CCP charter, members in a particular place should be led by the local party work committee, which meant Xinhua Hong Kong played the leadership role in Hong Kong. In 1983, there were about 6,000 party members in Hong Kong and Macao, and among the Hong Kong members, about half of them were local Hong Kong members. The ability and capacity of most of the members were considered limited. About 70 percent of them recruited before the Cultural Revolution were old, blue-collar, not well-educated and the party did not have cadres spread out in the community.[16]

Soon after Wang Kuang arrived in Hong Kong, he threw a big banquet and invited celebrities and influential figures in Hong Kong society in order to meet people. On 3 August, two Xinhua deputy directors—Li Jusheng and Luo Keming—attended the inauguration of new committee members of the Chinese Gold and Silver Exchange Society—the first time that Mainland representatives attended an event of a Hong Kong financial institution, thus giving a clear signal of Mainland interest in financial affairs.[17]

Hong Kong affairs would soon take an important turn, as the British pushed the Chinese in 1979 to discuss the future of the territory before Beijing was ready to tackle the issue.

The Question of Hong Kong

There are two major themes running through modern Chinese history: foreign occupation of Chinese territories (through the imposition of "unequal treaties" leading to anti-imperialist movements to reclaim territories) and the lack of international respect. In Sun Yat-sen's will, his charge to his followers was for the abolition of the unequal treaties to be carried into effect with "the least possible delay".[18] The KMT government in 1931 also stated that: "The Chinese people will not recognise the past unequal treaties."[19] Thus, resolving the issue of Hong Kong was always important to China. It was just a matter of time before China would move to recover a symbol of past humiliation.

The question of Hong Kong was brought up shortly after the People's Republic of China claimed the United Nations seat from Taiwan in October 1971. On 8 March 1972, Huang Hua, the Chinese ambassador to the United Nations (1971–1976) wrote formally to the United Nations Special Committee on the Declaration on Decolonisation asking it to remove Hong Kong and Macao from its decolonisation agenda on the ground that:

> The questions of Hong Kong and Macao belong to the category of questions resulting from the series of unequal treaties which the imperialists imposed on China. Hong Kong and Macao are part of Chinese territory occupied by the British and Portuguese authorities. The settlement of the question of Hong Kong and Macao is entirely within China's sovereign right and does not at all fall under the ordinary category of colonial territories. Consequently, they should not be included in the list of colonial territories covered by the declaration on the granting of independence to colonial countries and people. With regard to questions of Hong Kong and Macao, the Chinese government has consistently held that they should be settled in an appropriate way when conditions are ripe.[20]

Even prior to China's statement at the United Nations, the British government under Edward Heath had already identified that the question of the New Territories lease would have to be dealt with. Conservative MP, Anthony Royle, whom Heath appointed to the Foreign Office in 1970, set up an internal committee consisting of diplomats and Cabinet members to look into the matter. The committee believed that China gained significant benefits from Hong Kong and might want to maintain the status quo even beyond 1997. The question of the lease would have to be raised one day but the timing would be crucial. Since the matter was not urgent, it was placed on the back burner.[21]

The British did not object to China's statement in 1972 but it made them reassess Britain's relationship with Hong Kong. Heath's government thought that Hong Kong would have to be returned when China asked for it and arrangements would have to be negotiated. Indeed, the British saw good opportunities to improve Sino-British relations and the matter of Hong Kong should not stand in the way.[22] On 13 March 1972, China and Britain signed the Joint Communiqué on the Agreement on the Exchange of Ambassadors, the fruit of a year of negotiations. Was Britain's acquiescence to China's position on Hong Kong part of an understanding? It is hard to think that it was not, but British diplomats have insisted that the timing of the two events was a coincidence.[23] On 2 November 1972, the United Nations General Assembly removed Hong Kong and Macao from its list of colonial territories, as Britain and Portugal did not object. The practical effects of Huang Hua's move were that Britain ceased its 26-year-old practice of submitting information on Hong Kong's condition annually to the secretary general of the United Nations.[24]

As for the all-important question of when China would take Hong Kong back, Zhou Enlai said in reference to Hong Kong in an interview in October 1972 that: "A state must enter into negotiations when a treaty expires", that Britain would have to negotiate "at the appropriate time" and that China would not "embark upon such matters with undue haste".[25] Moreover, the word "colony" was replaced by "territory" in British official-speak. Hong Kong matters came under the purview of the Foreign Office. The Colonial Office and Commonwealth Relations Office were merged in 1966 and renamed the Commonwealth Office since most of the colonies had become independent countries. In 1968, the Commonwealth Office was folded into the Foreign Office, which was renamed the Foreign and Commonwealth Office (referred to as the Foreign Office in this book). As a gesture of goodwill to China, in 1973, the British government finally got the Hong Kong government to release the last of the prisoners from the 1967 riots.[26]

In Hong Kong, relations between the colonial government and Xinhua Hong Kong saw subtle changes too. Murray MacLehose, who had served in the colony as the political adviser[27] in the early 1960s, took over from David Trench as governor in 1971 and would serve until 1982. Previous governors had been appointed from the Colonial Office and MacLehose was the first diplomat sent from the Foreign Office. He had been the head of the Far Eastern Department, and he would have known about the committee Anthony Royle put together. Indeed, in a note to the Foreign Office in October 1971, MacLehose put forward ideas that looked remarkably similar to the one country, two systems concept, which Beijing would eventually propose.

> I think the best we could hope for would be some form of special status for Hong Kong under which sovereignty would return to China, but Hong Kong might be defined as a special administrative district to be managed in a way that would facilitate the continued residence of foreigners.[28]

In a subsequent report in 1972, MacLehose outlined how he saw China's position and why he wanted to embark on a social-building programme based around his predecessor's housing programme in Hong Kong:

> [Chinese leaders might] see merit in some continuing arrangement for Hong Kong whereby a special regime was established that nominally removed the colonial stigma ... [The formula could preserve] some of the economic and political benefits of the present status, save [China] from having to absorb a population with some different standard of living and attitude of mind, and preserve for foreigners a tolerable trading base while concentrating them in a single area where they did not affect life in the rest of China ... I think that [social reform] is the best contribution the Hong Kong government can make to achieving a satisfactory settlement, and for this it would need about 10 years.[29]

To some of those who worked with him, Murray MacLehose appeared to have had a personal desire to reconcile Hong Kong with the CCP.[30] A closer examination showed great caution in fact. Under MacLehose, senior civil servants stopped receiving daily intelligence reports on leftist activities. This was seen by some to be the reversal of a practice that treated the CCP as an inherently subversive organisation,[31] whereas the circulation of those reports probably was considered no longer necessary as they once were when the local leftists were causing disturbances (Chapter 6). Intelligence continued to be gathered and Special Branch continued to report to relevant senior officials on CCP activities up until 1995, when the unit was closed down as part of the British withdrawal from Hong Kong. Moreover, the Hong Kong government had previously liaised with CCP Hong Kong through the Information Services Department since Xinhua Hong Kong was supposedly a "news" organisation even though its party nature was known. Under MacLehose, that relationship was taken over by the political adviser's office. This brought CCP affairs closer to the governor. It was also under MacLehose that positive vetting was introduced to Hong Kong for the first time. This was a British technique to counter communist subversion that required candidates for civil service posts and important appointments to go through detailed security vetting. MacLehose introduced the most stringent form of barrier to the recruitment and promotion to senior positions of persons with any CCP connections, whether by choice or through their relatives, or with any significant Mainland connections in terms of family members. To pass a vetting, the official had to find at least two referees, who in a detailed review of the official, would have to convince the vetting officers that the official could not be subverted by the CCP. Seen in these terms, MacLehose was a cautious bureaucrat.

He was perhaps seen or remembered as a political "dove" because he went out of his way to sign the book of condolence at Xinhua's office on the death of Mao Zedong in 1976, and on 30 September 1978, he became the first governor to attend the annual National Day ceremony hosted by Xinhua Hong Kong on 1 October. Attending National Day celebrations became a customary practice for succeeding governors before the Handover. MacLehose was seen to have improved relations with Beijing, which led to an invitation. Over tea in Government House in December 1978, China's minister of foreign trade, Li Qiang, invited MacLehose to visit Beijing. A formal written invitation then followed—the first letter addressed to a governor in Hong Kong by a Chinese minister.

The Chinese intended to focus on economic relations. There was no plan of talking about the Hong Kong question. MacLehose made it known that he would go if he could meet important leaders, and when this was confirmed MacLehose advised the Foreign Office that Hong Kong's future should form a part of Britain's agenda for the trip. In 1977, MacLehose had tried to raise the issue of the lease with David Owen, the then foreign secretary, but Owen felt it was too early to raise the matter.[32] The idea was accepted as the British saw a possible opportunity to raise the question of Hong Kong's future at the highest level so as to test Beijing's reaction.[33] Would Beijing accept a "Macao solution" for post-1997 Hong Kong? After all, since

1967, an apt description for Macao was "Chinese sovereignty, Portuguese administration", as discussed in Chapter 6.

MacLehose visited Beijing in March 1979 with David Wilson, the political adviser, and Kan Yuet Keung, a member of the Legislative and Executive Councils. Wilson knew MacLehose from the time they both spent at the Far Eastern Department and both thought highly of each other. A decision had been made for MacLehose to take a "sidelong" approach to raise the issue of Hong Kong—that was to treat the matter as a technical one and observe the Chinese reaction. MacLehose would raise the question of land sub-leases in the New Territories from the perspective of facilitating long-term investment in the interest of Hong Kong. The logic was that there would be growing concern that as sub-leases got shorter and shorter, land purchasers and bankers would worry about mortgages more and more. Thus, if something could be done to blur the 1997 deadline it would be good for confidence.[34]

During preparation for the trip, when the Chinese side knew that MacLehose wanted to raise the issue of the New Territories lease, the Ministry of Foreign Affairs sought instructions from the CCP Central Committee on how to respond to the governor. MacLehose told the Chinese side that he wanted to raise with Deng Xiaoping his proposal of selling land in the New Territories with a 15-year lease as if there were no 1997 deadline.[35] The response was clear—China would resume Hong Kong, and MacLehose should not raise the matter with Deng Xiaoping because the Chinese were not ready for a discussion. The Chinese felt they were not ready for this discussion because they had not yet worked out a workable solution to resolve the question of Hong Kong.[36] MacLehose insisted that he would.[37] Jack Cater, the chief secretary (1978–1981), was against the governor raising the matter for two reasons: firstly, he saw the Chinese "as reactive, not proactive" and thus the questions should not be raised first by the British; and secondly, the worry over mortgages was "nonsense". Cater claimed there was no such worry in Hong Kong at the time. Kan Yuet Keung opposed MacLehose's raising the subject of the sub-leases for a different reason—he feared China would rebuff him, thereby causing panic to investors. David Wilson recalled that business people, particularly the Americans, were concerned about investing in property, and Chung Sze Yuen, by then the senior member of the Legislative Council, recalled that bankers were beginning to show concern.[38]

On 29 March, when MacLehose met Deng, the Chinese leader asked the governor to encourage investments in the Mainland, and the governor raised the issue of China controlling illegal immigration to Hong Kong better. Before the end of the meeting, MacLehose raised the issue of the New Territories. What happened next was a crucial but confused moment. When MacLehose made his prepared remarks about the New Territories sub-leases, the translator rendered his remarks as though the governor were suggesting Britain be allowed to extend the New Territories lease. David Wilson intervened to clarify the point but the atmosphere had changed. Deng Xiaoping seemed annoyed. According to one of those present, Deng was either "very fuzzy and he did not understand quite what was being asked of him, or he was very wily and he understood all too well". Deng said that China had sovereignty over Hong Kong and the colony would be recovered, but China would respect Hong Kong's special status, and in a negotiated settlement of its future, China would treat it as a special region and for a considerable period of time Hong Kong could practise capitalism while China continued its socialist path. CCP history notes Deng had in effect brought up the idea of one country, two systems at the meeting although it was not referred to as such.[39] When MacLehose pressed the point once more, Deng made it clear that whatever wording was used for land leases, it must avoid any reference to "British administration" and that China had not yet decided on the political structure for Hong Kong after 1997. Deng did not want to give the slightest impression that China would allow British rule beyond 1997, hence the insistence that British administration should not be mentioned. Deng also adopted an *ex cathedra* tone and said that investors should be told to "set their hearts at ease".[40]

In a subsequent meeting on the same day with Huang Hua, who was then the minister of foreign affairs (1976–1982), Huang said that it had been inappropriate for the British to have raised the question of land leases with Deng Xiaoping. It was a polite rebuke to the Hong Kong governor. When MacLehose said the problem of land leases was a real one, Huang replied that Deng Xiaoping's reassurance to investors should be sufficient.[41] MacLehose requested a meeting with Liao Chengzhi that evening and got 15 minutes. He tried to explain what he wanted to say to Deng Xiaoping. Liao's response was he could not say more than what Deng had already said.[42]

MacLehose had been rebuffed. He returned to Hong Kong trumpeting Deng's assurance that investors need not worry and said nothing else about the rest of the meeting. Kan Yuet Keung did not say anything about what happened at the meeting, not even to probing friends and colleagues.[43]

There are different interpretations of Deng Xiaoping's response. One interpretation is that he was unprepared for MacLehose raising the issue of the New Territories lease because he had not been briefed that the governor would bring it up. Deng essentially delivered China's official position in reply. Another interpretation is that as a revolutionary veteran, he saw it as his and the CCP's mission to reunify China so as to truly end imperialism. Another possibility could be Deng felt he had not yet fully consolidated power and the best approach was not to show any softness in regaining sovereignty. Deng certainly wanted to be remembered for taking a staunch patriotic approach as shown in the way he put matters some years later:

> No Chinese leaders or government would be able to justify themselves for [the failure to recover Hong Kong in 1997] before the Chinese people or before the people of the world. It would mean that the present Chinese government was just

like the government of the late Qing Dynasty and that the present Chinese leaders were just like Li Hongzhang!⁴⁴

Percy Cradock, who was the British ambassador in Beijing (1978–1984) and present at MacLehose's meeting with Deng Xiaoping, was also dissatisfied with the outcome of the meeting. Cradock was unsure if the Chinese understood what the British wanted to convey. He then had a meeting with China's vice-foreign minister to press the point once more but he was told not to pursue any proposal to extend British sovereignty beyond 1997.⁴⁵ Britain did however continue to raise the issue with Beijing on several other occasions.⁴⁶ The Chinese's impression then was that Britain was trying to force the issue to get Beijing to reveal its hand,⁴⁷ and perhaps British pushing also left an impression on the Chinese that Britain was unwilling to give up possession of Hong Kong. It seems beyond doubt that Beijing's decision to deal with the Hong Kong issue at that time was in response to the British continuing to press. The British proposal to split sovereignty and administration was alarming to the Chinese because it indicated the British did not wish to leave. It is anybody's guess what would have happened had Britain not pressed the point, although evidence all points to China resuming sovereignty. Xu Jiatun insisted in 1993 that, had MacLehose not gone to test the water with Deng Xiaoping, the talks on the future of Hong Kong might have taken place at a much later date with possibly a different outcome.⁴⁸ It is also useful to mark the recollection of Lu Ping in 1993, who was intimately involved in the whole affair at the Hong Kong and Macao Affairs Office:

> Since 1978, the question of recovering Hong Kong has been discussed [at the Hong Kong and Macao Affairs Office] and it was decided to take back Hong Kong. That was also the time of MacLehose. He had raised the New Territories issue and asked for the land lease to be extended beyond 1997. Naturally we did not agree, and although we did not recognise the unequal treaties, if only the New Territories were given back to China, Hong Kong would find it difficult to survive under British rule. Therefore the question of Hong Kong should be taken as a whole.⁴⁹

Historians will have to wait for the official archives to open to find out the full details so that they can speculate about what could otherwise have happened. Would a Macao solution have been possible for Hong Kong post-1997 had Britain not given an impression that it wanted to hang on to Hong Kong? For practical purposes today, it is all water under the bridge.

Available reports show the Politburo decided in March 1981 that China would recover sovereignty over Hong Kong in 1997, but there were arguments among the leaders over what would be the appropriate arrangements. Consensus among the top leaders was only reached in January 1982.⁵⁰ Thus, in April 1981, when Lord Carrington, the British foreign secretary (1979–1982), visited Beijing, Huang Hua did not want to discuss Hong Kong because there was no broad agreement yet among the top leadership. When the issue was put to Deng Xiaoping by Carrington,

Deng said he could not say more for now. However, Deng was most interested to talk about Taiwan.[51]

Indeed, in March 1979, when MacLehose raised the issue of the future of Hong Kong with Deng Xiaoping, Beijing was preoccupied with Taiwan. In January that year, Beijing had set out new principles for peaceful reunification. Liao Chengzhi, who was also at the meeting between MacLehose and Deng, was in the midst of working out the details of a formula for reunification with Taiwan. Thus, when Deng said to MacLehose that China would treat Hong Kong as a special region, he likely had a Taiwan-like solution in mind but he was not prepared to say more about it and did not want to be pressed. By 30 September 1981, Beijing had outlined a proposal for reunification with Taiwan. Ye Jianying spoke of the establishment of a special administrative region in a specific proposal for the KMT to consider.[52] However, the Taiwan problem proved too difficult to resolve quickly. Beijing decided to redirect its attention to Hong Kong instead. Perhaps if Hong Kong was reunified successfully, it would then be easier to reunify Taiwan.

Whilst Chinese leaders said little to the British for over two years, they had in fact been working on the issue of Hong Kong since early 1981. Deng Xiaoping wanted firm ideas that the CCP Central Committee could discuss, and he personally followed matters closely. Liao Chengzhi had the responsibility to formulate a policy and make a report to the party leadership. Liao's working group was made up of the State Council's Hong Kong and Macao Affairs Office and Xinhua Hong Kong, which provided an early opportunity for the party in Hong Kong to participate in providing reports, perspectives, and ideas. The Chinese also began to speak to numerous influential people from Hong Kong to collect views and test ideas.[53]

Liao Chengzhi's eventual report to the party leadership recommended that the resumption of sovereignty over Hong Kong should be based on three principles: stability and prosperity should be maintained; keep Hong Kong functioning as it was, which included its free port status and economic system; and Hong Kong's established political, social, and legal systems would remain in force.[54] The CCP's top leaders, including Zhao Ziyang, Hu Yaobang, Huang Hua, and Liao Chengzhi, reached a decision at the meeting of the Secretariat of the CCP Central Committee in December 1981 on how to recover Hong Kong in 1997. By then, Beijing had already prepared a draft amendment to the Chinese Constitution to supply the legal basis for the implementation of one country, two systems by empowering the state to set up special administrative regions and enabling them to pass laws different from those in the rest of the country. This amendment became Article 31 of the Chinese Constitution. A five-person study group was formed to work out details on how to resume sovereignty. Lu Ping would chair the group with two members from Xinhua Hong Kong. The group worked out a broad 12-point plan on China's Hong Kong policy post-1997 deriving ideas from China's Taiwan reunification plan, which would eventually form the basis of negotiation with the British.[55]

Thus, by December 1981, Beijing had decided on a specific policy approach. At a meeting in Beijing on 6 January 1982 between Prime Minister Zhao Ziyang and Humphrey Atkins, the junior minister who was responsible for Hong Kong at the Foreign Office (1981–1982), for once Zhao made solid comments—a distinct departure from the previous stonewalling. He talked about maintaining Hong Kong's prosperity and stability, as well as keeping it as a free port and business centre.[56] Zhao said China would discuss its position "with various circles in Hong Kong and take account of their views" in devising its plan.[57] When Atkins arrived in Hong Kong after Beijing and said that the Chinese realised that confidence would be endangered if the issue of Hong Kong was not resolved, that was read as the signal that Beijing was ready to negotiate with Britain on the future of Hong Kong. Beijing was in fact not quite ready to negotiate yet, but it was making preparations. The CCP needed time to explain and consult members on its policy on Hong Kong at the Twelfth Party Congress. After all, the top party leaders needed to bring members into agreement on offering a very special arrangement for Hong Kong that allowed capitalism to continue.[58]

MacLehose met Wang Kuang in January 1982 to put across the idea once more that Britain be allowed to continue administering Hong Kong for another 30 to 50 years. MacLehose left Hong Kong later that year and retired. He was made a life peer as Baron MacLehose of Beoch, of Maybole in the District of Kyle and Carrick and of Victoria in Hong Kong. He would return to Hong Kong to attend the Handover ceremony in 1997.

Beijing's Hong Kong

Both sides took cautious measures on the eve of the Sino-British negotiations. The Chinese focussed on bringing onto its side the Hong Kong elites by intensifying its united front activities; while the British sought to open up political participation at a modest level. Their respective steps marked the essential difference in their strategies for the entire period up until 1997.

The Hong Kong administration had published a Green Paper on improving district administration in 1980 to provide a forum for low-level political debate. The day before the release of the public consultation paper, the political adviser, David Wilson, spoke to Xinhua Hong Kong to inform the Chinese about it. This was the normal practice at the time for the British to inform the Chinese as a matter of courtesy. A subsequent policy White Paper was published in 1981 to create District Boards, which were to be formed through election.[59] The District Boards were introduced in 1982 to give advice to the government on various matters relating to the districts. The Chinese did not raise objections to their formation. In March that year, elections based on universal suffrage were held to return a third of the seats in the New Territories and then in September in the urban areas.[60] This move was a significant departure for colonial Hong Kong, where previously the only elections had been those for the Urban Council, and those on a highly restricted franchise. From then on, elections to the Urban Council and then the Regional Council were also based on universal suffrage. The impetus for the creation of the District Boards was unclear, as there did not appear to have been strong public pressure for change. On the face of it, the nature and timing of the proposal suggest it had something to do with anticipating that negotiations with China on the future of Hong Kong would start in the not too distant future. But the full story may only be known when the official archives are opened.[61]

Even as Beijing was considering a Hong Kong policy, the CCP machinery in Hong Kong had started to re-energise its united front work in the colony. An early task was to remind Hong Kong people through the left-wing media of the shameful period of history of the opium wars, how a weak China was forced to cede territory to Britain, and that it was now time to end imperialism. Another important task was to cultivate relations with prominent Hong Kong people in order to influence their thinking. From March to June 1982, Xinhua Hong Kong arranged for a stream of such people from Hong Kong to visit Beijing to meet Deng Xiaoping and other top leaders so that they could hear China's intention and position directly.[62] The united front strategy was to win influential people over by impressing upon them that the resumption of sovereignty was patriotic and inevitable.

During these audiences, the VIPs from Hong Kong did not find it easy to express their true feelings in a fulsome manner before the leaders. There were in fact many serious concerns over China's resumption of sovereignty of Hong Kong. In Xinhua Hong Kong's own gatherings of views, even people from left-wing organisations said that if a ballot were held, most of their members might not vote in favour of the resumption of sovereignty.[63] It seemed that the various concerns were not properly reflected to the leaders. Xu Jiatun, who became the director of Xinhua Hong Kong in July 1983, noted that the people who briefed him prior to his arrival in Hong Kong (the briefings would have been in May and June 1983) said all but a very few people were in favour of Hong Kong's return to China. After taking up his post, Xu soon discovered that although the leaders in Beijing had been told that Hong Kong people were patriotic and welcomed reunification, most were in fact sceptical and thousands were emigrating to Australia, Canada, the United States and other countries.[64] The problem of transmitting accurate and fulsome information about Hong Kong to CCP leaders in Beijing would continue even after 1997.

Thatcher's Beijing Visit

In May 1982, a new governor—Edward Youde (1982–1986)—took over from Murray MacLehose. His arrival marked a point in Hong Kong when its people became much more focussed on the territory's future. In welcoming him, the senior member of the Executive Council, Chung Sze Yuen (executive councillor, 1980–1988), said Youde's first priority should be the resolution of the question of the future of Hong Kong. One of his early tasks as governor was to brief and prepare Margaret Thatcher for her visit to Beijing in September that year, when Hong Kong would be on the agenda. Likewise, Percy Cradock was heavily involved with the trip and subsequent negotiations on the future of Hong Kong.

Thatcher arrived in Beijing on 22 September. The British position was that Hong Kong's prosperity and business confidence depended on a continuing British presence. In addition, the people of Hong Kong much preferred to keep the status quo and not be ruled by communists. In her memoirs, Thatcher acknowledged that her aim in Beijing was to "exchange sovereignty over the island of Hong Kong in return for continued British administration of the entire Colony well into the future".[65] Thatcher would remain deeply unhappy about negotiating the giving up of British territory, especially to a communist regime.[66] The tough-minded Thatcher, who felt invincible after winning the Falklands War in June 1982, would be upstaged completely by the even harder headed Deng Xiaoping.

Much to the British's irritation, the Chinese practised "megaphone diplomacy", whereby it announced its position through public statements prior to private talks with the British. It was Beijing's way to seize the initiative. It was also a way to show sovereignty was non-negotiable. Just before Margaret Thatcher left for Beijing, the Chinese had already released its negotiating position to the press in Hong Kong—China would inform Thatcher that it had decided to regain sovereignty in 1997, any kind of British administration beyond 1997 was unacceptable, but it was hoped that Britain and China would make efforts to promote prosperity before China regained sovereignty. Again, on 23 September, just before Thatcher and Zhao Ziyang started their meeting to discuss Hong Kong, Zhao turned to the press, as they were heading to the negotiation, to say that China would take back Hong Kong and would have policies and measures to ensure stability and prosperity. Everything that had happened up until this point showed Beijing's disregard for the diplomatic conventions of protocol and confidentiality. Beijing wanted to show who was in charge and what it thought about the issue of sovereignty. It did not matter that it would annoy the British.[67]

Thus, by 24 September, when Thatcher and Deng Xiaoping met, the atmosphere was already strained. Deng repeated that China would resume sovereignty, that there would be no place for continued British administration, and if Britain and China could not produce a transition agreement acceptable to China within a maximum of two years, then China would announce its own policies for Hong Kong. Hong Kong's capitalist system would be maintained, and existing laws could remain in force. The British had not expected a deadline to be set. The meeting between the two was "abrasive".[68] Thatcher had apparently said that the announcement of China's recovery of Hong Kong would create a "disastrous effect", and Deng's response was that the Chinese would face it squarely. Deng then warned:

> What I am concerned about is how to make a smooth transition over the next 15 years while the British remained in charge, as there may be major disturbances,

man-made disturbances. These could be created not just by foreigners but also by Chinese—but chiefly by Britons. It is easy to create disturbances. There must be no major disturbances in Hong Kong during the 15-year transition period.[69]

The Chinese were apparently prepared to take Hong Kong by force if there were unrest in Hong Kong prior to 1997.[70] They were very concerned about the transition period and Beijing's view was that it must prepare "against contingencies that we could not control".[71] Deng Xiaoping repeated his warnings to Geoffrey Howe, the British foreign secretary (1983–1989) in 1984 that the Chinese would "be paying close attention to developments during the remaining 13 years of the transition period" and that Beijing did not want to see the Hong Kong dollar being shaken, money being wasted on administrative expenses, increases in the number and pay of civil servants, administrators being imposed on the yet to be formed HKSAR government and British capital withdrawn from Hong Kong.[72] Beijing would give a public warning in July 1993 by releasing the Deng-Thatcher talk in 1982, as a countermeasure against Britain's plan for political reform. The talk, together with Deng's other utterances about Hong Kong, was republished after the massive demonstration against the Article 23 legislation on 1 July 2003 as a reminder again of how Beijing saw Beijing–Hong Kong relations.

It was after the meeting with Deng that Thatcher tripped on the steps of the Great Hall of the People, tumbling to her knees. Deng's worry about "major disturbances" and that the British could be the chief culprits to whip them up would colour Beijing–Hong Kong politics for a very long time to come.

The result of the Deng-Thatcher meeting was that negotiation would begin on the future of Hong Kong. Beijing had wanted Britain to acknowledge Chinese sovereignty over Hong Kong as a pre-condition for discussion but Britain refused. When Thatcher arrived in Hong Kong, she gave what became a famous press conference. She said that the unequal treaties were valid in international law, Britain had a "moral responsibility and duty" to Hong Kong, and then added: "If a country will not stand by one treaty, it will not stand by another."[73] In other words, Thatcher not only insisted that the treaties were valid—which she did to support the British position—but she also impugned China's trustworthiness. To some, her statements were disingenuous since, in 1981 with the passage of the British Nationality Act, Britain had already made sure Hong Kong British subjects were denied the right of abode in Britain and references to moral responsibility and duty rang hollow.[74]

The distrust between Britain and China was mutual. Thatcher's comments provoked Beijing to issue a special commentary to outline how it viewed Hong Kong, setting the rhetoric and tone for the transfer of sovereignty.[75] Beijing insisted that only the government of China had the right to claim responsibility for the people of Hong Kong. From Beijing's perspective, Hong Kong was a matter of national interest for China and the Chinese people as a whole, including the Chinese residents of Hong Kong.

It was against such a backdrop that Sino-British negotiation commenced in October 1982. Resumption of sovereignty was non-negotiable from the CCP's perspective but there could be various arrangements to be agreed with the British. The British position was that it could insist on treaty rights and retain sovereignty over Hong Kong Island and Kowloon (which was unlikely to work); Britain could exchange sovereignty for some kind of administrative presence in Hong Kong post-1997 (which should be explored); or Britain could simply go with the negotiations serving as a device for the discharge of its responsibilities towards Hong Kong (which was the bottom line, and in fact what happened).[76]

The Chinese had their own ideas on how to deal with Britain's two major arguments for there to be a British presence post-1997—the economic argument that a British presence was necessary for business confidence and prosperity, and public opinion was on the side of the British. These arguments were referred to as Britain playing the "economic card" and "public opinion card". Firstly, China could trump the economic argument by devising its own policies that would be good for business and the economy; and secondly, public opinion, especially those of the capitalist elites, could be turned round to support China's position through an intensive united front–propaganda campaign. Deng Xiaoping did not see why the Chinese could not rule Hong Kong just as well as the British.[77]

Between October 1982 and June 1983, China pushed Britain to acknowledge Chinese sovereignty over Hong Kong as a precondition to discussing substance. In January 1983, Chinese officials upped the ante by telling visitors from Hong Kong to Beijing that China had already worked out a plan for "Hong Kong people ruling Hong Kong", but they had not yet shown it to the British. By March it seemed the British became convinced that the Chinese would not change their minds. Thatcher wrote to Zhao Ziyang stating that if negotiations yielded arrangements acceptable to the people of Hong Kong, then she would be prepared to recommend it to Parliament on the transfer of sovereignty. There were two important messages in Thatcher's letter to Zhao. The first was the British did not want to concede the point on sovereignty just yet, but they also did not want to argue about it. The second was that a deal had to be palatable enough for the British Parliament to stomach since it would have to be debated openly in Britain. Zhao took the first point, but the second point would not be resolved until the very end, as events would show. The final concession from Beijing had to do with elections as the last sweetener.

The Chinese leaked Margaret Thatcher's letter in May and encouraged it to be understood as a concession on sovereignty. Nevertheless, the talks continued to be difficult, as the British continued to pursue post-1997 British administration. By the end of July 1983, the Chinese released details of a 12-point post-1997 plan. The level of jitters was rising in Hong Kong—it was obvious that things were not going well between Britain and China. After the next round of meetings on 23 September 1983 with no progress made, things in Hong Kong boiled over. The next day was a very Black Friday, followed by the equally depressing Black Saturday. The Hong Kong dollar hit a record low against the American dollar. The stock market plummeted. In London, Thatcher blamed it on the political uncertainty. In Beijing, Ji Pengfei said that China would make a statement concerning the future of Hong Kong by the end of 1984 if the negotiations had not produced a solution by then. The Hong Kong government pegged the Hong Kong dollar to the American dollar in mid-October, which was effective in reviving financial confidence.[78]

The British blinked first. By mid-November 1983, the British had dropped their position on British administration post-1997. The bottom line had been reached and Britain had to concede sovereignty and depart in 1997. After all, there was long-term Sino-British relations to consider. On 6 January 1984, Executive Councillor Lydia Dunn (a senior executive with the Swire Group) said publicly that a British presence was not necessary after 1997, and that she supported calls in Hong Kong for elections to the Legislative Council, and perhaps even the Executive Council.[79] This was the first time that an executive councillor openly supported elections, which signalled that, with the British having conceded sovereignty, it was time to consider post-Handover arrangements pragmatically to see how to guarantee the promised autonomy in the future. That also marked the moment when the political elites indicated their willingness to accept that Beijing was capable of preserving Hong Kong's systems.

Few people in Hong Kong were not worried about their future. Every family talked about what they could do and what options they had. Their anxiety was palpable. Beijing claimed it represented the Hong Kong Chinese and that the British did not. The British said they had a moral responsibility for Hong Kong but were unwilling to allow Hong Kong British subjects to have the right of abode in Britain. The people of Hong Kong knew they were squeezed between two powers both of whom claimed to speak for them but neither wanted to hear them out fully.[80] As late as 14 March 1984, the frustration felt by the Hong Kong community could be heard from the Legislative Council debate where the appointed legislators—who made up Hong Kong's then political elites—passed a motion stressing that: "This Council deems it necessary that any proposals for the future of Hong Kong should be debated by this Council before any final agreement is reached."[81] The Chinese side was unhappy about the raising of the motion because it pressed what Beijing labelled as the "three legged stool" concept that Hong Kong itself had a role in the Sino-British negotiations. The Chinese suspected the British were using the appointed legislators to strengthen their bargaining position while posing to represent public sentiments.[82] The extent of the people's isolation could be seen from statements made during the debate, which also spoke volumes about the colonial political system:

> I make no special claim for the extent to which the Council represents the will of the people of Hong Kong and so far as I am aware, no member of this Council has ever done so. It is not necessary to do so to establish that we have a responsibility

to address this issue, and the purpose of this motion is to reaffirm publicly our commitment to that responsibility.
—Roger Lobo

Our future is debated over our heads, it is remarkable that five-and-a-half million people should be expected to stay calm, confident and clueless for so long.
—Alex Wu

We have never claimed that we represent the people of Hong Kong. We have, however, always tried to reflect public opinions.
—Allen Lee

We were told that behind this motion there must be some sinister motive and [they] warned us not to revive the "three legged stool" concept and not to play the "opinion card". We were accused of rocking the boat simply through seeking to debate the issue in this Chamber. We were further told that because we have not been elected, we cannot claim to represent the people of Hong Kong, hence implying that there is no need for anyone to listen to whatever we have to say.
—Stephen Cheong

On 20 April 1984, Geoffrey Howe told the people of Hong Kong that continuing British administration was unrealistic but it might be possible to secure "a high degree of autonomy"—as the Chinese had been saying—under Chinese rule, where the way of life of Hong Kong people would be preserved. The British position shifted to extracting concessions from the Chinese and enshrining them in a binding agreement, but an enormous gulf existed between how the Chinese and British approached the drafting of an agreement: "We [the British] wanted to write a book—which would have looked rather like the *Encyclopaedia Britannica*—while the Chinese wanted about two to three sides of A4 paper."[83]

The Chinese wanted the shortest possible agreement, while the British wanted something as detailed as possible. The Hong Kong government had provided a tome of information containing all the things that were essential to the running of Hong Kong. The British felt details were needed to win the confidence of the Hong Kong community. The draft Sino-British Joint Declaration that was initialled on 26 September 1984 had a very short declaration and a series of annexes. The declaration was what the Chinese side wanted and the annexes were what the British side needed.[84] The declaration was clear that in terms of relations between the Central People's Government and the future Hong Kong Special Administrative Region, the latter "will be directly under the authority of the Central People's Government"—meaning Beijing will have overall or "comprehensive" jurisdiction over Hong Kong after 1997 (Chapter 10).

As far as the Chinese side was concerned, the one country, two systems principle meant socialism would not be practised in Hong Kong and that capitalism would operate there instead. Mainland theorists also explained the basic theory of the principle quoting Deng Xiaoping:

If the thought of one country, two systems is a meaningful thought to the world, it must be attributable to the Dialectic Materialism and Historical Materialism of Marxism. Using the words of Mao Zedong, it is seeking truth from facts . . . To respect facts and reality is to respect the reality of Hong Kong . . . We suggest keeping Hong Kong capitalism intact, that is to execute one country, two systems.[85]

Deng Xiaoping called the Sino-British Joint Declaration "a product of dialectic Marxism and historical materialism" while Margaret Thatcher described it as "an ingenious idea".[86] Percy Cradock, described it guardedly—"as comprehensive protection as could be devised and agreed".[87] In other words, it was the best that could be achieved, and it was a take-it-or-leave-it agreement, which greatly influenced how the people of Hong Kong looked at it. If there was no alternative, then it was obviously better to take it. When the Hong Kong Legislative Council debated it, only one member abstained for the reason that he did not think it was good enough for the people of Hong Kong.[88]

Throughout the 22 rounds of Sino-British talks, Beijing rolled out its propaganda–united front machinery to actively shape the result it wanted.[89] On 19 December 1984, when the treaty was formally signed in Beijing, a glimpse of the CCP's united front plan could also be seen from the 101 Hong Kong guests invited to witness the ceremony. These were their prime targets for co-option during the Sino-British negotiations, and relations with them would continue to be cultivated, as they were the elites Beijing needed to have on side during the transition period (Chapter 8 and Appendix II).

What both Beijing and Whitehall were unaware of was that the people of Hong Kong were undergoing a seismic shift in political consciousness. The events surrounding the Sino-British negotiations over the future of the territory and its people was having a politicising effect that would change Hong Kong forever.

8
The Shaping of Post-Colonial Hong Kong
From 1983 to 1989

The first words uttered by the Chinese Communist Party's new representative in Hong Kong as he stepped off the train from Guangzhou were: "I am here for the reunification of the motherland." Replacing Wang Kuang, Xu Jiatun arrived in Hong Kong on 30 June 1983, exactly fourteen years before the colony would become a Special Administrative Region of the People's Republic of China. In his role as the director of Xinhua Hong Kong, Xu was tasked with devising a strategy and an implementation plan for China to take back Hong Kong from the British. His time in Hong Kong shaped the early process for identifying the individuals and groups that would form the post-colonial political establishment. Beijing's position on recovering sovereignty over Hong Kong was based on certain assumptions about its understanding of Hong Kong's capitalist society, which continue to have an effect even today because the design of the post-1997 political system is based on them. Its united front strategy and tactics were likewise based on those assumptions.

The departure of Wang Kuang, the former director of Xinhua Hong Kong, in the midst of the Sino-British negotiation in May 1983 was a surprise to the leftist camp. Whilst it was said that Wang was replaced for health reasons, it was more likely that he was felt to have lacked the right credentials to deal with the complex issues arising from British to Chinese rule.[1] Wang was considered politically too conservative. Several of the top leaders had apparently thought Wang was "too left".[2] He was said to have disapproved of the establishment of the Special Economic Zones, and discouraged some infrastructure and philanthropic projects proposed by Hong Kong businessmen.[3] Nevertheless, during his time, Xinhua Hong Kong had begun to reach out to important figures in Hong Kong as part of its united front plan. For example, Xinhua Hong Kong extended an invitation to Chung Sze Yuen who was the senior member of the Executive Council by then, Kan Yuet Keung who had retired from politics, and T. K. Ann, the industrialist, to join the CPPCC in early 1982. Chung and Kan turned down the offer but Ann accepted. In March 1983, Xinhua Hong Kong extended the offer once more to Chung and said the offer would remain open indefinitely.[4] In addition, Xinhua Hong Kong was actively organising trips from the autumn of 1982 for businessmen to visit Beijing to meet top leaders.[5]

Xu Jiatun was the first secretary of the Jiangsu CCP, the top party cadre in the province. He was also a member of the CCP Central Committee, and thus a high-ranking official in the party hierarchy. While he had no Hong Kong or foreign affairs experience, he impressed Deng Xiaoping with his work in Jiangsu, which was why he was sought for the job in Hong Kong. To boost Xu's political authority, the CCP upgraded CCP Hong Kong to a provincial rank organ putting it directly under the CCP Central Committee. Thus, CCP Hong Kong and the State Council's Hong Kong and Macao Affairs Office became units of equal rank within China's political hierarchy. This lifted the importance of Xinhua Hong Kong to that of a first-rank, centrally controlled organisation. The head of the Hong Kong party organ enjoyed ministerial rank.[6] Moreover, Xu's seniority in the party meant that his position was on par with that of Ji Pengfei, who succeeded Liao Chengzhi as head of the Hong Kong and Macao Affairs Office although, having been foreign minister (1972–1974), Ji had greater prestige.

Xu's seniority gave him a lot of latitude to act as he saw fit. He reported directly to the CCP Central Committee or State Council depending on the subject and, where foreign affairs were involved, the Ministry of Foreign Affairs would be copied. This led to turf conflicts between Xu and the Hong Kong and Macao Affairs Office. There would be many differences of opinion between Xinhua Hong Kong under Xu Jiatun and the Hong Kong and Macao Affairs Office that sowed seeds of mutual distrust.[7] After Xu Jiatun's departure in 1990, Xinhua Hong Kong would be downgraded back to what it was prior to Xu's arrival (Chapter 9).[8] Xu disclosed that he had problems with Li Hou and Lu Ping at the Hong Kong and Macao Affairs Office, as well as Zhou Nan (who would succeed Xu in the future) at the Ministry of Foreign Affairs. In Xu's view, they were giving Beijing a carefully varnished view of Hong Kong, claiming that the public were impatient for reunification, when there was in fact plenty of scepticism.[9] Perhaps to admit that Hong Kong people felt otherwise would be an admission that the united front had failed in their job. The question of accuracy of briefing about Hong Kong would continue to be a challenge even after reunification.

To reabsorb Hong Kong—and also Macao and Taiwan in due course—insisting on the acceptance of communism would not do. Thus, practically, reunification must allow Hong Kong's capitalist system to continue. However, as Xu Jiatun observed, there was nothing in Marxist thinking that envisaged the practice of safeguarding a capitalist system over a long period of time under the leadership of a communist party. He acknowledged that the one country, two systems formula enshrined in the Sino-British Joint Declaration presented a brand new mission and a great challenge to the CCP, and it would require new thinking to get the job done.[10] Moreover, the Four Cardinal Principles, as Deng Xiaoping had said, would not be applied to Hong Kong. As Hong Kong would not operate a communist system, it could not be run by communists. Thus, the implementation of one country, two systems required "Hong Kong people ruling Hong Kong" and by definition, that meant an administration run by the bourgeoisie, not the working class. The future government structure should therefore be dominated by the capitalist class.[11] Interestingly, Xu Jiatun observed that cadres should therefore not be involved in running Hong Kong, but if a cadre (whose party identity was hidden) should take part in the administration of Hong Kong, he still had to implement non-communist policies, and even if the CCP should pass a contrary directive, he should refuse to execute it.[12] Perhaps it was this belief that got him into trouble in 1989 (Chapter 9).

Xu Jiatun had access to the Sino-British negotiations from June 1983, after his appointment, but just before he arrived in Hong Kong. He would continue to be briefed on how the British shaped their position. He could see how the British would use the economic card and the public opinion card to their advantage. It was his duty to help counter them. However, upon taking office, he soon found that CCP Hong Kong did not have an overall strategy to cope with the return of sovereignty to the Mainland. By November 1983, Xu had set out a work plan, which was discussed at a specially held meeting in Shenzhen with members of CCP Hong Kong, as well as representatives from various party branches and groups. The plan had six aspects and would guide their work in the coming years:

1. The priority was to win the trust of Hong Kong people.
2. During the transitional period, China's strategy was both to struggle against, as well as to unify with Britain in order to ensure the return of a stable and prosperous Hong Kong to Chinese rule.
3. The Hong Kong CCP would rely on the working class and a widely based patriotic united front to implement its plan.
4. The Hong Kong CCP would publicise patriotism, and promote one country, two systems. Criticism of communism and positive publicity about capitalism would be allowed.
5. For the prosperity of Hong Kong, the Hong Kong CCP would make the British *hongs* stay, appease the local Chinese businessmen, unify overseas Chinese businesses, and strengthen Mainland-financed companies.
6. The Hong Kong CCP would reorganise the teams of cadres in Hong Kong to meet the new challenges.[13]

A critical component of achieving the strategy required Xu Jiatun to rebuild the united front in Hong Kong and to extend it far and wide.

Internal Reorganisation

What was the legal status of Xinhua Hong Kong? Registered as a news organisation, it was an open secret that it was the front for the CCP in Hong Kong. Under Hong Kong law, any organised group was required to apply to the Registrar of Societies for registration. Exemption from registration might be granted by the Registrar to those societies that were established solely for charitable purposes. The law was explicit that the Registrar may deny approval and registration of any group if the society was a branch or affiliate or connected with any organisation or groups of a political nature established outside Hong Kong. The CCP did not seek registration or exemption from registration from the Hong Kong government, and the Hong Kong authorities did not make a fuss, otherwise each would find the other's position intolerable. On the one hand, why should the ruling party of China, which claimed sovereignty over Hong Kong, seek registration from an imperialist authority? On the other hand, why should the British have to accept formally the CCP's operation in the colony? It was better to ignore the issue of legality of the CCP's presence in Hong Kong altogether. It became the habit of all concerned not to speak about it at all. An interesting question was how the CCP's activities were funded in Hong Kong prior to 1997. While party work in Hong Kong would have formed part of China's national budget, it was likely that, because foreign exchange was involved, Xinhua Hong Kong received its funding from Mainland-controlled organisations in Hong Kong, such as the Hong Kong Branch of the Bank of China.[14]

During Xu Jiatun's time in Hong Kong from 1983 to 1990, the number of staff at Xinhua grew from about 100 to about 400 people. Xu had wanted 600 people. However, his successor, Zhou Nan, did build the workforce within Xinhua Hong Kong to 600 people by the time of the transition (Chapter 9). Xu built up a structure that approximated the Hong Kong government's key departments relating to economic affairs, finance, trade, air transport, education, culture, and sports as part of the takeover strategy, as well as restructuring Xinhua's departments for united front and its related work (see Table 2).

When he took up his post, he found morale low among Hong Kong cadres. Many of them took part in the 1967 riots out of a sense of patriotism and anti-imperialism, but they were then criticised and had been feeling disgruntled ever since. Membership had not been growing. Xu could see that the party was not in good shape to take on the work needed to implement one country, two systems and a major reshuffle was necessary. He announced four transformations and got to work immediately: he would revolutionise, rejuvenate, specialise, and intellectualise Xinhua Hong Kong.[15] Xu changed the name of the United Front Work Department to that of the Coordination Department. The term "united front" had a heavy communist-propagandist flavour, which he found put people off in Hong Kong. Xu also set up the Youth Work Leading Group and the Women Work Leading Group so as to target young people and women in Hong Kong as part of their united front efforts. Mostly importantly, the party set up three branches to launch work in the community on Hong Kong Island, in Kowloon Tong and in Shatin.[16]

As for intelligence work, Xu Jiatun unified it under the Security Department. Intelligence work was done in all sectors of the community, but there were possibly too many contacts and informants of low quality in Hong Kong. Mainland officials sent to manage intelligence work in Hong Kong were professionals mostly sent by the Ministry of Public Security and Ministry of National Security. The task of the personnel from Public Security was to take care of the security of Xinhua Hong Kong and other Mainland-owned institutions. A small number of them were also responsible for intelligence work. All those sent from National Security were involved in intelligence work. It was nevertheless agreed by the ministries that, after the merging of their operations, some particularly important "connections" (agents carrying out top secret missions) would still be directly controlled by them but the director of Xinhua Hong Kong would be kept informed. During Xu's time, agents under the Security Department were able to provide important information related to the Sino-British negotiations and were twice commended by the Ministry of National Security and Ministry of Foreign Affairs.[17]

There were other intelligence personnel in Hong Kong, which were harder for Xu Jiatun to control. The Central Military Commission, which had intelligence personnel in Hong Kong, did not agree to merge their agents within the Xinhua's new Security Department although it agreed to keep the director informed. Moreover, the national security departments of the coastal provinces, such as Jiangsu, Zhejiang and Fujian, as well as military regions, such as the Guangzhou and Nanjing military regions, also had agents in Hong Kong.[18] Thus, there were many intelligence agents in Hong Kong from a variety of Mainland units, who more often than not did not know each other nor were operating with the full knowledge of Xinhua Hong Kong. Xu Jiatun had also observed that agents were therefore not well managed.[19]

More importantly, Xu calculated that the Hong Kong authorities knew who the key cadres were and what Xinhua Hong Kong did in Hong Kong. The Hong Kong authorities tapped Xinhua's telephone calls around the clock and so could be assumed to know a lot about their activities. Whenever Xu had something important to report to Beijing, he would go to Shenzhen to make calls.[20] Thus, on the one hand, cadres might as well be allowed to attend public occasions, although they would not use their party affiliation since the CCP was, and remains, an underground organisation in Hong Kong. On the other hand, it was necessary to "develop an absolutely secret new organisation" to undertake upper level work.[21] Presumably this was done, although there is understandably no record of it.

Generally, Xu Jiatun appointed new and younger people, bringing the average age at Xinhua Hong Kong from 65 years down to 55 years. He requested high quality and experienced cadres for transfer from Guangdong, Fujian, Jiangsu, Zhejiang and Shanghai,[22] thereby changing the regional mix of Xinhua personnel, which used to be dominated by the Cantonese. He reduced the number of deputy directors from six to four.[23] Xu promoted two local Hong Kong party cadres as assistant deputy directors.[24] Xu Jiatun also separated the political functions and the news functions of Xinhua Hong Kong. He moved the news section from the Xinhua headquarters in Happy Valley to Sharp Street in Wan Chai. He introduced a degree of transparency to Xinhua Hong Kong. He allowed its organisational structure to be made public. In the past, since Xinhua Hong Kong was presented as a news agency, the personnel responsible for political work were all supposedly "journalists". After Xu's arrival, the titles of the various departments were changed to correspond with their actual functions.²⁵ The line-up at the most senior level of China's presence in Hong Kong after reorganisation in 1986 was as follows:

Director of Xinhua, and Secretary of CCP Hong Kong: Xu Jiatun.

Deputy Director of Xinhua, and Vice-Secretary of CCP Hong Kong: Zheng Hua.

Deputy Directors of CCP Hong Kong: Qiao Zhonghuai, Mao Junnian, Zhang Junsheng, and Pan Zengxi.

Assistant Deputy Directors of CCP Hong Kong: Wang Rudeng and Chen Fengying.

CCP Hong Kong member, CCP Macao Secretary, Director of Xinhua Macao: Zhou Ding.

Table 2 The Bureaucracy of CCP Hong Kong[26]

Leading Small Groups	Offices	Committees	Departments
United Front Work	General Office	Finance	Organisation (Personnel)
Taiwan Work	Policy Research	Trade	Foreign Affairs
Economic Work		Air Transport	Taiwan Affairs
Investigation and Research Work			Economic Security
Youth Work			Coordination (United Front)
Women's Work			Propaganda
			Culture & Education
			Arts & Sports
			Youth & Women

A Special Kind of United Front Work

When Xu Jiatun first arrived at Hong Kong, he stated that he hoped to perform a bridging role between Beijing and Hong Kong and make Beijing's policies accord with the practical situation of Hong Kong.²⁷ Safeguarding capitalism for a long time became the foundation of united front work in Hong Kong.

Deng Xiaoping had said that the goal of united front work in Hong Kong was to get people to "love the motherland and Hong Kong". It was not a prerequisite to "support socialism and the leadership of CCP" as practised on the Mainland. Deng further said that those cadres conducting united front work in Hong Kong had to be bold enough to make friends even with "right-wingers and spies". In CCP-speak, "right-wingers" were those in the upper strata of society who were pro-British, pro-American, and pro-Taiwan.²⁸ In other words, united front work in Hong Kong must include the establishment, not just the party's traditional targets of workers, intellectuals, teachers and students. That required a significant departure in ideological terms for the CCP, but oddly enough the CCP had never disdained the elites. Indeed, the party took their traditional targets for granted, and gave special attention and priority to cultivating the elites. Many businessmen would do well out of their Mainland connections.

Xu Jiatun's major united front targets were the leading figures among the Hong Kong political elites. Xu and his deputies held regular meetings to exchange views with several executive councillors—Chung Sze Yuen, Lydia Dunn (who would succeed Chung as the senior member in 1988), and Lee Quo Wei (chairman of the Hang Seng Bank)—throughout the Sino-British negotiations. The first meeting took place on 15 August 1983 at a dinner hosted by the vice-chancellor of the Chinese University of Hong Kong. After that, regular secret rendezvous were organised until the Sino-British Joint Declaration was concluded after which meetings became less frequent. After each meeting, while Chung reported the discussion to the governor, Xu reported to Beijing.[29] In the early days, the executive councillors suggested using a "company" approach to solve the Hong Kong problem. China should resume sovereignty and become like the chairman of a company's board of directors, and retain Britain as the general manager to continue the day-to-day running of Hong Kong.[30] In addition to smoothing communication between Beijing and Hong Kong, another function of these meetings was to assess acceptability and reaction to Beijing's ideas prior to making them public. As commented by Chung Sze Yuen, Xu "wanted to test its rhetoric on us inside the room and broadcast the same on the outside through its media".[31] Another person Xu cultivated was legislator Maria Tam, who also proposed the same company solution as the executive councillors.[32] Tam would turn out to be one of the most successful post-colonial elites as she was still relatively young at the time of reunification (Chapter 10).

The CCP's contacts with senior Hong Kong government officials also became more frequent. There was an active campaign to cultivate civil servants close to retirement and those who had just retired, in case there might be a need to call upon their services in the future. Moreover, having them on-side, created a sense that people who could administer Hong Kong could be called upon by Beijing to serve should it be necessary. Former civil servants who had been actively cultivated included Li Kwan Ha, a former commissioner of police, and Nicky Chan, a former secretary for lands and works. Converts included Donald Liao, a former secretary for home affairs, and Wilfred Wong, a former deputy secretary in the former Civil Service Branch. Wong, like Maria Tam, was relatively young and could expect to be useful after 1997. There were also two High Court judges—Arthur Garcia and Benjamin Liu, an Appeal Court judge—Simon Li, and a chief justice—T. L. Yang, who were cultivated. Interestingly, Garcia, Li, and Yang thought they had a chance to become the first Chief Executive. Garcia briefly put his name forward in 1996 as a candidate, Li actually did but did not get the required number of nominations (a minimum of 50 from among Selection Committee members) to get to the starting blocks, and Yang actually did get through to the selection, but lost to Tung Chee Hwa by a large margin. Tung invited Yang to sit on the Executive Council, which Yang accepted.

According to CCP Hong Kong's analysis of class in Hong Kong, the community had three main strata—the big capitalists, middle class, and workers. All of them wanted to protect and promote their interests after 1997. The party concluded that:

> The top political echelon of Hong Kong must adapt to its capitalist economic structure and class structure, so Hong Kong's future political system will have the local patriotic capitalists as the main body, and ally with other classes to form a non-socialist political system. At present, Hong Kong has already witnessed many prominent industrialists, businessmen, professionals, and their organisations actively participating in local political activities, reflecting this trend.[33]

Thus it was essential for the party to cultivate the big capitalists. Beijing's worry was not just over the potential for massive capital outflow and emigration from Hong Kong by these wealthy entrepreneurs, although they had legitimate reasons to be concerned. After all, Hong Kong provided two-thirds of total direct investments to the Mainland from 1979 to 1995. Beyond that, however, Chinese official analysis saw Hong Kong capitalism not just as a structure of competitive markets and institutions, but in terms of an economic and political system dominated by a small group of businessmen supported by pro-business government policies. Their research would have included the works of academics who have explained the success of colonial administration in terms of a process of "administrative absorption of politics by which the government co-opt[ed] the political forces, often represented by elite groups, into an administration decision-making body".[34] It may also be that they had viewed instances of mass, radical agitation—such as those times in the 1920s, 1950s and 1960s noted in Chapters 3, 5 and 6—as outcomes of overflowing patriotism and anti-imperialism rather than internally generated social discontent. They may have concluded that the workers' movement was relatively weak in Hong Kong, and in any case, the CCP already controlled the FTU and thus could count of its support when necessary.[35]

It was thought that if the major capitalists could be convinced of China's position, it would be less difficult to get the middle class to follow. Xu Jiatun noted that capitalists in Hong Kong could be grouped into factions, like the Guangdong, Shanghai and Fujian factions, and those with Southeast Asian backgrounds. The key targets were about a dozen of the top tycoons, including Pao Yue Kong, Li Ka Shing, Kwok Tak Sing, Run Run Shaw, and Cha Chi Min. Henry Fok could already be counted to be on-side in view of his longstanding connection to the Mainland, and was already a member of the CPPCC.

Xu perceived that a "businessman's political inclination is normally linked to his business. He would side with whomever would support him."[36] Thus, it was useful to nurture a group of patriotic businessmen. It would hit two birds with one stone. Bringing these capitalists on side would help China to deal with Britain's economic card since the capitalists could keep the economy chugging along, and their support would also counter the British public opinion card that Hong Kong people preferred the status quo. When a number of Hong Kong's prominent businessmen ran into financial trouble and sought Xu's help, he was willing to find ways to support them. They would no doubt feel they owed China a debt in the future when a favour needed to be called in. Xu was not the first to go out of his way to do this in fact. It is a part of Hong Kong's political lore that Beijing saved Tung Chee Hwa's shipping company from bankruptcy in the mid-1980s through a capital injection through Henry Fok, and the Bank of China provided a credit line as well.[37] Xu disclosed in his memoirs that he helped entrepreneur Fung King Hei for example when he had financial problems.[38]

As for the middle class, CCP Hong Kong's analysis of this group was that its constituents had a strong impulse to advance and that they were more or less satisfied with the existing social ladder, although there were signs of demands for a democratic environment with equal opportunities. To bring the middle class on-side, Xu Jiatun sought to improve CCP Hong Kong's policy toward left-wing organisation on the one hand and strengthen connections with civil society organisations on the other hand. New departments were set up at Xinhua Hong Kong to focus on united front work with the middle class with special emphasis on the science, technology, sports and cultural sectors. Moreover, teachers in middle and primary schools were to be targeted.

Xu Jiatun became a man to be seen around town and to be seen with. He sought the company of the rich, the famous, the infamous and entertainment stars. He attended many public and private functions, ranging from banquets, weddings, funerals to sports event and drama performances. He made speeches to business associations and at universities. He invited many guests to meals and friendly chats at the Xinhua Hong Kong office. He even attended the first anniversary celebration of Meeting Point, a new pro-democracy pressure group, which indicated that at the time, Xu was prepared to cultivate even pro-democracy activists in support of Hong Kong's return to China. Looking back at the CCP's united front history, such as noted in Chapter 4, of reaching out to as many people from all walks of life as possible, Xu was following in the party's pragmatic tradition. It was from 1985 that the CCP became anxious about the timing and extent of democratic reform, and the united front became more circumspect about nurturing democracy activists.

Xu Jiatun was a popular figure among Hong Kong journalists because of his willingness to make comments. He even made one of the most popular television stars of the time, Lisa Wang Ming Chuen, a delegate to the 7th NPC in an attempt to win the support of the cultural sector—a classic united front tactic to unite with leading figures in the arts.[39] A powerful tool that Xu had was the ability to organise trips to Beijing for those he wanted to cultivate, so that they could meet top Chinese leaders, including Deng Xiaoping. These pilgrimages to the Chinese capital proved most effective. For the ambitious, there was nothing like being close to the seat of power and to think one could influence the thinking and actions of the leaders.

However, the strategy of co-opting capitalists and upper middle class people led to criticisms within the traditional leftist camp that old faithfuls and the lower classes were neglected. "Xu Jiatun put too much emphasis on the united front work in the upper and middle classes, but he neglected the grassroots. Xu seemed to have an illusion that the grassroots people would support him, which was not true. The problem of such practice was that, first, the elite-mass gap would be enlarged and second, the problem of confidence crisis could not be directly solved."[40] Some leftists further remarked that Xu "looked down" on those from grassroots level and under his leadership "the eyes of the Xinhua News Agency only looked at upper class and business sector".[41]

Xu Jiatun's own writings indicated that he felt he needed to cultivate social contacts that the CCP did not have in Hong Kong, which required him to reach out to capitalists, entrepreneurs, middle-class professionals, and celebrities. Old-time leftists were unhappy that capitalists and the bourgeoisie would run Hong Kong. As such, Xu did not think that the existing cadres and supporters could deliver on the goal of safeguarding capitalism. Indeed, the left-wing unions in particular needed to be re-organised since they had become almost dormant after the 1967 riots. The unions should therefore stop pushing for the realisation of socialism and should work for the welfare of workers in Hong Kong instead, otherwise it would run counter to the need to safeguard capitalism. Where conflicts arose between workers and capitalists, the left-wing unions should adopt a policy that would be beneficial to both management and labour and seek a solution through consultation rather than resort to strikes. The left-wing labour unions could not be too happy about being put in such a straitjacket but they did not have much choice.

The party nurtured new and younger union leaders, such as Tam Yiu Chung and Chan Yuen Han in place of old ones. Tam would rise to become a legislator (1985–2016) and executive councillor (1997–2002), and Chan would become a member of the Legislative Council (1995–2008 and 2012–2016). Thus, when there was a taxi-driver strike in 1985, when strikers petitioned Xinhua Hong Kong, the strikers were urged to settle matters with the Hong Kong government. The Chinese did not want to be seen to be fomenting strikes, boycotts and riots, as the communists were seen to have done in 1922 with the Seamen's Strike, in 1925–1926 with the Guangdong–Hong Kong Strike-Boycott and in particular during the 1956 and 1967 riots (see Chapters 3, 5, and 6). Xu Jiatun even attempted to unify the three factions of unions in Hong Kong—those on the left, the right (pro-Taiwan) and those that were neither left nor right (referred to as "neutral") but it did not work.[42]

There were other voices emerging in Hong Kong that were of minor interest to Xinhua Hong Kong prior to the conclusion of the Sino-British Joint Declaration. These were not the voices of the then establishment representing business or the

British colonial authorities. These voices were mostly of Hong Kong Chinese who were born and raised in Hong Kong and strongly identified with Hong Kong as their home. They were on the whole better educated and some had lived overseas. They called for solid guarantees that a high degree of autonomy and Hong Kong people ruling Hong Kong meant the post-1997 political system would be underpinned by a democratic system of free and fair elections. For example, Meeting Point—mentioned above—was one such group. Many of its former members would become politicians in the coming years.[43] Another group was the Hong Kong Observers, a pressure group made up of young professionals. Some of their members would also become prominent politicians and opinion-shapers in the years to come.[44] In 1982, they commissioned Hong Kong's first detailed public opinion survey to ascertain the degree of concern over the future of Hong Kong, which neither the British nor the Chinese found to their liking. The Chinese did not want to hear that Hong Kong people had real concerns about Chinese rule and that keeping the status quo had majority support. The British did not want to know that Chinese sovereignty with real autonomy could nevertheless be acceptable.[45] Neither the British nor the Chinese needed to pay much attention to these inconvenient voices after they struck their deal in September 1984.

With the formal signing of the Sino-British Joint Declaration in Beijing on 19 December 1984, Beijing invited 101 VIPs from Hong Kong to witness the event. The list was agreed upon after "cordial consultations" between China and Britain.[46] The occasion was seen as a golden united front opportunity to cultivate important people, especially right-wingers and Hong Kong government officials. The list included senior Hong Kong civil servants, such as Nicky Chan and Anson Chan; British corporate leaders, such as Michael Miles of Swire & Sons and Michael Sandberg of the Hongkong & Shanghai Banking Corporation; Chinese tycoons, such as Pao Yue Kong, Li Ka Shing, Lee Quo Wei, Francis Tien, Lee Shau Kee, Gordon Wu, Stanley Ho, Cha Chi Ming, and Henry Fok; Hong Kong political figures, such as Chung Sze Yuen, Selina Chow, Maria Tam, Roger Lobo, and Stephen Cheong; Justice Simon Li; actress Liza Wang Ming Chuen; Hong Kong professional and community leaders, such as Martin Lee, Szeto Wah, Elsie Elliot (Tu), Mak Hoi Wah, and Lau Wong Fat, as well as people in leftists circles, including Percy Chen, Yeung Kwong, Fei Yi Ming, and Tam Yiu Chung.

For a list of the VIPs from Hong Kong, see Appendix II.

Preparing for Resumption of Sovereignty

After the Sino-British Joint Declaration was signed, Hong Kong entered into its transitional phase to Chinese rule. The most important task was to prevent any opposition to the resumption of sovereignty, and the second was to ensure Hong Kong continued to support the Mainland economically and financially. A third important task was to nurture a group of "status markers" who could populate the post-1997 political system under Chinese rule.⁴⁷ This would also be the group that would help to draft and provide views to the Basic Law drafting process. All of these tasks required continuous united front and propaganda work from the CCP to keep up confidence and to instil a belief that Hong Kong under Chinese rule would be even better than under British rule.

The status markers were familiar faces, as many of them were the same as those who had played a similar role under British rule. The need to preserve capitalism for half a century in post-1997 Hong Kong meant that some members of the business elites (from the families that owned banking, industrial, trading and real estate companies, together with the senior executives of major public companies, as well as leading professionals) would be chosen to help run Hong Kong. The drafting and consultation on the Basic Law involved most of the notable business and professional elites, making those processes a huge united front exercise the purpose of which was to give the post-1997 constitution a semblance of legitimacy.

The Sino-British Joint Declaration had served its purpose in embodying the political settlement on the question of Hong Kong. It would be referred to less and less, while the Basic Law would attempt to resolve the inherent contradictions between the Mainland, which operates a Leninist political system in which the supremacy of the CCP cannot be challenged, and Hong Kong's capitalist system underpinned by a liberal tradition, the rule of law and an independent judiciary.

Ji Pengfei promised that the drafting process would include "collecting the opinions of Hong Kong people so that the opinion of the majority would be reflected".⁴⁸ Influential Hong Kong people from various walks of life would have to be formally co-opted into the drafting process. It would be through their endorsement of both the process and the outcome that Beijing could claim the Basic Law was acceptable to Hong Kong. Furthermore, the elaborate drafting and consultative process to produce the Basic Law was essential to show the people of Hong Kong—as well as the people of Macao and Taiwan—that Beijing meant what it said, that there would be one country, two systems, a high degree of autonomy and the local people ruling themselves.

The creation of the Basic Law had three aspects. Firstly, there was the drafting of the post-1997 constitution itself. Secondly, there was the putting together and management of a drafting committee. Thirdly, there was the appointment of a broader consultative committee to show the eventual constitution had wide support. The whole exercise, which lasted from 1985 to 1989, was a massive united front–propaganda challenge, where the Xinhua Hong Kong and the Hong Kong and Macao Affairs Office played the most important roles. It was a highly controlled process, but there were many moments of drama, although at the end it was clear that real decision-making power was preserved in the CCP's hands.

Basic Law drafting instructions and strategy

The purpose of the Basic Law was never to dovetail with the Sino-British Joint Declaration. It is an instrument for Beijing to exert sovereignty post-1997. The CCP's policy was that there should be no substantial democratic development in Hong Kong. The drafting instructions for the Basic Law could be seen from the utterances of Deng Xiaoping on 16 April 1987 listing the overriding principles in drafting the post-1997 constitution:

- The provisions should not be too detailed. The key was to put down the principles. This was the same attitude adopted on the Chinese side with the Sino-British Joint Declaration (Chapter 7).
- The Hong Kong post-1997 system should not be a complete Western system. The separation of executive, legislative and judicial powers was inappropriate. The future HKSAR system should be an executive-led system.
- Universal suffrage should not take place immediately. Even if warranted, it should be introduced gradually and step-by-step.
- The central authorities in Beijing should monitor the HKSAR but it would not need to interfere directly. The Hong Kong executive organ would intervene. Only if major disturbances broke out would military forces be used.[49]

Deng Xiaoping elaborated that the key to political success was to devise and keep to the right policies and direction and as long as a legislative body stayed on track, it would avoid wrangling and society would prosper.[50]

While Hong Kong appointees were given a role on the drafting body to create the Basic Law, and Hong Kong appointees made up a large consultative committee to provide views, the invisible, and sometimes not so invisible, hand of the CCP was always there to control the outcome. The process for organising the drafting of the Basic Law followed the classic CCP operation method to create the impression and semblance that something had wide support. Referred to as the "two ups, two downs" process, selected Hong Kong people would be involved in initial work on the Basic Law draft, which would be submitted to Beijing, and Beijing would then send it back to Hong Kong for further consultation. More work would then be done and resubmitted to Beijing for promulgation. The method is based on Mao Zedong's idea of "from the masses to the masses", which requires the party to operate by:

> taking the ideas of the masses (scattered and unsystematic ideas) and concentrate them (... turn them into concentrated and systematic ideas), then go to the masses and propagate and explain these ideas until the masses embrace them as their own, hold fast to them and translate them into action.[51]

Basic Law Drafting Committee and Basic Law Consultative Committee

In June 1985, the creation of a Basic Law Drafting Committee (BLDC) was announced in Beijing. As a working group of the NPC, the BLDC was appointed by and reported to the national legislature. It had a total of 59 members, 36 from the Mainland and 23 from Hong Kong. The criteria for appointment were that the Mainland should be those who were familiar with Hong Kong, and some should be legal and constitutional experts, and the Hong Kong members should be patriotic, familiar with the situation of Hong Kong, and have professional knowledge of a particular sector. Xu Jiatun played a key role in deciding who from Hong Kong should be on the BLDC. In terms of selection of the Hong Kong members, it was supposed to reflect a balance of views,[52] so as to "let people with different political inclinations fully reflect the views of the Hong Kong Chinese people".[53] A key purpose was to "balance the opinions and interests of different people, especially for the purpose of realising the Sino-British Joint Declaration, and the spirit of the future Basic Law while following the principle of involving a majority of the people, with the ultimate goal of bringing stability and with stability, prosperity".[54]

However, the key positions on the BLDC were also held by either Chinese officials or people Beijing trusted. The chairman of the BLDC was Ji Pengfei. There were 8 vice-chairmen: Xu Jiatun, Wang Han Bin (secretary general of the NPC), Hu Sheng (director, Party Research Centre of the CCP Central Committee), Fei Xiaotong (one of China's most respected anthropologists and sociologists), T. K. Ann (an industrialist and member of the CPPCC),[55] Pao Yue Kong (a shipping tycoon), Fei Yi Ming (publisher of *Ta Kung Pao*, member of the NPC and member of the Legal Commission under the SCNPC), and David K. P. Li (chairman of the Bank of East Asia). The appointment of Pao and Li as vice-chairmen, together with that of T. K. Ann, showed Beijing's desire to form a political alliance with the capitalists. This deliberate strategy has been described as the "political absorption of economics".[56] Moreover, Ann and Pao represented the Shanghai and Li the Cantonese factions, two important business groups. All of the Hong Kong vice-chairmen were politically conservative, and therefore unlikely to object to Beijing's ideas for Hong Kong's future political arrangements.

In total, there were twelve tycoons among the Hong Kong members. Among the other Hong Kong appointees, besides pro-China figures, it could be seen that their appointments followed the classic united front formula of including a variety of sectors to show the BLDC represented many interests in Hong Kong. Those who represented the then establishment included two UMELCO[57] members (Maria Tam and Wong Po Yan, a prominent businessman) and an Appeal Court Judge (Simon Li). The Chinese side had sounded out the Hong Kong government on their appointments.[58] Other appointees included old faithfuls, such as the elderly Mok Ying Kwai (Chapter 5), the chairman of the Heung Yee Kuk (Lau Wong Fat); the vice-chancellors of two universities; a bishop to represent the religious sector; senior professionals; a left-wing trade unionist (Tam Yiu Chung), and even two liberal voices who had been calling for greater democracy (Martin Lee, a barrister and Szeto Wah, a teacher and head of the Professional Teachers Union). The inclusion of Lee and Szeto was in line with united front practice of offering membership

The Shaping of Post-Colonial Hong Kong   159

to a small number of vocal critics so that they could be controlled through rules of procedures.[59] Lee and Szeto would become two of Hong Kong's most famous politicians after 1989. In 1984, Xu Jiatun even invited Szeto to join the CCP, likely because Szeto had wanted to join the party when he was young. The invitation was declined.[60] Tam Yiu Chung and Lau Wong Fat would also enjoy longevity in Hong Kong politics—as legislators (both until 2016) and both had a stint as executive councillor. Of the thirty-six Mainland BLDC members, fifteen were officials concerned with various aspects of Mainland relations with Hong Kong, and eleven were legal specialists. With the number of Mainland members exceeding the number of Hong Kong members by a safe margin, Beijing had overwhelming numerical superiority on the committee. The members of the BLDC were divided into five sub-groups, each group focussing on one area of discussion.

The BLDC's Secretariat was located in Beijing and made up of the officials who worked directly on Hong Kong affairs. The secretary-general was Li Hou, the deputy director of the Hong Kong and Macao Affairs Office, and the two deputy secretary-generals were Lu Ping and Mao Junnian, a deputy director of CCP Hong Kong. At the request of the Hong Kong and Macao Affairs Office, a special Research Department was set up within Xinhua Hong Kong to gather all the comments, models and recommendations on political systems and political development put forward by people in society. The materials would be considered by CCP Hong Kong, the Research Department would prepare reports for the Hong Kong and Macao Affairs Office and the BLDC. The Research Department's heads were Mao Junnian and Qiao Zhonghuai, both deputy directors of CCP Hong Kong.[61]

At the first meeting of the BLDC on 1 July 1985 in Beijing, a plan was tabled by Ji Pengfei for a Basic Law Consultative Committee (BLCC) to be formed so that more people from Hong Kong could be involved. The more important BLDC was too small in size to accommodate all the prominent people in Hong Kong the united front wanted to cultivate. Twenty-five of the Hong Kong members of the BLDC formed a Sponsors' Committee to work on setting up the BLCC. The five BLDC vice-chairmen residing in Hong Kong, which included Xu Jiatun, were asked to take up the preparatory work for setting up the BLCC. Xinhua Hong Kong provided the necessary assistance. The Hong Kong BLDC members drafted the constitution of the BLCC, which would have one hundred and eighty members. Three of the tycoons on the committee provided the necessary funds to cover costs. The secretary of the BLCC was Mao Junnian, and T. K. Ann was the chairman. Mao was later replaced by Leung Chun Ying, a surveyor and obviously a young man who would go places in the future. The BLCC membership would be like a Who's Who list of VIPs in Hong Kong at the time with a handful of social activists.

Xu Jiatun had wanted to include senior British appointees to the Executive and Legislative Councils in the BLCC. Chung Sze Yuen, the most senior member of the Executive Council, and his counterpart in the Legislative Council, Lydia Dunn, were both approached since Xu had been cultivating relationship with them for some time. They both turned down the invitation. Chung noted that: "Dunn and I agreed that since we were both senior advisors to the Hong Kong governor and were privy to sensitive documents, including papers pertaining to Sino-British relations, we might diminish our roles were we to join the BLCC . . . If there were any leak of classified information one day . . . the blame for that would rest with us and affect our public standing."[62]

Table 3 BLCC Sectors Breakdown[63]

Sector	Sub-sectors	No. of BLCC Members
Industry & Commerce	Commerce, Industry, Tourism, Transportation	38
Finance and Real Estate	Banking, Insurance, Securities; Construction, Real Estate Development	18
Professionals	Accountants, Architects, Engineers, Lawyers & Judges, Planners, Surveyors	19
Media	Print, Radio, Television	12
Grassroots	Academics, Agriculture, Arts & Culture, City Management, Civil Servants, Community Groups, Education, Labour, Medical, Politics, Science & Technology, and Social Services	78
Religious	Leaders of six religions	6
BLDC Members	BLDC	5
Foreign Nationals		3
Others	Overseas Chinese	1
TOTAL		180

Xu Jiatun and the party machinery controlled membership to the BLCC although there were supposedly three ways for the selection of its members: certain associations and groups could recommend their people to be appointed; BLDC members could appoint members; and individuals and groups could apply to be considered. The final body that emerged had people from nine major sectors of interests. Most of them were identified by the BLDC as "representative organisations" in those sectors that took on a similar ring to that of the functional constituencies created for the 1985 Legislative Council election. For such a large body, it was important to include a number of social activists who were calling for a faster pace of democratic reform—such as Lee Wing Tat and Frederick Fung, who would both have long careers as legislators—but their voices could easily be overwhelmed by the majority, who were much more conservative.

The BLCC came to life on 18 December 1985 and immediately got mired in controversies. Firstly, it came to light that a liberal-minded unionist, Lau Chin Shek of the Christian Industrial Committee, was initially nominated by a labour joint conference to stand for selection among labour representatives to the BLCC. But Xu Jiatun essentially rejected Lau on the ground that "quite a few businessmen in Hong Kong resented him" and that including Lau would make him more famous.[64] This meant Lau would not have the FTU's support. He realised he would not win and decided to pull out of the election instead, which prompted independent unions to withdraw from the process as well. This incident illustrated how ill-prepared Xu was to accept someone the business elites did not like, with the result that the CCP's failed to co-opt the working class into the process.[65] Secondly, the hidden hand of the CCP was revealed over the selection of key BLCC positions. The BLCC constitution provided for seven officers to be elected from a nineteen-member executive committee, who were in turn to be elected by members. In effect, BLDC members Xu Jiatun and David Li had already selected who the seven officers should be. At the election of the BLCC executive committee, BLDC member, Pao Yue Kong, showed up to chair the meeting although he had no authority to do so not being a BLCC member. Pao ignored procedures and proceeded to read out a list of nineteen names and then directed the gathered members to elect them with a round of applause. This kind of arrangement was commonplace on the Mainland but not in Hong Kong and led to complaints. Whilst another meeting was called to rectify the violation of procedures, the same nineteen members were chosen. The seven officers were likewise also "elected".[66]

A new organisation became the dominant group within the BLCC. The business and professional elites of the BLDC and the BLCC, led by Vincent Lo, formed the Business and Professional Group of the Basic Law Consultative Committee. The group came into existence initially in April 1986 with 57 members and later added another two members, and became known as The Group of 89. Subsequently, another group—the Group of 19—sprung to life. It was made up of more liberal-minded community representatives, social workers and professionals in the BLCC but this group, being small by comparison and without the resources that the business elites commanded, never enjoyed the influence that the Group of 89 had.[67]

A full membership list of the BLDC and BLCC is available in Appendix III and the Biographies provide more information on BLDC and BLCC members.

"Election": What It Did Not Mean

During much of the Sino-British negotiations, democracy was not a key issue. Preservation of the existing systems and way of life in Hong Kong was the priority, and that socialism would not be practised. Thus, it was important to ensure the HKSAR would be invested with executive, legislative and independent judicial power, that the laws then in force would remain basically unchanged, the government would be composed of Hong Kong inhabitants and not sent from the Mainland, and rights and freedoms would be protected. It was the preservation of the existing systems that China signed up to for the post-1997 regime. The tycoons and businessmen did not push for democracy, nor did members of the Executive and Legislative Councils insist on a fully representative system of government for the future. The voices from the community calling for democracy did not have to be taken too seriously into account. It was only after Britain made clear that there would be no continued British presence in Hong Kong beyond the Handover that the issue of democracy came to the fore. The British government expressed to the Chinese that a commitment to democratic reform was crucial in securing parliamentary support for the eventual settlement. The British felt that a promise that Hong Kong could look forward to democratic development would to a large extent fulfil their moral obligation to the people of the territory. Margaret Thatcher's personal insistence on an elected legislature was crucial to prod the negotiations in that direction, since election was initially ignored by British and Hong Kong officials. The point they made to get Beijing to go along with it was that, while the Joint Declaration had already been initialled and then signed, it still had to be ratified by Parliament before it could come into effect.

Despite the importance of the subject to the six million people of Hong Kong, the parliamentary debate in the House of Commons on 5 December 1984 was poorly attended. An observer noted that only eight percent of the Members of Parliament bothered to show up and "even a good few of the forty-one MPs who had enjoyed trips to Hong Kong paid for by the Hong Kong Government saw no reason to return the courtesy".[68] On 11 December, the House of Lords debated the Hong Kong question. It was a better-attended affair than the insultingly sparse attendance at the House of Commons. Nevertheless, it was clear from the parliamentary debates that there was an understanding among the parliamentarians that introducing representative government in Hong Kong was part of the arrangements. Richard Luce, the minister of state in the Foreign and Commonwealth Office (1983–1985), told that House of Commons that Britain would "build up a firmly based, democratic administration in Hong Kong in the years between now and 1997". Baroness Janet Young, the minister of state, Foreign and Commonwealth Office (1983–1987), in the House of Lords, also stated on behalf of the British government that the planned democratic reform in Hong Kong was "entirely consistently with the provisions in the draft agreement which specified that the Legislature of the Hong Kong SAR shall be constituted by elections".[69]

The insertion of the phrase "constituted by elections" to describe the future Hong Kong legislature was one of the very last points that was agreed between Britain and China. A mere seven days before the draft Joint Declaration was submitted to both governments for approval, the British raised the question of Hong Kong internal governance and managed to insert in the post-1997 Legislative Council that it "shall be constituted by elections" and that the "executive authorities shall be accountable to the legislature".[70] However, details would be a matter for China to sort out in the Basic Law.

As to what "election" meant, it was understood by the British negotiators that it need not mean multiparty election by universal suffrage. The British accepted that "elections" might include indirect elections and election through a restricted franchise.[71] To the Chinese, "election" definitely did not mean universal suffrage. Elections for CCP bodies are selections where the candidates are pre-selected or approved by the party hierarchy in numbers equal or almost equal to the posts available. Since all the candidates are acceptable to the party an election could then take place. The favoured method of selection under the communist system is in fact "consultation", which in practice is the exercise of the party's discretion to choose whom it thinks fit. The Sino-British Joint Declaration is a bicultural document whose words reflect the values, meanings and understandings of two very different political and legal systems.[72] The first "election" of the executive committee of the BLCC noted above provided an example of the gulf of difference between the Mainland understanding of election and that understood in Hong Kong.

Green and White Papers

During the Sino-British negotiations, the Hong Kong government issued a Green Paper in July 1984 on representative government, which called for two months of public consultation on political reform "to develop progressively a system of government the authority of which is firmly rooted in Hong Kong, which is able to represent the view of the people of Hong Kong, and which is more directly accountable to the people of Hong Kong".[73] As it was published before China had agreed to the phrase "constituted by elections" to the post-Handover agreement, the paper was strong on principles and weak on details. When the White Paper was published in November, after agreement with China had been secured, more could be put forward. The plan was to restructure the Legislative Council through the creation of 12 seats for functional constituencies representing specific commercial and professional interests, and another 12 seats to be returned by an electoral college made up of local public bodies. The electoral college would become the Election Committee provided by the Basic Law, and the selection methods of that body would be functional in nature. In other words, functional elections underpinned much of the new electoral system.

Before functional constituencies were introduced in Hong Kong, the colonial government appointed people from various business and professional sectors to sit as unofficial members to the Legislative Council. It was thought that these people were capable of reflecting the views of the Hong Kong community and could contribute their "specialist knowledge and value expertise" to the legislature. The functional constituencies evolved this practice into a formal one using elected representatives, and the Basic Law would entrench this in the post-1997 political system.[74]

As for direct election, the Hong Kong government undertook to conduct a review in 1987 because:

There was little evidence of support in public comment on the Green Paper for any move towards direct election in 1985. With few exceptions the bulk of the public response from all sources suggested a cautious approach with a gradual start by introducing a very small number of directly elected members in 1988 and building up to a significant number of directly elected members by 1997.[75]

The CCP watched the events relating to the Green and White Papers closely and pondered what they meant. Their conclusion was the British wanted to establish a representative government in a bid to return the administration to the people of Hong Kong instead of to China, and to shift the Executive Council's policy-making power to the Legislative Council, which was a fundamental change to the colony's government structure—and, contrary to Deng Xiaoping's drafting instructions for the Basic Law. In other words, Britain was attempting to make many changes in the next 13 years of British rule that would make governing difficult for the HKSAR government in the future. In the eyes of Chinese officials, the devious British were about to launch a "democracy card" to spoil things for China. It would divide Hong Kong opinion and nurture pro-British elements so that post-1997 Hong Kong would be ruled by British agents without the direct presence of the British. In order to stop the British from moving ahead further, in October 1985, Ji Pengfei called upon the British to alter the Hong Kong political system prior to 1997 only in ways that "converged" with the Basic Law. The need for convergence was elevated to a principle by Xu Jiatun a month later. According to Xu, Deng Xiaoping said to him that, if nothing was done in time, the British would have pushed ahead with the plan and Hong Kong "would be in chaos".[76]

The British would give in. By reaching an understanding with Beijing, the British would ensure there would be no major political reform until the Basic Law was promulgated in 1990, and in return, Beijing would allow the Legislative Council formed in 1995 to straddle the transition to 1999 if the method of its formation conformed to the Basic Law. This understanding was referred to as the "through train" arrangement.[77]

Even though the British agreed to the principle of convergence in exchange for the through train, Xu Jiatun thought the British had played a "master stroke" by putting forth ideas of representative government because it had the effect of deepening "division and turmoil" in society. The middle class and grassroots were mobilising to take part in democratic politics. Their calls for democracy upset people in the capitalist class—whether Chinese or foreign, who were unready to participate in "the game of politics" and they also feared the "free lunch" and "high taxation" phenomena arising as democracy developed in Hong Kong. As Xu recounted, some of the capitalists and people in the upper strata of society thought they could rely on China to resist Hong Kong's democratic trend. If the trend could not be resisted, then it was important to slow the pace down. Xu had attempted to use the Hong Kong and Macao International Investment Company to bring together most of the capitalists so that they could consider getting involved in competitive politics, but there was no common wish to cooperate and the competitiveness among them within the BLDC and BLCC over the future political system was "fierce", as could be seen from the various proposals emanating from groups of members within those bodies.[78]

A former Xinhua Hong Kong deputy director, Huang Wenfang, thought Xu Jiatun was extremely conservative over the democratic process in Hong Kong. During the drafting of the Basic Law, Xu strongly opposed that idea that the number of directly elected seats in the legislature should exceed half. Xu feared that "one man, one vote" would make Beijing lose control of the situation in Hong Kong.[79] As the top cadre in Hong Kong, Xu's view on democracy had significant influence on Beijing, but whatever might have been his personal preference, he was most likely just following Deng Xiaoping's broad instructions closely. Deng had clearly been worried that democracy would bring chaos.

On 26 September 1985, the Hong Kong Legislative Council saw its first indirect elections when twelve functional constituency seats were elected. The barrister, Martin Lee, was elected to represent the Legal Functional Constituency, launching one of Hong Kong's most important political careers in the run-up to 1997. The Hong Kong government conducted another review in 1987 to assess whether an element of direct election should be introduced to the Legislative Council in 1988. The Green Paper published in May 1987 remains famous today for its design. It aimed to dampen earlier hopes that a number of directly elected seats would be introduced in the following year. The Hong Kong government set up a Survey Office to collect and collate public responses over a four-month period. The questions, options and sub-options put to Hong Kong people were confusing, leading to allegations that they were framed to obfuscate. The questionnaire was constructed in such a way that it was possible to say you were against direct election, but not possible to say unequivocally that you were in favour of them. The public was simply not given a clear choice for direct election in 1988.

Notably, in September 1987, the Group of 89 proposed that the future Chief Executive should be selected by an electoral college of 600 people made up mostly of business and professional circles. Their proposal also provided that, from 1992, the legislature should be expanded to 80 members with 25 members chosen by the electoral college, 25 members by functional constituencies, and 40 members by direct election.[80] The Group of 19 proposed that the HKSAR Chief Executive should be nominated by the Legislative Council and elected by universal suffrage. As for election to the Legislative Council, this group proposed that a quarter of the members should be returned by an electoral college, a quarter by functional constituencies and half by direct election.[81] These two groups represented the two ends of the spectrum within the BLCC.

The CCP Hong Kong mobilised left-wing organisations to express opposition to the introduction of direct election to ensure there would be many opposition voices. Organisations representing the capitalists' interests also submitted views to oppose implementing elections too quickly. Thus, the FTU and its 77 affiliated bodies, the Chinese General Chamber of Commerce and its 80-plus affiliated bodies were among those which got their networks to respond. The FTU asserted that "eating is more important than voting". Chinese enterprises also organised signature campaigns among their employees. It was also reported that the Bank of China arranged for its employees to watch a video, narrated by Ma Lik (who was then the vice-secretary general of the BLCC), explaining why the introduction of direct elections was a British conspiracy. Ma Lik would become a member of the Legislative Council. The Bank of China also prepared a printed pro-forma opposing letter for its employees to sign and send to the Survey Office.[82] The pro-democracy camp likewise organised people to sign petitions through street campaigns.

The Survey Office released its findings in October 1987. The Survey Office did not distinguish between pre-printed forms used for submissions and individual submissions. This had the effect of over-representing those opposed to direct elections. Of 60,706 submissions against direct elections in 1988, 50,175 came from pre-printed forms and 22,722 of them were from united front organisations. Of the 35,129 submissions that favoured direct elections, only 1,313 were on pre-printed forms. Moreover, 220,000 signatures with names and identity card numbers were excluded from the table altogether. If these had been on pre-printed forms, they would have been counted and there was no logic to exclude them except to manipulate a result the government wanted.[83]

The Hong Kong government concluded that there was overwhelming support for the introduction of direct elections to the Legislative Council, but not in 1988. Governor David Wilson (1987–1992) recalled events thus:

> it was convenient for us [the British], in terms of handling the transition with China, that we did not have ... overwhelming pressure from people in Hong Kong to move straight away into direct elections because we knew that doing that would be very difficult for the Chinese to accept.[84]

There were in fact many non-government surveys conducted during that time showing there was majority support in Hong Kong for direct elections to be introduced in 1988. A poll conducted by Survey Research Hong Kong in July 1987 showed 54 percent in favour of direction election in 1988, with 16 percent opposed, 22 percent unsure and 8 percent with no opinion. Another telephone survey conducted by Market Decision Research in August found 41 percent wanted to see some element of direct election in 1988, 20 percent wanted more indirectly elected members, 15 percent wanted no change and 24 percent had no opinion.[85]

Before releasing the White Paper in February 1988, David Wilson visited Beijing in December 1987 to exchange views with the Chinese on political developments in Hong Kong. It was believed that he and Chinese officials reached an understanding as to the pace of the democratisation process in Hong Kong.[86] When the White Paper was released afterwards, it stated that there would be 10 directly elected members to be introduced to the 56-seat Legislative Council in 1991, which the Chinese had already announced they would allow. In other words, there would be no direct election in 1988.[87]

Despite the slowing down of the timetable for direct election to be introduced in Hong Kong, the fact that it would happen meant the formation of political parties was inevitable. Up until 1986, Beijing was not in favour of party formation in Hong Kong. Li Hou even threatened that the CCP would participate in Hong Kong if party politics emerged.[88] However, from 1987 onwards, Beijing stopped publicly opposing the formation of political parties, which signalled the CCP had formed a new policy to deal with the onslaught of elections.

In April 1988, the BLDC released the first draft of the Basic Law for a five months' consultation. There were many criticisms of the draft.[89] On the issue of election to the Chief Executive and legislature, since there was no consensus among the drafters, various options were included as possible choices, including those of the Group of 89 and Group of 19 noted above. The formula proposed by the latter was the most democratic. T. S. Lo proposed splitting the legislature to create a bicameral system with the functional constituency members sitting in a second chamber (Chapter 9).

Looking at how the BLDC functioned, it was clear that the Mainland drafters' key concerns had to do with ensuring the Basic Law reflected the full recognition of Chinese sovereignty, and having adequate mechanisms provided so that the Central People's Government could exercise control where necessary. For the Mainland, having sovereignty meant having control, and the levers of control must be built into the future constitution. The Hong Kong drafters had mixed and divided interests. Some were willing to go with whatever was the Mainland position, while others wanted to protect their economic interests through emphasising specific business sectors and ensuring their representation would be entrenched. The issue of the distribution of power after 1997 was thus the key issue. There was a strong belief among a significant contingent of the Hong Kong BLDC and BLCC members that prosperity and stability could only be ensured if power was retained in the hands of the economic and political elites. In the 1980s, the political elites were the top civil servants and their appointees to the Executive and Legislative Councils and to the most important government consultative bodies. A large number of these appointees were members of the economic elite, who together formed the club that supposedly ran Hong Kong so successfully. In other words, the majority of the BLDC and BLCC members believed that the post-reunification institutional framework should be based on the past distribution of power under colonial rule. The draft Basic Law provoked a substantial public response with approximately 73,000 submissions.

In November 1988, BLDC member and co-convenor of the working group on political development, Louis Cha, put forward a political model that he thought could be a compromise model. He did not try to resolve the differences embodied in the various models over the pace and direction of democratisation. Instead, he tried to find a way that he thought could sustain Hong Kong's way of life and could also be acceptable to Beijing. He called this compromise model the Mainstream Model. Cha's idea was for directly elected members to be returned for 27 percent of the seats for the first term in 1997 to 1999, increasing to 50 percent by the third and fourth terms (2003 to 2007 and 2007 to 2011). A referendum might be held in 2011 to decide whether the Chief Executive and the Legislative Council should be elected by universal suffrage. This was the model that gained Beijing's backing and was approved by the BLDC. The BLDC also endorsed an amendment raised by Hong Kong businessman Cha Chi Min, who promoted that the referendum would only be held if it were approved by the Chief Executive, two-thirds majority of the legislators, and the SCNPC; and the result of the referendum would be valid only if it had the support of 30 percent of registered voters. The Mainstream Model and the amendment became known as the Cha-Cha Model.[90] They generated widespread criticism in Hong Kong. The gulf of difference between Beijing's concerns and Hong Kong's aspirations were too wide and confidence in Hong Kong was beginning to wane.[91] Unbeknown to anyone at the time, the most severe blow to confidence was yet to come in a few months.

Tiananmen: 15 April to 4 June 1989

China faced many challenges in promoting economic reforms at breakneck speed. Dissatisfaction arising from economic liberalisation that led to inflation, lay-offs at state-owned enterprises and official corruption created widespread grievances. China's intellectuals began to call for relaxation of social and political controls, as was happening under Mikhail Gorbachev's policy of *glasnost* in the Soviet Union.[92] The mix of pressures in China developed into a massive eruption of discontent in 1989.

Tiananmen Square is a large open space in the centre of Beijing, just south of the Forbidden City, flanked by the Great Hall of the People on one side and the Museum of Revolutionary History on the other side. There are also the monument to the martyrs of the Revolution and the Mao Zedong Memorial Hall in the vicinity. It has been the most potent political site in the Chinese history of the twentieth century. This was where emperors used to live, where students protested during the May Fourth Movement in 1919, where the CCP announced that it assumed power in 1949, and where Mao Zedong watched as throngs of Red Guards gathered at the start of the Cultural Revolution.

The Square came alive unexpectedly in 1989 on 15 April with the death of Hu Yaobang from heart attack. He was looked upon favourably by the people for overseeing the rehabilitation of thousands of those persecuted during the Anti-Rightist campaign and the Cultural Revolution. He was seen by the people as having encouraged significant political reform, including refusing to take a tough line against a period of student protests in 1986, for which he was made to resign as CCP general secretary (1980–1987) and make a self-criticism. Hu's time was remembered as a period of experiment and liberalism. Upon hearing his death, large numbers of people, including many students, appeared at Tiananmen Square spontaneous to commemorate the former leader. More people showed up still on the succeeding days. Their mourning turned into protests and demands for greater democracy and less corruption. The protests spread to other big cities and for the next seven weeks, the people's expressions of grievances touched almost every corner of China, with Hong Kong and the rest of the world watching with bated breath. What will happen?

On 22 April 1989, the Chinese government held an official ceremony to commemorate Hu Yaobang. Over 100,000 students assembled in Tiananmen Square. The students demanded a dialogue with the government, and after their demand was rejected, they started to boycott classes. On 26 April, the government used an editorial in the *People's Daily* to denounce the protests as a form of "turmoil" attempting to "fundamentally refute the leadership of the CCP and the socialist system". The editorial aroused a strong reaction from the people. On the following day, more than a million people demonstrated on the streets of Beijing. A meeting between party leaders and students on 29 April went badly, after which the students decided to organise a hunger strike on 13 May. The students received enormous support from Beijing residents, people from other Mainland cities, Hong Kong, as well as from overseas. On 18 May 1989, Premier Li Peng met the student leaders in the Great Hall of the People. He refused to acknowledge the protests were patriotic acts and not turmoil. On 20 May, Li Peng announced the imposition of martial law in Beijing.[93] Troops were sent and by 4 June, and the government claimed to have put down a "counter-revolutionary rebellion".

The dramatic and heart-breaking events of 4 June 1989 affected not only the Mainland but also touched the lives of the people of Hong Kong. Shortly after the protests started in April 1989, Hong Kong people from all walks of life started all kinds of activities to express their support for the students in Beijing. There were countless gatherings, signature campaigns, petitions and collection of donations for the students. The Members of the Executive and Legislative Councils too were swept up in the moment in May 1989. They agreed on a model for political reform that provided for direct elections for half of the seats in the Legislative Council by 1997 and all the seats by 2003, and for the Chief Executive of future HKSAR to be directly elected no later than 2003. The so-called OMELCO Consensus Model received widespread backing in Hong Kong but it would be rejected by the BLDC (Chapter 9).[94]

On the night of 20 May 1989, thousands assembled at Victoria Park in a strong tropical storm to protest the Chinese government's imposing martial law in Beijing. The next day over a million people marched to support the student movement. Despite the large numbers, it was a peaceful and solemn event. People from all backgrounds, including those from the left joined the march. A group of civil society activists formed the Hong Kong Alliance in Support of Patriotic Democratic Movements of China. People at Xinhua Hong Kong and Mainland-funded organisations also threw themselves into the marches on their own initiative. There was even a signature drive at Xinhua. After the imposition of martial law, the pro-Beijing *Wen Wei Po* in Hong Kong issued an editorial featuring only the phrase in large characters—"Deep Sorrow".[95]

Xu Jiatun, speaking in July 2007 remembered events thus:

> The patriotic feelings of Hong Kong people reached a climax during the Tiananmen Square protest. Except for a small number of people who opposed the Communist Party, the overwhelming majority were patriotic. They wanted to see progress in their country. Pro-Beijing groups were under enormous pressure from their own members to support the students. I decided they could participate in the June 4–related protests under certain conditions. They should not make public speeches, call for the downfall of leaders and chant inappropriate slogans. At one point, some Chinese-funded enterprises expressed the wish to hold commemorative services on their premises for June 4 victims. I decided we should not stop their staff from doing so if they acted on their own, but senior executives should not take part.[96]

The crackdown on 4 June 1989 changed Hong Kong, changed how Beijing looked at Hong Kong, changed Britain's attitude, and marked a turning point in Hong Kong people's political consciousness.

> People from all walks of life in Hong Kong were jittery about 1997. They were quick to associate the 4 June crackdown with their fate after 1997, and more and more people were keen to take part in the marches. The slogan "Today's Beijing will be Tomorrow's Hong Kong" expressed their frame of mind at a time when 1997 was drawing nearer.
>
> Xu Jiatun, 1993[97]

9
Passage to Reunification
From 1990 to 1997

The Chinese Communist Party wanted to ensure that the future Hong Kong Special Administrative Region government would be able to function without interference from subversive or unfriendly forces and for Beijing to be able to exert control should it be necessary. This outcome could only be assured if post-1997 power remains in the hands of patriots. A structure designed for control had to be put in place during the final years of colonial rule. The people who would work the system also had to be made ready. Once these were bolted down, Beijing could feel comfortable enough not to be seen to intervene after the transfer of sovereignty. The CCP referred to this as the *zhuada* concept (hold a firm grip on major things), and once this had been secured, it could tolerate minor things (*fangxiao*),[1] such as a few opposition legislators.

The final few years before reunification required the CCP to anticipate and deal with potential British "treachery". The threat to a smooth transition was the new British push for greater democracy after the events of Tiananmen. It was what the British needed to do to be able to leave Hong Kong with honour in the eyes of international opinion. There would be many conflicts between the British and the Chinese as they tried to achieve their respective goals. Although the CCP was ready to counter British efforts, the party could not have anticipated that it would have to deal with a new governor quite different from any of his predecessors. Beijing reserved the harshest criticisms for him.

Breaking off relations was not an appealing or workable option for either side because they needed each other to make the moment of the Reunification (for the Chinese) and the Handover (for the British) a confident affair. Although at one time, the Chinese had thought momentarily that the British and Chinese could each have their own ceremonies and it would be obvious to the world which one was more important.[2] Whatever the Chinese thought of the British, one country, two systems could not be allowed to fail since it was for China to implement and realise. The eyes of the world would be on Hong Kong. Macao would come back to the fold in 1999, and there was still the big prize of reunification with Taiwan in the future.

The CCP knew it needed to strengthen the post-1997 establishment that would serve the HKSAR, including producing the first HKSAR chief executive and appointing suitable members of the first Executive Council. To be on the safe side, the party also started to create a fifth column of Mainland foot soldiers in Hong Kong to protect Beijing's interests, especially during election time.

Post-Tiananmen Doubts

The Hong Kong community was devastated and drastically transformed by 4 June. The events were:

> so dramatic that it drew around the clock coverage by Hong Kong mass media, so emotional that it ignited the nationalistic feeling of many Hong Kong Chinese, so appealing that it rekindled the democratic aspiration of the local populace, and so tragic that it made most of the Hong Kong people moan, weep, and thunder.[3]

The CCP saw things quite differently, as was made clear by Ji Pengfei on 22 June:

> The counter-revolutionary riot in Beijing started out first as a student movement and later as turmoil. During this time Hong Kong compatriots expressed their different viewpoints in various manner. Some Hong Kong people went to the mainland and were involved in activities prohibited by the state constitution and law; in effect they provoked more riots. [Hong Kong should not] interfere or attempt to change the socialist system on the mainland. Nor should they allow some people to use Hong Kong as a base to subvert the people's government.[4]

In the aftermath of 4 June 1989, Beijing had many challenges, one of which was the struggle for political authority to succeed the aging leadership led by Deng Xiaoping. Holding tightly onto power at the party centre was essential to riding through the storm. The issue of a smooth transition for Hong Kong to Chinese rule became embroiled in that struggle. Toughness had to be displayed, as softness might have given the British and the Western powers the mistaken impression that CCP rule was vulnerable. Thus, those who showed sympathy to the demonstrators had to be purged, the most senior of whom was Zhao Ziyang, the general secretary of the CCP. He was expelled from the Standing Committee of the Politburo and put under house arrest for the rest of his life until his death in January 2005.[5] With Deng Xiaoping's blessing, Jiang Zemin, the then party secretary of Shanghai and a Politburo member, replaced Zhao, and eventually assumed the posts of the general secretary of the CCP, chairman of the Central Military Commission and president of the People's Republic of China. Jiang would stay in power as China's top leader until 2002.

Beyond the succession challenge and economic sanctions from the West imposed after 1989, Beijing had to deal with its pariah status in the world, the implications of the disintegration of the Soviet Union, as well as the collapse of communist regimes in Eastern Europe. In assessing world affairs, the CCP adopted a cautious and watchful outlook on foreign relations.[6] An early remedial effort by the CCP to mend its reputation was to use every attraction and sweetener to invite international guests and businessmen to visit Beijing in order to give the new leadership the appearance of acceptance. This was particularly important for Li Peng, who more than anyone else was seen to have been most associated with the implementation of the crackdown.[7]

Invitations were extended to Hong Kong business people to visit Beijing and meet top leaders. T. S. Lo was a most willing traveller there. He met Li Peng, which made him a man to note back in Hong Kong, as he might be heading for greater prominence since a post-1997 leader had to be identified and made ready to assume power.[8]

Crisis of Confidence

Hong Kong's despondency could be seen from the nervousness of even the tycoons and taipans.[9] Xu Jiatun disclosed an interesting twist to the post-Tiananmen saga. In a move to stave off control of Hong Kong by China in 1997, a group of Hong Kong's richest businessmen led by Helmut Sohmen, the Austrian son-in-law of shipping magnate Pao Yue Kong, tried to set up a plan to pay Beijing HK$10 billion to lease the territory for ten years from 1997 and for it to practise self-rule. Xu thought they were naïve and told them that there was a slim chance that the idea would be acceptable to the Chinese leadership, but he would pass it on nevertheless, but they had better not publicise it. After Jiang Zemin had become the general party secretary in June 1989, he interviewed Xu and supposedly asked Xu to send a report to him and Deng Xiaoping elaborating on the tycoons' idea. Jiang would eventually turn the proposal down. Lu Ping and Zhou Nan criticised Xu for sending the report, describing it as a move on Xu's part to seek power and wealth by selling the country.[10]

Xu must have faced a horrendous grilling by party officials for not having controlled the situation in Hong Kong. For example, the *Wen Wei Po* wrote unhelpful editorials. Long-time left-wing supporters, such as unionists Cheng Yiu Tong and Tam Yiu Chung, participated in marches. Worse, employees of Xinhua Hong Kong published a letter calling for Li Peng to step down.[11] For Xu, the head of the CCP in Hong Kong, to have allowed such acts was unforgivable.

Beijing was concerned that Hong Kong people might become difficult to deal with. Some of the Hong Kong BLDC members petitioned Beijing for a delay in the resumption of sovereignty and for the British to continue in administration. This was regarded as a top secret according to Lu Ping. Obviously, if the petition became public, it could gather steam and would put enormous pressure on Beijing. Lu sought the view of Jiang Zemin, who response was: "It is nothing. Stand firm. Don't let it happen."[12] On 11 July 1989, when Jiang Zemin met the leading figures of the BLDC and the BLCC, he used the opportunity to issue a warning to Hong Kong people—they should not interfere with Mainland politics—"the well water should not interfere with the river water".

Xu Jiatun knew that he did not have the trust of Jiang Zemin and Li Peng, as he had with Zhao Ziyang. Indeed, a reason he did not have the new leaders' trust was that he was considered too close to the deposed Zhao. According to former Xinhua deputy director, Huang Wenfang, Jiang and Li had taken over the handling of Hong Kong matters at the CPP Central Committee level with the help of Qian Qichen, who was foreign minister from 1988 to 1998. Matters of importance relating to the colony were first reported to Qian, and then Jiang and Li would be asked for their advice. The two top leaders divided Hong Kong work between them: Li handled most of the issues concerning government departments, while Jiang handled party affairs and decisions concerning overall decisions.[13]

Xu realised that his days in Hong Kong were numbered. Indeed, he was seen by Li Peng as part of the Zhao Ziyang faction—a definite disadvantage for Xu Jiatun in those difficult days following the Tiananmen crackdown.[14] In order to minimise the fallout, he asked that he be allowed to retire. On 15 January 1990, Beijing announced that Zhou Nan would replace Xu as the new director of Xinhua Hong Kong. Xu remembered events thus:

> [After retirement] I had intended to stay in Shenzhen. When it was made clear to me that Zhou had set up a special team to investigate me, I woke up to the real purpose of Mr Zhou's appointment. He was going to make me the whipping boy. I therefore decided to leave [China]. I called a friend in Hong Kong to come to see me in Shenzhen. I asked him to apply for a US visa for me in Hong Kong. The then US consul-general wondered whether it was true. It took a few days for them to issue a visa for me. I came to Hong Kong from Shenzhen by car and went to the airport. When I arrived, the Hong Kong government had made special arrangements for me to board the flight.[15]

Xu believed that he was facing an imminent purge and fled to the United States with three family members in May 1990. He passed away in Los Angeles in 2016. Beijing considered Xu's defection as traitorous because his escape was seen to have been assisted by Western forces to which Xu was prepared to disclose state secrets.[16] In March 1991, he was stripped of his party membership for "deserting the people". There must have been bad blood between Xu and his three colleagues—Lu Ping, Li Hou, and Zhou Nan. While he accused them of deceiving Beijing into thinking that Hong Kong people welcomed the reunification,[17] they saw Xu as disloyal. Xu Jiatun and Zhou Nan would continue to spar verbally even in 2007, when they reflected on the past. Zhou accused Xu of defecting to the United States with his mistress. Xu countered that the party had never been able to prove what he did wrong.[18]

Zhou Nan arrived in Hong Kong in February 1990 to take up the post of director at Xinhua Hong Kong. He was a vice minister at the Ministry of Foreign Affairs and had led the Chinese team in the reunification negotiations. The status of CCP Hong Kong was changed—it no longer carried provincial level status as it did under Xu's leadership. Unlike during Xu's tenure, when Deng Xiaoping and Zhao Ziyang were willing to decentralise power to CCP Hong Kong, Jiang Zemin's priority was to recentralise authority.

Some saw the power of initiating and formulating policy on Hong Kong going to the State Council's Hong Kong and Macao Affairs Office.[19] However, in 1994 Huang Wenfang made a point of clarifying the flow of authority, two years after he retired from Xinhua Hong Kong. He stressed that Xinhua Hong Kong and the Hong Kong and Macao Affairs Office were of equal status, both at ministerial level and that neither had leadership over the other. Xinhua was a top-level overseas post of the CCP, while the Hong Kong and Macao Affairs Office was a government office of the State Council handling Hong Kong and Macao work. Huang explained that a top-level party post meant that firstly, Xinhua Hong Kong was set up and controlled by the party; secondly, it represented and was responsible for the party's work that fell within its scope; and finally, it was the CCP's top organ in Hong Kong. When there was an important decision to be made about Hong Kong policy, CCP Hong Kong and the Hong Kong and Macao Affairs Office would meet and discuss it. If the issue concerned Sino-British relations, someone from the Ministry of Foreign Affairs would also join the discussion. If it concerned some other issue, such as an economic matter, then people from the relevant departments would join. Huang felt it was necessary to make this clarification because the media often referred to the Mainland's work relating to Hong Kong as a "three horse carriage" linking Xinhua Hong Kong, the Hong Kong and Macao Affairs Office, and the Hong Kong and Macao desk at the Ministry of Foreign Affairs. He also wanted to clarify that leadership over important decisions related to Hong Kong were made by top party leaders—Jiang Zemin, Li Peng, and Qian Qichen—not the Hong Kong and Macao Affairs Office at the State Council or the Ministry of Foreign Affairs.[20]

There was one issue however on which Zhou Nan followed in the footsteps of Xu Jiatun, that was to significantly expand the workforce within Xinhua Hong Kong. In 1983, shortly after Xu arrived in Hong Kong to take up his post, he had wanted to increase the number of staff to about 600. By the time he left, the size had increased from about 150 people to 400 people. During Zhou Nan's time by 1997, the workforce grew to 600 people.[21] (See Figure 6.) However, between 1990 when Zhou first took over Xinhua Hong Kong and August 1992, 180 middle- and low-ranking staff members were transferred back to the Mainland chiefly because of their participation in Tiananmen-related protests and parades in Hong Kong.[22]

Compromise on Political Reform

As a result of the massive crisis of confidence in Hong Kong as the events of 1989 unfolded, there was strong public sentiment that a faster pace of democratic reform was essential to guarantee the autonomy of the future political system. Even prior to the crackdown on 4 June,[23] there was an ongoing debate within the BLDC, the BLCC and Hong Kong society about the design of the future political structure. As

Figure 6 Xinhua Organisation under Zhou Nan[24]

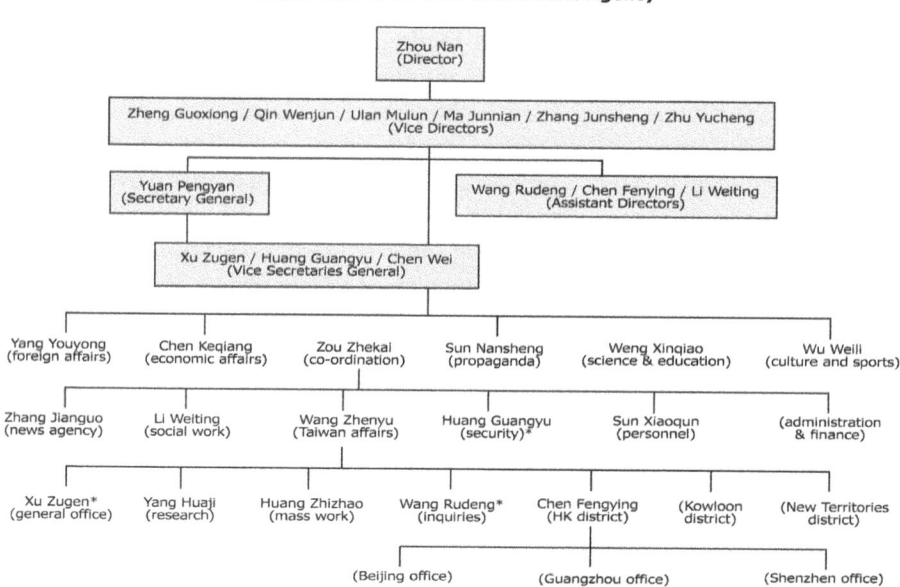

noted in Chapter 8, the OMELCO Consensus model, proposed in May 1989 by the members of the Executive and Legislative Councils, though popular in Hong Kong, was unacceptable to Beijing. The Group of 89 and the more liberal members within the BLCC proposed the new "4-4-2 model" that they thought was "pro–Hong Kong" and might be more acceptable to Beijing.

They also worked with the liberal wing among Hong Kong's opinion leaders at the time so that there could be wider agreement on what the future political model should be. This scheme provided for 40 percent of the seats in the Legislative Council to be directly elected, and the rest would be divided between functional constituencies (40 percent) and an electoral college (20 percent) from 1995 to 2001. Chinese officials rejected the 4–4–2 model.[25]

Beijing preferred T. S. Lo's bicameral model. This called for the legislature to be made up of a district and a functional chamber. For the first and second terms of office, members of the district chamber would be elected by District Boards and Municipal Councils, while the functional chamber would be selected by occupational groups. In the third term, legislators would decide whether the legislature's composition should be changed. There would be a split voting system for different categories of legislators. Members of the two chambers would vote as two separate blocks. All bills would need to be passed by both blocks to succeed. Lo's ideas of creating a split voting system in the legislature found its way into Annex II (II) of the Basic Law. Thus, while the post-1997 legislature is one house, it functions like a bicameral body where the directly elected members could be constrained.[26]

The initial momentum created by the OMELCO Consensus and the efforts of the Group of 89 dissipated. In time, the business community focussed on calling upon the British Government to grant British nationality to Hong Kong people instead of pushing for a much faster pace of democratisation.[27] Many of them were keen to both be on good terms with Beijing, as well as to obtain foreign passports as an insurance policy should they need to decamp from Hong Kong.

The events in Beijing from April to June 1989 greatly affected world opinion on Hong Kong's future. Britain could not be seen to be acting honourably and responsibly if it did not provide arrangements to guarantee "a high degree of autonomy" in post-1997 Hong Kong through Hong Kong people electing their own political leaders. Soon after the crackdown, British foreign secretary Geoffrey Howe wrote to Vice Premier Wu Xueqian stating that confidence in Hong Kong had been badly shaken, and that Britain was planning to reconsider the arrangements for the direct elections of 1991 in Hong Kong. Howe also asked Beijing to postpone the passing of the Basic Law. The Chinese reply marked the start of a long diplomatic row—China would not agree to any change concerning Hong Kong's political system by Britain.

The CCP's Conspiracy Theory

The CCP's assessment of Hong Kong in terms of world politics concluded that Britain had changed her policy towards China with respect to Hong Kong and the British were prepared to use Hong Kong to destabilise the CCP regime. From Zhou Nan's recollection, which reflected the dominant CCP's view at the time, Hong Kong was no longer a matter between China and Britain. It had become a plot organised by Western anti-China forces. For example, he considered Margaret Thatcher's call in October 1989 to the member states of the Commonwealth to "state unequivocally its support for Hong Kong and call on China to rebuild confidence there"[28] as an attempt to ask for international efforts to intervene in Hong Kong affairs.[29] Qian Qichen's reflection was more elegantly expressed. He thought Britain "considered that it had made excessive concessions over Hong Kong, and it wanted to regain lost ground".[30]

The CCP regarded the Hong Kong Alliance in Support of Patriotic Democratic Movements in China to have been an instrument of the anti-China forces. The fear was that the West would use Hong Kong as a subversive base against China. A crucial change after 1990 to CCP Hong Kong's united front policy under Zhou Nan was that it became much less inclusive. Pro-democracy groups and those of more liberal persuasion were excluded.[31]

It did not help that most of the leaders of the pro-democracy camp, such as Martin Lee and Szeto Wah, were key members of the Alliance, which had actively supported the student demonstrations in Beijing in 1989, and helped to smuggle many of the wanted activists out of the Mainland after the crackdown. The Alliance was branded a subversive group, and Martin Lee and Szeto Wah as subversives. Although Lee and Szeto had already resigned from the BLDC, they were formally expelled. A new provision was introduced to the draft post-1997 constitution to prohibit treason, sedition, secession, subversion, and theft of state secrets so as to strengthen Beijing's ability to control events in the future. The HKSAR government's attempt to legislate what Article 23 of the Basic Law requires would cause a massive demonstration in Hong Kong in 2003 that would change the CCP's policy towards Hong Kong once more (Chapter 10).

Hong Kong Pre-1997 Political Parties Formation
1989: Hong Kong Democratic Foundation
1990: United Democrats of Hong Kong
1990: Liberal Democratic Foundation
1992: Co-operative Resources Group, which became the Liberal Party in 1993
1992: Democratic Alliance for the Betterment of Hong Kong (DAB)
1994: Hong Kong Progressive Alliance (merged with the DAB in 2005)

There is one aspect of Article 23 worth noting. It also includes a provision that requires the HKSAR to pass legislation "to prohibit foreign political organisations or bodies from conducting political activities in the Region, and to prohibit political organisations or bodies of the Region from establishing ties with foreign political organisations or bodies".[32] While the Basic Law does not have a provision specifically about political parties, Article 23 tacitly acknowledges that political parties can exist but is specific that they must not have ties with foreign political bodies or organisations. This is to make it plain that Hong Kong parties must not have ties with hostile foreign forces.

In December 1989, Percy Cradock—who was by then Margaret Thatcher's special policy adviser—went to Beijing to deliver a long letter from the British prime minister to Jiang Zemin. The letter stated that Britain would follow the Sino-British Joint Declaration, had no intention to use Hong Kong as a base of subversion or to internationalise the question of Hong Kong. However, Britain was facing huge pressure to "increase substantially" the quota of directly elected legislators in 1991, pressure that could not be ignored. Thatcher expressed a hope that China would keep in step with Britain's arrangement when drafting the Basic Law. When Jiang met Cradock, the Chinese understood the British wanted elections in Hong Kong to be a precondition for putting Sino-British relations back on track. Jiang warned that the Chinese were not oblivious to what the West was thinking:

> In addition to domestic factors, the international environment also contributed to the political turmoil that happened in late spring and early summer in China this year. On the international stage, some people misinterpreted the situation. They

believed that various socialist countries had become chaotic enough that China too would collapse with a push.[33]

As for public opinion in Hong Kong, Beijing suspected British manipulation. Jiang commented that:

> As for public opinion, we have to find out if the views are being manipulated or genuinely expressed by the people. In Western countries, the so-called public opinion and the ruling power's "guidance" and intention are always closely related. Some people in Hong Kong believe they are representing public views, but I cannot agree with them. Those people either have their own agendas or they simply want to make trouble.[34]

Crisis of Legitimacy

Subsequent to the meeting between Jiang Zemin and Percy Cradock, Cradock also met China's foreign minister, Qian Qichen, to whom he gave a letter from the new British foreign minister, Douglas Hurd, detailing the British positions of the draft Basic Law. Qian saw Hurd's letter as evidence that the British had indeed changed its stance on Hong Kong. He recounted that there had been smooth cooperation between the two countries in drafting the Basic Law and the British had no objections to the first published draft but now the British were raising considerable disagreements, "especially the developments of Hong Kong's political system, and added more requirements, such as increasing drastically the proportion of directly elected members in the Hong Kong Legislative Council".[35]

Beijing believed the British were taking advantage of the negative international sentiments against China post-Tiananmen to push for a more rapid pace of democratic reform in Hong Kong. To put in place a representative government in Hong Kong was seen as unnecessary and part of a ploy to strike at China.[36] The British were seen to be attempting to change Hong Kong's longstanding executive-led political system, where power was focussed in the hands of the executive to a legislative-led one, so as to restrain the executive by enhancing the power and status of the legislature. The purpose of such a ploy was to transform the post-1997 Hong Kong into an "independent entity" in order to serve Britain's long-term political and economic interests.[37]

Despite strained relations and mutual distrust, China and Britain continued to negotiate. Qian Qichen and Douglas Hurd corresponded on Hong Kong's democratic reform arrangements over a series of seven letters. By February 1990, the two sides had reached a secret agreement as a result of Governor David Wilson's visit to Beijing and his meeting with Li Peng, where Wilson managed to persuade Beijing that without significant advance on direct election, Hong Kong would become ungovernable. The agreement reached was that the British would provide for 18 directly elected seats in 1991 to the Legislative Council (30 percent of total seats) using the "double seat, double vote" system, and in return, Beijing agreed that there would be 20 directly elected seats in 1997, 24 seats in 1999 and 30 seats in 2003. That voting system meant there would be double seat constituencies and voters could cast two votes for each of the seats.³⁸ This method was used to reduce the chance for the pro-democracy groups to sweep all the seats if a single-member system was adopted instead. If the arrangements were satisfactorily implemented, those elected to the Legislative Council in 1995 could ride on a through train and serve until 1999. That arrangement was enacted in Annex II (I) of the Basic Law promulgated in April 1990 by making an exception of the arrangements for the first legislature after 1997. In the end, it was Sino-British agreement that proved to be more important than the efforts of the BLDC and BLCC. The Sino-British through train agreement represented the best compromise that could be reached by the two sides.

Shoring Up Confidence amidst Suspicions

To shore up confidence in Hong Kong, the British government announced the British Nationality Scheme in December 1989, which offered 225,000 people or 50,000 qualified households in Hong Kong the right of permanent residency in Britain. As stated by Governor David Wilson, the purpose of the scheme was to "give those selected the confidence to stay in Hong Kong up to and beyond 1997".³⁹ Britain also asked other countries such as Australia and Canada to devise similar emigration scheme for Hong Kong people. From the CCP's point of view, rather than anchoring the people to stay, the scheme was a ploy to "internationalise" Hong Kong with the hidden agenda of turning Hong Kong Chinese into nationals of other countries.⁴⁰ In response, Beijing claimed that the scheme violated the Sino-British Joint Declaration and declared that it would not recognise such passport holders as foreign nationals. Thus, China would treat them as Chinese nationals within Chinese jurisdiction. Furthermore, Beijing inserted a provision into the Basic Law that the post-1997 Legislative Council shall be composed of Chinese citizens who are permanent residents of the Region with no right of abode in any foreign country. However, permanent residents of the Region who are not of Chinese nationality or who have the right of abode in foreign countries may also be elected members of the Legislative Council, provided that the proportion of such members does not exceed 20 percent of the total membership of the Council.⁴¹ The 20 percent would go to specific functional constituencies, such as the those representing the Hong Kong General Chamber of Commerce and Tourism, as a concession to businessmen and professionals, some of whom held foreign nationality or had right of abode overseas.

In October 1989, Governor David Wilson also announced a massive infrastructure project referred to as the Port and Airport Development Strategy. The whole project would cost HK$127 billion and the first phase, which included the building of a new airport on Lantau Island, was scheduled to be completed in 1997.

Announcing the project in his Annual Policy Address that year, Wilson said that: "despite the shocks we have experienced during the year, your Government is continuing to plan for the long-term future of Hong Kong. We have a clear vision of what we are trying to achieve. It is a vision that I hope will sustain Hong Kong during the present period of uncertainty and give us all confidence in our ability to overcome whatever problems confront us."[42] The British saw the new airport project as a way to instil confidence. The British and Hong Kong authorities had not expected problems because Chinese officials had voiced no objections in private briefings. Moreover, the Bank of China had also publicly welcomed the project immediately after its announcement and Xinhua Hong Kong even published the Bank of China's suggestion that the Land Fund could be used to fund the airport.[43] Thus, the decision on the part of Beijing to denounce the project was astonishing. Governor David Wilson recalled events thus:

> We had told the Chinese what we were going to do at several levels but as it came at a time when all high-level contact had been broken by the European Union, frankly I don't think anything was registered . . . the Chinese became highly suspicious of us, egged on, I fear to say, by some of their supporters in Hong Kong.[44]

The Chinese claimed that it would deplete Hong Kong's fiscal reserves and the British would give out all the contracts to their favoured parties.[45] Hence, Jiang Zemin publicly criticised the project as a British plot to "host an extravagant meal and leave China to pay for it".[46] Though Beijing also recognised that Hong Kong needed a new airport, it effectively blocked the project by refusing to give an undertaking on behalf of the future HKSAR government to repay loans. This strategy forced an agreement with the British that Britain and China would form a consultative body and the Hong Kong government would leave not less than HK$25 billion in reserves for the post-1997 government. In September 1991, John Major (prime minister, 1990–1997) flew to Beijing to sign the Memorandum of Understanding for the project with Li Peng.[47]

The controversy over the airport enabled Beijing to achieve its objective of having a say over pre-1997 affairs in Hong Kong. As early as January 1991, Beijing had wanted to find a way to assert itself. Wu Xueqian made the remark that "during the transition period, only the Central People's Government can, and is entitled to, speak on behalf of the people of Hong Kong".[48] In April 1992, Lu Ping, by then the head of the Hong Kong and Macao Affairs Office, made Beijing's intention very clear:

> In the latter half of the transition period, the Chinese government does not intend to intervene with the administrative affairs of the British-Hong Kong government. However, for matters related to the 1997 issue and smooth political transition, which require the future SAR government to bear responsibilities and obligations, the British-Hong Kong government should consult more often with the Chinese government. The Chinese government has the responsibility to consider and

participate in examining these matters. This practice is entirely consistent with the spirit of the Sino-British Joint Declaration. In the latter half of the transition period, if the British-Hong Kong government cannot obtain the support of the Chinese government, some matters would be very difficult to be accomplished.[49]

Indeed, from 1991, Chinese officials including those at Xinhua Hong Kong began to comment more frequently on Hong Kong affairs. For example, Xinhua Hong Kong objected to the proposed privatisation plan of Radio and Television Hong Kong, the public broadcaster. In 1991, after the landslide victory of the democratic camp in the first ever Legislative Council election with a number of directly elected seats, Beijing warned the Hong Kong government not to appoint any democrats to the Executive Council.[50] In March 1992, Lu Ping expressed concern that the Hong Kong government budget planned to raise taxes to pay for increased expenditure, and in Lu's view, this was against the principle of spending to be kept within revenue stated in the Basic Law.[51]

The Surprising Chris Patten

In 1992, John Major decided that David Wilson should step down as governor of Hong Kong. Major neither named a successor nor arranged another diplomatic posting for Wilson, who had another three years before he was to retire. Major also removed Percy Cradock as foreign policy adviser. To some observers, these personnel changes signalled that the British government was unhappy with its two most important experts on Hong Kong and how Sino-British affairs were proceeding.[52] What was a total surprise was the eventual appointment of Christopher Patten as the last governor of Hong Kong.

Chris Patten was a heavyweight in British politics, which gave him a special authority with the British political establishment. He was after all the chairman of the Conservative Party, who had just had the party re-elected. While he charted the party's re-election victory in 1992, he lost his own seat in the constituency of Bath and thus had to leave Parliament. Patten's appointment as governor of Hong Kong was an accident of history. His seniority and close relationship with John Major and Douglas Hurd gave him direct access to them to discuss Hong Kong matters. Patten arrived in Hong Kong in July 1992 and created a sense of curiosity all round, since Hong Kong had never had a politician as head of government. He knew his job was to ensure Britain could exit the colony and be considered by world opinion to have done its best for the people of Hong Kong.

During the earliest weeks of his governorship, Patten took measure of his closest advisers in the Executive Council. Lydia Dunn, the most senior member then, persuaded all the other members to offer their resignations in order to give the new governor a chance to restructure his cabinet. He took the opportunity not to reappoint some of the members. Rita Fan, Selina Chow, and Allen Lee were not invited back. They would become fierce opponents to Chris Patten, but would continue to enjoy long political careers in Hong Kong, including appointments to the NPC. Rita Fan would achieve the highest accolades post-1997. In March 2008, she was made one of the vice-chairmen of the SCNPC—a highly sought-after position. Most interesting, Patten added Tung Chee Hwa, a shipping tycoon to the Executive Council. Tung was in fact Beijing's nominee, and thus represented the voice of political conservatism and also that of Beijing.[53] It is unclear exactly when Beijing decided Tung was its choice for the HKSAR's first chief executive, but he was obviously already a contender in 1992. One report noted that by late 1995, Tung had become the top choice after a period of background checks by the Mainland security and political apparatus.[54]

Without anyone knowing what he would do at the time, Patten was going to surprise Hong Kong—and Beijing—with his first Policy Address in October 1992. Patten exploited grey areas and found room in the Basic Law to introduce more democratic elements in the system. Patten insisted that:

> What I have tried to do with these proposals is to meet two objectives which I understand represent the views of the community—to extend democracy while working within the Basic Law. All the proposals I have outlined would, I believe, be compatible with the provisions of the Basic Law. What these arrangements should give us, therefore, is a 'through train' of democracy running on the tracks laid down by the Basic Law.[55]

The Patten Proposals had seven elements:

1. Using of the "single seat, single vote" method for all three tiers of geographical constituency elections to the District Boards, Municipal Councils[56] and Legislative Council;
2. Lowering of the minimum voting age from 21 to 18;
3. Abolishing all appointed seats on the District Boards and Municipal Councils;
4. Removing the restrictions on local delegates to China's NPC to stand for elections;
5. Broadening the franchise of certain existing functional constituencies by replacing corporate voting with individual voting;
6. Introducing nine new functional constituency seats; and
7. Introducing of an Election Committee comprising of District Board members to return 10 members to the Legislative Council.[57]

A fortnight prior to the announcement, Douglas Hurd had given the details of the Patten Proposals to Qian Qichen. The Chinese side warned that in their view, some aspects of the plan were in violation of the Basic Law, and a legislature so elected would not be able to straddle across from 1997 to 1999. They emphasised that any arrangements for the 1995 Legislative Council election should be agreed by both side beforehand. Beijing saw the Patten Proposals as direct confrontation. To the Chinese, Patten had ignored the Seven Diplomatic Documents between Qian and Hurd, about which amazingly the Foreign Office had not briefed him. In other words, it had inexplicably withheld the information.[58]

Beijing made Patten the principal culprit of the trouble and the Chinese propaganda machine singled him out for attack. Lu Ping labelled Patten as "Sinner of a Thousand Years" at a press conference.[59] In Hong Kong, Xinhua officials used many occasions to criticise Patten. For example, Zheng Guoxiong, Xinhua Hong Kong's deputy director, said that:

> Patten insisted on confrontation by putting forward his reform proposals. This affected and harmed the prosperity of Hong Kong. Chris Patten did not have any sincerity to cooperate with China. His attitude was thoroughly confrontational, Chris Patten completely ignored the effort and attitude of the Chinese government and he brought harmful effects to the prosperity and stability of Hong Kong. He should be the one who bears all the responsibility.[60]

CCP Hong Kong's strategy was to galvanise Hong Kong people to oppose Patten and his reform package, and to persuade the people that China, not Britain, was the real protector of their long-term interests. Zhou Nan, in meeting with the chairmen of the District Boards, said that:

> More and more Hong Kong people have realised that Patten's political reform package is in serious violation of the Joint Declaration, the Basic Law and the previous agreements reached by Chinese and Britain. They also realised that by walking along this wrong path, Patten has already jeopardised and will continue to jeopardise the prosperity and stability of Hong Kong and a smooth transition. We have already taken and shall take all the necessary measures to maintain the stability and prosperity of Hong Kong, to ensure a smooth transition in 1997 and to protect the long-term interests of Hong Kong people. The only way out for Patten is he should immediately abandon his so-called political reform package and stop playing political tricks.[61]

It is interesting to speculate whether Chris Patten would have acted differently had he known about the seven diplomatic exchanges. Perhaps the packaging would be different, but the substance could well have been much the same because the totality of the Patten Proposals was in fact quite modest. The Chinese side appeared to have been so upset with the last governor that perhaps they saw the expert packaging for more than what it was.[62] Chris Patten had to be publicly humiliated whenever possible to show China would not bow to pressure. Thus, on one famous occasion in December 1993, Zhou Nan refused to shake Patten's hand at a public event.[63] In Beijing's view, the fight over Hong Kong's political system related to the integrity of Chinese sovereignty and China had to be tough.[64] However, the crudeness and rudeness did not go down well with the people of Hong Kong or in world opinion. Patten understood that if he submitted to Beijing's pressure, he would no longer have the credibility and authority to govern Hong Kong in the remaining years before 1997. For many Hong Kong people, while they may not have believed

Patten's way could change Beijing's mind, they still saw him as a champion for their cause. After all, there were not many people who could say no to Beijing.[65] According to the polls conducted by the Public Opinion Programme of Hong Kong University, Patten enjoyed high popularity ratings throughout his tenure in Hong Kong.[66]

In February 1993, Britain's foreign minister Douglas Hurd wrote to Qian Qichen for proposing negotiation "without preconditions". In March 1993, the Hong Kong government published Patten's political reform package in the official government gazette. On 22 April 1993, the two sides reached a decision that negotiations between them would start in Beijing. Jiang Enzhu, the deputy foreign minister, represented the Chinese side, and Robin McLaren, the British ambassador to China, represented the British side. Patten played an all important role in controlling the content of the negotiations. The two sides held seventeen rounds of talks on the arrangements for the 1994 District Boards and 1995 Legislative Council elections but were not able to reach agreement. Beijing blamed Britain for breaking off the talks.[67] Jiang Enzhu would become ambassador to London in 1995, and director of Xinhua Hong Kong from 1997 to 2000 before becoming the director of the Liaison Office of the Central People's Government in Hong Kong until 2002.

On 30 November, negotiations effectively came to an end when Douglas Hurd wrote to Qian Qichen that the British had decided to present the Patten Proposals to the Hong Kong Legislative Council for scrutiny. The Chinese saw that as "a declaration of a showdown with China".[68] Qian's reply was that it was a matter of principle to China that the opinions of the Hong Kong legislature could not supersede the discussion between the two governments and that if the British did indeed put the Patten Proposals to the legislature it would mean a breakdown in bilateral negotiations.

With the tabling of the Electoral Provisions (Miscellaneous Amendments) (No. 2) Bill 1993 (giving effect to the first four proposed reforms) and the Legislative Council (Electoral Provisions) (Amendment) Bill 1994 (giving effect to the last three proposed reforms) in the Legislative Council, CCP Hong Kong's role was to do its best to torpedo them. It was a close call for Chris Patten, but the two bills were passed on 24 February 1994 and 30 June 1994 respectively. Beijing made it clear that the last District Councils, the Urban Council, the Regional Council and the Legislative Council would be terminated with the expiration of British administration. The through train would not run and Beijing would organise matters separately.

Overt Route to Taking Charge

In preparing for the resumption of sovereignty, Beijing had to cultivate individuals and groups in Hong Kong to become part of the post-colonial establishment under Chinese rule. In light of the deteriorating relationship with the British since 1989, and especially after the arrival of Chris Patten, the CCP had to do its best to counter

British interest to promote political reform, derail the Patten Proposals, and put in place a shadow government to undermine the colonial authorities after the passage of the proposals.

Since Xu Jiatun's time, CCP Hong Kong had already begun to institutionalise the co-option mechanism by first focussing on the capitalist class to bring them onside in the belief that the business elites were the most crucial in maintaining prosperity. As many of the leading business people were already members of the political elite through appointments by the British into the colonial structure, the CCP's strategy was to win them over by giving them a place in the post-colonial establishment. As Xu had observed, businessmen were pragmatic and their first concern was always their business interests. The Hong Kong appointees to the BLDC and BLCC reflected the party's successful effort to recruit large numbers of influential business people. As noted in Chapter 8 and above, some of these voices cultivated by the Chinese side proved most useful in resisting demands for more liberal reforms, as shown by Louis Cha's mainstream model, and T. S. Lo's bicameral model. Moreover, appointments to the BLDC and BLCC provided useful experience for the CCP in working with the business elites and other opinion shapers. Indeed, from those appointments, many of the individuals have gone on to occupy important positions in post-colonial politics, and even their sons and daughters.

Local affairs advisers

Nevertheless, it was necessary for CCP Hong Kong to further expand its reach in the Hong Kong community after the promulgation of the Basic Law and to strengthen its ability to counter the British pursuit of political reform post-Tiananmen. Implementing an idea from Lu Ping, China created general honorific advisory positions in order to outreach to a larger number of people. Between March 1992 and April 1995, a total of 186 people were appointed for two years as Hong Kong affairs advisors in four batches. The appointments were given much fanfare by the State Council's Hong Kong and Macao Affairs Office and Xinhua Hong Kong. These advisors were appointed on individual basis and mainly consisted of prominent businessmen, pro-Beijing politicians and professionals, academics and labour union leaders.[69] Tung Chee Hwa, who would become the first chief executive of HKSAR, was appointed as one of the first batch of 44 advisors along with other tycoons like Henry Fok, T. K. Ann, Run Run Shaw, and Li Ka Shing. No one from the democratic camp was appointed. The Chinese officials emphasised that the appointment of these advisors was to "build a regular channel of communication with Hong Kong people and gather the wisdom of Hong Kong people" and they would not "undermine the administrative capacity of the Hong Kong government" nor "be a second power centre".[70] There was no formal work for the advisers. Another 667 district affairs advisers were appointed to bring in less important people who had influence within a narrower sphere such as District Board chairmen and Municipal Council members.⁷¹ Indeed, expanding its network would have been in China's interest whatever the state of Sino-British relations. These appointments had endorsement value, being of individuals who had respectable records of public service but who would not engage in the confrontations over democratic reforms that had occurred on the BLCC.⁷²

Preparing for elections

The CCP was prepared to be pragmatic. While it was not in favour of a faster pace for elections, once it became clear that an election was going to occur, the party begun to mobilise pro-China groups to take part. The appointment of district affairs advisers was an important step in fighting district elections. The CCP would need to find suitable people to stand for election, as well as people in the districts to drum up support. At the same time, CCP Hong Kong had actively to establish its power base at the grassroots level, cultivating relationships with such people as the leaders of *kaifongs*, mutual aid and area committees, members of District Boards, members of the Heung Yee Kuk, as well as urban councillors and regional councillors. To fight legislative elections, it needed to encourage both the grassroots leaders and the elites to form political parties and stand for direct and functional elections. Moreover, the party would also need to strengthen its traditional bases with left-wing trade unions, women's groups, youth groups and other satellite united front organs to mobilise support during campaigning. Examples of newer united front groups included the Federation of Women which was inaugurated in 1993 with 600 members with legislator and CPPCC delegate Peggy Lam as the chairperson, the Association of Chinese Enterprises (an organisation made up of Mainland companies in Hong Kong), the Association of Post-Secondary Students (a patriotic student union), and the Federation for the Stability of Hong Kong (made up of various politicians and Hong Kong affairs advisers, district affairs advisers, NPC and CPPCC deputies).⁷³

There was a flurry of activities among the younger members of the political elites to face upcoming elections. Maria Tam was the chairperson of the Liberal Democratic Federation. T. S. Lo founded the New Hong Kong Alliance, but it never got very far as Lo realised he would not become the first chief executive. A group of legislators formed the Co-operative Resources Group in 1992, which eventually morphed into the Liberal Party.⁷⁴ Tsang Yok Shing founded the DAB in 1992 with Tam Yiu Chung also becoming a member. Since the DAB was the pro-Beijing party, its role was to check the pro-democracy parties in elections prior to 1997, support the policies of the HKSAR government post-reunification, and act as a united front umbrella within the Hong Kong community.⁷⁵ When it was felt that the DAB was too grassroots and a middle-class pro-China party was needed, solicitor Ambrose Lau was encouraged by Xinhua Hong Kong to form the Hong Kong Progressive Alliance in 1994 through the merging of various groups that had heavier business and professional memberships.⁷⁶ While Maria Tam's party never got very far, she eventually joined the Hong Kong Progressive Alliance, and when that folded into the DAB in 2005 after its lacklustre performance in the 2004 legislative election, she became one of the DAB's vice-chairmen. The functional electoral system also ensured that the left-wing camp would win a number of seats through its allies in various functional constituencies, such as labour, and the Heung Yee Kuk.

In election campaigns, CCP Hong Kong functioned as a "behind-the-scene commander, orchestrating the co-ordination of pro-China candidates and mobilising satellite organisations".⁷⁷ In order to prepare for the 1994 District Board elections and the 1995 Legislative Council elections, Huang Zhizhao, the deputy secretary-general of Xinhua Hong Kong was given the responsibility of coordinating the fielding of candidates, and there was also a working group within Xinhua Hong Kong led by Zheng Guoxiong responsible for mapping out long-term strategies for its favoured candidates and groups in future elections.⁷⁸

Subsequent to the 1994 and 1995 elections, the election machinery would continue to expand to include the Federation of Hong Kong–Guangdong Community Organisations, Kowloon Federation of Associations and Hong Kong Island Federation. The older New Territories Association of Societies had already been established in 1985 and going forward, these bodies would play important coordination roles in election campaigns to assist the patriotic camp. Taking the Hong Kong Island Federation as an example, it has a number of affiliated organisations, including the Unified Associations of Central and Western District, Unified Associations of Wanchai District, Unified Associations of Eastern District, and Unified Associations of Southern District. These affiliates would play active roles as well in mobilising yet other affiliated groups and their members to vote for patriotic candidates and parties.⁷⁹

Up until today, the united front organs and their satellites implement top down, pyramid-like, mobilisation for the DAB or specific candidates the CCP supports by spreading messages of support to every corner of the networks. The satellites embedded in the community are like transmission belts for these messages to flow through. Moreover, the large united front organs, such as the FTU, also provide people and money to assist in campaigning. To ensure these organs work hard for the preferred parties and candidates, there are overlapping memberships between the DAB and the united front organs (Chapter 10 and Figure 7). For example, DAB leaders such as Tam Yiu Chung and Cheng Yiu Tong are long-time leaders in the FTU, and the DAB has also invited district leaders to join the party. For example, former legislator and District Councillor Chan Kam Lam represented the Kwun Tong Residents' Union, and District Councillor Suen Kai Cheong was once the leader of the Wanchai Federation of Associations.⁸⁰ The party also acts as mediator to reduce competition and conflicts among the parties and groups.⁸¹

Preliminary Working Committee

On 16 July 1993, just as the first two batches of Hong Kong Affairs Advisers had been appointed, and in the midst of the Sino-British row over the Patten Proposals, Beijing decided to create yet another body called the Preliminary Working Committee. The intention to form the committee was first made known publicly in March 1993. However, it seemed Beijing already thought some such body was necessary in order to prepare for the final phase of the transition, even before Chris Patten's appointment, but his reform proposals might just have provided opportunities to score bigger propaganda and diplomatic points. The row over the Patten Proposals enabled Beijing to issue a warning that unilateral action would result in the setting-up of a "second stove" and, when it was formed, to say it was an unfortunate product of British confrontation.[82]

The term "second stove" was used in reference to various Chinese folk tales in which a second wife sets up a separate stove or kitchen to rival that of the first wife. The term denoted the seizing of initiative to control the establishment of the post-1997 political system. As Zhou Nan acknowledged, the Chinese side wanted to take an early initiative to make arrangements for the setting up of the HKSAR government[83] although Beijing insisted that the Preliminary Working Committee was not a second power centre or a shadow administration. Chinese officials said it could not be so because it was an advisory body operating under the SCNPC in Beijing and not functioning in Hong Kong. Despite Beijing's denial, the committee was generally seen to be a shadow government.[84]

The forming of such a body was not envisaged by either the Sino-British Joint Declaration or the Basic Law. When the legality of setting up such a committee was raised, Beijing argued that a decision made by the NPC on 4 April 1990,[85] at the same time that the Basic Law was passed, provided that the NPC shall establish a Preparatory Committee for the HKSAR and that the Preliminary Working Committee was just preparation for the Preparatory Committee to be set up in 1996. It would "lay down the preparatory work for the future Preparatory Committee, including to the methods of forming the HKSAR government, legislature and other matters".[86]

The Preliminary Working Committee held its first meeting in July 1993 and ended its work in December 1995. It consisted of 57 members, of which 30 were from Hong Kong. The large number of Hong Kong members was to make it palatable to Hong Kong people, but the composition of the Mainland members and the seniority of them was what really mattered. It was a body that enabled Beijing to coordinate its takeover of Hong Kong among the various parts of the Chinese political hierarchy. The chairman was Qian Qichen and the six vice-chairmen consisted of four Mainland officials (Lu Ping, Zhou Nan, Jiang Enzhu, and Zheng Yi). Mainland members included those with vice-ministerial rank from the Ministry of Foreign Affairs, Hong Kong and Macao Affairs Office, Ministry of Public Security,

People's Liberation Army, Ministry of Foreign Trade and Economic Cooperation, People's Bank of China, and the CCP's United Front Work Department. Of the Hong Kong vice-chairmen, were two tycoons who were among the most trusted by Beijing (Henry Fok and T. K. Ann) and a judge (Simon Li). Other Hong Kong members consisted of many of those who were the targets of the united front, such as David Li, Li Ka Shing, T. S. Lo, and Maria Tam. Old faithfuls, such as Tsang Yok Shing, were also included.

Although there were five sub-groups focussing on various aspects of local affairs,[87] the main focus of work was to put forward proposals on political issues arising from the Reunification, in particular the formation of the first HKSAR government, the role of civil servants after 1997, and identifying existing laws that might contravene the Basic Law and to discuss what needed to be done. Beijing also expected the Preliminary Working Committee to work with other pro-Beijing organisations in Hong Kong, such as the Hong Kong delegates to the NPC and CPPCC, and the newly appointed affairs advisers, of which there were many overlapping memberships.[88]

Preparatory Committee

The Preparatory Committee was established on 26 January 1996. It consisted of 150 members with 94 Hong Kong appointees and 56 Mainland appointees. All the members of the Preliminary Working Committee were appointed to serve on the Preparatory Committee. The chairman was Qian Qichen. Lu Ping and Zhou Nan were two of the four vice-chairmen from the Mainland side. The five Hong Kong vice-chairmen were the familiar faces of Henry Fok, T. K. Ann, Tung Chee Hwa, Simon Li, and Leung Chun Ying. Mainland members included appointees from the Ministry of Foreign Affairs, the Hong Kong and Macao Affairs Office, the Joint Liaison Group,[89] the People's Bank of China, the Bank of China, the State Planning Commission, the State Economic and Trade Commission, the Ministry of Foreign Trade and Economic Cooperation, the State Council Special Economic Zones Office and the Ministry of Finance. Representatives from security agencies included the People's Liberation Army, the Ministry of Public Security, and the Ministry of State Security. There were also officials from united front organs like the CCP's United Front Work Department, the Association for Relations Across the Taiwan Strait and the State Council Overseas Chinese Affairs Office. Further, there were representatives from local authorities like the Shenzhen Communist Party Committee, the Guangdong People's Congress and the Beijing Communist Party Committee. For the Hong Kong members, a large proportion of them were businessmen, and the rest were professional, pro-Beijing politicians, and representatives of other social sectors. Many of them were previously appointed as Hong Kong affairs advisers or delegates to the NPC and CPPCC.[90]

The Preparatory Committee was responsible for implementation work related to the establishment of the HKSAR, including the prescription of the method for the formation of the first government and the first Legislative Council of the HKSAR. It was also responsible for preparing the establishment of a 400-member Selection Committee, which in turn was responsible for the selection of the first chief executive of the HKSAR.[91] Since the Preliminary Working Committee had in fact exceeded the parameters set for the Preparatory Committee in the Basic Law, the Preparatory Committee had a wider scope of work than the one set by the Basic Law. For example, it endorsed the Preliminary Working Committee's proposal for a Provisional Legislature to be formed; gave advice on how the Mainland's Nationality Law could be applied in Hong Kong; provided recommendations on how to interpret parts of the Basic Law; and recommended which existing laws contravened the Basic Law.

Selection Committee

The Selection Committee was created by the Preparatory Committee using a formula that represented the kind of selection method Beijing is most comfortable with. Under the Basic Law, the Selection Committee would have 400 members made up of Hong Kong permanent residents. The composition of this body required that membership be equally split among four broad functional sectors: industrial, commercial and financial; professional; labour, social services and religious; and politics (Hong Kong deputies to the NPC—those 26 members became members of the Selection Committee automatically, former political figures, and Hong Kong members of the National CPPCC). Three hundred members from the first three sectors were "elected" by all the members of the Preparatory Committee, and the number of candidates would be 20 percent more than the number of seats. Those from the first three sectors who wanted to be involved in the selection had to first submit his or her name to a body he or she was a member of (such as the Chinese Manufacturers' Association or professional institutes). After the applications were reviewed by the relevant bodies, they could then be nominated to the Preparatory Committee. The list of nominations was then edited by the Secretariat of the Preparatory Committee after the closing date for entering names on 30 September 1996. The list was then given to all members of the Preparatory Committee to solicit opinions. After that, names could be put forward as candidates. On the method of the election, all members of the Preparatory Committee could vote for members of every sector of the Selection Committee. The ballots were anonymous. Those who won the most votes were elected. Those belonging to the fourth (politics) sector, who wanted to take part in the Selection Committee, could enter their names to the organisations of their own sector, or other sectors. They could be nominated to the Preparatory Committee after relevant organisations reviewed their applications. They could also be nominated by five preparatory committee members. There were a total of 5,789 applicants who put their names forward. On 2 November 1996, the 400 members were elected by members of the Preparatory Committee.

The Selection Committee was responsible for recommending the candidate for the first chief executive through local consultations or through nomination and election after consultations. The ambit of the Selection Committee was later expanded by the Preparatory Committee to include responsibility for the selection of the 60 members of the Provisional Legislative Council.

For the selection of the chief executive, three candidates received enough nominations (50 nominations from members of the Selection Committee) to stand for selection—Tung Chee Hwa got the largest number of nominations; Peter Woo, believed he had a chance and offered his own candidacy and scraped through; and T. L. Yang, a former chief justice, was supposedly the candidate encouraged by Xinhua Hong Kong to run. Simon Li failed to get enough nominations, and T. S. Lo had already pulled out of the race on 16 October 1996, when he realised he was not Beijing's chosen one.[92] A voting process was held and Tung was declared the winner.

Tung's office and Executive Council

In setting up the Chief Executive's Office, Tung Chee Hwa appointed Chen Jianping, known to be Lu Ping's protégé and a former correspondent of Hong Kong's *Wen Wei Po* stationed in Beijing. A medium-level cadre, Chen's role was to act as liaison between Tung Chee Hwa and the Hong Kong and Macao Affairs Office. Chen would continue to serve beyond Tung's term to assist the other chief executives. Various mechanisms and channels were set up for Tung and his office to consult parts of the Central Authorities in Beijing ranging from hotlines between Tung's office and Beijing, to regular reporting trips to the capital.[93]

Tung Chee Hwa was reputed to have consulted Beijing on many things major and minor. He wanted to ensure he knew what the bottom lines were so that he would not transgress them on a variety of issues. There were even rumours that he consulted Beijing so often that some cadres suggested to him that he could be more autonomous. Examples included whether to allow the Democratic Party and democrats to use the balcony of the Legislative Council Building in the early hours of 1 July 1997 to make their "we will be back" proclamation, as well as whether to allow all secretary-level civil servants to continue to serve in his administration. Reputedly Lu Ping made the decision to let the democrats go ahead and the CCP leadership decided all the serving secretaries should continue.[94] Nevertheless, when the HKSAR government was planning to intervene in the market during the Asian Financial Crisis in 1998 and Tung asked Qian Qichen to send people to Hong Kong to discuss the government's plans, Qian refused because it was a local matter.[95]

Tung Chee Hwa would go on to appoint his first Executive Council in July 1997. Unsurprisingly, his closest advisory body was dominated by members of the business elite and professionals with longstanding relations with Beijing. They included

Leung Chun Ying, Henry Tang, who had inherited a textile business and was a member of the Liberal Party, Chung Shui Ming, a banker with the Bank of China and a member of the Hong Kong Progressive Alliance, Antony Leung, a banker, and Nellie Fong, an accountant. One DAB and FTU member were also appointed—Tam Yiu Chung, so as not to exclude a face that can claim to represent the grassroots. The most important aspect of Tung's Executive Council was that it was considered entirely patriotic by the CCP.

Provisional Legislature

In August 1994, the SCNPC decided that the Legislative Council elected in 1995 would be disbanded at the time of reunification because the election methods used did not comply with Sino-British agreement. Shortly afterwards, a sub-group of the Preliminary Working Committee proposed that a provisional legislature should be set up instead as a temporary measure until such time as new electoral legislation could be passed that conformed with the Basic Law. The Chinese side claimed that forming a provisional legislature was a necessary response to the breakdown of the through-train arrangement caused by the British side. In March 1996, the Preparatory Committee, with one dissenter, voted in favour of the establishment of a Provisional Legislative Council with similar powers to those provided for the Legislative Council under the Basic Law.[96] At about that time, Chinese officials had also let it be known in Hong Kong that any civil servant who wanted to participate in the post-1997 government must declare his or her support for the Provisional Legislative Council.[97]

The Provisional Legislative Council was created in December 1996 by block vote by the members of the Selection Committee. Among the 60 legislators so selected were 51 members of the Selection Committee (in other words, they voted to select themselves), 24 of whom were also members of the Preparatory Committee. Among them, 33 were legislators elected in 1995. Since the "pro-democracy" camp legislators stayed away because they regarded the Provisional Legislative Council as a body without proper legal foundation, those who filled the provisional body were essentially from the 'pro-Beijing' camp, which included 10 failed candidates in the 1995 election.[98] The DAB had 10 seats, the Hong Kong Progressive Alliance also had 10 seats, and the FTU had one seat. This was the solid pro-Beijing core, and together they controlled 21 seats in the provisional body. The business-friendly Liberal Party had 10 seats and the Liberal Democratic Federation occupied 3 seats. From among the pro-democracy camp, only the Association for Democracy and People's Livelihood, a small political party, was willing to serve in the provisional legislature (they had 4 seats but would not have as many seats in the legislature again).

For the 33 legislators who served on both legislatures, they had to scurry between Hong Kong and Shenzhen since the Hong Kong Government refused to allow the Provisional Legislative Council to conduct meetings in Hong Kong alongside the Legislative Council. The provisional body operated in Shenzhen before the Handover with logistics support from the Shenzhen Municipal Government. In his capacity as the chief executive designate, Tung Chee Hwa proposed the Public Order (Amendment) Bill 1997 and the Societies (Amendment) Bill 1997. They sought to revive various provisions that the colonial administration had repealed to liberalise laws that restricted freedom of assembly and association.[99] The provisional body passed the amendments even before the transfer of sovereignty, and with the passage of a special Reunification Ordinance enacted immediately after China resumed Hong Kong, these amendments were confirmed as laws of the HKSAR.

The Provisional Legislative Council moved to Hong Kong on 1 July 1997 and remained in office until the first HKSAR legislature assumed office in October 1998. During that year, it repealed or amended 25 pieces of legislation that were considered to have been in conflict with the Basic Law. The electoral laws based on the Patten Proposals were substantially changed, including the adoption of the proportional representation voting system using the Largest Remainder Formula. This was designed to enable the leftist camp to capture more seats in future legislative elections.[100] Zhou Nan asserted that those provisions enacted during Patten's time had the hidden intention of "undermining the governing capacity of the future HKSAR government".[101]

A feature of the Provisional Legislative Council was that, when Tung Chee Hwa spoke there, legislators sometimes clapped their hands to show deference and support. With the new elected Legislative Council in 1998, this particular feature resembling Mainland political practice stopped, despite many of the provisional legislators being returned.[102]

NPC and CPPCC: Pre- and post-1997

The national NPC is comprised of delegates elected by lower-level people's congresses in provinces and municipalities. Prior to 1997, the Hong Kong deputies to the NPC were chosen by Xinhua Hong Kong and endorsed by Beijing before being formally elected by the Guangdong Provincial People's Congress to form part of the provincial delegation to the national legislature. Election in Hong Kong to the NPC was not considered possible under British rule. The sorts of people who used to be appointed to the NPC were leading left-wing figures from the labour, education, cultural and patriotic business sectors. However, from 1984 onwards, appointments begun to shift to the elites who were never part of the left-wing camp. There was a clear preference for appointing business elites. In 1988 and 1993 for the Seventh and Eighth NPCs, there were 18 and 26 Hong Kong appointees respectively. In 1988, there were 7 appointees from the business sector and 5 professionals. In 1993, there were 10 from the business sector and 8 professionals. In both NPCs, labour, culture and publishing combined only had 5 appointees.[103]

The selection of Hong Kong deputies to the Ninth NPC in 1997 after reunification initially provided much public interest because it gave Hong Kong a side seat to witness how the Mainland political culture worked. How would Mainland officials organise an election in Hong Kong? Some scholars believe the selection process became the most open in terms of Mainland experience in the history of NPC elections.[104] A 424-member Electoral Conference was appointed by Beijing of which the 400-member Selection Committee made up the bulk of the electors. All in all, there were 22 NPC members, about 100 national CPPCC members, while another 50 or so were members of provincial people's congresses or consultative conference members. While anyone who could get 10 nominations from the Electoral Conference could compete for the 35 seats, members of the Democratic Party did not manage to get past the door even though the party was given a chance to enter the race, as Tung Chee Hwa's special adviser, Paul Yip Kwok Wah, publicly stated that if the Democratic Party wanted to enter the race he would be willing to be a nominator. This was an early olive branch from the CCP to the democrats, but it required them to be willing to enter the race and thereby signify their acceptance of the Mainland system. Their platform called for the end to one-party rule on the Mainland, which was a sign to the CCP that the Democratic Party remained in opposition and unpatriotic. Nominations became scarce for their three candidate and they eventually withdrew from the election altogether. Of the 35 deputies selected, the largest number of votes was won by Jiang Enzhu, the newly inaugurated director of Xinhua Hong Kong. His joining the race appeared nonsensical to the Hong Kong community since the people of the city did not ever consider Jiang able to represent them, but it provided Hong Kong with a quick lesson in Mainland politics. The NPC could not be equated with a parliament in the Western tradition. While it has formal law-making functions within the Chinese political structure, it is in effect "a concentrated manifestation of state power. Provincial interests were not so much represented there as 'reflected' in the formal presence of their delegations which were all headed by their provincial leaders."[105] In the HKSAR's case, in the absence of Tung Chee Hwa heading the team of NPC deputies, Jiang Enzhu was there to enable the HKSAR deputies to stand on an equal footing alongside other delegations in accordance with the usual Mainland practice. Among the next highest vote getters were Ng Hong Man, Tsang Tak Sing, Maria Tam, and Rita Fan.[106]

For the election of the Tenth NPC in 2002, the number of seats was increased to 36 but tight control was exerted by the CCP Hong Kong. One of the candidates was Wang Rudeng of the Liaison Office, the successor body to Xinhua Hong Kong after 2000. This time, the Electoral Conference was made up of 953 appointed members including the expanded 800-member Election Committee that would also select the second chief executive plus numerous other pro-government figures. A total of 78 candidates fulfilled the requirement of getting ten nominations. Four members of the Democratic Party and Frederick Fung of the Association for Democracy and People's Livelihood sought to stand and got the required number of nominations.

This caused some excitement in Hong Kong that Beijing might be prepared to accept a symbolic presence of the pro-democracy camp in the NPC. The Democratic Party candidates had toned down their platform and no longer called for the end to one-party rule. After the first round of voting to reduce the number of candidates to 54, the five democrats were eliminated. There were plenty of media stories that voters brought with them various lists of preferred candidates. For example, the DAB and FTU had preferred candidates. Insiders also claimed the Liaison Office had a recommended list. Topping the votes were Maria Tam, Wang Rudeng and Rita Fan. Some Liberal Party members did surprisingly well, and old timers like Tsang Tak Sing and Ng Hong Man only ranked relatively low but made the first cut. However, the second round of voting was what really mattered and it was this that showed the CCP's order of preference. There was a considerable amount of behind-the-scene calculations and mobilisation to ensure certain people won and the most favoured ones got high votes. Thus, almost all the deputies to the Ninth NPC were returned. Rita Fan and Wang Rudeng were the top two vote getters. Members of the DAB, FTU and Hong Kong Progressive Alliance took a total of 12 seats.[107]

In 2008, members of the Democratic Party still did not make any headway to join the Eleventh NPC, but an unexpected candidate who just waltzed in was the former permanent secretary for education, Fanny Law, who resigned from government after an official inquiry found that she had interfered with academic freedom.[108] This created an impression that the NPC seat was a consolation prize for a senior HKSAR government official whom the Mainland considered patriotic. In the past, favoured retired officials had been appointed to the CPPCC. In 2012, the Democratic Party did not bother to try to join the Twelfth NPC. Two minor members of the democratic camp made an attempt but they were never going to get anywhere.

While the NPC is an important body within the Mainland political system, the role of the Hong Kong deputies remains undefined. This problem arises because of how the deputies are chosen: essentially by an appointed election body. Moreover, there is also an attempt on the part of the Central Authorities to ensure the NPC deputies are not seen as a second power centre in Hong Kong. Thus, calls from the deputies for office and resource support have fallen on deaf ears. In March 2008, the SCNPC's deputy secretary, Qiao Xiaoyang, told the Hong Kong deputies they did not need "to hang up a signboard" referring to the request for an office to be established in the HKSAR. Instead, the Liaison Office would request additional manpower and resources instead.[109]

As already discussed in Chapter 2, the CPPCC is China's highest political consultative-advisory body and a national-level united front organ. It meets once a year in Beijing at the same time as the NPC sessions. The CPPCC is consulted on important political policies and major problems. Appointments of Hong Kong members in the run up to reunification formed part of China's overall united front strategy to win hearts and minds, and it seems an understanding had been reached between the Liaison Office and the HKSAR government to involve CPPCC members more in local affairs through appointments to various bodies.[110] In 1998, Hong Kong had two members among the 31 vice-chairmen of the Ninth CPPCC—Henry Fok and T. K. Ann. Henry Fok was the ultimate pro-China business tycoon—there was no one quite like him or who could match his patriotic credentials. His connections with China went back to the 1950s during the Korean War. He had never been part of the colonial establishment, never received any British honours and had always been low-key and low-profile. He had been a member of the CPPCC since the Fifth CPPCC in 1978 and vice-chairmen since the Eighth CPPCC. Fok had also been a member of the NPC since 1988. Indeed, he was the only person who served on the NPC, CPPCC and the Preparatory Committee concurrently, although already in his mid-70s by then, making him the most important and honoured person in the pro-China camp. T. K. Ann was a recruit from 1984 as a member of the Sixth CPPCC. His example is of particular interest for study. He was a successful textile industrialist in the 1950s and a member of the Legislative Council from 1970 to 1974. He was a member of the Executive Council under Governor Murray MacLehose from 1974 to 1979. He was awarded an OBE and later a CBE. In early 1982, Ann was invited by Xinhua Hong Kong to join the national CPPCC. During a trip to Tokyo together with Chung Sze Yuen and Kan Yuet Keung in February 1982, they discovered that all three had been so invited. Chung and Kan would decline the invitation but they provided the following analysis to their friend T. K. Ann:

> [he] had already retired from the Legislative and Executive Councils, and later also from the chairmanship of the Trade Development Council. He was, however, still engaged in public affairs and was very knowledgeable about the operations of the Hong Kong Government. He could, and would, contribute his insights to the Chinese cause.[111]

T. K. Ann accepted the appointment to serve on the Sixth CPPCC in 1983, continued to serve in the Seventh CPPCC in 1988, and in 1993, he was elevated to become one of the vice-chairmen, a position that is considered a leader within the Chinese political hierarchy. He was among the first batch of Hong Kong affairs advisers' appointments, and played an important role in the run up to reunification serving as one of the vice-chairmen of the BLDC and as chairmen of the BLCC. Ann was one of three vice-chairmen of the Preliminary Working Committee and one of five vice-chairmen of the Preparatory Committee. By then he was 85 years old.

Beyond the number of high-profile people from Hong Kong sitting on the national NPC and CPPCC are also many appointees to the equivalent provincial and local bodies. It is hard to keep track of all these other appointees, who are less important in the united front pecking order but are nevertheless part of the CCP's overall work to influence the elites in Hong Kong. For example, in 2008, there were 51 Hong Kong and Macao members on the Shenzhen People's Political Consultative

Conference.¹¹² The extensiveness of the united front penetration can be seen from the Board of Directors (2008–2009) of Po Leung Kuk, a longstanding charitable organisation that provides support for orphaned children, as well as education and social services. Of the 20 members of its board 8 served on one or more of the Mainland's people's political consultative conferences. Some of them also were members of other united front bodies. Similarly, of the 19 members of the Board of Directors (2017–2018) of the Tung Wah Group of Hospitals, another longstanding charitable body, at least 10 of them served on various people's political consultative conferences or overseas Chinese friendship or youth associations.¹¹³

The Hong Kong deputies to the NPC and CPPCC at whatever level are part of the CCP's united front. The most politically significant is perhaps the overlapping memberships between members of the Hong Kong Legislative Council and the NPC and CPPCC. These appointments are there to facilitate the smoother implementation of Beijing's governing strategy towards Hong Kong. While members to the NPC and CPPCC can no doubt voice their views on national issues, they are part of the binding web of the united front apparatus, the first purpose of which is to transmit and gain support for Beijing's and pro-government policies in the HKSAR, as responding positively to them is the ultimate test of patriotism.

There are also the occasional rewards apart from enjoying the prestige of being members of the NPC and CPPCC and being given the post-1997 HKSAR government's Bauhinia medals. An example of a special reward is the group that was selected to carry the Olympic torch in 2008 during the relay in Hong Kong. Apart from the city's top athletes, sports managers and a number of talents in other fields, torch-bearers also included tycoons (or their proxies from their companies) and members of the old united front circles and new political order. Thus, the 74-year-old Tsang Hin Chi, a businessman and former SCNPC member, was rewarded with a place even though he had to be in a wheelchair. The list included a number of second-generation tycoon family members, such as Timothy Fok, the son of Henry Fok and also the president of the Hong Kong Olympic Committee; Victor Li, son of Li Ka Shing; Pansy Ho, daughter of Stanley Ho; as well as those from political circles, such as Li Gang, deputy director of the Liaison Office; the director of the New Territories Association of Societies; two representatives from the Hong Kong Youth Association; the chairman of the DAB's youth wing; a number of patriotic district councillors; the head of Bank of China (Hong Kong); Liza Wang Ming Chuen, Leung Chun Ying, and Rita Fan.

For a list of the 120 torch-bearers and their affiliations, see Appendix IV.

Public Perception of the Pro-China Elites

It could be seen that the CCP used a series of official appointments to identify the post-colonial, patriotic elite. By the time of the transition in mid-1997, there were at least a thousand Hong Kong residents with some form of official Mainland title.

Between them, they shared an even larger number of Mainland appointments and titles conferred by the Chinese government from 1992. As already noted in Chapter 8, the building blocks of this group started with appointments to the BLDC and BLCC, and to the creation of the Hong Kong affairs advisers and district affairs advisers, before establishing the Preliminary Working Committee, Preparatory Committee and Section Committee. Post reunification, the first Executive Council is also a part of this group.[114]

Despite the CCP's united front efforts and its hard work in propaganda, it was difficult for it to establish legitimacy and maintain public credibility of the united front organisations and the pro-China camp. Contemporaneous public opinion polls showed that 37 percent of the respondents thought that the members of the Preliminary Working Committee could not represent Hong Kong, 40 percent also said those members did not speak their minds, and that the Legislative Council was a much more trusted body than those created by Beijing. Overall, the Hong Kong community saw the pro-China elites as mouthpieces and yes-men of the Mainland.[115]

Table 4 The Mainland's Hong Kong Appointees[116]

Body	Total Hong Kong Members	Business and Professionals	Previous Executive and Legislative Councillors	NPC or CPPCC Members
Hong Kong Affairs Advisers	185	133	41	37
District Affairs Advisers	667	368	13	1
Preliminary Working Committee	37	25	16	14
Preparatory Committee	94	66	29	39
Selection Committee	400	291	60	102
Provisional Legislative Council	60	37	41	10
1st Executive Council	11	9	6	0

Covert Route to Taking Charge

In view of the fact that China was about to embark on a brand new one country, two systems experiment, and that the CCP had to be flexible, it was nevertheless important for the party to consolidate power in Hong Kong. As an underground organisation, this posed an unusual challenge. The party would have to deal with Hong Kong as if it was enemy territory and old-time revolutionary tactics would have to be rolled out. It might not be sufficient to just depend on the overt institutional framework in place populated mainly by pro-government people. There had also to be "an iron fist".[117]

Apart from overtly creating the post-colonial establishment and institutions discussed above, there was a fifth-column operation going on at the same time. The basic idea was to infiltrate Hong Kong society. In early 1983, the Organisation Department of the CCP Central Committee was instructed to oversee a programme, in consultation with the relevant ministries and agencies, to send cadres to Hong Kong with one-way permits as immigrants for "family reunion". Unlike two-way permit holders, who went to Hong Kong on working visas and must leave after their work ends, the one-way permit holders could stay for the long term. There were five major sponsoring bodies on the Mainland responsible for identifying and managing people to send to Hong Kong—the State Council's Hong Kong and Macao Office, the Ministry of State Security, the United Front Department, the Overseas Chinese Office, and the Taiwan Affairs Office. Candidates were apparently mostly in their 30s and 40s, with good education and skills. Once the fifth columnists arrived in Hong Kong, they were supposed to contact Xinhua Hong Kong and the relevant sponsoring bodies so that they could maintain contact.

In the early years, the mission of the fifth column was initiated as an insurance policy as the British were still to be in power for more than a decade. It was seen as useful to have one's own people dotted around Hong Kong, who could be called to action if need be. The need for an insurance faded somewhat during 1985–1989 when Sino-British relations were good, with transition arrangements proceeding relatively smoothly. However, the Tiananmen crackdown changed Beijing's mood substantially and fifth column-building became important once more. The results of the 1991 Legislative Council election, the Patten Proposals put forward in 1992 and the results of the 1995 Legislative Council election made Beijing feel it was critical to have enough votes that it could control in post-1997 elections. Thus, the mission for the fifth column became one of acting as a voting bloc for the pro-government camp. This was felt to be necessary because while the CCP had considerable influence in the upper levels of Hong Kong society through having co-opted many of the elites, the party had little leverage on the general public, who made up the electorate for the election to the Legislative Council.

Yin Qian, a scholar who has done research on the fifth column noted that recruitment of fifth columnists saw two peaks in the 13 years between 1983 and 1997. The first peak was in 1986–1987 and the second in 1991–1993. Interestingly, Xu Jiatun had said in 1988 that the Chinese could mobilise a force of 50,000 "sons of the people" to oppose proposals of Hong Kong implementing direction elections in 1988, which would indicate that around the time of the first peak this was the strength of the fifth column.[118]

Yin Qian also had this to say about how things had turned out by the time of the Reunification:

> Despite constant denials of its existence by both the Chinese and British governments, the fifth column in Hong Kong was an open secret. In fact, the selection of fifth columnists represented such a lucrative business, and was so pervasive among

officials at various levels, that many depended on it for continuing personal prosperity. Strong resistance could therefore be expected from the bureaucracy should the operation be scrapped. In addition, the fifth columnists, hand-picked by various party agencies, represented an elite group within the Chinese system. For the CCP, the operation of the fifth column policy served various interests: on the one hand it strengthened Beijing's position in Hong Kong by grooming its new generation of proxies; on the other hand, it further cemented and expanded the patron/client relationship between the party and certain individuals/families/groups, thereby further consolidating the CCP's domestic political control and leverage.[119]

Yin Qian's estimated that around 20 percent of the total family reunion immigrants to Hong Kong from China during the period 1983–1997 were fifth columnists, a figure of more than 83,000.

Changing identity

Hong Kong has always been a place where people from the Mainland went to settle. There have been many surveys and analyses done over time on how Hong Kong people saw their identity. The one-way permit scheme noted above continued after 1997, which allowed about 55,000 Mainlanders to settle in Hong Kong each year. After seven years of residency, they could apply for permanent residency status, after which they could vote at elections. After the reunification, various talent and investment schemes also enabled other Mainlanders to obtain permanent residency in Hong Kong. Surveys showed that Hong Kong residents born on the Mainland were generally more politically conservative, and recent migrants were more pro-Beijing and pro-government. The Hong Kong Transition Project offered useful insights because it had traced how Hong Kong people described themselves since 1993. In that year, the bulk of Hong Kong people saw themselves as either "Hong Kong Chinese" or "Hong Kong person" and the numbers of these two groups were similar. Between 1997 and 2007, the identity of "Hong Kong person" was stronger than "Hong Kong Chinese". What was most interesting was the emergence of a new self-categorised group of "Chinese Hong Konger" appearing in 2010 that cut across all age groups. This may signal an identity that is more Chinese than "Hong Kong Chinese". Between 2010 and 2014, this group became larger than "Hong Kong Chinese" and on par with "Hong Kong person".[120] The identity of Hong Kong may be subtly shifting and these two groups will contend over defining the identity of Hong Kong people in the years to come.

10

Reunification, Patriotism, and Political Disorder

From 1997 to 2017

British rule ended in Hong Kong at the stroke of midnight on 30 June 1997. The return of this lost territory marked the beginning of a new era of Chinese Communist Party activities. The party built the new regime and fashioned a new political order to support "one country, two systems". While the party could begin to look directly at things from inside Hong Kong, interpreting events and the mood of the Hong Kong community would prove challenging. The Mainland's roots of suspicion of the former colonial entity, where people had lived under foreign influence for so long, ran deep. As such, the CCP's disposition to distrust Hong Kong people, especially those whom they saw as having British or other Western connections, remained high. The underlying assumptions of how Mainland cadres saw Hong Kong and the world, and how Hong Kong people saw themselves and their worldview remained far apart. Hong Kong people also needed to get used to the fact that the HKSAR is no longer a faraway colony of a foreign power. After 1997, Hong Kong became a part of the People's Republic and is important in national politics. Understandably, the CCP takes an intense interest in the HKSAR as part of a national political experiment.

The CCP could never quite forgive the British for changing Hong Kong's depoliticised governing formula at the eleventh hour before their departure by insisting on elections. From its perspective, Hong Kong's elections had to be managed to reduce the risk of surprise (i.e., unacceptable results). After 1997, extremely complex sub-sector elections select the chief executive, and similarly complex functional elections elect half of the legislators. These methods supposedly produce "balanced participation" in the political affairs of Hong Kong. In fact, they have entrenched many vested interests directly into the political system. The problem of legitimacy and fairness continues to plague the politics of Hong Kong.

The two post-reunification decades may be divided into three periods—with the eras of the three chief executives as the dividing lines. Between 1997 and 2003, the CCP took a hands-off approach with Tung Chee Hwa as chief executive. The CCP realised that it had a political crisis on hand after the seminal 1 July 2003 protest over the attempt to legislate national security laws required by Article 23 of the Basic Law. Its chosen leader for Hong Kong had effectively been deposed by a show of people power. The people were demanding a faster pace of democratic reform in the belief that it would underpin good governance. In 2005, the new era with Donald Tsang as chief executive started with high hopes for both the party and Hong Kong. Surprisingly, his administration lost popularity within a short time. By 2008, the CCP had already changed its approach to Hong Kong; and by 2009, the Hong Kong community got wind that there was a "second governing team" functioning alongside the HKSAR government. The era of Leung Chun Ying that started in 2012 was marked by several troubling mass movements. The younger generations promoted "localism" and ignited a surge of demand for autonomy, the most radical among them calling for "self-determination" and "independence". This era was also marked by political disorder in the Legislative Council.

Twenty years after the reunification, the CCP has effectively "come out" in Hong Kong. Officials from the second governing team are visibly active. While the CCP could claim a measure of success in promoting its values and outlook in Hong Kong, the people there are girded by a different set of norms and they remain wary of being "mainlandised". This is especially true of the younger generations, who have yet to reconcile with Chinese rule. The change in leadership in Beijing after the 18th National Party Congress in 2012 also had an impact on party leaders' view on Hong Kong, as regime and national security became the most important objective in a politically volatile world. When Xi Jinping visited Hong Kong for the twentieth anniversary of the reunification, he emphasised that Beijing's commitment to "one country, two systems" had never wavered. However, he asked Hong Kong people to be guided by a sense of "one country" but conceded that the "two systems" would not be neglected. He also drew a clear red line—Hong Kong must not use its privileged autonomy and freedoms to challenge state sovereignty, security, and development interests. Similar sentiments were expressed in Xi's political report at the opening of the 19th National Party Congress in October 2017.

Mainland Institutions and Hong Kong

Hong Kong and Macao Affairs Office

Soon after the reunification, Lu Ping retired as head of the Hong Kong and Macao Affairs Office and was replaced by Central Committee member Liao Hui, the son of Liao Chengzhi, whose previous job was head of the Overseas Chinese Affairs Office. Its prime responsibility after 1997 was to be the liaison and coordination channel between the HKSAR government and Mainland authorities and to act as the gatekeeper to prevent ministries and regional chiefs from interfering with Hong Kong. Liao's policy was referred to as the "three nos"—"don't criticise the HKSAR; don't criticise the policies of the HKSAR; and don't harp on about the bureaucratic links between the Hong Kong and Macao Affairs Office and the HKSAR".[1]

The CCP's policy over Hong Kong was reassessed and changed after the 1 July 2003 demonstration. Cao Erbao, head of the research department at CCP Hong Kong, wrote in 2008 in *Study Times*, a Central Party School publication, of there being two "governing teams" working to implement "one country, two systems". The first was the local administration made up of the chief executive, political appointees, the civil service, and judicial personnel responsible to actualise the promise of "Hong Kong people ruling Hong Kong". The second group was the Mainland team with responsibilities for Hong Kong affairs. This team was rather large and beyond the ambit of the Hong Kong and Macao Affairs Office. These included "central government departments specialising in or are responsible for Hong Kong affairs; representative offices of the central government; other central government ministries responsible for national affairs and policies; and officials specialising in Hong Kong–related issues in the government and party provincial committees, autonomous regions and municipalities that are related to Hong Kong". Cao described this second team as an "important governing force" and an "important outward expression of the 'one country' principle". He stated that there were "matters that concern China's sovereignty or come within the responsibilities of the Central Authorities or relationship between the Central Authorities and the HKSAR". In other words, the second team supplements what the HKSAR government cannot deal with. Most notably, he argued that the Mainland team should operate legally and openly in Hong Kong, which would "reflect the significant historical change in the party's role in Hong Kong".[2] His essay signalled that the CCP would be more explicit in its work in Hong Kong in the future. Cao's description was not so different from Xu Jiatun's idea of how the party might operate after 1997 (see "Introduction"). A commentary in a Macao newspaper noted that Cao's essay spelled the "complete abandonment" of the Hong Kong and Macao Affairs Office's gatekeeping role and that under Hu Jintao's leadership, the emphasis was on active engagement of the Mainland's government and party functionaries in Hong Kong affairs rather than Jiang Zemin's hands-off approach.[3]

Roles of the organs of state in Hong Kong

Post-reunification, there are three organs of state in the HKSAR.[4] Apart from the party organ (Xinhua Hong Kong), the Ministry of Foreign Affairs and the People's Liberation Army established themselves in Hong Kong after 1997. Though each is a separate body with no supervisory relationship, the party organ exercises de facto leadership over them. In July 1999, when President Hu Jintao visited Hong Kong to celebrate the second anniversary of the reunification, he spelt out their respective roles:

> Xinhua Hong Kong has maintained a close relationship with Hong Kong, facilitated communication and cooperation between Hong Kong and the Mainland,

and also effectively handled Taiwan-related matters and other matters assigned by the Central Government. The Commissioner's Office of China's Foreign Ministry assisted the HKSAR government in handling a large amount of foreign affairs matters, strengthened the connection and cooperation in economic and cultural areas between the HKSAR and foreign countries, regions, and international organisations. The Hong Kong Garrison of the Chinese People's Liberation Army has performed its duties in accordance with the law and established a good reputation. It has protected the national sovereignty and unity, territorial integrity, and the safety of Hong Kong.[5]

From Xinhua Hong Kong to Liaison Office

It was no secret that Lu Ping of the Hong Kong and Macao Affairs Office and Zhou Nan, who headed Xinhua Hong Kong prior to 1997, had major disagreements over Hong Kong policy during the final years of the transition. Zhou was seen to be more intolerant than Lu, and the fact that the two institutions had overlapping functions made a turf battle inevitable, as it had been between Xu Jiatun and Ji Pengfei. As 1997 approached, the debate in Beijing was about the role of Xinhua Hong Kong post-reunification. Lu Ping and Tung Chee Hwa favoured a much smaller Xinhua presence; otherwise, it would be seen as the "hidden power" behind the HKSAR. After all, post-reunification, liaison and coordination between the Hong Kong and the Mainland authorities was supposed to be handled by the Hong Kong and Macao Affairs Office.[6] The Central Authorities decided to scale down Xinhua gradually after 1997 by 60 percent.[7]

Zhou Nan retired in August 1997[8] and was succeeded by Jiang Enzhu, the Chinese representative in the Sino-British negotiations in 1993 and the Chinese ambassador to the United Kingdom from December 1995. Jiang said Xinhua Hong Kong was not another power centre and would not interfere in affairs that were within the autonomy of the HKSAR. He also indicated that the responsibilities of Xinhua Hong Kong had to be adjusted and that it would cooperate with, and support, the HKSAR government.[9] However, scaling down Xinhua Hong Kong substantially did not happen. Instead, Jiang gave it a new lease of life through reframing its responsibilities.[10] Moreover, Xinhua Hong Kong still needed to provide support to the DAB, FTU, Hong Kong Progressive Alliance, and other patriotic bodies.[11]

The status of Xinhua Hong Kong was raised. In January 2000, Xinhua Hong Kong changed its name to the Liaison Office of the Central People's Government in the HKSAR and relocated from Happy Valley to a new site in the Western District. The change was to reflect its official status as Beijing's representative organisation in Hong Kong. The inclusion of the central government in the new name served to bolster its status. By the end of 2000, the number of staff had been trimmed down from 600 to about 400, much less than the 60 percent originally envisaged.[12] After restructuring, there were 22 departments dealing with a wide range of activities, including research, culture, media and propaganda, education, youth, law, finance, security, Hong Kong Island, Kowloon, the New Territories, Taiwan, etc.[13]

In 2002, Gao Ziren, the deputy director, succeeded Jiang Enzhu as the next director. A key task for the Liaison Office was to help Tung Chee Hwa pass the Article 23 legislation so that Hong Kong would have laws to prohibit treason, secession, sedition, subversion, theft of state secrets, and ties with foreign political bodies. The Liaison Office's responsibilities involved mobilising supporters, neutralising the majority, and defeating the "small" number of opponents. When the HKSAR government put forward the legislative proposal, Gao described it as "very lenient".[14] Tung Chee Hwa framed the passing of the proposed legislation thus: "it is the common responsibility of you and me as Chinese citizens to implement Article 23 of the Basic Law".[15] Maria Tam even said that anyone who did not support the Article 23 legislation was not fit to be Chinese.[16] The left-wing press mounted a propaganda campaign to denounce opponents as traitors. Business tycoons, such as Li Ka Shing, Stanley Ho, and Gordon Wu felt they had to publicly support the bill.[17] Various leftist groups organised seminars and wrote supporting submissions to the government. Twenty-seven pro-government organisations formed the Grand Coalition to Support the Enactment of Legislation to Protect National Security. The convener of coalition was the FTU's Cheng Yiu Tong, who had been appointed to the Executive Council by Tung Chee Hwa. Senior local patriotic figures like Xu Simin, Tsang Hin Chi, and Chan Wing Kee joined a mass assembly where the coalition claimed more than 40,000 people from 1,500 organisations participated.[18]

From 2 April 2003, Hong Kong's attention was momentarily diverted by the arrival of a new infectious disease—severe acute respiratory syndrome. However, once it had begun to subside, public attention turned back to the Article 23 legislation. Those opposing it called for more time for public consultation and amendment of certain provisions. The HKSAR government did not give way since its assessment was that it had enough votes in the Legislative Council to pass the bill on the scheduled date of 9 July 2003. The government's insistence provoked a massive public demonstration on 1 July when more than 500,000 people took part in the protest. This was the seminal event that would change the CCP's policy on Hong Kong. Many scholars have explored the events leading up to the demonstration. It suffices to say here that the civil society and pro-democracy groups that organised the march made sure the focus was on Tung Chee Hwa and his officials and not the CCP or the Chinese government to avoid direct confrontation with Beijing.[19]

Zou Zekai, the deputy director of the Liaison Office, used the Cultural Revolution as an example and said that street protests and demonstrations would eventually lead to the complete collapse of Hong Kong's economy.[20] The Liaison Office apparently thought the demonstrators were paid to protest. It had reported internally that each demonstrator was paid HK$300 to march, while those who shouted slogans were paid HK$500 each. And to make the foreign connection clear, it had reported that the money was channelled through the American investment bank, Morgan Stanley.[21] If such a report had indeed been made, it would have been blatantly untrue but it could have perpetuated the longstanding belief within the CCP that foreign forces were trying to destabilise Hong Kong.

Within days of 1 July, the Politburo convened an enlarged meeting and decided that Hong Kong should keep to the original schedule to pass the bill.[22] Gao Siren echoed that there should be no delay; and Mainland enterprises issued an open letter opposing postponement.[23] However, with the Liberal Party supporting a delay, Tung Chee Hwa had no choice but to abort passage of the bill as the HKSAR government would not have sufficient votes to push it through.[24] Gao then changed his tone and said he respected Tung's decision.[25] He added that the Tung administration should reprioritise efforts to address economic issues instead.[26]

The 1 July demonstration was a serious setback for the Liaison Office. It had seriously underestimated feelings in Hong Kong and the number of protesters joining the march. People were unhappy not just because of the Article 23 legislation but the community had been through several years of a weak economy and deflation, and the public mood had turned negative. Beijing must have received conflicting information just prior to the protest ranging from a relatively low turnout to figures well over 200,000. Premier Wen Jiabao, who was in Hong Kong between 29 June and 1 July, left for Shenzhen after the official reunification anniversary celebrations that morning and watched what happened in the afternoon from Shenzhen. Wen was apparently enraged by the Liaison Office for not getting matters right.[27] Even the veteran leftist Xu Simin criticised the Liaison Office for not having done enough united front work in Hong Kong. Moreover, Xu said that after the 1 July 2003, the Liaison Office "just disappeared after things went wrong".[28]

Personnel and structural changes were made at the Liaison Office. In 2009, Gao Siren was succeeded by his deputy, Peng Qinghua, an experienced cadre who had once served in the CCP's Organisation Department. He had already been made a member of the Central Committee of the CCP in 2007. In 2012, Zhang Xiaoming, deputy director of the Hong Kong and Macao Affairs Office, succeeded Peng. In the same year, he was made an alternate member of the Central Committee of the CCP, which is one rank lower than all previous directors of CCP Hong Kong—and one rank below Wang Guangya, the director of the Hong Kong and Macao Affairs Office, who was his former boss. This signalled that decisions were made in Beijing and the Liaison Office was expected to implement them. Zhang was made the head of the Hong Kong and Macao Affairs Office soon after the twentieth anniversary of the reunification and was also elevated to full membership of the Central Committee of the CCP at the 19th National Party Congress. His successor at the Liaison Office is Wang Zhimin, former head of the Liaison Office in Macao, who was also made a full member of the Central Committee. Wang used to be a deputy director at the Hong Kong Liaison Office (2005–2009) in charge of youth affairs. Their promotion to the Central Committee signalled the importance the party places on Hong Kong matters.

The Liaison Office's responsibilities are:

1. Liaising with the Commissioner's Office of China's Foreign Ministry in the HKSAR and the Hong Kong Garrison;
2. Liaising and assisting relevant Mainland authorities to manage the Chinese enterprises in Hong Kong;
3. Facilitating cooperation between Hong Kong and the Mainland on the economic, education, scientific, cultural and sports areas etc.
4. Connecting with local people from various sectors, facilitating communication between Hong Kong and the Mainland, and reflecting Hong Kong people's views on Mainland affairs;
5. Handling matters related to Taiwan; and
6. Handling other duties assigned by the Central People's Government.[29]

It is unclear how many people work at the Liaison Office today. The Office had bought many residential properties worth hundreds of millions of dollars,[30] presumably for staff and visitors, indicating that increasing numbers of Mainland cadres and officials go to Hong Kong for work and visits. Rita Fan revealed in 2017 that all the staff at the Liaison Office were from the Mainland—mostly from Guangdong with the rest from Fujian and other places. She suggested that the Liaison Office should hire Hong Kong staff so that it could understand local culture better.[31] Her statement was a sign that even among those who were closest to the CCP in Hong Kong, there were still sentiments that Mainland officials in Hong Kong did not understand how the local people think and thus were unable to reflect matters fully or accurately to Beijing.

Commissioner and commander

The Office of the Commissioner of China's Ministry of Foreign Affairs has a major presence in the HKSAR.[32] The first commissioner was Ma Yuzhen, a diplomat, who was ambassador to the United Kingdom from 1991 to 1995, and vice-minister at the State Council Information Office prior to going to the HKSAR. Generally, the Commissioner's Office operated in a low-profile manner. Nevertheless, occasional comments about local affairs were made. For example, Ma warned that Hong Kong should not be used as an "operation base" by the Falun Gong, which Beijing had declared an "evil cult".[33] In 2000, when Chris Patten (then a European Union commissioner) remarked on various local issues when visiting Hong Kong, the Commissioner's Office issued a statement criticising Patten for commenting on China's internal matters.[34] Likewise, it criticised the United States government for interfering in Chinese affairs after the Department of State released its China Country Report on Human Rights Practices, which included sections on Hong Kong and Macao.[35] The Commissioner's Office also responded to foreign news articles to emphasise the Chinese government's "zero tolerance" for "Hong Kong independence in whatever form".[36]

The stationing of the Hong Kong Garrison in the HKSAR is provided for in Article 14 of the Basic Law, as well as the Mainland's Law on the Garrison of the HKSAR. Advance Garrison personnel arrived in Hong Kong between April and May 1997 to prepare for the transfer of defence responsibility from the British, and 500 advance troops entered Hong Kong on 30 June 1997. A 4,000 contingent of ground, navy, and air personnel arrived on 1 July 1997. Its headquarters is at the Chinese People's Liberation Army Forces Hong Kong Building (previously known as the Prince of Wales Building) at Tamar and it also controls former British army sites. The Garrison is led by both a military commander and a political commissar. The cost of keeping the Garrison in Hong Kong is borne by the Central People's Government. Its main responsibilities are to prepare against and resist aggression, safeguard the security of the HKSAR, carry out defence duties, control military facilities, and handle foreign-related military affairs. Upon the request of the HKSAR government, the Garrison may provide assistance in the maintenance of public order and disaster relief.[37] In 2012, there were 15 squads in the Garrison, which had increased to 20 squads by 2017. The Garrison is part of a larger national army and has become a well-equipped combat-ready force. While it is under the direct leadership of the Central Military Commission, administrative control rests with the Southern Theatre Command (former known as the Guangzhou Military Region).[38] The Garrison can also play a role in international affairs. For example, in November 2016, its officers took part in the first ever joint military exercise overseas with their Malaysian counterparts,[39] and on 5 June 2017, it conducted an air and naval patrol off Hong Kong waters, likely to show China's determination to protect what China regards to be Chinese waters in the South China Sea.[40]

The Garrison had initial difficulties adapting to Hong Kong. In 2002, Commander Xiong Ziren said that Hong Kong had "a variety of political groups, social organisations and factions. They have different political views and inclinations. Hostile forces inside and outside the country always tried to take every opportunity to corrupt, befriend and instigate the Garrison", Xiong then provided a standard Mainland description of Hong Kong—that Hong Kong had been separated from the Mainland for a long time, people had a colonial education, and there were "anti-China and extreme rightist forces" both within the territory and on the outside. These characteristics resulted in Hong Kong people holding biases and misunderstanding about the CCP and Chinese government.[41] It could equally be said that in perpetuating this line of thinking, the party sustained biases and misunderstandings about Hong Kong and its people.

The garrison had to flex its muscles from time to time to send signals to Hong Kong people. It held the biggest military parade outside Beijing on 1 August 2004 to mark China's Armed Forces Day with 3,000 troops and armoured vehicles. On that occasion, Commander Wang Jitang stated his support for the then beleaguered Tung Chee Hwa.[42] On 24 January 2014, the Garrison staged a first air-and-sea drill across Victoria Harbour, providing a warning sign after several activists had broken into the Tamar headquarters on 26 December 2013, waving a colonial-era flag and calling on the PLA to "get out".[43] On 1 July 2014, the garrison opened its doors to the public at three bases, as demonstrators gathered to stage their annual march for democracy.[44] The garrison held a live-fire exercise at the Castle Peak Range on 4 July 2015.[45] A major land-sea-air drill was staged on 31 October 2016, soon after two winners of the 2016 Legislative Council election used their oath swearing to promote independence.[46]

Over time, the garrison was also assigned united front work. An early example was in May 2005, when legislators from the democratic camp were invited to visit the military camp on the garrison's Open Day. The invitation was widely seen as an attempt by Beijing at reconciliation with the democrats after Tung Chee Hwa stepped down.[47] The garrison's overall united front work had been extensive. Since 1997, it had allowed over 620,000 people to visit army sites, trained young people at military summer camps, planted tens of thousands of trees, donated blood, and assisted thousands of seniors and children in care homes. Its military marching band and artistic team also performed for local residents on many occasions.[48] It was no small feat that the garrison developed a reasonable image in Hong Kong as could be seen from public opinion surveys in 2004 and 2015.[49]

Political Disorder and Governance

A constant feature of post-reunification Hong Kong between 1997 and 2017 was disorder. While the CCP fashioned a new regime filled mainly by "patriots", the post-1997 government faced many difficulties and Hong Kong people remained generally dissatisfied. The legitimacy and authority of the chief executives and their governing teams came under repeated challenge. The Hong Kong community saw the electoral system as manifestly unfair. There was a chance in 2015 to take a step forward but it was lost due to miscalculations by the democrats. Civil servants were also thought to be insufficiently supportive of the chief executives.

Dealing with elections

"Elections" was one of the very last points agreed between Britain and China and the British knew that the Chinese never bought into Western-style free elections. The bicultural nature of the Sino-British Joint Declaration meant that the word "elections" reflected the values, meanings, and understandings of two very different political systems (Chapter 8). The Basic Law, finalised after the trauma of 4 June 1989, spelt out the post-1997 framework on elections. The CCP's concern has always been that political power in Hong Kong must rest with "patriots" (Chapter 9). The compromises in the Basic Law did not mean the inherent contradiction in how "elections" is understood had been resolved—only that they would come to the fore after 1997.

The Basic Law provides that the "ultimate aim" is the election of the chief executive and all legislators by universal suffrage with the proviso that the pace of change would depend on "the actual situation" and that "the principle of gradual and orderly progress" had to be taken into account. The Basic Law provides that the methods for elections could change after 2007 but the drafters ensured that the bar is set high—it would need the support of a two-thirds majority in the Legislative Council, the chief executive's consent, and the "approval" of the SCNPC in the case of change of electoral method for the chief executive, and "reporting for the record" in the electoral method of the legislature.

For Hong Kong, Beijing promised universal suffrage but the goal posts kept being moved. Democrats wanted universal suffrage to be achieved in 2007 for the chief executive election and in 2008 for the whole legislature. For Beijing, it was too soon. Another opportunity arose for the chief executive election in 2017 to be by universal suffrage. When discussion started in 2013, the Central Authorities were willing to allow Hong Kong voters to directly elect the chief executive, but there would need to be a nomination process to screen out candidates unacceptable to Beijing. For the CCP, this was a major concession. A screening device was essential because who becomes chief executive is a matter of national security. The pro-democracy camp wanted a nomination process without filter. The eventual proposal was voted down in 2015 to the disappointment of many people. Almost immediately, the pro-democracy camp asked for talks on electoral reform to start again. It may be assumed that if the timing and details of reform could not be agreed between Beijing and Hong Kong, Beijing would simply not allow election by universal suffrage to take place.[50] It is inconceivable to the CCP that the position of chief executive is not filled by a trusted person. From time to time, Chinese officials repeat Deng Xiaoping's explanation from the mid-1980s—the post-1997 political model would be an "executive-led system" and not a Western model with "separation of powers".[51] What it means is that the Central People's Government governs the HKSAR via the chief executive.

The election of the Legislative Council is a balancing exercise between direct election on a geographical basis and election through functional constituencies. The CCP's approach is to ensure that patriots win a majority of the seats. The assumption was that the patriotic majority would ensure smooth conduct of government business through the legislature. That assumption proved to be wrong.

Patriots, elections, and opposition voters

Between 1984 and 2004, the CCP used various occasions to describe what it took to pass the patriotism test. It included loving China and Hong Kong, respecting the Chinese nation, supporting the resumption of sovereignty over Hong Kong, not impairing Hong Kong's prosperity and stability, not subverting the authority of the Central Authorities, not supporting Taiwan and Tibet independence, not colluding with foreign powers to interfere with China's internal affairs, and not endangering state security by opposing the Article 23 legislation.[52] In 2013, in discussing the nomination process for selecting chief executive candidates for the 2017 election, Qiao Xiaoyang, chairman of the NPCs Law Committee, said that no person who "confronts" Beijing could lead the HKSAR;[53] and Zhang Xiaoming said politically undesirable candidates should be excluded.[54] In June 2014, the State Council made it absolutely clear why being patriotic is important:

> Hong Kong must be governed by Hong Kong people with patriots in the mainstay, as loyalty to one's country is the minimum political ethic for political figures . . . [otherwise] the practice of "one country, two systems" in the HKSAR will deviate from its right direction, making it difficult to uphold the country's sovereignty, security and development interests, and putting Hong Kong's stability and prosperity and the wellbeing of its people in serious jeopardy.[55]

To the CCP, democracy is not the end goal but a means to choose safe hands—"patriots"—to run Hong Kong. The electoral systems for the chief executive and half the legislators have a congenital design flaw, however. They are dominated by various vested interests for which Hong Kong pays a heavy price in efficiency, innovation, and competitiveness. Moreover, the public see the electoral systems as grossly unfair, as vested interests take precedence over the public interest; and here lies a crucial part of the people's discontent.

Among Hong Kong voters, there is a hardcore group that supports the opposition. The 2010 by-election showed the size of this group, as well as the strategising capability of the CCP. The League of Social Democrats floated the idea in July 2009 that the democrats should provoke a by-election and use it as a de facto referendum of public desire for universal suffrage to be achieved at the 2012 elections for both the chief executive and the legislature. The League of Social Democrats and the Civic Party joined hands in this enterprise. Five legislators from the two parties resigned in January 2010 to trigger the by-election, which was held on 16 May 2010. The CCP's counter-strategy was not to field candidates thereby minimising voter turnout so that the by-election could not be considered a referendum. Beijing adopted this strategy because it was unsure whether the pro-government side would do well enough to make a direct punch-up worthwhile. Moreover, a full-scale battle ran the risk of allowing the democrats to claim the by-election was effectively a referendum. Tactically, the pro-government camp questioned whether the by-election violated the Basic Law and attacked the perpetrators for destabilising Hong Kong and wasting time and resources. With no credible opponents, the one-sided by-election returned the five legislators who resigned. The turnout rate was 17.19 percent representing 579,795 voters, the bulk of whom may be said to be hardcore opposition voters.[56]

Election of the chief executive

Members of the chief executive Election Committee are made up of ex officio members from political bodies and representatives from business, community, and the professions. Except for the ex officio members, Election Committee members are chosen from various sub-sectors, which are both corporate and personal in nature. Corporate sub-sectors include such bodies as chambers of commerce, employers' federation, manufacturers' association, enterprises association, banks, and associations made up of property-related companies and even transport-related bodies. The nature of corporate voting is that those who control a member corporation effectively control its vote. Those sub-sectors that are personal in nature are tied to specified professions. For example, the accountancy sub-sector is made up of certified public accountants. Likewise, the legal, engineering, medical, and education sub-sectors are made up of members of those professions. The idea for functional elections was the creation of the pre-1997 colonial administration, designed to co-opt the then pro-establishment business and professional elites when election to the Legislative Council was first introduced in the 1980s.

Over the course of the post-1997 years, more political bodies and sub-sectors were added to expand the size of registered electors and members of the Election Committee. By the 2017 chief executive election, there were 38 sub-sectors, and the number of registered electors grew from under 132,000 to over 230,000. The size of the Election Committee expanded from 800 members in 2002 to 1,200 members in 2012. The HKSAR government worked out all the eligibility details. In the eyes of the CCP, the election of the chief executive became increasingly democratic because "such a composition is an expression of equal participation and broad representativeness".[57] Along this line of thinking, having the overwhelming support from the Election Committee is the proxy for having the support of Hong Kong society. Thus, the driving force for the CCP in chief executive elections is to ensure its candidate has the overwhelming support of the Election Committee.

In the case of Tung Chee Hwa's re-election in 2002, while it was unchallenged, the party had to show that Tung had strong support. While a candidate only needed 100 nominations, Tung got over 700 nominations. Party officials made it clear that to maintain "stability and continuity" it was best that Tung served a second term.[58] Hong Kong NPC and CPPCC members, business tycoons, and leftist leaders were mobilised to show support, some of whom felt pressured, fearing that non-cooperation would be reported to the Liaison Office.[59] In gratitude, Tung later described the Liaison Office as the "HKSAR government's best friend".[60] After Tung stepped down in 2005, an election had to be organised. Beijing decided that Donald Tsang, the then chief secretary, should be the successor. Tsang was the only valid candidate and got 674 nominations.

Donald Tsang's re-election in 2007 was more challenging. The pro-democracy camp participated in sub-sector elections to win seats to the Election Committee by relying on sub-sectors for the professions. The democrats fielded Alan Leong of the Civic Party. Donald Tsang secured 641 nominations. Alan Leong got 132—enough to get to the starting line. Even though Tsang would win, the CCP knew some Election Committee members had reservations. The party wanted to minimise blank votes since it would show internal division. A good occasion to wheel out "big guns" to lobby for Tsang was in March 2007 in Beijing, when many of the Election Committee members were there for the annual meetings of the NPC and CPPCC. The head of the United Front Department, Liu Yandong, hosted meetings to consolidate votes.[61] In the end, Donald Tsang got 649 votes and Alan Leong got 123 votes. There were 11 blank votes and six Election Committee members did not vote. The most memorable aspect of the 2007 election was two widely watched televised debates, where the sure winner had to justify his policies and governance style—a welcomed experience for Hong Kong.

The 2012 chief executive election was more gripping. The punch-up was between two high-profile patriots—Henry Tang, a second-generation tycoon, who was Donald Tsang's chief secretary—and Leung Chun Ying, who had been the secretary of the Basic Law Consultative Committee in the 1980s and served on the Executive Council under Tung Chee Hwa and Donald Tsang. In July 2011, Wang Guangya articulated Beijing's criteria for the next chief executive: the person should be patriotic and love Hong Kong, be able to govern, and be broadly acceptable to the people.[62] Unlike before, Beijing did not express a preference. As the size of the Election Committee had been increased to 1,200 members, candidates had to obtain 150 nominations to get to the starting line. Henry Tang got 390 nominations and Leung Chun Ying got 305. The democrats fought for seats to the Election Committee, like they did in 2007, and fielded legislator Albert Ho of the Democratic Party. Ho garnered 188 nominations but was a side show. There was no clear indication of preference from Beijing even by the annual meetings of the NPC and CPPCC. There was much speculation about why Beijing did not indicate a preference, and why Wang added public acceptability as a criterion. One line of thinking was that leaders had different preferences, or that either was acceptable. Another line of thinking was that the public acceptability criterion was put forward because Leung Chun Ying's supporters in Beijing thought he was the more popular candidate and it was an indirect way of showing support early in the race without articulating a preference. Tang and Leung fought a bruising battle. The media revealed Tang's marital infidelities and that he had an unauthorised underground extension in his home. Tang claimed at a televised debate that Leung had suggested at a confidential meeting to use the riot police and tear gas against protesters in 2003, which Leung denied. Tang's claim could not be substantiated and he breached the confidentiality of high-level government meetings. The CCP threw its weight behind Leung after that debate. Leung reaped 689 votes, Henry Tang got 286 votes, and Albert Ho received 76 votes.

The 2017 chief executive election had many surprises. Veteran DAB member Tsang Yok Sing sought but failed to get Beijing's support to run.[63] Long-time patriot, Regina Ip, failed to get to the starting line but Woo Kwok Hing, a retired judge, did.[64] Leung Chun Ying did not seek re-election.[65] John Tsang, the financial secretary, said a reason he sought the top job was that he had an unexpected handshake with Xi Jinping in 2015.[66] The democrats managed to grab 325 Election Committee seats and decided to back Tsang.[67] A *Wen Wei Po* commentary described Tsang as the proxy of the opposition.[68] Lo Man Tuen, the vice-chairman of the CPPCCs foreign affairs sub-committee, added two further reasons why Tsang was unacceptable to Beijing: he "lacked principle on major issues"—referring to his non-committal attitude to mass protests and he ignored signals from Beijing urging him not to run.[69] Carrie Lam, the chief secretary, who was preparing for retirement, became Beijing's candidate. She received 579 nominations. Woo Kwok Hing and John Tsang garnered 179 and 160 nominations respectively. The televised debate on 14 March 2017 did not have the high drama of 2012. The most notable aspect of the other televised debate organised by the Election Committee on 19 March 2017 was how few Election Committee members bothered to show up. Only 507 members attended. With more than 200 from the opposition camp targeting Lam, she had a tough ride.[70] In the end, she got 777 votes. John Tsang received 365 votes and Woo Kwok Hing got 21 votes.

Bernard Chan, executive councillor and the campaign director for Carrie Lam, noted what it was like to run in Hong Kong's chief executive election. It provides a window into how the vested interests lobby for their causes:

> We needed to win over a majority – and preferably a sizable one – of the ... Election Committee ... In theory, it should not be too difficult to lobby for votes ... In practice, it is impossible to address the committee as a single group. It is a small body, so every individual vote counts. Yet the body is splintered into 38 subsectors, many of which are fairly narrow constituencies. Every candidate must visit all of them, listen to their concerns and give them reasons why they should back him or her. This electorate is not simply split into two or three broad factions. Many of these groups have very specific positions on issues to do with their industries or professions. Quite a few have very detailed demands. In some cases, the demands are impossible to meet. And some are contradictory.[71]

Strategising and mobilising for elections

The CCP has been successful in mobilising the united front forces at elections and strategising for the best outcomes through optimising the placement of candidates in constituencies. Its success has been built upon investing time and resources to turn the DAB into the dominant party, assisting other pro-government parties, and maintaining alliances among patriotic bodies to turn out the vote. In other words,

Xinhua Hong Kong and its successor body, the Liaison Office, is the mastermind behind elections for the pro-government camp.

The DAB was established in 1992 with 56 members. Even by the 1999 District Councils election, it was already the best organised political party in Hong Kong. By 2005, it had absorbed the moribund Hong Kong Progressive Alliance. By 2017, the DAB had over 32,000 members, including 117 district councillors, 12 legislators, as well as 7 NPC and 25 CPPCC deputies.[72] Just how close the DAB is to the Liaison Office could be seen from its biannual fundraising event. In 2014, the event raised nearly HK$70 million. Zhang Xiaoming donated a piece of his own calligraphy that sold for HK$13.8 million. In 2016, the DAB raised HK$60 million that included another piece of Zhang's calligraphy that fetched HK$18.8 million. Pro-Beijing business people were extremely generous in opening their wallets.[73]

Overlapping memberships among the DAB, FTU, and key united front bodies result in a "triple alliance" among them to count on each other for campaigning support.[74] The Liaison Office also supported "independent" candidates to win seats at district and legislative elections. For example, in the 2015 District Council elections, out of 943 candidates, 384 of them declared themselves to be independent

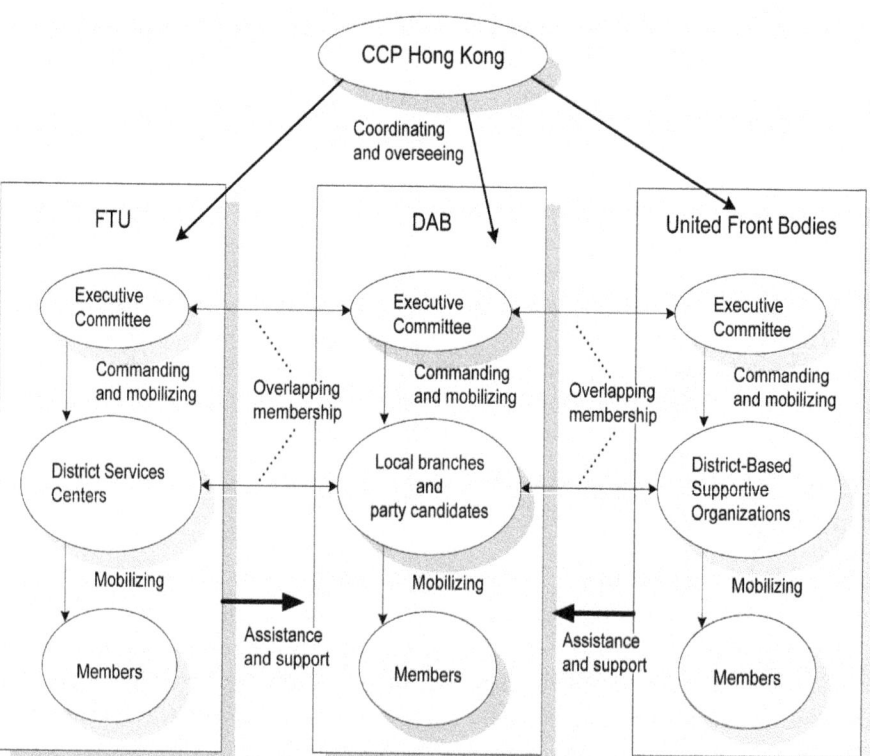

Figure 7 Triple alliance between DAB, FTU, and key united front bodies[75]

or non-affiliated candidates but 88 of them were found to be active members of pro-government political groups.[76]

In 1999, a part of the electoral landscape was changed to disadvantage the opposition. The elected Urban Council and Regional Council were dissolved. These bodies had executive power and budgets to run sanitation services, fresh food markets, and sports and cultural events. Doing away with them not only centralised power within the HKSAR government but also removed the electoral bases of many opposition councillors. At the same time, the advisory District Boards (Chapter 7) were transformed into the District Councils. Tung Chee Hwa brought back a number of appointed seats to the District Councils between 1999 and 2015 (appointed seats were eliminated before 1997), which was another way to dilute the influence of the opposition. There are 18 District Councils with 458 elected seats for the 2016–2019 term of office. District Councils election are on a first-past-the-post basis.

When sacrifices had to be made, it was clear who had priority. In the 2008 Legislative Council election, the Liaison Office's last minute "get out the vote" effort went to the DAB–Heung Yee Kuk alliance over the Liberal Party.[77] Extra effort also went to the DAB instead of the FTU in the 2016 election, which veteran unionist Wong Kwok Hing believed led to his defeat.[78] Favouritism at election no doubt hurt the feelings of those who felt they did not get sufficient help.

Ideologically, the FTU represents grassroots and blue-collar workers' interests while the DAB represents lower-middle and middle-income interests. The Liberal Party is pro-business and aligns with upper economic circles. Internal strive caused the Liberal Party to split after the 2008 election. Over time, through reorganisation and rebranding among pro-business patriotic politicians, the Business and Professional Alliance for Hong Kong was formally created as a political party in 2012. The New People's Party, founded by Regina Ip in January 2011, is also part of the pro-government camp. Michael Tien left the New People's Party in 2017 to form the Roundtable Pragmatism.

Pro-Government Forces in 2016–2020 Legislative Council and Year of Formation

1948: Hong Kong Federation of Trade Unions (FTU)
1992: Democratic Alliance for the Betterment of Hong Kong (DAB)
1993: Liberal Party
1999: New Century Forum
2011: New People's Party
2012: Business and Professional Alliance for Hong Kong
2017: Roundtable Pragmatism

Fragmentation and veto power

The Legislative Council is made up of geographical and functional members in equal proportion. To ensure the DAB could win more seats in the geographical constituencies, the pre-1997 first-past-the-post election system was replaced by proportional representation using the Largest Remainder Formula from the 1998 election. This kind of system favours weaker parties, which was what the DAB needed at the time. Functional elections are like sub-sector elections described above for the chief executive election.[79] A mark of functional constituencies is the high frequency of there being just one candidate who is automatically elected in the business-related seats. In other words, these are seats that are spoken for, where the vested interests agree who should represent them, such as in real estate.[80] While functional seats are mainly held by pro-government lawmakers, the opposition has been able to hold on to various constituencies with individual voting, such as for teachers and lawyers.

The combination of the proportional representation method for geographical election and functional elections has enabled the patriotic forces to win a majority of the legislative seats from election to election but the same system is also limiting the advance of both the pro-government and pro-democracy forces. What cannot grow tends to fragment.[81] Proportional representation enables even small groups to have a chance to win. On the pro-democracy side, small parties have grabbed seats, such as the League of Social Democrats and People Power. In the 2016 election, new opposition groups—Demosistō, Democracy Groundwork, Land Justice League, and Civic Passion—each won a seat, and Youngspiration won two seats. They have also split the pro-democracy camp between the traditional democrats and a radical faction. A further observation can be made: despite the fierce battle for seats, the overall result between the pro-government and pro-democracy camps is about winning or losing at the margins that affect a very small number of seats.

The opposition's ability to retain one-third of the seats enabled the democrats to veto government proposals to change the electoral system, as the Basic Law requires a two-thirds majority in such cases. On 18 June 2015, the Legislative Council voted down the HKSAR government's electoral proposal for the chief executive to be elected by universal suffrage in 2017. It was expected that the package would not pass as there was insufficient support for the two-thirds majority needed. What will not be forgotten in Hong Kong's legislative history is the bungling of the vote by the pro-government camp. Only eight pro-government legislators voted for the proposal, as the others walked out in the mistaken belief that the vote would be adjourned while they waited for Lau Wong Fat of the Heung Yee Kuk to arrive. Confusion was caused by the spur-of-the-moment request from Jeffrey Lam of the Business and Professional Alliance to the president of the Legislative Council to adjourn the vote, which prompted the DAB's Ip Kwok Him to signal to pro-government lawmakers to leave the chamber. In fact, the voting process had already been initiated.[82] Not only was the pro-government camp unable to blame the opposition for rejecting reform, they were widely ridiculed for getting things so wrong. There were tears and apologies.[83] Beijing was surprised by the walkout. A Mainland official admitted what happened was "embarrassing".[84]

Filibuster and disorder

The bungling of the crucial vote on 18 June 2015 illustrated a recurrent problem with the pro-government camp. Like the pro-democracy camp, it is also fragmented and pluralised. While it is common for parliamentarians to time their presence in the chamber to when they expect to speak or cast their vote, opposition lawmakers in Hong Kong had exploited the lack of resolve of pro-government lawmakers to stay in their seats by using the filibuster to delay or stop legislative proceedings. The pro-government lawmakers could have minimised the filibuster by being present during legislative meetings to discourage time-wasting quorum, division, and adjournment calls. The efforts of just a handful of the more radical lawmakers to sustain tedious filibustering proved most effective. Through perfecting the art of filibustering during the Leung Chun Ying administration, the opposition substantially affected government business.[85] From the HKSAR government's perspective, the cost to effective governance was enormous:

> This is already the fourth year in which Members put forward loads of amendments to the Appropriation Bills and made incessant quorum calls . . . driving the Government to the verge of a "fiscal cliff" . . . [Other] meetings . . . have also been affected by individual Members' filibusters from time to time. The objective result is a serious congestion of agenda items.[86]

The financial secretary made a point of noting on 26 April 2017 in relation to the 2017–2018 Budget that:

> In the past four fiscal years . . . on average, over 16 meeting days are required each year for the passage [of the Budget] . . . which is six times the average time needed for scrutinising the same bill . . . since 1997.[87]

The pro-government camp is in fact just a mixed bag and motley crew with different interests. Its deficiencies were colourfully described by the head of the Central Policy Unit, Shiu Sin Por, in March 2016. He criticised its lawmakers for "messing around" with their own agendas and failed to fulfil their duties, while still collecting a decent pay cheque every month. He highlighted their poor communication, inability to work together, and unwillingness to sit through meetings to prevent filibustering.[88] Tung Chee Hwa suggested in June 2016 that the HKSAR government might work more closely with the pro-government camp to solve the problem of lack of unity. He lamented that all three chief executives could not run an "executive-led" government:

As a result, past administrations have been unable to achieve what they aspired to. The problem is that . . . the chief executive does not lead any political parties, while the lawmakers are popularly elected. Of the lawmakers, some are non-affiliated while even more are attached to different political parties. They represent different interest groups, and have thus constantly disputed with one another and the SAR government. Therefore, the chief executives found it difficult to effectively execute the executive-led governance model as stipulated under the Basic Law, resulting in even greater friction . . . The government should work even closer with the pro-establishment camp, build a closer partnership relationship with them, and allow them to get more involved in the implementation and discussion of government policies. At the same time, the pro-establishment camp not only should consider the interests of their voters, but also should think about the interests of the whole of Hong Kong.[89]

Chief executive and civil service

The CCP's assumption was that with Tung Chee Hwa as chief executive, supported essentially by the senior ranks of pre-1997 civil servants, the administration of the HKSAR would function effectively from day to day. Yet, this did not happen. There were two sets of circumstances which casted doubts about the competence of the first post-1997 government. Firstly, the Asian Financial Crisis in 1997 and its aftermath drained confidence, as stock and property markets collapsed. The HKSAR government took aggressive and courageous actions to defend the Hong Kong dollar against speculative attack and bought stocks to support the market. The many opinions at the time on whether the HKSAR government took appropriate actions created doubts in the minds of the public about the competence of the governing team.[90] Secondly, Tung and the civil servants had their differences. He was seen by the seasoned bureaucrats as an inexperienced politician. The civil servants felt Tung did not always listen to them and Tung felt he was not supported. The government appeared poorly joined up and the public blamed Tung Chee Hwa.[91] Mainland officials, from Hu Jintao to officers of the Liaison Office, had to repeatedly voice support for him. As Tung's popularity did not improve, the Liaison Office was asked by Beijing to investigate the reasons for the widespread discontent. The Liaison Office reported that Tung's problems were mainly caused by the chief secretary, Anson Chan, who had not been fully supportive of him.[92] Chan was the quintessential successful "administrative officer"—a generalist class of bureaucrats under the colonial system groomed for the senior ranks. In September 2000, Chan was asked to visit Beijing where Qian Qichen gave her a dressing-down. He emphasised that Chan and the civil service should do better to support the chief executive.[93] Anson Chan announced in January 2001 that she had decided to step down and left in April. She later revealed that there had been considerable disagreement between her and Tung:

If you are not able to influence the course of events, particularly events that you very much disagreed with, you must make your choice. So I decided to step down and not be forced out. Mr. Tung and I may not have agreed on how to tackle particular issues. The difficulties were compounded by the introduction of the political appointee system.[94]

Tung Chee Hwa established a new ministerial system in 2002, where the chief executive would appoint ministers to support his policy direction. Civil servants would then be politically neutral rather than be politicians and administrators at the same time. As with any new system, there were many teething problems with the ministers and how the system functioned. Its implementation did not make governing easier for Tung.[95] After Donald Tsang was re-elected in 2007, he appointed mainly civil servants to be ministers and added deputy ministers and political assistants. Questions arose about the need for having yet more layers of inexperienced appointees, how they worked as a team, and their division of responsibility with the civil servants. Tsang also expanded and embedded more administrative officers in the bureaucracy since he believed the supposedly multi-skilled administrators—part of the colonial governing structure—were the ones who would know how to solve problems. Leung Chun Ying relied on both civil servants and external appointees to make up his team. Carrie Lam too had to rely mostly on civil servants as ministers. It was difficult to attract external talent at a time when the political environment was highly charged with officials being frequently vilified and pilloried. While a ministerial system could not solve the problems of legitimacy for the post-1997 chief executives, it did show that the CCP had to accept people from outside the traditional patriotic camp in the creation of ministerial teams. Some of the appointees served more than one term and some were promoted from deputy ministers to ministers. New systems take time to take root and Hong Kong's ministerial system will no doubt continue to evolve.

There has been little attempt to reform the civil service, led by administrative officers, for Hong Kong to stay competitive and cope with a fast-changing world, including technological, financial, managerial, and communication developments. The highly segmented and stratified bureaucratic structure of the Hong Kong civil service made working across disciplines and departments difficult. The lack of legitimacy and toxic political environment discouraged initiatives that are considered politically "risky". The speed of getting things done was not helped by extended filibusters in the legislature. Moreover, dealing with the Mainland did not come naturally to the Hong Kong civil service. Speaking Putonghua remains a challenge for many bureaucrats. Not only is the Mainland a very different system, but the People's Republic of China is also a rising world power with a large and expanding economy with significant research, policy, military, scientific, technology, and innovation capabilities. Beijing has strategies and plans to play an increasingly significant part in global affairs and Mainland officials are ambitious. The HKSAR civil service's outlook of Hong Kong and its role within the nation and the world seems parochial by comparison.

Another area of discomfort for civil servants is that Beijing takes an intense interest in the HKSAR because it is a part of the nation. In the past, Hong Kong was a faraway afterthought for the British. The attitude of senior civil servants in supporting the chief executive became an issue for Beijing. In May 2017, Politburo member Zhang Dejiang emphasised that Beijing's "implicit powers" includes "supervising whether [Hong Kong's civil servants] uphold the Basic Law, and whether they pledge allegiance to the country and [Hong Kong]".[96] This means Beijing has a say in not only the appointment of ministers but also the most senior civil servants in terms of their suitability. In his speech on 1 July 2017 in Hong Kong, Xi Jinping specifically stated that the "awareness of the constitution and the Basic Law" needed to be raised "among civil servants"; and he called upon the Carrie Lam administration, which included the senior bureaucrats, to "advance with the times, actively perform your duties, and continue to improve government performance".[97]

United front supporting cast

The CCP's mobilisation of united front groups when needed has become a part of Hong Kong's post-1997 politics, such as when the HKSAR government consulted the public or the Legislative Council called deputations on public order or electoral reform issues. The language used and positions adopted were highly similar, which pointed to the likelihood that the CCP machinery played a coordination role. The united front forces include the Hong Kong Island Federation, Kowloon Federation of Associations, New Territories Association of Societies, and the Federation of Hong Kong, as well as a wide range of bodies, such as the Shaukeiwan and Chaiwan Residents Fraternal Association, Hong Kong Federation of Women, Fukien Athletic Club, Youth Executive Subcommittee of the Chinese General Chamber of Commerce, Hong Kong Federation of Students, Hong Kong Swatow Merchants Association, Hong Kong Clerical Grades Civil Servants General Union, Personal Care Workers and Home Helpers Association, Kowloon Elderly Progressive Association, and Hong Kong Overseas Chinese General Association.[98] Scholars estimated that the united front machinery covers more than 600 organisations,[99] and it has cultivated as many as 4,000 to 6,000 civic groups over the years.[100]

Since 2012, the united front legions became more muscular. An early example was the Hong Kong Youth Care Association that went head-to-head with the Falun Gong. For many years, the Falun Gong put up banners and exhibits at street sides frequented by Mainland tourists. In 2013, the Hong Kong Youth Care Association put up anti–Falun Gong banners at the same locations with slogans like "Boycott Falun Gong evil cult", "Build a harmonious Hong Kong", and "Taiwan Falun Gong get out of Hong Kong".[101] A recent development was the appearance of a range of new groups to counter the actions of the opposition, including Caring Hong Kong

Power, Voice of Loving Hong Kong, Hong Kong Youth Care Association, Hong Kong Justice League, Defend Hong Kong Campaign, Silent Majority for Hong Kong, and Alliance for Peace and Democracy.[102] For example, Voice of Loving Hong Kong organised the *Love Hong Kong, Support Government* rally on New Year Day in 2013 to counter anti-government demonstration organised by Civil Human Rights Front. Silent Majority for Hong Kong was formed in 2013 to oppose the Occupy Movement. The Alliance for Peace and Democracy formed in 2014, which included Silent Majority for Hong Kong, countered the Occupy and Umbrella Movements. The alliance organised signature campaigns, a run for democracy, and a parade. Patriotic groups also got together to denounce the two Youngspiration legislators-elect, Leung Chung Hang and Yau Wai Ching, for their insulting oath swearing in October 2016. The groups called their alliance the Anti-China-Insulting, Anti-Hong Kong Independence Alliance.[103] On 29 November 2016, Zhang Dejiang received Silent Majority for Hong Kong in Beijing and praised its efforts.[104]

Mass Movements and Beijing–Hong Kong Relations

Mass movements in Hong Kong since the reunification have changed Beijing–Hong Kong relations from the initial hands-off attitude to a hands-on approach. Two high-level edicts from Beijing sought to stress what the CCP wanted Hong Kong people to mull over. In effect, the protests and edicts were head-on collisions between Beijing and Hong Kong. Prior to 1997, there was a buffer provided by the British presence. After reunification, there was no intermediary to absorb the impact. Despite the long transition period from British to Chinese sovereignty, the real transition only really started in 1997.

After the 1 July 2003 demonstration, the CCP sent many foot soldiers to Hong Kong to understand the situation. Party leaders had to show support for Tung Chee Hwa and buy time to figure out what to do. By mid-July, a reassessment process was in place with Politburo member Zeng Qinghong leading the review. Heads of the various CCP departments, relevant ministries, the judiciary and military, Hong Kong and Macao Affairs Office, and the Liaison Office were all involved.[105] By 16 September, Zeng had toured South China to explore ways to deepen the economic interdependence of Hong Kong and Guangdong, after which he summoned Tung Chee Hwa for a discussion in Hangzhou.[106] The rising tide of public support resulted in strong wins for the democrats at the November District Council elections, which worried the CCP—the clamour for "double universal suffrage" to be achieved in 2007 and 2008 had to be stopped. A plan emerged. On 3 December 2003, when Tung Chee Hwa went to Beijing to brief leaders on his work, Hu Jintao used the occasion to send a special message couched in a seemingly innocuous news report:

> the president and the central government is very much concerned with the development of the Hong Kong political system with a clear-cut but position of principle

... The central government holds the view that the political system of the HKSAR must proceed ... in line with the Basic Law.¹⁰⁷

In party-speak, the reference to "principle" means the Central Authorities would not give way. Beijing had worked out a chain of actions. The first step was for Tung Chee Hwa to repeat and stress Beijing's concern in his annual policy address on 7 January 2004.¹⁰⁸ He announced at the same time the formation of a Task Force on Constitutional Development with Chief Secretary Donald Tsang as the head. Tsang explained on the same day that:

> [t]aking into consideration our duty to uphold the Basic Law, as well as political reality, we believe that we need to first initiate discussions with the Central Authorities before determining the appropriate arrangements for the constitutional review. At the most basic level, this will avoid the Central Authorities and the Hong Kong community reaching different understandings of those Basic Law provisions regarding constitutional development. Such a scenario could cause serious confrontation between the Hong Kong community and our sovereign government. Obviously, we do not want to precipitate such a situation.¹⁰⁹

In other words, Beijing had to be consulted first. The Task Force met officials in Beijing from 8 to 10 February 2004 and upon its return to Hong Kong, repeated all the issues once more.¹¹⁰ On 25 February, the propaganda machinery ratcheted up the debate with *Wen Wei Po* in Hong Kong providing a refresher course on patriotism, as noted earlier in this chapter. Just as the patriotism debate was subsiding, the final piece of the jigsaw was dropped into place. On 26 March, another innocuous-sounding Xinhua news report stated that the agenda of the next SCNPC meeting on 2–6 April was discussed and it would include a draft interpretation of two specified sections of the Basic Law.¹¹¹ No one had expected such a move. An interpretation was provided on 6 April 2004. The CCP had delivered the final knock-out punch.

National education

When Hu Jintao visited Hong Kong for the tenth anniversary of the reunification in 2007, he stressed the need to put more emphasis on national education. Donald Tsang pledged to do so and announced the development of moral and national education as an independent, standalone subject in his 2010 policy address.¹¹² It would be introduced progressively from the 2012–2013 school year and would become compulsory in primary schools in 2015–2016 and in secondary schools the following year. Tsang's term ended on 30 June 2012. Leung Chun Ying inherited the launch of the new subject. Three days after Leung assumed office, news broke that a teaching handbook, called *The China Model*, created by authors with close ties to the Mainland, lauded the CCP as a progressive, selfless, and united ruling party but described the American election system in derogatory terms. The handbook was condemned as political brainwashing. This led to the first mass protest during the Leung Chun Ying era.[113]

The protest started on 29 July where 90,000 people participated. This was a campaign led by students, parents, and teachers—not the pan-democrats. The organisers did not want their movement to be hijacked by politicians. Large crowds continued to besiege government headquarters for days. The HKSAR government eventually backed down—moral and national education would not be compulsory. The most significant outcome from this period was the emergence of post-90s activists, one of whom, Joshua Wong, became an international celebrity, and another, Nathan Law, ran for legislative election in 2016 and won. Their group, Scholarism, attracted many young members and it was a major force during the subsequent mass movements. By 2014, the youngsters had become seasoned activists. On 10 April 2016, Scholarism transformed itself into the political party, Demosistō, with Nathan Law as its chairman.[114] The party promoted self-determination and proposed Hong Kong to hold a referendum in a decade's time so that Hong Kong people could decide their own fate beyond 2047.[115] Leung Chun Ying responded that the HKSAR was an inalienable part of the country with no time limit. He said the phrase in the Basic Law that the HKSAR would "remain unchanged for 50 years" referred to the capitalist system and way of life of Hong Kong—it did not mean that the sovereignty could be changed.[116]

The young had an irresistible quality and media-attractiveness lacking in tired politicians. They were energetic, fearless, creative, stubborn, self-righteous, and disrespectful of authority. They hated being belittled as ignorant kids. The young, their parents, and teachers were also furious at being labelled as "black hands" of political forces. The energy released from their campaign captured the attention of students, setting the stage for more activism. The national education debate also brought out the fear of political indoctrination of the education system.[117] Another strand was mixing political values with "China". Disapproval of the CCP's outlook became associated with "China", "Mainland", and even "Mainlanders". Horace Chin captured the mood of the young through his writings. He argued that Hong Kong should become an autonomous city-state.[118] The CCP saw these developments in Hong Kong as a dangerous "political duel" between national identity and Hong Kong independence with foreign interference lurking in the background.[119] Hu Jintao highlighted the Politburo's concern at the 18th CCP Congress in November 2012:

> The underlying goal of the principles and policies adopted by the central government concerning Hong Kong and Macao is to uphold China's sovereignty, security and development interests and maintain long-term prosperity and stability of the two regions… The central government will also firmly support the chief executives and governments of the two special administrative regions in promoting the unity of our compatriots in Hong Kong and Macao under the banner of loving both the motherland and their respective regions and in guarding against and forestalling external intervention in the affairs of Hong Kong and Macao.[120]

Xi Jinping repeated that China's sovereignty, security, and development interests must be upheld when he gave his address on 1 July 2017 at the twentieth anniversary of the reunification. He also emphasised the importance "to raise awareness and enhance guidance, especially to step up patriotic education of the young people".[121] The contrasting attitude between Chinese leaders and Hong Kong parents and students was stark.

Edicts from Beijing

Beijing issued *The Practice of the "One Country, Two Systems" Policy in the Hong Kong Special Administrative Region*, a White Paper published by the State Council on 10 June 2014. The paper states that Beijing has "comprehensive jurisdiction" over the HKSAR and can "directly exercises" that jurisdiction. Hong Kong's autonomy is "not an inherent power, but one that comes solely from the authorisation by the central leadership". In other words, "a high degree of autonomy" never meant full autonomy and not even decentralised power. It means that Hong Kong only has "the power to run local affairs as authorised" by Beijing.[122]

Lawyers were particularly sensitive and upset by references in the White Paper to describe judges as "administrators" and having to be patriotic. Some 1,800 lawyers wore black and marched in silence. Judges too had to make sense of the White Paper. Chief Justice, Geoffrey Ma, stressed that judges in Hong Kong acted independently: "and the reality matches this".[123] Judge Joseph Fok noted that the "administration" in generic terms included judges but the judicial oath was clear that judges "administer justice without fear or favour". Furthermore, he stressed that "the oath of allegiance taken by judges . . . in Hong Kong is not inconsistent with judicial independence".[124]

The White Paper was the prelude to another SCNPC decision on electoral reform—Hong Kong could achieve universal suffrage for the election of the chief executive in 2017 with "corresponding institutional safeguards"—a nominating committee to ensure candidates were patriotic.[125] Legal scholar Benny Tai at the University of Hong Kong proposed using civil disobedience to pressurise Beijing and the HKSAR government to give way. He named the campaign Occupy Central with Love and Peace.[126] University students and Scholarism staged coordinated class boycotts and organised public events, which eventually morphed into the Occupy and Umbrella Movements.[127]

Since the 1 July 2003 demonstration, the subsequent wave after wave of protests had both toughened the resolve of the Central Authorities, as well as politicised the younger generations in Hong Kong. The moral and national education debate in 2012 penetrated primary and secondary schools. University students and young graduates were the main participants in the Occupy and Umbrella Movements in 2014. Teachers were squeezed between a rock and a hard place since the HKSAR government did not wish to see pro-independence activities at schools while students pushed to be allowed to do what they wanted. Some schools issued internal guidelines to help principals and teachers navigate the minefield. Wang Zhenmin of the Liaison Office said independence debates should not take place in schools because it would "poison" students' minds.[128]

Birth of social movements

Over time, a generational change had taken place in Hong Kong, which affected the community's attitude on many issues. This was evidenced by the heightened public interest in a range of new demands. An important factor that riled the young was the unfairness in Hong Kong society, where income inequality had risen sharply over the course of two decades. Popular causes also related to lifestyle, such as expanding open spaces, walking and cycling, protecting the environment, supporting local culture, and reviving farming. The contours of the "post-80s", "post-90s", and "millennial" generations as a political force became clearer after 2007. Generally, they lean towards liberal ideas and are savvy with e-mobilisation methods. For example, they took part in the Anti-High Speed Rail Movement against the Hong Kong-Shenzhen-Guangzhou Express Rail Link. On 18 December 2009, thousands of protesters gathered outside the Legislative Council while legislators debated the funding for the project. The debate had to be adjourned. Protestors gathered at the Legislative Council on 15 January as the debate resumed. The protesters used social media means, such as chat rooms, SMS, Twitter, YouTube, and Facebook, to spread their message and rally people. They used simple but eye-catching means to get media attention, such as doing the prostrating walk (苦行). Funding was approved after 25 hours. Protestors blocked government officials and lawmakers from leaving and delayed their departure for many hours.[129] Such activities fertilised young people's consciousness and gave birth to "localism".

Law, Order, and Politics

It was bound to happen. The two very different political and legal systems of the Mainland and Hong Kong would clash. The Basic Law was promulgated by China under its constitution. Elsie Leung said, "from 1 July 1997 . . . a page has turned in our legal history. The common law must now operate under the Basic Law."[130] The Hong Kong Police Force had to deal with constant protests, and yet Hong Kong remained one of the safest cities in the world. The Occupy and Umbrella Movements in 2014 and the Mong Kok Riots of 2016 left so much frustration among rank-and-file policemen that they too had to let off steam in March 2017, while judges looked philosophically at their challenges.

An unexpected case

A case that the CCP could not have expected was Jiang Enzhu being sued by legislator Emily Lau. In 1996, Lau took advantage of the new Personal Data (Privacy) Ordinance to seek information from Zhou Nan on whether Xinhua Hong Kong held information on her and if so to provide it. It was widely believed in Hong Kong that the CCP had files on many people. The law requires organisations being asked for information to respond within 40 days or it commits an offence. Lau did not receive a timely response, which prompted her to lodge a complaint to the Privacy Commissioner, as she was entitled to do under the ordinance. After the Privacy Commission contacted Xinhua Hong Kong, Lau received an unsigned response that it did not have a file on her. By then, ten months had elapsed. Since a prima facie breach of the law had been established the Privacy Commission passed the case to the secretary of justice, Elsie Leung, for her to decide whether to prosecute. Leung decided not to do so.[131] Lau then brought a private prosecution against Jiang. He sought a judicial review to have the case thrown out. The court found Jiang had not committed the offence as he was not in Hong Kong at the time. The ruling provided for Lau to pay Jiang's costs.[132] The CCP no doubt found the case annoying. The interest in the case was its attempt to test the status of Xinhua Hong Kong on the applicability of laws to state organs in the HKSAR, which remains a complex and evolving legal issue.[133]

Basic Law interpretations

Prior to reunification, Hong Kong's highest court was the Judicial Committee of the Privy Council in Britain, which hears appeals from overseas territories and colonies. After 1997, the highest appellate court is the Court of Final Appeal in Hong Kong but the SCNPC has the final power of interpretation of the Basic Law. While the full NPC meets once a year in March, the SCNPC is a permanent body that convenes usually every other month. The Chinese Constitution provides that the NPC has the power to amend the constitution and enact and amend basic laws; and its Standing Committee has power to interpret the constitution, enact and amend laws other than those that must be enacted by the full NPC, and supplement and amend laws enacted by the NPC.[134] In the case of Hong Kong's Basic Law—a national law— before giving an interpretation, the Standing Committee is required to consult the Committee of the Basic Law of the HKSAR, a subcommittee of the SCNPC. The Mainland system considers constitutional and legal interpretation to be a legislative, not judicial, function. The chairman of the NPC is usually the third-ranking Politburo member, who also oversees the work of the SCNPC. There was concern in Hong Kong prior to 1997 about how the SCNPC would function in playing its Basic Law interpretation role. This issue came "alive" after reunification. There were five interpretations in the 20 years since 1997.

The first case had to do with the right of abode. The Court of Final Appeal decided in 1999 that according to the Basic Law, all children born of Hong Kong permanent residents, no matter where they were born, had the right of abode in Hong Kong. The HKSAR government estimated that 1.6 million Mainlanders could immigrate to Hong Kong over a ten-year period. Tung Chee Hwa wrote to the State Council requesting an interpretation of the relevant Basic Law provisions. This was unexpected because the plain reading of the Basic Law provided that the court, not the executive, could request an interpretation. The SCNPC's interpretation was that the court's ruling was "inconsistent with the legislative intent" of the Basic Law—a contrived reason—but it was clear that the HKSAR government wanted to close a potential immigration floodgate. Lawyers were concerned that in future the chief executive could trigger the interpretation process to overturn an inconvenient court ruling. However, the interpretation was popular with the Hong Kong public, as it reduced the number of possible Mainland immigrants to around 170,000 people.[135]

Without being requested by either the court or the HKSAR government, the SCNPC announced its second interpretation of the Basic Law on 6 April 2004 on electoral reform. The interpretation made new law by spelling out a five-step process for electoral methods to be changed. The chief executive must provide a report to the SCNPC about whether there is a need for change, and the SCNPC would then decide "in light of the actual situation" and in accordance with the "principle of gradual and orderly progress".[136] The interpretation was widely condemned in Hong Kong.

The third and fourth interpretations did not attract much public attention. The third interpretation in 2005 arose when Tung Chee Hwa stepped down. The then acting chief executive, Donald Tsang, sought an interpretation to clarify whether the term of the re-election would be for the remainder of the term or for a fresh five years. The plain reading of the Basic Law indicated a fresh five years. The SCNPC's interpretation was for the remainder of the term only.[137] The fourth interpretation was sought by the Court of Final Appeal in 2011 to clarify whether a sovereign nation was immune to prosecution in Hong Kong. The SCNPC ruled that Hong Kong should follow China's law on state immunity as the issue related to foreign affairs.[138]

The fifth interpretation arose after two pro-independence legislators-elect, Leung Chung Hang and Yau Wai Ching, used the occasion of their oath taking to assume office on 12 October 2016 to throw insults about, including racial slur against China. They also had a banner bearing the words "Hong Kong is not China". While on previous occasions, some pro-democracy legislators had also been theatrical when they swore their oaths, no one had gone so far. The theatrics were such that the secretary-general of the Legislative Council, who had to administer the oath for all legislators, held that the oaths from Leung and Yau were invalid. The president of the legislature then decided to allow the two to retake the oaths the following week. However, the HKSAR chief executive and secretary of justice filed a judicial review application to stop them from doing so. While Leung and Yau were widely condemned for their behaviour, arguments arose as to whether the government could intervene in the affairs of the Legislative Council. The government's case against Leung and Yau was that they had in effect declined to take the oath and that the president of the legislature could not allow them to retake it because they had already vacated their seats. On 7 November, the SCNPC delivered an interpretation of Article 104 of the Basic Law on swearing allegiance when assuming public office. Alongside the interpretation, the SCNPC issued an explanation to show the gravity of the matter:

> In recent years, some people of Hong Kong society openly advocate the notion of "Hong Kong independence" or notions of the same nature, such as "the independence of Hong Kong", "Hong Kong national self-determination", etc. which have caused grave concern, anxiety and anger among people of the whole country, including the vast majority of Hong Kong residents. The inherent nature of "Hong Kong Independence" is secession. Words and conduct advocating "Hong Kong Independence" seriously contravene the policy of "one country, two systems", seriously contravene the Constitution of the country, the Basic Law . . . and the relevant legal provisions of the HKSAR, seriously undermine national unity, territorial integrity and national security, and also have a serious impact on the long-term prosperity and stability of Hong Kong.[139]

On 15 November 2016, the High Court ruled that the chief executive could bring proceedings as he had a constitutional duty under the Basic Law to see to its proper implementation; and that the circumstances showed that Leung Chung Hang and Yau Wai Ching had automatically vacated their office as they had effectively declined to take the oath. The president of the legislature could not allow the retaking of the oath where it had already been declined and the office vacated. The court also noted that the outcome of the case would be the same with or without referring to the SCNPC's interpretation, as the court's decision was based on interpreting local laws.[140] Leung and Yau appealed but failed to overturn the decision. That was not the end. In December 2016, the chief executive and the secretary for justice lodged another legal bid to disqualify four more legislators in how they took their oaths. The High Court stripped Leung Kwok Hung of League of Social Democrats, Lau Siu Lai of Democracy Groundwork, Nathan Law of Demosistō, and Edward Yiu, the functional member for surveying, planning, and landscaping, of their seats on 14 July 2017.[141] By-elections would have to be organised.[142]

The Liaison Office's Wang Zhenmin and Hong Kong and Macao Affairs Office's former deputy director Chen Zuo'er thought there were as many as 15 lawmakers who had taken their oaths in manners that were insincere or insulting. Wang said they used the occasion as opportunity for performance and not to pledge loyalty and support to the nation. At a seminar in Shenzhen on 9 November 2016, Chen listed the acts he thought were unacceptable—adding words, tearing up constitutional documents, chanting self-determination, raising an umbrella, taking too long to finish reading the oath, pronouncing the People's Republic of China in wrong tones, hitting a tambourine, and turning the national and HKSAR flags upside down.[143] Politicians will no doubt be careful to observe their oath swearing in the future.

Rise of identity politics

The CCP had been concerned about anti-Mainland feeling brewing in Hong Kong. The economic rise of the Mainland had created a sense of anxiety that Mainlanders were buying up property, using up maternity ward facilities, and even amassing infant milk powder in Hong Kong to the detriment of local people. Mainlanders were referred to as "locusts" for sucking up Hong Kong's resources.[144] High-profile incidents, including activists unfurling the colonial flag and demonstrating outside the PLA's barracks at Tamar (noted above), as well as Hong Kong soccer fans jeering the Mainland team in during qualifying rounds of the World Cup in 2015 and showing disrespect when the national anthem was played,[145] gave vent to the frustration of Hong Kong being overwhelmed by the Mainland. At the same time, Mainlanders felt unhappy about Hong Kong people's behaviour too.

Anti-Mainland sentiments led Hong Kong people, especially the young, to assert and cultivate their own identity but it was the surprise rebuke by Leung Chun Ying in his policy address in January 2014 that made it a public matter:

> The 2014 February issue of "Undergrad", the official magazine of the Hong Kong University Students' Union, featured a cover story entitled "Hong Kong people deciding their own fate". In 2013, a book named "Hong Kong Nationalism" was published by "Undergrad". It advocates that Hong Kong should find a way to self-reliance and self-determination. "Undergrad" and other students, including student leaders of the occupy movement, has misstated some facts. We must stay alert. We also asked political figures with close ties to the leaders of the student movement to advise them against putting forward such fallacies.[146]

The Hong Kong National Party was formed in March 2016 with mainly student activists and recent graduates explicitly to build an independent Hong Kong. The Hong Kong and Macao Affairs Office, Liaison Office, and HKSAR government issued statements asserting that the Hong Kong National Party had touched the "bottom-line" of "one country, two systems"; that independence advocacy was against the Basic Law; that such suggestions would not be conducive to the overall interest of Hong Kong; and that it would not be tolerated.[147] The birth of the Hong Kong National Party ignited a debate about the limits of free speech. The HKSAR government's view was that:

> Article 1 of the Basic Law clearly points out that the HKSAR is an inalienable part of the PRC . . . any views that advocate the independence of Hong Kong . . . are wrong, and are in themselves in contravention of "one country, two systems" and the Basic Law, and in complete disregard of the well-being of seven million Hong

Kong people . . . The Secretary of Justice has also made it clear that any action to advocate "Hong Kong independence" is in breach of the relevant provisions of the Basic Law and incompatible with the legal status and the overall interests of the HKSAR. Just as all acts that contravene the Basic Law or those that may constitute criminal offences, the Department of Justice will keep a close watch and maintain close contact with the relevant law enforcement agencies, and the HKSAR Government will take appropriate action when necessary.[148]

News broke in mid-April that Zhang Dejiang would visit Hong Kong. He arrived on 17 May for a three-day visit. In a high-profile speech, he defined "localism" as fondness for one's hometown and its lifestyle but separatism was dangerous.[149] Despite top-level warning from Beijing leaders, and the HKSAR government's attempt to bar pro-independence candidates from standing in the 2016 Legislative Council election through requiring candidates to pledge to uphold the HKSAR as an inalienable part of China, Leung Chung Hang and Yau Wai Ching slipped through the net.[150] When they stepped over the mark during their oath taking, the HKSAR government and the SCNPC took action. The gravity of the case from the Central Authorities' perspective cannot be overemphasised. At the NPC and CPPCC meetings in Beijing in March 2017, Zhang Dejiang, in his position as NPC chairman, and Yu Zhengsheng, the fourth-ranking Politburo member in his position as chairman of the CPPCC, listed the SCNPC interpretation and the CPPCC's support for it among their major achievements in the past year. Likewise at the opening of the NPC session, Li Keqiang, the premier and second-ranking Politburo member, made a point of saying in his annual government work report that the "one country, two systems" policy would be applied "without being bent or distorted", and that "separatism is never an option in Hong Kong".[151] In April 2017, the CCP Central Committee's influential *Qiushi Journal* identified separatist activities in Hong Kong (and Taiwan) were eroding the foundation of the party's rule and that it would be a focus of China's national security strategy.[152]

Detentions and missing persons

Meshed into the complexity of Basic Law interpretations, Beijing–Hong Kong relations and the rising political consciousness of the young were several incidents that made Hong Kong jittery. These were cases embroiled in the politics of the Mainland. To Hong Kong people, they illustrated the nature of the Mainland's system that they most feared—extended detention, forced confession, or even extraterritorial abduction.

The first case was that of veteran reporter Ching Cheong, who was detained on 22 April 2005 in Shenzhen. Hong Kong people recalled the case of Xi Yang, a Mainland reporter working for *Ming Pao*, who was arrested in 1993, prosecuted and sentenced to 12 years' imprisonment for trafficking financial state secrets.[153] In Ching's case, for 1,020 days, he experienced residential surveillance, detention, and imprisonment. Ching was considered an "insider" although not a CCP member, having been deputy editorial manager at *Wen Wei Po*. He was working for Singapore's *The Straits Times* when he was detained for leaking state secrets. He was later charged and convicted of the more serious charge of espionage and sentenced to five years' imprisonment. Like in Xi's case, Ching's plight became a *cause celebre*. Both incidents touched Hong Kong people's fear about Article 23 and the nebulous crime of theft of state secrets. Ching had wide friendships in Hong Kong and many people, including Donald Tsang, pleaded his case to Beijing. On 5 February 2008, Ching was released on parole. He wrote:

> throughout the course of my interrogation, I was never asked about the state secrets that I was suspected of stealing or leaking. Since the legal reasons—that is, reasons that can be brought out into the open and debated—are not the true reasons for my arrest, I can only look for the real reasons in the political realm ... I have come to believe that I had become embroiled in the power struggle in the upper echelons of the CCP. I had been used by one faction to deal a blow to another.[154]

The second case had to do with five employees of Mighty Current Publishing House that published, distributed, and sold books critical of the CCP and its leaders, many of which were "quickie" books that were gossipy and salacious but popular with tourists from the Mainland. Each of the five people went missing between October and December 2015, which had the effect of shutting down the market for these books. Ching Cheong thought the CCP leadership was concerned that the book market in Hong Kong had become an extension of elite party politics where political factions regularly leaked information to embarrass their rivals.[155]

The first person to go missing was Gui Minghai, who disappeared from his home in Thailand. Three others then went missing in Guangdong, followed by Lee Bo, the fifth person. They all turned up in detention on the Mainland. The case of greatest concern in Hong Kong was that of Lee Bo. He appeared in a video saying that he left Hong Kong voluntarily to assist an investigation. The question was whether he was in fact kidnapped by Mainland agents. Article 22 of the Basic Law is clear that no part of any authority on the Mainland may interfere in the affairs of the HKSAR. Four of the people eventually returned to Hong Kong at different times. The last to return was Lam Wing Kee—the founder of Mighty Current Publishing House—on 14 June 2016. He held a press conference two days later stating that he was detained by Mainland security agents and was interrogated for months about the identities of the authors and buyers of books, and his televised confession was forced. Lam spoke out because "[t]his is not just about me. This is about the freedom of Hong Kong people."[156] On 17 June, a spokesman for the Ministry of Foreign Affairs stated that Lam was a Chinese national and that he had violated Mainland law on the Mainland.[157] In response to widespread condemnation that these cases had jeopardised "one country two systems", Wang Guangya said:

the books published aren't about Hong Kong affairs ... but about the Mainland's affairs. [Lam Wing Kee] publishes ... books in Hong Kong and brings them back to sell on the Mainland. This is his understanding of 'one country, two systems'—this 'one country, two systems', we'd rather not have it.[158]

Mass protests and frustrated policemen

On 22 February 2017, more than 33,000 policemen and their families gathered at the Police Sports and Recreation Club to show support for seven police officers who were sentenced to two years' imprisonment for assaulting an activist in 2014 during the Occupy and Umbrella Movements. Policemen thought the sentences were too heavy and rank-and-file officers used the occasion to let off steam about having to endure insults from protesters as part of their job.[159] The assault in question took place on 15 October after the activist was arrested for pouring liquid onto police officers.

Hong Kong has been described as the "City of Protests". Police data from 2007 to 2016 showed that the number of public processions and public meetings increased from 3,824 to 13,158.[160] Between 2012 and 2016, the police had to deal with a chain of mass movements. The moral and national education protests were relatively mild and short. The Occupy Movement started as a civil disobedience movement but morphed into the Umbrella Movement on 28 September 2014 when the police used teargas to warn and disperse a growing crowd of protesters. The Umbrella Movement lasted 79 days and blocked much of Admiralty, eventually spilling over to Causeway Bay and Mong Kok. The movement became a global sensation and is well documented.[161] The protests petered out when injunctions were ordered by the court arising out of private law suits based on public nuisance initiated by nearby building owners and bus and taxi operators. Some protesters argued that they did not need to obey the law as they were engaged in civil disobedience. Some ignored the injunctions and waited until the bailiffs enforced the court orders before vacating the roads. By then public sentiments was clear—defiance of the court injunctions was eroding the rule of law. The roads were finally cleared and normal life resumed.

Hong Kong's protest culture up until then was peaceful. Nevertheless, the Occupy and Umbrella Movements were long and draining for the entire police force. However, the short but riotous incident in Mong Kok during Lunar New Year on 8 and 9 February 2016 was violent. Sympathisers claimed that hawker control officers wanted to clear unlicensed hawkers; activists sought to protect them because the food they sold, such as fish balls, were seen to be a part of local culture. In other words, the rise of "localism" and the unhappiness of young people with what they saw as "unfair" government policy was the trigger. Hong Kong Indigenous and Civic Passion, militant groups established respectively in 2012 and 2015, participated in the riot. The HKSAR government saw things quite differently:

> [T]he Mong Kok riot ... was an incident of serious criminal violence by rioters with a collective intention to break the law, involving offences such as riot, unlawful assembly, arson, criminal damage, assaulting police officers and possession of offensive weapon etc.... The rioters ... claimed to defend ... "localism" ... violence is not a solution to problems, but only a trigger for more violence.[162]

Judges and judgements

Hong Kong's political disorder spilled over to the courts. Those who did not like the outcome of judicial rulings complained about acquittals and sentences that were too light or too heavy. There have also been complaints from the pro-government side about the frequent use of judicial review by opposition lawmakers and community groups to challenge public projects and pro-government efforts to end filibustering in the Legislative Council. The chief justice, Geoffrey Ma, stressed that one should not just look at the outcome of cases:

> whenever the government loses a case, it is said that the rule of law is alive and well; the opposite when the government wins ... what is really meant is that the outcome of the cases has not been to certain people's liking. And yet, if one is analysing cases determined by the courts, the more pertinent question must of course surely be whether the court has applied the law and acted in accordance with the law, as opposed to applying extraneous factors (meaning non-legal matters such as political consideration).[163]

Media Control

Controlling and influencing the media is second nature to the CCP (Chapter 2) but it has to navigate a very different media culture in Hong Kong. It had to launch campaigns "to regain the Hong Kong media" in 1989 after Tiananmen and again at critical times, such as after the 1 July 2003 demonstration, and the various mass movements from 2012. Prior to 1997, the party sought to influence Hong Kong media through binding media owners to the Mainland political system. After 1997, it became easier to expand Mainland-owned media outlets. Mainland interests have also bought into Hong Kong's traditional media outlets, as well as three major bookstores—Chung Hwa Book Co, the Commercial Press, and Joint Publishing Hong Kong, which together control a sizable portion of the book publishing, distribution, and retail businesses.[164]

Two media cultures

The Mainland and Hong Kong media exist in very different cultures. A good example that illustrates the difference was on 27 October 2000, after a Hong Kong reporter asked Jiang Zemin if Tung Chee Hwa was the "emperor's choice" to serve a second term. Jiang said:

> I'm addressing you as an elder. I'm not a reporter. But I have seen too much and it's necessary to tell you. In reporting, if there are errors you must be responsible. You ask me whether we support Mr. Tung? If we don't support him, how could he be chief executive?[165]

Following the outburst, Jiang Zemin turned his back on the reporters and muttered that they were "naïve". The incident illustrated the cultural gulf between the Mainland and Hong Kong. It was no doubt "naïve" to ask the powerful general secretary such a question but Hong Kong reporters often ask obvious questions to elucidate the obvious answer so that there is an acknowledgment and public record of a particular state of affairs.

Media ownership

Hong Kong used to have a variety of media organisations with different sympathies, including pro–Hong Kong government, pro-Beijing, pro-Taiwan, independent, and irreverent tabloids. From the mid-1990s, the pro-Taiwan newspapers pulled out as 1997 drew near while Mainland-owned media outlets expanded. The CCP-controlled *Ta Kung Pao* and *Wen Wei Po* merged in February 2016 to become the Ta Kung Wen Wei Media Group although the two daily papers continue to be published separately. *China Daily*, another state-owned organisation, publishes an English edition in Hong Kong; the *Hong Kong Commercial Daily* is owned by the Shenzhen Press. Over the years, non-government Mainland business had also invested in Hong Kong media organisations and the assumption is that the owners keep friendly relations with the Mainland authorities. These include *Sing Pao*, *South China Morning Post*, and *Phoenix Satellite Television*. A stake in *Television Broadcast* (TVB) was sold in 2011 to a Hong Kong company that had a shareholding agreement with a Mainland investor who could control the company, the arrangement for which came to light in May 2017.[166]

Another common feature among the owners of Hong Kong's major media organisations was their appointments to Mainland political bodies—an effective way to integrate them into the Mainland political system.[167] For example, the previous and current owners (respectively Sally Aw Sian and Charles Ho) of the Sing Tao Holdings Limited, which publishes *Sing Tao Daily* and the English-language *The Standard*, were appointed to the CPPCC. Other media owners who were made members of Mainland political bodies included Ma Ching Kwan of the Oriental Press Group; Peter Woo, whose family controls Wharf (Holdings) Limited, which in turn controlled iCable Communications Limited (which held Cable TV); Victor Li, the elder son of Li Ka Shing and the Li empire owns Metro Broadcast Corporation;

Richard Li, the younger son who has built PCCW, controls NOW Broadband TV, and also owns the *Hong Kong Economic Journal*.[168]

Losing investments

Some of the tycoons were even willing to buy loss-making media businesses that made little commercial sense. Sing Tao Holdings Limited and Asia Television (ATV) stood out. The previous chairman of Sing Tao Holdings was Sally Aw Sian, then a CPPCC member. When three of the group's senior executives were charged with conspiracy to defraud by falsifying circulation figures in 1998, the group's business was already in bad shape. Aw was named as a co-conspirator but was not charged.[169] In June 1999, the business was sold to the investment bank Lazard Asia, where Charles Ho of Hong Kong Tobacco played a crucial part. He was Sally Aw Sian's biggest creditor and as part of the deal, she would get a loan from Lazard Asia to repay her debts and he dropped bankruptcy proceedings against her.[170] The ownership history of ATV is truly fascinating. ATV used to be called Rediffusion (RTV) prior to 1981 with British and Australian ownership. In July 1982, the Far East Group, owned by tycoon Deacon Chiu, took a stake in the company and the company was renamed ATV. The business was not a financial success, but in 1984 the Chiu family bought all the shares in the company. In 1987, Chiu put the shares up for sale, which were sold in 1989. The buyers were tycoons Lim Por Yen, Cheng Yu Tung, and Stanley Ho. The new ownership consisted of the Lim family with one-third of the shares, his company Lai Sun with a sixth, Cheng Yu Tung's New World group owning half, and Stanley Ho's Sociedade de Turismo e Diversões de Macau joining as a minority shareholder. In 2002, Lai Sun sold its shares to the industrialist, Chan Wing Kee. In 2007, together with Liu Changle, chairman of Phoenix Satellite Television Holdings Limited, they bought most of ATV's shares, after which Cha Chi Min's family took a 58 percent stake in the company and the Mainland's CITIC group took 15 percent, leaving Chan and Liu still holding 27 percent. During this whole period, ATV remained a loss-making business. The company was seriously bleeding at the rate of HK$1 million a day. The Cha family tried to improve day-to-day management.[171] From the time of Deacon Chiu, all the major Hong Kong owners were appointed to important pre-reunification bodies and/or the NPC or CPPCC. Chiu was a member of the CPPCC. Lim Por Yen, Cheng Yu Tung, and Chan Wing Kee were all Hong Kong affairs advisers and Preparatory Committee and Selection Committee members, and Chan Wing Kee was also an NPC member. In 2008, he was appointed to the CPPCC and its prestigious Standing Committee. Cha Chi Min was a BLDC member, Hong Kong affairs adviser, Preliminary Working Committee member, and Preparatory Committee and Selection Committee member. As Joseph Wong, a former senior civil servant noted, there was a "force behind [ATV] that does not want it to close down".[172] The saga continued for years. Taiwanese and Mainland businessmen invested in ATV and there were many arguments among them over management. All the while, the quality of the station declined. ATV finally stopped transmission on 1 April 2016 but the story of tycoons taking up loss-making media outlets did not end there. Peter Woo's Wharf (Holdings) announced in March 2017 that it would close the unprofitable cable business (that included the iCable News Channel), but a rescuer stepped in a month later. The "white knight" is a consortium made up of David Chiu and Henry Cheng—the sons of Deacon Chu and Cheng Yu Tung.[173]

Among the major media businesses in Hong Kong, Jimmy Lai of the Next Media Group, which published the high circulation *Apple Daily*, is the *bête noire* as far as Beijing is concerned and is considered "unfriendly". His publications do not receive advertising from Mainland businesses, Beijing-friendly tycoons' companies, and even other companies have pulled advertising.[174]

Crossing the line

Prior to 1997, Lu Ping told a group of Hong Kong journalists that "I don't want to create any illusion for you. After 1997, it will not be possible for you to advocate two Chinas, or one China and one Taiwan, or Hong Kong independence, or Taiwan independence, or Tibet independence. The press will not be allowed to do so."[175] On 12 April 2000, the Liaison Office commented on how Hong Kong needed to deal with Taiwan-related issues, in light of Chan Shui-bian of the pro-independence Democratic Progressive Party having won the presidential election the month before. Wang Fengchao, the deputy director, warned journalists that the media should not handle Taiwanese independence in the same way as ordinary news stories. He urged that news reports should be beneficial to the cause of national unification. His remarks came in response to a Hong Kong media interview carrying statements by the then Taiwan vice president, Annette Lu, on Taiwan independence.[176] Taiwan's Sunflower Student Movement, which lasted 23 days between March and April 2014, inspired student activists in Hong Kong during the Umbrella Movement. By early 2016, Scholarism and Federation of Hong Kong Students went as far as suggesting that Tsai Ing-wen, Taiwan's newly elected president from the Democratic Progressive Party, should see Hong Kong as a partner so that the two places could face the Mainland together.[177] More galling still to the CCP was in June 2017 when three Hong Kong legislators—Raymond Chan of People Power, Nathan Law of Demosistō, and Eddie Chu of Land Justice League, as well as activists Joshua Wong and Alex Chow—went to Taiwan to attend the launch press conference of the Taiwan Congressional Hong Kong Caucus, formed by 18 pro-independence lawmakers to foster closer ties with the pro-democracy camp in Hong Kong. Their action provoked a strong statement from Beijing opposing collusion between pro-independence forces from Taiwan and Hong Kong.[178]

The landscape in cyberspace

The media landscape since 1997 has changed enormously all over the world. Globalisation, new technologies, fierce competition, ownership changes, and financial pressure have created conditions that challenge the traditional media outlets to find new business models. People are constantly online and they are able to seek, receive, and send information through a large variety of means. The difference between the Mainland and Hong Kong is that in the HKSAR, people have full media and information access from around the world while many overseas websites are blocked on the Mainland as part of the country's censorship policy.

The Hong Kong Journalists Association sees cyberspace as the new battleground over press freedom but the most basic challenge is survival. Producing quality journalism and constantly updating reports is expensive. Finding a business model where that can be done has thus proved difficult, as online media outlets open and close. A notable case was the saga of *House News*, a content aggregator and blog launched in 2012, modelled along the lines of *Huffington Post* in the United States. Co-founder, Tony Choi, backed the Occupy Movement. He was also the chief executive officer of an electronics company with manufacturing on the Mainland. The popular site, reputedly had over 100,000 readers, was closed in July 2014. Choi issued a statement blaming the closure on fear and political pressure. Nevertheless, he created *The Stand News* in December 2014 using a public donation model, but it was less successful than its predecessor. *Hong Kong Free Press*, an English online newspaper, established in late 2015, also used the non-profit model. These and other sites like them survive on small donations, a few paid staff, and volunteer writers. *Citizens News* was launched in early 2017 by several veteran local journalists, well-known for their commitment to professional journalism. The site uses crowdfunding to cover its operational costs of HK$5 million per year. *HK01* was an exception. Launched in January 2016, its investors had set aside HK$300 million to get it up and running and seemed ready to use profits from other businesses to subsidise the media business.[179]

Curious case of Sing Pao

The otherwise pro-Beijing and little-read *Sing Pao* caused a surprising stir in Hong Kong. The chairman of Sing Pao Media Enterprises, Gu Zhuoheng, a businessman, bought the paper when it ran into financial trouble in 2015. The paper published inflammatory articles between 30 August 2016 and late March 2017. The first bombshell was a front-page commentary that described Leung Chun Ying as the true inciter of Hong Kong independence. It claimed that raising the subject was a plot and that under the Liaison Office's orchestration, the "ultra-left camp and leftist media" exaggerated the independence phenomenon.[180] Mainland media described Gu as a "fugitive" wanted for his involvement in illegal money lending.[181]

Undeterred, *Sing Pao* ran another commentary saying that the "Gang of Four", made up of Zhang Xiaoming, head of the Ta Kung Wen Wei Media Group, Jiang Zaizhong, Leung Chung Ying, and an unnamed individual (subsequently intimated to be Tung Chee Hwa) was destabilising Hong Kong.[182]

Sing Pao also made many accusations related to the 2017 chief executive election, including bribery. Articles in September 2016 claimed that assistance and resources were provided to Youngspiration to run against Scholarism, and that Leung Chun Ying and the Liaison Office were behind it.[183] There was a court case in July 2016 when it came to light that a man called Cheng Wing Kin offered money to localists to run in District Council elections in 2015. Cheng and two others were convicted in October for offering bribes to candidates to stand in specified constituencies. Among those offered money was Leung Chung Hang of Youngspiration (which he did not accept). The court heard that Cheng believed he was instructed by someone he believed to be an official from the United Front Work Department who wanted to investigate election conspiracies between localists and pan-democrats.[184] After Leung Chun Ying announced on 9 December 2016 that he would not seek re-election, *Sing Pao* claimed the Liaison Office would back Regina Ip (which did not happen).[185]

Sing Pao claimed that Zhang Dejiang had let the Liaison Office run amuck and that the Liaison Office engaged in corrupt practices. The paper urged the CCP's Central Commission for Discipline Inspection to investigate.[186] It turned out that Li Gang, a former deputy director of the Liaison Office (2003–2014), who went on to head the Macao Liaison Office (2014–2016), was being investigated for corruption and subsequently removed from a recently appointed post at the Overseas Chinese Affairs Office (2016–2017).[187] Moreover, *Sing Pao* likely knew that the commission had already inspected the Hong Kong and Macao Affairs Office back in July and August 2016 and that it was about to issue a report. On 14 October, a report was indeed issued that criticised the Hong Kong and Macao Affairs Office for weak leadership, poor implementation of decisions from higher-up, lax management, and a list of other deficiencies, including the need to pay more attention to the "corruption risks" in its leadership and subordinates, as well as step up monitoring on the use of funds.[188] Furthermore, in November 2016, the Central Authorities had already approved the setting up of a special team to investigate suspected corruption involving CPPCC delegates, including deals in securing Hong Kong delegates to the CPPCC; and the number of Hong Kong CPPCC delegates to various provinces and municipalities would be reduced from over 2,000 to some 700 after a revamp.[189] In June 2017, Pan Shengzhou became a deputy director of the Hong Kong and Macao Affairs Office, representing the party's Central Commission for Discipline Inspection, which likely meant corruption prevention became a high priority.[190] The general feeling in Hong Kong was that *Sing Pao*'s commentaries were part of a power struggle among different factions in Beijing and that they used Hong Kong to attack their enemies. The commentaries provided an interesting peep into the Mainland's political machination.

A Report Card: The CCP and the HKSAR

The CCP has achieved what it set out to do. A historical injustice was settled with Hong Kong's reunification with China in 1997. British and international assessments tend to focus on the characteristics of Hong Kong before the transition but the Chinese focus on its view of colonial history. Xi Jinping made a point of saying on 1 July 2017 that the people of Hong Kong "enjoy more extensive democratic rights and freedoms than at any other time".[191] For the CCP, the Sino-British Joint Declaration was the diplomatic tool to transfer sovereignty and it stated that Hong Kong "will be directly under the authority of the Central People's Government". As unpalatable as it may be for Hong Kong, Beijing has "comprehensive jurisdiction" over the HKSAR. China considers the treaty to have served its purpose and that Britain has no further role.[192] The Basic Law is what matters post-1997. Nevertheless, Beijing finds it necessary to repeat again and again what Deng Xiaoping said in the 1980s because that was when the CCP's vision and structure for the HKSAR was decided and China had made it clear that it did not envisage a liberal democracy for Hong Kong. If there was perhaps a time in the 1990s when CCP leaders saw democratisation as a possible option for China, that time had passed. Chinese leaders today do not see free elections as the default option for all jurisdictions even as their economies develop and advance. Previous talk in the world about the inevitability of Western-style liberal democracy—the "end of history" thesis[193]—has been replaced by a much more sceptical one. China argues that its regime is legitimate because it is effective in improving people's lives. The CCP has also hardened its position since the 18th National Party Congress, which was re-emphasised at the 19th National Party Congress. Cadres are expected to reject "universal values" such as free speech, democracy, and separation of powers that could undermine one-party rule, and therefore threaten regime and national security.[194] Under such an atmosphere, the insistence that Hong Kong deserves a Western-style political system is unpersuasive to CCP leaders.

Elections, democracy, and governance

Even if Hong Kong people concede that it is not unreasonable for Beijing to move cautiously towards universal suffrage in Hong Kong, there is another serious problem for the CCP—the people of Hong Kong want a political system that can solve longstanding socio-economic problems. If their political leaders cannot be fully legitimised through the ballot box so that voters take the responsibility for those they voted in, leaders are still expected to deliver a government that can gain performance legitimacy. Xi Jinping acknowledged that Hong Kong "faces quite a few challenges", that "Hong Kong's traditional strengths start to lose the edge while new drivers of growth are yet to emerge", and "housing and other issues that affect the daily life of the people have become more serious".[195] The problem for Beijing is the united front strategy that it successfully used to co-opt the capitalist class and to keep the "previous system" has become a barrier to change and societal advancement. Sub-sectors and functional elections prevent the HKSAR government from solving many problems, such as land use, small houses, rich public housing tenants, low wages, retirement protection, working hours, medical reform, and taxi services, because of the strong vested interest lobbies directly entrenched in the political system. The privileged interests can make demands of the chief executive, legislators, and political parties to favour them. This system makes Hong Kong less efficient, less innovative, and uncompetitive because it is hard to budge the vested interests. The privileged folks may be regarded as politically "safe" from the party's perspective but it sacrifices the public interest. The incessant demand for fairness and democracy arises from this design flaw in the post-1997 political system.

The second team

A longstanding concern is whether Mainland officials understand Hong Kong people's sense of identity, outlook, and thinking. The justification for having a second team is the need for management of the relationship between Mainland authorities and the HKSAR, but if they cannot truly understand Hong Kong, their reporting and analysis would be deficient. United front activities and the more muscular counter-actions against mass movements are often clumsy and unappetising, adding to the sense that Beijing wants to press its views without understanding Hong Kong people's sensitivities and sensibilities. The CCP should be concerned that its counter-actions have not only failed to bridge differences but also widened contention. Another challenge is to convince parents and students that national education is not "brainwashing".

No doubt the second team can help to deal with Hong Kong issues related to the Mainland, but since it works hard to help patriots win elections, it is not unreasonable that the people see the CCP as having responsibility for the unfair electoral system. It may be that the vote share of the pro-democracy camp has dropped from a height of 60 percent in 1998 to 55 percent in 2016 for various reasons,[196] and that there may be a subtle identity shift of increased "Chineseness" in the population (Chapter 9), but an unfair election system that cannot solve glaring problems will continue to cause contention. The pro-government camp has so far not been able to play a leadership role. They have tended to play the role of "explaining" the Mainland's position but parroting is not what is needed. United front work 20 years after reunification cannot be about keeping the capitalists and vested interests on side to the detriment of the public interest. The HKSAR government—the first team—is responsible for running the day-to-day affairs within its autonomy, but it has one hand tied behind its back arising from the sub-sectors and functional election systems, and the talent-deficient pro-government establishment.

The Hong Kong experiment

The CCP sees its creation of the HKSAR as a great experiment, which is indeed the case. There are many aspects of the experiment that are truly unique. While neither the CCP nor the people of Hong Kong want the experiment to fail, their perspectives on autonomy versus control are different. Seen from Beijing, not holding the line on control when activities threaten regime and national security would be seen as failure. Seen from Hong Kong, clamping down on freedom of expression would likewise be seen as failure. Nevertheless, Beijing's sensitivity to the fuzzy line between what it can tolerate as free speech versus advocacy challenging sovereignty and security is not something Hong Kong should ignore.

Young activists' promotion of "self-determination" and "independence", if persisted, will not be tolerated by Beijing, especially if they get too friendly with Taiwan's pro-independence advocates. The defence that it is free speech in Hong Kong will not be able to withstand the primacy of "national security". The warning has been made at the very highest level—Hong Kong must not use its autonomy and freedoms to promote separatism. Xi Jinping said on 1 July 2017 in Hong Kong that "any attempt to endanger China's sovereignty and security, challenge the power of the central government . . . or use Hong Kong to carry out infiltration and sabotage activities against the Mainland is an act that crosses the red line, and is absolutely impermissible".[197] Xi repeated the party's warning when he delivered his political report at the opening of the 19th National Party Congress: "We will never allow anyone, any organisation, or any political party, at any time or in any form, to separate any part of Chinese territory from China."[198]

Moreover, patience is wearing thin in Beijing that Hong Kong still needs to pass Article 23 legislation. Treason and sedition are crimes already on Hong Kong's statute book so it should be possible to start a discussion about how to update them sooner rather than later. As for secession and subversion, Hong Kong could start a discussion on what activities to criminalise while still respecting freedom of expression conducted peacefully. As for theft of state secrets, Hong Kong's existing laws governing official secrets should suffice. The legal community could play a useful role to promote dispassionate discussion. No one would want to see the Central Authorities apply national security laws to the HKSAR but it is not beyond the realm of possibility as Beijing loses patience. There is also the issue of legal cooperation between Hong Kong and the Mainland. Article 95 of the Basic Law enables law enforcement bodies to "render assistance to each other" but arrangements remain informal. The Mainland does not want to see people suspected or convicted of crimes to use Hong Kong as a refuge. Recent cases of the booksellers and Mainland businessman Xiao Jianhua[199] show that the Mainland could use irregular means to pursue Chinese nationals whom it sees as having contravened its laws outside Mainland territory as a part of its anti-corruption drive. This is one of the toughest issues for Hong Kong to deal with. Nevertheless, the HKSAR government has the duty to sort out structured mutual assistance arrangements, and the legal community can also help to promote discussion in a difficult area.

Discussing such matters is hard, which is why it has been avoided. While many Hong Kong people do not deny that the Mainland has made tremendous strides since the 1980s, and they may even support Mainland policies in many areas, it is a tough sell to get Hong Kong's younger generations to see a one-party authoritarian state in a favourable light. Their identity is tied to liberal values, which is why they emphasise the "two systems" against "one country", or Hong Kong versus the Mainland, or "Hongkongers" versus "Mainlanders". The traditional united front voices and methods are repugnant to many people in Hong Kong and they are ineffective to solve the "them and us" problem. The younger generations want to improve Hong Kong and they are the most strident in demanding fairness and democracy. Independence is not the answer. But, as long as the CCP and the HKSAR government cannot bring about a fairer society in Hong Kong, where the economic gains are shared widely, it will be hard to persuade young people that they should reconcile themselves with "one country".

Appendix I

Survey of Public Opinion about the Chinese Communist Party 2007

A survey was conducted by Hong Kong Transition Project about the Hong Kong people's attitude towards the CCP in June 2007. A total of 810 people were successfully surveyed.

Place of birth

*Out of 810 respondents, 541 were Hong Kong–born (66.8%), 230 were born in China (28.4%), 38 elsewhere (4.7%).

Respondents' identities

*Out of 810 respondents, 290 said they were "Hong Kong Chinese" (35.8%), 227 said they were "Chinese" (28%), and 267 said they were "Hong Kong Person" (33%).

Questions asked

1. Are you currently satisfied or dissatisfied with the PRC government in ruling China?

Place of birth vs. Satisfaction with PRC government in governing China
- About 1/4 of Hong Kong–born respondents stated that they were somewhat dissatisfied with PRC government's performance in ruling China.
- Over half of Hong Kong–born respondents stated that they were somewhat satisfied with PRC government's performance in ruling China.
- About 59% of Hong Kong–born respondents were either somewhat satisfied or very satisfied with PRC government's performance in ruling China. [PRC-born: 60%]
- Compared to Hong Kong–born respondents, more PRC-born respondents (in terms of % and absolute number) said that they were very satisfied with PRC government's performance in ruling China.
- About 17% PRC-born respondents said they did not know. [Hong Kong–born: 12%]
- About 22% of PRC-born respondents said they were either very dissatisfied or somewhat dissatisfied with PRC government's performance in ruling China.

2. **Are you currently satisfied or dissatisfied with the PRC government in ruling China?**

All respondents
    Very dissatisfied – 54 (6.6%)
    Somewhat dissatisfied – 198 (24.4%)
    Somewhat satisfied – 330 (40.7%)
    Very satisfied – 27 (3.3%)
    Don't know – 201 (24.8%)

Cross tabulation: Place of birth
- For those who are either very dissatisfied or somewhat dissatisfied (31%) with the CCP's general performance, over 70% are Hong Kong–born.
- Over 41% Hong Kong–born respondents stated they were somewhat satisfied with the CCP's general performance, while over one-third said they were somewhat dissatisfied or very dissatisfied.
- 45% of PRC-born respondents said they were either somewhat satisfied or very satisfied with the CCP's general performance.

Cross tabulation: Respondents' identities (Hong Kong Chinese, Chinese, Hong Kong Person, etc.)
- 37% of those who were very dissatisfied with the CCP's general performance were Hong Kong Person. Another 35% of those very dissatisfied were Hong Kong Chinese.
- About 39% of those who were somewhat dissatisfied with the CCP's general performance were Hong Kong Person. Another 38% of those somewhat dissatisfied were Hong Kong Chinese.
- In terms of somewhat satisfied, the frequency distribution was less extreme among Hong Kong Chinese, Chinese and Hong Kong Person. About 36% of somewhat satisfied were Hong Kong Chinese, 32% were Chinese, and 30% were Hong Kong Person.
- 56% those who said they were very satisfied with the CCP's general performance were Chinese.
- 43% of Hong Kong Chinese, 52% of Chinese, and 39% of Hong Kong Person were either very satisfied or somewhat satisfied with the CCP's general performance.
- Cross tabulation: Feelings towards Hong Kong's future prospects as a part of China.
- For those who were very satisfied with the CCP's general performance, none of them said that they were very pessimistic about Hong Kong's future prospects as part of China.
- One-third of those who said they were very dissatisfied with the CCP's general performance stated they were pessimistic about Hong Kong's future prospects as part of China. Another one-third stated they were neutral about Hong Kong's future prospects as part of China.
- 22.8% of all respondents said they were somewhat satisfied with the CCP's general performance and optimistic about Hong Kong's future prospects as part of China [highest frequency distribution.]

Appendix I

- About one-fifth of those who said they were optimistic about Hong Kong's future prospects as a part of China said that they were somewhat dissatisfied with the CCP's general performance. About 30% of "optimistic" people did not know whether they were satisfied with the CCP's general performance or not.

3. How well do you think the CCP understands Hong Kong people's views?

All respondents
    Very well – 86 (10.6%)
    Somewhat well – 296 (36.5%)
    Not well – 268 (33.1%)
    Not well at all – 66 (8.1%)
    Don't know – 94 (11.6%)

Cross tabulation: Place of birth
- 46.7% of Hong Kong–born respondents said the CCP understood Hong Kong people's views very well or somewhat well, while 45% said CCP understood Hong Kong people's views not well or not well at all.
- 46.5% of PRC-born respondents said the CCP understood Hong Kong people's views very well or somewhat well.
- About 19% of PRC-born said they did not know.

Cross tabulation: Respondents' identities (Hong Kong Chinese, Chinese, Hong Kong Person, etc.)
- 48% of Hong Kong Chinese believed that the CCP understood Hong Kong people's views very well or somewhat well, while 40% said not well or not well at all.
- 38% of Hong Kong Person stated the CCP understood Hong Kong people's views very well or somewhat well, while 51% said not well or not well at all.
- 57% of Chinese said the CCP understood Hong Kong people's views very well or somewhat well, while 31% said not well or not well at all.
- Cross tabulation: Feelings towards Hong Kong's future prospects as a part of China.
- For those who said the CCP did not understand Hong Kong people's views well (i.e., the "not well" option), about 44% said they were optimistic about Hong Kong's future prospects as a part of China.
- About 60% of those who said CCP understood Hong Kong people's views "somewhat well" said they were optimistic about Hong Kong's future prospects as a part of China.
- About half of those who were "neutral" towards Hong Kong's future prospects as a part of China said CCP did not understand Hong Kong people's views well ("not well").
- None of the "very pessimistic" respondents said they did not know whether the CCP understood Hong Kong people's views or not

4. **Since it is now 10 years after Hong Kong's reunification, do you think that the operation of CCP members in Hong Kong can be more open, like declaring that they are members or should it continue as now, with no open declarations of CCP membership?**

All respondents
    Openly declare membership – 293 (36.1%)
    Continue as now – 379 (46.8%)
    Consider open declaration sometime in future – 23 (2.8%)
    Don't know – 103 (12.7%)
    Too sensitive – 12 (1.5%)

Cross tabulation: Place of birth
- 46.8% Hong Kong–born respondents said the operation of CCP members should continue as now, while 46.5% of PRC-born thought the same way. Only 0.3% difference between Hong Kong–born and PRC-born respondents.
- About 40% of Hong Kong–born respondents said CCP members in Hong Kong should openly declare their membership.
- Over one-fifth of PRC-born said they did not know.

Cross tabulation: Respondents' identities (Hong Kong Chinese, Chinese, Hong Kong Person, etc.)
- 38% of Hong Kong Chinese and 42% of Hong Kong Person said CCP members in Hong Kong should openly declare their membership. Only 26% of Chinese thought the same way.
- 42% of Hong Kong Chinese, 56% of Chinese and 43% of Hong Kong Person believed the operation of CCP members should continue as now.
- Only about 1% of Chinese thought the issue was too sensitive.

Cross tabulation: Feelings towards Hong Kong's future prospects as a part of China
- 23.7% of all respondents said they were optimistic about Hong Kong's future prospects as a part of China AND CCP members in Hong Kong should continue as now (re membership declaration).
- About 62% of those who were very optimistic said CCP members in Hong Kong should continue as now (re: membership declaration).
- About 48% of those who were optimistic said in Hong Kong should continue as now (re: membership declaration).
- A bit more than one-third of those where who were optimistic said CCP members in Hong Kong should openly declare their membership.
- Over 54% pessimistic respondents and one-quarter of very pessimistic respondents said CCP members in Hong Kong should openly declare membership.

Appendix I

5. Do you think CCP members in Hong Kong are currently influencing the Hong Kong government?

All respondents
    A great deal – 123 (12.5%)
    Somewhat – 317 (39.1%)
    Not so much – 164 (20.2%)
    None at all – 58 (7.2%)
    Don't know – 148 (18.3%)

Cross tabulation: Place of birth
- About 44% of Hong Kong–born respondents thought Hong Kong CCP members had somewhat influence over Hong Kong government.
- Only 5% Hong Kong–born believed Hong Kong CCP members had no influence over Hong Kong government at all.

Cross tabulation: Respondents' identities (Hong Kong Chinese, Chinese, Hong Kong Person, etc.)
- 41% of Hong Kong Chinese, 35% of Chinese and 41% of Hong Kong Person thought Hong Kong CCP members had somewhat influence over Hong Kong government.
- 23% of Hong Kong Chinese, 20% of Chinese and 18% of Hong Kong Person thought Hong Kong CCP members had not so much influence over Hong Kong government.
- Only 4% of Hong Kong Chinese believed Hong Kong CCP members had no influence over Hong Kong government at all but 11% of Chinese thought this way.

Cross tabulation: Feelings towards Hong Kong's future prospects as a part of China
- About 40% of those who were optimistic about Hong Kong's future prospects as a part of China said CCP members in Hong Kong are somewhat influencing the Hong Kong government.

6. Are you currently worried or not worried about these specific aspects affecting you, your family or Hong Kong: CCP interference in Hong Kong affairs?

All respondents
    Not worried – 412 (50.9%)
    Slightly worried – 197 (24.3%)
    Somewhat worried – 96 (11.9%)
    Very worried – 80 (9.9%)
    Don't know – 25 (3.1%)

Cross tabulation: Place of birth
- About 48% of Hong Kong–born respondents said they were not worried about CCP's interference in Hong Kong affairs.
- About 55% of PRC-born respondents said they were not worried about CCP's interference in Hong Kong affairs.
- Slightly over one-quarter of Hong Kong–born and 19% of PRC-born said they were slightly worried about CCP's interference in Hong Kong affairs.

Cross tabulation: Respondents' identities (Hong Kong Chinese, Chinese, Hong Kong Person, etc.)
- 49% of Hong Kong Chinese, 63% of Chinese and 43% of Hong Kong Person stated they were not worried about CCP's interference in Hong Kong affairs.
- 28% of Hong Kong Chinese, 18% of Chinese and 27% of Hong Kong Person said they were slightly worried about CCP's interference in Hong Kong affairs.
- 11% of Hong Kong Chinese and 12% of Hong Kong Person stated they were very worried about CCP's interference in Hong Kong affairs. BUT only about 5% of Chinese thought the same way.

Cross tabulation: Feelings towards Hong Kong's future prospects as a part of China
- About 36% of total respondents were either very optimistic or optimistic about Hong Kong's future prospects as a part of China AND not worried about CCP's interference in Hong Kong affairs.
- 11% of total respondents were neutral towards Hong Kong's future AND not worried about CCP's interference in Hong Kong affairs.
- 75% very optimistic, 58% optimistic and 39% neutral respondents were not worried.

7. Who do you think has influence over Hong Kong's development of democracy? Local CCP members?

All respondents
    Very great deal – 97 (12.0%)
    Somewhat – 277 (34.2%)
    Not so much – 168 (20.7%)
    None at all – 80 (9.9%)
    Don't know – 188 (23.2%)

8. Who has the most influence do you think of these groups over Hong Kong's development of democracy?

Two respondents reported that they thought local CCP members had the most influence.

Appendix II

The VIPs Invited to Witness the Signing of the Sino-British Joint Declaration

1. 方心讓　　　Harry Fang
2. 王寬誠　　　Wong Kwan Cheng
3. 王澤長　　　Peter C. Wong
4. 包玉剛　　　Pao Yue Kong
5. 司徒華　　　Szeto Wah
6. 田元灝　　　Francis Tien
7. 白　朗　　　Bill Brown
8. 列顯倫　　　Henry Litton
9. 何文法　　　Ho Man Fat
10. 何世柱　　　Ho Sai-chu
11. 何佐芝　　　George Ho
12. 何承天　　　Edward Ho Sing-Tin
13. 何鴻超　　　Ho Hung Chiu
14. 何鴻燊　　　Stanley Ho
15. 何鴻鑾　　　E. P. Ho
16. 利國偉　　　Q. W. Lee
17. 利黃瑤璧　　Li Wong Yiu Pik
18. 李子誦　　　Li Tse Chung
19. 李兆基　　　Lee Shau Kee
20. 李伯忠　　　P. C. Lee
21. 李柱銘　　　Martin Lee
22. 李葉慧璣　　Lee Yip Wai Kay
23. 李嘉誠　　　Li Ka Shing
24. 李福善　　　Simon Li
25. 李盧玉蟬　　Lee Lo Yuk Sim
26. 李啟明　　　Lee Kai Ming
27. 李澤培　　　J. P. Lee
28. 李連生　　　Lee Lin Sang

29.	沙理士	A. de O. Sales
30.	沈 弼	M. G. R. Sandberg
31.	汪明荃	Liza Wang Ming Chuen
32.	周梁淑怡	Selina Chow
33.	林光宇	Albert Lam
34.	邱德根	Deacon Chiu
35.	查濟民	Cha Chi Min
36.	胡應湘	Gordon Wu
37.	胡漢輝	Wu Hon Fai
38.	胡鴻烈	Hu Hung Lick
39.	范華達	T. G. Freshwater
40.	倪少傑	Ngai Shiu Kit
41.	唐驥千	Jack Tang
42.	夏永豪	Timothy Ha Wing Ho
43.	梁就茂	Liang Jiu Mao
44.	莫華釗	Christopher Mok Wah Chiu
45.	郭元漢	Kwok Yuen Hon
46.	郭志權	Philip Kwok
47.	陸冬青	Anthony Luk Tung Chin
48.	彭炳棠	Pang Bing Tong
49.	程源鏘	Y. K. Ching
50.	馮秉芬	Kenneth Fung
51.	馮若婷	Feng Ruo Ting
52.	葉文慶	Henrietta Ip
53.	杜葉錫恩	Elsie Tu
54.	鄔維庸	Raymond Wu Wai Yung
55.	廖烈文	Liu Lit Man
56.	廖瑤珠	Liu Yiu Chu
57.	鄧國容	Tang Kwok Yung
58.	黎敦義	Denis C. Bray
59.	霍士傑	H. M. G. Forsgate
60.	霍英東	Henry Fok
61.	霍偉釗	Huo Wei Zhao
62.	戴宏志	L. M. Davies
63.	羅 保	Roger Lobo
64.	羅桂祥	Lo Kwee Seong
65.	譚耀宗	Tam Yiu Chung
66.	釋覺光	Rev. Sik Kwok-Kwong

Appendix II

67.	劉皇發	Lau Wong Fat
68.	劉廼強	Lau Nai Keung
69.	孫方中	Sun Fang Zhong
70.	張一帆	Zhang Yi Fan
71.	張五常	Stephen Cheung
72.	張有興	Hilton Cheong-Leen
73.	張建忠	Cheung Kin Chung
74.	張振國	Zhang Sheng Guo
75.	張鑑泉	Stephen Cheong Kam Chuen
76.	楊　光	Yeung Kwong
77.	楊鳴章	Rev. Yang Ming Zhang
78.	簡福飴	Kan Fook Yee
79.	脫維善	Wilson Tuet
80.	謝志偉	Daniel Tse
81.	譚惠珠	Maria Tam
82.	費彝民	Fei Yimin
83.	鄧統元	Deng Tong Yuan
84.	鄺廣傑	Kwong Kong Kit
85.	鄭家純	Cheng Kar Shun
86.	鍾士元	Chung Sze Yuen
87.	陳乃強	Nicky Chan
88.	陳方安生	Anson Chan
89.	陳丕士	Percy Chen
90.	陳有慶	Robert Chan
91.	陳祖澤	John Chan
92.	陳莫榮真	Winnie Chan
93.	陳慶祥	Robert H. C. Chan
94.	馬　臨	Ma Lin
95.	麥海華	Mak Hoi Wah
96.	麥理士	Michael Miles
97.	黃允畋	Wong Wan Tin
98.	黃克立	Huang Ke Li
99.	黃廷芳	Huang Ding Fang
100.	黃偉雄	Wong Wai Hong
101.	黃肇焯	Wong Siu Cheuk
102.	黃禮泉	Wong Lai Chuen

Note: There are 102 names here whereas according to the government press release only 101 VIPs were invited because newspapers reports showed an additional name.

Appendix III

Members of the Basic Law Drafting Committee and Basic Law Consultative Committee

BASIC LAW DRAFTING COMMITTEE

Chairman: Ji Pengfei 姬鵬飛

Vice-Chairmen: T. K. Ann 安子介, Y. K. Pao 包玉剛, Xu Jiatun 許家屯, Fei Yimin 費彝民, Hu Sheng 胡繩, Fei Xiaotong 費孝通, Wang Hanbin 王漢斌, David Li 李國寶

Secretary: Li Hou 李後

Deputy Secretaries: Lu Ping 魯平, Mao Junnian 毛鈞年

All Members:

Cha Chi-min 查濟民
Chen Chu 陳楚
Chen Xin 陳欣
Cheng Ching-fun 鄭正訓
David Li 李國寶
Duanmu Zheng 端木正
Fei Xiaotong 費孝通
Fei Yimin 費彝民
Fok Ying-tun 霍英東
Guo Dihuo 郭棣活
Hu Sheng 胡繩
Ji Pengfei 姬鵬飛
Jia Shi 賈石
Ke Zaishuo 柯在鑠
Lau Wong-fat 劉皇發
Lei Jieqiong 雷潔瓊
Li Hou 李後
Li Ka-Shing 李嘉誠
Li Yumin 李裕民
Liao Hui 廖暉

Lin Hengyuan 林亨元
Liu Yiu-chu 廖瑤珠
Louis Cha 查良鏞
Lu Ping 魯平
Ma Lin 馬臨
Mao Junnian 毛鈞年
Maria Tam 譚惠珠
Martin Lee 李柱銘
Mo Yinggui (Mok Ying Kwai) 莫應溎
Qian Changzhao 錢昌照
Qian Weichang 錢偉長
Qiu Shaoheng 裘劭恆
Raymond Wu 鄔維庸
Rayson Huang 黃麗松
Rev. Peter Kwong 鄺廣傑
Rev. Sik Kwok-Kwong 釋覺光
Rong Yiren 榮毅仁
Rui Mu 芮沐
Sanford Yung 容永道
Shao Tianren 邵天任

Simon Li 李福善
Szeto Wah 司徒華
T. K. Ann 安子介
Tam Yiu-chung 譚耀宗
Wang Hanbin 王漢斌
Wang Shuwen 王叔文
Wang Tieya 王鐵崖
Wong Po-yan 黃保欣
Wu Dakun 吳大琨
Wu Jianfan 吳建璠

Xiang Chunyi 項淳一
Xiao Weiyun 蕭蔚雲
Xu Chongde 許崇德
Xu Jiatun 許家屯
Y. K. Pao 包玉剛
Yong Longgui 勇龍桂
Zhang Youyu 張友漁
Zheng Weirong 鄭偉榮
Zhou Nan 周南

BASIC LAW CONSULTATIVE COMMITTEE

All Members:

ANN, Tse-Kai 安子介
AU, Sing Wai Eric 歐成威
CHA, Louis 查良鏞
CHA, Veronica W. 查伍小貞
CHAN, Cheng-Chun 陳誠存
CHAN, Chi-Kwan Peter 陳子鈞
CHAN, Hip Ping 陳協平
CHAN, Pun 陳彬
CHAN, Siu-Kam 陳少感
CHAN, Wing Kee 陳永棋
CHAN, Ying Lun 陳英麟
CHANG, Denis Khen-Lee 張健利
CHANG, Ka Mun 張家敏
CHANG, Wan-Fung 張雲楓
CHAR, Nee Quin 謝宜均
CHEN, Edward K. Y. 陳坤耀
CHEN, Thomas Tseng-Tao 陳曾燾
CHENG, Chung Wai 鄭鐘偉
CHENG, Kai Nam 程介南
CHENG, Mignonne 鄭陶美蓉
CHENG, Yiu Tong 鄭耀棠
CHENG, Yu Tung 鄭裕彤
CHEONG, Stephen Kam-Chuen 張鑑泉
CHEUNG, Chun Kwok 張振國
CHEUNG, Lun 章麟

CHEUNG, Pak Chi 張栢枝
CHEUNG, Sai Lam 張世林
CHEUNG, Tommy Yu Yan 張宇人
CHEUNG, Yau Kai 張佑啟
CHING, Yuen-Kai 程源鎧
CHOW, Kenneth Charn Ki 鄒燦基
CHOW, Nelson Wing Sun 周永新
CHOY, Tak Ho 蔡德河
CHU, Fee-Loong Aloysius 朱飛龍
CHU, Lawrence C. H. 朱祖涵
CHUANG, Siu Leung Andrew 莊紹樑
CHUNG, Chi Yung 鍾期榮
CHUNG, King Fai 鍾景輝
DEVESON, Patrick Charles Samuel 戴維信
FOK, Timothy Tsun-Ting 霍震霆
FOK, Wah Pun 霍華彬
FUNG, Daniel R. 馮華健
FUNG, Ho-Keung 馮可強
FUNG, Kin Kee Frederick 馮檢基
FUNG, Wai Kwong 馮煒光
FUNG, William Kwok Lun 馮國綸
FUNG, Wing Cheung Tony 馮永祥
GAIRNS, David Wylie 簡大偉
GRIFFIN, Nick 李奇
HA, Louis E. Keloon 夏其龍

HA, Man-Ho Anthony 夏文浩
HARILELA, Hari N. 夏利萊
HO, Edward Sing-Tin 何承天
HO, Man Fat 何文法
HO, Raymond Chung Yai 何鍾泰
HO, Stanley 何鴻燊
HO, Ting Kwan 何定鈞
HU, Chu-Jen 胡菊人
HU, Fa-Kuang 胡法光
HUANG, Raymond 黃維城
HUANG, Rayson Lisung 黃麗松
IP, Henrietta Man Hing 葉文慶
IP, Yeuk-Lam 葉若林
KADOORIE, Lawrence 嘉道理
KAN, Fook Yee 簡福飴
KO, Chan Gock William 高贊覺
KO, Gra Yee 高家裕
KO, Siu Wah 高苕華
KONG, Tak Yan 江德仁
KU, Sze Chung 顧思聰
KUNG, Chi Keung 龔志強
KWOK, Man Cho 郭文藻
KWOK, Philip Chi-Kuen 郭志權
KWOK, Yuen-Hon 郭元漢
KWONG, Peter Kong Kit 鄺廣傑
LAM, Kwong Yu 林光宇
LAMBOURN, John Stove 林邦莊
LAU, Nai Keung 劉迺強
LEE, Jung-Kong 利榮康
LEE, Kai Ming 李啟明
LEE, Kai Yu Paul 李啟宇
LEE, Lin Sang 李連生
LEE, Peter Chung-Yin 李仲賢
LEE, Wing Tat 李永達
LEONG, Che-Hung 梁智鴻
LEUNG, Chun Ying 梁振英
LEUNG, Lam Hoi 梁林開
LEUNG, Siu Tong 梁兆棠
LI, Arthur Kwok-Cheung 李國章

LI, Richard King Hang 李景行
LI, Ronald Fook Shiu 李福兆
LI, Siu Kei 李紹基
LIU, Ching Leung 廖正亮
LIU, Lit-Man 廖烈文
LIU, Yong Ling 劉永齡
LO, Hong Sui Vincent 羅康瑞
LO, King-Man 盧景文
LO, Tak Shing 羅德丞
LOK, John Hsiao Pei 陸考佩
LUK, Tung Chin Anthony 陸冬青
MA, Joseph Ching Chung 馬清忠
MACCALLUM, I. R. A. 麥嘉霖
MAK, Chan 麥燦
MAK, Hoi Wah 麥海華
MAN, Hon Ming 文漢明
MAN, Sai Cheong 文世昌
MILES, Michael 麥理士
MAO, Junnian 毛鈞年
MONG, William Man Wai 蒙民偉
NG, Agnes Mung Chan 吳夢珍
NG, Hong Man 吳康民
NG, Kam Tsuen 吳錦泉
NG, Steve Siu Pang 吳少鵬
NG, Tor Tai 吳多泰
NG, Yiu Tung 吳耀東
POON, Chun Leung 潘振良
POON, Chung Kwong 潘宗光
PUN, Chiu Yin 潘朝彥
PUN, Kwok Shing 潘國城
ROGERS, Anthony Gordon 羅傑志
SALES, A. de O. 沙理士
SETO, Fai 司徒輝
SHAO, You Bao 邵友保
SHEK, Wai 石慧
SHEN, Peng Ying 沈本瑛
SHU, Tse Wong 舒慈煌
SHUM, Choi Sang 岑才生
SHUNG, Jih-Chong 沈日昌

SOHMEN, Helmut 蘇海文
SOMERVILLE, Michael Neale 沈茂輝
SUN, Samson 孫秉樞
SUN, Sheng Tsang 孫城曾
TAM, Ling Kwan 談靈鈞
TANG, Hing Yee 鄧卿意
TANG, Hsiang-Chien 唐翔千
TAO, Edwin Hsueh-Chi 陶學祁
TIEN, James Pei-Chun 田北俊
TISDALL, Brian H. 戴斯德
TO, Shui Moon 堵綏滿
TSANG, Hin Chi 曾憲梓
TSANG, Jeffrey Y. S. 曾翼生
TSANG, Kwong To 曾光道
TSE, Daniel Chi Wai 謝志偉
TSE, Jacob Wai Chee 謝懷志
TSIN, Sai Nin 錢世年
TSO, Wung-Wai 曹宏威
TSUI, Sze-Man (Xu, Simin) 徐四民
TSUI, William H. C. 徐慶全
TU, Elsie 杜葉錫恩
TUET, Kasim Wilson Wai-Sin 脫維善
TUNG, Chee-Hwa 董建華
VAN, Lau 文樓
WAN, Kwok Shing 溫國勝
WONG, David Edward Leslie Yat-Huen 黃日煊

WONG, Hong Yuen 黃匡源
WONG, Kong Hon 黃光漢
WONG, Kwan Cheng 王寬誠
WONG, Lai Chuen 黃禮泉
WONG, Philip Yu-Hong 黃宜弘
WONG, Po Yan 黃保欣
WONG, Ronnie Man Chiu 王敏超
WONG, Wan Tin 黃允畋
WONG, Ying Wai Wilfred 王英偉
WOO, Peter Kwong-Ching 吳光正
WRANGHAM, Peter J 雷興悟
WU, Annie Suk-Ching 伍淑清
WU, Harold T. 吳坦
WU, Wai Yung Raymond 鄔維庸
WUT, Chiu 屈超
YANG, T. L. 楊鐵樑
YAU, Eddy Shik Fan 邱錫蕃
YEE, Ewan Lup Yuen 余立仁
YEUNG, Yue Man 楊汝萬
YIP, Luke Jing Ping 葉敬平
YOUNG, Howard 楊孝華
YU, Wai Mui Christina 姚偉梅
YUEN, Philip Pak Yiu 阮北耀
YUNG, Lincoln Chu-Kuen 榮智權
ZEE, Kwoh Kung 徐國炯
ZEE, Sze-Yong 徐是雄

Appendix IV
Olympic Torch-Bearers 2008

No.	Surname	Given name	中文姓名	Occupation/Affiliation
1	Lee	Lai Shan	李麗珊	retired athlete (windsurfing)
2	Li	Ching	李　靜	athlete (table tennis)
3	Ko	Lai Chak	高禮澤	athlete (table tennis)
4	Lau	Tak Wah, Andy	劉德華	artist
5	Yip	Pui Yin	葉姵延	athlete (badminton)
6	Fong	Lik Sun	方力申	retired athlete (aquatics)/artist
7	Chen	Kelly	陳慧琳	artist
8	Ku	Kui Kei	古巨基	artist
9	Chiu	Wing Yin, Rebecca	趙詠賢	athlete (squash)
10	Yu	Chui Yee	余翠怡	paralympic athlete (wheel-chair fencing)
11	Chan	Siu Tong	陳少棠	elected member, Yau Tsim Mong District Council
12	Chiang	Wai Hung	蔣偉洪	athlete (athletics)
13	To	Yu Hang	杜宇航	athlete (wushu)
14	Chan	Chi Ho, Johnny	陳志豪	engineer
15	Yu	Hing Lung	余慶龍	athlete (volleyball)
16	Tsang	Hing Hung	曾慶鴻	athlete (rugby)
17	Tam	Wai Yeung	譚偉洋	athlete (basketball)
18	Yiu	Chun Kan	姚俊勤	undergraduate, CUHK
19	Chan	Sung Ip	陳崇業	ex-officio member, Tsuen Wan District Council
20	Wong	King Fai, Peter	黃景輝	managing director, Hutchison Telecommunication (Hong Kong)
21	Leung	Chun Ying	梁振英	member, Executive Council
22	Chan	Chi Wan, Stephen	陳志雲	general manager, Television Broadcasting Ltd.

Appendix IV

No.	Surname	Given name	中文姓名	Occupation/Affiliation
23	Wong	Fai	王　輝	athlete (shooting)
24	Mak	So Ning, Tania	麥素寧	athlete (triathlon)
25	Li	Tzar Kuoi, Victor	李澤鉅	managing director, Cheung Kong Group
26	Chen	Wen Yan	陳文彥	vice chairman, Hong Kong Youth Federation
27	Ho	Shuk Ting	何淑婷	school teacher
28	Chan	Kwok Yue	陳廣裕	athlete (handball)/school teacher
29	Yu	Hiu Tung	余曉東	athlete (tennis)
30	Cheung	Kwok Kwan	張國鈞	chairman, Youth Democratic Alliance Betterment
31	Chan	Yun To	陳潤韜	athlete (bodybuilding)
32	Law	Hiu Fung	羅曉鋒	athlete (rowing)
33	Chan	Kwok Ming	陳國明	athlete (snooker)
34	Hung	Chao Hong	洪祖杭	president, South China Athletic Association; Hong Kong Dancesport Association
35	Chiu	Chung Hei	趙頌熙	athlete (table tennis)
36	Chow	How Chen	周厚澄	chairman, Community Sports Committee of HAB appointed member, Tsuen Wan District Council
37	Yeung	Chui Ling	楊翠玲	athlete (fencing)
38	Kwok	Ping Kong	郭炳江	managing director, Sun Hung Kai Group
39	Ng	Ching Fai	吳清輝	principal, Hong Kong Baptist University
40	Cheng	Yuk Han, Bjork	鄭玉嫻	athlete (fencing)/undergraduate
41	Sy	Ethan Timothy	施懿庭	CEO, Telecommunications Ltd. (absent)
42	Lim	Kiah Meng	林家名	president, SIS International Limited
43	Kong	Chak Fung	江澤峰	student
44	Leung	Siu To	梁兆燾	information technology consultant
45	Lam	Shun Chiu, Dennis	林順潮	faculty dean, CUHK
46	Lam	Tai Fai	林大輝	supervisor, Lam Tai Fai College
47	Tai	Hei Yan, Diane	戴希恩	medical practitioner
48	Fan	Tak Ming, Eric	樊德明	manager

No.	Surname	Given name	中文姓名	Occupation/Affiliation
49	Kok	Pak Kuan, Michael	郭伯鈞	chief executive, Dairy Farm Group
50	Tsang	Hin Chi	曾憲梓	president, Gold Lion Group
51	Ma	Koon Sang	馬觀生	coach (dragon boat)
52	Chan	Kok Wah	陳國華	elected member, Kwun Tong District Council
53	Chui	Hong Sheung	崔康常	principal, Hang Seng College of Commerce
54	Chan	Yik Hei	陳易希	undergraduate, HKUST
55	Lam	Heung Yeung, Herman	林向陽	general manager, Microsoft Hong Kong Limited
56	Lee	Wing See	李穎詩	consultant (commerce)
57	Chan	Yuk Chi	陳旭智	soccer player
58	Wong	Kam Chi	黃金池	elected member, Wong Tai Sin District Council
59	Zeng	Guang	曾　光	undergraduate
60	Yu	Sum Yee	余心怡	athlete (artistic cycling)
61	Yuen	Yuen Kin	阮元健	school teacher
62	Cheng	Lai Hin, Michael	鄭禮騫	athlete (soccer)
63	Wan	Kin Yee	溫健儀	athlete (athletics)
64	Sze	Hang Yu	施幸余	athlete (aquatics)
65	Tie	Yana	帖雅娜	athlete (table tennis)
66	Koon	Wai Chee	官惠慈	athlete (badminton)
67	Saeed	Farooq	沙飛露	athlete (hockey)
68	Lee	Ka Kit	李家傑	vice chairman, Henderson Group
69	Zilo	Lily	丘莉莉	athlete (equestrian)
70	Ip	Sik On, Simon	葉錫安	chairman, Hong Kong Equestrian Federation
71	Ho	Kim Fai	何劍輝	retired athlete (rowing)
72	Lam	Tak Kwan	林德坤	student
73	Mak	Pui Hin, Christina	麥珮軒	athlete (squash)
74	Cheng	Ka Ho	鄭家豪	athlete (wushu)
75	Lee	Wai Kong, Sunny	李惠光	director, Information Technology, Hong Kong Jockey Club
76	Arena	Alexander Anthony	艾維朗	group managing director, PCCW Limited
77	Chu	Ching Wu	朱經武	president, HKUST
78	Chan	Cho Chak, John	陳祖澤	chairman, Hong Kong Jockey Club

Appendix IV

No.	Surname	Given name	中文姓名	Occupation/Affiliation
79	So	Wa Wai	蘇樺偉	paralympic athlete (athletics)
80	Yip	Siu Hong, Nelson	葉少康	paralympic athlete (equestrian)
81	Lee	Tze Hau, Michael	利子厚	steward, Hong Kong Jockey Club
82	Cheng	Yue Tin	鄭雨滇	jockey
83	Chan	Lim Chee, Amy	陳念慈	retired athlete (badminton)
84	Cheng	Man Kit, Kenneth	鄭文傑	athlete (equestrian)
85	Lee	Ka Man	李嘉文	athlete (rowing)
86	Shek	Wai Hung	石偉雄	student
87	Lau Kun	Lai Kuen, Stella	劉靳麗娟	principal, Diocesan Girl's School
88	Wang	Ming Chuen, Liza	汪明荃	artist and chairperson, Chinese Opera Performers Association
89	Li	Ki Kwong	李奇光	undergraduate, HKU
90	Li	Gang	李 剛	deputy director, Chinese Liaison Office in Hong Kong
91	Kim	Byung Wook	金炳昱	managing director, Samsung (Hong Kong) Limited
92	Wong	Ken	黃建恒	general manager, Lenovo Group (Hong Kong and Taiwan)
93	Ng	Gar Loc, Fenella	吳家樂	retired athlete (rowing)
94	Yuen	Wai Sun	阮維新	senior correctional services officer
95	Leung	Kar Ming	梁嘉銘	director, New Territories Association of Societies
96	Yip	Wing Sie	葉詠詩	Music Director, Hong Kong Sinfonietta
97	Li	Fai	李 暉	retired athlete (wushu)
98	Li	Kwok Wah	李國華	Agriculture Services
99	Xu	Jian	許 健	vice president, VolksWagen Group, China
100	Ho	Chiu King, Pansy Catilina	何超瓊	director, Hong Kong Ballet
101	Wu	Hsiao Li	吳小莉	deputy director, Phoenix TV Station
102	Kwok	Chun	郭 俊	secretary general, Hong Kong Youth Federation
103	Hu	Shao Ming, Herman	胡曉明	chairman, Major Event Committee of HAB
104	Fung	Shek Kong	馮錫江	merchant
105	Fan Hsu	Lai Tai, Rita	范徐麗泰	president, Legislative Council

No.	Surname	Given name	中文姓名	Occupation/Affiliation
106	He	Guangbei	和廣北	deputy managing director and chief executive, Bank of China (Hong Kong) Ltd.
107	Wong	Man Chiu, Ronnie	王敏超	Retired Athlete (Aquatics)
108	Fung Ma	Kit Han, Jenny	馮馬潔嫻	chairman, Paralympic Committee and Sports Association for the Physically Disabled
109	Chung	Kin Man	鍾建民	athlete (mountaineering)
110	Sin	Sin Chau	冼仙舟	vice chairman, Southern District Recreation and Sports Association
111	Ng	Shuit Kwai	伍雪葵	retired athlete (athletics)
112	Chiu	Chi Keung	趙資強	elected member, Eastern District Council
113	Chan	Yik Shun, Eason	陳奕迅	artist
114	Chung	Kwok Leung	鍾國樑	student
115	Chan	Kee Sun, Tom	陳紀新	managing director, Consumer Group, PCCW Limited
116	Cheung	Hok Yau, Jacky	張學友	artist
117	Tsai	Hiu Wai	蔡曉慧	athlete (aquatics)
118	Wang	Chen	王　晨	athlete (badminton)
119	Fok	Tsun Ting, Timothy	霍震霆	president, Sports Federation and Olympic Committee of Hong Kong, China
120	Wong	Kam Po	黃金寶	athlete (cycling)

Note: Torch-bearer Mr. Sy Ethan Timothy for leg no. 41 of the torch relay in Hong Kong could not join the relay because of flight delay. The torch-bearer for leg no. 40, Ms. Cheng Yuk-han, took up Mr. Sy's leg in addition to her own.

Sources:
http://www.lcsd.gov.hk/TorchRelay/en/torchbearer.php
http://www.districtcouncils.gov.hk
http://www.lcsd.gov.hk/TorchRelay/b5/torchbearer.php?page=6#name

Notes

Introduction

1. For a summary of the contradiction, see Kevin P. Lane, *Sovereignty and the Status Quo*, pp. 5–9.
2. Hu Jintao's Work Report, 17th National Party Congress, section X, *Carrying Forward the Practice of "One Country, Two Systems" and Advancing the Great Cause of Peaceful National Reunification*, http://www.china.org.cn/english/congress/229611.htm#10.
3. 中央統戰網，〈如何理解保持香港澳門長期繁榮穩定是我們黨治國理政面臨的嶄新課題（專題）〉,《第二十次全國統戰工作會議》, 3 June 2008, http://wztz.66wz.com/system/2008/06/03/100559627.shtml.
4. Ibid.
5. Subsequent to the publication of Cao Erbao's essay, the *Sing Tao Daily* appeared to have been the only Hong Kong media organisation to have reported on it: 紀曉華，〈管治力量一分為二〉,《星島日報》, 1 February 2008. The next time the issue was publicly addressed was on 16 April 2009, Christine Loh, "One City, Two Teams", *South China Morning Post*, before many more news and commentary pieces had begun to appear.
6. In 2002, at the 16th Party Congress, the CCP formally redefined its status as the "party in power" and no longer as a "revolutionary party", which was how it had always described itself.
7. Wei Pan, "Crossing the River: Legalism, Reform, and Political Change", *Harvard International Review*, p. 42.
8. In 2002, the Chinese Constitution was amended to add in the ideology of the Three Represents.
9. Kellee S. Tsai, "China's Complicit Capitalists", *Far Eastern Economic Review*, p. 15; and David Goodman, "Why China's Middle Class Supports the Communist Party", *Huffington Post*, 2013.
10. Huang Yasheng's central argument in *Capitalism with Chinese Characteristics* is that since the 1990s, the development model favoured rapid urban development, which in turn favoured creating massive state-owned enterprises and big foreign multinational corporations, leaving rural and private enterprise starved of funds that became a limit to their growth. By 2014, Nicholas Lardy concluded in *Markets over Mao: The Rise of Private Business in China* that the private sector produced two-thirds of China's GDP.
11. Since economic liberalisation in the late 1970s, China has grown astonishingly, raising 660 million people out of poverty but the fruits of the growth have not been widely shared

across society; Serhan Cevik and Caroline Correa-Caro, "Growing (Un)equal: Fiscal Policy and Income Inequality in China and BRIC+", *International Monetary Fund*, March 2015.

12. Kellee S. Tsai, "China's Complicit Capitalists", *Far Eastern Economic Review*, p. 15.
13. The number of poor households in Hong Kong reached 460,000 in 2015. Wealth disparity in Hong Kong is now worse than other developed regions in the world; Oxfam Hong Kong, "Local Wealth Inequality Worsens as Richest Earn 29 Times More Than Poorest", 11 October 2016, http://www.oxfam.org.hk/en/news_5160.aspx.
14. Statement by Chen Zuoer, November 1995, see Fanny W. Y. Fung and Albert Wong, "Veteran Head of HK and Macau Office Steps Down after 14 years", *South China Morning Post*, 9 April 2008, quoting various statements from him.
15. Stephen Brown, Edward Fung, Christine Loh, Kylie Uebergang, and Steve Xu, *The Budget and Public Finance in Hong Kong*, pp. 6–10.
16. Donald Tsang, *My Declaration Speech: Building a New Hong Kong, Creating Quality Life Together*, 1 February 2007.
17. For a discussion about the policy assumptions of the Donald Tsang administration, see Christine Loh and Carine Lai, *Reflections of Leadership*, pp. 189–90.
18. Lau Siu-kai has an expanded list of ten features, see "In Search of a New Political Order", in Yue-man Yeung, *The First Decade*, pp. 140–41.
19. Almost one in five people in Hong Kong, especially younger people, preferred independence after 2047; Public Opinion and Political Development in Hong Kong, Survey Result, Press Release, Centre for Communication and Public Opinion Survey, The Chinese University of Hong Kong, 24 July 2016.
20. 〈中共在港地下黨大老〉,《開放雜誌》, November 2008.
21. Emily Lau, "Where's the Party?", *Far Eastern Economic Review*, 12 June 1986, p. 16.
22. The debates were both raised by the author, when she was a member of the Legislative Council. The quotes are from the Official Proceedings of the Legislative Council, 26 April 1995, pp. 3317–46; and 5 March 1997, pp. 164–84.
23. Yu Kwok-chun asked Tung Chee Hwa, "If you became the Chief Executive of the HKSAR, what would your relationship be with Xinhua?" Tung replied, "Xinhua is one of the Central Authorities' organisations in Hong Kong. Other than Xinhua, there will also be the PLA and Foreign Ministry in Hong Kong. I will communicate with them in this regard and will frequently stay in touch with them. For Xinhua's scope of work, I think the Central Authorities will define it. I will surely communicate with them. I know the Chief Executive of the HKSAR is accountable to the Central People's Government. I know that you and many other people would like to know if Hong Kong would have a 'king of kings' in the future. I know that Hong Kong will not have such a 'king of kings' because the Central Authorities, Hong Kong and everyone will definitely implement 'One Country, Two Systems' and a 'high degree of autonomy', as well as act according to the Basic Law", *Wen Wei Po*, 27 November 1996.
24. The four rumoured underground CCP members were the DAB-FTU's Tam Yiu Chung (譚耀宗), Leung Chun Ying (梁振英), Antony Leung (梁錦松), and the Hong Kong Progressive Alliance's Chung Shui Ming (鍾瑞明);《開放雜誌》, May 1997, p. 54.
25. 牛虻,〈從反英暴動到紅頂商人——左派社團「學友社」的一段歷史〉,《開放雜誌》, February 1997, p. 50.

26. These two rumoured CCP members were Elsie Leung (梁愛詩), the then Secretary for Justice, and Tsang Tak Shing (曾德成), then a consultant to the Central Policy Unit and later the Secretary for Home Affairs; 童行,〈董建華身邊的港共名單〉,《開放雜誌》, August 2003, p. 38.
27. Albert Wong, "DAB's Tsang Still Silent on Communist Membership", *South China Morning Post*, 8 October 2008.
28. Yau Chui-yan, "Voice of Reason", *South China Morning Post*, 4 February 2009.
29. 吳康民,〈共產黨形象全是負面嗎?〉, *Ming Pao*, 13 October 2008.
30. Public Opinion and Political Development in Hong Kong, Survey Result, Press Release, Centre for Communication and Public Opinion Survey, The Chinese University of Hong Kong, 24 July 2016.
31. 許家屯,《許家屯香港回憶錄(上、下冊)》(香港:香港聯合出版社,1993)。This is referenced from here on as Xu Jiatun, *Memoirs*, p. 470.
32. Xu Jiatun, *Memoirs*, p. 69.
33. In a footnote to "Beijing's Fifth Column and the Transfer of Power in Hong Kong: 1993–1997", in Robert Ash, *Hong Kong in Transition*, p. 129, Yin Qian noted that Jonathan Mirsky, East Asia editor of *The Times* (London), told him that the information leaked by a friend in the pre-Handover Special Branch indicated that there were 23,000–28,000 party members in Hong Kong. There he also quoted a smaller estimate from Willy Wo-lap Lam of about 15,000.
34. Ibid., pp. 113–14.
35. Deng Xiaoping,〈中國不允許亂〉, 4 March 1989,《鄧小平文選第三卷》. http://web.peopledaily.com.cn/deng/.

Chapter 1

1. In Vladimir Lenin's *What Is to Be Done?*, he argued that the people can only achieve revolutionary consciousness through a vanguard party made up of professional revolutionaries, practising democratic centralism, *Collected Works*, Vol. 5., pp. 347–530.
2. For a short description of the CCP's basic structure, see Ching Cheong, "China's Administration over Hong Kong: The New China News Agency and the Hong Kong and Macau Affairs Office", in Nyaw Mee-kau and Li Si-ming, *The Other Hong Kong Report 1996*, pp. 111–14.
3. Ibid., p. 113. The chart shows that at every administrative level, the party organs are placed slightly above the government ones.
4. Ibid., p. 114.
5. Ibid.
6. Since 1977, party congresses have occurred about every five years, where party delegates nationwide gather in Beijing to select a new term of the CCP Central Committee.
7. Alternate CCP Central Committee members do not have the right to vote on the final party decisions or resolutions at the plenary meetings and are lower in rank than full members. Only full members are selected into the Politburo.
8. The core cluster of departments includes the General Office and four departments—Organisation, Propaganda, United Front Work, and International Liaison. There are also

three centres for policy support—Policy Research, Party History Research, and Party Documents Research—and two publications that publish in the name of the CCP Central Committee—*People's Daily* and the journal *Seeking Truth*. The Central Party School is also a core party organ. Beyond the core organs are committees with responsibility for social order, secrecy, and guiding spiritual civilisation construction.

9. Ching Cheong, "China's Administration over Hong Kong: The New China News Agency and the Hong Kong and Macau Affairs Office", in Nyaw Mee-kau and Li Si-ming, *The Other Hong Kong Report 1996*, p. 116.
10. Ching Cheong refers to the Hong Kong and Macao Affairs Office as the Hong Kong and Macao Office; ibid., pp. 119–23. Official references all use the former name however.
11. There are 4,000 to 5,000 top-level cadres, who make up the core ruling elite in the party; see Suizhou Li, "The CCP, the State and the Cadres in China", *Chinese Public Administration Review*, p. 50.
12. John P. Burns, *The Chinese Communist Party Nomenklatura System: A Documentary Study of Party Control of Leadership Selection*, and his "Strengthening Central CCP Control of Leadership Selection: The 1990 *Nomenklatura*", *The China Quarterly*, pp. 458–91; and Suizhou Li, "The CCP, the State and the Cadres in China", *Chinese Public Administration Review*, pp. 47–56.
13. John P. Burns, "The Structure of Chinese Communist Party Control in Hong Kong," *Asian Survey*, pp. 748–65.
14. Ching Cheong, "China's Administration over Hong Kong: The New China News Agency and the Hong Kong and Macau Affairs Office", in Nyaw Mee-kau and Li, Si-ming, *The Other Hong Kong Report 1996*, pp. 114–15.
15. Ibid., p. 116.
16. Ibid., p. 115. The Joint Liaison Group mentioned in this chart refers to the Sino-British Joint Liaison Group created after the signing of the Sino-British Joint Declaration. It was set up for liaison, exchange of information, and consultation relating to transition issues, and it continued it until 1 January 2000.
17. Laszlo Ladany, *The Communist Party of China and Marxism*, pp. 7–8.
18. Marxism regards dialectical materialism as the doctrine that history progresses in stages that are based solely on the supremacy of different economic classes: feudalism replaced aristocracy, capitalism replaced feudalism, and socialism or communism will replace capitalism—all according to immutable laws. The party regards its role as to lead the masses to expedite the march of history to communism.
19. Chapter 22 on Ideological Totalism, in Robert Jay Lifton, *Thought Reform and the Psychology of Totalism*, provides a discussion on thought reform and coercion.
20. The phrase is considered a part of the official ideology of "socialism with Chinese characteristics". It means to look for practical solutions rather than those based on political ideology such as during Mao Zedong's time. The origins of this attitude stemmed from Deng's utterance: "I don't care if it's a white cat or a black cat. It's a good cat so long as it catches mice."
21. How the CCP has viewed democratic centralism can be seen from such official pronouncements as the *Documents of the 13th National Congress of the CCP*, 1987, p. 95.
22. Kenneth Lieberthal, *Governing China*, pp. 193–94.

23. "China's Private Sector Contributes Greatly to Economic Growth: Federation Leader", *China Daily*, 6 March 2018, http://www.chinadaily.com.cn/a/201803/06/WS5a9e7735a3106e7dcc13fef8.html.
24. In 1983, the Organisation Department of the CCP published a book entitled *250 Questions and Answers on the Work of the Party Organisation*, quoted in Laszlo Ladany, *The Communist Party of China and Marxism*, pp. 514–16.
25. Xu Jiatun, *Memories*, pp. 24–25.
26. 余錦賢,〈中共在港地下黨大老〉,《開放雜誌》, 8 November 2008.
27. Social Indicators of Hong Kong, "Number of Society Registered under the Society Ordinance, Cap. 151", http://www.socialindicators.org.hk/en/indicators/strength_of_civil_society/3.1.
28. Yongshun Cai, "Managing NGOs in China", *China Policy Institute Analysis*, 2017.

Chapter 2

1. Adapted from Michael Saward, *Co-optive Politics and State Legitimacy*, pp. 1–2.
2. Charter of the CPPCC. See the official website of the National Committee of the CPPCC: http://www.cppcc.gov.cn/English/cppcc/.
3. Zhou Enlai, *Selected Works of Zhou Enlai*, Vol. 1, p. 405.
4. See the Official Website of CPPCC: http://www.cppcc.gov.cn.
5. Fanny W. Y. Fung and Albert Wong, "Veteran Head of HK and Macao Office Steps Down after 14 Years", *South China Morning Post*, 9 April 2008.
6. See the Official Website of CPPCC: http://www.cppcc.gov.cn.
7. Peggy Lam, speech in the Legislative Council, Official Proceedings of the Legislative Council, 26 April 1995, p. 3339.
8. Gary Cheung and Eva Wu, "City Liaison Office Deputy Defends HK Delegates", *South China Morning Post*, 19 March 2000; Mary Ma, "No Truth to Power Sharing", *The Standard*, 25 March 2009; and Joseph Wong, "Liaison Office Must Put Out Fire Raging over Delegates", *South China Morning Post*, 25 March 2009.
9. The definitions of "persuasion" and "propaganda" used in the box in this chapter are taken from G. S. Jowatt and V. O'Donnell, *Propaganda and Persuasion*.
10. Anne-Marie Brady, *Marketing Dictatorship*, p. 1.
11. Ibid., p. 12.
12. Ibid., quoting Ding Guangen (丁關根 1929), who headed the United Front Department from 1990 to 1992 and the Propaganda Department from 1992 to 2002, pp. 13–14.
13. For a thorough discussion, see He Qinglian, *The Fog of Censorship*.
14. Other national party newspapers are the *Guangming Daily* and the English-language *China Daily*, which are both controlled by the Propaganda Department, and the *Economic Daily*, which is controlled by the State Council. These organisations carry the rank of vice-ministries.
15. For a wider discussion, see Anne-Marie Brady, *Marketing Dictatorship*, and Alex Chan, "From Propaganda to Hegemony: *Jiaodian Fangtan* and China's Media Policy", *Journal of Contemporary China*, pp. 35–51.

16. Anne-Marie Brady, *Marketing Dictatorship*, p. 80.
17. For a detailed discussion, see Suisheng Zhao, "A State-Led Nationalism: The Patriotic Campaign in Post-Tiananmen China", *Communist and Post-Communist Studies*, pp. 287–302.
18. Anne-Marie Brady, *Marketing Dictatorship*, p. 50.
19. Wang Zhenghua, "Hong Kong to View Buddhist Finger Bone Treasure", *China Daily*, 20 May 2004.
20. "HK Holds Grand Opening Ceremony for Veneration of Buddha *Sarira*", Xinhuanet, 26 May 2004, http://english.sina.com/special_report/040526buddha.shtml.
21. Ibid.
22. Ibid.
23. Donald Tsang, Policy Address 2007–2008, paragraphs 116–20.
24. Ambrose Leung, "Fury at DAB Chief's Tiananmen Tirade", *South China Morning Post*, 16 May 2007.
25. Anne-Marie Brady, *Marketing Dictatorship*, pp. 101 and 104. The use of regulation as a means of control is discussed in pp. 104–9.
26. 《新編黨的宣傳工作實用手冊》, 2003.
27. Anne-Marie Brady, *Marketing Dictatorship*, pp. 80, 82, 88–89, and 98.
28. Ibid., pp. 107–8.
29. Ibid., pp. 118–19.
30. Ibid., pp. 124–25.

Chapter 3

1. Other early Hong Kong activists included four students and three workers, see Chan Lau Kit-ching, *From Nothing to Nothing*, pp. 29–30.
2. 楊少平,〈中共香港黨(團)組織的建立及其早期活動〉,《廣東黨史》, p. 28.
3. Chan Lau Kit-Ching, *From Nothing to Nothing*, p. 30.
4. The Chinese Socialist Youth League (changed into the Communist Youth League in 1959) was formed in 1922 in Guangzhou and it is "a mass organisation of advanced youth led by the CPC, a school for the broad masses of youth to study communism in practice and an assistant and reserve of the CPC." See the official website of the Communist Youth League: http://www.cycnet.com/chinayouth/index.htm.
5. For detailed discussion of the works of the Chinese Socialist Youth League in its early days, see Chan Lau Kit-ching, *From Nothing to Nothing*, pp. 38–45.
6. Ibid., p. 47.
7. Chan Ming Kou, "Labor and Empire: The Chinese Labor Movement in the Canton Delta 1895–1927", doctoral dissertation, Stanford University, 1975, quoted in Chan Lau Kit-ching, *From Nothing to Nothing*, p. 22.
8. For a longer discussion of the Mechanics' Strike of 1920, see John M. Carroll, *A Concise History of Hong Kong*, pp. 96–97.
9. Chan Lau Kit-ching, *From Nothing to Nothing*, p. 48.

10. Leo F. Goodstadt noted that the expatriates' closest relationships were confined to their own racial group. What united them was "the common desire to overcome the strains they felt while living in an alien environment"; *Uneasy Partners*, pp. 21–22.
11. Steve Tsang provides a detailed account of the cadets system, which morphed into the administrative officers system, in *Governing Hong Kong*.
12. The Chinese seamen were grossly underpaid (their wages were only about a quarter of that of European seamen) and they had to work 14 hours per day. They also suffered from the recruitment agency system through which they had to pay an initial bribe to the agents in order to be employed by the shipping companies. See Rosemarie Chung Lu Cee, "Study of the 1925–26 Canton–Hong Kong Strike-Boycott", p. 41.
13. The Chinese Seamen's Union had a strong historical connection with Sun Yat-sen. It originated from a secret organisation which had assisted Sun Yat-sen in passing news from port to port in his early revolutionary attempts. The name Chinese Seamen's Union was given to the union by Sun Yat-sen. Sun also sent a personal representative to Hong Kong to attend the inauguration of the union in February 1921. Because of this close relationship, there were allegations that the Seamen's' Strike was in fact contrived by Sun, though he strongly denied it. See Rosemarie Chung Lu Cee, "Study of the 1925–26 Canton–Hong Kong Strike-Boycott", pp. 32–33.
14. Philip Snow, *The Fall of Hong Kong*, p. 7.
15. Ta Chen, "Shipping Strike in Hong Kong", *Monthly Labour Review*, May 1922, in David Faure, *Society*, pp. 160–62.
16. Fourteen different shipping companies suffered at least HK$5 million loss in total because of cargoes held up in the harbour. The cost of rice rose more than 100% during the strike. The cost of other foodstuffs like fish, beef, and pork also rose by 30% to 50%. See Rosemarie Chung Lu Cee, "Study of the 1925–26 Canton–Hong Kong Strike-Boycott", p. 57.
17. Ta Chen, "Shipping Strike in Hong Kong", *Monthly Labour Review*, May 1922, in David Faure, *Society*, pp. 162–66.
18. Chan Lau Kit-ching, *From Nothing to Nothing*, p. 26. Chen and Sun disagreed on the direction of reform.
19. Ta Chen, "Shipping Strike in Hong Kong", *Monthly Labour Review*, May 1922, in David Faure, *Society*, p. 162.
20. Ibid., pp. 162–66.
21. John M. Carroll, *A Concise History of Hong Kong*, p. 98.
22. Frank Welsh, *A History of Hong Kong*, pp. 370–71.
23. Colonial Office 129/474, Stubbs to Devonshire, 18 March 1922. Other reports, such as by Ta Chen in David Faure, *Society*, noted three people were killed and eight wounded; see pp. 162–66.
24. Kevin P. Lane, *Sovereignty and the Status Quo*, pp. 31–32.
25. Steve Tsang, *A Modern History of Hong Kong*, p. 89; and John M. Carroll, *A Concise History of Hong Kong*, p. 99. For another account, see Michael Share, *Where Empires Collided*, pp. 60–61.
26. Chan Lau Kit-ching, *From Nothing to Nothing*, pp. 23–26.
27. Ibid., p. 26. Chan Lau Kit-ching argued that while the Communists claimed that the Manifesto was instrumental in steering the strike, it was unlikely to have had much

impact as most of the strikers were illiterate. Furthermore, given the nascent and limited CCP's presence in Guangdong, the party could not have had that much of an impact, pp. 23–26.

28. For example, the FTU's Cheng Yiu Tong, in his speech celebrating the 80th anniversary of Hong Kong Seamen's Strike in March 2002, described the strike as "a national struggle against the deprivation and oppression by the foreign shipping capitalists and British-Hong Kong government", "with clear patriotic and anti-colonialism nature" and "a significant patriotic and anti-imperialism victory of the Chinese working class" (香港海員爭取和維護權益的鬥爭，是中國海員反抗外國輪船資本家和港英的剝削壓迫的民族鬥爭，帶有鮮明的愛國反帝反殖的性質，罷工的勝利也就是中國工人階級愛國反帝的偉大勝利)。See http://www.ftu.org.hk/view.php?Tid=502. "People Net"《人民網》also described the strike as "a political struggle against imperialism" and the strikers "successfully assault the arrogant imperialists and advanced the labour movement in China" (罷工從要求增加工資的經濟鬥爭，發展成為反抗帝國主義壓迫的政治鬥爭罷工的勝利，有力地打擊了帝國主義者的氣焰，推動了中國工人運動的發展)。See http://politics.people.com.cn/BIG5/8198/65833/66255/4471229.html.

29. There was a wave of labour disputes after the Seamen's Strike, involving a large number of workers such as bakers, motor bus drivers, Chinese restaurant employees, and Hong Kong Electric Company's employees. See Rosemarie Chung Lu Cee, "Study of the 1925–26 Canton–Hong Kong Strike-Boycott", p. 59.

30. Sun Yat-sen sought the assistance from the Soviets. Under Comintern influence, the manifesto of the First National Congress of the KMT of 26 January 1924 declared an anti-imperialist policy, condemning foreign imperialism and blaming it for China's plight and quasi-colonial status; Edmund Fung, "The Sino-British Rapprochement, 1927–1931", *Modern Asian Studies*, p. 80. See also Michael Share, *Where Empires Collided*, pp. 62–71, for a long discussion on the Comintern's activities in Hong Kong between 1921 and 1927.

31. During the Seamen's Strike, Lau Chu Pak (劉鑄伯 1867–1922, a prominent Chinese leader and a member of the Legislative Council at the time) said in a Legislative Council meeting that the labour unions "had strong Bolshevist support". Shouson Chow (周壽臣 1861–1956), also asked the governor not to make concession to the strikers and supported the suppression of all labour guilds. See Chan Lau Kit-Ching, "The Perception of Chinese Communism in Hong Kong 1921–1934", *The China Quarterly*, pp. 1046–48.

32. The number of people reportedly killed and wounded vary; see Steve Tsang, quoted from Japanese sources and noted nine deaths and dozens injured, *A Modern History of Hong Kong*, p. 92; Stephen Uhalley Jr. noted ten deaths, *A History of the Chinese Communist Party*, p. 27, while Hu Sheng noted thirteen deaths, *A Concise History of the Communist Party of China*, p. 66.

33. 楊少平,〈中共香港黨（團）組織的建立及其早期活動〉,《廣東黨史》, p. 29.

34. Steve Tsang, *A Modern History of Hong Kong*, p. 93.

35. According to the *South China Morning Post*, "the trouble started with the Queen's College strike", 20 June 1925; Chan Lau Kit-Ching, "The Perception of Chinese Communism in Hong Kong 1921–1934", *The China Quarterly*, pp. 1051–52.

36. 中共廣東省委黨史研究室,《中國共產黨廣東地方史（第一卷）》, p. 120.

37. Subsequent investigations failed to establish beyond doubt which side began the clash that led to the shootings, shots were fired by the British and French sentries as well as by Chinese demonstrators. Among the 52 deaths, 51 were Chinese and only one Frenchman,

and among the injured were eight Europeans and one Japanese, see Steve Tsang, *A Modern History of Hong Kong*, p. 94, and Frank Welsh, *A History of Hong Kong*, pp. 371–72.

38. Liu Shuyong, *An Outline History of Hong Kong*, pp. 94–95; and Hu Sheng, *History of the Communist Party of China*, pp. 67–68.
39. See 中共廣東省委黨史研究室,《中國共產黨廣東地方史（第一卷）》, p. 120. See also Ming K. Chan, *Precarious Balance*, p. 48. The demand that the Chinese should be able to live anywhere in Hong Kong was a response to the Chinese being barred from living on the Peak as a result of the Peak District Reservation Ordinance 1904, which provided that no Asiatic could rent property there, and by the Peak District (Residence) Ordinance 1918, which required that all applications to live on the Peak needed to be approved by the authorities. Philip Snow noted that "No Chinese could so much as visit the Peak unless they had been invited or were delivering goods"; *The Fall of Hong Kong*, p. 3.
40. Ming K. Chan, *Precarious Balance*, p. 48.
41. Philip Snow, *The Fall of Hong Kong*, p. 12.
42. Chan Lau Kit-Ching, "The Perception of Chinese Communism in Hong Kong 1921–1934", *The China Quarterly*, pp. 1053–54.
43. John M. Carroll, *Edge of Empires*, p. 143. See also John M. Carroll, *A Concise History of Hong Kong*, pp. 99–105. The Soviets were involved in supporting the strike-boycott, see Michael Share, *Where Empires Collided*, pp. 62–72.
44. John M. Carroll, *Edge of Empires*, pp. 147–49; and Philip Snow, *The Fall of Hong Kong*, pp. 12–13.
45. Rosemarie Chung Lu Cee, "Study of the 1925–26 Canton–Hong Kong Strike-Boycott", pp. 100–108; Frank Welsh, *A History of Hong Kong*, pp. 372–73; Liu Shuyong, *An Outline History of Hong Kong*, pp. 96–97; Steve Tsang, *A Modern History of Hong Kong*, pp. 95–96; and Chan Lau Kit-ching, "The Perception of Chinese Communism in Hong Kong 1921–1934", *The China Quarterly*, p. 1054.
46. Rosemarie Chung Lu Cee, "Study of the 1925–26 Canton–Hong Kong Strike-Boycott", p. 125.
47. Ming K. Chan, *Precarious Balance*, p. 47.
48. See Hong Kong Annual Report 1924 and 1926.
49. For a detailed discussion of the economic impact of the boycott on Hong Kong, see Rosemarie Chung Lu Cee, "Study of the 1925–26 Canton–Hong Kong Strike-Boycott", pp. 128–41.
50. Chan Lau Kit-Ching, "The Perception of Chinese Communism in Hong Kong 1921–1934", *The China Quarterly*, pp. 1052–53.
51. John M. Carroll, *Edge of Empires*, pp. 145–46, and John M. Carroll, *A Concise History of Hong Kong*, p. 102.
52. Governor Stubbs gave HK$100,000 to help Chen Jiongming stage a coup in Guangdong, which had not been authorised by London, and he also proposed a naval blockade of the Pearl River, which was rejected, see Steve Tsang, *A Modern History of Hong Kong*, p. 96; Liu Shuyong, *An Overall History of Hong Kong*, p. 97, noted that Stubbs paid Chen and another warlord, Deng Benyin (鄧本殷) to serve British interests. Although there were initial successes, they eventually failed. Philip Snow, *The Fall of Hong Kong*, p. 13, noted that Shouson Chow and Robert Kotewall raised HK$50,000 from the Tung Wah Hospital

Committee to pay yet another warlord, Wei Bangping (魏邦平), to lead a coup against the KMT-CCP regime in Guangzhou that failed.

53. John M. Carroll, *Edge of Empires*, pp. 149–52.
54. The Northern Expedition (1925–1926) was a military campaign which brought the KMT to power in 1927. It began in Guangzhou. Halfway through the expedition, the KMT and CCP pact fell apart.
55. Steve Tsang, *A Modern History of Hong Kong*, pp. 96–97.
56. John M. Carroll, *Edge of Empires*, pp. 153–56. Chow and Kotewall were both appointed members of the Legislative Council.
57. John M. Carroll, *Edge of Empires*, pp. 182–86, and Oliver Lindsay, *The Battle for Hong Kong*, p. 222.
58. Two councils were created—the Chinese Representative Council and the Chinese Cooperative Council consisting of Hong Kong's leading business and professional elites, including Chow and Kotewall, see John M. Carroll, *Edge of Empires*, pp. 183–86. Carroll notes that by 1944, when it appeared that the war was not going well for Japan, local leaders began to avoid their duties on these councils, and Kotewall even withdrew for health reasons.
59. Paul Gillingham, *At the Peak*, pp. 33, 43–44.
60. Barbara Barnouin and Yu Changgen, *Zhou Enlai*, pp. 34–39.
61. Steve Tsang, *A Modern History of Hong Kong*, pp. 98–100.
62. The settlement, in essence, was that the colonial government did not oppose the imposition of a tax of 2.5% on all imports and 5% on luxury goods from Hong Kong by the KMT and the revenues would be used to subsidise the strikers after the strikes.
63. Chan Lau Kit-ching, *From Nothing to Nothing*, p. 67.
64. 中共廣東省委黨史研究室，《中國共產黨廣東地方史（第一卷）》，pp. 119–20. At that time, Hong Kong had more than 130 labour unions in which seamen, printing and tram unions were already under the control of the CCP activists and CCP members tried to infiltrate the other unions. Eventually, those CCP controlled labour unions started the strike first and dozens of other labour unions joined the strike later, involving more than 250,000 workers during the entire period of the strike-boycott. Hong Kong had a population of about 750,000 then.
65. Norman Miners, *Hong Kong under Imperial Rule*, p. 19.
66. Chan Lau Kit-Ching, "The Perception of Chinese Communism in Hong Kong 1921–1934", *The China Quarterly*, pp. 1054–55.
67. Norman Miners, *Hong Kong under Imperial Rule*, p. 20.
68. Butters, Report on Labour and Labour Conditions in Hong Kong, 1939, referred to in Ming K. Chan, *Precarious Balance*, p. 53.
69. For a useful discussion, see H. L. Fu and Richard Cullen, "Political Policing in Hong Kong", *Hong Kong Law Journal*, 2003, pp. 199–230.

Chapter 4

1. Many Guangdong communist and labour leaders like Liu Ersong (劉爾崧), Deng Pei (鄧培), Li Qihan (李啓漢), and Xiao Chunu (蕭楚女) were arrested and executed. A number

Notes to pages 53–56

of communist activists who had close connection to Hong Kong, like Peng Yuesheng (彭月笙), Zhang Ruicheng (張瑞成), and He Yaoquan (何耀全) were also killed. See Chan Lau Kit-ching, *From Nothing to Nothing*, p. 78.

2. The Nanchang uprising on 1 August 1927 was the first CCP military revolt in its history. Its purpose was to seize the local government from the KMT. Many prominent CCP leaders and generals like Zhou Enlai, Zhu De (朱德), He Lung (賀龍), and Ye Ting (葉挺) were all involved in this military uprising. However, the CCP was quickly defeated and many members had to flee to Hong Kong and Shanghai. The date 1 August is regarded by the CCP as the anniversary of the founding day of the PLA. See Chan Lau Kit-ching, *From Nothing to Nothing*, p. 84.
3. Chan Lau Kit-ching, *From Nothing to Nothing*, pp. 86–89.
4. Michael Share, *Where Empires Collided*, p. 8.
5. For details of the arrests and raids made by Hong Kong Police against CCP members, see 中共廣東省委黨史研究室,《中國共產黨廣東地方史（第一卷）》, pp. 339–43. See also John M. Carroll, *A Concise History of Hong Kong*, p. 102.
6. Ho Chi Minh was arrested in Hong Kong in June 1931 and jailed until 1933. The first party congress of the Vietnamese Communist Party was held in Macao in 1935.
7. Chan Lau Kit-ching, *From Nothing to Nothing*, p. 123.
8. Chan Lau Kit-Ching, "The Perception of Chinese Communism in Hong Kong 1921–1934", *The China Quarterly*, p. 1060.
9. Robert Cottrell, *The End of Hong Kong*, pp. 20–24; and Philip Snow, *The Fall of Hong Kong*, p. 17.
10. Japan had already occupied Manchuria in 1931. On 7 July 1937, the Japanese army telegraphed the KMT forces saying that a Japanese soldier was missing and demanded that its army be allowed to enter Beijing to search for the soldier, who was later found unharmed. Some historians believe that this was an unintentional accident while others believe that the incident was fabricated and used as a pretext for the invasion of central China.
11. The fall of Shanghai and Nanjing were in October and December 1937 respectively. Guangzhou was occupied by the Japanese army in October 1938.
12. Zhang Xueliang was put under house arrest by the KMT for 54 years. Chiang Kai-shek took him to Taiwan when he fled in 1949. When Zhang turned 90 he was allowed to leave Taiwan (15 years after Chiang died). Zhang went to Hawaii, where he lived out his days. He outlived everyone of importance of that era except Madam Soong Meiling, Chiang's wife, who died in 2003.
13. Mao Zedong, *Selected Works of Mao Zedong*, Vol. 3, p. 252.
14. Margaret Macmillan, *Seize the Hour*, p. 43.
15. Philip Snow, *The Fall of Hong Kong*, p. 27.
16. At the beginning of the Sino-Japanese war, Whitehall adopted an ambiguous attitude towards the Japanese invasion of China. The British allowed the passing of military supplies through Hong Kong to the Chinese army. At the same time, Whitehall was carefully not to do anything openly to anger Japan. For example, despite calls from the local Chinese community, the colonial government refused to provide financial assistance to China for the relief of war victims. See Norman Miners, *Hong Kong under Imperial Rule*, p. 26.
17. John M. Carroll, *Edge of Empires*, p. 161.

18. John M. Carroll, *A Concise History of Hong Kong*, p. 117.
19. 楊漢卿，〈八路軍駐香港辦事處的統戰工作〉，《廣東黨史》，p. 53; and Philip Snow, *The Fall of Hong Kong*, p. 28.
20. Chan Sui-jeung, *East River Column*, p. 29.
21. The CCP Central Southern Bureau organised leftist writers like Xia Yan (夏衍) and Zhang Youyu (張友魚) from Guilin and Chongqing to go to Hong Kong, and under the direction of Liao Chengzhi, started publications like《華商報》,《大眾生活》,《筆談》,《文藝陣地》,《耕耘》,《世界知識》,《青年知識》,《大地畫報》, etc. See 葉漢明、蔡寶瓊,〈殖民地與革命文化霸權：香港與四十年代後期的中國共產主義運動〉,《中國文化研究所學報》, p. 195.
22. 楊漢卿，〈八路軍駐香港辦事處的統戰工作〉，《廣東黨史》，p. 53. "司徒慧敏等上海電影工作者和香港電影工作者合作，拍攝了《血濺寶山血》 and《游擊進行曲》等一系列抗日影片。"
23. 楊漢卿，〈八路軍駐香港辦事處的統戰工作〉，《廣東黨史》，pp. 54–55.
24. Song Qingling successfully invited the wife of the colonial government's chief medical officer Situ Yongjue (司徒永覺) and Professor Norman of Hong Kong University to be the honorary secretary and treasury of the League respectively. On an international level, she successfully appealed to the mother of US President Roosevelt for support. Further, many medical staff from Western countries were organised to go to the war zones on the Mainland to provide medical services. See 楊漢卿,〈八路軍駐香港辦事處的統戰工作〉,《廣東黨史》, pp. 56–57.
25. The overseas Chinese in Southeast Asia were mainly from Guangdong and Fujian. The Hakkas are identified with the counties of Meixian, Huizhou, Bao'an, and Huiyang as their main homes. See Chan Sui-jeung, *East River Column*, pp. 9–14 and 20–21.
26. Vivienne Poy, speech "Hong Kong, 1941–1945" to the China and Hong Kong History, Philately and Culture Society, 1 May 1999. Poy spoke about the Japanese Occupation and the East River Guerrillas, see http://www.viviennepoy.ca/english/speeches/1999Speeches/09-010599_HK_Stamp_Soc_e.pdf.
27. Philip Snow, *The Fall of Hong Kong*, pp. 27–28.
28. John M. Carroll, *A Concise History of Hong Kong*, p. 117.
29. Oliver Lindsay, *The Battle for Hong Kong*, p. 48.
30. Chan Sui-jeung, *East River Column*, p. 38.
31. Ibid., p. 41.
32. Ibid., pp. 24 and 81.
33. Ibid., p. 67.
34. Chan Sui-jeung, *East River Column*, pp. 38–39. The Hong Kong–Kowloon Independent Brigade is also referred to as the Hong Kong Independent Battalion or the Hong Kong–Kowloon Independent Company in some publications.
35. Ibid., pp. 81–83.
36. See Vivienne Poy, speech "Hong Kong, 1941–1945", 1 May 1999; and *East River Column*, p. 50.
37. Chan, Sui-jeung, *East River Column*, pp. 44–49.
38. Ibid., and 張雷鋒,〈香港大營救〉,《軍事歷史》, p. 60.

39. The British Army Aid Group (BAAG) was formed by Lindsay Ride, a British prisoner of war who had escaped from Hong Kong. For accounts of the guerrillas, see Sally Blyth and Ian Wotherspoon, *Hong Kong Remembers*, pp. 17–23; Lau Kam Man, a former guerrilla recalled the guerrillas and the BAAG worked closely throughout the war; see also accounts by Liu Shuyong, *An Outline History of Hong Kong*, pp. 111–13; Frank Welsh, *A History of Hong Kong*, pp. 420–21; and Chan Sui-jeung, *East River Column*, pp. 49–56; also Vivienne Poy's speech "Hong Kong, 1941–1945", 1 May 1999.
40. Ride's report to the British War Office praised the guerrillas, whom he referred to as "our guerrillas", see Vivienne Poy's speech, "Hong Kong, 1941–1945", 1 May 1999.
41. For a full account, see Chan Sui-jeung, *East River Column*, pp. 49–64.
42. Ibid., pp. 79–80.
43. Vivienne Poy's speech "Hong Kong, 1941–1945", 1 May 1999.
44. Ibid.
45. Ibid.
46. Wellington Koo was a member of the Chinese delegation to the Paris Peace Conference in 1919. He demanded that Japan returned Shandong to China, which was turned down by the Western powers. China did not sign the Treaty of Versailles.
47. R. W. Louis, "Hong Kong: The Critical Phase 1945–1949", *American Historical Review*, p. 1062.
48. For a full account, see Philip Snow, *The Fall of Hong Kong*, pp. 229–60, and Steve Tsang, *A Modern History of Hong Kong*, pp. 124–26. Tsang argues that Britain decided to keep Hong Kong for three reasons: it was British effort that had built Hong Kong; Hong Kong was even more important post-war as a base for trade; and having lost the colony to Japan, it was a point of national honour to recover Hong Kong, see p. 132.
49. John M. Carroll, *A Concise History of Hong Kong*, p. 127.
50. Ibid., p. 128.
51. For a detailed account of events, see Philip Snow, *The Fall of Hong Kong*, pp. 245–48. See also Steve Tsang, *A Modern History of Hong Kong*, pp. 134–38. The future of Hong Kong was the most contentious issue between Chiang Kai-shek and the British before 1949. Chiang raised the issue at a meeting with the British ambassador in June 1946. He maintained relations with Britain would not be "satisfactory" or conducted with "mutual confidence" while the question of Hong Kong remained "without some solution". For an account of the issue of Hong Kong between the KMT and Britain, see S. R. Aston, "Keeping a Foot in the Door: Britain's China Policy: 1945–50", *Diplomacy and Statecraft*, p. 88.
52. Liu Shuyong, *An Outline History of Hong Kong*, pp. 175–77.
53. Philip Snow, *The Fall of Hong Kong*, p. 248. Kevin P. Lane also provides an account of the nationalist government struggle for the return of Hong Kong, *Sovereignty and the Status Quo*, pp. 41–60.
54. Lau Kam Man, a former guerrilla said the KMT had soldiers in Hong Kong, in Sally Blyth and Ian Wotherspoon, *Hong Kong Remembers*, pp. 21–22, but it could not have been a significant presence; Philip Snow did not refer to a KMT military presence in *The Fall of Hong Kong*.
55. Philip Snow, *The Fall of Hong Kong*, p. 248. For a detail account, see Chan Sui-jeung, *East River Column*, pp. 85–106.

56. On 16 August 1945, Grimson left Stanley Prison and took charge from the Japanese as acting governor. He organised all the former officials to form a provisional government. On 27 August, he made a radio announcement that the provisional government had been established. Grimson was made governor of Singapore in 1946. For an account of events, see Frank Welsh, *A History of Hong Kong*, pp. 430–34; and Philip Snow, *The Fall of Hong Kong*, pp. 249–51.
57. 袁小倫，〈戰後香港進步文化革命〉，載於中共廣東省委黨史研究室，《香港與中國革命》，p. 263.
58. Chan Sui-jeung provides extensive discussion on the events and the personalities in *East River Column*.
59. 港九獨立大隊史編寫組，《港九獨立大隊史》，pp. 184–85.
60. Chan Sui-jeung, *East River Column*, p. 102. See also 周奕，《香港英雄兒女——東江縱隊港九大隊抗日戰史》，p. 217, "別了！親愛的港九新界同胞們！今天，我們離開港九了，但我們關心你們的自由幸福仍和以前一樣。經過了長期困苦鬥爭以後，我們希望你們能獲得香港政府的救濟，重建家業，改善生活。我們希望你們光榮的鬥爭能引起國際人士應有的尊敬，獲得應有自由，和平與幸福的生活。"
61. Chan Sui-jeung, *East River Column*, pp. 103–5. 人民網：http://www.people.com.cn/BIG5/paper464/16721/1471723.html.
62. For a full discussion about relations with the KMT, see Steve Tsang, *Democracy Shelved*, pp. 50–55.
63. Ibid., pp. 29 and 55–57.
64. John M. Carroll, *A Concise History of Hong Kong*, pp. 182–86; and Philip Snow, *The Fall of Hong Kong*, pp. 253–60.
65. For a thorough discussion of this period of history, see Steve Tsang, *Democracy Shelved*, pp. 24–31.
66. Chan Sui-jeung noted that the pressure on landowners and cadres responsible for implementing land reform was such that in February 1953, 805 landowners were driven to suicide, and in the Spring of 1953 in west Guangdong alone that 1,165 cadres committed suicide. By 1953, it was estimated that as many as 7,000 senior Guangdong cadres had been punished. For a detail discussion about the fate of the members of the East River Column, see *East River Column*, pp. 135–58.
67. Chan Sui-jeung, *East River Column*, pp. 158–61.
68. The Hong Kong War Memorial Pensions Ordinance was amended in 1999 so that a Brigade member (or his spouse) is eligible for pension benefits if the member sustained injury, was killed in action, or was captured by the Japanese authority and held in captivity between 7 and 25 December 1941. As the Brigade was only formed in February 1942, the law was amended to cover the period of the Brigade's activities between February 1942 and September 1945.
69. Lindsay Rides' archives, see http://library.hku.hk/record=b2379733.
70. For an account of the Chongqing negotiations, see Barbara Barnouin and Yu Changgen, *Zhou Enlai*, pp. 101–7.
71. Diana Lary, *China's Republic*, p. 164.
72. Hu Sheng, *A Concise History of the Communist Party of China*, pp. 337–39.
73. Mao Zedong, *On Guerrilla Warfare*.

74. Some scholars see the loss of Yenan as a fiasco, and that the communists were then forced to operate on the move, but the loss of Yenan was subsequently explained away by the CCP as a deliberate strategy, see Diana Lary, *China's Republic*, pp. 166–67.
75. Diana Lary, *China's Republic*, p. 168.
76. Stephen Uhalley Jr., *A History of the Chinese Communist Party*, pp. 66–78.
77. 袁小倫，〈戰後初期中共利用香港的策略運作〉，《近代史研究》，p. 127.
78. 劉子健，〈中共中央香港分局對華南革命鬥爭的指導〉，載於中共廣東省委黨史研究室，《香港與中國革命》，pp. 226–27.
79. Zhou Enlai said at a CCP Central Committee meeting in December 1946 that: "香港地位日漸重要，不但對兩廣、南洋方面，對歐美聯絡方面也日見重要。華南工作甚繁，領導機構需要適當解決，以便統一領導公開和秘密工作"，周恩來年譜（1898–1949），p. 708; and see 中共廣東省委黨史研究室，《中國共產黨廣東地方史（第一卷）》，p. 611.
80. "推動反美反蔣統一戰綫，支援解放區戰爭……英美間及統治階層內部矛盾極多，各種政治關係又極複雜。你們要善於掌握這一複雜環境，倚靠人民力量，在長期鬥爭中爭取勝利"，see 中共廣東省委黨史研究室，《中國共產黨廣東地方史（第一卷）》，p. 612.
81. According to Zhang Zhiyi (張執一), former deputy minister of the Central United Front Ministry (中央統戰部副部長), though the Shanghai Central Branch Bureau was assigned with the task of directing the work of Hong Kong Central Branch Bureau, it never worked that way. The CCP secret radio station in Hong Kong could contact the CCP Central directly, whereas the Shanghai Central Branch Bureau could not always keep in touch with the Central CCP because of its poor technical conditions, see 張執一，〈中央上海局和香港分局從事地下工作〉，《潮流月刊》，p. 67.
82. John P. Burns, "The Structure of the Chinese Communist Party Control in Hong Kong", *Asian Survey*, p. 749.
83. 中共廣東省委黨史研究室，《中國共產黨廣東地方史（第一卷）》，p. 613.
84. 劉子健，〈中共中央香港分局對華南革命鬥爭的指導〉，載於中共廣東省委黨史研究室，《香港與中國革命》，pp. 228–29.
85. Ibid., p. 234.
86. 葉漢明、蔡寶瓊，〈殖民地與革命文化霸權：香港四十年代後期的中國共產主義運動〉，p. 203. See also 劉田夫、吳南生及楊應彬，〈方方主持中共香港分局展開政治鬥爭〉，《潮流月刊》，p. 64.
87. The intellectuals who formed the league included Chen Junru (沈鈞儒) and Zhang Bojun (章伯鈞), see 劉子健，〈中共中央香港分局對華南革命鬥爭的指導〉，載於中共廣東省委黨史研究室，《香港與中國革命》，pp. 234–35.
88. Moreover, He Xiangning became the vice-chairman of the First and Second CPPCC and vice-chairman of the Standing Committee of the Second and Third NPC. Chen Junru was the then president of the Supreme People's Court; Zhang Bojun was the vice-chairman of the Second CPPCC and minister of transportation.
89. Foreign Office, Secret Memorandum by Mr. Bevin on the Situation in China, CP(49)39[CAB 129/32], 4 March 1949, collected in Rohan Butler and M. E. Pelly, *Documents on British Policy Overseas*.
90. With the financial assistance of some Chinese businessman, the CCP opened the Heung To Middle School (香島中學), Pui Kiu Middle School (培僑中學), and Hon Wah Middle

School (漢華中學) in early 1946. See 葉漢明、蔡寶瓊,〈殖民地與革命文化霸權:香港四十年代後期的中國共產主義運動〉,《中國文化研究所學報》, p. 201.

91. Steve Tsang, *Democracy Shelved*, p. 86.
92. 袁小倫,〈戰後香港進步文化活動〉,載於中共廣東省委黨史研究室,《香港與中國革命》, p. 271.
93. For detailed discussion of the focus of these publications, see 袁小倫,〈戰後香港進步文化活動〉,載於中共廣東省委黨史研究室,《香港與中國革命》, pp. 265–69.
94. 葉漢明、蔡寶瓊,〈殖民地與革命文化霸權:香港四十年代後期的中國共產主義運動〉,《中國文化研究所學報》, p. 198.
95. 袁小倫,〈戰後香港進步文化活動〉,載於中共廣東省委黨史研究室,《香港與中國革命》, p. 268.
96. See Xinhua News Agency Official Website: http://203.192.6.89/xhs/lsyg.htm.
97. Qiao Guanhua returned to the Mainland after 1949 and worked as a diplomat. He became the PRC's ambassador to the United Nations in 1971 and foreign minister in 1974. See http://www.fmprc.gov.cn/eng/ziliao/wjrw/3606/t44160.htm.
98. 茆貴鳴,《喬冠華傳》, pp. 308–9.
99. Steve Tsang, *Democracy Shelved*, p. 56.
100. The British journalist was Gordon Harmon, and what Mao reportedly said to him was recorded in FO371/63318, Boyce (Peking) to Chancery (Nanking) 30 December 1946, see Steve Tsang, *A Modern History of Hong Kong*, p. 153.
101. "我們現在不提出立即歸還的要求,中國那麼大,許多地方都沒有管理好,先急於要這塊小地方幹嗎?將來可按協商辦法解決",毛澤東,〈同三位西方記者的談話(一九四六年十二月九日)〉,載於毛澤東,《毛澤東文集》,第4卷, p. 207. See also 毛澤東思想網:http://mzdthought.com/html/mxzz/mzdwj/4/816.html.
102. 葉漢明、蔡寶瓊,〈殖民地與革命文化霸權:香港四十年代後期的中國共產主義運動〉,《中國文化研究所學報》, p. 202.
103. James Tang, "World War to Cold War: Hong Kong's Future and Anglo-Chinese Interactions, 1941–55", in Ming K. Chan, *Precarious Balance*, p. 115.
104. Foreign Office, Minute by China Department on the Communist Threat in Hong Kong (F 15770/154/10), 19 October 1948, collected in Rohan Butler and M. E. Pelly, *Documents on British Policy Overseas*.
105. Li Shian, "Britain's China Policy and the Communists, 1942 to 1946: The Role of Ambassador Sir Horace Seymour", *Modern Asian Studies*, pp. 49–50.
106. "一方面(英國)和蔣介石拉得很緊。另外,他對我們也不拒絕",茆貴鳴,《喬冠華傳》, p. 307.
107. 杜俊偉,〈論抗戰時期周恩來「求同存異」國際統戰策略與實踐〉,《中共四川省委黨校學報》, pp. 69–70.
108. Li Shian, "Britain's China Policy and the Communists, 1942 to 1946: The Role of Ambassador Sir Horace Seymour", *Modern Asian Studies*, p. 63.
109. For a fuller account, see Steve Tsang, *Democracy Shelved*, pp. 81–87.
110. Ministry of Defence, Top Secret Report by the Joint Intelligence Committee on the Military Situation in China, JIC (48) 30 (0) Final (Annex) 13 May 1948, Rohan Butler and M. E. Pelly, *Documents on British Policy Overseas*.

111. Report on Communist Activities in Hong Kong, Alexander Grantham to Secretary of State, Secret, 23 February 1949. FO 371/75779, quoted in Wm R. Louis, "Hong Kong: The Critical Phase, 1945-1949", *American Historical Review*, p. 1077.
112. 葉漢明、蔡寶瓊，〈殖民地與革命文化霸權：香港四十年代後期的中國共產主義運動〉，《中國文化研究所學報》，pp. 209-10.
113. Colonial Office, "Memorandum by Mr. Creech Jones on Hong Kong", CP (49) 120, 23 May 1949, Rohan Butler and M. E. Pelly, *Documents on British Policy Overseas*.
114. Ibid.
115. 劉蜀永，〈英國對香港的政策與中國的態度（1948-1952）〉，《中國社會科學》，p. 184.
116. Foreign Office, "Minute by China Department on the Communist Threat to Hong Kong" [F 15770/154/10], 19 October 1948, Rohan Butler and M. E. Pelly, *Documents on British Policy Overseas*.
117. Ministry of Defence, "Top Secret Report by the Joint Intelligence Committee on the Military Situation in China", JIC (48) 30 (0) Final (Annex), 13 May 1948, Rohan Butler and M. E. Pelly, *Documents on British Policy Overseas*.
118. Steve Tsang, *Democracy Shelves*, p. 105, and Kevin P. Lane, *Sovereignty and the Status Quo*, p. 63.
119. Xu Jiatun, *Memoirs*, p. 194.
120. Mark Roberti, *The Fall of Hong Kong*, p. 38.
121. Ibid.
122. John M. Carroll, *A Concise History of Hong Kong*, pp. 135-36; see also Steve Tsang, *Democracy Shelved*, p. 105. In August 1949, public security legislation was passed to give the governor even wider powers of control.
123. "我們在這場鬥爭中必須有所取捨。在公開宣傳上，我們不能反對國民黨收復香港，以免在政治上處於被動；而一旦國民黨收復香港，又將使我黨處於十分不利的地步。只要能在香港站穩腳跟就可以對其利用。因此，黨中央指示我們，應利用國、英、美之間的矛盾，利用我黨在抗戰期間打下的基礎，迫使港英當局實現若干民主改良，造成便利民主分子活動之條件，並將其建設成為華南民主運動的基地"，譚天度，〈抗戰勝利後我參加的香港中英談判〉，載於中共中央黨史研究室、中央檔案館編，《中共黨史資料》第62輯，p. 60, disclosed by a veteran CCP member who was responsible for the united front work in the Hong Kong Work Committee in the 1940s.
124. Steve Tsang, *Hong Kong*, p. 71.
125. James Tang, "World War to Cold War: Hong Kong's Future and Anglo-Chinese Interactions, 1941-55", in Ming K. Chan, *Precarious Balance*, p. 114.
126. Grantham, *Via Ports*, pp. 179-180. See also John M. Carroll, *A Concise History of Hong Kong*, pp. 137-39.

Chapter 5

1. FO371/75779, Enclosure from Heathcote-Smith to Lamb, 2 December 1948.
2. Foreign Office, Minute by Mr. Burgess on Communist documents captured in Hong Kong, F9267/1016/10, 25 June 1949. The CCP's official history notes the PLA in Shenzhen

could have recovered Hong Kong if the CCP had wanted to do so in 1949 but it was the party's policy not to do so at the time,《中共黨史重大事件述評》, p. 351.
3. 黃文放,《解讀北京思維》, p. 47.
4. 金堯如,《香港五十年憶往》, pp. 30–32.
5. Ibid., pp. 33–34. 金堯如 noted that "香港的政策是東西方鬥爭全局的戰略部署……不能用狹隘的領土主權原則來衡量的".
6. Leo F. Goodstadt, *Profits, Politics and Panics*, p. 82.
7. Ibid., p. 87.
8. Steve Tsang, *Democracy Shelved*, pp. 124–25.
9. Ibid., p. 136.
10. Li Hou became the deputy director of the State Council Hong Kong and Macao Office in 1980.
11. 國世平、錢學君,《九七後中港新關係》, p. 49.
12. 鍾仕梅,〈中共如何管理香港〉,《當代雜誌》, p. 20.
13. Peter Wesley-Smith, "Chinese Consular Representation in British Hong Kong", *Pacific Affairs*, p. 370. See also Richard Hughes, *Borrowed Place Borrowed Time*, p. 39.
14. Robert Cottrell, *The End of Hong Kong*, p. 27.
15. Gary Catron, "Hong Kong and Chinese Foreign Policy, 1955–60", *China Quarterly*, p. 410.
16. 黃文放,《中國對香港恢復行使主權的決策歷程與執行》, p. 34.
17. See 鍾仕梅,〈工委遷港統一領導〉,《當代雜誌》, p. 20.
18. For background, see John P. Burns, "The Structure of Communist Party Control in Hong Kong", *Asian Surveys*, pp. 749–51; and Cindy Yik-Yi Chu, "Overt and Covert Functions of the Hong Kong Branch of the Xinhua News Agency, 1947–1984", *The Historian*, pp. 31–37.
19. The Cold War was the term used to describe a state of hostility between the Soviet Union and the US (and their respective allies) between 1945 and the early 1990s when the Soviet Union collapsed. The Korean War was the first armed conflict of the Cold War. After the Second World War, the Korean peninsula had been divided into Soviet and American spheres of influence with the 38th parallel as the demarcation line between North and South Korea. On 25 June 1950, Kim Il-Sung of North Korea attacked South Korea, which resulted in the United Nations sending in a US-led force to aid South Korea. The UN force commander, General Douglas MacArthur, indicated that he wanted to unify the Korean peninsula, and perhaps even take the fight into China. In 1951, President Truman dismissed MacArthur for his impetuosity. As troops came close to the border with China, Beijing warned that it would intervene. By the end of November, China sent 300,000 "volunteers" into Korea and pushed the United Nations forces to retreat beyond Seoul. Over time, more troops had to be sent. Fighting eased by the end of 1951 but it took another two years before an armistice was signed, see Graham Hutchings, *Modern China*, pp. 254–55.
20. Dean Acheson, US secretary of state to the British foreign secretary, quoted in Margaret Macmillan, *Seize the Hour*, p. 103. Macmillan provides a good summary of US-China relations between 1949 and 1972, pp. 95–110.
21. Leo F. Goodstadt, *Profits, Politics and Panics*, p. 88.
22. Margaret Macmillan, *Seize the Hour*, pp. 106–7.

23. Alexander Grantham, *Via Ports*, p. 169.
24. Frank Welsh, *A History of Hong Kong*, pp. 451–52.
25. Cheung Yan Lung, a leader among the New Territories indigenous villagers, in Sally Blyth and Ian Wotherspoon, *Hong Kong Remembers*, p. 38. In *The Times*, the London Newspaper, Zhao Guanji, a State Council official, described Hong Kong as providing a "lifeline" to China during the Korean War, 17 November 1980, noted in Robert Cottrell, *The End of Hong Kong*, p. 27.
26. 金堯如,《香港五十年憶往》, pp. 33–34. He noted that "香港留在英國人手上，我們反而主動……使英國不能也不敢對美國的對華政策和遠東部署跟得太緊……可以擴大和利用英美在遠東問題上的對華政策的矛盾……香港對我們大有好處，大有用處……最大限度地發展最廣泛的愛國統一戰線工作……突破以美國為首的西方陣營對我國實行封鎖禁運的前沿陣地。"
27. Ibid.,"重大的戰略意義" and "要維護香港的現狀和地位，包括英國的殖民地主義經濟和資本主義制度", p. 34.
28. 齊鵬飛,"長期打算，充分利用：1949年至1978年新中國對於香港問題和香港的特殊政策",《中共黨史研究》；《中共黨史重大事件述評》, p. 353.
29. Leo F. Goodstadt, *Profits, Politics and Panics*, pp. 90–94.
30. 黃文放,《解讀北京思維》, p. 47.
31. 周恩來,〈關於香港問題〉,《周恩來統一戰綫文選》, pp. 353–55. Zhou noted: "香港要完全按資本主義制度辦事，才能存在和發展，這對我們是有利的。……香港應該化為經濟上對我們有用的港口……要進行社會主義建設，香港可作為我們同國外進行經濟聯繫的基地。可以通過他吸收外資，爭取外匯。" See also 人民網，周恩來著作選: http://cpc.people.com.cn/GB/69112/75843/75874/75992/5181257.html.
32. 黃文放,《中國對香港恢復行使主權的決策歷程與執行》, p. 49.
33. Sir Robert Black to Duncan Sandys, secretary of state for the colonies, 16 March 1964, CO1030/1590, quoted in David Faure, *Colonialism and the Hong Kong Mentality*, pp. 191–94.
34. Ibid., p. 194.
35. The three unequal treaties were the Treaty of Nanking in 1842 (ceding of Hong Kong Island to Britain); the Convention of Peking in 1860 (ceding of Kowloon); and the Second Convention of Beijing in 1898 (New Territories 99-year lease). For a discussion, see Kevin P. Lane, *Sovereignty and the Status Quo*, pp. 1–29 and 61–67.
36. 齊鵬飛,〈長期打算，充分利用：1949年至1978年新中國對於香港問題和香港的特殊政策〉,《中共黨史研究》, p. 27.
37. Robert Cottrell, *The End of Hong Kong*, p. 27. See also Chi-Kwan Mark, *Hong Kong and the Cold War*, p. 29.
38. Robert Cottrell, *The End of Hong Kong*, p. 27.
39. Zhou Enlai described Taiwan as a "great wound" to Henry Kissinger in July 1971, see Margaret Macmillan, *Seize the Hour*, p. 240.
40. Steve Tsang, *Democracy Shelved*, p. 132.
41. Frank Welsh, *A History of Hong Kong*, pp. 447–49, and John M. Carroll, *A Concise History of Hong Kong*, pp. 142–43.
42. Steve Tsang, *Democracy Shelved*, p. 175.

43. Steve Tsang believed Zhou Enlai knew about the attempt on his life and he did not in fact have an operation: "Target Zhou Enlai: The Kashmir Princess Incident of 1955", *China Quarterly*, pp. 776–82. According to Xu Jiatun, Taiwan's action was known to China, and the US was informed. The British apparently did not believe it, see Xu Jiatun, *Memoirs*, p. 52. *China Daily* reported on 21 July 2004 that declassified documents showed "Zhou, who was the main target, did not board the plane. His travel plans had been kept secret . . . The secrecy surrounded Zhou's travel plans saved his life and doomed the Kashmir Princess."
44. Xu Jiatun, *Memoirs*, p. 52.
45. Frank Welsh, *A History of Hong Kong*, pp. 456–58, and Kevin P. Lane, *Sovereignty and the Status Quo*, pp. 72–73.
46. Kevin P. Lane, *Sovereignty and the Status Quo*, pp. 73–74.
47. The statement reads: "不要設想對香港群眾進行社會主義教育。把國內的一套搬出去是不妥當的……同英國的鬥爭要有理，有利，有節。" It was said by Liao Chengzhi to Liang Weilin in November 1958. See 劉子健、彭建新、梁威林,〈談香港工作20年體會〉,《廣東黨史》, p. 7.
48. 劉子健、彭建新、梁威林,〈談香港工作20年體會〉,《廣東黨史》, p. 7. The statement reads: "要區別國內和香港的環境。你們的工作任務不是為了收回香港，而是充份利用香港。在10年內不考慮這個問題，除非它在香港乒乒乓乓打起來。因此，你們的工作要從長遠打算，不要搞得過份緊張，過份暴露，對英是要鬥爭的，但鬥了之後，要適可而止，頭腦始終要保持冷靜，不要發熱。" It was said by Liao Chengzhi to Liang Weilin in December 1958.
49. 廖承志,〈港澳和海外出版工要因地制宜〉, May 1956.《廖承志文集（上冊）》, p. 324. The statement reads: "在內容方面應注意不要觸犯當地的政策，法令，不要出版當地禁止出版的東西，也要照顧華僑的政治和文化水平。"
50. 李子誦,〈教我如何不想他：廖公〉,《當代雜誌》, p. 18.
51. Chi-Kwan Mark, *Hong Kong and the Cold War*, p. 15.
52. 劉子健、彭建新、梁威林,〈談香港工作20年體會〉,《廣東黨史》, p. 6 ("平時要團結各種各樣朋友，到需要時使用" and "各項工作的立足點和出發點").
53. "Marco Polo's Mixer", *Time*, 10 January 1972.
54. Richard Charles Lee was a member of the prominent Hysan Lee (利希慎) family involved in real estate and other businesses.
55. From 1870, the Mok family had served as comprador for Butterfield and Swire until 1931. See Christine Loh, *A Preferred Future*, pp. 19–39. Mok Ying Kwai was deported to Guangdong in 1952, where he was appointed to the Guangdong CPPCC.
56. Ho Yin was the father of Edmund Ho, the first chief executive of Macao (1999–2009).
57. Henry Fok was possibly the most influential businessmen with China in his time. He reportedly smuggled arms into China during the Korean War, which he denied, but he admitted to violating the embargo by smuggling steel, rubber and other raw materials to China, see Jonathan Cheng, "A life that reflected change", *The Standard*, 30 October 2006. Fok was appointed a vice-chairman of the CPPCC in 1993, had served as a Standing Committee member of the NPC, and also served as a member of the Basic Law Drafting Committee and the Preparatory Committee.
58. 劉子健、彭建新、梁威林,〈談香港工作20年體會〉,《廣東黨史》, pp. 7–8.
59. Ibid., p. 8.

60. This figure was referred to in Yiu Yan Nang, "Trade Union Policy and Trade Union Movement in Hong Kong", p. 76.
61. HKSAR Government, Archive, Document CO1030/1107. An undated secret report.
62. See《香港工人運動簡史》, http://www.hkctu.org.hk/1aboutctu/1/1.htm.
63. HKSAR Government, Archive, Document CO1030/1106, Hong Kong Local Intelligence Committee Intelligence Report, December 1960.
64. HKSAR Government Archive, Document CO1030/1106, Hong Kong Police Special Branch Report, November 1960. The information was obtained by agents who had infiltrated the unions.
65. Chan Lau Kit-ching, *From Nothing to Nothing*, pp. 11–12.
66. Steve Tsang, *Democracy Shelved*, p. 133.
67. HKSAR Government Archive, Document CO 1030/1107, an undated confidential memo entitled "the Communist Controlled Schools".
68. HKSAR Government Archive, Document CO 1030/1107, Letter from the governor of Hong Kong to the secretary of state for the colonies, August 1960.
69. Huang Wenfang, "Former Party Man Recalls Xinhua's Early Days and Zhou Enlai's Role", *Eastern Express*, 15 June 1994.
70. HKSAR Government Archive, Document CO 1030/1107. Hong Kong Police Special Branch Report, February 1960.
71. Heung To Middle School, allegedly a communist hardcore school, applied for exemption from building restrictions in 1961 in order to expand. The colonial government refused the application on town planning grounds, but at the same time stated "the requirements of town planning thus supported the political argument against facilitating expansion of a Communist school". See HKSAR Government Archive, Document CO 1030/1107, Hong Kong Local Intelligence Committee Monthly Intelligence Report, January 1961.
72. 周奕,《香港左派鬥爭史》, pp. 178–79.
73. Ibid., pp. 173–76.
74. HKSAR Government Archive, Document CO 1030/1107, Hong Kong Local Intelligence Committee Monthly Intelligence Report, February 1962.
75. According to Huang Wenfang, in the early 1960s, the daily circulation figures of *Hong Kong Commercial Daily*, *Ching Pao Daily*, and *New Evening Post* reached 50,000–60,000 and the sales of *Wen Wei Po* and *Ta Kung Pao* were also quite respectable and stable. See 文灼非,〈香港新華社如何透過左報做宣傳工作（1949–1982）〉,《信報財經月刊》, p. 13.
76. For a detail account of the Tung Tau Village incident, see Alan Smart, *The Shek Kip Mei Myth*, pp. 73–94. See also John M. Carroll, *A Concise History of Hong Kong*, p. 137; Frank Welsh, *A History of Hong Kong*, pp. 454–55; and Steve Tsang, *Democracy Shelved*, pp. 177–78.
77. Alexander Grantham, *Via Ports*, p. 159.
78. Steve Tsang, *Democracy Shelved*, pp. 177–78.
79. *Hong Kong Standard*, 2 March 1952.
80. John M. Carroll, *A Concise History of Hong Kong*, p. 137; Frank Welsh, *A History of Hong Kong*, pp. 454–55; and Steve Tsang, *Democracy Shelved*, pp. 178–79.

81. 劉蜀永，〈英國對香港的政策與中國的態度（1948-52）年〉，《中國社會科學》，pp. 185-86.
82. 廖承志，〈堅持愛國主義的辦報方針〉，5 December 1959.《廖承志文集》，pp. 396-97. "我們辦的報紙有兩類。主要的一類是進行社會主義教育，為社會主義建設服務，這是國內的報紙……另一類報紙，是我們在香港和海外辦的報紙……在華僑中辦的報紙，是以愛國主義為方針的……能不能在香港辦一家社會主義的報紙？不可能，也不必要……香港報紙的任務就是要對大多數同胞進行愛國主義教育……銷路愈多愈好……要面對港澳大多數群眾，為他們所愛看，為他們所懂……我們的報紙不要脫離香港大多數人的覺悟程度。"
83. "若要你們在香港辦黨報，倒不如叫人民日報去搞一個分社，乾脆把人民日報拿到香港去印發"，金堯如，《香港五十年憶往》，p. 47.
84. 劉子健、彭建新、梁威林，〈談香港工作20年體會〉，pp. 7-8.
85. James Lilley, *China Hands*, p. 84.
86. Ibid., p. 86.
87. Barclay Crawford, "CIA Agents Saw HK as Window on Communist Party", *South China Morning Post*, 28 June 2007.
88. James Lilley, *China Hands*, p. 95.
89. Alexander Grantham, *Via Ports*, p. 169.
90. Steve Tsang, *Democracy Shelved*, p. 134.
91. Xu Jiatun, *Memoirs*, pp. 52-53. The senior police officer mentioned by Xu was Ceng Zhaohe (曾昭科), an assistant superintendent of the Hong Kong Police in 1961. See 〈前高級警官被指中國間諜逐出境　曾昭科盼董特首昭雪〉，《星島日報》，6 March 2002.
92. 鍾仕梅，〈工委政策偏離中央方針〉，《當代雜誌》，6 January 1990, pp. 34-35.
93. Ibid., pp. 34-35.
94. Mao Zedong's view of remoulding Chinese society was laid out in his essay *On the People's Democratic Dictatorship*, 30 June 1949. In Mao's words, "democratic dictatorship" means democracy is practised by the "people" (led by the party), not the "reactionaries" so that "democracy for the people and dictatorship over the reactionaries is the people's democratic dictatorship". Mao also said that if things were not done that way the revolution would fail. Read essay from http://www.marxist.org/reference/archive/mao.
95. The CCP saw the land reform programme as a success because the landlord class and its power was destroyed and replaced by cadres and middle peasants, who benefited the most from the reform. Middle peasants were those who were not the poorest or the richest peasants.
96. According to party history, by the spring of 1953, land reform had basically been accomplished throughout the country. Nationwide, more than 300 million peasants had been allotted land: "Ownership by the landlord class, the foundation of the feudal system that had continued for several thousand years in China, was by that time thoroughly eliminated. This meant a great, historic victory"; Hu Sheng, *A Concise History of the Communist Party of China*, pp. 417-18. Chan Sui-jeung discussed Guangdong's land reform implementation in considerable detail, and includes the role of Fang Fang and Ye Jianying, *East River Column*, pp. 136-54.
97. The Suppression of Counterrevolutionaries is considered in CCP history as one of the party's "great movements" in the early period of the founding of the PRC. It targeted those

with KMT connections, religious leaders, as well as secret society members. By October 1951, party history records that the counter-revolutionaries had been "basically wiped out", Hu Sheng, *A Concise History of the Communist Party of China*, pp. 420–21.
98. According to party history, problems included the "lawless elements among the capitalists, not satisfied with ordinary profits gained by normal methods, tried hard to grab high spoils by illegal means such as bribing state functionaries", capitalists evading taxes, and stealing of economic information. The campaign supposedly enabled the party "to gain complete political and economic initiative and bring about rapid economic restoration and development"; Hu Sheng, *A Concise History of the Communist Party of China*, pp. 430–32.
99. A leading work on the Thought Reform Campaign is that of psychologist Robert Jay Lifton's *Thought Reform and the Psychology of Totalism*, published in 1961, where he described in detail various methods used to change people's minds coercively, see Chapter 22.
100. Party history notes the party's "policy of uniting and remoulding intellectuals"; Hu Sheng, *A Concise History of the Communist Party of China*, p. 460.
101. Mao Zedong, "On the Correct Handling of the Contradiction among the People", *Selected Works of Mao Zedong*, 27 February 1957.
102. According to party history, the Hundred Flower Campaign resulted in criticisms and comments, "some of which were erroneous", but the party sought to rectify "contradictions" by listening to criticisms, "well over 90 percent" were beneficial in helping the party improve its work. However, "a few bourgeois Rightists" launched attacks of the party and the socialist system, which led to the anti-Rightist movement; Hu Sheng, *A Concise History of the Communist Party of China*, pp. 520–27.
103. There are two schools of thought about Mao's true intention in calling the Hundred Flower Campaign. One view, including that of the Soviet leader, Nikita Khrushchev, suspected Mao called for open criticism to induce dissenters to reveal themselves so he could identify and eliminate them (this is also the view of Jung Chang and Jon Halliday in *Mao*); whereas the other view is that Mao was genuinely surprised by the intensity of the dissent, see Lucian W. Pye, *China*, p. 235.
104. For a short account of the Great Leap Forward, see Graham Hutchings, *Modern China*, pp. 164–66.
105. For an account of the collectivisation of the countryside, see Justin Yifu Lin, "Collectivization and China's Agricultural Crisis 1959–1961", *Journal of Political Economy*, pp. 1228–52.
106. See John M. Carroll, *A Concise History of Hong Kong*, p. 150, and David Faure, *Society*, pp. 274–80.
107. Nikita Khrushchev served as the first secretary of the Communist Party of the Soviet Union after Stalin's death in 1953 and until 1964. From 1958 until 1964, he was also the premier (chairman of the Council of Ministers). Khrushchev had attacked Stalin and his cult of personality in 1956, and revised Leninist doctrine by proclaiming that the war between communism and imperialism was not inevitable. These and other Soviet actions eventually led to the cooling of relations between China and the Soviet Union, see Roderick MacFarquhar and Michael Schoenhals, *Mao's Last Revolution*, pp. 3–13.

Chapter 6

1. There is scholarly debate about when the Cultural Revolution started. The earliest date was in September 1965 with a speech made by Lin Biao, or on 16 May 1966 when senior party leaders were criticised by Mao Zedong.
2. On that day, Hua Guofeng, who was Mao Zedong's anointed successor, with Ye Jianying, moved with lightning speed. With the help of Mao's long-time bodyguard and the guard unit, they arrested the members of the Gang of Four and several of their principal supporters. The struggle between the Gang of Four and the moderates that everyone had expected was suddenly precluded.
3. *Decision Concerning the Great Proletarian Cultural Revolution*, adopted 8 August 1966 by the Central Committee of the CCP.
4. Ibid.
5. The first Red Guard organisation was formed on 29 May 1966 by students at the middle school attached to Tsinghua University, Robert MacFarquar and Michael Schoenhals, *Mao's Last Revolution*, p. 87.
6. Frank Welsh, *A History of Hong Kong*, p. 469.
7. For a definitive account of the Cultural Revolution, see Robert MacFarquar and Michael Schoenhals, *Mao's Last Revolution*; and also Laszlo Ladany, *The Communist Party of China and Marxism*, pp. 289–350.
8. David Bonavia, *Hong Kong 1997*, pp. 33–36.
9. 金堯如，《香港五十年憶往》, p. 123.
10. 冉隆勃、馬繼森，《周恩來與香港「六七暴動」內幕》, pp. 63–64.
11. Robert MacFarquhar and Michael Schoenhals, *Mao's Last Revolution*, p. 115.
12. 金堯如，《香港五十年憶往》, p. 95.
13. For example, 司馬文森, a cultural counsellor stationed in France, was persecuted and imprisoned after returning to China. See 張家偉，《香港六七暴動內情》, pp. 216–17. Cheung's book is also available in English, *Hong Kong's Watershed: The 1967 Riots*.
14. Robert Cottrell, *The End of Hong Kong*, p. 28.
15. See the comments made by Liang Shangyuan (梁上苑), the former deputy director of Hong Kong Xinhua News Agency in 張家偉，《香港六七暴動內情》, p. 19. Some commentators noted CCP members and supporters from grassroots backgrounds were keen to emulate Red Guard—like activities in Hong Kong, 梁慕嫻，〈六七暴動惡花今結果〉，《開放雜誌》, http://www.open.com.hk/0708p53.html. See also Gary Ka-wai Cheung, *Hong Kong's Watershed: The 1967 Riots*, pp. 16–20.
16. David Wilson, interview, 19 September 2003, p. 18, http://chu.cam.ac.uk/archives/collections/BDOHP/Wilson.pdf. David Wilson worked at the Foreign Office in London at the time of the 1967 riots, and was governor of Hong Kong, 1987–1992.
17. David Bonavia, *Hong Kong 1997*, pp. 36–37.
18. Quoted in Ian Scott, *Political Change and the Crisis of Legitimacy*, p. 97. For a scholarly analysis of the impact that Macao had on Hong Kong, see Robert Bickers, "On Not Being Macao (ed) in Hong Kong: British Official Minds and Actions in 1967", in *May Days in Hong Kong*, pp. 54–67.
19. The group's full name in English is the Cultural Revolution Group of the Chinese Communist Party's Central Committee. The Central Committee consisted of the

Politburo and its Standing Committee, as well as the Secretariat. In 1964, Mao Zedong had a group formed to carry out the rectification campaign in the arts and literary circles and to prepare reports and policy documents. In May 1966, the group was renamed the Central Cultural Revolution Group directly under the Politburo's Standing Committee. In August 1966, the Group became the authority responsible for the Cultural Revolution. By January 1967, as a result of various purges, the Secretariat of the Central Committee ceased to function, and by the following month the Group also replaced the Politburo. The Group shared power with the CCP Central Committee, State Council and Central Military Commission. Jiang Qing and her supporters became the centre for power, and they controlled the Group. The Group was dissolved in 1969, see Kwok-sing Li, *A Glossary of Political Terms*, pp. 583–85. See also Robert MacFarquhar and Michael Schoenhals, *Mao's Last Revolution*, pp. 80, 99–101; and Gao Wenqian, *Zhou Enlai*, pp. 115–16 and 153–55.

20. David Wilson, interview, pp. 19–21, http://chu.cam.ac.uk/archives/collections/BDOHP/Wilson.pdf, 19 September 2003. Barbara Barnouin and Yu Changgen, *Zhou Enlai*, pp. 252–58 on Chen Yi and pp. 258–60 on foreign affairs; and Gao Wenqian on Zhou Enlai and Chen Yi, *Zhou Enlai*, pp. 170–79.
21. John P. Burns, "The Structure of Communist Party Control in Hong Kong", *Asian Survey*, p. 751.
22. One view is that Zhou Enlai was still in control of the Hong Kong matters during the Cultural Revolution and the revolution by the CCP in Hong Kong was in fact orchestrated by him, see 余長更,〈周恩來遙控「反英抗暴」內幕〉, 載冉隆勃、馬繼森,《周恩來與香港「六七暴動」內幕》, pp. 2–55. Another view was that Zhou had lost control by August 1967 when he was denounced by Wang Li of the Central Cultural Revolution Small Group, see Steve Tsang, *A Modern History of Hong Kong*, pp. 184–85.
23. 金堯如,《香港五十年憶往》, p. 128, the Hong Kong CCP was told to "重新走上革命道路"。
24. Barbara Barnouin and Yu Changgen, *Zhou Enlai*, p. 225.
25. John P. Burns, "The Structure of Communist Party Control in Hong Kong", *Asian Survey*, p. 751.
26. Cindy Yik-Yi Chu, "Overt and Covert Functions of the Hong Kong Branch of the Xinhua News Agency, 1947–1984", *The Historian*, p. 38.
27. Jack Cater, who was secretary for defence, thought "[t]here was nothing happening in Hong Kong in early 1967"; Wong Cheuk Yin, "The 1967 Leftists Riots and Regime Legitimacy in Hong Kong", http://www.hku.hk/hkcsp/ccex/ehkcss01/issue3_ar_lawrence_wong.htm.
28. *Kowloon Disturbances, 1966, Report of Commission of Inquiry*. For a summary of the report, see Ian Scott, *Political Change and the Crisis of Legitimacy in Hong Kong*, pp. 82–96.
29. Steve Tsang, *A Modern History of Hong Kong*, p. 186.
30. Robert Bickers and Ray Yep, *May Days in Hong Kong*, p. 7.
31. Steve Tsang, *A Modern History of Hong Kong*, pp. 173 and 184.
32. Gary Ka-wai Cheung, *Hong Kong's Watershed: The 1967 Riots*, pp. 28–29.
33. Ian Scott, *Political Change and the Crisis of Legitimacy in Hong Kong*, p. 100; and Gary Ka-wai Cheung, *Hong Kong's Watershed: The 1967 Riots*, pp. 29–42.
34. Hong Kong Government, *The Face of Confrontation*, February 1968.

35. 張家偉, 香港六七暴動內情《香港六七暴動內情》, "有計劃, 有組織, 有預謀的對我國愛國工人和愛國同胞進行瘋狂的迫害", p. 34.
36. Ma Jisen, *The Cultural Revolution in the Foreign Ministry of China*, pp. 179–80.
37. Editorial, *Ta Kung Pao*, 12 May 1967.
38. Hong Kong Government, *Hong Kong Disturbances, 1967*, pp. 48–52.
39. Ibid.
40. John Cooper, *Colony in Conflict*, p. 62.
41. 張家偉,《香港六七暴動內情》, pp. 42–43.
42. 金堯如,《香港五十年憶往》, pp. 132–33.
43. Wong Cheuk Yin, "The 1967 Leftists Riots and Regime Legitimacy in Hong Kong", http://www.hku.hk/hkcsp/ccex/ehkcss01/issue3_ar_lawrence_wong.htm. Wong's thesis gives the impression that Jack Cater contacted Zhou Enlai in Beijing to ascertain China's intention. That would have been unlikely since it was uncommon for Hong Kong officials to contact Mainland officials directly, but there would have been messages being carried back and forth from various go-between, such as the senior representatives of Bank of China.
44. 張家偉,《香港六七暴動內情》, p. 47.
45. The HKSAR Government awarded Yeung Kwong a Grand Bauhinia Medal in 2001, which aroused much controversy.
46. 張家偉,《香港六七暴動內情》, pp. 45–46, "港英當局對中國同胞還在進行瘋狂的民族迫害, 這場反迫害鬥爭就是一場民族鬥爭。用毛澤東思想武裝起來的各業工人和各界同胞一定要把反迫害鬥爭升級一定要粉碎港英的迫害陰謀, 不獲全勝, 誓不收兵。"
47. Ibid., pp. 46–47.
48. Hong Kong Government, *Hong Kong Yearbook 1967*, p. 12. See also Denis Bray, *Hong Kong Metamorphosis*, p. 125. The Information Services Department was housed in a low-rise building on the other side of Queen's Road, where the Cheung Kong Centre is today.
49. Hong Kong Government, *Hong Kong Disturbances, 1967*, pp. 48–52.
50. David Bonavia, *Hong Kong 1997*, p. 39.
51. 張家偉,《香港六七暴動內情》, p. 47.
52. David Wilson, interview, p. 18, http://chu.cam.ac.uk/archives/collections/BDOHP/Wilson.pdf.
53. Roderick MacFarquhar and Michael Schoenhals, *Mao's Last Revolution*, pp. 224–27; Barbara Barnouin and Yu Changgen, *Zhou Enlai*, p. 261; and Ma Jisen, *The Cultural Revolution in the Foreign Ministry of China*, p. 180.
54. Ma Jisen, *The Cultural Revolution in the Foreign Ministry of China*, p. 181.
55. 金堯如,《香港五十年憶往》, p. 134, "不敢鬥爭, 不敢勝利".
56. 張家偉,《香港六七暴動內情》, p. 61.
57. Hong Kong Government, *The Face of Confrontation*, February 1968.
58. 劉武生,《文革中的周恩來》, p. 330. Ma Jisen, *The Cultural Revolution in the Foreign Ministry of China*, noted the Hong Kong delegation only arrived in Beijing on 25 May (p. 181) but 劉武生 noted meetings took place on 24 and 27 May.
59. Ma Jisen, *The Cultural Revolution in the Foreign Ministry of China*, pp. 181–83.

60. 張家偉，《香港六七暴動內情》，p. 63.
61. Hong Kong Government, *Hong Kong: Report for the Year 1967*, p. 18.
62. John M. Carroll, *A Concise History of Hong Kong*, p. 156.
63. The *People's Daily* editorial on 3 June 1967 was entitled "Strike Back Resolutely at the Provocation of British Imperialism" （堅決反擊英帝國主義的挑釁）。The original Chinese text reads: "英帝國主義是香港萬惡的殖民統治者，是香港四百萬中國同胞的敵人，七億中國人民的敵人……一百多年來，英帝國主義在香港幹盡了壞事，血債累累，罪惡滔天，必須清算！……目前，擺在香港愛國同胞面前的任務，就是再接再厲，把這場反英抗爭堅持下去，奪取偉大的勝利。為了實現這個目標，就應該放手地發動群眾，以工人階級為核心，團結香港，一切可以團結的反帝愛國力量，不斷鞏固和壯大反英抗暴鬥爭的隊伍。"
64. John Cooper, Colony in Conflict, p. 82.
65. 張家偉，《香港六七暴動內情》，p. 61; and Ma Jisen, *The Cultural Revolution in the Foreign Ministry of China*, pp. 183–84.
66. Maynard Parker, "Reports: Hong Kong", *The Atlantic*, November 1967, www.theatlantic.com/issues/67nov/hk1167.htm.
67. 張家偉，《香港六七暴動內情》，ibid., p. 71.
68. Ibid., p. 71. "除了被港九愛國同胞和中國人民打得粉身碎骨之外，絕不會有別的下場。"
69. John M. Carroll, *A Concise History of Hong Kong*, p. 176.
70. 金堯如，《香港五十年憶往》，p. 153.
71. David Bonavia, *Hong Kong 1997*, p. 41.
72. Steve Tsang, *A Modern History of Hong Kong*, p. 186.
73. Leo F. Goodstadt, *Uneasy Partners*, p. 77.
74. 張家偉，《香港六七暴動內情》，pp. 74–75.
75. Ibid., p. 81. "頭昏腦脹，大滅敵人的威風。"
76. Denis Bray, *Hong Kong Metamorphosis*, pp. 126–28. See also John Cooper, *Colony in Conflict*, p. 105; David Bonavia, *Hong Kong 1997*, p. 43; and Wong Cheuk Yin, "The 1967 Riots and Regime Legitimacy in Hong Kong". According to Ma Jisen, Zhou Enlai was very unhappy about the incident, *The Cultural Revolution in the Foreign Ministry of China*, p. 186.
77. Wong Cheuk Yin, "The 1967 Riots and Regime Legitimacy in Hong Kong". Wong's thesis gives the impression Cater had talked directly with Zhou Enlai, which was unlikely, see footnote 43 above.
78. Ibid., and 張家偉，《香港六七暴動內情》，p. 89.
79. The veteran leftist is Xu Simin （徐四民）。See 李谷城，《香港新華社的功能與角色》，http://202.76.36.61/vol%2018/vol18Doc1_2.htm.
80. 張家偉，《香港六七暴動內情》，p. 92. "把刀鋒對準港英法西斯強盜及其走狗，窮追猛打，決不留情。"
81. Official Report of Proceedings of the Meeting of Legislative Council on 12 July 1967, pp. 367–68. The acting colonial secretary was Michael David Irving Gass. The records show typographical mistakes where square brackets are used in the quotation, but it is clear what the right words should be.

82. FCO 40/112, *Hong Kong Confrontation*, 12 July 1967. The author wishes to thank Ray Yep for pointing out the existence of this reference. For an analysis of how the governor saw matters, see Ray Yep, "The 1967 Riots in Hong Kong: The Domestic and Diplomatic Fronts of the Governor", *May Days in Hong Kong*, pp. 22–36, especially p. 185, footnote 33.
83. John Cooper, *Colony in Conflict*, p. 156.
84. These are the statistics claimed by the Anti-Persecution Struggle Committee. See 張家偉，《香港六七暴動內情》, p. 96. For details of the raids, see John Cooper, *Colony in Conflict*, Chapter 10.
85. John Cooper, *Colony in Conflict*, p. 158.
86. 張家偉，《香港六七暴動內情》, p. 270.
87. Denis Bray, *Hong Kong Metamorphosis*, p. 128.
88. *Ta Kung Pao*, 21 July 1967, referred to in 張家偉，《香港六七暴動內情》, p. 98.
89. Ibid., p. 99.
90. Hong Kong Government, *Report of the Year 1967*, p. 16.
91. Ibid., p. 176.
92. John Cooper, *Colony in Conflict*, p. 176.
93. 張家偉，《香港六七暴動內情》, p. 100.
94. John Cooper, *Colony in Conflict*, p. 183; and John M. Carroll, *A Concise History of Hong Kong*, p. 156.
95. 張家偉，《香港六七暴動內情》, p. 104.
96. John Cooper, *Colony in Conflict*, p. 183; Denis Bray, *Hong Kong Metamorphosis*, p. 130; and "Hong Kong 1967 Leftist Riots", http://en.wikipedia.org/wiki/Hong_Kong_1967_riots.
97. Lau Kit-wai, "Vocal Support", *South China Morning Post*, Section C, front page, 2 July 2008.
98. John M. Carroll, *A Concise History of Hong Kong*, p. 156; and Roderick MacFarquar and Michael Schoenhals, *Mao's Last Revolution*, p. 225. A month later, in retaliation, the Chinese authorities arrested Reuter's correspondent in Beijing, Anthony Grey.
99. The three newspapers were the *Tin Fung Yat Pao* (田豐日報), *Afternoon News* (新午報), and *Hong Kong Evening News* (香港夜報); see also Roderick MacFarquar and Michael Schoenhals, *Mao's Last Revolution*, p. 225.
100. Interview with Denis Bray in Wong Cheuk Yin, "The 1967 Riots and Regime Legitimacy in Hong Kong".
101. Britain recognised the People's Republic of China in 1950. The two sides reached an agreement to exchange *charges d'affaires* on 17 June 1954, after which Britain set up its mission in Beijing. A full embassy was only set up after the Sino-British Joint Communiqué on the Agreement on the Exchange of Ambassadors was signed on 13 March 1972.
102. Percy Cradock, *Experiences of China*, p. 64.
103. Barbara Benouin and Yu Changgen, *Zhou Enlai*, p. 263.
104. Leo F. Goodstadt, *Profits, Politics and Panic*, p. 78. Laszlo Ladany noted that in the first half of 1967, the economy was still functioning, but by the second half, when the Cultural Revolution reached the workers, there were nationwide strikes and clashes between workers and Red Guards with many factories shutting because there was no coal and therefore no power to keep production running, *The Communist Party of China and Marxism*, p. 315.

105. Ma Jisen, *The Cultural Revolution in the Foreign Ministry of China*, p. 188.
106. 金堯如,《香港五十年憶往》, p. 190.
107. Ibid., p. 166.
108. John M. Carroll, *A Concise History of Hong Kong*, p. 156.
109. John Cooper, *Colony in Conflict*, p. 229; and John M. Carroll, *A Concise History of Hong Kong*, p. 157.
110. John Cooper, *Colony in Conflict*, p. 222.
111. 金堯如,〈香港反英抗暴的內幕〉, 載於冉隆勃、馬繼森,《周恩來與香港「六七暴動」內幕》, p. 73.
112. Ma Jisen, *The Cultural Revolution in the Foreign Ministry of China*, p. 189.
113. Hong Kong Government, *Report of the Year 1967*, p. 44.
114. John Cooper, *Colony in Conflict*, p. 275.
115. Hong Kong Government, *Report of the Year 1967*, p. 53. For more details, see Catherine R. Schenk, "The Banking and Financial Impact of the 1967 Riots in Hong Kong", *May Days in Hong Kong*, pp. 105–26.
116. 張家偉,《香港六七暴動內情》, p. 6.
117. For a discussion on the failure of the colonial political system including its appointment system, see Christine Loh, "Government and Business Alliance: Hong Kong's Functional Constituencies", in *Functional Constituencies*, pp. 29–30.
118. The Commission of Inquiry set up to look into the causes of the 1966 riots reported that the rioters were male, young, low-paid, under-privileged, uneducated or poorly educated with little outlet for their energy, and frustrated with their working and living conditions, Hong Kong Commission of Inquiry, *Kowloon Disturbances, 1966, Report of Commission of Inquiry*. While this was a government-appointed body, its recommendations were not all accepted by the government, such as putting in place a social insurance and benefits programmes, as had been created in some colonies, for example, Singapore.
119. Denis Bray, *Hong Kong Metamorphosis*, p. 133. The City District Office scheme was a copy of the District Offices in the New Territories introduced in 1910. The New Territories was relatively quiet during the 1967 riots the reason for which was attributed to better communications between the government and indigenous villagers; see pp. 133–40.
120. Official Report of Proceedings on 14 February 1967, Hong Kong Legislative Council, p. 20.
121. For a discussion of the City District Office scheme, see Ian Scott, *Political Change and the Crisis of Legitimacy*, pp. 107–10; and Steve Tsang, *Governing Hong Kong*, pp. 94–99.
122. The phrase was coined by Ambrose King in "Administrative Absorption of Politics in Hong Kong: Emphasis on the Grass Roots Levels", *Asian Survey*, pp. 422–39.
123. Ian Scott, *Political Change and the Crisis of Legitimacy in Hong Kong*, pp. 113–17.
124. Official Report of Proceedings on 14 February 1967, Hong Kong Legislative Council, pp. 34–38.
125. Ian Scott, *Political Change and the Crisis of Legitimacy in Hong Kong*, pp. 121–26.
126. Leo F. Goodstadt, "Red Guards in Hong Kong?", *Far Eastern Economic Review*, 20 July 1967, referred in William Heaton, "Maoist Revolutionary Strategy and Modern Colonialism: The Cultural Revolution in Hong Kong", *Asian Survey*, p. 844.
127. Wong Cheuk Yin, "The 1967 Riots and Regime Legitimacy in Hong Kong".

128. 張家偉,《香港六七暴動內情》, pp. 85–86.
129. Xu Jiatun, *Memoirs*, p. 52.
130. Wong Cheuk Yin, "The 1967 Riots and Regime Legitimacy in Hong Kong".
131. John Cooper, *Colony in Conflict*, p. 155.
132. Ibid.
133. Comments by 廖一原, member of the Standing Committee of the Anti-Persecution Committee. See 張家偉,《香港六七暴動內情》, p. 218.
134. 張家偉,《香港六七暴動內情》, p. 105.
135. Florence Leung Mo Han, *My Time in Hong Kong's Underground Communist Party*, 2012.
136. 〈六七暴動派反殖傳單入獄〉,《明報》, 14 June 2007. http://www.mingpaovan.com/htm/News/20070614/HK-gaa2.htm.
137. Tsang Yok Sing remembers in Sally Blyth and Ian Wotherspoon, *Hong Kong Remembers*, pp. 95–98.
138. Andrew Li, "Red Sun over Stanley", *Far Eastern Economic Review*, 25 July 1968, pp. 207–11. For an analysis of social conditions in Hong Kong then, see David Clayton, "The Riots and Labour Laws: The Struggle for an Eight-Hour Day for Women Factory Workers, 1967–71", *May Days in Hong Kong*, pp. 127–44.
139. Xu Jiatun, *Memoirs*, p. 40.
140. Ibid., pp. 75–76.
141. 金堯如,《香港五十年憶往》, p. 184.
142. 《工商日報》, 10 September 1968, "該校曾被警方搜出非法武器,以及指派學生投擲炸彈等事實……實人神之所共嫉,天地之所不容……漢華中學經過鬥爭失敗之餘,即改頭換面,包藏禍心,企圖死灰復燃……本區鄉民世代過慣寧靜生活,如一旦有此搗亂份子,在此設校授徒,鼓吹鬥爭邪說……勢必喧擾不堪,使鄉民驚心動魄,寢食不安,危害地方。"
143. Tsang Yok Sing, "The Leftist Community", *Tsang Yok Sing Straight Talk*, pp. 157–58.
144. Gao Wenqian, *Zhou Enlai*, pp. 3, 110, 138, and 143.
145. Roderick MacFarquar and Michael Schoenhals, *Mao's Last Revolution*, pp. 221–22; and Gao Wenqian, *Zhou Enlai*, pp. 167–70.
146. Barbara Barnouin and Yu Changgen, *Zhou Enlai*, pp. 260–63; and Gao Wenqian, *Zhou Enlai*, pp. 174–79.
147. 張家偉,《香港六七暴動內情》, p. 259.
148. 梁上苑,《中共在香港》, p. 164.
149. 金堯如,〈香港反英抗暴的內幕〉, 載於冉隆勃、馬繼森,《周恩來與香港「六七暴動」內幕》, p. 74.
150. 金堯如,《香港五十年憶往》, p. 184.
151. See interviews with Hu Dizhou (胡棣周) and Luo Fu (羅孚). Hu was member of the Anti-Persecution Committee and publisher of the leftist press *Hong Kong Evening Post* (香港夜報). He was arrested in August 1967 and that caused the burning of British Diplomatic Mission in Beijing by the Red Guards. Luo was an editor of a leftist press and was responsible for the CCP united front work in the literature area in Hong Kong. See 張家偉,《香港六七暴動內情》, pp. 197 and 252.
152. See interviews with Liao Yiyuan (廖一原) and Luo Fu, 張家偉,《香港六七暴動內情》, pp. 217 and 253.

153. 張家偉，《香港六七暴動內情》, p. 9.
154. In Relation to the Party's Resolution on Historical Issues since the Founding of the People's Republic of China, passed by the 11th CCP Central Committee on 27 June 1981.
155. Roderick MacFarquhar and Michael Schoenhals, *Mao's Last Revolution*, pp. 456–58.
156. The interview was in English on RTHK:

> —Host: I was struck by one phrase at the end of the policy address, towards the end of the conclusion, you say, we promote democratic development without compromising social stability or government efficiency, that kind of implies that democratic development does compromise social stability or government efficiency?
>
> —Donald Tsang: It can, it can, if we go to the extreme, people go to the extreme, and you have a Cultural Revolution, for instance, in China. When people take everything into their hands, then you cannot govern the place . . .
>
> —Host: But the Cultural Revolution wasn't really an extreme example of democracy.
>
> —Donald Tsang: What is it? People taking power into their own hands! Now, this is what it means by democracy, if you take it to the full swing. In other democracies, even if you have an elected person, then you overturn the policy in California, for instance, you have initiative number, number, number what, then you overturn policy taken by the government, that's not necessarily conducive to efficient government.

See *Ming Pao* website: http://www.mpinews.com/htm/INews/20071012/gb52236a.htm for the full text.

157. "I am very sorry that I made an inappropriate remark concerning the Cultural Revolution during a radio interview yesterday, and I wish to retract that remark. Hong Kong people treasure democracy and hope to implement universal suffrage as soon as possible. I share the same aspirations. I reiterate that I will honour my pledge in the Policy Address to do my utmost in resolving the question of universal suffrage in Hong Kong during my current term." See Government Information Service, http://www.info.gov.hk/gia/general/200710/13/P200710130147.htm.
158. Raymond Yeung, "Give Justice to Those Killed in the 1969 Riots, Leftist Workers Say", *South China Morning Post*, 8 May 2017.

Chapter 7

1. A good example is Wei Jingsheng. He asked that there should be a Fifth Modernisation—democracy—and was arrested for treason (corresponding with foreigners about the Chinese-Vietnamese War 1979) and sentenced to 15 years in prison. He was released in 1993 and then re-arrested. He was finally released "for medical reasons" and deported to the US in 1997, where he has remained.
2. In 1978, Deng Xiaoping made clear that Marxism "undoubtedly involves the revision of some outmoded principles". He chose "realism" as the guiding principle and "practice"—not ideology—became the sole criterion for truth. He insisted this was "not revisionism".

Revisionism was a high crime during the Cultural Revolution and during the earlier years of communist rule. Deng was in effect putting revisionism to bed.

3. Documents of the 13th National Congress of the CCP; and the Constitution of the PRC 1982. The Four Cardinal Principles were written into the CCP charter, as well as the Chinese Constitution in 1982 and thus are still relevant today.

4. Deng Xiaoping, summary of talks with members of a Hong Kong industrial and commercial delegation and with Chung Sze Yuen and other Hong Kong figures on 22 and 23 June 1984, recorded in Deng Xiaoping, *Deng Xiaoping on 'One Country, Two Systems'*, pp. 17.

5. 鄧小平,〈鄧小平在武昌、深圳、珠海、上海等地的談話要點〉(18 January to 21 February 1992),《鄧小平文選》,第三卷,《人民日報》, see http://web.peopledaily.com.cn/deng.

6. Documents of the Third Plenary Session of the 11th CCP Central Committee held in December 1978.

7. 陳新,〈中共在香港的經濟動向〉,《七十年代》, Issue 104, September 1978, p. 22.

8. When Deng Xiaoping decided to revive party work in Hong Kong, he said that "it is now the time to refurnish the temple, and Liao Chengzhi will be the Buddha in it" ("廟要修了,由廖承志來當菩薩"),〈鐵竹傳〉,《廖承志傳》, p. 489.

9. 〈魯平揭秘辛1990:回歸前最大危機〉,《文匯報》, 26 June 2007.

10. David Wilson, interview, 19 September 2003.

11. Wang Kang and Liang Weilin both came from Guangdong and had known each other since the 1930s with Wang having been Liang's protégé. Wong would thus make a good pair of "eyes and ears" in Hong Kong for Liang, see 李谷城,《香港的新華社功能與角色》, see http://202.76.36.61/vol%2018/vol18Doc1_2.htm.

12. Abridged from John P. Burns, *The Structure of Communist Party Control in Hong Kong*, pp. 756–57, quoting from Mainland materials.

13. 軒轅輅,《新華社透》, pp. 22 and 52.

14. Xu Jiatun, *Memoirs*, Chapters 2 and 8, and John P. Burns, *The Structure of Communist Party Control in Hong Kong*, p. 752.

15. Ching Cheong, "China's Administration over Hong Kong: The New China News Agency and the Hong Kong–Macau Affairs Office", in Nyaw Mee-kau and Li Si-ming, *The Other Hong Kong Report*, p. 199.

16. Xu Jiatun, *Memoirs*, pp. 69–70.

17. 陳新,〈中共在香港的經濟動向〉,《七十年代》, September 1978, Issue 104, p. 22.

18. Sun Yat-sen's will was written on 20 February 1925 and signed on 11 March 1925, Sun Yat-sen, *San Min Chu I: The Three Principles of the People*, p. i.

19. KMT National People's Convention, Manifesto Concerning the Abrogation of Unequal Treaties, 1931, pp. 461–65.

20. The original Chinese text reads: "香港和澳門是被英國和葡萄牙當局佔領的中國領土的一部分,解決香港,澳門問題完全屬於中國主權範圍內的問題,根本不屬於通常的所謂殖民地範疇,因此不應列入反殖宣言中適用的殖民地地區的名單之內。對香港和澳門問題,中國政府一貫主張在條件成熟的時候,用適當方式加以解決。聯合國無權討論這一問題。" See http://big5.china.com.cn/book/zhuanti/hyl/2007-10/25/content_9124238.htm.

21. Mark Roberti, *The Fall of Hong Kong*, pp. 9–10.
22. Ibid., p. 10.
23. Robert Cottrell, *The End of Hong Kong*, p. 33.
24. James Tang and Frank Ching, "The MacLehose–Youde Years: Balancing the 'Three-Legged Stool' 1971–86", in Ming K. Chan, *Precarious Balance*, pp. 153–54.
25. Robert Cottrell, *The End of Hong Kong*, pp. 32–33.
26. John M. Carroll, *A Concise History of Hong Kong*, p. 177. It was also likely that the prisoners were close to having served out their terms.
27. The political adviser to the governor on foreign affairs was a transfer from the British diplomatic service. The political adviser worked as a mini-Foreign Office in the Hong Kong government dealing with Mainland and Southeast Asian affairs. It had a person from the Foreign Office backed up by someone from the Hong Kong government or later by a second Foreign Office person, see David Wilson, interview, 2003.
28. Gary Cheung reported on new information obtained from recently declassified documents from the British National Archives, "MacLehose Thought of SAR Idea 11 Years before Deng's Plan", *South China Morning Post*, 25 June 2007.
29. MacLehose wrote a report to Sir Alec Douglas—Home in 1972. See Gary Cheung, "MacLehose Thought of SAR Idea 11 Years before Deng's Plan", *South China Morning Post*, 25 June 2007.
30. Robert Cottrell related an observation from a senior Hong Kong civil servant of MacLehose, *The End of Hong Kong*, p. 36; and Jonathan Dimbleby described MacLehose as "an unabashed enthusiast for China", *The Last Governor*, p. 39.
31. Robert Cottrell, *The End of Hong Kong*, p. 37.
32. Mark Roberti, *The Fall of Hong Kong*, pp. 13–14.
33. Xu Jiatun noted that it was the British who wanted to bring the issue of Hong Kong up, not the Chinese, *Memoirs*, pp. 82–83. Robert Cottrell thought it had to do with the British government's Export Credit Guarantee Department that was about to have to start writing loan guarantees that extended beyond 1997, *The End of Hong Kong*, pp. 41–44. Jonathan Dimbleby quoted Percy Cradock's recollection that the Foreign Office thought there would come a point when fears about the future would begin to overshadow Hong Kong's prosperity if the future of Hong Kong was not sorted out; see *The Last Governor*, pp. 40–41.
34. The main lease was the lease on the New Territories granted by China to Britain which would expire in 1997, thus the Hong Kong government sold land on sub-leases. Robert Cottrell noted that MacLehose was to ask the Chinese during his visit to Beijing: "whether the expiry date of 27 June 1997, which was written into all New Territories sub-leases sold by the Hong Kong government, could be replaced with a statement that such leases were valid 'for so long as the Crown administers the territory'", *The End of Hong Kong*, p. 51. See also Steve Tsang, *A Modern History of Hong Kong*, pp. 212–14. He noted that what drove MacLehose to want to bring up the issue of the future of Hong Kong was a sense of responsibility to Hong Kong. See also Mark Roberti, *The Fall of Hong Kong*, pp. 18–20.
35. Chung Sze-yuen, *Hong Kong's Journey to Reunification*, p. 31.
36. 《中共黨史重大事件述評》, pp. 351–55.
37. Xu Jiatun, *Memoirs*, Vol. I, pp. 82–83; and David Wilson, interview, 19 September 2003.

38. Jonathan Dimbleby related what Jack Cater said on mortgages: "This is nonsense. We did not even have mortgages at the time—or at least in no great number. And I'd certainly not heard about it and obviously I would have done", *The Last Governor*, pp. 40–41. Mark Roberti noted Cater was worried about a rebuff from China, and urged that the matter be first discussed by the Executive Council, *The Fall of Hong Kong*, pp. 18–20. Robert Cottrell also detected little concern about mortgages among leading businessmen at the time, *The End of Hong Kong*, pp. 41–43. A voice of concern was that of Jimmy McGregor, the then director of the Hong Kong General Chamber of Commerce, who in 1976 said investors would need assurances from China before making long-term investments in Hong Kong, John M. Carroll, *A Concise History of Hong Kong*, p. 177. David Akers-Jones, a former civil servant who served as chief secretary from 1985 to 1987, noted that by the end of the 1970s the expiry of the New Territories lease "was getting too close to enable property developers to go to the banks for money for plans would take many years to come to fruition" but he also said that "land in the New Territories . . . continued to be sold on a lease expiring three days before the end of June 1997", *Feeling the Stones*, p. 108. David Wilson made a point of highlighting the concerns of the Americans, Interview, 19 September 2003. Chung Sze Yuen noted that: "Banks would be imprudent to lend and indeed, companies, particularly the capital intensive electric power stations, would be reluctant to invest until they could clear away the uncertainties", *Hong Kong's Journey to Reunification*, pp. 28–29.
39. 《中共黨史重大事件述評》, p. 352.
40. Robert Cottrell, *The End of Hong Kong*, pp. 54–55; and Jonathan Dimbleby, *The Last Governor*, p. 43. Huang Wenfang also added that Deng Xiaoping said he did not want the British to bring up the future of Hong Kong too early, 黃文放,《中國對香港恢復行使主權的決策歷程與執行》, p. 4. See also Mark Roberti, *The Fall of Hong Kong*, pp. 20–23.
41. Robert Cottrell, *The End of Hong Kong*, p. 56.
42. Mark Roberti, *The Fall of Hong Kong*, p. 23.
43. Chung Sze Yuen noted that Kan Yuet Keung never spoke about what happened in Beijing, particularly about the meeting between MacLehose and Deng Xiaoping, *Hong Kong's Journey to Reunification*, p. 30.
44. This was what Deng Xiaoping told Margaret Thatcher on 24 September 1982, Deng Xiaoping, *Deng Xiaoping on 'One Country, Two Systems'*, pp. 1–2.
45. Jonathan Dimbleby, *The Last Governor*, p. 42.
46. In July 1979, Percy Craddock sent a memorandum on the issue of the sub-leases to the Chinese Foreign Ministry, which responded in September that the British idea of extending the sub-leases "for so long as the Crown administers the territory" was unnecessary. In November 1979, the new prime minister, Margaret Thatcher, mentioned Hong Kong to Hua Guofeng, China's then premier (1976–1980) when he visited Britain. In December 1979, Peter Carrington raised it with Huang Hua when Huang visited Britain, and in May 1980, James Callaghan, a former prime minister, sought to discuss Hong Kong on his visit to Beijing. See 李後,《回歸的歷程》, p. 68; and Robert Cottrell, *The End of Hong Kong*, pp. 61–62.
47. Robert Cottrell noted a meeting and discussion between Liao Chengzhi and Hong Kong financier Fung King Hey in March 1981, *The End of Hong Kong*, p. 63.
48. Xu Jiatun, *Memoirs*, pp. 82–83.
49. Lu Ping, comments in *Window*, 2 July 1993, p. 33.

50. Steve Tsang noted that the Politburo took the decision to take back Hong Kong in March 1981. Li Xiannian was initially unhappy with allowing Hong Kong to remain capitalist and that it took until January 1982 for Deng Xiaoping to achieve consensus among the top leaders, *A Modern History of Hong Kong*, p. 217.
51. Deng Xiaoping supposedly said that "對這個問題現在不能說更多的話"; see 黃文放，《中國對香港恢復行使主權的決策歷程與執行》, p. 6; and Robert Cottrell noted that Deng wanted to discuss China's plan for reunification with Taiwan, *The End of Hong Kong*, p. 63.
52. Beijing's nine-point plan for Taiwan reunification stated *inter alia* that Taiwan could enjoy a high degree of autonomy as a special administrative region, retain its armed forces, its social-economic system and way of life, and that Beijing would not interfere with Taiwan's local affairs. Talks should be held between the CCP and KMT to accomplish reunification.
53. Xu Jiatun noted that Deng Xiaoping, Hu Yaobang, Zhao Ziyang, and Liao Chengzhi spoke to a dozen or so Hong Kong figures, *Memoirs*, p. 88. Robert Cottrell noted that between November–December 1981, the Chinese side received a flurry of Hong Kong visitors in Beijing, *The End of Hong Kong*, p. 66.
54. 黃文放，《中國對香港恢復行使主權的決策歷程與執行》, p. 13.
55. 李後，《回歸的歷程》, p. 74; and 黃文放，《中國對香港恢復行使主權的決策歷程與執行》, p. 14.
56. Atkins had gone to Beijing to prepare for the new British prime minister, Margaret Thatcher, to visit China. The news that Thatcher would visit Beijing was announced after Atkins's meeting with Zhao on 6 January 1982.
57. Robert Cottrell, *The End of Hong Kong*, p. 67.
58. Mark Roberti, *The Fall of Hong Kong*, p. 39.
59. Hong Kong Government, *White Paper: District Administration in Hong Kong*, January 1981.
60. During the early days of District Boards election, a third of the seats were elected by universal suffrage and the rest were appointed.
61. Ian Scott noted difficulty in tracing the source of the impetus for setting up the District Boards, *Political Change and the Crisis of Legitimacy in Hong Kong*, p. 28; and Shiu-hing Sonny Lo drew a similar conclusion, *The Politics of Democratization in Hong Kong*, pp. 73–81. Norman Miners noted how radical it was to adopt universal suffrage for the District Boards election; *The Government and Politics of Hong Kong*, pp. 170–71.
62. These people included tycoons, long-time prominent leftists, publishers, etc., e.g., Henry Fok (霍英東), Richard Charles Lee (利銘澤), K. S. Li (李嘉誠), Gordon Wu (胡應湘), T. K. Ann (安子介), Fung King Hei (馮景禧), Rayson Huang (黃麗松), Fei Yimin (費彝民), Xu Simin (徐四民), Ng Hong Min (吳康民), Louis Cha (查良鏞), and others. See 李後，《回歸的歷程》, pp. 76–77.
63. 黃文放，《中國對香港恢復行使主權的決策歷程與執行》, p. 12.
64. Xu Jiatun, *Memoirs*, pp. 89–90; and Xu Jiatun's interview with *Ming Pao Monthly*, August 2007.
65. Margaret Thatcher, *Downing Street Years*, p. 259. Thatcher also wrote: "By the time I visited the Far East in September 1982 Britain's standing in the world, and my own, had been transformed as a result of the victory in the Falklands".

66. David Wilson, interview, http://chu.cam.ac.uk/archives/collections/BDOHP/Wilson.pdf, 19 September 2003.
67. For an account of what happened, see Mark Roberti, *The Fall of Hong Kong*, pp. 46–47.
68. Robert Cottrell, *The End of Hong Kong*, pp. 87–92.
69. Deng Xiaoping's talk with Margaret Thatcher on 24 September 1982, Deng Xiaoping, *Deng Xiaoping on 'One Country, Two Systems'*, pp. 1–5.
70. Margaret Thatcher had said that Deng Xiaoping told her at the meeting that: "I could walk in and take the whole lot this afternoon", to which she replied: "There is nothing I could do to stop you but the eyes of the world would now know what China is like." Lu Ping disclosed that the Chinese were ready to resort to "requisition by force" if the Sino-British negotiations had set off unrest in the colony, see Michael Sheridan, "China Plotted Hong Kong invasion", *The Australian*, 25 June 2007.
71. Qian Qichen, *Ten Episodes in China's Diplomacy*, p. 271.
72. Deng Xiaoping's talk with Geoffrey Howe on 31 July 1984, Deng Xiaoping, *Deng Xiaoping on One Country, Two Systems*, pp. 19–21.
73. Mark Roberti, *The Fall of Hong Kong*, p. 51.
74. In 1981, Britain passed the British Nationality (Hong Kong) Act, which turned Hong Kong British subjects into "British Dependent Territory Citizens" and excluded them from enjoying the right of abode in Britain. The issue of British nationality in relation to the Hong Kong British subjects remained a sore point with the people of Hong Kong throughout the transition period. For a discussion on the effort and time it took for Britain to grant full British nationality to the ethnic minorities who would otherwise become stateless, see Christine Loh, *Being Here*, pp. 260–66.
75. On 30 September 1982, Xinhua News Agency published a commentary entitled "China's Solemn Stand on Hong Kong", which included a section on China's view on the unequal treaties.
76. David Faure provides an interesting perspective in *Colonialism and the Hong Kong Mentality*, pp. 79–84.
77. Deng Xiaoping, summary of talks with members of a Hong Kong industrial and commercial delegation and with Chung Sze Yuen and other Hong Kong figures on 22 and 23 June 1984, recorded in Deng Xiaoping, *Deng Xiaoping on 'One Country, Two Systems'*, p. 16.
78. The architect of the peg, John Greenwood, has now written about the experience in *Hong Kong's Link to the US Dollar*.
79. Cindy Yik-yi Chu, "The Origins of the Chinese Communist Alliance with the Business Elite in Hong Kong: The 1997 Question and the Basic Law Committees, 1979–1985", *Modern Chinese Society of Hong Kong Bulletin*, p. 54.
80. The Chinese side insisted that the governor of Hong Kong, who was a member of the negotiating team, represented Britain and not Hong Kong.
81. The debate on 14 March 1984 was raised by the then most senior member of the Legislative Council, Roger Lobo, and was referred to as the "Lobo Motion", *Hansard*, 14 March 1984, pp. 702–58.
82. Sze-yuen Chung, *Hong Kong's Journey to Reunification*, p. 80.
83. David Wilson in Sally Blyth and Ian Wotherspoon, *Hong Kong Remembers*, p. 179.

84. The use of the word "declaration" instead of "agreement" was significant. As China had never accepted the validity of the treaties ceding Hong Kong and Kowloon and leasing the New Territories, there was no need for the Chinese side to reach an agreement with the British on the exercise of sovereignty. Moreover, once China has exercised its sovereignty it would not need the British to agree to its policies.
85. Xiao Weiyun quotes Deng Xiaoping in *One Country, Two Systems*, p. 4. Xiao was a BLDC and senior Mainland legal expert and in his book, no explanation is given to the meaning of "dialectical materialism" and "historical materialism". It seems politically important to link these longstanding Marxist terms to the "one country, two systems" concept, pp. 4–6.
86. John M. Carroll, *A Concise History of Hong Kong*, p. 181.
87. Percy Cradock, *Experiences of China*, p. 209.
88. John Swaine, a barrister, abstained.
89. Robert Cottrell provides a detail account of the negotiations in *The End of Hong Kong*. For a shorter account, see Steve Tsang, *A Modern History of Hong Kong*, pp. 218–224. For an atmospheric recount, see David Bonavia's *Hong Kong 1997*. For a Chinese account, see Xu Jiatun, *Memoirs*, Chapter 3, on the negotiations.

Chapter 8

1. 李谷城，《香港的新華社功能與角色》，see http://202.76.36.61/vol%2018/vol18Doc1_2.htm.
2. Xu Jiatun, *Memoirs*, p. 23.
3. 盧育儀、麥慰宗、鍾仕梅，〈統戰工作有功，錯在重資輕勞〉，《當代雜誌》，13 January 1990, p. 14.
4. Chung Sze-yuen, *Hong Kong's Journey to Reunification*, pp. 39–43.
5. Ibid., pp. 63–67.
6. 鍾仕梅，〈對港方針，政出多門〉，《當代雜誌》，9 December 1989, p. 20.
7. Xu Jiatun's *Memoirs* provided examples, such as disagreements over what Mainland enterprises in Hong Kong could and could not do, conduct of Sino-British relations, style in operating united front work in Hong Kong, etc. For a discussion, see Shiu-hing Sonny Lo, "The Chinese Communist Party Elite's Conflicts over Hong Kong, 1983–1990", *China Transformation*, pp. 6–8.
8. Xu Jiatun's *Memoirs* recorded considerable conflicts between himself and Hong Kong and Macao Affairs Office over turf, see Chapter 8. See also Cindy Yik-Yi Chu, "Overt and Covert Functions of the Hong Kong Branch of the Xinhua News Agency, 1947–1984", *The Historian*, pp. 39–40; and John P. Burns, "The Structure of Communist Party Control in Hong Kong", *Asian Survey*, pp. 755–56.
9. Xu Jiatun's interview with *Ming Pao*, August 2007.
10. Xu Jiatun, *Memoirs*, p. 120.
11. Ibid., p. 141.
12. Ibid., pp. 470–71.
13. Ibid., pp. 64–65.
14. John P. Burns, *The Structure of Communist Party Control in Hong Kong*, p. 754, footnote 19.

15. Xu Jiatun, *Memoirs*, Chapter 2.
16. Ibid., p. 76.
17. Ibid., p. 55.
18. Ibid., p. 54. The Chinese military was divided into 7 military regions—Guangzhou, Nanjing, Chengdu, Jinan, Lanzhou, Beijing, and Shenyang.
19. Ibid., p. 54.
20. Ibid., p. 63.
21. Ibid., pp. 76–77.
22. Ibid., p. 223. Xu disclosed that Zhu Rongji, a future premier, had been identified as a possible transfer to Hong Kong, but the CCP Central Committee decided to make Zhu the mayor of Shanghai instead.
23. Xu Jiatun, *Memoirs*, p. 78.
24. The two local cadres were Wang Rudeng (王如登) and Chen Fengying (陳鳳英). See 軒轅輅，《新華社透視》, p. 52.
25. Chu Yik-yi, "Overt and Covert Functions of the Hong Kong Branch of the Xinhua News Agency, 1947–1984", *The Historian*, p. 41.
26. John P. Burns showed the structure which was adapted from Deng Feng, "Xianggang xinhuashe—gongwei cai gang de waiyi", *Contemporary*, No. 4, 16 December 1989, p. 19, in *The Structure of Communist Party Control in Hong Kong*, p. 754. The Security Department, which Xu Jiatun talked about in his *Memoirs*, has been included.
27. 李約 quoted Xu Jiatun saying, "我希望把中央、國務院的政策與香港的實際情況結合起，務求港人滿意，各界人士都滿意安心",〈獨家訪問許家屯〉,《廣角鏡》, Issue 129, June 1983, p. 6.
28. Xu Jiatun, *Memoirs*, p. 122.
29. Chung Sze-yuen's account of those meetings show the difficulties UMELCO members were put in vis-à-vis their loyalty, *Hong Kong Journey to Reunification*, pp. 95–97.
30. Ibid., pp. 96 and 139.
31. Ibid., p. 139.
32. Xu Jiatun, *Memoirs*, p. 97.
33. Teresa Ma, "Capitalism, China-Style", *Far Eastern Economic Review*, 1 March 1982; and Cindy Yik-yi Chu, "The Origins of the Chinese Communist Alliance with the Business Elite in Hong Kong: The 1997 Question and the Basic Law Committees, 1979–1985", *Modern Chinese History Society of Hong Kong Bulletin*, pp. 58–60.
34. Ambrose Y. C. King, "Administrative Absorption of Politics in Hong Kong: Emphasis in the Grass Roots Level", in Ambrose King and Rance P. L. Lee, *Social Life and Development in Hong Kong*, pp. 129–30.
35. For discussions about Beijing's perception of what made Hong Kong economically successful, see Leo F. Goodstadt, "China and the Selection of Hong Kong's Post-Colonial Political Elite", *China Quarterly*, pp. 727–28; and Wai-kwok Wong, "Can Co-optation Win over the Hong Kong People? China's United Front Work in Hong Kong Since 1984", *Issues & Studies*, pp. 116–18.
36. Xu Jiatun, *Memoirs*, pp. 130–31.
37. Nick Seward, "The Tung Kin Gulf: Rescue Plans Call for the Stripping of OOCL's Public Assets", *Far Eastern Economic Review*, p. 98; Guy Sacerdoti, "On Separate Tracks: Two

38. Xu Jiatun, *Memoirs*, p. 131. Xu Jiatun said Fung King Hei contacted him when he had financial problems and Xu arranged meetings with the Bank of China and others to help. After Fung died, Xu noted China still assisted his son.
39. Xu Jiatun, *Memoirs*, Chapter 4; and 軒轅輅,《新華社透視》, p. 96.
40. Interview with Yeung Yiu Chung (楊耀忠) dated 30 May 2002, see Wan Kwok Fai, "Beijing's United Front Policy Toward Hong Kong", p. 54.
41. 盧育儀 and 鍾仕梅 said that "整個新華社的眼睛不是向下望而是看著上層和工商界",〈統戰工作有功,錯在重資輕勞〉,《當代雜誌》, 13 January 1990, p. 14. Xu Jiatun said he did not neglect the old leftists, and that he reassessed the definition of "working class" in Hong Kong, *Memoirs*, Chapters 4 and 5.
42. Xu Jiatun, *Memoirs*, Chapter 5.
43. Meeting Point was formed in 1983. It was the first group in Hong Kong that formally considered itself to be a political party. In 1990, it merged with the United Democrats to become the Democratic Party. Meeting Point member, Anthony Cheung, became the Secretary for Transport and Housing (2012–2017). Other new groups that focused on Hong Kong's future included New Hong Kong Society, Hong Kong Prospect Institute, and Hong Kong Belongers' Association.
44. Hong Kong Observers effectively became defunct around 1988. Members included Christine Loh and Anna Wu who became legislators. Leung Chun Ying was active for a short period around 1981–1982. After her time in the Legislative Council (1993–1995), Wu was appointed the chairperson of the Equal Opportunities Commission after 1997, and then as an Executive Councillor in 2009–2017. Loh became the Under Secretary for the Environment in the Leung Chun Ying's administration (2012–2017).
45. For a record of the Hong Kong Observers Poll, see *Pressure Points*, pp. 196–209. For a discussion about the Hong Kong Observers, see Christine Loh, *Being Here*, pp. 171–85.
46. The Hong Kong government released a list of names of 101 invited guests and the newspapers also published a list of names. There appeared to have been a total of 102 invitees. Appendix II provides all the names that appeared from both lists. See also Press release, Government Information Service, 16 December 1984. There were in fact discrepancies between the government's press release and the names from newspapers. There may have been more than 101 invitees. Appendix II shows 102 names, which included the 101 names in the press release and another name that appeared in newspapers at the time.
47. The term "status marker" was used by Leo F. Goodstadt in "China and the Selection of Hong Kong's Post-Colonial Elite", *China Quarterly*, p. 722.
48. Ching Cheong noted that the BLDC would seek and collect Hong Kong people's views widely and that there would be quite a number of Hong Kong people in the BLDC, "廣泛地徵求和收集香港人的意見並反映大多數人的民意",〈基本法起草委員會將包括多名港人〉, *Wen Wei Po*, 11 March 1985.
49. Deng Xiaoping's speech at a meeting with Member of the BLDC in Beijing on 16 April 1987, *Deng Xiaoping on 'One Country, Two Systems'*, pp. 67–78. See also Xu Jiatun's comments on the overriding drafting principles set out by Deng Xiaoping, *Memoirs*, Chapter 6.
50. Ibid.

51. Steve Tsang, *A Modern History of Hong Kong*, p. 241.
52. Ching Cheong noted that "起草委員會的內地成員，應包括一些比較熟悉香港的人士，一些主管港澳工作的以及一些法律界人士，特別是制憲專家……香港地區人選則應具備愛祖國，愛香港，熟悉香港情況，並且在某個領域具有專業知識，同時又能採取「持平態度」的人士來出任"，〈基本法起草委員會怎樣產生？〉，*Wen Wei Po*, 12 April 1985.
53. 〈許家屯談成立起草委會〉，Xu Jiatun suggested "吸收香港的代表多參加，讓不同傾向的人能夠充分反映香港同胞的願望"，*Wen Wei Po*, 5 April 1985.
54. Ching Cheong et al defined "balance" as "所謂「持平」，就是能平衡各方意見和利益的人。持平的主張就是要能符合中英聯合聲明和將來基本法的精神，符合大多數人參與的原則。只有持平才能有穩定，有穩定才能有繁榮"，〈基本法起草委員會怎樣產生？〉，*Wen Wei Po*, 12 April 1985. The importance of "balance" is derived from three factors: (1) Hong Kong is a diverse society with complicated class relationships and a wide range of business sectors. To maintain such a society along with its diversity, it requires an attitude that encourages the participation of all the different parties（大家認為香港是一個多元化的社會，無論是階級關係，行業類別都是十分複雜的，因為要維持這樣一個社會的性質不變，就必須讓各方都有參與的機會，此其一）; (2) there is a common political goal of maintaining stability and prosperity in Hong Kong, and under this premise, people with various political inclinations should cooperate; "balance" is exactly to remain open to all different political inclinations（大家都有一個共同的政治目標，就是保持香港的繁榮的穩定，在這個大前提下，各種政治傾向的人都應互相合作，持平就是要能夠對各種政治傾向的兼容並蓄，此其二）; (3) along with the changes in Hong Kong as 1997 approaches, people's political inclinations would change and at an increasing pace; "balance" is to avoid dwelling in the past, and instead, cater to the circumstances today and in the future（隨著香港形勢的變化，人們的政治傾向也在不斷的變化中，而且距九七年越近，這種變化就越大，因此，不應去追究某人在過去歷史上曾抱對甚麼態度，更重要的是看今天和以後的態度，此其三）。
55. T. K. Ann was a member of the national CPPCC's Standing Committee.
56. Ambrose Y. C. King coined the term, quoted in Cindy Yik-yi Chu, "The Origins of the Chinese Communist Alliance with the Business Elite in Hong Kong: The 1997 Question and the Basic Law Committees, 1979–1985", *Modern Chinese History Society of Hong Kong Bulletin*, pp. 62–63.
57. Up until 1985, UMELCO stood for the Unofficial Members of the Legislative Council. At the time, the legislature only had appointed members and civil servant appointees were referred as the official members, thus UMELCO was used to distinguish between the official and unofficial members.
58. Xu Jiatun, *Memoirs*, Chapter 6.
59. Xu noted in his *Memoirs* that including Martin Lee would be preferable to excluding him as it would be easier to control him within the BLDC's confidential working structure than outside it, p. 157.
60. Staff reporters, "Xu Jiatun: The Communist Cadres Who Reached Out to All Sectors in Hong Kong", *South China Morning Post*, 29 June 2016. Szeto revealed in his autobiography, *Yangtze River Flows Eastward*, that he had wanted to join the party in his youth. He was a co-founder of the Hok Yau Club in 1949 (a left-leaning student group) and joined the New Democracy Youth League in September 1949 (which subsequently was renamed the Communist Youth League in 1957).

Notes to pages 159–168

61. Xu Jiatun, *Memoirs*, Chapter 6.
62. Chung Sze-yuen, *Hong Kong's Journey to Reunification*, p. 169.
63. Adapted from Ma Ngok, *Political Development in Hong Kong*, p. 41.
64. Xu Jiatun, *Memoirs*, pp. 162–63.
65. Shiu-hing Sonny Lo, "The Politics of Co-optation in Hong Kong: A Study of the Basic Law Drafting Process", *Asian Journal of Public Administration*, pp. 13–15.
66. Ibid., p. 10, and Steve Tsang, *A Modern History of Hong Kong*, p. 240.
67. Mark Roberti, *The Fall of Hong Kong*, pp. 176–78.
68. David Bonavia, *Hong Kong 1997*, p. 144.
69. Steve Tsang, *The Modern History of Hong Kong*, p. 115, and Robert Cottrell, *The End of Hong Kong*, pp. 181–82.
70. Basic Law, Annex I (I), and see Jonathan Dimbleby, *The Last Governor*, p. 52.
71. Robert Cottrell, *The End of Hong Kong*, p. 180.
72. There are other phrases that also show the difference in understanding between the British and Chinese. For example, the meaning of the right of "final adjudication" vested in the HKSAR does not mean the HKSAR has the ultimate power to interpret the Basic Law, which in fact rests with the SCNPC.
73. Hong Kong Government, *Green Paper: The Future Development of Representative Government in Hong Kong*, July 1984.
74. Functional constituencies and the functional electoral system are extensively discussed in Christine Loh and Civic Exchange, *Functional Constituencies*.
75. Hong Kong Government, *White Paper: The Further Development of Representative Government in Hong Kong*, November 1984.
76. Xu Jiatun, *Memoirs*, Chapter 6, pp. 169–73. See also Shiu-hing Sonny Lo, *The Politics of Democratization in Hong Kong*, pp. 90–93.
77. Steve Tsang, *Hong Kong*, p. 126.
78. Xu Jiatun, *Memoirs*, p. 190.
79. 黃文放，《解讀北京思維》，pp. 98–99.
80. The Group of 89, *A Proposal for the Future Structure of the Hong Kong SAR Government*, September 1987.
81. Mark Roberti, *The Fall of Hong Kong*, p. 177.
82. 何立，〈直選民意大結算〉，《九十年代》，October 1987, p. 40.
83. Ian Scott, *Political Change and the Crisis of Legitimacy in Hong Kong*, pp. 294–95.
84. David Wilson, interview, 19 September 2003.
85. For a short summary of the events of that period, see Ian Scott, *Political Change and the Crisis of Legitimacy in Hong Kong*, pp. 284–98.
86. 胡泰然，〈白皮書跳不出北京的框框〉，《九十年代》，January 1988, p. 44.
87. Steve Tsang, *Hong Kong*, p. 128.
88. Emily Lau, "Where's the Party?", *Far Eastern Economic Review*, 12 June 1986, p. 16.
89. For a summary of the criticisms, see Ian Scott, *Political Change and the Crisis of Legitimacy in Hong Kong*, pp. 301–5.
90. Shiu-hing Sonny Lo, *The Politics of Democratization in Hong Kong*, p. 121.

91. Steve Tsang, *Hong Kong*, pp. 242–43.
92. *Glasnost* is associated with Mikhail Gorbachev's liberalizing period in the history of the Soviet Union, starting from around 1985.
93. For detailed descriptions of the chronology of events, see 程翔，《天安門的反思》, and the official website of the Hong Kong Alliance in Support of Patriotic Democratic Movements of China: http://www.alliance.org.hk/english/historyblood.htm.
94. OMELCO stood for the Office of the Members of the Executive and Legislative Councils.
95. 〈新華社香港分社退職員工聲明〉,《九十年代》, July 1990, p. 42.
96. Interview with Xu Jiatun, "The Go-between", *South China Morning Post*, 6 July 2007.
97. Xu Jiatun, *Memoirs*, p. 380.

Chapter 9

1. The *zhuada fangxiao* strategy was first used in relations to reforming the state-owned enterprises but was then also applied to the CCP strategy in Hong Kong to gain control of the major things so that it could tolerate minor ones, Willy Wo-lap Lam, "Beijing's Hong Kong Policy in the First Year of the Transition", in Chris Yeung, *Hong Kong China*, p. 25.
2. Private communication from a former senior Hong Kong official in 2006.
3. Leung Sai-Wing, "The China Factor and Voters' Choice in the 1995 Legislative Council Election", in Lau Siu-kai and Louie Kin-shuen, *Hong Kong Tried Democracy*, p. 201.
4. *Xinhua News Agency News Bulletin*, 22 June 1989. The term "subversive base" carries the same meaning as an "anti-communist front" or "anti-China front".
5. Other top leaders included Hu Qili (胡啟立 1929), another member of the Standing Committee of the Politburo, who was also removed because he abstained from voting in favour of the imposition of martial law. He was rehabilitated and became the deputy minister of Machine-Building and Electronics Industry in 1991. Wan Li (萬里 1916), the chairman of the NPC, was temporarily under house arrest immediately upon his return from a visit to the North America during which he expressed sympathy towards the student demonstrations.
6. The challenge required a new orientation in foreign policy terms. Beijing expressed it using 28 characters: "Watch and analyse calmly; secure our positions; act with confidence; conceal our capacities; keep a low profile; do not lead; make contributions."
7. Xu Jiatun's memoirs talked about the importance to the CCP of getting people to accept invitations to visit Beijing, and his efforts to invite Hong Kong guests to Beijing particularly to meet Li Peng, *Memoirs*, pp. 425–26.
8. 高繼標,《香港最後一個政治貴族：羅德丞政海浮沉錄》, pp. 40–41.
9. Nevertheless, there was little evidence of the Hong Kong tycoons and taipans pulling sizable investments from either the Mainland or Hong Kong post-Tiananmen. It may have been that new investments were slowed temporarily.
10. Xu Jiatun, *Memoirs*, p. 435; and Scarlett Chiang, "Worried Bosses Tried to Lease HK for $10b", *The Standard*, 4 July 2007.
11. Xu's *Memoirs* noted that he was criticised by the party, and evidence of his faults would likely have included the events noted here. For an account of the Tiananmen crackdown, see Alvin Y. So, *Hong Kong's Embattled Democracy*, pp. 156–61.

12. Ambrose Leung, "Shaken by '89, Beijing Rethought Handover", *South China Morning Post*, 27 June 2007. Lu Ping and Xu Jiatun essentially had a similar experience. Both took ideas from Hong Kong people to the top leaders on essentially delaying Chinese rule. It may even have involved some of the same people making the suggestion. Xu did not refer to Lu's revelation in his memoirs. It is unclear whether the HK$10 billion offer from the tycoons and the petition were related or separate, and whether Xu knew about the latter.
13. Huang Wenfang, extracts from his memoirs, "Xinhua: The Inside Story", *Eastern Express*, 22 June 1994.
14. For a discussion of the hardline versus softline factions, see Shiu-hing Sonny Lo, "The Chinese Communist Party Elite's Conflicts over Hong Kong, 1983–1990", *China Transformation*, pp. 1–5.
15. Chris Yeung, interview with Xu Jiatun, "The Go-between", *South China Morning Post*, 6 July 2007. Xu revealed the name of the friend in Hong Kong who helped him in the interview—金堯如, a pro-Beijing figure, who died in 2005.
16. 宗道一等編著，周南修訂，《周南口述：身在疾風驟雨中》, p. 356.
17. Xu Jiatun's interview in *Ming Pao Monthly*, August 2007.
18. Chris Yeung, "Tycoons' Plan for Self-rule 'Treasonous'", *South China Morning Post*, 4 July 2007.
19. John P. Burns, "The Role of the New China News Agency and China's Policy Towards Hong Kong", in "Hong Kong and China in Transition", *Canada and Hong Kong Papers* No. 3, pp. 35–36. See also Wai-kwok Wong, "Can Co-optation Win Over the Hong Kong People? China's United Front Work in Hong Kong Since 1984", *Issues and Studies*, pp. 118–19.
20. Huang Wenfang, extracts from his memoirs, "Former Party Man Recalls Xinhua's Early Days and Zhou Enlai's Role", *Eastern Express*, 15 June 1994; and "Xinhua: The Inside Story", *Eastern Express*, 22 June 1994.
21. 〈新華社今正名「中聯辦」　姜恩柱：不干預港事務〉, *Ming Pao*, 18 January 2000.
22. Shiu-hing Sonny Lo, "The Chinese Communist Party Elite's Conflict over Hong Kong, 1983–1990", *China Transformation*, pp. 8–9.
23. Hong Kong people suffered a serious loss of confidence over the future of Hong Kong after 4 June. In an opinion poll conducted in late June 1989, 37% of the respondents said that they were seriously considering leaving Hong Kong, and among the category of professionals, executives, and entrepreneurs, 64% of them were prepared to leave. Another survey conducted by the Federation of Hong Kong Industries shortly after 4 June 1989 also showed that 75% of the manufacturers interviewed were either planning or considering emigration. See Joseph Cheng, "Prospects for Democracy in Hong Kong after the Beijing Massacre", *Australian Journal of Chinese Affairs*, pp. 166–67.
24. Huang Wenfang, extracts from his memoirs, "Xinhua: The Inside Story", *Eastern Express*, 22 June 1994.
25. For a discussion of the various models at the time, see Shiu-hing Sonny Lo, *The Politics of Democratization in Hong Kong*, pp. 121–29.
26. The Basic Law, Annex II, Part II.
27. Alvin Y. So provides a summary of the events surrounding the OMELCO Consensus, *Hong Kong's Embattled Democracy*, pp. 161–63 and pp. 168–69.

28. 宗道一等編著，周南修訂，《周南口述：身在疾風驟雨中》, p. 348, where Zhou Nan said: "僅從香港的局部看香港，往往看不清，如果從更大的形勢來看，可能看得更清楚", and also p. 350.
29. Speech made by the British prime minister Margaret Thatcher in the Commonwealth Heads of Government Meeting in October 1989. Referring to Hong Kong, she said: "I doubt whether the Chinese fully realise even now the impact on world opinion of events in Tiananmen Square. They try to pretend nothing untoward happened, whereas we know from very carefully gathered evidence that something like two to three thousand people were killed in and around the Square. Many of us thought that, after the experience of the Cultural Revolution in which many of the present Chinese leadership and their families suffered, we would not again see indiscriminate oppression in China. We were wrong. It also underlies the tenuous nature of opposition in China: there is nothing to compare with the history of *refuseniks* and *Samizdat* that was evident for years in the Soviet Union. These developments have inevitably been a set-back for co-operation between the five Permanent Members of the UN Security Council which had been increasingly successful. It will take some time to overcome this. It also creates serious worries over Hong Kong. The people of Hong Kong suffered a very severe shock from what happened in China and are desperately in need of reassurance as 1997 draws closer. We of course remain responsible for Hong Kong right up until that date and shall do all we can to safeguard its stability and prosperity. It would be very helpful if CHOGM could state unequivocally its support for Hong Kong and call on China to rebuild confidence there". See Margaret Thatcher Foundation, http://www.margaretthatcher.org/speeches/displaydocument.asp?docid=107792.
30. Qian Qichen, *Ten Episodes in China's Diplomacy*, p. 278.
31. Wai-kwok Wong, "Can Co-optation Win Over the Hong Kong People? China's United Front Work in Hong Kong Since 1984", *Issues and Studies*, pp. 118–19.
32. Article 23, Basic Law.
33. 〈香港必須有一個平穩的過渡期〉, 6 December 1989, 〈江澤民會見英國特使柯利達時的講話〉,《江澤民文選第一卷》, p. 82. The original wording is: "今年春夏之交中國發生政治風波，除國內因素外，確實也有國際背景。國際上有些人錯誤地估計了形勢，以為有些社會主義國家亂得差不多了，中國也只要推一下就倒了。" See also Qian Qichen's explanation of what happened, *Ten Episodes in China's Diplomacy*, pp. 257–58.
34. Ibid., p. 81. The original wording is: "民意問題，要看究竟是民眾真正自發表達的意願還是有人操縱。在西方國家，所謂民意也往往同當權者的引導和意圖貫徹密切相關。香港有的人說代表民意，我看他就不能代表民意，一是他有一定的個人目的，二是他唯恐天下不亂。"
35. Qian Qichen, *Ten Episodes in China's Diplomacy*, pp. 259–60.
36. 〈保持香港穩定繁榮是我們的基本國策〉, 20 March 1990, 〈江澤民會見新加坡國會議員，總理政治秘書吳博韜時談話的要點〉.《江澤民文選第一卷》, p. 118. Jiang Zemin's words were: "港督長期集大權於一身，現在卻大叫特叫民主，他們突然這樣做，沒有別的解釋，就是覺得國際氣候有，可以「敲打」中國。"
37. Qian Qichen, *Ten Episodes in China's Diplomacy*, p. 261.
38. Speech of Chief Secretary David Ford on 21 March 1990. See Official Report of Proceedings of Legislative Council, 21 March 1990, pp. 33–34. http://www.legco.gov.hk/yr89-90/english/lc_sitg/hansard/h900321.pdf.

39. Official Report of Proceedings of Legislative Council, 10 October 1990, p. 15.
40. 〈保持香港穩定繁榮是我們的基本國策〉，20 March 1990,〈江澤民會見新加坡國會議員，總理政治秘書吳博韜時談話的要點〉，《江澤民文選第一卷》，p. 118.
41. Basic Law, Article 67.
42. See paragraph 99 of the Policy Address 1989–1990. Official website of the Legislative Council: http://www.legco.gov.hk/yr89-90/english/lc_sitg/hansard/h891011.pdf.
43. The HKSAR Government Land Fund Trust was established on 13 August 1986 to facilitate the management of the HKSAR's share of revenue obtained from land sales during the period commencing from the entry into force of the Sino-British Joint Declaration (27 May 1985) until 1 July 1997, on which the assets of the trust were vested in the HKSAR government.
44. David Wilson, interview, http://chu.cam.ac.uk/archives/collections/BDOHP/Wilson.pdf.
45. Lu Ping,〈香港回歸的回顧〉,《縱橫》, p. 31.
46. 〈保持香港穩定繁榮是我們的基本國策〉，24 March 1990,〈江澤民會見新加坡國會議員，總理政治秘書吳博韜時的談話〉，《江澤民文選第一卷》，p. 118.
47. Leo F. Goodstadt noted that had British and Hong Kong officials taken account of the Chinese context and experience in project management it could have averted many problems. Thus, had financial presentations been made to Chinese officials about the airport project at the appropriate time, it could have allayed concerns about expensive showcase pieces that could be mismanaged, which was often what happened to large projects on the Mainland; "Prospects for the Rule of Law: The Political Dimension", in Steve Tsang, *Judicial Independence and the Rule of Law in Hong Kong*, p. 188.
48. Barbara Basler, "Furor Erupts over Hong Kong Plan", *New York Times*, 21 January 1991. See also analysis by Steve Tsang, *Hong Kong*, p. 180.
49. 國務院港澳辦主任魯平，29 April 1999 會見香港及澳門工會「五一」代表團時所作的表示。 See 趙睿、張明瑜（主編），宋瑩、張培忠（編者），《中國領導人談香港》，p. 404.
50. 中方首席代表郭豐民大使一九九二年六月十八日在中英聯合聯絡小組第二十三次會議舉行記者招待會時的講話。See 趙睿、張明瑜（主編），宋瑩、張培忠（編者），《中國領導人談香港》, p. 428. The original text is: "過渡時期後半段，中國政府無意干預港英政府的行政事務，但是涉及一九九七年與一九九七年政治順利交接有關的，需要特別行政區政府承擔的責任和義務的事情，港英政府應該與中國政府多磋商，中國政府有責任過問並參與審議，這完全符合中英聯合聲明精神。在過渡期的後半段，如果得不到中國政府的支持，港英政府有些事情也很難做到。"
51. John P. Burns, "Hong Kong in 1992: Struggle for Authority", *Asian Survey*, pp. 24–25.
52. Steve Tsang, *Hong Kong*, pp. 181–82.
53. Jonathan Dimbleby, *The Last Governor*, p. 324.
54. Willy Wo-lap Lam, "Government: Beijing's Hong Kong Policy in the First Year of Transition", in Chris Yeung, *Hong Kong China*, p. 26.
55. Official record of proceedings of the Legislative Council, 7 October 1992, p. 48. http://www.legco.gov.hk/yr92-93/english/lc_sitg/hansard/h921007.pdf.
56. The Municipal Councils were the Urban Council and the Regional Council, which were abolished by Tung Chee Hwa in 1999.
57. Eva Liu and S. Y. Yue, *Political Development in Hong Kong since the 1980s*.

58. Qian Qichen, *Ten Episodes in China's Diplomacy*, pp. 266–67. Extraordinarily, it seemed no one had briefed Chris Patten on the Seven Diplomatic Documents. An account of this gap in the governor's knowledge is recounted by Jonathan Dimbleby, who noted that the documents were withheld from Patten by the Foreign Office, *The Last Governor*, pp. 139–54.

59. 〈原國務院港澳辦主任魯平回憶香港回歸歷程〉，11 June 2007, http://news.sina.com/c/2007-06-11/170413203794.shtml.

60. 新華社香港分社副社長鄭國雄一九九二年十二月二日發表的談話。See 趙睿、張明瑜（主編），宋瑩、張培忠（編者），《中國領導人談香港》，p. 435. Original wording: "彭定康堅持對抗，一意孤行推行其「政改方案」，影響和破壞了香港繁榮的局面。彭定康絲毫沒有與中方合作的誠意，完全是對抗的態度……但彭定康完全不理會中方的努力和態度，給香港的繁榮穩定帶來了影響和破壞，責任完全在彭定康身上。"

61. 新華社香港分社社長周南在一九九二年十二月一日會見香港十五位區議會主席時所作的講話。See 趙睿、張明瑜（主編），宋瑩、張培忠（編者），《中國領導人談香港》，p. 256. Original wording: "現在已有愈來愈多的香港居民看清楚了彭定康政改方案是嚴重違反聯合聲明，違反基本法和中英已達成的協議……他們也認識到，彭定康沿著錯誤的道路走下去，已經並將繼續造成破壞香港穩定繁榮和平穩過渡的惡果……我們已經和將要採取的一切措施都是為了維護香港的穩定繁榮，保障一九九七年的平穩過渡和維護香港居民的長遠利益。擺在彭定康面前的唯一出路是立即拋棄他的所謂政改方案，不要再繼續玩弄政治把戲。"

62. For a discussion of the Patten Proposals, see Steve Tsang, *A Modern History of Hong Kong*, pp. 254–61.

63. The occasion was at the opening of the Tian Tan Buddha (天壇大佛) on Lantau Island, where Zhou Nan refused Patten's outstretched hand by putting his own hands together in a Buddhist greeting gesture instead, see 宗道一等編著，周南修訂，《周南口述：身在疾風驟雨中》，p. 382.

64. Zhou Nan said: "The controversy relating to the Hong Kong political system is not about whether we want democracy or not, it is about whether we should honour our words. From a deeper level, it is a sovereignty issue. Any matter touched upon the cardinal principle of sovereignty, Chinese people will not surrender to any foreign pressure." Original wording: "現在有關香港政制問題的爭論，並不是要不要民主之爭，而是要不要守信義之爭。從更深層次上來說，仍然是主權之爭。在涉及國家主權這樣重大的原則問題上，中國人民是決不會屈服於任何外部壓力的。"〈周南在1994年3月13日在人大廣東團大會上的發言〉。See 趙睿、張明瑜（主編），宋瑩、張培忠（編者），《中國領導人談香港》，p. 257. Douglas Hurd's view was that what angered Beijing was not so much the content of the Patten Proposals but that Patten had failed to conduct negotiations with Beijing beforehand in secret; and Cradock's view was that the Chinese would only speak to the British and take no account of Hong Kong's view, Jonathan Dimbleby, *The Last Governor*, p. 146.

65. Steve Tsang, *Hong Kong*, p. 194.

66. See the official website of the Hong Kong University Public Opinion Programme: http://hkupop.hku.hk/english/archive/poppolls/chris/hyear/chart/hyear1.gif.

67. Qian Qichen, *Ten Episodes in China's Diplomacy*, p. 269. For a detailed account of the 17 rounds of talks from the British perspective, see Jonathan Dimbleby, *The Last Governor*, pp. 177–210.

68. Qian Qichen, *Ten Episodes in China's Diplomacy*, p. 275.
69. The four batches of a total number of 186 Hong Kong advisors were appointed in March 1992, April 1993, May 1994, and April 1995 respectively.
70. 〈國務院港澳辦公室主任魯平，新華社香港分社社長周南一九九二年二月二十九日在北京香港就聘請香港事務顧問一事發表的談話〉。 See 趙睿、張明瑜（主編），宋瑩、張培忠（編者），《中國領導人談香港》, p. 356. Original wording: "建立一個與港人經常溝通的渠道，集中港人的智慧，為實現平穩過渡創造良好的條件，不會影響港英在過渡時期負責香港行政管理的能力，也不存在所謂第二個權力中心的問題。"
71. District Boards were the precursors to District Councils and the Municipal Councils were the Urban Council and Regional Council, which were abolished by Tung Chee Hwa in 1999.
72. An excellent report on Beijing cultivation of its post-colonial elites from which the authors have drawn upon extensively is Leo F. Goodstadt's "China and the Selection of Hong Kong's Post-Colonial Political Elite", *China Quarterly*, pp. 721–41.
73. Shiu Hing Sonny Lo and Donald Hugh McMillen, "A Profile of the 'Pro-China Hong Kong Elite': Images and Perceptions", *Issues and Studies*, pp. 117–18.
74. The members of the Cooperative Resources Centre were Allen Lee (convenor), Stephen Cheong, Selina Chow, Ngai Siu Kit, Lau Wong Fat, Edward Ho, Peggy Lam, and Peter Wong.
75. Shiu-hing Sonny Lo, *Governing Hong Kong*, p. 202.
76. The 52-member Hong Kong Progressive Alliance was formed in April 1994 through the merging of the Federation of Stability for Hong Kong, the Hong Kong Chinese Reform Association and the New Hong Kong Alliance.
77. Shiu-hing Sonny Lo, Yu Wing-yat, and Wan Kwok-fai, "The 1999 District Councils Elections", in Ming K. Chan and Alvin Y. So, *Crisis and Transformation in China's Hong Kong*, p. 154.
78. Shiu-hing Sonny Lo and Donald Hugh McMillen, "A Profile of the 'Pro-China Hong Kong Elites' Images and Perceptions", *Issues & Studies*, p. 117. The authors quoted from 10 January 1994, *South China Morning Post*, that Huang Zhizhao was the deputy secretary-general and Zheng Guoxiong was the leader of the working group at Xinhua Hong Kong.
79. Shiu-hing Sonny Lo, Wing-yat Yu, and Kwok-fai Wan, "The 1999 District Councils Elections", in Ming K. Chan and Alvin Y. So, *Crisis and Transformation in China's Hong Kong*, p. 163, footnote 43.
80. Suen Kai Cheong is an appointed district councillor in Wanchai (2007 District Council appointee), and he has run in legislative elections in the past under the DAB banner.
81. Kwong Hoi Ying, "Party-Group Relations in Hong Kong: Comparing the DAB and the DP".
82. Leo F. Goodstadt noted that a CPPCC member stated that Lu Ping informed him of plans for a preliminary working body in March 1992, which was before Chris Patten's appointment as governor, "China and the Selection of Hong Kong's Post-Colonial Political Elite", *China Quarterly*, p. 731.
83. 宗道一等編著，周南修訂，《周南口述：身在疾風驟雨中》, p. 378.
84. Norman Miners, *The Government and Politics of Hong Kong*, p. 237.

85. Decision of the National People's Congress on the Method for the Formation of the First Government and the First Legislative Council of the Hong Kong Special Administrative Region adopted at the Third Session of the Seventh National People's Congress on 4 April 1990.
86. 〈國務院港澳辦公室主任魯平一九九三年四月二十日在會見香港外國基金訪問團時的講話〉。See 趙睿、張明瑜（主編），宋瑩、張培忠（編者），《中國領導人談香港》, p. 361.
87. Five sub-groups were set up—the Political, Economic, Legal, Social and Security, and Cultural Sub-groups. The PWC held six plenary sessions and a number of meetings and seminars were also conducted by the sub-groups. The last plenary session was held in December 1995.
88. 〈新華社香港分社社長周南一九九三年七月九日在新華社香港分社會見香港地區的全國人大代表，全國政協委員和港事顧問時的談話〉。See 趙睿、張明瑜（主編），宋瑩、張培忠（編者），《中國領導人談香港》, p. 363.
89. The Joint Liaison Group (JLG) was created in 1985 in accordance with the terms of the Sino-British Joint Declaration to handle matters relating to Hong Kong in the run-up to the resumption of the exercise of sovereignty by China. Annex II of the Joint Declaration sets out the functions of the JLG as follows: (a) to conduct consultations on the implementation of the Joint Declaration; (b) to discuss matters relating to the smooth transfer of government in 1997; and (c) to exchange information and conduct consultations on such subjects as may be agreed to by the two sides. The JLG was an organ of liaison and not an organ of power. It met in Hong Kong, London, and Beijing, at least once a year at each venue. The term of the JLG ended on 1 January 2000. The JLG had held 47 plenary meetings between 27 May 1985 and 1 January 2000, see the official website of the Constitutional and Mainland Affairs Bureau: http://www.cmab.gov.hk/en/issues/joint2.htm/.
90. Jamie Allen, *Seeing Red*, pp. 288–89.
91. Decision of the National People's Congress on the Method for the Formation of the First Government and the First Legislative Council of the Hong Kong Special Administrative Region adopted at the Third Session of the Seventh National People's Congress on 4 April 1990. It had seven sub-groups dealing with the Selection Committee, the first chief executive, the Provisional Legislative Council, legal matters, economic affairs, celebration activities, and the first HKSAR Legislative Council.
92. Lo Tak Shing was seen to be a hardliner. He was also unpopular with many people including members of the Selection Committee. Simon Li had said he would not stand for election if Lo was running, but with Lo pulling out, Li decided to enter the race but failed to get to the starting block, Chris Yeung, "Lessons for the Hardliners", *The Standard*, 20 October 1996.
93. Willy Wo-lap Lam, "Government: Beijing's Hong Kong Policy in the First Year of Transition", in Chris Yeung, *Hong Kong China*, pp. 25–27.
94. Ibid., pp. 29–30.
95. Joyce Ng, "Beijing refused to step in during 1998 Hong Kong financial crisis, former city chief reveals", *South China Morning Post*, 7 July 2017.
96. See the official website of the Provisional Legislative Council, http://legco.gov.hk/yr97-98/english/resp/resp.htm.

97. Qian Qichen recorded that the British wrote to him to complain about Chinese officials making it known that civil servants who wanted to serve in the new government had to declare support for the Provisional Legislative Council and that Qian did not bother to reply to Foreign Secretary Malcolm Rifkind's letter, *Ten Episodes in China's Diplomacy*, pp. 276–77.
98. They were Tsang Yok Shing, Tam Yiu Chung, Cheng Kai Nam (DAB), Peggy Lam, Elsie Tu, Lau Kong Wah, Wong Siu Yee, Tang Siu Tong, Raymond Ho, and Ho Sai Chu.
99. Cap. 245 and Cap. 151. The amendments require demonstrations with more than 30 participants should seek the prior approval of the police, and that an association must first register, with government approval, before it could become a lawful entity. The concept of "national security" was also introduced as a criterion upon which the police would consider whether to approve a demonstration or an association. See Benny Y. T. Tai, "Chapter 1 of Hong Kong's New Constitution: Constitutional Positioning and Repositioning", in Ming K. Chan and Alvin Y. So, *Crisis and Transformation in China's Hong Kong*, pp. 198–99.
100. See Electoral Affairs Commission, Guidelines on Election-Related Activities in Respect of the 1998 Legislative Council Election, Part VII, http://www.elections.gov.hk/elections/legco1998/elecgu.htm.
101. These civil liberties provisions were in the Public Order Ordinance, Societies Ordinance, and Bill of Rights Ordinance. See 宗道一等編著，周南修訂，《周南口述：身在疾風驟雨中》, pp. 381–82. The labour laws included ones on collective bargaining, namely, the Employee's Rights to Representation, Consultation and Collective Bargaining Ordinance.
102. Willy Wo-lap Lam, "Government: Beijing's Hong Kong Policy in the First Year of Transition", in Chris Yeung, *Hong Kong China*, pp. 33–34.
103. Anthony B. L. Cheung and Paul C. W. Wong, "Who Advised the Hong Kong Government? The Politics of Absorption before and after 1997", *Asian Survey*, p. 884, Table 2.
104. Suzanne Pepper, "Hong Kong Joins the National People's Congress: A First Test for One Country with Two Political Systems", *Journal of Contemporary China*, p. 319.
105. Ibid., p. 328.
106. Ibid., for a detail discussion, pp. 319–43.
107. For a detail discussion of the Tenth NPC election, see Shiu-hing Sonny Lo, "The Election of the Hong Kong Deputies to the National People's Congress"; see also Shiu-hing Sonny Lo, *The Dynamics of Beijing–Hong Kong Relations*, pp. 185–98.
108. Polly Hui, Liz Gooch, and Albert Wong, "Fanny Law Quits over 'Interference'", *South China Morning Post*, 21 June 2007. Fanny Law resigned as the Permanent Secretary for Education and Manpower after a commission of inquiry into alleged government interference at the Hong Kong Institute of Education delivered negative verdict on her conduct. However, a court held she did not violate the institute's right to academic freedom.
109. Fanny W. Y. Fung and Celine Sun, "NPC Official Rejects HK Delegates' Plan for an Office in the City", *South China Morning Post*, 10 March 2008; and Fanny W. Y. Fung, "HK Deputies' Role Stuck in Limbo, 10 Years On", *South China Morning Post*, 16 March 2008.
110. Gary Cheung and Eva Wu, "City Liaison Office Deputy Defends HK Delegates", *South China Morning Post*, 19 March 2009.
111. Chung Sze-yuen, *Hong Kong's Journey to Reunification*, pp. 42–43.

112. He Huifeng, "Shenzhen Conference to Discuss 'Liberation' of Cross-Border Ties", *South China Morning Post*, 8 April 2008. This news report noted that the 51 Hong Kong and Macao members of the Shenzhen People's Political Conference lobbied for a position laid out by Guangdong's new party secretary.
113. Many of the Po Leung Kuk board members sat on political consultative bodies in Chongqing, Zhuhai, Hubei, Hebei, Qingyuan, Fujian, Guangdong, and Jiangxi, and several of the board members also served on other united front bodies such as the All-China Federation of Returned Overseas Chinese Association, Hong Kong Federation of Overseas Chinese, All China Youth Federation, and Hong Kong Federation of Women; information from the advertisement of the Po Leung Kuk's Inauguration of the Board of Directors 2008–2009, *South China Morning Post*, 8 April 2008, p. A11. Many of the Tung Wah Group of Hospitals board members sat on political consultative bodies in Beijing, Shenzhen, Guangxi, Chongqing, and the national CPPCC, as well as such bodies as the Hong Kong Overseas Chinese General Youth Association, Hong Kong CPPCC Youth Association, Shenzhen Overseas Friendship Association, Liaoning Youth Federation etc.; information from the advertisement of the Tung Wah Group of Hospitals' Inauguration of the Board of Directors 2017–2018, *South China Morning Post*, 6 April 2017, p. A9.
114. Leo F. Goodstadt, "China and the Selection of Hong Kong's Post-Colonial Political Elite", *China Quarterly*, p. 737.
115. Shiu-hing Sonny Lo and Donald Hugh McMillen, "A Profile of the 'Pro-China Hong Kong Elite': Images and Perceptions", *Issues and Studies*, p. 119.
116. Leo F. Goodstadt, "China and the Selection of Hong Kong's Post-Colonial Political Elite", *China Quarterly*, p. 737.
117. Much of the rest of this section is based on the research of Yin Qian, who has interviewed fifth columnists in Hong Kong, "Beijing's Fifth Column and the Transfer of Power in Hong Kong: 1983–97", in Robert Ash, *Hong Kong in Transition*, pp. 113–32.
118. Yin Qian, "Beijing's Fifth Column and the Transfer of Power in Hong Kong: 1983–97", in Robert Ash, *Hong Kong in Transition*, p. 116; and Hansard, 26 April 1995, speech by Emily Lau, p. 3330.
119. Ibid.
120. Hong Kong Transition Project, *Constitutional Reform: Confrontation Looms as Hong Kong Consults*, April 2014, http://hktp.org/list/constitutional-reform.pdf. See also Stan Hok-Wui Wong, Ngok Ma, and Wai-man Lam, "Migrants and Democratization: The Political economy of Chinese Immigrants in Hong Kong", *Contemporary Chinese Political Economy and Strategic Relations: An International Journal* 2, no. (September 2016): 9089–40.

Chapter 10

1. Willy Wo-lap Lam, "Government: Beijing's Hong Kong Policy in the First Year of Transition", in Chris Yeung, *Hong Kong China*, pp. 30–31.
2. 曹二寶，〈一國兩制條件下香港的管治力量〉，《學習時報》（第422期），1 January 2008.
3. 永逸，〈中聯辦正積極發揮澳門第二支管治力量作用〉，《新華澳報》，5 February 2008.

Notes to pages 204–206

4. The term "state organ" is defined as those that carry out functions of the Central People's Government (CPG) or functions for which the CPG has responsibility for under the Basic Law; it does not carry out commercial functions, and it is acting within the scope of authority and functions delegated to it by the CPG or the Central Authorities, see LC Paper No. CB(2) 629/98–99(02) Panel of Constitutional Affairs, Legislative Council.
5. 〈胡錦濤讚董建華港人治港做得好〉, *Ming Pao*, 1 July 1999. Hu Jintao said: "新華社與香港保持密切的聯繫,促進了香港與內地的交流與合作,並且有效地處理了涉台事務和中央交辦的其他事務。外交部駐港特派員公署協助特區政府處理了大量的對外事務,有力地促進了特區在經濟,文化等領域與世界各國,各地區和國際組織的聯繫與合作。中國人民解放軍駐港部隊在依法履行職責,以威武文明之師的良好形象,維護了國家的主權,統一,領土完整和香港的安全。"
6. LC Paper No. CB(2) 629/98–99(02) Panel of Constitutional Affairs, Legislative Council.
7. Willy Wo-lap Lam, "Government: Beijing's Hong Kong Policy in the First Year of Transition", in Chris Yeung, *Hong Kong China*, p. 32.
8. He was diagnosed with stomach cancer. See 宗道一等編著,周南修訂,《周南口述:身在疾風驟雨中》, p. 395.
9. Jiang Enzhu said, "新華社香港分社不干預香港特別行政區高度自治範圍內的事務……香港回歸祖國後,新華社香港分社的職能將作出適當的、必要的調整……對特區政府的工作給予配合和支持"。宗道一,〈香江之水通海牙──記新華社香港分社社長姜恩柱與他的夫人朱曼黎〉,《黨史博覽》, pp. 13–17.
10. "姜恩柱社長接受中通社記者訪問時指出香港新華社乃中央授權工作機構重申該社不干預香港特區自治範圍內事務", *Wen Wei Po*, Hong Kong, 31 October 1997.
11. Willy Wo-lap Lam, "Government: Beijing's Hong Kong Policy in the First Year of Transition", in Chris Yeung, *Hong Kong China*, pp. 31–33.
12. 〈新華社今正名「中聯辦」 姜恩柱:不干預港事務〉, *Ming Pao*, 18 January 2000.
13. The 22 departments were 辦公廳,研究部,人事部,宣傳文體部,協調部,社團聯絡部,青年工作部,經濟部,社會工作部,教育科技部,台灣事務部,行政財務部,監察室,信息咨詢室,保安部,警務聯絡部,港島工作部,九龍工作部,新界工作部,北京辦事處,廣東聯絡部,深圳辦事處. Two more departments were added after the 1 July 2003 demonstration to deal with police liaison and social affairs. See official website of the Liaison Office of the Central People's Government: http://www.locpg.gov.cn.
14. 〈中聯辦主任高祀仁:燒國旗應檢控議員炮轟斥予港府政治壓力〉, *Ming Pao*, 2 October 2002; and 〈高祀仁曾憲梓力撐「不說就是偷」推論〉, *Ming Pao*, 19 October 2002.
15. Tung Chee Hwa, Hansard, 10 October 2002, http://www.legco.gov.hk/yr02-03/english/counmtg/hansard/cm1010ti-translate-e.pdf, p. 270.
16. Jimmy Cheung, "Anson Chan Provokes Outcry after Her Latest Veiled Attack", *South China Morning Post*, 30 December 2002.
17. Gary Cheung, "Six Tycoons Weigh in with Support for the Administration's Proposals", *The Standard*, 23 January 2003.
18. 〈四萬人集會挺廿三條 76輛旅巴接送否認威迫利誘〉, *Ming Pao*, 23 December 2002.
19. In particular, see the many essays in Joseph Y. S. Cheng (ed.), *The July 1 Protest Rally*, and Sonny Lo, "Hong Kong, 1 July 2003—Half a Million Protestors: The Security Law, Identify Politics, Democracy, and China", *Behind the Headlines*. For a contemporaneous report,

see Q/A with Christine Loh, *Uncharted Territory*, CLSA Emerging Markets, 7 July 2003, http://www.civic-exchange.org/eng/upload/files/200307_HKPolitics.pdf.

20. 〈籲以文革為鑑　莫「整天上街遊行」　中聯辦：港勿變動亂之都〉, *Ming Pao*, 7 August 2003.
21. Frank Ching, "Self-Deceit", *South China Morning Post*, 10 February 2004.
22. Zheng Hanliang, *China Times*, 7 July 2003.
23. 〈高祀仁：不容再拖　鄔維庸：恐得寸進尺〉, *Ming Pao*, 6 July 2003.
24. The events leading up to the Liberal Party backing the public call for a delay was the result of its chairman, James Tien, who was an Executive Councillor, going to Beijing to meet Liao Hui, where he got the mistaken impression that Beijing was willing to delay passage of the bill. When he returned to Hong Kong he told the public that a delay was possible. When it became clear to Tien that Tung Chee Hwa planned to push ahead Tien had no choice but to resign from the Executive Council. With the Liberal Party's votes uncertain, Tung announced that he would delay passage, Q/A with Christine Loh, *Uncharted Territory*, CLSA Asia-Pacific Markets, 7 July 2003, http://www.civic-exchange.org/eng/upload/files/200307_HKPolitics.pdf.
25. Gao Siren said: "中聯辦尊重董建華的特區政府押後二讀的決定，並說這段時間政府要加強與市民溝通"。〈尊重押後二讀〉, *Ming Pao*, 8 July 2003.
26. Gao Siren said: "押後二讀國安條例草案，不會影響政府管治威信。香港現時經濟不景氣，市民受到失業，負資產所困擾，特區政府現階段應該制訂有利經濟發展的措施，以及改善民生，紓解民困"。陳冬,〈解讀中聯辦的救港藥方〉, *Ming Pao*, 7 July 2003.
27. 〈疑洩江澤民去年訪港行程　中聯辦：蔡小洪案屬冰山一角〉, *Ming Pao*, 20 December 2003.
28. Xu Simin said: "出問題便不見了人"。〈訪京團「補中聯辦不足」〉, *Ming Pao*, 28 October 2003.
29. See the official website of the Liaison Office of the Central People's Government: http://www.locpg.gov.cn.
30. Staff reporter, "Liaison Office Buys Block in Sai Ying Pun for HK$480m", *South China Morning Post*, 17 February 2015; and 〈中聯辦半年4000萬購高樂德福8伙　近兩年共6億買71伙港住宅〉, *Ming Pao*, 12 August 2016.
31. Phila Su, "Beijing's Liaison Office in Hong Kong Should Recruit Locals Who Understand City, Political Heavyweight Says", *South China Morning Post*, 10 March 2017.
32. The Commissioner's Office of China's Foreign Ministry was established on 1 July 1997 in accordance with Article 13 of the Basic Law. Its official functions include: (1) upholding state sovereignty and the supreme interests of the nation; (2) supporting and assisting the HKSAR in its exchanges and cooperation with other parts of the world to enhance its international status and influence; (3) protecting the legitimate rights and interests of the overseas Hong Kong compatriots; and (4) promoting long-term prosperity and stability of Hong Kong. There are five departments in the office: (1) General Affairs Department responsible for office administration and protocol. It also handles applications for flights to Hong Kong by foreign aircraft, visits to Hong Kong by foreign military vessels and the use of radio frequencies; (2) Policy Research Department for studying foreign policies relating to Hong Kong and putting forward policy proposals to assist and support Hong Kong in conducting overseas cooperation. It also follows trends in economic and

financial development and regional cooperation in the Asia Pacific; (3) Department of International Organisations and Conferences coordinates matters concerning Hong Kong's relations with international organisations, including its participation in or hosting of international conferences, joining international organisations and the setting up of offices in Hong Kong by international organisations; (4) Department of Treaties and Law responsible for handling matters relating to bilateral and multilateral treaties and other legal issues concerning Hong Kong; (5) Consular Department handles matters relating to the setting up of foreign consular missions in Hong Kong and the application of consular treaties between China and foreign countries in Hong Kong and provides consular protection and other services for Chinese nationals from Hong Kong in foreign countries; (6) Department of Media and Public Relations in charge of information releases as well as public relations and media issues, see Commission's official website: http://www.fmcoprc.gov.hk/eng/gywm/tpy/default.htm. In 1998, there were about 130 personnel working in the office. 〈馬毓真特派員在香港美國商會午餐會上的演講〉, *Ta Kung Pao*, 29 April 1998.

33. Ma said: "不能把香港作為一個基地". 〈難解何以「獨厚」法輪功〉, *Ming Pao*, 15 December 1999.
34. 〈港事務與臺問題屬中國內政　外交部責彭定康說三道四〉, *Ta Kung Pao*, 20 October 2000.
35. 〈外交部駐港公署：美人權報告對港人權狀況的指責毫無道理〉, 中國新聞社, 1 March 2000.
36. Office of the Commissioner of China's Ministry of Foreign Affairs, "Office Spokesperson Submits Letter to Wall Street Journal Refuting Self-Determination", 17 November 2016.
37. See Article 14, Basic Law and Articles 2, 3, 5, and 9 of the Law of the PRC on the Garrisoning of the HKSAR. See also Research Division Information Note, "The Hong Kong Garrison of the Chinese People's Liberation Army", Legislative Council Secretariat, 17 January 2011.
38. Minnie Chan, Stuart Lau, and Naomi Ng, "Xi Jinping Inspects 20 Squads at Garrison in Biggest Military Parade since City's Handover", *South China Morning Post*, 1 July 2017.
39. Ibid.
40. Nectar Gan and Tony Cheung, "Hong Kong's PLA Garrison No Longer Just Symbolic, Top Brass Says", *South China Morning Post*, 16 June 2017.
41. Xiong Ziren said: "香港的各種政治團體，社會組織和黨派林立，政治觀點和傾向各異，國內外各種敵對勢力時刻伺機對駐軍人員進行腐蝕，拉攏，策反活動等等……由於香港與祖國大陸政治分離百多年，長期接受英國殖民主義教育，加上境內外反華和極右勢力的造謠中傷，使香港居民對我軍普遍不了解，甚至存有不同程度的偏見和隔閡，影響了對我們黨和政府形象的看法", 〈港政團腐蝕駐港解放軍〉, *Ming Pao*, 21 June 2002.
42. 〈駐港部隊首度閱兵挺董施政〉,《都市日報》, 2 August 2004; and Tonny Chan, "Hong Kong Cheers First Garrison Parade", *China Daily*, 2 August 2004.
43. Jeffie Lam and Minnie Chan, "PLA Drill in Victoria Harbour Seen as Warning to Hong Kong Protesters", *South China Morning Post*, 25 January 2014.
44. Nikki Sun and Adam Rose, "On Day of Hong Kong Mass Protests, China's Army Open Barracks to Public", *Reuters*, 1 July 2014.
45. "PLA holds Military Drill in HK, Locals Invited to Observe", *Xinhua*, 4 July 2015.

46. Shirley Zhao, "People's Liberation Army Holds Military Drill in Hong Kong's New Territories", *South China Morning Post*, 31 October 2016.
47. 〈民主派8議員訪軍營　盼與中方更多交流〉, *Ming Pao*, 2 May 2005.
48. LegCo Question No. 4, Involvement of the Hong Kong Garrison of the People's Liberation Army in training youngsters, Legislative Council, 4 February 2015; and "PLA HK Garrison Wins Hearts and Minds", *China Daily*, www.ecns.cn, 21 June 2017.
49. 〈逾六成市民滿意駐港部隊〉, *Wen Wei Po*, 1 August 2001. In August 2004, according to a poll done by the Hong Kong University Public Opinion Programme, 60% of the respondents were satisfied with the performance of the garrison in Hong Kong. See also Hong Kong University Public Opinion Programme, "Popularity Survey of Hong Kong Disciplinary Forces and the PLA Hong Kong Garrison", 8 December 2015, http://www.hkupop.hku.hk/english/release/release1309.htm.47.
50. Kimmy Chung, "No Chance Beijing Will Reform Hong Kong Electoral Frame work in Next Five Years", *South China Morning Post*, 3 May 2017 and updated on 4 May 2017.
51. Zhang Xiaoming, "A Correct Understanding of the Characteristics of the Political System of the Hong Kong Special Administrative Region", speech on 12 September 2016 at a seminar on the 25th anniversary of the promulgation of the Basic Law, English translation, *South China Morning Post*, 16 September 2016.
52. For a useful summary about patriots and patriotism, see "Looking into the Past to Ensure the Future", *China Daily*, 23 February 2004, http://www.chinadaily.com.cn/english/doc/2004-02/23/content_308316.htm.
53. Gary Cheung and Joshua But, "Qiao Xiaoyang says Beijing Forced into Universal Suffrage Debate", *South China Morning Post*, 26 March 2013.
54. 〈張曉明以「篩箕」論特首篩選　堅決反對佔中〉, *Hong Kong Economic Journal*, 16 July 2013.
55. Information Office of the State Council, *The Practice of the "One Country, Two Systems" Policy in the Hong Kong Special Administrative Region*, June 2014, pp. 46–47.
56. For details of the by-election, see the Electoral Affairs Commission report, http://www.eac.gov.hk/en/legco/2010lcbe_detailreport.htm.
57. Information Office of the State Council, *The Practice of the "One Country, Two Systems" Policy in the Hong Kong Special Administrative Region*, June 2014, p. 22.
58. 〈知名人士紛挺董〉, *Ming Pao*, 11 December 2001; and 〈高祀仁：家和萬事興〉, *Ming Pao*, 22 October 2001.
59. 〈人大政協擬聯署挺董〉, *Ming Pao*, 12 December 2001; and 〈知名人士紛挺董〉, *Ming Pao*, 11 December 2001.
60. 〈董讚中聯辦政府摯友〉, *Ming Pao*, 17 September 2002.
61. Ambrose Leung, "Tell All to Get on to the Tsang Bandwagon", *South China Morning Post*, 15 March 2007.
62. Andrea Deng, "Beijing States Priorities for HKSAR's Next CE", *China Daily*, 11 July 2011.
63. Kimmy Chung, "Beijing Did Not Want Me in Hong Kong Leadership Race, Jaspar Tsang Reveals", *South China Morning Post*, 15 March 2017. Tsang said he wanted to ensure there would be competition against the unpopular Leung Chun Ying.
64. Regina Ip wanted to run in the 2012 chief executive election but did not have sufficient support among the patriotic camp. She was the secretary for security under Tung Chee

Hwa's administration with responsibility for the Article 23 legislation, and she was a member of Leung Chun Ying's Executive Council. Her consolation prize was to be invited on Carrie Lam's Executive Council, which she accepted.

65. Jeffie Lam and Joyce Ng, "Hong Kong Chief Executive CY Leung Will Not Seek Reelection Due To Family Reasons", *South China Morning Post*, 9 December 2016. Leung said he wanted to spare his family from suffering the pressure arising from electioneering. He dismissed speculations that his decision was due to Beijing not supporting his re-election bid.

66. Ng Kang Chung and Jeffie Lam, "Handshake with Chinese President Xi Jinping among Reasons John Tsang Decided to Run for Hong Kong Leadership", *South China Morning Post*, 3 February 2017.

67. Joyce Ng, Jeffie Lam, Tong Leung, and Stuart Lau, "Pro-democracy Camp Takes Record Quarter of Seats on Election Committee That Will Choose Chief Executive", *South China Morning Post*, 12 December 2016.

68. 〈反對派為「造王」扭曲選委意願〉, Editorial, *Wen Wei Po*, 16 March 2017.

69. Kimmy Chung and Joyce Ng, "Beijing 'Doesn't Trust John Tsang Because He Ignored Its Warning Not to Run' in Hong Kong Chief Executive Election", *South China Morning Post*, 24 March 2017, updated on 25 March 2017.

70. Ng Kang Chung, "Pro-establishment no-shows at Hong Kong CE race debate caused Lam to feel the heat", *South China Morning Post*, 20 March 2017.

71. Bernard Chan, "Can Carrie Wow with Style and Substance?", *South China Morning Post*, 31 March 2017.

72. The DAB's website, http://www.dab.org.hk. For a discussion about the DAB, see also Shiu-hing Sonny Lo, *Competing Chinese Political Visions: Hong Kong vs. Beijing on Democracy*, pp. 176–89.

73. Fanny Fung, "HK$13.8 Million Buys 'Successful Future' Calligraphy by Beijing's Top Representative in Hong Kong", *South China Morning Post*, 16 April 2014; and Ng Kang Chung, "Hong Kong Businessman Bids HK$18.8 Million for Calligraphy by Beijing Official at DAB Fundraiser", *South China Morning Post*, 22 November 2016.

74. Shiu-hing Sonny Lo, Wing-yat Yu, and Kwok-fai Wan, "The 1999 District Council Elections", in Ming K. Chan and Alvin Y. So, *Crisis and Transformation in China's Hong Kong*, pp. 139–65, especially pp. 154–55.

75. Shiu-hing Sonny Lo, Wing-yat Yu, and Kwok-fai Wan, "The 1999 District Council Elections", in Ming K. Chan and Alvin Y. So, *Crisis and Transformation in China's Hong Kong*, pp. 139–65; the chart is adapted from the one on p. 155.

76. Brian C. H. Fong, "In-between Liberal Authoritarianism and Electoral Authoritarianism: Hong Kong's Democratization under Chinese Sovereignty, 1997–2016", *Democratization*, 2016, pp. 7–10, http://dx.doi.org/10.1080/13510347.2016.1232249.

77. 〈『懲戒』自由黨誤中田北俊〉, *Ming Pao*, 12 September 2008. For a discussion about the Liberal Party, see Shiu-hing Sonny Lo, *Competing Chinese Political Visions: Hong Kong vs. Beijing on Democracy*, pp. 191–200.

78. Tony Cheung, "Trade Union Veteran Wong Kwok-hing Blames Legco Defeat on 'Rumours' and Dishonest Tactics", *South China Morning Post*, 11 September 2016 and updated on 12 September 2016.

79. For a detail discussion about subsectors elections, see Simon N. M. Young and Richard Cullen, *The Chief Executive Election in the HKSAR*; and for functional constituencies, see Christine Loh and Civic Exchange, *Functional Constituencies: A Unique Feature of the Hong Kong Legislative Council*.
80. In 1998, 10 seats were unchallenged; in 2000, there were 9 such seats; in 2004, there were 11; in 2008 there were 14; in 2012, there were 16; and in 2016, there were 10 uncontested seats. Some lawmakers in these constituencies were unchallenged for several elections in a row. For the details, see the Electoral Affairs Commission's website, http://www.eac.gov.hk.
81. For a discussion on proportional representation, see Ngok Ma, "Increased Pluralization and Fragmentation: Party System and Electoral Politics in the 2012 Elections", in Joseph Y. S. Cheng, *New Trends of Political Participation in Hong Kong*, pp. 185–209.
82. What happened was recorded in the Official Record of Proceedings of the Legislative Council, 18 June 2015, pp. 13464–67, http://www.legco.gov.hk/yr14-15/english/counmtg/hansard/cm20150618-translate-e.pdf.
83. Tony Cheung, "Key Figure in Botched Hong Kong Reform Vote Walkout Apologises for Fiasco", and Tony Cheung and Lai Ying-kit, "We're Sorry: Hong Kong Pro-establishment Lawmakers Apologise for Reform Vote Walkout", *South China Morning Post*, 19 June 2015.
84. Staff reporters, "Hong Kong Reform Package Rejected as Pro-Beijing Camp Walk out in 'Miscommunication'", *South China Morning Post*, 18 June 2015 and updated on 19 June 2015.
85. Owen Fung and Ng Kang Chung, "'A Colossal Waste of Money': Legco Quorum Calls Cost Hongkongers HK$45.6 Million", *South China Morning Post*, 15 July 2016.
86. LegCo Question No. 6, Impacts of filibusters on Government's implementation of policies and HK society, Legislative Council, 18 May 2016.
87. Financial Secretary, 26 April 20017, http://www.info.gov.hk/gia/general/201704/26/P2017042600635.htm.
88. 〈邵善波評暴亂：政治鬥爭無關管治　年輕人看不見前景　非換特首可解決〉, *Sing Tao Daily*, 14 March 2016; and interview with 〈邵善波：社會困局 換特首不能解決〉, *Hong Kong Economic Times*, 14 March 2016.
89. Tung Chee Hwa's speech to the Our Hong Kong Foundation, 13 June 2016, http://www.scmp.com/news/hong-kong/politics/article/1974752/extracts-former-hong-kong-chief-executive-tung-chee-hwas.
90. Zhou Xin, "How Beijing and Hong Kong Sent Billionaire George Soros Packing the Last Time He Attacked Asian Markets", *South China Morning Post*, 27 January 2016 and updated on 30 May 2016.
91. There are scholarly publications on the relationship between Tung Chee Hwa and the civil service, see Joseph Y. S. Cheng, ed., *The July 1 Protest Rally: Interpreting a Historic Event*; Joseph Y. S. Cheng, ed., *The Hong Kong Special Administrative Region in Its First Decade*; and Yue-man Yeung, *The First Decade: The Hong Kong SAR in Retrospective and Introspective Perspectives*.
92. 〈北京不滿助董不力〉, *Ming Pao*, 13 January 2001.

93. Qian Qichen supposedly said: "陳方安生司長和特區政府全體公務員一起，更好地支持行政長官的工作"。〈北京促陳太更好地挺董　陳方安生主動澄清不和傳言〉, *Ming Pao*, 27 September 2000.
94. Anson Chan, "Ten Years on Eyewitness", *South China Morning Post*, 1 July 2007. On 27 November 2007, Chan also said on RTHK's Backchat: "I resigned chiefly (there were a number of other concerns) because I was not able to go along with CH's proposal to introduce the accountability system. I thought in the absence of universal suffrage to introduce a layer of political appointees would not be efficient, would affect the operation of the civil service. I thought there were other ways of grooming political talents. I spent a year trying to persuade CH not to go down this road. But as I did not succeed and I felt I could not defend this package, I chose to leave."
95. For discussions about the Principle Officials Accountability System, see Christine Loh and Richard Cullen, *Accountability Without Democracy*, http://www.civic-exchange.org/publications/2002/POASE.pdf; Christine Loh and Carine Lai, *Reflections of Leadership*, pp. 78–84; and Brian C. H. Fong, "Ten Years of Political Appointments in Hong Kong: The Challenges and Prospects of Developing a Political Appointment System under a Semi-Democratic Regime, 2002–12", *New Trends of Political Participation in Hong Kong*, pp. 67–103.
96. Stuart Lau, "State Leaders Zhang Dejiang Declares Beijing's Power to 'Supervise' Hong Kong Civil Servants' Allegiance", *South China Morning Post*, 27 May 2017; and Stuart Lau, "Beijing Signals Tighter Grip", *South China Morning Post*, 28 May 2017.
97. Translation of Xi Jinping's full speech in Hong Kong on 1 July 2017, *South China Morning Post*, 2 July 2017.
98. For typical submissions to the Legislative Council, see the website of the Hong Kong Legislative Council, Security Panel Papers Year 2001–2011; and for a discussion, see Shiu-hing Sonny Lo, *Governing Hong Kong*, pp. 241–42.
99. Brian C. H. Fong, "One Country, Two Nationalisms: Center-Periphery Relations between Mainland China and Hong Kong, 1997–2016", *Modern China*, p. 9, http://journals.sagepub.com/doi/abs/10.1177/0097700417691470.
100. Joseph Y. S. Cheng, "The Occupation Campaign in Hong Kong: A Participant's View", *Contemporary Chinese Political Economy and Strategic Relations: An International Journal*, p. 690.
101. "Row over Anti-Falun Gong Banners", *South China Morning Post*, 9 January 2013; and Hong Kong Journalists Association, "Dark Clouds on the Horizon: Hong Kong's Freedom of Express Faces New Threats", *Annual Report 2013*, p. 3.
102. Brian C. H. Fong, "In-between Liberal Authoritarianism and Electoral Authoritarianism: Hong Kong's Democratization under Chinese Sovereignty, 1997–2016", *Democratization*, 2016, pp. 10–12, http://dx.doi.org/10.1080/13510347.2016.1232249.
103. Ng Kang Chung, Naomi Ng, Raymond Cheng, Peace Chiu, and Raymond Yeung, "Angry Crowd Demands Youngspiration Oath Pair to Quit Hong Kong Legco", *South China Morning Post*, 26 October 2016 and updated on 30 November 2016.
104. Alex Lo, "Silent Majority Have Ears in High Places", *South China Morning Post*, 1 December 2016.
105. Ching Cheong, "Beijing May Shelve New HK Law", *The Straits Times*, 15 August 2003.

106. "Chinese Vice-President Calls for Further Cooperation between Mainland, HK and Macao", 17 September 2003, http://www.chinaembassy.at/det/xwdt/t104837.htm.
107. *China Daily*, 4 December 2003.
108. Policy Address 2004–2005, paragraph 77.
109. Press Release, HKSAR government, Task Force on Constitutional Review, 7 January 2004, http://www.legco.gov.hk/yr03-04/english/panels/ca/papers/ca0216cb2-920-1e.pdf.
110. Press Release, HKSAR government, Chief Secretary concludes Beijing visit, 10 February 2004, http://www.info.gov.hk/gia/general/200402/10/0210205.htm.
111. "China's Top Legislature Will Deliberate a Draft Interpretation of Clause 7 of Annex I and Clause 3 of Annex II of the Basic Law of the Hong Kong Special Administrative Region (HKSAR) in Its Next Meeting from April 2 to 6", Xinhuanet, 26 March 2004, archived at http://www.article23.org.hk/english/newsupdate/mar04/0326e3.htm.
112. Policy Address 2010–2011, paragraph 161.
113. For details of this episode, see Steven C. G. Fung, "Political Participation of Students in Hong Kong: A Historical Account of Transformation", Joseph Y. S. Cheng, *New Trends of Political Participation in Hong Kong*, pp. 270–73.
114. For a discussion about Scholarism and students' activism, see Benson Wai-Kwok Wong and Sanho Chung, "Scholarism and Hong Kong Federation of Students: Comparative Analysis of Their Development after the Umbrella Movement", *Contemporary Chinese Political Economy and Strategic Relations: An International Journal*, pp. 865–84; and Ben Bland's *Generation HK* is also useful.
115. Jeffie Lam, "Self-Determination, Elections on Agenda for New Party", *South China Morning Post*, 11 April 2016.
116. Joseph Li, "Leung, Most HK People Support 'One Country'", *China Daily Asia*, 15 September 2016.
117. For a scholarly discussion on the moral and national education mass movement, see Karita Kan, "Lessons in Patriotism", *China Perspectives*, no. 2012/4, pp. 63–69.
118. Horace Chin (陳雲根), a.k.a. Wan Chin (陳雲), is the author of *On the Hong Kong City State* published in 2011. Chin advocates Hong Kong to be a polity with total autonomy and only be affiliated with the Mainland in name. For a discussion about Chin's work, see Che-po Chan, "Post-Umbrella Movement: Localism and Radicalism of the Hong Kong Student Movement", *Contemporary Chinese Political Economy and Strategic Relations: An International Journal*, Vol. 2, No. 2, September 2016, pp. 885–908.
119. Keung Kai-hing, "HK Independence Attempt a Display of Political Naiveté", *China Daily*, 18 October 2012.
120. Hu Jintao's report at the 18th Party Congress, 17 November 2012, http://news.xinhuanet.com/english/special/18cpcnc/2012-11/17/c_131981259.htm.
121. Translation of Xi Jinping's full speech in Hong Kong on 1 July 2017, *South China Morning Post*, 2 July 2017.
122. Information Office of the State Council, *The Practice of the "One Country, Two Systems" Policy in the Hong Kong Special Administrative Region*, June 2014, Section V.
123. Geoffrey Ma, "Strength and Fragility in Tandem: The Rule of Law in Hong Kong", Annual International Rule of Law Lecture 2015, The Bar Council of England and Wales, http://www.hkcfa.hk/filemanager/speech/en/upload/130/Strength%20and%20Fragility%20in%20tandem%20-%20The%20Rule%20of%20Law%20in%20Hong%20Kong.pdf.

124. Joseph Fok, "Demonstrating Judicial Independence in Increasingly Politicized Times", Commonwealth Law Conference 2017, 21 March 2017, http://www.hkcfa.hk/filemanager/speech/en/upload/183/C2%20Independence%20of%20the%20Judiciary%20and%20Legal%20Profession.pdf.
125. Decision of the SCNPC adopted on 31 August 2014.
126. Occupy Central with Love and Peace Manifesto, see http://oclp.hk/index.php?route=occupy/book_detail&book_id=11.
127. For details of the events, see Joseph Y. S. Cheng, "The Occupation Campaign in Hong Kong: A Participant's View", *Contemporary Chinese Political Economy and Strategic Relations: An International Journal*, Vol. 2, No. 2, September 2016, pp. 699–734; and Jermain T. M. Lam, "The Occupy Central Movement and Political Reform in Hong Kong", in Joseph Y. S. Cheng, *New Trends of Political Participation in Hong Kong*, pp. 450–81.
128. Flora Chung, "School Off-limits to Independence 'Poison'", *The Standard*, 17 August 2016.
129. For discussions about the evolution of civil society activities in Hong Kong, see Eliza Wing-yee Lee, "Civic Society Organisations and Local Governance in Hong Kong", in Stephen Wing-kai Chu and Siu-lun Wong, *Repositioning the Hong Kong Government: Social Foundations and Political Challenges*, pp. 147–64; Daniel Garrett and Wing-chung Ho, "Hong Kong at the Brink: Emerging Forms of Political Participation in the New Social Movement", in Joseph Y. S. Cheng, *New Trends of Political Participation in Hong Kong*, pp. 347–83; and Calvin H. M. Lau, "Political Participation of the Post-80s Generation: Their Protest Activities and Social Movements in Recent Years in Hong Kong", in Joseph Y. S. Cheng, *New Trends of Political Participation in Hong Kong*, pp. 387–415.
130. Elsie Leung, "Why the Government Must Seek an Interpretation of BL53(2) from the NPCSC", http://www.doj.gov.hk/eng/archive/pdf/sj20050419e.pdf, 15 April 2005.
131. To be fair, there were several other cases where the secretary for justice had also decided not to prosecute. For a longer discussion, see Christine Loh, "Human Rights in the First Year—Genuine Restraint, or Buying Time?", in Nyaw Mee-kay and Li Si Ming, *The Other Hong Kong Report 1998*, pp. 65–67.
132. *Jiang Enzhu vs. Emily Lau Wai-Hing*, HCAL27/98, 8 June 1999, https://www.hongkong-caselaw.com/jiang-enzhu-v-lau-wai-hing-emily/.
133. On 7 April 1998, the Provisional Legislature passed the Adaptation of Laws Ordinance, which exempted state organs from the application of a number of Hong Kong laws, similar to the immunity enjoyed by the Crown prior to 1997. Crown immunity is a judicial doctrine stemming from the concept that "the monarch can do no wrong". Like for Crown immunity prior to the transition, state immunity post-transition confers on state organs immunity from suit and execution in the Hong Kong courts. The common law had extended the meaning of the Crown from the monarch to all bodies and persons acting as servants and agents of the Crown. In resuming the debate on the bill, the issue of the status of Xinhua Hong Kong was discussed, see http://www.legco.gov.hk/yr97-98/english/counmtg/general/yr9798.htm. The issue of state immunity and the circumstances that it could be claimed by a state organ was discussed in *Intraline Resources SDN BHD vs. The Owners of the Ship or Vessel 'Hua Tian Long'* (2010) 3 HKLRD. 67.
134. Functions and Powers of the SCNPC, http://www.npc.gov.cn/englishnpc/Organization/2007-11/15/content_1373018.htm.
135. Decision of the SCNPC, 26 June 1999. For a discussion of the case, see Albert H. Y. Chen, "The Court of Final Appeal's Ruling in the 'Illegal Migrant' Children Case: Congressional

Supremacy and Judicial Review", *Hong Kong's Constitutional Debate: Conflict over Interpretation*, edited by Johannes M. M. Chan et al., pp. 73–96.

136. Decision of the SCNPC, 26 April 2004. For a discussion, see Albert H. Y. Chen, "The Constitutional Controversy of Spring 2004", *Hong Kong Law Journal*, 2004, pp. 215–26, https://hub.hku.hk/bitstream/10722/74855/1/content.pdf?accept=1.

137. Decision of the SCNPC, 27 April, 2005. See also Elsie Leung, "Why the Government Must Seek an Interpretation of BL53(2) from the NPCSC", 19 April 2005, http://www.doj.gov.hk/eng/archive/pdf/sj20050419e.pdf.

138. Decision of the SCNPC, 26 August 2011.

139. Explanations on the draft interpretation of Article 104 of Basic Law of Hong Kong SAR, 7 November 2016, http://news.xinhuanet.com/english/2016-11/08/c_135812367.htm.

140. Judgment HCSL185-2016, 15 November 2016, http://legalref.judiciary.hk/lrs/common/ju/ju_frame.jsp?DIS=106799&currpage=T.

141. High Court judgment, 14 July 2017, http://legalref.judiciary.hk/doc/judg/html/vetted/other/en/2016/HCAL000223_2016_files/HCAL000223_2016ES.htm.

142. The first set of by-elections was held on 11 March 2018. Another two seats still had to be dealt with.

143. Tony Cheung, "First Two, Now 15 Hong Kong Lawmakers Face Prospect of Being Expelled from Legislative Council", *South China Morning Post*, 9 November 2016 and updated on 10 November 2016.

144. "Hong Kong Advert Calls Chinese Mainlanders 'Locusts'", *BBC News*, 1 February 2012. For an interesting essay, see Feng Chi-shun, "I'm Proud to Be a 'Locust'", *China Daily Asia*, 8 July 2015.

145. For a discussion, see Brian Bridges, "Booking the National Anthem: Hong Kong's Identities through the Mirror of Sport", *Contemporary Chinese Political Economy and Strategic Relations: An International Journal*, Vol. 2, No. 2, September 2016, pp. 819–43.

146. Policy Address, 14 January 2015, paragraph 10. See also Tong Cheung and Peter So, "Hong Kong Nationalism Flies off the Shelves Following Leung Chun Ying's Policy Address Criticism", *South China Morning Post*, 21 January 2015.

147. Phila Siu, "Beijing Slams Creation of Hong Kong Independence Party, Saying It Endangers National Security", *South China Morning Post*, 30 March 2016 and updated on 31 March 2016; and Kenneth Lau, "Party Ideas 'Cannot Be Tolerated'", *The Standard*, 1 April 2016.

148. LegCo Question No. 4: Views and acts advocating independence of Hong Kong, 20 April 2016, http://www.info.gov.hk/gia/general/201604/20/P201604200307.htm.

149. Luis Liu and Shadow Li, "Top Legislator Zhang Hails 'One Country, Two Systems'", *China Daily Asia*, 19 May 2016.

150. Candidates already had to declare in the nomination form to uphold the Basic Law and pledge allegiance to the HKSAR. On 14 July 2016, the Electoral Affairs Commission announced that an extra confirmation was needed to declare acceptance that Hong Kong was an inalienable part of China. The HKSAR government explained that the new requirement was to help candidates better understand the law, their legal liability and consequences of breach, as well as help voters to understand the candidates. Returning officers were given the responsibility to invalidate non-compliant candidates. It was widely discussed in the media that the requirement was aimed at pro-independence Edward Leung of Hong Kong Indigenous who got some 60,000 votes in the New Territories East

by-election in February and was likely to win. Despite this controversial requirement, Leung Chung Hang and Lau Wai Ching of Youngspiration and Cheng Chung Tai of Civic Passion had their nominations validated and got elected even though Edward Leung was barred. See Press Release, HKSAR government, 30 July 2016, http://www.info.gov.hk/gia/general/201607/30/P2016073000700.htm.

151. Li Keqiang's Work Report, 15 March 2017, http://chinaplus.cri.cn/news/politics/11/20170316/1585.html.
152. 鍾國安，〈以習近平總書記總體國家安全觀為指引　譜寫國家安全新篇章〉，《求是》，2017/8, http://www.qstheory.cn/dukan/qs/2017-04/15/c_1120788993.htm. See also Frank Tang, "Party Points to HK Separatist Threat", *South China Morning Post*, 16 April 2017.
153. For a detailed discussion of the Xi Yang's case, see Carol P. Lai, *Media in Hong Kong*, pp. 50–77. Xi was released back to Hong Kong on parole, see *Dui Hua Human Rights Journal*, 4 March 2008, http://www.duihua.org/hrjournal/2008_03_01_archive.html.
154. Ching Cheong, *My 1,000 Days Ordeal: A Patriot's Torture*, pp. 38–39.
155. Juliana Liu, "Hong Kong's Missing Booksellers and 'Banned' Xi Jinping Book", *BBC News*, 4 February 2016.
156. Transcript of Lam Wing Kee's opening statement at the press conference, 17 June 2016, http://www.scmp.com/news/hong-kong/law-crime/article/1976598/full-transcript-lam-wing-kees-opening-statement-his-hong.
157. Phila Siu and Tony Cheung, "Bookseller Is a Chinese National Who Broke Mainland Law and Beijing Has the Right to Deal with Him, Ministry Declares", *South China Morning Post*, 17 June 2016.
158. Jennifer Ngo and Jeffie Lam, "Beijing Official Accuses Bookseller of 'Destroying' Hong Kong's Governing Policy", *South China Morning Post*, 2 July 2016.
159. Niall Fraser and Danny Mok, "33,000 Gather in Support of Hong Kong Officers Jailed for Beating up Occupy Protester Ken Tsang", *South China Morning Post*, 22 February 2017 and updated on 23 February 2017.
160. Public order events and statistics, Hong Kong Police, http://www.police.gov.hk/ppp_en/09_statistics/poes.html.
161. Jason Y. Ng, *Umbrellas in Bloom: Hong Kong Occupy Movement Uncovered*; and Joseph Y. S. Cheng, and Emile K. K. Yeoh (eds.), "From Handover to Occupy Campaign: Democracy, Identity and the Umbrella Movement", *Contemporary Chinese Political Economy and Strategic Relations: An International Journal*, August/September 2016.
162. LCQ5: Mongkok Riots, 2 March 2017, http://www.info.gov.hk/gia/general/201603/02/P201603020594.htm.
163. Geoffrey Ma, "Strength and Fragility in Tandem: The Rule of Law in Hong Kong", Annual International Rule of Law Lecture 2015, The Bar Council of England and Wales, http://www.hkcfa.hk/filemanager/speech/en/upload/130/Strength%20and%20Fragility%20in%20tandem%20-%20The%20Rule%20of%20Law%20in%20Hong%20Kong.pdf.
164. Hong Kong Journalists Association, "Dark Clouds on the Horizon: Hong Kong's Freedom of Expression Faces New Threats", *Annual Report 2013*, and "Two Systems Under Siege: Beijing Turns the Screws on Hong Kong", *Annual Report 2017*, provide useful background information on issues raised in this paragraph.

165. 〈訓斥記者四分鐘　指提問天真　「I am angry」　江：支持連任不等同欽點〉, *Ming Pao*, 28 October 2000.
166. Shirley Yam, "Behind the TVB Façade Lies the True Identity of Its Owner", *South China Morning Post*, Business Section, 17 May 2017. The owner, Li Ruigang, responded in Peggy Sito and Eric Ng, "Media Chief Questions HK's Shares System", *South China Morning Post*, 24 June 2017.
167. For a discussion on integrating media owners to the Mainland's political system, see Hong Kong Journalists Association, *Rising Nationalism*, 2008, p. 10; *Dark Clouds on the Horizon*, 2013, pp. 15–16; and *One Country, Two Nightmares*, 2016, pp. 5–7.
168. Hong Kong Journalists Association, *Rising Nationalism*, p. 10.
169. Speech by the secretary for justice explaining the decision not to prosecute, 24 May 1999, http://www.info.gov.hk/gia/general/199903/24/0324147.htm. It might have been that the decision not to prosecute was taken at a higher level.
170. Hong Kong Journalists Association and Article 19, *The Ground Rules Change*, pp. 20–21.
171. "Wong Exit Shows No Two Tigers Can Co-exist", *South China Morning Post*, 24 December 2008.
172. Joseph Wong (王永平), 〈中央，亞視，政治，生意〉, *Economic Journal*, 31 December 2008.
173. Eric Ng, "i-Cable shareholders accept white knight, vote for rights issue to be raised funds, continue operations", *South China Morning Post*, 29 May 2017.
174. Michael Forsythe and Neil Gough, "Hong Kong Media Worries Over China's Reach as Ads Disappears", *New York Times*, 11 June 2014.
175. Carol Lai and Andy Ho, "Press: How Free Is the Press?", in Chris Yeung, *Hong Kong China*, p. 200.
176. Wang Fengchiao said: "報道台獨觀點不能作為一般新聞處理後", 〈「傳媒有責任維護家統一和領土完整」王鳳超為報道台獨言論設限〉, *Ming Pao*, 13 April 2000.
177. Students in Taiwan occupied the Legislative Yuan in the spring of 2014 and created the Sunflower Student Movement. They sought to delay implementation of a trade in services agreement with the Mainland. See Tony Cheung, "The Sunflower and the Umbrella: Hong Kong Activists Travel to Taiwan, Call for Closer Ties, New Policies for Incoming Government", *South China Morning Post*, 17 January 2016.
178. Kimmy Chung, "Pro-independence Taiwanese lawmakers launch support group for Hong Kong democracy", *South China Morning Post*, 12 June 2017.
179. For a discussion about online media, see Hong Kong Journalists Association, "Dark Clouds on the Horizon", *Annual Report* (2013), pp. 16–17; "Grave Threats to Freedom of Expression in Hong Kong", *Annual Report* (2014), pp. 21–24; and "One Country, Two Nightmares," *Annual Report* (2016), pp. 11–14.
180. 〈煽風點火「港獨」鬧劇　梁振英播「獨」〉, *Sing Pao*, 30 August 2016.
181. Ernest Kao, "Red notice issued for Sing Pao's chief's arrest on behalf of Shenzhen authorities", *South China Morning Post*, 9 March 2017 and updated on 10 March 2017.
182. 〈「亂港四人幫」　薄熙來追隨者等搞局　香港之亂始於2012年〉, *Sing Pao*, 12 September 2016.
183. 〈炮製激進政團鞏固利益　中聯辦梁振英禍港捧青年新政扮港獨〉, *Sing Pao*, 3 September 2016.

Notes to pages 240–243   325

184. See *HKSAR Government vs.* 鄭永健, 顧家豪, 陳建隆, 24 October 2016, http://legalref.judiciary.hk/lrs/common/search/search_result_detail_frame.jsp?DIS=107097&QS=%2B&TP=RV.
185. 〈瓦解「西環寶藥黨」 小明不見了 太陽如常升起 中聯辦換班在望〉, *Sing Pao*, 11 December 2016.
186. 〈張德江巴結中聯辦用「錢」買權 打造全國人大貪腐之路〉, *Sing Pao*, 3 October 2016.
187. Choi Chi-yuk, Kimmy Chung, and Tong Cheung, "Overseas Chinese Affairs Office Deputy Li Gang Removed from His Post", *South China Morning Post*, 1 September 2017.
188. Joyce Ng and Gary Cheung, "HK Affairs Office in the Cross Hairs", *South China Morning Post*, 16 October 2016.
189. 〈中聯辦被爆黑幕 查政協買賣 大削港區委員〉, *Oriental Daily*, 18 November 2016.
190. Joyce Ng, "Cadre from Xi's Reform Body Joins Beijing's HK Office", *South China Morning Post*, 9 June 2017.
191. Translation of Xi Jinping's full speech in Hong Kong on 1 July 2017, *South China Morning Post*, 2 July 2017.
192. According to Richard Ottaway, the chairman of the British Parliament's Foreign Affairs Committee, Ni Jian, deputy Chinese ambassador to Britain, conveyed to him the message that the Sino-British Joint Declaration "is now void and only covered the period from the signing in 1984 until the handover in 1997. Foreign Ministry spokesperson, Hua Chunying, echoed that: "Britain has no sovereignty over Hong Kong that has returned to China, no authority and no right to oversight". See Danny Lee and Gary Cheung, "Beijing tells Britain it has no 'moral responsibility' for Hong Kong, *South China Morning Post*, 31 December 2016 and updated on 12 September 2015. On 30 June 2017, the Foreign Ministry stated that the Sino-British Joint Declaration was a "historical document that no longer has any realistic meaning". It stated that: "It also does not have any binding power on how the Chinese central government administer Hong Kong. Britain has . . . no supervising power over Hong Kong". See Joyce Ng, "Joint declaration 'no longer has meaning', China says", *South China Morning Post*, 1 July 2017, and Joyce Ng, "1984 treaty 'still binding, but UK cannot meddle'", *South China Morning Post*, 9 July 2017.
193. Francis Fukuyama proposed that what the world was witnessing in the 1990s was "the end of history . . . the end point of mankind's ideological evolution and the universalization of Western liberal democracy as the final form of human government"; *The End of History and the Last Man*, 1992.
194. "Communique on the Current State of the Ideological Sphere", *Central Committee of the CCP's General Office*, 22 April 2013, see translation http://www.chinafile.com/document-9-chinafile-translation#start.
195. Translation of Xi Jinping's full speech in Hong Kong on 1 July 2017, *South China Morning Post*, 2 July 2017.
196. Joyce Ng, "Pan-democrat Vote Share Slides", *South China Morning Post*, 3 July 2017.
197. Translation of Xi Jinping's full speech in Hong Kong on 1 July 2017, *South China Morning Post*, 2 July 2017.
198. The reference is Xi Jinping's Political Report, 19th National Party Congress, 18 October 2017.
199. Julia Hollingsworth, "The Hong Kong Luxury Hotel Turned Tycoon Hideout Away from Prying Mainland Chinese Eyes", *South China Morning Post*, 2 February 2017.

Biographies

Abbreviations

BLCC	Basic Law Consultative Committee
BLDC	Basic Law Drafting Committee
BPA	Business and Professional Alliance for Hong Kong
CPPCC	Chinese People's Political Consultative Conference
DP	Democratic Party
ExCo	Hong Kong Executive Council
FTU	Federation of Trade Unions
HKAA	Hong Kong Affairs Advisor
HKMAO	Hong Kong and Macao Affairs Office
HKPA	Hong Kong Progressive Alliance
LegCo	Hong Kong Legislative Council
LP	Liberal Party
NPC	National People's Congress
PC	Preparatory Committee
PL	Provisional Legislature 1996–1998
PWC	Preliminary Working Committee
SC	Selection Committee 1996–1997
4th	NPC and CPPCC 1975–1978
5th	NPC and CPPCC 1978–1983
6th	NPC and CPPCC 1983–1988
7th	NPC and CPPCC 1988–1993
8th	NPC and CPPCC 1993–1997
9th	NPC and CPPCC 1998–2002
10th	NPC and CPPCC 2003–2007
11th	NPC and CPPCC 2008–2012
12th	NPC and CPPCC 2013–2018

Mainland Leaders and Officials

Chen Yi (陳毅 1901–1972). Veteran revolutionary; also served as China's Foreign Minister.

Deng Xiaoping (鄧小平 1904–1997). Paramount leader of the post-Mao era and chief architect of "one country, two systems".

Biographies

Hu Jintao (胡錦濤 b. 1942). General Secretary of the CCP, President of China, and Chairman of the Central Military Commission 2002–2012.

Hu Yaobang (胡耀邦 1915–1989). CCP leader considered a reformer; died of a heart attack in 1989.

Huang Hua (黃華 1913–2010). Ambassador to the UN 1971–1976 and Minister of Foreign Affairs 1976–1982.

Ji Pengfi (姬鵬飛 1910–2000). Foreign Minister 1972–1974; head of HKMAO, and BLDC.

Jia Qinglin (賈慶林 b. 1940). Politburo member.

Jiang Qing (江青 1914–1991). Mao Zedong's fourth wife. Played a critical role during the Cultural Revolution as a member of the Gang of Four.

Jiang Zemin (江澤民 b. 1926). Became the top leader after the Tiananmen crackdown.

Li Changchun (李長春 b. 1944). Politburo member.

Li Keqiang (李克強 b. 1955). Premier from 2013.

Li Peng (李鵬 b. 1928). Premier 1988–1998.

Li Qiang (李強 1905–1996). Minister of Foreign Trade; invited MacLehose to Beijing in 1978.

Li Xiannian (李先念 1909–1992). President of China 1983–1988.

Liao Chengzhi (廖承志 1908–1983). Had longstanding connection with Hong Kong. Purged in 1968 but released in 1972. He regained power over Hong Kong affairs in 1978.

Lin Biao (林彪 1907–1971). In 1969 he became the next most powerful person after Mao. Lin supposedly planned a failed coup and during his escape, his plane crashed in Mongolia.

Liu Shaoqi (劉少奇 1898–1969). He was in Guangzhou in 1925 during the strike-boycott. Chairman of China and Head of State from 1959 to 1968 but purged during the Cultural Revolution and died.

Liu Yandong (劉延東 b. 1945). Head of United Front Department until elected to the Politburo in 2007. Her replacement is Du Qinglin (杜青林).

Liu Yunshan (劉雲山 b. 1947). Director of Propaganda Department 2002–2012; Politburo Standing Committee 18th Party Congress.

Luo Guibo (羅貴波 1908–1995). Chinese Vice-Foreign Minister 1957–1970.

Mao Zedong (毛澤東 1893–1976). Led the CCP to victory over the KMT and was the leader of China up until his death.

Peng Zhen (彭真 1902–1997). Veteran revolutionary, who fell out of favour with Mao Zedong in 1966 but was rehabilitated by Deng Xiaoping and was Chairman of the 6th NPC (1983–1988).

Qian Qichen (錢其琛 1928–2017). Foreign Minister 1988–1998 and Vice-Premier 1993–2003 with substantial involvement in Hong Kong affairs.

Qiao Xiaoyang (喬曉陽 b. 1945), PC, Deputy Secretary SCNPC and Chairman of the NPC's Law Committee.

Tao Zhu (陶鑄 1908–1969). Replaced Fang Fang as the Director of the Provincial Land Reform Committee of the party in Guangdong in 1952. Tao's assistant was Zhao Ziyang.

Wang Hanbin (王漢斌 b. 1925). 6th to 8th SCNPC, Secretary General of the NPC, and BLDC Vice-Chairman.

Wen Jiabao (溫家寶 b. 1942). Premier from 2003 to 2013.

Wu Xueqian (吳學謙 1921–2008). Foreign Minister 1982–1988 and Vice-Premier 1988–1993.

Xi Jinping (習近平 b. 1953). Vice-President in 2008; took over from Zeng Qinghong on Hong Kong matters at the Politburo before becoming General Secretary in 2012 and President and Chairman of the Central Military Commission in 2013.

Ye Jianying (葉劍英 1897–1986). A Hakka and veteran soldier and military hero; first Party Secretary of Guangdong and held many high offices, including Chairman of the 5th NPC (1978–1983).

Yu Zhengsheng (俞正聲 b. 1945). Politburo member and Chairman of the CPPCC from 2013.

Zeng Qinghong (曾慶紅 b. 1939). Politburo member, Vice-President 2003–2008, and oversaw Hong Kong affairs.

Zhang Dejiang (張德江 b. 1946). Politburo member since 2012 with responsibility for Hong Kong affairs, and Chairman of SCNPC of the 12th NPC.

Zhang Hanfu (章漢夫 1906–1972). Vice-Foreign Minister in the 1950s.

Zhao Ziyang (趙紫陽 1919–2005). General Secretary of the CCP and signed the Sino-British Joint Declaration. He was put under house arrest from 1989 until he died.

Zhou Enlai (周恩來 1898–1976). Foreign Minister 1949–1958 and first Premier of the PRC. He played a unique and vital role in defining Hong Kong policy and relations throughout his career.

Xinhua Hong Kong/Liaison Office, HKMAO, and Mainland officials stationed in the HKSAR

Directors, Xinhua Hong Kong (renamed Liaison Office after 2000) (in chronological order)

Qiao Guanhua (喬冠華 1913–1983). First Director of Xinhua Hong Kong, and Foreign Minister 1974–1976.

Huang Zuomei (黃作梅 1916–1955). Second Director of Xinhua Hong Kong. Also known as Raymond Wong, he was the interpreter and director of international relations for the East River Column and thus a CCP-British go-between. He was invited by the British government to join the victory parade in London in May 1946 and was awarded a medal by King George VI and an MBE. He died when the *Kashmir Princess* crashed in 1955.

Liang Weilin (梁威林 1911–2008). Third Director of Xinhua Hong Kong 1958–1977, a former guerrilla, he directed the 1967 riots.

Wang Kuang (王匡 1917–2003). Fourth Director of Xinhua Hong Kong 1978–1982. Member of the 5th, 6th, and 7th CPPCC Standing Committee.

Xu Jiatun (許家屯 1916–2016). Fifth Director of Xinhua Hong Kong 1983–1989. Former Party Secretary for Jiangsu 1977–1983, Vice-Chairman BLDC.

Zhou Nan (周南 b. 1927). Sixth Director of Xinhua Hong Kong 1990–1997, previously served as Vice-Foreign Minister, and Ambassador to the UN. He headed the Chinese negotiation team on the Hong Kong's transfers of sovereignty, and BLDC.

Jiang Enzhu (姜恩柱 b. 1938). Seventh Director of Xinhua, he oversaw the transition to the Liaison Office 1997–2002. A former Vice-Foreign Minister, a member of the Sino-British negotiations team, and Ambassador to Britain 1995–1997, PWC, Deputy Director of the PC.

Gao Siren (高祀仁 b. 1944). Eighth Director of Xinhua, 2002–2009. Headed various party posts in Guangdong before becoming a Deputy Director of Xinhua from 1999 then transferring to the Liaison Office.

Biographies

Peng Qinghua (彭清華 b. 1957). Ninth Director of Xinhua, 2009–2012. Before becoming Director, he was a Deputy Director of the Liaison Office from 2003.
Zhang Xiaoming (張曉明 b. 1963). Tenth Director 2012–2017. Before becoming Director, he was a Deputy Director of HKMAO.
Wang Zhimin (王志民 b. 1957). Eleventh Director appointed in 2017. He had worked as a deputy director on youth affairs before taking up the directorship of Macao's Liaison Office.

Other officials at Xinhua Hong Kong (renamed Liaison Office after 2000)

Cao Erbao 曹二寶
Chen Daming 陳達明
He Zhiming 何志明
Huang Shimin 黃施民
Huang Wenfang 黃文放
Huang Zhizhao 黃智超
Li Gang 李剛
Li Guikang 黎桂康
Li Jusheng 李菊生
Liang Shangyuan 梁上苑
Luo Keming 羅克明
Mao Junnian 毛鈞年, Deputy Secretary BLDC.
Pan Zengxi 潘曾錫
Qi Feng 祁烽
Qiao Zhonghuai 喬宗准, son of Qiao Guanhua.
Wang Fengchao 王鳳超
Wang Rudeng 王如登
Wang Zhenmin 王振民, became head of legal department in 2014; former Dean of Tsinghua University's law school.
Zeng Guoxiong 鄭國雄
Zhang Junsheng 張浚生
Zheng Hua 鄭華
Zhou Ding 周鼎, CCP Macao Secretary, Director of Xinhua Macao.
Zhu Manping 朱曼平
Zou Zhekai 鄒哲開

Hong Kong and Macao Affairs Office (see also Mainland Leaders and Officials)

Chen Zuoer (陳佐洱 b. 1942). Deputy Director, retired in 2008.
Li Hou (李後 b. 1923). Secretary General HKMAO, Secretary to BLDC, and Deputy Director HKMAO.
Liao Hui (廖暉 b. 1942). Son of Liao Chengzhi. Director 1997–2010.
Lu Ping (魯平 1927–2015). Deputy Secretary BLDC and Director of HKMAO 1990–1997.

Pan Shengzhou (潘盛洲 b. 1957). Deputy Director since June 2017.
Wang Guangya (王光亞 b. 1950). Director of HKMAO from 2010.

Others

Lu Xinhua (呂新華). Second Commissioner of China's Foreign Ministry in the HKSAR.
Ma Yuzhen (馬毓真). Seasoned diplomat and first Commissioner of China's Foreign Ministry in the HKSAR.
Wang Jitang (王繼堂). Third Commander of the Hong Kong Garrison.
Xiong Ziren (熊自仁). First Commander of the Hong Kong Garrison.
Zheng Yi (鄭義). Vice-chairman of the Preliminary Working Committee.

East River Guerrillas and Agents

Cai Guoliang (蔡國樑). Leader of the Hong Kong–Kowloon Independent Brigade.
Chen Daming (陳達明). A guerrilla who went on to do party work in Beijing and then transferred to Xinhua Hong Kong as Deputy Director in 1982.
Fang Fang (方方 1904–1971). Directed guerrilla activities on the Mainland from Hong Kong during the civil war up until 1949 and became a Vice-Chairman of the CCP in Guangdong with responsibility for land reform. He was detained in 1966 during the Cultural Revolution, tortured and died in 1971.
Huang Zuomei (黃作梅 1916–1955). Became second Director of Xinhua Hong Kong, see above.
Li Cheng. A guerrilla agent during the Japanese occupation.
Liang Weilin (梁威林 1911–2008). A guerrilla leader who became the longest serving head of Xinhua Hong Kong (see above).
Tan Gan. A guerrilla who then worked for Xinhua Hong Kong as an editor.
Ya Wen. She observed boat movements in the harbour during the Japanese occupation.
Yang Qi (楊奇). A guerrilla who was purged in the 1950s but then transferred to Xinhua Hong Kong to head the regular news section. In 1982, he became the Secretary General at Xinhua Hong Kong before taking over as Publisher of *Ta Kung Pao* in 1984.
Zeng Sheng (曾生 1910–1995). A principal organiser and Secretary of the Seamen's Union, who became General and Commander-in-Chief of guerrilla forces in Guangdong. He became Deputy Governor of Guangdong and Mayor of Guangzhou in 1960. He was arrested in 1967 during the Cultural Revolution and incarcerated until 1974. In 1975 he was appointed Vice-Minister of Communications and became Minister in 1979. He retired in 1983 and died in Guangzhou in 1995.

Colonial Governors of Hong Kong

(In chronological order)

Reginald Stubbs (1919–1925)
Cecil Clementi (1925–1930)
Mark Young (1941 and 1946–1947)

Alexander Grantham (1947–1957)
Robert Black (1958–1964)
David Trench (1964–1971)
Murray MacLehose (1971–1982)
Edward Youde (1982–1986)
David Wilson (1987–1992)
Chris Patten (1992–1997)

British Officials and Politicians

Humphrey Atkins (1922–1996). Junior Foreign Office Minister with responsibility for Hong Kong 1981–1982.
Peter Carrington (1919–2007). Foreign Secretary 1979–1982.
Archibald Clark-Kerr (1882–1951). Ambassador to China 1938–1942.
Percy Cradock (1923–2005). *Charge d'Affaires* Beijing 1966–1969. From 1978 to 1984 he was the Ambassador to China, where he opened and led the negotiations on the Hong Kong. From 1984 to 1992 he was the Prime Minister's Foreign Policy Adviser.
Edward Heath (1916–2005). Prime Minister 1970–1974.
Geoffrey Howe (b. 1926). Foreign Secretary 1983–1989.
Douglas Hurd (b. 1930). Foreign Minister 1989–1995.
Richard Luce (b. 1936). Junior Foreign Office Minister with responsibility for Asia, including Hong Kong 1983–1985.
John Major (b. 1943). Prime Minister 1990–1997.
Robin McLaren (b. 1934). Ambassador to China 1991–1994.
David Owen (b. 1938). Foreign Secretary 1977–1979.
Anthony Royle (1927–2001). Junior Foreign Office Minister with responsibility for Asia, including Hong Kong 1970–1974.
Horace James Seymour (1885–1978). Ambassador to China 1942–1946.
Lord Malcolm Shepherd (1918–2001). Visited Hong Kong during the 1967 riots as Minister of State, Foreign Office 1967–1970.
Margaret Thatcher (1925–2013). Prime Minister 1979–1990.
Baroness Janet Young (1926–2002). Leader of the House of Lords 1983–1987.

Hong Kong and Macao Chief Executives

Edmund Ho (何厚鏵 b. 1955). Son of Ho Yin (何賢 1908–1983), who was influential in Macao. First Chief Executive of Macao, served two terms (1999–2009).
Carrie Lam (林鄭月娥 b. 1957). Civil servant. Former Chief Secretary before becoming the Fourth Chief Executive of Hong Kong in 2017.
Leung Chun Ying (梁振英 b. 1954). Surveyor. HKAA, Secretary-General BLCC, PWC, PL, ExCo 1997–2012, 10th and 11th CPPCCs. Third Chief Executive of Hong Kong (2012–2017), and made a Vice-Chairman of the 12th CPPCC in March 2017.
Donald Tsang (曾蔭權 b. 1944). Civil servant. Former Financial Secretary and Chief Secretary before becoming Chief Executive of Hong Kong (2005–2012).

Tung Chee Hwa (董建華 b. 1937). Shipping tycoon. HKAA, BLCC, ExCo 1992–1996, 8th CPPCC, and PC. First Chief Executive of Hong Kong (1997–2005) and a Vice-Chairman of 11th and 12th CPPCC.

Hong Kong Tycoons

T. K. Ann (安子介 1912–2000). LegCo 1970–1977, ExCo 1974–1978. BLDC, BLCC, HKAA, PWC, and PC. Several CPPCC terms.

Sally Aw (胡仙 b. 1932). Former owner of Sing Tao Publishing. 8th CPPCC.

Cha Chi Min (查濟民 1916–2007). BLDC, HKAA, PWC, PC, and SC.

Laura Cha (查史美倫 b. 1952) Daughter-in-law of Cha Chi Min. Vice-Chairperson China Securities Regulatory Commission 2001–2004. ExCo 2004 to present, 11th to 12th NPCs.

Payson Cha (查懋聲 b. 1943). Son of Cha Chi Min. SC and 9th to 11th CPPCC. His former wife, Veronica Cha (查伍小貞), served on BLCC.

Bernard Chan (陳智思 b. 1965). Son of Robin Chan, who served on 7th to 10th NPCs, PWC and PC, LegCo 1998–2008, ExCo 2012 to present, and 11th and 12 NPCs.

Chan Wing Kee (陳永棋 b. 1947). BLCC, HKAA, PWC, PC, SC, 8th and 9th NPCs, 10th to 12th CPPCCs, and Standing Committee of the 11th and 12th CPPCCs.

Henry Cheng (鄭家純 b. 1946). Son of Cheng Yu Tung, chairman of New World Development Ltd., 11th and 12th CPPCCs, and Standing Committee of 11th and 12th CPPCCs.

Cheng Yu Tung (鄭裕彤 1925–2016). New World Development Ltd., BLCC, HKAA, PWC, PC, and SC.

David Chiu (邱達昌 b. 1954). Son of Deacon Chiu.

Deacon Chiu (邱德根 1925–2017). Far East Group and former ATV chairman; 9th CPPCC.

Henry Fok (霍英東 1923–2006). BLDC, HKAA, PWC, PC, and SC. Served several NPC and CPPCC terms including his last, the 10th CPPCC when he was a Vice-Chairman.

Timothy Fok (霍震霆 b. 1952). Son of Henry Fok. BLCC, SC, LegCo 1998–2012 and several CPPCCs. Member of the International Olympic Committee (2001–2016 and made Honorary Member since 2017) and President, National Olympic Committee of Hong Kong.

Fung King Hei (馮景禧 1922–1985). Xu Jiatun disclosed that when Fung had financial problems, he made arrangements for Mainland institutions to help him.

Charles Ho (何柱國 b. 1949). Chairman of Sing Tao News Corporation. 9th to 12th CPPCCs.

Stanley Ho (何鴻燊 b. 1921). Shun Tak Holdings Ltd. and Sociedade de Turimo e Diversôes de Macau with many businesses related to gambling in Macao. BLCC, SC, and 9th and 10th CPPCCs.

Kwok Tak Sing (郭得勝 1911–1990). Founder of Sun Hung Kai Properties.

Jimmy Lai (黎智英 b. 1948). Founder of Next Media (includes *Apple Daily*, considered "unfriendly" by the CCP).

Lee Quo Wei (利國偉 1918–2013). Chairman Hang Seng Bank 1988–1997. LegCo, ExCo, HKAA, and SC.

Lee Shau Kee (李兆基 b. 1928). Henderson Land Development Co. Ltd. HKAA.

David Li (李國寶 b. 1939). Bank of East Asia. BLDC Vice-Chairman, HKAA, PWC, PC, LegCo 1985–1997, PL, LegCo 1998–2012, and ExCo 2005–2008.

Li Ka Shing (李嘉誠 b. 1928). Founder of Cheung Kong Holdings, BLDC, HKAA, PWC, PC, and SC.
Richard Li (李澤楷 b. 1966). Younger son of Li Ka Shing, CPPCC of Beijing since 2000.
Victor Li (李澤鉅 b. 1964). Elder son of Li Ka Shing, HKAA, 9th to 12th CPPCCs.
Lim Por Yen (林百欣 1914–2005). Lai Sun Group, and at one time the largest shareholder of ATV. HKAA.
Vincent Lo (羅康瑞 b. 1948). Shui On Holdings Ltd., BLCC, HKAA, PWC, PC, SC, and 9th to 12th CPPCCs.
Ma Ching Kwan (馬澄坤). Oriental Press Group, 10th to 11th CPPCCs.
Pao Yue Kong (包玉剛 1918–1991). Shipping tycoon, BLDC Vice-Chairman.
Run Run Shaw (邵逸夫 1907–2014). Shaw Brothers and founder of TVB, HKAA, and SC.
Helmut Sohmen (b. 1939). Son-in-law of Pao Yue Kong and a shipping magnate in his own right. BLCC and LegCo 1985–1988.
Francis Tien (田元灝 1916–1992). Industrialist, LegCo 1971–1985, and father of James and Michael Tien.
Tsang Hin Chi (曾憲梓 b. 1934). Industrialist, BLCC, HKAA, PWC, PC, SC, and 7th and 10th NPCs.
Peter Woo (吳光正 b. 1946). Son-in-law of Pao Yue Kong and chairman of Wharf Holdings and Wheelock and Co. BLCC, HKAA, and 9th to 12th CPPCCs, Standing Committee member. Ran for selection as the first Chief Executive.
Gordon Wu (胡應湘 b. 1935). Chairman of Hopewell Holdings. HKAA, SC, and 6th to 11th CPPCCs.

Hong Kong Officials, Judges, Executive Councillors, and Legislators

Jack Cater (1922–2006). Secretary for Defence; became the Deputy Colonial Secretary (Special Duties) to tackle the 1967 riots. Chief Secretary 1978–1981.
Anson Chan (陳方安生 b. 1940). Chief Secretary until 2001. Ran for election to LegCo in the 2007 by-election and won but did not seek re-election in 2008.
Chan Kam Lam (陳鑑林 b. 1949). DAB, SC, PL, LegCo 2000–2016, and 10th to 12th CPPCCs.
Nicky Chan (陳乃強 1931–2003). Secretary for Lands and Works 1983–1986.
Raymond Chan (陳志全 b. 1972). People Power. LegCo 2012–2016. He retained his seat in the 2016 election but his oath was invalidated in 2017.
Chan Yuen Han (陳婉嫻 b. 1946). FTU, DAB, HKAA, PL, LegCo 1995–2008 and 2012–2016, and 10th to 12th CPPCCs.
Cheng Yiu Tong (鄭耀棠 b. 1948). FTU, DAB, BLCC, HKAA, PWC, PC, SC, LegCo 1995–1997, PL, ExCo 2000–2017 and 7th to 11th NPCs.
Stephen Cheong (張鑑泉 1941–1993). Business executive. BLCC, HKAA and LegCo 1985–1993.
Anthony Cheung (張炳良 b. 1952). Academic. Former member of DP. LegCo 1995–1997 and ExCo 2005–2017. Secretary for Transport and Housing (2012–2017).
Selina Chow (周梁淑怡 b. 1945). LegCo 1981–1997, PL, LegCo 1998–2008, ExCo 1991–1992 and 2003–2008, and 11th to 12th CPPCCs.

Chow Shouson (周壽臣 1861–1959). Major political figure of his time. ExCo and a close adviser to the Hong Kong government during the strike-boycott in 1925–1926 working with Robert Kotewall.

Chow Tse-ming (周梓銘). In 1955, Chow Tse-ming was the janitor who worked on the aeroplane *Kashmir Princess*. He was thought to have planted a bomb on the airplane, which exploded in mid-air killing Huang Zuomei and others who were on board. He is believed to have disappeared to Taiwan.

Choy So Yuk (蔡素玉 b. 1950). DAB, LegCo 1997–2008, CPPCC Fujian Province, and 11th to 12th NPCs.

David Chu (朱幼麟 b. 1944). HKPA, HKAA, PWC, PC, SC, LegCo 1995–1997, PL, LegCo 1998–2004, and 10th NPC.

Eddie Chu (朱凱廸 b. 1977). Social activist. Land Justice League, won a seat to LegCo in 2016.

Chung Shui Ming (鍾瑞明 b. 1951). Bank director, senior researcher for Xinhua News Agency, Chief Executive of Government Land Fund, Member of Sino-British Land Commission. DAB, ExCo 1997–2002, and 11th to 12th CPPCCs.

Chung Sze Yuen (鍾士元 b. 1917). LegCo 1968–1978, ExCo 1972–1988, HKAA, PC, and ExCo 1997–1999.

Lydia Dunn (鄧蓮如 b. 1940). Senior executive with the Swire Group, and the senior member of ExCo under David Wilson and Chris Patten. She left Hong Kong after 1997 to live in London.

Rita Fan (范徐麗泰 b. 1942). ExCo under David Wilson but was not reappointed by Chris Patten. She resigned her appointed seat in LegCo and established close ties with China serving on the 9th and 10th NPCs. She served on the PL, then was elected via the Election Committee before standing for direct election in 2004. LegCo President from 2000 to 2008. She did not seek re-election, but became a Vice-Chairperson of 11th to 12th NPCs.

Joseph Fok (霍兆剛 b. 1962). Court of Appeal judge.

Nellie Fong (方黃吉雯 b. 1949). LegCo 1988–1991, HKAA, PWC, PC, and ExCo 1997–2002 and 10th to 12th CPPCCs.

Frederick Fung (馮檢基 b. 1953). Hong Kong Association for Democracy and People's Livelihood. BLCC, and PC, LegCo 1991–1997, PL, and LegCo 2000–2016.

Arthur Garcia (賈施雅 b. 1924). High Court judge.

Albert Ho (何俊仁 b. 1951). Solicitor. DP and Chairman 2006–2012, LegCo 1995–1997 and 1998–2016. Ran in Chief Executive selection in 2012.

Ip Kwok Him (葉國謙 b. 1951). DAB, LegCo 1995–1997, PL, LegCo 1998–2004 and 2006–2016, and 10th to 12th NPCs.

Regina Ip (葉劉淑儀 b. 1950). Secretary for Security until 2003. Ran in LegCo 2007 by-election and lost to Anson Chan but won in 2008. Founded New People's Party in 2011. Ran in 2017 Chief Executive selection but failed to get enough nominations. ExCo 2012 to present.

Kan Yuet Keung (簡悅強 1913–2012). LegCo 1961–1972 and ExCo 1966–1980. Travelled to Beijing with Murray MacLehose in 1979 and met Deng Xiaoping.

Robert Kotewall (羅旭和 1849–1949). Worked closely with Chow Shouson during the strike-boycott of 1925–1926 to advise the Hong Kong government. He was appointed to ExCo in 1936 when Chow stepped down.

Biographies

Jeffrey Lam (林健鋒 b. 1951). Businessman. Formerly LP, BPA, LegCo 2004 to present, ExCo 2012 to present.

Peggy Lam (林貝聿嘉 b. 1928). District Council 1985-2003, LegCo 1988-1995, PWC, PC, SC, PL, and Chairman, Hong Kong Federation of Women.

Ambrose Lau (劉漢銓 b. 1947). HKPA, HKAA, PWC, PC, LegCo 1995-1997, PL, LegCo 1998-2004, 9th to 12th CPPCCs.

Emily Lau (劉慧卿 b. 1952). Journalist. Founder member of the Frontier, which merged with the DP in 2009 and was a Vice-Chairperson before becoming Chairperson (2012-2016). LegCo 1991-1997 and 1998-2016.

Lau Chin Shek (劉千石 b. 1944). Unionist. LegCo 1991-1997 and 1998-2008.

Lau Wong Fat (劉皇發 1946-2017). Heung Yee Kuk, HKAA, BLDC, PWC, PC, LegCo 1985-1997, PL, LegCo 1998-2016, ExCo 2009-2012, 10th and 11th CPPCCs.

Fanny Law (羅范椒芬 b. 1953). Permanent Secretary, Education and Manpower Bureau until 2007. ExCo 2012 to present. Member of 11th to 12th NPC.

Allen Lee (李鵬飛 b. 1940). Businessman. Former LP member and founding Chairman. LegCo 1978-1997, and 1998-2000, HKAA, PC, PL 1997-1998, ExCo 1985-1992, and 9th to 10th NPCs.

Martin Lee (李柱銘 b. 1938). Barrister. Founding Chairman of DP. BLDC (until 1989), LegCo 1991-1997 and 1998-2008.

Richard Charles Lee (利銘澤 1905-1983). ExCo and LegCo.

Lee Wing Tat (李永達 b. 1955). Social activist. DP, BLCC, LegCo 1991-1997 and 1998-2012.

Alan Leong (梁家傑 b. 1958). Barrister. Chairman of Civic Party since 2016. LegCo 2004-2012. He ran against Donald Tsang in the 2007 Chief Executive selection.

Antony Leung (梁錦松 b. 1952). Banker. PC, ExCo 1997-2002. Financial Secretary 2002-2003.

Elsie Leung (梁愛詩 b. 1939). Solicitor. DAB, HKAA, Guangdong Provincial People's Congress 1983-1988, SC and Secretary for Justice 1997-2005.

Leung Kwok Hung (梁國雄 b. 1956). League of Social Democrats. LegCo 2004-2016. He retained his seat in 2016 but was disqualified due to improper oath taking.

Andrew Li (李國能 b. 1948). A reporter during the 1967 riots, who became a barrister and then Chief Justice of the HKSAR, 1997-2010.

Li Kwan Ha (李君夏 b. 1937). Retired Police Commissioner. 10th CPPCC.

Simon Li (李福善 1922-2013). Appeal Court judge. HKAA, BLDC, PWC, and PC. Ran in first Chief Executive selection.

Donald Liao (廖本懷 b. 1929). Civil servant, held posts as Secretary for Housing, and Secretary for Home Affairs, HKAA.

Benjamin Liu (廖子明 b. 1931): High Court judge.

Lo Tak Shing (T. S. Lo 羅德丞 1935-2006). Solicitor. LegCo 1974-1985, ExCo 1980-1985, BLCC, and 10th CPPCC.

Roger Lobo (羅保 1923-2015). LegCo 1972-1985 and ExCo 1978-1985.

Geoffrey Ma (馬道立 b. 1956). Chief Justice since 2010.

Ma Lik (馬力 1952-2007). DAB, HKAA, Deputy Secretary General BLCC, SC, LegCo 2004-2007, and 9th NPC.

Siu Sin Por (邵善波 b. 1949). HKAA, Deputy Secretary General PC, SC, Head of Central Policy Unit 2012-2017, and several CPPCCs.

Szeto Wah (司徒華 1931–2011). Teacher and former head of the Professional Teachers' Union. Chairman of Hong Kong Alliance in Support of Patriotic Democratic Movements in China. BLDC (resigned in 1989), LegCo 1985–1997 and 1998–2004.
Maria Tam (譚惠珠 b. 1945). Barrister. DAB, LegCo 1981–1991 and ExCo 1983–1991, BLDC, HKPA, Basic Law Committee, 9th to 12th NPCs.
Tam Yiu Chung (譚耀宗 b. 1949). FTU, DAB, HKAA, BLDC, PWC, PC, PL, LegCo 1998–2016, ExCo 1997–2002, 10th to 12th CPPCCs.
Henry Tang (唐英年 b. 1952). Son of industrialist Tang Hsiang Chien (唐翔千, BLCC). 7th to 9th CPPCCs, LP, LegCo 1991–1997 and 1998–2002 and PL. Secretary for Commerce, Industry and Technology 2002–2004, Financial Secretary 2004–2007, and Chief Secretary 2007–2011. He ran for Chief Executive in 2012 and lost.
James Tien (田北俊 b. 1947). Son of Francis Tien. Chairman of LP succeeding Allen Lee (and resigned as Chairman after the 2008 LegCo election due to the party's poor results), BLCC, LegCo 1993–1997, PL, LegCo 1998–2008, ExCo 2002–2003, 10th to 11th CPPCCs, and LegCo 2012–2016.
Michael Tien (田北辰 b. 1950). Son of Francis Tien. Resigned from LP, joined New People's Party but resigned in 2017 and created Roundtable, LegCo 2012 to present, 11th to 12th NPCs.
Tsang Lai Yu (曾勵予). Sister of Tsang Yok Sing and Tsang Tak Shing, was jailed for a month for participating in the riots in 1967.
Tsang Tak Shing (曾德成 b. 1949). Chief Editor of *Ta Kung Pao* in 1988 before joining the HKSAR government's Central Policy Unit in 1998. Secretary for Home Affairs 2007–2015, and 7th to 10th NPCs.
Tsang Yok Sing (曾鈺成 b. 1947). Teacher. DAB founding Chairman (until 2003). Guangdong Provincial People's Congress 1983–1988, HKAA, PWC, PC, PL, LegCo 1998–2016, and President 2008-20-16, ExCo 2002–2008, 8th NPC, and 10th to 11th CPPCCs.
Elsie (Elliot) Tu (杜葉錫恩 1913–2015). Urban Councillor. BLCC, LegCo 1988–1997, SC, PL 1997–1998.
Joseph Wong (王永平 b. 1948). Secretary for Civil Service (2000–2006) and then Secretary for Commerce, Industry and Technology (2006–2007) before retiring.
Wong Kwok Hing (王國興 b. 1949). FTU, DAB, LegCo 2004–2016.
Philip Wong (黃宜弘 b. 1938). HKAA, BLCC, LegCo 1991–1997, PL, LegCo 1998–2012, and 9th to 10th NPCs.
Wong Po Yan (黃保欣 b. 1923). Businessman. LegCo 1979–1988, HKAA, BLDC, BLCC, PWC, PC, SC, and 9th NPC.
Wilfred Wong (王英偉 b. 1952). Former Deputy Secretary, Civil Service Branch and Managing Director of Shui On Holdings Ltd. Member of BLCC, PWC, PC, 9th to 11th NPCs
Woo Kwok Hing (胡國興 b. 1946). Retired judge. Ran for Chief Executive selection in 2017.
Alex Wu (吳樹熾 1920–2005). Businessman. LegCo 1975–1985, and HKAA.
T. L. Yang (楊鐵樑 b. 1929). Chief Justice 1988–1996, BLCC and ExCo 1997–2002. Ran in first Chief Executive selection.

Others

Louis Cha (查良鏞 b. 1924). Famous author, founder, and former publisher of *Ming Pao*. BLDC, BLCC, PC.

Chen Duxiu (陳獨秀 1879–1942). An intellectual and founder of the CCP.

Chen Jianping (陳建平). Known to be Lu Ping's protégé and a former correspondent of Hong Kong's *Wen Wei Po* stationed in Beijing. A medium-level cadre, Chen acted as liaison between Tung Chee Hwa and the Hong Kong and Macao Affairs Office. He stayed on to serve Donald Tsang, promoted to be Senior Special Assistant by C. Y. Leung, and continues to serve Carrie Lam.

Chen Jiongming (陳炯明 1878–1933). The head of the Guangdong administration and a rival of Sun Yat-sen.

Percy Chen (陳丕士 1901–1989). In 1947, he established a private law practice in Hong Kong as a barrister. In 1956, he founded the Marco Polo Club. He was invited to witness the signing of the Sino-British Joint Declaration in 1984. Member of the 6th CPPCC.

Cheng Wing Kin (鄭永健). Convicted for offering bribes to District Council election candidates in 2915.

Chiang Kai-shek (蔣介石 1887–1975). When Sun Yat-sen died in 1925, Chiang took control of the KMT and became the overall leader of the Republic of China in 1928. He lost the civil war to the CCP and escaped to Taiwan.

Horace Chin Wan Kan (陳雲根 b. 1961). Also known as Chin Wan (陳雲). Author of various works advocating localism.

Ching Cheong (程翔 b. 1949). Vice-editorial manager of *Wen Wei Po*. After 4 June 1989, Ching resigned in protest and, with others, founded *Commentary*. In 1996, he joined the *Straits Times*. In 2005, he was detained on the Mainland charged with spying for Taiwan and sentenced to imprisonment for five years. He was released on 5 February 2008.

Tony Choi (蔡東豪 b. 1964). Founder of *House News* and *The Stand News*.

Alex Chow (李大釗 b. 1990). Student activist.

Fei Xiaotong (費孝通 1910–2005). Distinguished Chinese social scientist and anthropologist. BLDC Vice-Chairman.

Fei Yiming (費彝民 1908–1988). Publisher of *Ta Kung Pao*. BLDC Vice-Chairman and 2nd to 5th CPPCCs and 5th to 7th NPCs.

Fu Qi (傅奇). Famous movie star turned director and producer.

Franklin Charles Gimson (1890–1975). Colonial administrator, who briefly served as the Colonial Secretary of Hong Kong before the surrender to the Japanese on 25 December 1941. He established a short-lived provisional government after the liberation of Hong Kong.

Gu Zhenghong (顧正紅 1905–1925). A worker and CCP member who was killed on 15 May 1925 in Shanghai that sparked riots.

Gu Zhuoheng (谷卓恒). Chairman of Sing Pao Media Enterprises.

Cecil Harcourt (1892–1959). Rear Admiral. He received the surrender from the Japanese after the war.

He Xiangning (何香凝 1872–1972). A KMT official who broke with the nationalists and formed the KMT Revolutionary Committee in Hong Kong.

Hsueh Ping (薛平). A reporter at Xinhua News Agency sentenced to imprisonment during the 1967 riots.

Hu Sheng (胡繩 1918–2000). Director, Party Research Centre of the CCP Central Committee, and BLDC Vice-Chairman.

Jiang Zaizhong (姜在忠). Head of Ta Kung Wen Wai Media Group.

Lt. Donald W. Kerr. Member of the US Air Force, who was rescued after his aeroplane was shot down in 1944 in Hong Kong.

Ko Cheuk Hung (高卓雄 1902–1987). Chairman of the Hong Kong Chinese General Chamber of Commerce in the early 1950s. Early CPPCC member.

Wellington Koo (顧維鈞 1887–1985). Member of the Chinese delegation to the Paris Peace Conference in 1919. He was subsequently the Chinese Ambassador to Britain.

Lam Bun (林彬 1930–1967). A radio talk show host who was assassinated by a death squad of leftists in 1967.

Lam Wing Kee, Lee Bo, and other booksellers (林榮基 and 李波). The five staff of Mighty Current Publishing who went missing included Gui Minhai (桂民海), Lui Bo (呂波), and Cheung Jiping (張志平).

Nathan Law (羅冠聰 b. 1993). Student activist. Chairman of Demosistō, who won a seat to LegCo in 2016 but had his oath invalidated in 2017.

Lau Siu Lai (劉小麗 b. 1976). Lecturer. Founder of Democracy Groundwork, who won a seat to LegCo in 2016 but had her oath invalidated in 2017.

Baggio Leung Chung Hang (梁頌恆 b. 1986). Youngspiration candidate who won a seat to LegCo in 2016 but failed to take his oath.

Li Dazhao (李大釗 1888–1927). Founder of the CCP with Chen Duxiu.

Li Jichen (李濟深 1885–1959). A KMT high-ranking military official who broke with the nationalists and formed the KMT Revolutionary Committee in Hong Kong. He was appointed to the SCNPC in 1954.

Li Weimen (林偉民 1887–1927). A union leader who became a CCP member in the 1920s.

Li Zisong (李子誦). Former chief editor of *Wen Wei Po* in Hong Kong.

Lian Guan (連貫 1906–1991). A CCP leader in Hong Kong during the 1940s and the Secretary of the Eighth Route Army's party branch office in Hong Kong.

Liao Zhongkai (廖仲愷 1877–1925). A Hakka and the KMT's finance chief. He provided the CCP with considerable funds to support the Hong Kong strikers in Guangzhou during the strike-boycott of 1925–1926. Father of Liao Chengzhi and grandfather of Liao Hui.

Lin Junwei (林君蔚). School inspector with the Education Department, who together with Zhang Rendao (張仁道), a graduate of the well-known high school, Queen's College, and Li Yibao (李義保), a primary school teacher, founded *Zhenshanmei Magazine* (真善美雜誌) in 1920.

Ling Wanyan (凌宏仁). Headmaster of the left-wing Sai Kung Public School in the 1960s.

Liu Bocheng (劉伯承 1892–1986). Together with Deng Xiaoping, they gave an order to blockade the Yangtze, intending to hold the *Amethyst* at bay.

Liu Changle (劉長樂 b. 1951). Chairman of Phoenix Satellite Television Holdings Ltd. who, together with Chan Wing Kee, invested in ATV.

Lo Man Tuen (盧文端 b. 1948). DAB, Vice-Chairman of CPPCC'S foreign affairs sub-committee.

Henry Luk (陸海安). Editor of the right-wing newspaper *Chun Pao* (真報) during the 1960s.

Mak Hoi Wah (麥海華). Social activist and BLCC.

Mok Ying Kwai (莫應溎 1901–1997). Businessman from a prominent comprador family who became a committed CCP supporter and was appointed to the BLDC.

Ng Hong Man (吳康民 b. 1926). NPC from 4th NPC, BLCC, and HKAA.

Lt. Col. Lindsay Ride (1898–1977). With the help of Francis Lee Yiu Piu, who made arrangements with the guerrillas, Ride established the British Army Aid Group (BAAG) in South China to help escapees and to smuggle medicines into the POW camps in Hong Kong

Shi Hu (石慧). A famous "leftist" movie star in the 1960s.

Song Jiaoren (宋教仁 1882–1913). An anti-Qing revolutionary and a founder of the KMT together with Sun Yat-sen. He was assassinated.

Song Qingling (宋慶齡 1893–1981). Wife of Sun Yat-sen. She formed the Defend China League (保衛中國同盟) in Hong Kong in June 1938 and was quite successful in rallying support for the resistance.

Su Zhaozheng (蘇兆徵 1885–1929). A union leader who became a CCP member in the 1920s.

Suen Kai Cheong (孫啟昌 b. 1953). DAB, Member of Wanchai District Council 1991–1993, Urban Council 1994–1999, SC 1996–1997, Wanchai District Council 2000–2003. Lost the 2003 election and was an appointed District Councillor in Wanchai in 2007.

Sun Yat-Sen (孫中山 1866–1925). Founder of the KMT and considered father of the revolution by both the KMT and CCP.

Benny Tai (戴耀廷 b. 1964). Legal scholar who came up with the idea of Occupy Central with Love and Peace in 2013.

Tang Bingda (湯秉達). A key committee member of the Anti-Persecution Committee.

Edward Tyrer. Hong Kong's Police Commissioner who was replaced in July 1967.

Liza Wang (汪明荃 b. 1947). Singer and entertainer. Member of the 7th to 11th CPPCCs.

Wong Jo Fun. Principal of Chung Wah Middle School who was arrested and detained during the 1967 riots.

Joshua Wong (黃之鋒 b. 1996). Student activist. Founder of Scholarism, and General Secretary of Demosistō.

Xi Yang (席揚). Reporter for *Ming Pao* who was convicted of trafficking financial state secrets in 1993. A banker, Tian Ye, was convicted of passing financial state secrets to Xi Yang.

Xu Simin (徐四民 1914–2007). Chairman of *The Mirror*. Member of BLCC, HKAA, PWC, PC, SC 1996–1999, 5th to 9th CPPCCs.

Yau Wai Ching (游蕙禎 b. 1991). Youngspiration candidate who won a seat to LegCo in 2016 but failed to take her oath.

Yeung Kwong (楊光). FTU leader and chairman of Hong Kong–Kowloon All Sectors Anti-Persecution Committee.

Edward Yiu (姚松炎 b. 1964). Surveyor. He won a seat to LegCo in 2016 but had his oath invalidated in 2017.

Zhang Xueliang (張學良 1900–2001). Warlord of Manchuria who kidnapped Chiang Kai-shek on 12 December 1936.

Bibliography

Rola Luzzatto and Rennie Remedios, *Hong Kong Whos Who: An Almanac of Personalities and Their Histories, 1958–1960*.

Rola Luzzatto and Joseph Walker, *Hong Kong Whos Who: An Almanac of Personalities and Their Comprehensive Histories, 1970–1973*.

"Who's Who", *South China Morning Post*, 1979.

Who's Who in Hong Kong, Database Publishing, 1984 edition.

Who's Who in Hong Kong, Hoi Nam Publishing, 1997.

Whos Who in the HKSAR, PA Professional Consultants Ltd., 2001.

Who's Who in the HKSAR, Sing Tao Publishing Ltd., 2004.

Web research using Basic Law Collection (Basic Law Library), Google, and Baidu.

Bibliography

Books

Allen, Jamie. *Seeing Red: China's Uncompromising Takeover of Hong Kong*. Singapore: Butterworth-Heinemann Asia, 1997.

Akers-Jones, David. *Feeling the Stones: Reminiscences by David Akers-Jones*. Hong Kong: Hong Kong University Press, 2004.

Ash, Robert. *Hong Kong in Transition: The Handover Years*. New York: Palgrave Publishers, 2000.

Barnouin, Barbara, and Yu Changgen. *Zhou Enlai: A Political Life*. Hong Kong: Chinese University Press, 2006.

Bickers, Robert, and Ray Yep, eds. *May Days in Hong Kong: Riot and Emergency in 1967*. Hong Kong: Hong Kong University Press, 2009.

Bland, Ben. *Generation HK*. Hawthorn, Australia: Penguin Books, 2017.

Blyth, Sally, and Ian Wotherspoon. *Hong Kong Remembers*. Hong Kong: Oxford University Press, 1996.

Bonavia, David. *Hong Kong 1997: The Final Settlement*. Hong Kong: South China Morning Post, 1985.

Brady, Anne-Marie. *Marketing Dictatorship: Propaganda and Thought Work in Contemporary China*. Lanham, MD: Rowman and Littlefield, 2008.

Bray, Denis. *Hong Kong Metamorphosis*. Hong Kong: Hong Kong University Press, 2001.

Burns, John P. *The Chinese Communist Party Nomenklatura System: A Documentary Study of Party Control of Leadership Selection*. New York: M. E. Sharpe, 1989.

Butler, Rohan, and M. E. Pelly, and assisted by J. J. Yasame. *Documents on British Policy Overseas: Series 1*, Volume 8. London: H.M.S.O., 1984.

Carroll, John M. *A Concise History of Hong Kong*. Hong Kong: Hong Kong University Press, 2007.

Carroll, John M. *Edge of Empires: Chinese Elites and British Colonials in Hong Kong*. Hong Kong: Hong Kong University Press, 2007.

Chan Lau, Kit-ching. *From Nothing to Nothing: The Chinese Communist Movement and Hong Kong 1921–1936*. Hong Kong: Hong Kong University Press, 1999.

Chan, Ming K., ed. *Precarious Balance: Hong Kong between China and Britain 1842–1992*. Hong Kong: Hong Kong University Press, 1994.

Chan, Ming K., and Alvin Y. So, eds. *Crisis and Transformation in China's Hong Kong*. Hong Kong: Hong Kong University Press, 2002.

Chan, Sui-jeung. *East River Column: Hong Kong Guerrillas in the Second World War and After*. Hong Kong: Hong Kong University Press, 2009.
Chang, Jung, and Jon Halliday. *Mao: The Unknown Story*. London: Jonathan Cape, 2005.
Cheng, Joseph Y. S., ed. *The July 1 Protest Rally: Interpreting a Historic Event*. Hong Kong: City University of Hong Kong Press, 2005.
Cheng, Joseph Y. S. *New Trends of Political Participation in Hong Kong*. Hong Kong: City University of Hong Kong Press, 2014.
Cheung, Gary. *Hong Kong's Watershed: The 1967 Riots*. Hong Kong: Hong Kong University Press, 2009.
Ching, Cheong. *My 1,000 Days Ordeal: A Patriot's Torture*. Singapore: Straits Times Press, 2012.
Chow, Tse-Tsung. *The May 4th Movement: Intellectual Revolution in Modern China, 1915–1924*. Cambridge, MA: Harvard University Press, 1963.
Chung, Sze-yuen. *Hong Kong's Journey to Reunification: Memoirs of Sze-yuen Chung*. Hong Kong: Chinese University Press, 2001.
Cooper, John. *Colony in Conflict: The Hong Kong Disturbances, May 1967–January 1968*. Hong Kong: Swindon Book Company, 1970.
Cottrell, Robert. *The End of Hong Kong: The Secret Diplomacy of Imperial Retreat*. London: John Murray, 1993.
Cradock, Percy. *Experiences of China*. London: John Murray, 1994.
Deng, Xiaoping. *Deng Xiaoping on 'One Country, Two Systems'*. Hong Kong: Joint Publishing, 2005.
Deng, Xiaoping. *Selected Works of Deng Xiaoping 1975–1982*. Beijing: Foreign Languages Press, 1984.
Dimbleby, Jonathan. *The Last Governor*. London: Little, Brown and Company, 1997.
Faure, David. *Colonialism and the Hong Kong Mentality*. Hong Kong: Hong Kong University Press, 2003.
Faure, David, ed. *A Documentary History of Hong Kong: Society*. Hong Kong: Hong Kong University Press, 1997.
Gao, Wenqian. *Zhou Enlai: The Last Perfect Revolutionary: A Biography*. New York: PublicAffairs, 2007.
Gillingham, Paul. *At the Peak: Hong Kong between the Wars*. London: Macmillan, 1983.
Goodstadt, Leo F. *Profits, Politics and Panics: Hong Kong's Banks and the Making of a Miracle Economy, 1935–1985*. Hong Kong: Hong Kong University Press, 2007.
Goodstadt, Leo F. *Uneasy Partners: The Conflict between Public Interest and Private Profit in Hong Kong*. Hong Kong: Hong Kong University Press, 2005.
Grantham, Alexander. *Via Ports: From Hong Kong to Hong Kong*. Hong Kong: Hong Kong University Press, 1965.
Greenwood, John. *Hong Kong's Link to the US Dollar: Origins and Evolution*. Hong Kong: Hong Kong University Press, 2008.
Groot, Gerry. *Managing Transitions: The Chinese Communist Party, United Front Work, Corporatism, and Hegemony*. New York and London: Routledge, 2004.
He, Qinglian. *The Fog of Censorship: Media Control in China*. New York: Human Rights in China, 2008.

Hong Kong Observers. *Pressure Points: A Social Critique by The Hong Kong Observers*. 2nd edition. Hong Kong: Summerson (HK) Research Centre, Summerson Eastern Publishers Ltd., 1983.
Hu, Sheng. *A Concise History of the Communist Party of China*. Beijing: Foreign Languages Press, 1994.
Huang, Yasheng. *Capitalism with Chinese Characteristics*. Cambridge: Cambridge University Press, 2008.
Hughes, Richard. *Borrowed Place, Borrowed Time*. 2nd edition. London: Andre Deutsche, 1976.
Hutchings, Graham. *Modern China: A Companion to a Rising Power*. London: Penguin Books, 2000.
Jowatt, G. S., and V. O'Donnell. *Propaganda and Persuasion*. Beverley Hills: Sage, 1986.
King, Ambrose Y. C., and Rance P. L. Lee, eds. *Social Life and Development in Hong Kong*. Hong Kong: Chinese University Press, 1981.
Ladany, Laszlo. *The Communist Party of China and Marxism 1921–1985: A Self-Portrait*. London: C. Hurst and Company, 1988.
Lai, Carol P. *Media in Hong Kong: Press Freedom and Political Change 1967–2005*. Oxford: Routledge, 2007.
Lane, Kevin P. *Sovereignty and the Status Quo: The Historical Roots of China's Hong Kong Policy*. Boulder, CO: Westview Press, 1990.
Lardy, Nicholas. *Markets over Mao: The Rise of Private Business in China*. Washington DC: Petersen Institute for International Economics, 2014.
Lary, Diana. *China's Republic*. Cambridge: Cambridge University Press, 2007.
Lau, Siu-kai, and Louie Kin-Shuen, eds. *Hong Kong Tried Democracy: The 1991 Elections in Hong Kong*. Hong Kong: Chinese University Press; Hong Kong Institute of Asia-Pacific Studies, 1993.
Lenin, Vladimir. *What Is to Be Done?* Vol. 5. Moscow: Foreign Languages Publishing House, 1961.
Leong, Sow-Theng. *Sino-Soviet Diplomatic Relations 1917–1926*. Honolulu: University Press of Hawai'i, 1976.
Li, Kwok-sing. *A Glossary of Political Terms of the People's Republic of China*. Hong Kong: Chinese University Press, 1995.
Lieberthal, Kenneth. *Governing China: From Revolution through Reform*. New York: W. W. Norton, 2004.
Lifton, Robert Jay. *Thought Reform and the Psychology of Totalism: A Study of "Brainwashing" in China*. Chapel Hill: University of North Carolina Press, 1989.
Lilley, James. *China Hands: Nine Decades of Adventure, Espionage, and Diplomacy in Asia*. New York: Public Affairs, 2004.
Lindsay, Oliver. *The Battle for Hong Kong 1941–1945: Hostage to Fortune*. Hong Kong: Hong Kong University Press, 2005.
Liu, Shuyong. *An Outline History of Hong Kong*. Beijing: Foreign Languages Press, 1997.
Lo, Shiu-hing Sonny. *Competing Chinese Political Visions: Hong Kong vs. Beijing on Democracy*. Santa Barbara, CA: Praeger, 2010.
Lo, Shiu-hing Sonny. *The Dynamics of Beijing–Hong Kong Relations: A Model for Taiwan?* Hong Kong: Hong Kong University Press, 2008.

Lo, Shiu-hing Sonny. *Governing Hong Kong: Legitimacy, Communication and Political Decay.* New York: Nova Science Publishers Inc., 2001.
Lo, Shiu-hing Sonny. *The Politics of Democratization in Hong Kong.* London: Macmillan, 1997.
Loh, Christine. *Being Here: Shaping a Preferred Future.* Hong Kong: South China Morning Post, 2006.
Loh, Christine, and Civic Exchange, eds. *Functional Constituencies: A Unique Feature of the Hong Kong Legislative Council.* Hong Kong: Hong Kong University Press, 2006.
Loh, Christine, and Carine Lai. *Reflections of Leadership: Tung Chee Hwa and Donald Tsang 1997–2007.* Hong Kong: Civic Exchange, 2007.
Ma, Jisen. *The Cultural Revolution in the Foreign Ministry of China.* Hong Kong: Chinese University Press, 2004.
Ma, Ngok. *Political Development in Hong Kong: State, Political Society, and Civil Society.* Hong Kong: Hong Kong University Press, 2007.
MacFarquhar, Roderick, and Michael Schoenhals. *Mao's Last Revolution.* Cambridge, MA: Harvard University Press, 2006.
Macmillan, Margaret. *Paris 1919: Six Months That Changed the World.* New York: Random House, 2002.
Macmillan, Margaret. *Seize the Hour: When Nixon Met Mao.* London: John Murray, 2006.
Mann, James. *The China Fantasy: Why Capitalism Will Not Bring Democracy to China.* Seattle, WA Penguin, 2008.
Mao, Zedong. *On Guerrilla Warfare.* Baltimore: Nautical and Aviation, 1992.
Mao, Zedong. *Selected Works of Mao Tse-tung.* Beijing: Foreign Languages Press, 1961.
Mark, Chi-Kwan. *Hong Kong and the Cold War: Anglo-American Relations 1949–1957.* Oxford: Oxford University Press, 2004.
Miners, Norman. *The Government and Politics of Hong Kong.* 5th edition. Hong Kong: Oxford University Press, 2000.
Miners, Norman. *Hong Kong under Imperial Rule 1912–1941.* Hong Kong: Oxford University Press, 1987.
Ng, Jason Y. *Umbrellas in Bloom: Hong Kong Occupy Movement Uncovered.* Hong Kong: Blacksmith Books, 2016.
Nyaw, Mee-kau, and Li Si-ming, eds. *The Other Hong Kong Report 1996.* Hong Kong: Chinese University Press, 1996.
Pei, Minxin. *China's Trapped Transition: The Limits of Developmental Autocracy.* Cambridge, MA: Harvard University Press, 2006.
Pike, Fredrick B., and Thomas Stritch, eds. *The New Corporatism: Social-Political Structures in the Iberian World.* Notre Dame: University of Notre Dame Press, 1974.
Pye, Lucian W. *China: An Introduction.* 2nd edition. New York: Little, Brown and Company, 1978.
Qian, Qichen. *Ten Episodes in China's Diplomacy.* New York: HarperCollins, 2005.
Roberti, Mark. *The Fall of Hong Kong: China's Triumph & Britain's Betrayal.* New York: John Wiley and Sons, 1994.
Saward, Michael. *Co-optive Politics and State Legitimacy.* Aldershot: Dartmouth, 1992.
Schmitter, Phillipe C., and Gerhard Lehmbruch, eds. *Trends towards Corporatist Intermediation.* Beverly Hills: Sage Publications, 1979.

Scott, Ian. *Political Change and the Crisis of Legitimacy in Hong Kong*. Hong Kong: Oxford University Press, 1989.
Scott, Ian. *Public Administration in Hong Kong: Regime Change and Its Impact on the Public Sector*. Singapore: Marshall Cavendish International, 2005.
Share, Michael. *Where Empires Collided: Russian and Soviet Relations with Hong Kong, Taiwan, and Macao*. Hong Kong: Chinese University Press, 2007.
Smart, Alan. *The Shek Kip Mei Myth: Squatters, Fires and Colonial Rule in Hong Kong, 1950–1963*. Hong Kong, Hong Kong University Press, 2006.
Snow, Philip. *The Fall of Hong Kong: Britain, China and the Japanese Occupation*. New Haven: Yale University Press, 2003.
So, Alvin Y. *Hong Kong's Embattled Democracy: A Societal Analysis*. Baltimore: Johns Hopkins University Press, 1999.
Sun Yat-sen. *San Min Chu I: The Three Principles of the People*. Taipei: Government Information Office, 1990.
Tang, James Tuck-Hong. *Britain's Encounter with Revolutionary China 1949–1954*. London: Macmillan, 1992.
Thatcher, Margaret. *Downing Street Years*. New York: HarperCollins, 1993.
Tsang, Steve. *Democracy Shelved: Great Britain, China and Attempts at Constitutional Reform in Hong Kong 1945–1952*. Hong Kong: Oxford University Press, 1988.
Tsang, Steve. *Governing Hong Kong: Administrative Officers from the Nineteenth Century to the Handover to China*. Hong Kong: Hong Kong University Press, 2007.
Tsang, Steve. *Hong Kong: Appointment with China*. London and New York: I.B. Tauris, 1997.
Tsang, Steve, ed. *Judicial Independence and the Rule of Law in Hong Kong*. Hong Kong: Hong Kong University Press, 2001.
Tsang, Steve. *A Modern History of Hong Kong*. Hong Kong: Hong Kong University Press, 2004.
Tsang, Yok Sing, *Tsang Yok Sing Straight Talk: A Collection of Essays on Hong Kong Affairs*. Hong Kong: Cosmos Books Ltd., 1995.
Uhalley, Stephen, Jr. *A History of the Chinese Communist Party*. Stanford: Hoover Institution Press, 1988.
Van Slyke, Lyman P. *Enemies and Friends: The United Front in Chinese Communist History*. Stanford: Stanford University Press, 1967.
Welsh, Frank. *A History of Hong Kong*. Updated edition. London: Harper Collins, 1997.
Wilson, Dick. *Chou: The Story of Zhou Enlai 1898–1976*. London: Hutchison, 1984.
Worthing, Peter. *A Military History of Modern China: From the Manchu Conquest to Tian'anmen Square*. Westport and London: Praeger Security International, 2007.
Xiao, Weiyun. *One Country, Two Systems: An Account of the Drafting of the Hong Kong Basic Law*. Beijing: Peking University Press, 2001.
Yeung, Chris, ed. *Hong Kong China: The Red Dawn*. Sydney: Prentice Hall, 1998.
Yeung, Yue-man, ed. *The First Decade: The Hong Kong SAR in Retrospective and Introspective Perspectives*. Hong Kong: Chinese University Press, 2007.
Zhou, Enlai. *Selected Works of Zhou Enlai*, Vol. 1. Beijing: Foreign Languages Press, 1981.

Journals, Manuscripts, Transcripts, and Reports

Aston, S. R. "Keeping a Foot in the Door: Britain's China Policy: 1945–1950". *Diplomacy and Statecraft* 15, no. 1 (2004): 79–94.
Brodsgaard, Erik. "Improving Party Cadre System to Better Govern China". *East Asia Institute EAI Bulletin* (September 2001). Singapore: National University of Singapore.
Brown, Stephen, Edward Fung, Christine Loh, Kylie Uebergang, and Steven Xu. *The Budget and Public Finance in Hong Kong*. Hong Kong: Civic Exchange, March 2003.
Burns, John P. "The Role of the New China News Agency and Chain's Policy Towards Hong Kong". In "Hong Kong and China in Transition", *Canada and Hong Kong Papers* No. 3, 17–60. Toronto: Joint Centre for Asia Pacific Studies, 1994.
Burns, John P. "Hong Kong in 1992: Struggle for Authority". *Asian Survey* 33, no. 1 (January 1993): 22–31.
Burns, John P. "The Structure of the Chinese Communist Party Control in Hong Kong". *Asian Survey* 30, no. 8 (August 1990): 749–63.
Burns, John P. "Strengthening Central CCP Control of Leadership Selection: The 1990 Nomenklatura". *The China Quarterly* no. 138 (June 1994): 458–91.
Cai, Yongshun. "Managing NGOs in China". *China Policy Institute Analysis*. 2017. https://cpianalysis.org/2017/02/17/managing-ngos-in-china/.
Catron, Gary. "Hong Kong and Chinese Foreign Policy, 1955–60". *The China Quarterly* no. 51 (July–September 1972): 405–24.
Cervik, Serhan, and Correa-Caro, Caroline. "Growing (Un)equal: Fiscal Policy and Income Inequality in China and BRIC+". International Monetary Fund (IMF Working Paper March 2015) WP15/68.
Chan, Alex. "From Propaganda to Hegemony: *Jiaodian Fangtan* and China's Media Policy". *Journal of Contemporary China* 11, no. 30 (2002): 35–51.
Chan Lau Kit-Ching. "The Perception of Chinese Communism in Hong Kong 1921–1934". *The China Quarterly* no. 164 (December 2000): 1044–61.
Chan, Ming K. "Labor and Empire: The Chinese Labor Movement in the Canton Delta 1895–1927". Doctoral dissertation, Stanford University, 1975.
Cheng, Jie. "The Story of a New Policy". *Hong Kong Journal* (Fall 2009). http://www.hkjournal.org/archive/2009_fall/1.htm.
Cheng, Joseph Y. S. "Prospects for Democracy in Hong Kong after the Beijing Massacre". *The Australian Journal of Chinese Affairs* no. 23 (January 1990): 161–85.
Cheng, Joseph Y. S., and Emile K. K. Yeoh, eds. "From Handover to Occupy Campaign: Democracy, Identity and the Umbrella Movement". *Contemporary Chinese Political Economy and Strategic Relations: An International Journal* 2, no. 2 (August/September 2016).
Cheung, Anthony B. L., and Paul C. W. Wong, "Who Advised the Hong Kong Government? The Politics of Absorption before and after 1997". *Asian Survey* 44, no. 6 (2004): 874–94.
Chinese University of Hong Kong. Public Opinion and Political Development in Hong Kong, Survey Result. Press Release. Centre for Communication and Public Opinion Survey. 24 July 2016.
Chu, Cindy Yik-Yi. "The Origins of the Chinese Communist Alliance with the Business Elite in Hong Kong: The 1997 Question and the Basic Law Committees, 1979–1985". *Modern Chinese History Society of Hong Kong Bulletin* nos. 9–10 (October 1999): 51–67.

Chu, Cindy Yik-Yi. "Overt and Covert Functions of the Hong Kong Branch of the Xinhua News Agency, 1947–1984". *The Historian* 62, no. 1 (Fall 1999): 31–46.

Chung, Lu Cee Rosemarie. "Study of the 1925-26 Canton-Hong Kong Strike-Boycott". Master's thesis, University of Hong Kong, 1969.

Dicks, Anthony. "Treaty, Grant, Usage or Sufferance? Some Legal Aspects of the Status of Hong Kong". *The China Quarterly* no. 95 (September 1983): 427–55.

Fong, Brian C. H. "In-between Liberal Authoritarianism and Electoral Authoritarianism: Hong Kong's Democratization under Chinese Sovereignty, 1997–2016". *Democratization*. 2016. http://dx.doi.org/10.1080/13510347.2016.1232249.

Fong, Brian C. H. "One Country, Two Nationalisms: Center-Periphery Relations between Mainland China and Hong Kong, 1997–2016". *Modern China* (2017). http://journals.sagepub.com/doi/abs/10.1177/0097700417691470.

Fu, H. L., and Richard Cullen. "Political Policing in Hong Kong". *Hong Kong Law Journal* (2003): 199–230.

Fung, Edmund. "The Sino-British Rapprochement, 1927–1931". *Modern Asian Studies* 17, no. 1 (1983): 79–105.

Goodman, David. "Why China's Middle Class Supports the Communist Party". *Huffington Post*. 2013.

Goodstadt, Leo F. "China and the Selection of Hong Kong's Post-Colonial Political Elite". *The China Quarterly* 163 (September 2000): 721–41.

The Group of 89. *A Proposal for the Future Structure of the Hong Kong SAR Government* (September 1987).

Heaton, William. "Maoist Revolutionary Strategy and Modern Colonialism: The Cultural Revolution in Hong Kong". *Asian Survey* 10, no. 9 (September 1970): 840–57.

Hong Kong Commission of Inquiry. *Kowloon Disturbances 1966*. Hong Kong: Government Printer, 1967.

Hong Kong Government. *The Face of Confrontation*. Hong Kong: Government Printer, 1968.

Hong Kong Government. *Hong Kong Disturbances 1967: Report of Commission of Inquiry*. Hong Kong: Government Printer, 1967.

Hong Kong Government. *Hong Kong: Report for the Year 1967*. Hong Kong: Government Printer, 1968.

Hong Kong Government. *Hong Kong Yearbook 1967*. Hong Kong: Government Printer, 1967.

Hong Kong Government. *White Paper: District Administration in Hong Kong*. Hong Kong: Government Printer, 1981.

Hong Kong Government. *White Paper: The Further Development of Representative Government in Hong Kong*. Hong Kong: Government Printer, 1984.

Hong Kong Journalists Association. "Dark Clouds on the Horizon: Hong Kong's Freedom of Expression Faces New Threats". *Annual Report*. 2013.

Hong Kong Journalists Association. "Grave Threats to Freedom of Expression in Hong Kong". *Annual Report*. 2014.

Hong Kong Journalists Association. "The Ground Rules Change: Freedom of Expression in Hong Kong Two Years after the Handover to China". *Annual Report*. 1999.

Hong Kong Journalists Association. "One Country, Two Nightmares: Hong Kong Media Caught in Ideological Battleground". *Annual Report*. 2016.

Hong Kong Journalists Association. "Rising Nationalism: A Potential Threat to Hong Kong's Freedom of Expression". *Annual Report*. 2008.

Hong Kong Journalists Association. "Shrinking Margins: Freedom of Expression in Hong Kong Since 1997". *Annual Report*. 2007.
Hong Kong Journalists Association. "Two Systems under Siege: Beijing Turns the Screws on Hong Kong". *Annual Report*. 2017.
Hong Kong Legislative Council. "The Hong Kong Garrison of the Chinese People's Liberation Army". Research Division Information Note. 17 January 2011.
Hong Kong Legislative Council. LC Paper No. CB(2) 629/98-99(02) Panel of Constitutional Affairs. 2002.
Hong Kong Transition Project. "Constitutional Reform: Confrontation Looms as Hong Kong Consults". April 2014. http://hktp.org/list/constitutional-reform.pdf.
Hopkinson, Lisa, and Mandy Man Lei Lao. *Rethinking the Small House Policy*. Hong Kong: Civic Exchange, 2003.
Information Office of the State Council. *The Practice of the "One Country, Two Systems" Policy in the Hong Kong Special Administrative Region*. June 2014.
Kan, Karita. "Lessons in Patriotism". *China Perspectives*, no. 2012/4: 63–69.
King, Ambrose. "Administrative Absorption of Politics in Hong Kong: Emphasis on the Grass Roots Levels". *Asian Survey* 15, no. 5 (May 1975): 422–39.
KMT National People's Convention Manifesto Concerning the Abrogation of Unequal Treaties, 1931.
Kwong, Hoi Ying. "Party-Group Relations in Hong Kong: Comparing the DAB and the DP". Master's thesis, Hong Kong University of Science and Technology, 2004.
Lague, David. "Standing up to the Boss". *Far Eastern Economic Review*, 25 July 2002.
Lau, Emily. "Where's the Party?" *Far Eastern Economic Review*, 12 June 1986.
Li, Andrew. "Red Sun over Stanley". *Far Eastern Economic Review*, 25 July 1968.
Li, Shian. "Britain's China the Communists, 1942 to 1946: The Role of Ambassador Sir Horace Seymour". *Modern Asian Studies* 26, no. 1 (February 1992): 49–63.
Li, Suizhou. "The CCP, the State and the Cadres in China". *Chinese Public Administration Review* 4, no. 1/2 (September/December 2007): 47–56.
Lin, Justin Yifu. "Collectivization of China's Agricultural Crisis 1959–1961". *Journal of Political Economy* 98, no. 6 (December 1990): 1228–52.
Liu, Eva Liu, and S. Y. Yue. *Political Development in Hong Kong since the 1980s*. Hong Kong: Research and Library Services Division, Legislative Council Secretariat, September 1996.
Lo, Shiu Hing Sonny. "The Chinese Communist Party Elite's Conflict over Hong Kong, 1983–1990". *China Transformation* 8, no. 4 (Spring 1994): 1–14.
Lo, Shiu Hing Sonny. "The Politics of Co-optation in Hong Kong: A Study of the Basic Law Drafting Process". *Asian Journal of Public Administration* 14, no. 1 (June 1992): 3–24.
Lo, Shiu Hing Sonny, and Donald H. McMillen. "A Profile of 'Pro-China' Hong Kong Elite: Images and Perceptions". *Images & Studies* 31, no. 6 (June 1995): 98–127.
Lo, Sonny. "Hong Kong 1 July 2003—Half a Million Protestors: The Security Law, Identify Politics, Democracy, and China". *Behind the Headlines* 60, no. 4 (2004). Canadian Institute of International Affairs.
Loh, Christine, and Richard Cullen. *Accountability without Democracy: The Principal Officials Accountability System in Hong Kong*. Hong Kong: Civic Exchange and National Democratic Institute for International Affairs, September 2002.

Loh, Christine, and Richard Cullen. "Politics without Accountability: A Study of the New Principal Official Accountability System in Hong Kong". *San Diego International Law Journal* 4 (2003): 127–88.
Louis, R. W. "Hong Kong: The Critical Phase 1945–1949". *American Historical Review* 102, no. 4 (October 1997): 1052–84.
Ma, Teresa. "Capitalism, China-style". *Far Eastern Economic Review*, 1 March 1982.
Mao, Zedong. "On the People's Democratic Dictatorship". Speech, 30 June 1949. http://www.fordham.edu/halsall/mod/1949mao.html.
National Democratic Institute. "The Promises of Democratization in Hong Kong: The 2008 Legislative Council Election, 7 September 2008". *NDI Hong Kong Report* 13 (15 October 2008).
Oxfam Hong Kong. "Local Wealth Inequality Worsens as Richest Earn 29 Times More Than Poorest". 11 October 2016. http://www.oxfam.org.hk/en/news_5160.aspx.
Parker, Maynard. "Reports: Hong Kong". *The Atlantic On-Line* (November 1967), www.theatlantic.com/issues/67nov/hk1167.htm.
Pepper, Suzanne. "Hong Kong Joins the National People's Congress: A First Test for One Country with Two Systems". *Journal of Contemporary China* 8, no. 21 (1999): 319–43.
Sacerdoti, Guy. "On Separate Tracks: Two Shipping Groups Negotiate with Banks to Stay Afloat". *Far Eastern Economic Review* 133, no. 35 (11 September 1986).
Seward, Nick. "The Tung Kin Gulf: Rescue Plans Call for the Stripping of OOCL's Public Assets". *Far Eastern Economic Review* 130, no. 48 (5 December 1985).
Sheridan, Michael. "China Plotted Hong Kong Invasion". *The Australian*, 25 June 2007.
Social Indicators of Hong Kong. "Number of Society Registered under the Society Ordinance Cap. 151". http://www.socialindicators.org.hk/en/indicators/strength_of_civil_society/3.1.
Tsai, Kellee S. "China's Complicit Capitalists". *Far Eastern Economic Review* 171, no. 1 (Jan/Feb 2008): 15.
Tsang, Steve, "Target Zhou Enlai: The 'Kashmir Princess' Incident 1955". *The China Quarterly* no. 139 (September 1994): 766–82.
UNDP Report on *Social Inequality in China*. United Nations, December 2005.
The University of Hong Kong, Hong Kong University Public Opinion Programme. "Popularity Survey of Hong Kong Disciplinary Forces and the PLA Hong Kong Garrison". 8 December 2015. http://www.hkupop.hku.hk/english/release/release1309.htm. 47.
Van Rafghem, Marcos, and Anson P. Lau. *Past and Future Justifications of Functional Constituencies: An Analysis through the Performance of Functional Constituencies Legislators (2004–2006)*. Hong Kong: Civic Exchange, 2006.
Waldron, Stephen Edward. "Fire on the Rim: A Study in Contradictions in Leftwing Political Mobilization in Hong Kong 1967". PhD thesis, Syracuse University, 1976.
Wan, Kwok Fai. "Beijing's United Front Policy Toward Hong Kong: Application of Merilee Grindle's Model". Master's thesis, University of Hong Kong, 2003.
Wei, Pan. "Crossing the River: Legalism, Reform, and Political Change". *Harvard International Review* 25, no. 2 (Summer 2003): 42–47.
Wesley-Smith, Peter. "Chinese Consular Representation in British Hong Kong". *Pacific Affairs* 71, no. 3 (Autumn 1998): 359–75.

Wilson, David Clive (Lord Wilson of Tillyorn). DOPH Interview Index and Biographical Details. 19 September 2003. http://www.chu.cam.ac.uk/archives/collections/BDOPH/Wilson.pdf.

Wong, Cheuk Yin. "The 1967 Leftists Riots and Regime Legitimacy in Hong Kong". Master's thesis, University of Hong Kong, 2000. http://www.hku.hk/hkcsp/ccex/ehkcss01/issue3_ar_lawrence_wong.htm.

Wong, Stan Hok-Wui, Ngok Ma, and Wai-man Lam. "Migrants and Democratization: The Political Economy of Chinese Immigrants in Hong Kong". *Contemporary Chinese Political Economy and Strategic Relations: An International Journal* 2, no. 2 (September 2016): 9089–40.

Wong, Wai-kwok. "Can Co-optation Win over the Hong Kong People? China's United Front Work in Hong Kong since 1984". *Issues & Studies* 33, no. 5 (May 1997): 102–37.

Yiu, Yan Nang. "Trade Union Policy and Trade Union Movement in Hong Kong". Master's thesis, University of Hong Kong, 1980.

Zhao, Suisheng. "A State-Led Nationalism: The Patriotic Campaign in Post-Tiananmen China". *Communist and Post-Communist Studies* 31, no. 3 (September 1998): 287–302.

Zweig, David. "Undemocratic Capitalism: China and the Limits of Economism". *The National Interest*, no. 56 (Summer 1999): 63–72.

Chinese Publications

中央統戰網,〈如何理解保持香港澳門長期繁榮穩定是我們黨治國理政面臨的嶄新課題(專題)〉,《第二十次全國統戰工作會議》,2008年6月3日,http://wztz.66wz.com/system/2008/06/03/100559627.shtml。
中共廣東省委黨史研究室,《香港與中國革命》,廣州:廣東人民出版社,1997。
中共中央黨史研究室、中央檔案館編,《中共黨史資料》,北京:中共黨史出版社,1997。
中共廣東省委黨史研究室,《中國共產黨廣東地方史(第一卷)》,廣州:廣東人民出版社,1999。
毛澤東,〈湖南農民運動考察報告〉,《毛澤東選集》,第一卷,北京:人民出版社,1991。
毛澤東,《毛澤東文集》第4卷,北京:人民出版社,1996。
文灼非,〈香港新華社如何透過左報做宣傳工作(1949–1982)〉,《信報財經月刊》,1996年1月,第19卷,第10期。
牛虻,〈從反英暴動到紅頂商人——左派社團「學友社」的一段歷史〉,《開放雜誌》,1997年2月,頁50。
永逸,〈中聯辦正積極發揮澳門第二支管治力量作用〉,《新華澳報》,2008年2月5日。
冉隆勃、馬繼森,《周恩來與香港「六七暴動」內幕》,香港:明報出版社,2001。
江澤民,〈香港必須有一個平穩的過渡期〉,1989年12月6日,〈江澤民會見英國特使柯利達時的講話〉,《江澤民文選第一卷》。
何立,〈直選民意大結算〉,《九十年代》,1987年10月。
余錦賢,〈中共在港地下黨大老〉,《開放雜誌》,2008年11月8日。
李子誦,〈教我如何不想他:廖公〉,《當代雜誌》,1989年12月23日。
李谷城,〈香港的新華社功能與角色〉,http://202.76.36.61/vol%2018/vol18Doc1_2.htm。
李後,《回歸的歷程》,香港:三聯書店,1997。
李約,〈獨家訪問許家屯〉,《廣角鏡》,1983年6月,第129期。
杜俊偉,〈論抗戰時期周恩來「求同存異」國際統戰策略與實踐〉,《中共四川省委黨校學報》,2002年12月,第4期。
周奕,《香港左派鬥爭史》,香港:利文出版社,2002。

周奕，《香港英雄兒女——東江縱隊港九大隊抗日戰史》，香港：利文出版社，2004。
周恩來，〈關於香港問題〉，《周恩來統一戰綫文選》，北京：人民出版社，1984。
《周恩來年譜（1898–1949）》，北京：中央文獻出版社、人民出版社，1989。
金堯如，《香港五十年憶往》，香港：金堯如紀念基金出版，2005。
宗道一等編著，周南修訂，《周南口述：身在疾風驟雨中》，香港：三聯書店，2007。
宗道一，〈香江之水通海牙——記新華社香港分社社長姜恩柱與他的夫人朱曼黎〉，《黨史博覽》，1998年，第2期，頁13–17。
胡泰然，〈白皮書跳不出北京的框框〉，《九十年代》，1988年1月。
茆貴鳴，《喬冠華傳》，江蘇文藝出版社，2007。
袁小倫，〈戰後初期中共利用香港的策略運作〉，《近代史研究》，2002年，第6期。
軒轅輅，《新華社透視》，香港：廣角鏡出版社，1987。
高繼標，《香港最後一個政治貴族：羅德丞政海浮沉錄》，香港：博益出版集團有限公司，2007。
許家屯，《許家屯香港回憶錄（上、下冊）》，香港：香港聯合出版社，1993。
國世平、錢學君，《九七後中港新關係》，香港：太平洋世紀出版社，1998。
張家偉，《香港六七暴動內情》，香港：太平洋世紀出版社，2000。
張執一，〈中央上海局和香港分局從事地下工作〉，《潮流月刊》，1990年9月15日，第43期。
張雷鋒，〈香港大營救〉，《軍事歷史》，2005年，第10期。
曹二寶，〈一國兩制條件下香港的管治力量〉，《學習時報》，2008年1月1日，第422期。
梁上苑，《中共在香港》，香港：廣角鏡出版，1985。
梁慕嫻，《我與香港地下黨》，香港：開放出版社，2016。
郭德宏、李玲玉（主編），柳建輝（副主編），《中共黨史重大事件述評》，北京：中共中央黨校出版社，2005。
陳新，〈中共在香港的經濟動向〉，《七十年代》，1978年9月，第104期。
港九獨立大隊史編寫組，《港九獨立大隊史》，廣州：廣東人民出版社，1989。
港九各界同胞反對港英迫害鬥爭委員會編，《香港風暴》，1967。
程翔，《天安門的反思》，香港：勵志出版社，1990第一章。
童行，〈董建華身邊的港共名單〉，《開放雜誌》，2003年8月，頁38。
黃文放，《解讀北京思維》，香港：經濟日報出版社，2001。
黃文放，《中國對香港恢復行使主權的決策歷程與執行》，香港：香港浸會大學林思齊東西學術交流研究所，1997。
〈新華社香港分社退職員工聲明〉，《九十年代》，1990年7月。
《新編黨的宣傳工作實用手冊》，北京：紅旗出版社，2003。
楊少平，〈中共香港黨（團）組織的建立及其早期活動〉，《廣東黨史》，1996年5月。
楊漢卿，〈八路軍駐香港辦事處的統戰工作〉，《廣東黨史》，2005年6月。
葉漢明、蔡寶瓊，〈殖民地與革命文化霸權：香港與四十年代後期的中國共產主義運動〉，《中國文化研究所學報》，2001年，新第10期，頁191–215。

趙睿、張明瑜（主編），宋瑩、張培忠（編者），《中國領導人談香港》，香港：明報出版社，1997。

《廖承志文集》編輯辦公室，《廖承志文集（上冊）》，香港：三聯書店，1990。

齊鵬飛，〈長期打算，充分利用：1949–1978新中國對於香港問題和香港的特殊政策〉，《中共黨史研究》，1997年第2期。

劉子健、彭建新、梁威林，〈談香港工作20年體會〉，《廣東黨史》，1997年3月。

劉田夫、吳南生及楊應杉，〈方方主持中共香港分局展開政治鬥爭〉，《潮流月刊》，1990年10月15日。

劉武生，《文革中的周恩來》，香港：三聯書店，2006。

劉蜀永，〈英國對香港的政策與中國的態度（1948–1952）年〉，《中國社會科學》，1995年，第2期。

鄧峰，〈香港新華社——工委在港的外衣〉，《當代雜誌》，1989年12月16日。

盧平，〈香港回歸的回顧〉，《縱橫》，2007年，第9期。

盧育儀、麥慰宗、鍾仕梅，〈統戰工作有功，錯在重資輕勞〉，《當代雜誌》，1990年1月13日。

鍾仕梅，〈中共如何管理香港〉，《當代雜誌》，1989年11月25日。

鍾仕梅，〈工委遷港統一領導〉，《當代雜誌》，1989年12月2日。

鍾仕梅，〈對港方針，政出多門〉，《當代雜誌》，1989年12月9日。

鍾仕梅，〈工委政策偏離中央方針〉，《當代雜誌》，1990年1月6日。

鍾國安，〈以習近平總書記總體國家安全觀為指引　譜寫國家安全新篇章〉，《求是》，2017/8, http://www.qstheory.cn/dukan/qs/2017-04/15/c_1120788993.htm.

鐵竹偉，《廖承志傳》，北京：人民出版社，1998。

www.ingramcontent.com/pod-product-compliance
Ingram Content Group UK Ltd.
Pitfield, Milton Keynes, MK11 3LW, UK
UKHW021843140426
5217IPUK00022B/1566